WHAT INSPIRATIONAL LITERATURE

DO I READ NEXT?

WHAT INSPIRATIONAL LITERATURE

DO I READ NEXT?

GALE GROUP

Detroit
San Francisco
London
Boston
Woodbridge, CT

Pamela Willwerth Aue

Henry L. Carrigan, Jr.,
Contributing Editor

Pamela Willwerth Aue

Henry L. Carrigan, Jr., Contributing Editor

Gale Group Staff:

Senior Editor: Kathleen J. Edgar
Associate Editor: Ellice Engdahl
Contributing Editors: Kathleen Meek, Charles B. Montney
Contributing Associate Editors: Robert Franzino, Elizabeth Manar
Contributing Assistant Editor: Prindle LaBarge
Managing Editor: Debra M. Kirby

Composition Manager: Mary Beth Trimper
Assistant Production Manager: Evi Seoud
Manufacturing Manager: Dorothy Maki
Buyer: Stacy L. Melson
Product Design Manager: Cynthia Baldwin
Graphic Designer: Michelle DiMercurio
Cover Photography: Bridget A. Barrett

Manager, Technical Support Services: Theresa Rocklin
Senior Programmer/Analyst: Dan Bono
Programmer/Analyst: David J. Mosorjak

ISBN 0-7876-3942-7
ISSN 1526-6818

Printed in the United States of America

10 9 8 7 6 5 4 3 2

Contents

Preface

by Pamela Willwerth Aue

What Inspirational Literature Do I Read Next? is a tool designed to help readers find fiction and non-fiction titles that reflect their beliefs and interests, affirm their personal values, describe the beliefs of others, provide motivational and uplifting stories, profile religious and spiritual leaders, and answer questions about spiritual matters. From devotionals and religious commentaries to historical fiction and romances, *What Inspirational Literature Do I Read Next?* offers the reader both contemporary and classic recommendations in religious, spiritual, and inspirational literature.

Highlights

• An overview essay that describes the development of the inspirational literature market, including its status as we enter the twenty-first century.

• Ten indexes to help readers locate certain authors or titles, as well as books with specific series names, awards won, time periods, geographic settings, categories, subjects, character names, or character descriptions.

• A selection of titles that includes both classic favorites and contemporary examples of inspirational, spiritual, and religious fiction and nonfiction for readers of all ages.

• Publication information that indicates the first date of publication for each title, unless a specific revised edition of the work is being recommended. For classic titles, the original date of issue is provided to give readers useful information about the origin of the work. Many of these classic titles are available today in new and revised editions.

• A glossary of terms to help readers understand unfamiliar words they may encounter in descriptions, and to clarify the usage of other terms within the context of inspirational literature.

Details on More Than 1,000 Titles

This first edition of *What Inspirational Literature Do I Read Next?* contains entries on more than 1,000 inspirational books ranging from ancient scriptural texts to contemporary novels. Many of the books profiled in this volume are considered classics within their cultural and religious heritages. Some, including the *Koran*, the *Bible*, and the *Torah*, are considered divinely inspired writings upon which major world religions are based. There are books for readers of all ages, and works representing both major and lesser-known religious traditions of the world.

The entries are listed alphabetically by author. If an author has more than one title included, the books are then arranged alphabetically by title. The following information is provided for each title (when applicable):

• **Author's or editor's name** and real name if a pseudonym is used. Names of co-authors, co-editors, and illustrators are also given.

• **Book title.**

• **Date and place of publication; name of publisher.**

• **Category:** Lists one or two categories that best describe the book (i.e., Mystery, Morality Play, Theology, etc.).

• **Series:** The name of the series the book is in.

• **Subject(s):** Lists up to three themes or topics covered in the title.

• **Age range(s):** Indicates the age level for which the title is best suited. Categories include Children (up to age 10), Young Adult (11-17), and Adult (18+), as well as combinations of these groups.

• **Major character(s):** Names of main characters featured in the book, with brief descriptions of each.

• **Time period(s):** Identifies when a fictional story takes place or the years covered by nonfiction titles.

• **Locale(s):** Identifies the geographic setting of the title.

• **Summary:** A brief plot synopsis or description of the book and its origins.

• **Selection of awards the book has won.**

• **Other books by the same author:** Titles and publication dates of other books the author has written. This is useful for those wanting to read more by a particular writer.

• **Other books you might like:** Titles by other authors written on a similar theme or in a similar style as the main entry. For example, the entry for an autobiography may include recommendations of biographies or critical works written about the same person, or autobiographies written by people in the same profession as the author of the main entry title. Recommended titles often reflect the same religious or spiritual traditions and doctrines as those represented by the main title, but not always. Suggested fiction titles may share similar plot lines, historical settings, or genre characteristics.

Indexes Answer Readers' Questions

The ten indexes in *What Inspirational Literature Do I Read Next?* can be used separately or in conjunction with each other to create many pathways to featured titles, answer general questions, and locate specific titles. For example:

"What are the books in Jan Karon's Mitford series?"
The SERIES INDEX lists entries by the name of the series of which they are a part.

"Are there any plays that have won the Pulitzer Prize?"
The AWARDS INDEX lists awards and honors received by both classic and current fiction and nonfiction titles.

"Do you know of any books set during the U.S. Civil War?"
The TIME PERIOD INDEX is a chronological listing of the time settings in which the main entries take place. This can help readers find books about a particular period in history or those set during a specific era or decade.

"Are there any novels set in Jerusalem?"
The GEOGRAPHIC INDEX lists titles by their locale. This can help readers pinpoint an area in which they may have a particular interest, such as their hometown, another country, or an imaginary place.

"I'm looking for an autobiography. Can you help me find one?"
The CATEGORY INDEX lists books by their type, including Autobiography, Devotionals, Historical Fiction, Religious Commentaries, Romance, New Age (Fiction), and New Age (Nonfiction).

"I like novels about family life. What do you suggest?"
The SUBJECT INDEX lists books by the topics they cover. This can help readers find titles associated with a particular religious tradition or its adherents (e.g. Buddhism, Catholicism, Mennonites, or Baptists) or a subject of interest (e.g. Monasticism, End-Times, Family Life, or Prayer).

"I read a novel about a girl named Corrie Belle Hollister. Is she in any other books?"
The CHARACTER NAME INDEX lists the major characters named in the entries. This can help readers who remember some information about a book, but not its author or title.

"Can you recommend some good books about biblical figures or teachers?"
The CHARACTER DESCRIPTION INDEX identifies major characters by occupation (e.g. Teacher, Journalist) or persona (e.g. Angel, Biblical Figure).

"What has Judith Pella written recently?"
The AUTHOR INDEX contains a listing of all authors of main entries as well as those listed under "Other books you might like." This index can help identify additional titles for readers who remember the name of an author whose work they've already enjoyed or who they've heard about from friends.

"I enjoyed reading *Stone Tables* by Orson Scott Card. Are there similar books I might like?"
The TITLE INDEX includes in one alphabetical listing all main entry titles as well as all titles recommended under "Other books by the same author" and "Other books you might like." By searching for a specific title, readers can find out what other books are similar to a title they like.

The indexes can also be used to narrow down or broaden choices. A reader interested in stories about family life set in Ireland could consult the SUBJECT INDEX and the GEOGRAPHIC INDEX to see which titles appear in both under the appropriate headings. Someone interested in Westerns set in the 1860s could compare titles listed under that decade in the TIME PERIOD INDEX with titles listed under "Westerns" in the CATEGORY INDEX. And with the AUTHOR and TITLE indexes, which include all books listed under "Other books by the same author" and "Other books you might like," it is easy to compile an extensive list of titles for further reading, not only with the titles recommended in a main entry, but also by seeing other titles to which the main entry or its recommended titles are similar.

About the Authors

Contributing Editor Henry L. Carrigan, Jr. is editorial director at Trinity Press International. From 1994 to 1999, he was Religion Book Review Editor at *Publishers Weekly*. From 1991 to 1994, he wrote columns about spiritual reading and Christian fiction for the *Library Journal*. He has written numerous articles about the field of religious publishing and has led workshops at the local and national level on religion collection development for public and seminary libraries. Based on his expertise in the field of religious and spiritual literature, Carrigan created the list of main entry titles for this premier volume of *What Inspirational Literature Do I Read Next?* Carrigan's knowledge of the religious and inspirational book market also informs his introductory essay following this section.

Pamela Willwerth Aue is a writer and editor in the fields of contemporary literature, spirituality, and education. Between 1993 and 1998, she was employed by Gale Research, where she worked in a variety of roles, including managing editor of publications focusing on twentieth-century authors and their works. Her professional interest in inspirational literature is a natural extension of a life-long love for reading, learning, and helping others find encouragement and motivation through books, music, and other resources. Ms. Aue received a Bachelor of Arts degree in English, French, and Russian from Central Michigan University and a Master's degree in Education from Wayne State University.

Acknowledgments

Many thanks to Dr. Paul I. Willwerth and Patricia G. Willwerth for a lifetime of love, encouragement, and inspiration. Your lifelong examples of faith and integrity in all circumstances offered valuable motivation during the preparation of this manuscript. Many thanks, also, to Craig S. Aue, who uncomplainingly provided countless pizza and take-out dinners, and to Ashley and Taylor Aue, who willingly relinquished Internet time with their friends to allow me to use more than my fair share of research and online correspondence time. Thanks are offered to all who shared books and recommendations with me. Grateful kudos are also due for the support, encouragement, and copyediting excellence offered by Kathleen Edgar and Ellice Engdahl of the Gale Group.

The editors, in turn, would like to extend special thanks to Susan E. Edgar and Nancy A. Edgar for their contributions to this work.

Also Available Online

The entries in *What Inspirational Literature Do I Read Next?* will also be available in the online version of *What Do I Read Next?* on GaleNet. This electronic product encompasses more than 83,000 books, including genre fiction, mainstream fiction, and nonfiction. All the books included in *What Do I Read Next?* online are recommended by librarians or other experts or appear on bestseller or award lists. The user-friendly functionality allows readers to refine their searching by using several criteria, while making it easy to identify similar titles for further research and reading. The online version is updated with new information on a quarterly basis. For more information about *What Do I Read Next?* online, please contact the Gale Group.

Suggestions Are Welcome

The editors welcome any comments and suggestions for enhancing and improving *What Inspirational Literature Do I Read Next?* Please address correspondence to:

Editors
What Inspirational Literature Do I Read Next?
Gale Group, Inc.
27500 Drake Road
Farmington Hills, MI 48331-3535
Phone: 248-699-GALE
Toll-Free: 800-347-GALE
Fax: 248-699-8074

Introduction

by Henry L. Carrigan, Jr.

"Of making many books there is no end, and much study is a weariness of the flesh."
—Ecclesiastes 12:12

Although the writer of Ecclesiastes did not have the current boom in religion publishing in mind when he wrote these words, he well could have. Since the early 1990s, requests for religion books have come steadily flooding into libraries and bookstores in an unstoppable stream. As the twenty-first century begins, there appears to be no end to the flood of religion books streaming into the market. Indeed, religion is the second fastest growing category in publishing, and it should continue such growth, according to the Book Industry Study Group, for at least another five years. One Gallup poll projects an 82 percent growth in religion/spirituality books by the year 2010 over the year 1987, the largest sales increase in nonfiction books.

Of course, libraries want to keep up with the demand for the latest spirituality or religion titles, but, like most bookstores, they have limited space. While bookstores can solve this problem simply by returning the books, libraries find themselves confronted with another set of issues. In the first place, librarians want to keep as many books on the shelves as possible for their patrons. Although the usefulness of the multitude of books about angels that were published in the early 1990s continues to diminish, there will be patrons who want to find out more about angels and will come to the library to find it. Secondly, most librarians want to have balanced materials for their public. When a patron wants to find out more about Wicca or Scientology or about the history of a small sect in America, he or she comes to the library hoping to find all kinds of information—books that neither simply condemn a religious practice nor overtly praise that practice. Finally, librarians want to have in their core collections those religion books that are indispensable reference tools—like Mircea Eliade's *The Encyclopedia of Religion* and the most recent edition of Frank Mead's *Handbook of Denominations in the United States*—and those that are classics—like Catherine Marshall's *Christy*, Thomas Merton's *The Seven Storey Mountain*, and Augustine's *Confessions*.

Perhaps the greatest challenge libraries face is maintaining the balance between classic religion titles—many of which are now out of print—and popular religion titles whose usefulness may diminish after six months. Another challenge libraries face is how to categorize many of these more popular religion titles. Although this question arises most frequently when dealing with fiction—should it be called "Christian fiction," "spiritual fiction," "inspirational fiction"?—it also occurs in increasing frequency with nonfiction. Is Deepak Chopra a religious writer, or does he write self-help books? Are works about Tae-Bo about spirituality? While the Dewey Decimal system solves this problem for catalogers, it does not aid the patron who is searching the shelves for a book he or she thinks is a "spirituality" title only to find the book in the health and nutrition section. For libraries that use labels on their books, what label should they put on the spine of the latest Thich Nhat Hanh book or the most recent monastery cookbook or the newest book on spiritual gardening? Are they religion books? Spirituality books? Inspirational books?

In contemporary America, many people associate religion with an institutional expression of faith replete with the trappings of liturgy and dogma. Religion conjures up the image of their Sabbath days as children when their parents forced them to sit through long and incomprehensible mutterings about God and the universe. For people outside any religious tradition, the word often signifies a dogmatic institution more interested in rules and regulations than in fostering a vital relationship between people and the sacred. Spirituality, on the other hand, encourages personal experience and encounters with the transcendent—what William James referred to as the "More"—that are not subject to the regulatory channels of traditional religious institutions. Because of its focus on individuality, spirituality does not require involvement or upbringing in a religious tradition but merely a seeking after connection to this "More." People are free to pursue spiritual lives outside of a religious community and apart from any religious rules or institutional regulations. Pollster, analyst, and author George Barna characterizes 1990s religion in America as "a personalized, customized form of faith views which meet personal needs, minimize rules and absolutes, and which bear little resemblance to the pure form of any of the world's major religions." Some have remarked that a religious person attends church while a spiritual person attends workshops. Thus, many librarians do not like to use the word religious to describe these popular books because many people associate religion with narrowness and dogmatism. On the other hand, while spirituality captures the experiential character of contemporary religious expression, it neglects the rich tradition out of which many of these spiritual practices arise.

Some librarians have suggested using the word "inspirational" as a catchall category for these popular books. The advantage of this word is that it captures the generic character of many popular books written from a particular spiritual worldview. For example, Rodger Kamenetz's *Stalking Elijah*, an autobiographical lesson in finding Jewish faith by looking outside of Judaism, is a book that moves people to lead dramatically different lives. It is inspiring. But, this way of talking about books could just as well be applied to Dale Carnegie's *How to Win Friends and Influence People*, to novels like Jack Kerouac's *On the Road*, or to Peter Mayle's travel books on Provence. All these books are inspiring, too, but would anyone think of them as having a spiritual character? Another disadvantage of the word "inspirational" is its implicit neglect of the classical texts of a religious tradition. Many contemporary readers have difficulty reading such texts simply because of their sometimes archaic language and complex religious ideas. Because of the tremendous difference between the classical text's instructions on being religious and the contemporary reader's religious sensibility, many readers do not find these texts inspiring but frightening and threatening. Still another disadvantage of this word is its Western, and really Christian, bias. The Greek root word from which our word inspiration comes is *pneuma*, or *pneumatos*. The word itself means spirit or breath, but it is most often translated as Holy Spirit.

However, we have decided to use the word "inspirational" in this book to try to capture as wide a range of "spiritual" materials as possible—including sacred texts of the world's religions as well as classic texts from those traditions—and to avoid the narrowness many readers and librarians associate with religion. Thus, the present volume contains entries that describe the sacred texts of Judaism, Christianity, Hinduism, Buddhism, and Islam. It also includes entries that offer details about classic literature from various traditions like the *Talmud* and John Bunyan's *The Pilgrim's Progress*. In addition, the entries in the volume range from histories of American Christianity (Martin E. Marty's *Pilgrims in Their Own Land*), Wiccan studies (Starhawk's *The Spiral Dance*), spiritual psychology (Paul Tournier's *The Meaning of Persons*), and theology (Dietrich Bonhoeffer's *Letters and Papers from Prison*) to the pop psychology and quasi-spirituality of M. Scott Peck's *The Road Less Traveled*, Ernest Becker's *The Denial of Death*, and Harold S. Kushner's *When Bad Things Happen to Good People*. The volume contains entries for fiction titles as well as nonfiction, and the fiction entries range from the genre fiction of popular Christian writers like Janette Oke and Gilbert Morris to the literary fiction of John Updike and Doris Betts. There are entries here for devotional books—actually some of the first religion bestsellers—books of sermons, autobiographies and biographies of great religious leaders, and poetry.

Although this wave of attention to religion and spirituality seems novel to many people, it is hardly a new phenomenon. Americans have been seeking ways of being religious in a secular society ever since governor John Winthrop called his Massachusetts Bay Colony a "New Jerusalem." By the nineteenth century, the desire among European immigrants to hold on to their indigenous religions resulted in the rise of denominationalism in America. During these years, religion publishing developed. At first, such publishing was confined primarily to denominational presses like the Methodist Book Concern (founded in 1789), Augsburg (1848), and Broadman House (then a division of the Southern Baptist Convention's Sunday School Board, founded in 1898). These publishers issued devotional books, curriculum resources, and hymnals for a niche audience of clergy and laity.

Some of the earliest inspirational materials in America were pamphlets of sermons by the great revivalists Billy Sunday and Dwight L. Moody. These preachers sold copies of their books at their revival meetings. Moody sold his line so well that he was able to establish his own company, Fleming H. Revell Co. In 1896, preacher Charles M. Sheldon produced one of the first religious bestsellers when he collected his Sunday evening sermons asking "What would Jesus do?" in his book *In His Steps*. Since 1897, the book has sold 22 million copies and provides the impetus behind the contemporary WWJD (What Would Jesus Do?) publishing trend.

Until the 1960s, denominational presses dominated most of the religion publishing in the United States. For much of the nineteenth and twentieth centuries, the main audience for religion books was clergy. In addition, these denominational houses published materials for use by their own constituents. A Lutheran house would never have thought of publishing a Baptist book. By the 1940s, the audience for inspirational books began to grow beyond the boundaries of the denomination. In 1925, Bruce Barton's *The Man Nobody Knows* became a huge bestseller, and by the 1930s and 1940s the works of preacher Harry Emerson Fosdick, whose sermons often discussed social justice rather than individual salvation, gained a huge following. By the early 1950s, Catherine Marshall's *A Man Called Peter*, Dale Evans Rogers' *Angel Unaware*, Norman Vincent Peale's *The Power of Positive Thinking*, Billy Graham's *The Secret of Happiness*, Fulton J. Sheen's *Peace of Soul*, and Anne Morrow Lindbergh's *Gift From the Sea* dominated bestseller lists.

Inspirational publishing moved into the mainstream in the 1960s when trade houses like Macmillan, Farrar, Straus & Giroux, Bobbs-Merrill, Harper & Row, and New Directions began to release titles that appealed to disaffected churchgoers. The success of Harvey Gallagher Cox's *The Secular City* (1965), which sold more than 250 million copies, caught the attention of trade publishers. These publishers began trying to capture those readers who had become disenchanted with traditional, institutional religious authority. These readers had turned away from what they perceived as rigid authoritarianism and were moving toward religious expressions that fostered introspection, individuality, and creativity. Harper & Row published the writings of Catholic social worker Dorothy Day as well as Sam Keen's celebratory paean to the body and its role in Christian faith and worship, *To a Dancing God*.

American religion was also reshaped in the 1960s by its encounter with Eastern religions, as various forms of Buddhism (most notably Zen) became alternatives to the model of American society that sociologist that Will Herberg had dubbed "Protestant-Catholic-Jew." The increasing eastward turn led to the founding of publishing houses like Shambhala, Tuttle, and Parallax Press, which offered books on the practices of various Buddhist traditions, the spirituality of Hinduism, the writings of American Zen teacher Alan Watts, and manuals on yoga. This new syncretistic spirit, which wove together Eastern spiritual traditions with Western spirituality, gave rise to the New Age movement. Publishers like Blue Dove, Quest, and Bear & Co. and, later, imprints like Riverhead represented this new movement.

By the 1970s and 1980s, the religious and spiritual excitement of the 1960s had waned. Many Americans traveled through these years seeking not so much spiritual renewal as individual gratification. The Jesus People movement and liberation theology demonstrated the turn from God-centeredness to self-centeredness and individual experience so characteristic of these years. The self-help and recovery movements of the 1980s eventually bore a significant influence on religion publishing through titles like M. Scott Peck's *The Road Less Traveled* and Harold S. Kushner's *When Bad Things Happen to Good People*.

In the 1970s, the growth of evangelical Christian publishing surprised many. Driven by the popularity among young people of new forms of Christianity, publishers like Tyndale House and Zondervan began to publish books that would appeal to this new generation. Tyndale House's *The Living Bible, Paraphrased* (1971) sold three million copies in its first year, and Zondervan hit the jackpot with Hal Lindsey's apocalyptic thriller *The Late Great Planet Earth* (1972). Moreover, these houses were not associated with particular denominations and so could publish books that would have appeal to Christians across denominational lines. Catholic publishing also saw the rise of new presses and imprints like Paulist Press, Orbis Books, and Doubleday's Image Books that published Catholic theology, titles on social activism in the Church, and classics of Catholic spirituality for popular audiences.

In the 1990s, the Baby Boomers who were shaped by the 1960s, 1970s, and 1980s made up the largest segment of book buyers. As they entered middle age and began to confront their own mortality, their spiritual search intensified. Today, religion and spirituality fill the radio and television airwaves, and it appears that the religion that appeared marginal or absent in the 1970s and 1980s has resurfaced with a new urgency.

Who could have guessed that a simple and sentimental little inspirational book called *Chicken Soup for the Soul* would sell millions of copies in trade bookstores and spawn a whole series of books for various kinds of "souls": women, teenagers, Christians? Who could have known that a biography of God, written by a journalist turned academic, would win the Pulitzer Prize? Who can explain the incredible popularity of the new *Catechism of the Catholic Church*, whose paperback editions share space in airport kiosks alongside the romances of Danielle Steel? How could anyone predict that HarperSanFrancisco's 1992 edition of Sogyal Rinpoche's *The Tibetan Book of Living and Dying*, a fairly specialized treatise on Tibetan Buddhism, would sell 220,000 copies? Thirty years ago many of these books would have been published by sectarian religious or academic publishers, if they were published at all. Their enormous popularity today represents not only the resurgence of the popularity of religion in America today but also the depth at which trade publishers are involved in capitalizing on the popularity of inspirational titles.

Indeed, trade publishers have entered the inspirational market at a dramatic rate. In response to the growing demand for religion and spirituality titles, many of these publishers have established their own inspirational imprints to reach this steadily growing audience. As they recognized the tremendous potential for publishing to this niche market, publishers like Doubleday, Crown, Penguin/Putnam, and Harlequin began to establish imprints that would supply titles for this inspirational market. While Doubleday had already established Image Books in the 1960s to publish classic spiritual texts—like Georges Bernanos' *The Diary of a Country Priest*—for a Catholic audience, in the 1990s Doubleday established WaterBrook to capture the surging evangelical Christian market. Penguin/Putnam responded to the growing interest in Buddhism and Eastern religion by establishing its Riverhead line, and Putnam's Tarcher imprint publishes books both for audiences interested in liturgical spirituality and New Age spirituality. Crown's Bell Tower imprint reaches out to the general spirituality crowd, and Harlequin entered the inspirational fiction market with its Steeple Hill imprint. Finally, Viking's Arkana books recover not only classic texts of the Eastern mystical traditions but also esoteric Western texts that provide the foundations for the paths of many spiritual seekers. As they develop their religion collections in the twenty-first century, librarians need to look as much to trade publishers as religion publishers.

The large presence of trade publishers in the inspirational publishing business in many ways mirrors the changes that marked American attitudes toward religion and spirituality in the 1990s. As the decade was born, many Americans began to discover that the material wealth they had focused on accumulating in the 1980s did not provide them with the spiritual sustenance they craved. All of a sudden people started to talk about "dysfunction" and "stress" as they tried to describe the spiritual brokenness and frenetic pace of living lives of getting and spending. Thus, the first wave of inspirational books in the 1990s suggested very general ways of trying to reunite the soul with the body. These books drew on Native American spirituality, Wiccan spirituality, alchemy, Eastern religious traditions, Western esoteric sciences, magic, ritual, myth, psychology, holistic medicine, Celtic spirituality, animistic religions, and shamanism as sources for their spiritual solutions. Searching for any suggestions they could find to help them fill their spiritual hunger, readers of these books fashioned a syncretistic spirituality or exchanged one spirituality for another when one style failed to meet their demands. From the beginning of the decade to its midpoint, this surge of interest in spirituality continued unabated and turned the heads of pollsters and publishers.

During the last five years of the 1990s, this swelling wave of spirituality began to take on a different face. The early years confirmed that the interest in religion was not just a blip on the cultural radar screen that was going to disappear soon. For many, the interest in spirituality was simply a revival of the 1960s way of life that urged spiritual connections with the world through music, drugs, literature, politics, Eastern religions, and community. In one sense, then, the early 1990s did not represent much of a departure from the aura of Woodstock and the Summer of Love. For many people, though, the turn to spirituality was a return to a way of being in the world that they had left behind long ago. As the Baby Boomers began to raise their own children, they sought not just a rootless spirituality but a spirituality rooted in the religious tradition in which they were raised but which they had long ago left. The major difference, however, between this way of being religious and their childhood way of being religious is that they would like to recover their early religious traditions outside of these traditions. Community life in an institution still does not appeal to these readers, and this group is seeking its tradition-based spirituality in books. Consequently, bestselling inspirational books of the late 1990s included spiritual memoirs about growing up in a particular religious tradition, guidebooks on religious pilgrimages, how-to books that suggest various methods for incorporating the spiritual rules of monastic communities, the principles of religious teachings and doctrine, and the meanings of sacred texts in everyday life.

Perhaps the most startling and welcome change in the late 1990s was the demand for sophisticated books on religion. While the early years of the decade were marked by sentimental and simplistic inspirational books—from books on angels to New Age books to the *Chicken Soup for the Soul* books—the latter years of the 1990s were marked by more complex books that are intellectually challenging and spiritually satisfying. Bestsellers like Jack Miles' *God: A Biography*, which takes readers on a tour de force of academic biblical criticism and history, represent these new kinds of books.

Many reasons explain the surge in popularity in inspirational titles. Perhaps the most prominent is the changing face of American society. In the 1950s, sociologist of religion Will Herberg could remark that the dominant religious model in America was "Protestant-Catholic-Jew" (the title of his famous book). However, at the turn of the twenty-first century, the fastest growing religions in America are Buddhism and Islam. This growth is generated not only by the number of immigrants bringing their indigenous religions into the United States but also by the number of Americans who have joined these groups in their search for spiritual satisfaction. According to some reports, by the year 2005 Asians will be the dominant cultural group in America. This statistic only confirms that Buddhism in the United States will continue to grow well into the twenty-first century. Many Baby Boomers have also grabbed on to Zen Buddhism for its holistic ways of thinking about the world, body, and spirit. Books by Vietnamese Buddhist monk Thich Nhat Hanh and the Tibetan spiritual leader the Dalai Lama continue to remain atop bestseller lists at the beginning of the new millennium. Book about various world religions remain popular as readers try to become more acquainted with the faiths of their neighbors. Books like Arthur Magida's *How to Be a Perfect Stranger* and Gayle Colquitt White's *Believers and Beliefs* offer readers a chance to get to know various faiths on the personal level of practice.

Yet another reason for the popularity of inspirational titles stems from the desire for individualistic expression of faith. In the 1990s readers were searching for ways to weave their own experiences of the sacred into their everyday lives. Kathleen Norris' *The Cloister Walk* urges individuals to incorporate the spiritual practices of a Benedictine monastery into their ordinary lives. Norris' book has become so popular simply because she, herself, tells the story of the ways she accomplished this in her life. Books by Thich Nhat Hanh and Deepak Chopra maintain their popularity because of their syncretism. These authors show readers that you can draw your spirituality from the threads of multiple religious traditions to forge a spiritual expression that is suited to your own life. Thus, a Christian might draw upon Hindu yogic practices and Buddhist meditation teachings to fashion a spirituality that he or she can express through his or her everyday life.

Still another reason for the popularity of inspirational books as the new millennium begins stems from the return to traditions. Although much of the spirituality of the early 1990s was very generic and rootless, the spirituality of recent years has been more rooted in tradition. Many Baby Boomers are returning to the faiths of their childhoods and are trying to become reacquainted with the principles and practices of those faiths. More important, they are seeking the lessons that can be taught by the sacred texts of those traditions. Thus, Vintage Books, Paraclete Press, Paulist Press, and St. Martin's are all actively publishing series of classic texts—ranging from Augustine's *Confessions* to Teresa of Avila's *The Way of Perfection*—as a response to this interest. Even here, though, syncretism is at work. Many of those who are engaged in this tradition-based spirituality are weaving the threads of one religious tradition with the threads of another to create a religious expression that suits their own personal lives. Rodger Kamenetz, for example, illuminated and deepened his own Jewish faith through a deep engagement with Buddhist teachers. All of these factors play a tremendous role in the current popularity of religion.

As we enter the new millennium, the popularity of inspirational books continues to grow. Several trends will mark inspirational publishing in the coming years. First, there will be more and more books that seek the intersections of religion and science. Many of these books will continue the debate between creationists and evolutionists, but many of them will be asking questions about the ways that a person can be moral or religious when evolutionary psychology, sociobiology, and genetic science has determined that humans are motivated simply by their animalistic urges. Contemporary language theory and the theory of consciousness will spark debate about whether humans even have a soul. Advances in biotechnology, especially cloning and embryo research, will challenge many religious people's ideas about what it means to be human. Second, as the population ages there will be more and more books that examine religious perspectives on aging and death. Third, as denominationalism in America declines, there will be a number of books about the future shape of religious community. Finally, religion fiction will continue to grow, and the quality of the fiction will continue to increase. Much inspirational fiction has for many years been little more than a veiled sermon. In 1999, though, both religion houses and trade houses started to publish quality fiction that has strongly drawn characters and complex plots. The desire for more realistic approaches to fiction motivates this trend.

Developing a religion collection in a public library has never been more challenging. The need to maintain a balanced and thoughtful collection is foremost in most librarians' minds, yet the steady influx of new and popular material makes collection development a daunting task. If libraries can maintain a core circulating and non-circulating collection of classic and contemporary texts, patrons will benefit tremendously. We hope this book will be useful to both readers and the libraries that serve them, not only as a readers' advisory tool, but also as a tool for collection development. The books listed here provide the core of a good library religion collection, and the suggestions about what to read next offer valuable guidance for both readers and librarians in an area that is constantly changing.

Glossary

Afterlife: In religious terms, an existence that follows one's earthly death is referred to as "the afterlife." Afterlife beliefs vary among and within religious traditions. Some faith systems teach that there are particular places to which souls are transported at the moment of death; in some cases, practitioners of these beliefs expect an eventual resurrection of their earthly bodies, as well. Other traditions teach that souls will inhabit earthly bodies, one after the other (and not always human ones), until they have been perfected. Most religious systems that include doctrines about the afterlife also teach that a person's earthly beliefs, choices, and actions determine the nature of that person's afterlife experience.

Agnosticism: The belief that the existence of God, or any invisible, supreme being, can neither be proved nor disproved. An agnostic does not necessarily deny the possibility of such existence. Agnosticism is often confused with atheism, which is the denial of the existence of any supreme being such as God. See also **Atheism**.

Allah: The foundation of the Islamic religion is submission to the will of Allah, the Supreme Being, the eternal and all-powerful creator, and the source of eternal reward or punishment. Prayers are made directly to Allah, without human or divine mediators. Adherents of Islam believe that the *Koran*, the holy scripture of Islam, is the word of Allah revealed through the prophet Muhammad.

Amish: The Amish are Protestant Christians whose conservative, agricultural communities—primarily located in Pennsylvania, Ohio, Indiana, and Canada—can trace their earliest roots back to the sixteenth century in Europe. Although there are other Amish groups that are less conservative, it is the Old Order Amish whose distinctive style of plain dress and rejection of modern technology are recognized throughout the United States. The Amish lifestyle at the beginning of the twenty-first century is very similar to that of the eighteenth century Amish who came to America to escape persecution in their homelands.

Anglicans: Anglicans are members of an Anglican Church. The Anglican Church is the branch of Christianity that became the official Church of England following the Protestant Reformation of the sixteenth century. The Angli-

can tradition in the United States can be found in the Episcopal Church, which shares general doctrine and worship style, as well as the Book of Common Prayer, with the Church of England.

Apartheid: The policy of racial division followed in South Africa from 1948 until the early 1990s. The laws of apartheid separated people into racial groups: White, black African (or Bantu), Coloured (mixed descent), and Asian (Indians and Pakistanis). Apartheid laws dictated where people could live and restricted representation in the national government to whites only.

Apocalypse: A Jewish form of literature characterized by highly symbolic descriptions and predictions of future events. In religious terms, "apocalypse" refers both to prophetic writings that foretell the destruction of the world and the ultimate salvation of believers by a Messiah, and to the prophesied event itself. In Christian writings, the Book of Revelation is referred to as an apocalyptic text, and the end-of-the-world vision it proclaims is often called the Apocalypse. See also **End-Times**.

Apocrypha: A collection of texts that date from between 300 BC to about AD 100, the books of the Apocrypha are included in the scriptures of the Roman Catholic and Orthodox Christian churches. The Apocryphal texts include Judith, the Wisdom of Solomon, Tobit, Sirach (Ecclesiasticus), Baruch, and the two books of the Maccabees. In non-Orthodox Protestant Christianity, these texts, along with two books of Esdras and several additional writings, are not considered part of the *Bible* itself, and are referred to as "the Apocrypha." The Apocryphal writings were part of the Greek version of the Old Testament in the fifth century, but were not included in the Hebrew *Bible*, which became the Old Testament used by the Protestant branch of Christianity.

Apologetics: A branch of theology centered on the defense or proof of the divine origins and absolute truth of a particular doctrine or system of belief. Apologetics consists of formal, structured, logical arguments offered by scholars in their particular religion, most commonly Christianity.

Ashram: A religious retreat or learning center, usually but not exclusively referring to the residence of a Hindu guru and the guru's disciples or community.

Atheism: Atheism is a doctrine that denies the existence of a supreme being, creator, or deity of any kind. Atheism is often confused with agnosticism, which is a doctrine of belief that the existence of a supreme or divine being can neither be proved nor disproved. See also **Agnosticism**.

Baptists: Protestant Christians who accept the basic principles of Protestantism that resulted in its division from Catholicism, Baptists additionally believe in baptism, or ritual affirmation of the individual's membership in the church by immersion in water, as well as the autonomy of the individual church. Therefore, although many churches may be part of a larger denomination such as the Southern Baptist Convention or the American Baptist Churches in the U.S.A., each congregation is subject to its own standards and structures of governance and practice. The first Baptist church in America was founded in Rhode Island in 1639 by English Puritan Roger Williams. The Baptist denomination split over slavery in the nineteenth century, resulting in a general division of North and South among Baptist congregations. See also **Southern Baptists**.

Bar Mitzvah/Bat (or Bas) Mitzvah: All branches of modern Judaism—Conservative, Reform, and Orthodox—recognize the age of maturity in young men at 13 with the religious ceremony of Bar Mitzvah. At this time, boys are expected to observe all the commandments and participate in religious life as adults. In Conservative and Reform Judaism, the religious adulthood of girls is recognized between the ages of 12 and 14 with a similar ceremony known as Bat (or Bas) Mitzvah.

Bible: The collection of ancient writings that form the doctrinal foundation of Christianity is known as the *Bible*. Consisting of two main parts—the Old Testament and the New Testament—the *Bible*'s contents include books of Jewish law and history, the teachings of pre-Christian prophets, letters to early Christian believers from apostles who were followers of Jesus, and many examples of poetry, songs, and wisdom writings. The canon of Biblical works in the Roman Catholic tradition includes six books that do not appear in the Protestant *Bible*. These six works, along with six more texts—some original, some considered additions to Biblical writings—form what is known as the Protestant Apocrypha. The Jewish scriptures, which include the books of the Protestant Old Testament (albeit differently ordered), are also sometimes called the Hebrew *Bible*. The *Bible* has been translated into more languages than any other book in the world. See also **Christianity**.

Buddhism: A major world religion, Buddhism was founded in northeastern India and is based on the teachings of Siddhartha Gautama, better known as the Buddha or the Enlightened One. Buddhism has been influential not only in India, but in Tibet, Nepal, and Mongolia, and the eastern and southeastern Asian countries of China, Japan, Taiwan, Korea, and Vietnam, as well. Buddhist practices are observed in many different forms throughout the world, including in the United States and other Western countries, even among adherents of other faith traditions. See also **Tibetan Buddhism** and **Zen Buddhism**.

Catholicism: The history, doctrines, and practices of the Roman Catholic Church and its adherents are generally referred to as Catholicism. The Roman Catholic Church is the largest single branch of Christianity, and among its doctrines is the belief that the supreme earthly authority in matters of faith is the bishop of Rome, better known as the pope. Roman Catholicism has had a profound impact on the history and cultures of the world, particularly in Europe, the United States, and Latin America.

Channeling: A New Age term that refers to supernatural communication from an unseen entity, usually a deceased person, through the body or voice of a living person who is typically in a trance or a trance-like state. The living person is said to be an intermediary, or channel, through which such communication may occur.

Christianity: A major world religion with adherents and practitioners on all continents and in most countries of the world, Christianity is built around the life, death, and return to life of Jesus Christ. Although there are several main branches of Christianity, including Orthodox, Roman Catholic, and Protestant, and countless subdivisions within these major categories, there are certain elements of the religion that appear, in one form or another, throughout the range of Christian belief systems. The holy writings of Christianity are known as the *Bible*. Major religious observances in Christianity include Easter, which commemorates the death and resurrection—coming back to life—of Jesus; Pentecost, which celebrates the revelation of the Holy Spirit of God to the earliest groups of Christian believers; and Christmas, which marks the birth of Jesus Christ. See also ***Bible*, Catholicism**, and **Protestantism**.

Christian Science: Founded in Boston in 1879 by Mary Baker Eddy, Christian Science is a religion based on the healings attributed to Jesus in the New Testament. Eddy taught that these healings were simply the working of God through spiritual law, rather than divine or miraculous interventions, and that believers could rely on prayer, rather than on conventional medicine, for physical healing. The teachings and doctrines of Christian Science are based on three texts: the *Bible*; Eddy's treatise, *Science and Health*, which was first published in 1875; and her *Manual of the Mother Church*, written in 1895.

Conservative Judaism: A branch of American Judaism that integrates Jewish law and heritage with modern life in the tradition of Eastern European Jews. Conservative

Judaism was founded by Solomon Schechter, a Romanian-American scholar whose research and teaching in both England and the United States in the late nineteenth and early twentieth centuries led to the founding of the United Synagogue of America, which remains one of the primary institutions of Conservative Judaism. Elements of Conservative Judaism include respect for the cultural and scriptural heritage of Judaism, flexibility in applying Judaic law, and community among Jewish believers. See also **Judaism**.

Creationism: A wide range of beliefs about the origins and subsequent development of the universe and of life on earth, all of which are based upon on the actions of a miraculous, omnipotent, supreme being by whose power all life was created. While creationists as a group reject the theory of evolution, they do not agree among themselves on all aspects of creationist theories. Some creationists use scientific evidence to support their beliefs.

Creeds: A religious creed is the summarization of the main articles of faith of a particular belief system. In Christianity, the Apostles' Creed, dating to the second century, was the first formal statement of doctrine. It is still used by many Christian churches at the beginning of the twenty-first century, with some revisions and adaptations.

Cults: In religious terminology, a cult is a group of people who share a set of beliefs or practices that are generally considered extremist and are led by a charismatic, often authoritarian, leader. Membership in a cult usually results in a major lifestyle change, and cult members are often required to cease all contact with friends and family members who are not also members of the cult.

Deacons: In Christian churches, the role of deacon ranges from that of an ordained minister or assistant in ministry to that of an unordained, but specially commissioned, volunteer. In Catholicism, deacons assist priests in worship services, particularly through the reading of scripture. In Protestant churches, deacons are generally not ordained, and they usually assume a role in congregational leadership or assistance with mission and outreach programs.

Denominations: Within Protestant Christianity, there are many denominations, or large groups of churches that share a common name, similar worship style, or doctrinal beliefs. Each denomination may embody a range of unique subdivisions, as well. Examples of Protestant denominations are Baptist, Episcopal, Lutheran, Methodist, and Presbyterian. Denominations are sometimes referred to as sects, but that term is more appropriately applied to much smaller, individualized groups that deliberately separate themselves from a larger denominational identity in terms of doctrine, orthodoxy, and practice.

Dogmatics: "Dogma" is a doctrine or a collection of doctrines associated with a particular belief system. Dogmatics is an aspect of theology that focuses on the study and explication of these doctrines.

Dutch Reformed: A Christian tradition with theological roots in the Protestant Reformation of the sixteenth century and ethnic roots in the Netherlands and Germany. The first Dutch Reformed church in America was founded in 1628, but today most American churches based in this movement are considered separate from those in Europe. See also **Protestantism**.

Eastern Orthodoxy: A branch of Christianity, separate from Catholicism and Protestantism, whose rites, traditions, and practices originated in the fifth-century church of the Byzantine Empire. In Eastern Orthodoxy, the patriarch of Constantinople, an office similar to the papacy in Catholicism, is recognized as the honorary head of the church on earth. Christianity's first major split occurred during the Byzantine Empire, resulting in the Eastern church, which was centered in Constantinople, and the Western church, which was centered in Rome.

End-Times: In biblical terms, the years preceding and following the prophecied return of Jesus to earth are called the End-Times. Particularly in fundamentalist, conservative Christian denominations, the New Testament book of Revelation is considered to be a guide to what will happen to believers just before and after the second coming of Christ. Although the text was written during the first century, some believers in each generation interpret the geopolitical, economic, and scientific events of their time within the context of the book of Revelation as signs of the End-Times. See also **Apocalypse** and **Revelation**.

Evangelism: The organized dissemination of religious ideas, through preaching, printed materials, electronic media, and other means. It is practiced in numerous religious traditions, both in local communities and through worldwide programs (including missionary work).

Fundamentalism: In Protestantism in the late nineteenth century, a conservative movement called Fundamentalism began to promote religious doctrines including the literal truth of the *Bible*, the virgin birth of Jesus Christ, and the physical resurrection of Christ. The fundamentalist movement cut across denominational lines in response to an increase in scientific, rather than spiritual, views of the world, especially the theory of evolution and the study of the *Bible* from a literary and historic perspective. Although the impact of Fundamentalism weakened during the 1930s, it remains an element of conservative Christianity in the United States today.

Gnosticism: The second and third centuries saw the development of the doctrines of Gnosticism, a religious movement with roots in Christianity but practices and philosophies that differed significantly from those of orthodox Christianity. The Gnostics believed that the divine nature of God was trapped in the lesser nature of human bodies, and that spiritual salvation of the imprisoned soul was dependent on the mystical, esoteric acquisition of divine knowledge through faith.

Gospels: In the New Testament of the *Bible*, the Gospels are the four accounts of the life, teachings, death, and resurrection of Jesus Christ. Three of the texts—Matthew, Mark, and Luke—are called the "Synoptic Gospels" because they provide the same general portrayal of the life of Christ. The fourth of the Gospels is John. The term "gospel" is also used occasionally to refer to the teachings of religious leaders.

Hinduism: One of the major world religions, Hinduism is a widely varied collection of philosophical and religious ideas and cultural practices that originated in India. Central to the essence of Hinduism is a belief in reincarnation and the worship of a supreme being that can manifest itself in many forms. The holy writings of Hinduism include the *Vedas*, the oldest of which may date back to 1300 BC, and the *Upanishads*, dating to c. 600 BC.

Islam: Islam, a major world religion, has its roots in the teachings of Muhammad about Allah, as revealed through the holy text known as the *Koran*. Those who practice Islam are called Muslims. Islam was founded in Arabia and is practiced worldwide, particularly in the Middle East and other parts of Africa and Asia, as well as portions of Europe. In Islam, there is only one God—Allah—whose roles include the creation, maintenance, direction, and judgment of the world. See also ***Koran*** and **Muslims**.

Judaism: One of the oldest religions of the world, Judaism originated in what is now the Middle East. Many of its doctrines about an omnipotent, creator God are shared by Christianity. Judaism consists of a cultural and religious system of laws, customs, and rituals that have evolved over thousands of years, based on the writings of the *Torah*, or scriptural texts, and the teachings of the *Talmud*, rabbinical writings that reflect historical commentary on the scriptures. In America, contemporary Judaism takes on three basic forms: Reform, which is the most liberal; Conservative, which seeks to integrate modern life and traditional Jewish law; and Orthodox, which includes a spectrum of traditional groups that seek to preserve the separateness and rituals of Jewish religion and culture. See also ***Talmud*** and ***Torah***.

Koran: The sacred scripture of the Islamic religion, the *Koran* contains the revelations of Allah to Muhammad, as recorded by the followers of Muhammad. The earliest collection of writings that would become the *Koran* was compiled in the 630s, after the death of Muhammad. The Koran includes 114 chapters that cover Islamic codes of behavior and belief for religious, military, legal, commercial, and civil life. Doctrinal teachings of the *Koran* hold that there is only one God and one true religion, that all of humankind will experience a final judgment, and that throughout history, God has sent prophets to turn people back to the truth. In the Islamic tradition, the *Koran* is believed to be the complete and holy word of Allah, and copies of the *Koran* are handled with the utmost reverence. See also **Islam**.

Lutherans: In the sixteenth century, German monk Martin Luther tried to reform the Western Christian church, but his efforts resulted instead in the division of the church into Roman Catholicism, from which he was excommunicated, and Protestantism, of which Lutheranism was one of the original four subgroups. Lutherans are members of any of several Lutheran denominations worldwide, all of which are founded on the principles of the Protestant Reformation as initiated by Martin Luther.

Mandala: A geometric design, usually circular, which is used as a meditation tool in Buddhism and Hinduism. Buddhist religious texts called tantras describe many different mandalas, each of which is designed for a unique type of practitioner. Despite individual differences that exist from one mandala to another, the basic structure and purpose of all mandalas is essentially the same.

Martyr: One who remains loyal to religious principles and beliefs in the face of persecution, suffering death in defense of his or her faith. In many religious traditions, martyrdom is considered the ultimate practice of faith and is worthy of recognition and admiration on the part of the faithful.

Mennonites: Protestant Christians with roots in the Anabaptist movement of sixteenth century Switzerland and Holland, which, among other things, urges separation of church and state, views the Bible as the ultimate authority, and rejects the concept of infant baptism. Mennonites traditionally refuse to be involved in military activity, reject a state-sanctioned religion, and embrace a community-centered lifestyle of faith and simplicity. More conservative Mennonite groups may be recognized by plain dress and a separateness from society that is similar to but not as complete as that of the Amish. Mennonite communities are historically located in rural farm areas of the United States, particularly in Pennsylvania and the southern Great Lakes states, as well as in Germany and the Netherlands.

Methodists: Methodists are Protestant Christians whose doctrines and style of worship, study, and service originated in the early eighteenth century in England. Methodism was transported to the United States in the years preceding the American Revolution, and it was spread throughout the country and the frontier through the ministry of circuit riders—preachers who traveled from town to town to establish and develop congregations—as well as through periodic revival meetings. The United Methodist church is one of the mainline Protestant Christian denominations in the United States.

Monasticism: Monasticism is a way of contemplative religious life that requires practitioners to withdraw from the world, either alone or as part of a monastic community such as a monastery or convent, so as to seek spiritual perfection. Monastic communities exist in Buddhism and Christianity, and the practice of becoming a hermit in order to seek truth is an accepted expression of faith in upper caste Hinduism.

Morality: A system of ideas and directives that govern personal or societal conduct, as based on a set of beliefs that judge certain actions as right and others as wrong. Many religious traditions include morality as a component of creed or practice, but not all traditions share the same principles of morality.

Mormons: Members of the Church of Jesus Christ of Latter-Day Saints are also called Mormons. Mormonism was founded in 1830 in the United States by Joseph Smith. Both the *Bible* and the *Book of Mormon* are believed to be the inspired word of God. Although Mormon beliefs are founded on principles of the Judeo-Christian tradition, certain historic and modern doctrines differ sharply from those of mainline Christianity. Family life, worldwide mission work, and the preservation of a conservative, church-centered lifestyle are important components of contemporary Mormonism.

Muslims: Followers of the Islamic faith. See also **Islam**.

Mysticism: An experientially based approach to understanding God or the supreme reality of a given religious tradition through meditation (personal reflection and contemplation) or other intuitive practice. Many religious traditions acknowledge a mystical aspect of theology or practice, although most do not mandate—or in some cases, willingly embrace—such expressions of faith. The practice of mysticism is generally intended to result in serenity, spiritual growth, and an increased harmony between one's inner life and one's outer circumstances. The outward form of mysticism varies among religions, and the authenticity of a mystical experience is generally evaluated by the degree to which the practitioner's life is enhanced as a result of the experience, rather than by the outward appearance of the experience itself.

Near-Death Experience: People who have experienced moments of what may be called clinical death before being medically revived often report having been transported through a tunnel into a bright light where they spoke with divine entities or departed loved ones. Occasionally these experiences involve the memory of scenes from the room in which they were unconscious patients, but from a disembodied, spirit-like state. Called near-death experiences, these events are believed by some to prove the existence of a benevolent God and a peaceful afterlife.

New Age: A term used to categorize a variety of beliefs, practices, and expressions of spirituality that fall outside the mainstream of Western religious and philosophical traditions. The earliest roots of New Age thinking in the United States may be attributed to the founding of the Theosophical Society in 1875, which promoted a spiritualistic, mystical approach to understanding the nature of God. Ancient, pre-Christian pagan traditions and the consciousness-raising philosophies of the 1960s countercul-

ture are also considered to be major influences on New Age thinking. The New Age movement of the 1980s and 1990s is reflected in music, art, literature, politics, philosophy, medicine, and spiritual practice. The "New Age" label is loosely applied to diverse philosophies including Wicca, Zen Buddhism, agnosticism, atheism, and feminism, and to such practices as channeling, psychic communication, meditation, and yoga.

Occult: In religious terms, "the occult" is used to refer to spiritual or ritualistic beliefs and activities related to supernatural and unexplained or secret phenomena that are outside the realm of Christian beliefs. New Age philosophies and practices are often labeled "occult" by conservative Christians. "Occult" also means secret or mysterious, and it is sometimes used to describe ancient secret rituals in Judaism or Orthodox Christianity.

Orthodox Judaism: A branch of Judaism that embraces as modern law the writings of the *Torah*, as interpreted by ancient rabbis and sages in the *Talmud*. In Orthodox Judaism, men and women have prescribed roles in public, private, and religious life, and Jews are required to observe the lifestyle laws set forth in the sacred writings of the religious tradition, which often set them apart from the rest of the modern world. See also **Judaism**, *Talmud*, and *Torah*.

Orthodoxy: In religious terms, "orthodoxy" generally refers to a specific religious tradition, such as Orthodox Judaism or the Eastern Orthodox Church. It may also refer to the traditional and conventional doctrines or practices of a particular religion, as compared to more liberal interpretations or doctrines that challenge or significantly alter any of the basic tenets of that faith system.

Paganism: A general term for pre-Christian, usually nature-based, religious traditions. In Christianity, "pagan" refers to a person who rejects the tenets of the Christian faith. In New Age terminology, a pagan is one who practices any of a variety of ancient traditions, including Wicca, whose roots are found in the rural, seasons-centered rituals and practices of pre-Christian Europe. See also **Wicca**.

Papacy: The Roman Catholic system of church structure and government headed by an ordained clergy member in the office of the Pope. In Roman Catholicism, each elected Pope is believed to be part of the direct line of succession from the apostle Peter, the disciple charged by Jesus Christ with spreading Christianity. The authority of the Pope is supreme within the Roman Catholic tradition. All ordained clergy and communicant members of the Roman Catholic church are to abide by the decrees and doctrines set forth by the Pope.

Paranormal: Phenomena that are outside the range of measurable, scientific proof or explanation, including mental or spiritual abilities that are not commonly shared by the majority of a given population. Mental telepathy, psychic powers, and channeling—serving as a medium for communication with the deceased—are examples of paranormal phenomena often associated with New Age spiritual beliefs and practices. See also **Channeling**.

Pentecostal: Christian congregations or individual believers whose worship experience includes outward displays of "being filled" with the Holy Spirit (part of the Christian Trinity, along with the Father and the Son). This is in reference to the New Testament description of the occasion of Pentecost, during which the apostles and other believers in Jesus received God in the form of the Holy Spirit. Characteristics of Pentecostal worship often but not always include "speaking in tongues," which is audible prayer or singing in languages unknown to either the speaker or the hearer; divine healing by the "laying on of hands"; and exuberant clapping and singing that increases in intensity and emotional fervor. Pentecostalism is found in a variety of denominations that do not share a common set of doctrines or practices. The roots of Pentecostalism in the United States can be traced to Los Angeles and the revival movement of the Negro Holiness Church there in 1906.

Presbyterians: Presbyterianism is a type of Protestant Christian church structure and government that bases its theology and worship on the Reformation traditions of John Calvin, a Swiss theologian of the sixteenth century. The church is governed by elders and presbyters in a structure that balances power between clergy and church members and between individual congregations and larger bodies of churches known as a presbyteries, synods, and a general assembly of churches worldwide. Presbyterians are members of individual Presbyterian churches, which are considered mainline Protestant churches in the United States. The first American Presbyterian congregations began meeting in New York and New England in the 1640s.

Protestantism: During the sixteenth century, several European Christian clergymen and theologians unsuccessfully tried to reform what was then known as the Western Church. Instead, what would later be called the Protestant Reformation resulted in a division of the Western Church into Roman Catholicism, which continued to be led by the Pope, and Protestantism, which rejected the supremacy of the Pope and believed in salvation by faith rather than by works. Protestantism itself was soon subdivided into four major traditions: Lutheran, based on the doctrines of Martin Luther; Calvinist, upon which Presbyterianism is based; Anabaptist, from which emerged both the Mennonite and Amish traditions; and the Anglican, which is the root of the Church of England and the Episcopal Church in the United States.

Redemption: In Christian theology, redemption is a term applied to the salvation from sin that is available to believers as a result of the sacrifice of the life of Jesus Christ. Within this context, Jesus is called the Redeemer, and believers may be called the Redeemed.

Reform Judaism: A branch of Judaism that embraces historical Judaism but does not require adherents to follow strictly the traditional religious rites and laws in the context of modern life. See also **Judaism**.

Revelation: The final text of the New Testament, the book of Revelation is believed to have been written between AD 81 and 96. It is an apocalyptic writing, filled with allegory and symbolism, that foretells the coming of justice for Christian believers who were at the time being persecuted under the Roman emperor Domitian. The book of Revelation has always been the subject of much interpretation and controversy within the Christian church as scholars and clergy in every generation have re-interpreted the meaning of the text to fit the context of their times. See also **Apocalypse**.

Salvation: In Christian theology, salvation is the deliverance of believers from the control or consequence of sin by the supernatural intervention of God through the death and resurrection of Jesus. In many conservative Protestant traditions, "being saved" means that one has personally accepted this intervention by making a public commitment to follow the teachings of Jesus. In other religious traditions, "salvation" refers to deliverance or protection from danger, problems, or other negative consequences by a supreme being, higher power, or system of thought and belief.

Santeria: With roots in West Africa and the Caribbean, Santeria is a religion similar to Voodoo practiced in parts of the United States. Santeria became a recognized religious tradition during the nineteenth century as West Africans from the Yoruba culture were sent to Cuba as slaves. As in Voodoo, Santeria combines elements of Roman Catholicism and the animism and magic of West African spiritual traditions. The ritual slaughter of animals for ceremonies has led to controversy in parts of the United States where Santeria is practiced. See also **Voodoo**.

Satyagraha: The policy of nonviolent resistance pioneered by Mohandas K. (Mahatma) Gandhi in India as a way to seek political reform. Martin Luther King, Jr., adopted many of the basic tenets of satyagraha for use during the early years of the civil rights movement in the United States.

Shamanism: An animistic religion found in certain Native American groups and within some groups in northern Asia. Shamanism's basic tenet is that there are individuals—shamans—who are born to be mediators between the visible and spirit worlds. To become a shaman, an individual must endure fasts, seclusion, and other difficult circumstances that result in visions and dreams. The shaman may be called upon to heal and provide guidance to the people as a medium through which the spirits of ancestors communicate with the visible world.

Shinto: Over the course of thousands of years, Shinto, an ancient Japanese religion, evolved from a collection of spiritual practices without a name into a national religion with patriotic components by the nineteenth century. In the sixth century, the name Shinto was designated to distinguish traditional native practices from Buddhism and Confucianism (the doctrine of social interaction and inner virtue set forth by Confucius), both of which had been introduced to Japan through China. Buddhist and Shinto practices merged in the ninth century, and in the eighteenth century, a revival of Shinto as the state religion took place. In the aftermath of World War II, nationalistic Shinto doctrines were eliminated from school teachings and public life, but the spiritual aspects of Shinto continue to be part of the religious fabric of Japanese culture.

Snake-Handling: A worship and faith practice engaged in by certain rural, usually Appalachian, fundamentalist Christian denominations. The successful handling of poisonous snakes as a part of public worship is considered to be a test of holiness and faith in God among these Christians. When snake bites result in death, it is said to be the will of God.

Southern Baptists: In the Baptist tradition, congregations may structure and govern themselves according to local standards. During the nineteenth century, American Baptist churches split along North-South lines, primarily over the issue of slavery. In 1845, the churches of the South formed the Southern Baptist Convention. In 1907, the Baptist churches in the North formed the Northern Baptist Convention, which is now known as the American Baptist Churches in the U.S.A. Although the denominations are not limited by geographic boundaries, there tend to be more churches of the Southern Baptist Convention in the South, and those congregations continue to be more conservative in theology and politics than are the churches of the former Northern Convention. See also **Baptists**.

Stigmata: An unusual phenomenon associated with religious ecstasy or hysteria, generally in a person who has devoted his or her life to contemplative or other cloistered Christian service. Blood or sores appear on the body of an individual in ways that clearly resemble the crucifixion wounds of Jesus Christ. Observations of this supernatural occurrence include marks on the hands, feet, and side, and sometimes wounds that correspond to those that would have been made by whips, scourges, and the crown of thorns placed on the head of Jesus. St. Francis of Assisi (c.1181-1226), founder of the Franciscan Order, is the first known person to show signs of the stigmata.

Sufism: A mystical aspect of Islam, Sufism came into conflict with traditional Islamic theology during the seventh century, but by the early twelfth century, Sufism was reconciled with and integrated into orthodox Islam. The Sufi mystic's path to spiritual maturity involves seven stages of separating from the world that include repentance, abstinence, renunciation, poverty, patience, trust in Allah, and obedience to the will of Allah. Poetry, dance, meditation, and music are characteristic expressions of Sufism.

Syncretism: The fusion of multiple beliefs or practices from different philosophical or religious traditions.

Talmud: A collection of Jewish rabbinical writings about the *Torah* and the laws that govern Jewish life. The *Talmud* includes the Mishnah, which dates from around AD 200, and the Gemara, the second part of the *Talmud*, which is primarily commentary about the first. Together, these comprise the foundation of religious authority and rabbinical wisdom governing Orthodox Judaism. See also **Judaism** and *Torah*.

Tibetan Buddhism: Sometimes called Lamaism, Tibetan Buddhism is the traditional religion of Tibet and Mongolia. Worship components include the recitation of prayers and sacred writings, and the chanting of holy songs accompanied by drums, trumpets, and horns of other kinds. Rituals include meditation, yoga, and mystical incantations. Sacred writings include more than 1000 works from India and China said to contain the teachings and wisdom of the Buddha. The religious leaders are known as lamas, and their supreme earthly leaders are the Dalai Lama and the Panchen, or Bogodo, Lama.

Torah: The foundation text of Jewish law and lifestyle, the *Torah* is sometimes called the Pentateuch, referring to the first five books of the Old Testament, or Hebrew Bible. The term "Torah" is sometimes applied to the entire canon of Jewish scriptural writings that include law, religious guidance, and rabbinic commentary on the scriptures themselves. See also **Judaism** and *Talmud*.

Voodoo: A religion associated primarily with Haiti but also practiced in Brazil, Trinidad, Cuba, and parts of the southern United States, especially Louisiana, Voodoo synthesizes elements of Catholicism with animism and magic from western African religious traditions. Components of Voodoo include ancestor worship, drumming, dancing, dreams, trances, rituals, and belief in a high god, Bon Dieu, who rules over local saints and deities.

Wicca: A nature and fertility-centered religion, Wicca is based on the lore and rituals of European paganism. The practices of Wicca are also known as witchcraft. The modern revival of this pre-Christian religion can be traced to the 1950s in England and the 1960s in the United States. Along with Wicca, similar neopagan religions with roots in ancient Celtic, Egyptian, Greek, and Nordic beliefs and practices have also been revived during the twentieth century as part of what is called the New Age movement. See also **Paganism**.

Zazen: A Japanese word for the silent, sitting meditation associated with Zen Buddhism. See also **Zen Buddhism**.

Zen Buddhism: Zen Buddhism is a set of Chinese and Japanese doctrines that deny faith and devotion as the ways to enlightenment, pointing instead to the practices of meditation, self-contemplation, and intuition as the keys to one's spiritual health and well-being.

Zionism: The worldwide effort in the late nineteenth and early twentieth centuries to re-establish a Jewish state in Palestine was known as Zionism. Jews from all parts of the world participated in a massive and voluntary relocation that resulted in the 1948 creation of the modern state of Israel. Contemporary Zionism is centered on the continued development and defense of Israel.

Non-Fiction Titles

1

PETER R. ACKROYD, Editor
C.F. EVANS, Co-Editor
S.C. GREENSLADE, Co-Editor
G.W.H. LAMPE, Co-Editor

The Cambridge History of the Bible

(London: Cambridge University Press, 1963-1970)

Category: Religious Commentaries
Subject(s): Bible; History
Age range(s): Adult

Summary: A work in three volumes, *The Cambridge History of the Bible* is one of the most comprehensive and respected reference sources available to biblical scholars. Volume One covers the period of time from the first writings through the time of Jerome; Volume Two is titled ''The West from the Fathers to the Reformation''; Volume Three covers the West from the Reformation to the mid-20th century.

Other books you might like:

Julio Trebolle Barrera, *The Jewish Bible and the Christian Bible: An Introduction to the History of the Bible*, 1998
F.F. Bruce, *The History of the Bible in English: From the Earliest Versions*, 1978
Laurence M. Vance, *A Brief History of English Bible Translations*, 1993

2

MARGOT ADLER

Drawing Down the Moon: Witches, Druids, Goddess-Worshippers and Other Pagans in America Today

(New York: Viking, 1979)

Category: New Age (Nonfiction)
Subject(s): Wicca; Witches and Witchcraft
Age range(s): Young Adult-Adult

Summary: Adler's book remains the single best overview and introduction to Wicca and goddess religions in America. Written at a time when Wiccan religion and the pagan religions had not yet generated very much attention, Adler's book contains interviews with practitioners of Wiccan art and goddess worship that reveal lively and dynamic religious movements. Adler's book is an indispensable history of paganism in contemporary America.

Other books by the same author:
Heretic's Heart: A Journey through Spirit and Revolution, 1997

Other books you might like:

Zsuzsanna E. Budapest, *Grandmother Moon: Lunar Magic in Our Lives: Spells, Rituals, Goddesses, Legends, and Emotions under the Moon*, 1991
Scott Cunningham, *Wicca: A Guide for the Solitary Practitioner*, 1988
Marian Green, *Natural Magic*, 1997
Shekhinah Mountainwater, *Ariadne's Thread: A Workbook of Goddess Magic*, 1991
Starhawk, *The Spiral Dance: A Rebirth of the Ancient Religion of the Great Goddess*, 1979

3

MORTIMER J. ADLER

The Angels and Us

(New York: Macmillan, 1982)

Category: Theology
Subject(s): Angels; Philosophy; Religion
Age range(s): Adult

Summary: In *The Angels and Us*, Mortimer J. Adler considers the images of angels throughout history, particularly in religious and philosophical thought. The philosopher discusses whether or not angels exist, and explores the hierarchies of angels as they are evident in literature, art, and religious teachings.

Other books by the same author:
Desires, Right and Wrong: The Ethics of Enough, 1991
Truth in Religion: The Plurality of Religions and the Unity of Truth, 1990
Reforming Education: The Opening of the American Mind, 1988
Six Great Ideas: Truth, Goodness, Beauty, Liberty, Equality, Justice: Ideas We Judge by, Ideas We Act On, 1981

Other books you might like:
Sophy Burnham, *A Book of Angels: Reflections on Angels Past and Present and True Stories of How They Touch Our Lives*, 1990
Massimo Cacciari, *The Necessary Angel*, 1994
Matthew Fox, *The Physics of Angels: Exploring the Realm Where Science and Spirit Meet*, 1996
Deborah R. Geis, *Approaching the Millennium: Essays on Angels in America*, 1997
Nancy Grubb, *Angels in Art*, 1995

4

MORTIMER J. ADLER

How to Think about God: A Guide for the 20th-Century Pagan

(New York: Macmillan, 1980)

Category: Theology
Subject(s): Religion; Philosophy; God
Age range(s): Adult

Summary: Mortimer J. Adler, well-known 20th-century philosopher and thinker, offers an approach to belief in God that circumvents science, faith, and mysticism as foundations for the existence of God. He returns to the arguments offered by Aristotle and Catholic theologian Aquinas, updating them for contemporary times. He uses the process of rational thought to lead the reader to see that it is not necessary to simply accept the existence of God through the suspension of disbelief.

Other books by the same author:
Desires, Right and Wrong: The Ethics of Enough, 1991
Truth in Religion: The Plurality of Religions and the Unity of Truth, 1990
Reforming Education: The Opening of the American Mind, 1988
Six Great Ideas: Truth, Goodness, Beauty, Liberty, Equality, Justice: Ideas We Judge by, Ideas We Act On, 1981

Other books you might like:
Francis A. Schaeffer, *The Church at the End of the Twentieth Century*, 1970
Francis A. Schaeffer, *The God Who Is There: Speaking Historic Christianity into the Twentieth Century*, 1968
Paul Tillich, *What Is Religion?*, 1969

5

MOLLY EMMA AITKEN, Editor
SIMON CHAPUT, Illustrator

Meeting the Buddha: On Pilgrimage in Buddhist India

(New York: Riverhead Books, 1995)

Category: Essays
Subject(s): Travel; Buddhism; Pilgrims and Pilgrimages
Age range(s): Young Adult-Adult

Summary: The seven most important destinations of Buddhist pilgrimages in India are highlighted in this collection of writings and photographs. Essays from modern writers including the Dalai Lama, Allen Ginsberg, and Anne Waldman mingle with centuries-old accounts of Buddhist pilgrims and writings from sacred Buddhist texts. The spiritual aspects of sacred pilgrimages over the course of many centuries are illuminated through pictures and words.

Other books you might like:
Peter Gold, *Tibetan Pilgrimage*, 1988
Corneille Jest, *Tales of the Turquoise: A Pilgrimage in Dolpo*, 1993
    Margaret Stein, translator
Robert Thurman, *Circling the Sacred Mountain: A Spiritual Adventure through the Himalayas*, 1999
    Tad Wise, co-author
Jennifer Westwood, *Sacred Journeys: An Illustrated Guide to Pilgrimages around the World*, 1997

6

ROBERT AITKEN

Taking the Path of Zen

(San Francisco: North Point Press, 1982)

Category: Doctrine
Subject(s): Buddhism; Meditation
Age range(s): Adult

Summary: *Taking the Path of Zen* offers a handbook for practicing Zen meditation. Robert Aitken provides instruction and inspiration to both experienced and novice practitioners, with guidance for developing and maintaining correct posture and breathing, as well as explanations of Zen Buddhism's Three Treasures and Ten Precepts. Aitken's text addresses common problems encountered in practicing *zazen* (Zen meditation).

Other books by the same author:
The Dragon Who Never Sleeps: Adventures in Zen Buddhist Practice, 1990
The Mind of Clover: Essays in Zen Buddhist Ethics, 1984

Other books you might like:
Charlotte Joko Beck, *Nothing Special: Living Zen*, 1993
    Steve Smith, co-editor
Nelson Foster, *The Roaring Stream: A New Zen Reader*, 1996
    Jack Shoemaker, co-editor

Philip Kapleau, *Awakening to Zen: The Teachings of Roshi Philip Kapleau*, 1997
Polly Young-Eisendrath, Rafe Martin, editors

7

MITCH ALBOM

Tuesdays with Morrie: An Old Man, a Young Man, and Life's Greatest Lesson

(New York: Doubleday, 1997)

Category: Biography; Autobiography
Subject(s): Death; Illness; Teacher-Student Relationships
Age range(s): Young Adult-Adult
Time period(s): 1990s
Locale(s): West Newton, Massachusetts; Detroit, Michigan

Summary: What would you do if you suddenly discovered you had only a short time to live? And even more difficult to answer: What would you do if you found out someone who had mentored you in your formative years but whom you'd since lost touch with was this dying man? A chance television appearance on "Nightline" reunites award-winning sports columnist Mitch Albom with his former college professor Morrie Schwartz during the latter's fight with amyothropic lateral sclerosis (ALS), also known as Lou Gehrig's Disease. Morrie manages in the last few months of his life to provide Mitch with a final lesson-this one about the importance of savoring life. Through weekly conversations, recorded by Albom, the dying man shares his experiences and inspires both his student and the reader.

Awards the book has won:
Christopher Award, Books for Adults, 1998

Other books by the same author:
Fab Five: Basketball, Trash Talk, the American Dream, 1993
The Live Albom: The Best of Detroit Free Press Sports Columnist Mitch Albom, 1988

Other books you might like:
Jane Bluestein, *Mentors, Masters, and Mrs. MacGregor: Stories of Teachers Making a Difference*, 1995
Kenny Kemp, *Dad Was a Carpenter: A Memoir*, 1999
N. Michael Murphy, *The Wisdom of Dying: Practices for Living*, 1999
Samuel Lee Oliver, *What the Dying Teach Us: Lessons on Living*, 1998
Morrie Schwartz, *Morrie: In His Own Words*, 1999
Joseph Sharp, *Living Our Dying: A Way to the Sacred in Everyday Life*, 1996
Jeff Spoden, *To Honor a Teacher: Students Pay Tribute to Their Most Influential Mentors*, 1999
Ken Standley, *From This High Place: Reflections on Living a Life of Courage and Purpose*, 1997

8

PAT ALEXANDER, Editor

Eerdmans' Book of Christian Poetry

(Grand Rapids, Michigan: Eerdmans, 1981)

Category: Poetry

Subject(s): Christianity; Faith
Age range(s): Children-Adult

Summary: Containing poetry that spans the history of Christianity, *Eerdmans' Book of Christian Poetry* is a classic collection of much-loved inspirational literature. A handy feature of this anthology is an index of first lines, often more memorable than a poem's title. Poems to please people of all ages, plus photos and illustrations throughout, make this a collection that the whole family can enjoy.

Other books by the same author:
What a Wonderful World, 1999
Amazing Bible Mysteries, 1996
My Own Book of Bible Stories, 1993
Eerdman's Family Encyclopedia of the Bible, 1978

Other books you might like:
Donald Davie, *New Oxford Book of Christian Verse*, 1988
Catherine De Vinck, *A Basket of Bread: An Anthology of Selected Poems*, 1997
Thomas P. McDonnell, *Classic Catholic Poetry*, 1988
Lois Rock, *Glimpses of Heaven: Poems and Prayers of Mystery and Wonder*, 1998
Thomas H. Troeger, *Borrowed Light: Hymn Texts, Prayers and Poems*, 1994

9

DANTE ALIGHIERI

The Divine Comedy

(c. 1310)

Category: Poetry
Subject(s): Christianity; Sin
Age range(s): Young Adult-Adult

Summary: "Midway along the journey of our life/I woke to find myself in a dark wood,/for I had wandered off from the straight path," says Dante the pilgrim in the famous opening lines of this epic poem. The action of the poem begins on Maundy Thursday, 1300, and ends one week later. Soon after Dante finds himself in this dark wood, the poet Virgil appears to lead him through the Inferno and Purgatory. In the Inferno, Dante encounters unrepentant sinners being punished appropriately for their crimes. At first, Dante feels pity for these people, but he soon proclaims that they are getting what they deserve. As he climbs into Purgatory, Dante discovers repentant sinners who are trying to make their way to Paradise. In Paradise, Dante finds that everyone concentrates his or her attention on God. Dante's spectacular poem creates a mythic view of heaven and hell that generations of Christians have interpreted literally.

Other books by the same author:
La Vita Nuova, c. 1290

Other books you might like:
Augustine, *Confessions*, c. 400
John Bunyan, *The Pilgrim's Progress*, 1678-1684
Geoffrey Chaucer, *The Canterbury Tales*, c. 1386
John Milton, *Paradise Lost*, 1667
Edmund Spenser, *The Faerie Queene*, c. 1590

10

ROSEMARY ALTEA

Proud Spirit: Lessons, Insights & Healing From "The Voice of the Spirit World"

(New York: Eagle Brook, 1997)

Category: New Age (Nonfiction)
Subject(s): Spiritualism; Afterlife
Age range(s): Young Adult-Adult

Summary: Spiritual medium Rosemary Altea is known for her spirit world communication, acting as a medium for the deceased to send messages to their loved ones left behind on earth. In stories culled from her professional experiences, as well as from her own circumstances, Altea offers answers to questions people ask about what happens in the spirit world beyond death. In addition, she examines many of the world's religious teachings about life, death, and earthly behavior, including the Ten Commandments, and suggests that such formal guidelines may no longer be relevant.

Other books by the same author:
Give the Gift of Healing: A Concise Guide to Spiritual Healing, 1997
The Eagle and the Rose, 1995

Other books you might like:
Bill Guggenheim, *Hello From Heaven!: A New Field of Research Confirms That Life and Love Are Eternal*, 1995
Joel Martin, *Love Beyond Life: The Healing Power of After-Death Communications*, 1997
Joel Martin, *We Don't Die: George Anderson's Conversations with the Other Side*, 1988
James Van Praagh, *Reaching to Heaven: A Spiritual Journey through Life and Death*, 1999

11

ROBERT ALTER, Editor
FRANK KERMODE, Co-Editor

The Literary Guide to the Bible

(Cambridge, Massachusetts: Harvard University Press, 1987)

Category: Religious Commentaries
Subject(s): Criticism; Literature; Bible
Age range(s): Adult

Summary: Renowned literary critics Robert Alter and Frank Kermode turn an analytical and interpretive eye to the writings of the Old and New Testaments in *The Literary Guide to the Bible*. Rather than interpreting meaning from a religious perspective, Alter and Kermode discuss theme, technique, and literary structure as they affect a reader's understanding of various portions of the Bible. Their essays enlighten and educate while drawing the reader into an exploration of the form, origin, and historical significance of each genre of scriptural writing found in the Bible.

Other books by the same author:
The World of Biblical Literature, 1992
The Invention of Hebrew Prose: Modern Fiction and the Language of Realism, 1988

The Art of Biblical Poetry, 1985
The Art of Biblical Narrative, 1981

Other books you might like:
John B. Gabel, *The Bible as Literature: An Introduction*, 1996
Norman K. Gottwald, *The Hebrew Bible: A Socio-Literary Introduction*, 1985
Stephen Prickett, *Words and the Word: Language, Poetics, and Biblical Interpretation*, 1986

12

JOAN WESTER ANDERSON

An Angel to Watch over Me: True Stories of Children's Encounters with Angels

(New York: Ballantine, 1994)

Category: Essays
Subject(s): Poetry; Angels; Children
Age range(s): Children-Adult

Summary: Interest in the personal experiences of children with angels led Joan Wester Anderson to collect material for *An Angel to Watch Over Me*, a follow-up to her bestselling *Where Angels Walk*. The stories in this volume were gathered by visiting with children whose angel visits ranged from a comforting presence during illness to active protection from bodily harm. Prayers, illustrations, and poetic language combine in a book that can be enjoyed at multiple levels by several generations.

Other books by the same author:
The Power of Miracles: Stories of God in the Everyday, 1998
Angels We Have Heard on High: A Book of Seasonal Blessings, 1997
Where Wonders Prevail: True Accounts That Bear Witness to the Existence of Heaven, 1996
Where Miracles Happen: True Stories of Heavenly Encounters, 1994
Where Angels Walk: True Stories of Heavenly Visitors, 1992

Other books you might like:
Nathalie Ladner-Bischoff, *An Angel's Touch: True Stories about Angels, Miracles, and Answers to Prayers*, 1998
Sophy Burnham, *Angel Letters*, 1991
Donna Gates, *The ABCs of Angels*, 1992
Ann Spangler, *An Angel a Day: Stories of Angelic Encounters*, 1994
Nancy Willard, *An Alphabet of Angels*, 1994

13

TERRY A. ANDERSON

Den of Lions: Memoirs of Seven Years

(New York: Crown, 1993)

Category: Autobiography
Subject(s): Hostages; Survival; Loneliness
Age range(s): Adult
Time period(s): 1980s; 1990s (1985-1993)
Locale(s): Lebanon

Summary: A gripping account of seven years in captivity, *Den of Lions: Memoirs of Seven Years* chronicles the experiences of American journalist Terry Anderson, who was taken hostage by Shiite extremists in Lebanon in 1985. During his confinement, Anderson was chained, beaten, and fearful that each day could be his last. However, he found the strength to rise above his circumstances and fight to stay alive, sane, and hopeful. He longed to be reunited with his family, including his daughter, as well as his fiancee who was pregnant at the time of his abduction. Meanwhile, back home, efforts were underway to secure his freedom. Anderson's sister, Peggy Say, and the Associated Press kept the journalist's plight in the public eye.

Other books you might like:

David Jacobsen, *Hostage: My Nightmare in Beirut*, 1991
    Gerald Astor, co-author
Brian Keenan, *An Evil Cradling*, 1992
Anne Maguire, *For Brian's Sake: The Story of the Keenan Sisters*, 1991
Peggy Say, *Forgotten: A Sister's Struggle to Save Terry Anderson, America's Longest-Held Hostage*, 1991
    Peter Knobler, co-author
Terry Waite, *Taken on Trust*, 1993

14

ANONYMOUS

Bhagavad-Gita
(c. 400 BC - AD 400)

Category: Scripture
Subject(s): Hinduism
Age range(s): Young Adult-Adult

Summary: *The Bhagavad-Gita* is one of the most powerful scriptures of Hinduism. The poem itself is a section of the larger Hindu epic called the *Mahabharata*. In the final battle of the Mahabharata, the hero Arjuna is getting ready to go to war with his cousins and uncles. As he prepares, however, he is repulsed by the horrors of war. Krishna, an avatar (incarnation) of the god Vishnu, who is also serving as Arjuna's charioteer, persuades him that by accepting fighting as his dharma (duty), he will be rewarded for his faith. Krishna also explains the love (bhakti) between God and humanity. This discourse between Krishna and Arjun forms the text of the *Bhagavad Gita*. The original texts date back to between 400 BC and AD 400.

Other books you might like:

Anonymous, *Rig Veda*,
    c. 1500 B.C. - 900 B.C.
Juan Mascaro, *The Upanishads*, 1965
    editor; original texts written between 1500 and 200 B.C.
Jagadish Chandra Chatterji, *The Wisdom of the Vedas*, 1980
Diana L. Eck, *Encountering God: A Spiritual Journey From Bozeman to Banaras*, 1993
Wendy Doniger O'Flaherty, *Hindu Myths: A Sourcebook*, 1975

15

ANONYMOUS

The Cloud of Unknowing
(c. 1300)

Category: Devotionals
Subject(s): Christianity; Mysticism
Age range(s): Adult

Summary: This anonymous 14th-century mystical writing claims that God can be known only by the heart and not by the intellect. Thus, the attempt of the human soul to achieve unity with God through prayer and contemplation involves an element of ignorance. Numerous editions appear in English translation, including two versions in 1997.

Other books you might like:

Meister Eckhart, *The Best of Meister Eckhart*, 1993
    Hacyon Backhouse, editor
Saint John of the Cross, *Dark Night of the Soul*, 1619
William A. Meninger, *The Loving Search for God: Contemplative Prayer and the Cloud of Unknowing*, 1994
Saint Teresa of Avila, *Interior Castle*, c. 1572
    E. Allison Peers, translator
Simone Weil, *Waiting for God*, 1951
    Emma Craufurd, translator

16

ANONYMOUS

A Course in Miracles
(Mill Valley, California: Foundation for Inner Peace, 1978)

Category: New Age (Nonfiction); Self-Help
Subject(s): Miracles; Faith; Self-Esteem
Age range(s): Adult

Summary: Taking its wisdom from a combination of 12-step programs and many other self-esteem programs of the last thirty years, this popular course attempts to help people to see the miraculous in the ordinary. The original text was compiled by Helen Schucman between 1965 and 1972 by a process she called "internal dictation." The original work has inspired many supplemental materials and spin-offs during the 1980s and 1990s.

Other books you might like:

Karen Casey, *Daily Meditations on Practicing the Course*, 1995
Joan M. Gattuso, *A Course in Love: Powerful Teachings on Love, Sex, and Personal Fulfillment*, 1997
Ann Lasater, *Affirming Miracles (How to Use Affirmations to Change Your Life)*, 1998
D. Patrick Miller, *Complete Story of the Course: The History, the People, and the Controversies Behind a Course in Miracles*, 1997
Kenneth Wapnick, *Absence From Felicity: The Story of Helen Schucman and Her Scribing of a Course in Miracles*, 1991
Marianne Williamson, *A Return to Love: Reflections on the Principles of a Course in Miracles*, 1992

17

ANONYMOUS

Little Flowers of St. Francis
(c. 1300)

Category: Devotionals
Subject(s): Christianity; Prayer
Age range(s): Young Adult-Adult

Summary: To signal his conversion to Christianity, the wealthy Francis (c. 1182-1226) gave up all of his worldly possessions, including his clothes, and began to live according to vows of poverty, chastity, and obedience. The poems and prayers in this collection of popular legends about the saint's life capture Francis' intense nature, mysticism, and his overwhelming love of God. Originally written in Italian, the work has appeared in numerous English translations.

Other books you might like:
Julien Green, *God's Fool: The Life and Times of Francis of Assisi*, 1985
  Peter Heinegg, translator
Thomas a Kempis, *The Imitation of Christ*, 1932
William Law, *A Serious Call to a Devout and Holy Life: Adapted to the State and Condition of All Orders of Christians*, 1729
  Numerous revised editions of this classic by Law (1686-1761) are available.
John Michael Talbot, *The Lessons of St. Francis: How to Bring Simplicity and Spirituality into Your Daily Life*, 1997
Helen Waddell, *The Desert Fathers*, c. 1936
  This volume by Waddell (1889-1965) is part of the series of Vintage Spiritual Classics, a set of classic religious literature.

18

ANONYMOUS

Ramayana
(c. 400 BC - AD 400)

Category: Scripture
Subject(s): Hinduism
Age range(s): Young Adult-Adult

Summary: Written more than 2,000 years ago, the *Ramayana* is one of the two great epics of Hinduism. The *Mahabharata* is the other. The *Ramayana* tells the tale of King Rama, who is an avatar (incarnation) of Lord Vishnu, who must rescue Sita, his queen, from the evil demon Ravanna. The epic recounts Rama's numerous valiant struggles to overcome seemingly impossible obstacles to defeat Ravanna. These exploits make Rama an ideal of honor and morality, and the epic is often reenacted in popular plays and festivals.

Other books you might like:
Anonymous, *Bhagavad-Gita*,
  c. 400 B.C. - 400 A.D.
Alain Danielou, *The Myths and Gods of India: The Classic Work on Hindu Polytheism From the Princeton Bollingen Series*, 1991

Diana L. Eck, *Darsan: Seeing the Divine Image in India*, 1981
Eva Jansen, *The Book of Hindu Imagery: Gods, Manifestations and Their Meanings*, 1993
Wendy Doniger O'Flaherty, *Other People's Myths: The Cave of Echoes*, 1988

19

GEORGE APPLETON, Editor

The Oxford Book of Prayer
(New York: Oxford University Press, 1985)

Category: Prayer
Subject(s): Christianity; Judaism; Islam
Age range(s): Young Adult-Adult

Summary: *The Oxford Book of Prayer* is a comprehensive collection of prayers in English from many faith traditions. The majority of prayers included represent Christianity in categories such as prayer of adoration, prayers from Scripture, prayers of Christians (famous and not), prayer as listening, and prayers of the church, which constitute denominationally characteristic prayers from the spectrum of Christianity. World religions represented in prayers from their traditions include Judaism, Hinduism, Buddhism, Islam, Baha'i, and Native American.

Other books by the same author:
Prayers From a Troubled Heart, 1983
The Quiet Heart: Prayers and Meditations for Each Day of the Year, 1983
Daily Prayer and Praise, 1978

Other books you might like:
E.M. Bounds, *The Complete Works of E.M. Bounds on Prayer*, 1990
Elizabeth Roberts, *Earth Prayers From around the World: 365 Prayers, Poems, and Invocations for Honoring the Earth*, 1991
James Melvin Washington, *Conversations with God: Two Centuries of Prayers by African Americans*, 1994
Esther Burns Wilkin, *The Golden Books Treasury of Prayers From around the World*, 1999

20

DAVID S. ARIEL

What Do Jews Believe?: The Spiritual Foundations of Judaism
(New York: Schocken Books, 1995)

Category: Doctrine; Theology
Subject(s): Judaism
Age range(s): Young Adult-Adult

Summary: Judaism is both a religion that predates all other Western faith traditions and a living religion that continues to evolve. That is the message of Ariel's *What Do Jews Believe?*. Each chapter focuses on a key aspect of Jewish belief, including God, prayer, Jewish identity, and the problem of good and evil. Ariel traces the evolution of thought and practice for each concept in the writings of scripture and the wisdom of Jewish sages from ancient times to modern day scholarship.

Other books by the same author:

Spiritual Judaism: Restoring Heart and Soul to Jewish Life, 1998

The Mystic Quest: An Introduction to Jewish Mysticism, 1988

Other books you might like:

Hayim Halevy Donin, *To Be a Jew: A Guide to Jewish Observance in Contemporary Life*, 1972

Larry Dossey, *Living Judaism*, 1995

Alfred J. Kolatch, *The Jewish Book of Why*, 1981

Milton Steinberg, *Basic Judaism*, 1947

21

KAREN ARMSTRONG

A History of God: The 4000-Year Quest of Judaism, Christianity, and Islam

(New York: Knopf, 1993)

Category: Theology
Subject(s): Christianity; Islam; Judaism
Age range(s): Adult

Summary: In this comparative history of three major world religions, the author integrates historical, philosophical, and theological perspectives to explore the roots and development of Judaism, Christianity, and Islam. A former Roman Catholic nun and well-known religious scholar, Armstrong applies intellectual and scientific discipline to her subject. She traces the growth of each faith, examining all three within various historical contexts, and concluding that, together and individually, these faith traditions have created the idea of a personal God similar to ourselves who is the central focus of religious belief. She delineates the degrees of correlation among the three faiths, particularly noting that their mystical traditions reflect and affirm one another.

Other books by the same author:

In the Beginning: A New Interpretation of Genesis, 1996

Muhammad: A Biography of the Prophet, 1992

Other books you might like:

David S. Ariel, *What Do Jews Believe?: The Spiritual Foundations of Judaism*, 1995

Owen Chadwick, *A History of Christianity*, 1996

Mircea Eliade, *A History of Religious Ideas*, 1978-1985

Jack Miles, *God: A Biography*, 1995

V.S. Naipaul, *Among the Believers: An Islamic Journey*, 1981

22

KAREN ARMSTRONG

In the Beginning: A New Interpretation of Genesis

(New York: Knopf, 1996)

Category: Religious Commentaries
Subject(s): Criticism; Bible; God
Age range(s): Adult

Summary: Karen Armstrong's examination of the Old Testament book of Genesis focuses less on a literal interpretation of the text than on a meditative exploration of writings that reveal a culture trying to define what it means to be people of the God of Abraham and Moses. Armstrong characterizes this work as a ''wrestling'' with God and the Scriptures, and suggests that instead of applying primarily a scientific, western approach to studying biblical writings, contemporary readers should pay meditative, intuitive attention to the works and the cultural context in which they were written

Other books by the same author:

A History of God: The 4000-Year Quest of Judaism, Christianity, and Islam, 1993

Muhammad: A Biography of the Prophet, 1992

Other books you might like:

Henri Blocher, *In the Beginning: The Opening Chapters of Genesis*, 1984

Stuart Briscoe, *The Communicator's Commentary: Genesis*, 1987

23

KAREN ARMSTRONG

Muhammad: A Biography of the Prophet

(San Francisco: HarperSanFrancisco, 1992)

Category: Biography; Theology
Subject(s): Islam; Muhammad
Age range(s): Adult

Summary: In this biography of Muhammad, Karen Armstrong focuses on the historical evidence that exists about the life of the founding prophet of Islam. Directing attention to the context in which Muhammad lived and exploring the human aspects of Muhammad as a historical as well as a religious figure, Armstrong portrays multiple dimensions of a leader whose following continues to grow more than 1,400 years after he lived on Earth.

Other books by the same author:

In the Beginning: A New Interpretation of Genesis, 1996

A History of God: The 4000-Year Quest of Judaism, Christianity, and Islam, 1993

Other books you might like:

Clinton Bennett, *In Search of Muhammad*, 1998

Uri Robin, *The Eye of the Beholder: The Life of Muhammad as Viewed by the Early Muslims*, 1995

24

LAUREN ARTRESS

Walking a Sacred Path: Rediscovering the Labyrinth as a Spiritual Tool

(New York: Riverhead Books, 1995)

Category: New Age (Nonfiction)
Subject(s): Meditation; Religious Life; Spirituality
Age range(s): Adult

Summary: Walking a labyrinth as a meditative practice predates Christianity. The use of labyrinths in religious life was adopted by Christians and continued until the 1500s. In *Walking a Sacred Path*, Lauren Artress introduces this ancient spiritual tool to a new century. She traces the history of labyrinth use, noting that labyrinths were laid into the stone floors of numerous medieval cathedrals in Europe. She explains how she used a large canvas to recreate the labyrinth from the Chartres cathedral in France for use at the Grace Episcopal Cathedral in San Francisco. Artress notes that the labyrinth metaphorically reminds practitioners of their spiritual journey, no matter what their faith tradition may be, and functions as a framework for the renewal of Christian mysticism.

Other books you might like:

Jacques Attali, *Labyrinth in Culture and Society: Pathways to Wisdom*, 1998

Helmut Jaskolski, *The Labyrinth: Symbol of Fear, Rebirth, and Liberation*, 1997

William Henry Matthews, *Mazes and Labyrinths: Their History and Development*, 1922

Jill Purce, *The Mystic Spiral: Journey of the Soul*, 1974

ISAAC ASIMOV

Asimov's Guide to the Bible

(Garden City, New York: Doubleday, 1968-69)

Category: Religious Commentaries
Subject(s): Bible; History; Science
Age range(s): Adult

Summary: Isaac Asimov takes a scholarly, secular approach in this reference guide to the Bible, yet manages to avoid an antireligious tone. In two volumes and more than 1200 pages, Asimov synthesizes scholarly findings and commentaries from multiple disciplines, including history, anthropology, and archaeology. Asimov offers possible scientific explanations for some of the miraculous events recorded in the Old and New Testaments, as well as a hypothetical astronomical scenario to explain the Star of Bethlehem. He also analyzes the philosophical, psychological, and sociological significance of relationships between people in Scripture, including Cain and Abel.

Other books by the same author:

Asimov's Chronology of the World, 1991

The Relativity of Wrong, 1988

Beginnings: The Story of Origins—of Mankind, Life, the Earth, the Universe, 1987

Other books you might like:

John Drane, *Introducing the New Testament*, 1990

Donald E. Gowan, *Theology of the Prophetic Books: The Death and Resurrection of Israel*, 1998

Victor Harold Matthews, *The Old Testament: Text and Context*, 1997

James E. Smith, *The Wisdom Literature and Psalms*, 1996

26

AUGUSTINE

Confessions

(c. 400)

Category: Autobiography
Subject(s): Christianity
Age range(s): Adult

Summary: In this classic story of conversion and the religious life, Augustine narrates his youthful struggles with God. From a mature spiritual perspective, Augustine recalls his early sinfulness, and he reflects on the religious meanings of those events. In these lively reflections, we follow Augustine's spiritual development as he overcomes temptations, experiences conversion, and engages in theological controversies. The original texts date to c. 400; many translations and editions have since been published.

Other books by the same author:

On Christian Doctrine, c. 400

The City of God, c. 400

Other books you might like:

Frederick Buechner, *The Sacred Journey*, 1982

John Bunyan, *The Pilgrim's Progress*, 1678-1684

Will D. Campbell, *Brother to a Dragonfly*, 1977

Thomas Merton, *The Seven Storey Mountain*, 1948

Henri J.M. Nouwen, *The Genesee Diary: Report From a Trappist Monastery*, 1976

27

MARILOU AWIAKTA

Selu: Seeking the Corn-Mother's Wisdom

(Golden, Colorado: Fulcrum, 1993)

Category: Essays
Subject(s): Indians of North America; Culture; Spirituality
Age range(s): Young Adult-Adult

Summary: *Selu: Seeking the Corn-Mother's Wisdom* is a collection of essays, stories, and poems introducing and celebrating the story of the Corn-Mother, a life-giving spirit in Native American traditions. The Corn-Mother, named Selu by the Cherokee nation, imparts important life values including strength, respect, cooperation, balance, and adaptability for living harmoniously with people and with the earth.

Other books by the same author:

Rising Fawn and the Fire Mystery, 1983

Abiding Appalachia: Where Mountain and Atom Meet, 1978

Other books you might like:

Michael Garrett, *Walking on the Wind*, 1998

Charles Hudson, *Elements of Southeastern Indian Religion*, 1984

Joyce Sequichie Hifler, *Cherokee Feast of Days: Daily Meditations*, 1992

Dhyani Ywahoo, *Voices of Our Ancestors: Cherokee Teachings From the Wisdom Fire*, 1987

28
ROLAND H. BAINTON

Here I Stand: A Life of Martin Luther
(New York: Abingdon-Cokesbury Press, 1950)

Category: Biography
Subject(s): History; Religion; Lutherans
Age range(s): Adult
Time period(s): 15th century; 16th century (1483-1546)
Locale(s): Germany

Summary: Martin Luther, German theologian, preacher, and professor, holds a pivotal role in the history of Christianity as the father of the Protestant Reformation. Roland H. Bainton's *Here I Stand* is a classic and authoritative biography of the man whose interpretation of the New Testament compelled him to take a stand against the religious structure of the Papacy. His actions forced a division in Christianity between adherents of the Roman tradition, Catholicism, and adherents of a newer faith tradition within Christianity, Protestantism. Bainton's historically rich accounting of the life of Martin Luther is illustrated with engravings and woodcuts from the sixteenth century, evoking a sense of time and place that adds depth to his assessment of Luther.

Other books by the same author:
Yesterday, Today and What Next?: Reflections on History and Hope, 1978
Studies on the Reformation, 1966
Early Christianity, 1960
The Age of the Reformation, 1956
The Reformation of the Sixteenth Century, 1952

Other books you might like:
Mike Fearon, *Martin Luther*, 1986
Bernard Lohse, *Martin Luther: An Introduction to His Life and Work*, 1986
Heiko A. Oberman, *Luther: Man between God and the Devil*, 1989
Ernest G. Schweibert, *Luther and His Times: The Reformation From a New Perspective*, 1950

29
SARAH BAN BREATHNACH

Simple Abundance: A Daybook of Comfort and Joy
(New York: Warner, 1995)

Category: New Age (Nonfiction); Devotionals
Subject(s): Spirituality; Self-Confidence; Meditation
Age range(s): Young Adult-Adult

Summary: Breathnach offers a different kind of daily devotional with this book. The entries contain short inspirational quotations and stories designed to bring peace, joy, and comfort into the reader's day. With each entry, Breathnach suggests directions for reflective writing to help readers fold the lessons of the daily meditation into their lives. Although the book is designed primarily for women, it is useful for anyone seeking to live a spiritually abundant life.

Other books by the same author:
Simple Abundance Companion: Following Your Authentic Path to Something More, 2000
Something More: Excavating Your Authentic Self, 1998

Other books you might like:
Caroline Myss, *Anatomy of the Spirit: The Seven Stages of Power and Healing*, 1996
M.J. Ryan, *A Grateful Heart: Daily Blessings for the Evening Meal From Buddha to the Beatles*, 1994
Benjamin Shield, *For the Love of God: Handbook for the Spirit*, 1997
Iyanla Vanzant, *One Day My Soul Just Opened Up: 40 Days and 40 Nights Toward Spiritual Strength and Personal Growth*, 1998
Marianne Williamson, *Illuminata: Thoughts, Prayers, Rites of Passage*, 1994

30
ARNOLD J. BAND, Editor

The Tales: Nahman of Bratslav
(New York: Paulist Press, 1978)

Category: Devotionals
Subject(s): Judaism; Mysticism; History
Age range(s): Adult

Summary: Rabbi Nahman of Bratslav (1772-1810) is one of the greatest storytellers in all of Jewish history. *The Tales* are a collection of his retellings of stories from the *Talmud* and the *Torah*. Many of his followers believe that the great Hasidic master is the Messiah. This anthology is a fine introduction to Nahman's writings.

Other books you might like:
Arthur Green, *Tormented Master: A Life of Rabbi Nahman of Bratslav*, 1979
Lawrence A. Hoffman, *My People's Prayer Book: Traditional Prayers, Modern Commentaries*, 1997
Curt Leviant, *The Man Who Thought He Was Messiah: A Novel*, 1990
Emmanuel Levinas, *Nine Talmudic Readings*, 1990
   Translated and introduced by Annette Aronowicz.
Marc-Alain Ouaknin, *The Burnt Book: Reading the Talmud*, 1995
   Llewellyn Brown, translator

31
WILLIAM BARCLAY

The Daily Study Bible Series
(Philadelphia: Westminster, 1975-1976)

Category: Religious Commentaries
Subject(s): Bible; Christianity
Age range(s): Adult

Summary: William Barclay's 18-volume *Daily Study Bible* was first published between 1953 and 1959. In its revised form, Barclay's reference series is considered a classic and authoritative New Testament study resource for teachers, students, clergy, and laypeople. Written as both a commentary on the original Greek texts and a devotional guide to the reading of the New Testament, Barclay's masterwork serves as a scholarly and a spiritual guide to the writings of Christianity.

Other books by the same author:
Great Themes of the New Testament, 1979
The Character of God, 1977
The Plain Man's Guide to Ethics: Thoughts on the Ten Commandments, 1973
A New Testament Workbook, 1955

Other books you might like:
Paul William Barnett, *Behind the Scenes of the New Testament*, 1991
C.L. Rawlins, *The Daily Bible Study Series*, 1979
Robert A. Spivey, *Anatomy of the New Testament: A Guide to Its Structure and Meaning*, 1996
Spiros Zodhiates, *The Complete Wordstudy New Testament*, 1991

32

JOAN D. BARGHUSEN

Cults

(San Diego: Lucent Books, 1998)

Category: Religious Encyclopedias/Dictionaries
Subject(s): Cults; Religious Communes; Religious Life
Age range(s): Young Adult
Time period(s): 20th century

Summary: *Cults* offers a balanced introduction to the subject of religious cults. The author defines the word "cult" as it is used to describe non-traditional religious organizations and explains what life in various cults may include. She also discusses a variety of reasons that people tend to join cults and addresses the generally negative relationship that exists between cults and mainstream society. *Cults* identifies the characteristics of cult leadership and mentions the Hare Krishna movement and the Unification Church as examples of familiar and widespread religious cults. The Charles Manson "family" is offered as an example of a smaller group that demonstrates the typical characteristics of a religious cult. The violent or suicidal deaths often associated with cults are discussed in terms of the Branch Davidians of Waco, Texas; the Heaven's Gate community led by Marshall Applewhite; and the mass suicide of hundreds of people at Jim Jones' People's Temple in Jonestown, Guyana. The author provides a glossary of terms and suggestions for further reading on the topic.

Other books you might like:
Willa Appel, *Cults in America: Programmed for Paradise*, 1983
Daniel Cohen, *Cults*, 1994
John J. Collins, *Cult Experience: An Overview of Cults, Their Traditions, and Why People Join Them*, 1991
James R. Lewis, *Cults in America: A Reference Handbook*, 1998
Robert Emmet Long, *Religious Cults in America*, 1994
J. Gordon Melton, *Encyclopedic Handbook of Cults in America*, 1992

Kay Marie Porterfield, *Straight Talk about Cults*, 1995

33

COLEMAN BARKS, Editor

The Hand of Poetry: Five Mystic Poets of Persia

(New York: Omega, 1993)

Category: Poetry
Subject(s): Islam; Sufism; Allah
Age range(s): Young Adult-Adult

Summary: Hazrat Inayat Khan introduced Sufism to the West in the early part of the 20th century. Much of Sufi conversation about Allah takes the form of beautiful lyric poetry. This book, translated and compiled by Coleman Barks, contains poems by the great Sufi poets Rumi, Sanai, Attar, Saadi, and Hafiz. It also contains Khan's lectures on Sufi poetry. These lectures provide biographical information on each poet.

Other books you might like:
Denise Breton, *Love, Soul, and Freedom: Dancing with Rumi on the Mystic Path*, 1998
Andrew Harvey, *Perfume of the Desert: Inspirations From the Sufi Wisdom*, 1999
Abu Abdullah Ghulam Moinuddin, *The Book of Sufi Healing*, 1991
Jelaluddin Rumi, *Rumi: In the Arms of the Beloved*, 1997
Jonathan Star, translator
Jelaluddin Rumi, *Look! This Is Love: Poems of Rumi*, 1996
Annemarie Schimmel, translator

34

DAVID B. BARRETT, Editor

World Christian Encyclopedia: A Comparative Study of Churches and Religions in the Modern World, AD 1900-2000

(New York: Oxford University Press, 1982)

Category: Religious Encyclopedias/Dictionaries
Subject(s): Christianity; History; Religion
Age range(s): Young Adult-Adult

Summary: David B. Barrett's comprehensive guide to twentieth-century Christianity provides a detailed yet compact compendium of data about churches worldwide between 1900 and 2000 A.D. Among the features of Barrett's encyclopedia are: a country-by-country examination of the Christian church in more than 200 nations worldwide, with statistical information, prose text, and photos; a cultural overview of the evolution of Christianity and its present-day cultural impact; and a chronology of evangelism throughout the course of Christianity. Barrett provides an atlas, dictionary, and bibliography, as well as multiple indexes for finding specific information quickly. A second, updated edition of *World Christian Encyclopedia* is scheduled for publication in February 2000.

Other books by the same author:
*Seven Hundred Plans to Evangelize the World: The Rise of a
   Global Evangelization Movement*, 1988
World-Class Cities and World Evangelization, 1986
*Kenya Churches Handbook: The Development of Kenyan
   Christianity, 1498-1973*, 1973

Other books you might like:
Everett Ferguson, *Encyclopedia of Early Christianity*, 1999
Norman L. Geisler, *Baker Encyclopedia of Christian Apolo-
   getics*, 1999
Alister McGrath, *The Blackwell Encyclopedia of Modern
   Christian Thought*, 1993

35

KARL BARTH

Evangelical Theology: An Introduction
(New York: Holt, Rinehart and Winston, 1963)

Category: Theology
Subject(s): Christianity; Protestantism; Bible
Age range(s): Adult

Summary: Karl Barth remains the greatest Protestant theologian of the 20th century. In all of his work Barth challenges
the Liberal theology of the late 19th century and places the
Bible at the center of theology and worship. This book provides an outline of Barth's theological program, and underscores his seminal idea that God reveals Himself to humanity
through Scripture rather than humanity's discovering God
through science. He explores topics ranging from the Holy
Spirit and faith to doubt and love. The book offers Barth's
own account of how he has arrived at his theological beliefs.
The work was translated by Grover Foley.

Other books by the same author:
The Epistle to the Romans, 1933
The Word of God and the Word of Man, 1928

Other books you might like:
Dietrich Bonhoeffer, *The Cost of Discipleship*, 1948
David E. Demson, *Hans Frei and Karl Barth: Different Ways
   of Reading Scripture*, 1997
Donald K. McKim, *How Karl Barth Changed My Mind*, 1986
Reinhold Niebuhr, *Moral Man and Immoral Society: A Study
   in Ethics and Politics*, 1932

36

STEPHEN BATCHELOR

*Buddhism Without Beliefs: A
Contemporary Guide to Awakening*
(New York: Riverhead, 1997)

Category: Theology
Subject(s): Buddhism; Religious Life
Age range(s): Young Adult-Adult

Summary: Stephen Batchelor is a former monk with experience in both Zen and Tibetan Buddhism. In *Buddhism without
Beliefs*, he proposes that the theology of Buddhism can be
separated from its practices, so that the benefits of Buddhist

ways of life are accessible to people of all faith traditions. He
explores concepts of Buddhism including awakening, integrity, awareness, compassion, and imagination, and offers suggestions and examples for tapping into each of these qualities
without adopting the theological and structural tenets of traditional Buddhism.

Other books by the same author:
*The Awakening of the West: The Encounter of Buddhism and
   Western Culture*, 1994
Alone with Others: An Existential Approach to Buddhism,
   1983

Other books you might like:
Sylvia Boorstein, *It's Easier than You Think: The Buddhist
   Way to Happiness*, 1995
Steve Hagen, *Buddhism Plain and Simple*, 1997
Alan Watts, *The Way of Zen*, 1957

37

R. PIERCE BEAVER, Editor

*Eerdmans' Handbook to the World's
Religions*
(Grand Rapids, Michigan: W.B. Eerdmans, 1982)

Category: Religious Encyclopedias/Dictionaries
Subject(s): World Religions; Culture; History
Age range(s): Young Adult-Adult

Summary: *Eerdmans' Handbook to the World's Religions*
offers an overview of the development of religious traditions
and beliefs worldwide. In sections including ''Ancient Religions,'' ''Living Religions of the East'' and ''People of a
Book,'' R. Pierce Beaver examines the history of religious
belief and its myriad evolutions over thousands of years. The
culminating chapter, ''Religion: Or the Fulfillment of Religion?'' offers a final overview of Christianity. Beaver's emphasis on Christian belief as the ultimate end of all religious
searching is evident in the structure of the guide and in the
treatment of other religions as compared to Christianity.

Other books by the same author:
Introduction to Native American Church History, 1983
*American Protestant Women in World Mission: History of the
   First Feminist Movement in North America*, 1980
*The Native American Christian Community: A Directory of
   Indian, Aleut, and Eskimo Churches*, 1979
*Envoys of Peace: The Peace Witness in the Christian World
   Mission*, 1964
*From Missions to Mission: Protestant World Mission Today
   and Tomorrow*, 1964

Other books you might like:
Liz Flower, *The Elements of World Religions*, 1997
Dean Halverson, *The Compact Guide to World Religions*,
   1996
Philip Novak, *The World's Wisdom: Sacred Texts of the
   World's Religions*, 1994
Huston Smith, *The World's Religions: Our Great Wisdom
   Traditions*, 1991
   revised updated edition of *The Religions of Man*, 1958

38

ERNEST BECKER

The Denial of Death
(New York: Free Press, 1973)

Category: Theology
Subject(s): Psychology; Death
Age range(s): Adult

Summary: Becker confronts one of the most common questions humans ask themselves: ''Why do we die and how can we avoid death?'' He uses a deeply psychological approach to investigate the many strategies people use to deny death. In addition, he argues that our awareness of death and its role in life can heighten our spiritual lives. His is among several books from the same time period that focus on the darker side of the human psyche and its relationship to the spiritual.

Other books by the same author:
Escape From Evil, 1975

Other books you might like:
Norman O. Brown, *Life Against Death: The Psychoanalytical Meaning of History*, 1959
Sam Keen, *Faces of the Enemy: Reflections of the Hostile Imagination*, 1986
Elizabeth Kubler-Ross, *On Death and Dying*, 1969
Charles Taylor, *Sources of the Self: The Making of Modern Identity*, 1989
Paul Tillich, *The Courage to Be*, 1952

39

SUE BENDER, Author/Illustrator
RICHARD BENDER, Illustrator

Everyday Sacred: A Woman's Journey Home
(San Francisco: HarperSanFrancisco, 1995)

Category: Autobiography
Subject(s): Spirituality; Self-Perception; Amish
Age range(s): Adult

Summary: In *Plain and Simple*, Sue Bender described the spiritual journey of living with the Amish in the midwest, far from her work and family life in New York. In *Everyday Sacred*, Bender chronicles the next stages of her spiritual odyssey. Back at home, Bender shares her experience of incorporating the lessons she learned during her stay with the Amish into life in the world of computers, automobiles, and high-pressure careers. With gentle prose accompanied by line drawings, Bender shares how she finds meaning in the small act of drinking a cup of coffee and keeps balance in her life by learning to be realistic about what she expects from herself each day.

Other books by the same author:
Plain and Simple Wisdom, 1995
Plain and Simple: A Woman's Journey to the Amish, 1989

Other books you might like:
Sarah Ban Breathnach, *Simple Abundance: A Daybook of Comfort and Joy*, 1995

Jann Mitchell, *Home Sweeter Home: Creating a Haven of Simplicity and Spirit*, 1996
Louise Stoltzfus, *Amish Women: Lives and Stories*, 1994

40

SAINT BENEDICT OF NURSIA

The Rule of St. Benedict
(c. 520)

Category: Devotionals
Subject(s): Christianity; Monasticism
Age range(s): Adult

Summary: Repelled by the corruption and evil of Roman society, Benedict of Nursia (c. 480-543) withdrew into a cave and began to live the life of a hermit. He was soon joined by such a large number of followers that he formed a monastic order. His ''Rules'' established administrative as well as spiritual order in his monastery and became the standard for many later monastic rules. Various versions have been published in English, including a 1998 edition edited by Timothy Fry.

Other books you might like:
Joan D. Chittister, *Wisdom Distilled From the Daily: Living the Rule of St. Benedict Today*, 1990
Esther De Waal, *Seeking God: The Way of St. Benedict*, 1984
Hugh Feiss, *Essential Monastic Wisdom: Writings on the Contemplative Life*, 1999
Kathleen Norris, *The Cloister Walk*, 1996
Norvene Vest, *Friend of the Soul: A Benedictine Spirituality of Work*, 1997

41

WILLIAM J. BENNETT, Editor

The Book of Virtues: A Treasury of Great Moral Stories
(New York: Simon & Schuster, 1993)

Category: Morality Tales
Subject(s): Customs; Virtues; Ethics
Age range(s): Young Adult-Adult

Summary: Former Secretary of Education Bennett believes that society would be better off than it is now if everyone possessed a common set of virtues. In this book he collects stories and legends, mostly from western sources, whose heroes possess the virtues Bennett thinks are important for a smoothly run and well-regulated society. High among Bennett's list of virtues are loyalty, friendship and courage, and he chooses numerous stories in which heroes portray these virtues. He hopes that parents will read these stories to their children as a way of teaching their young ones to acquire and live by these core virtues.

Other books by the same author:
The Moral Compass: Stories for a Life's Journey, 1995

Other books you might like:
H. Jackson Brown Jr., *Life's Little Instruction Book*, 1991

Jack Canfield, *Chicken Soup for the Soul: 101 Stories to Open the Heart and Rekindle the Spirit*, 1993

Eric Carle, *Eric Carle's Treasury of Classic Stories for Children by Aesop, Hans Christian Andersen, and the Brothers Grimm*, 1988

Ellen Frankel, *The Classic Tales: 4,000 Years of Jewish Lore*, 1989

Ronald H. Isaacs, *Sacred Moments: Tales From the Jewish Life Cycle*, 1995

42

HERBERT BENSON
MARG STARK, Co-Author

Timeless Healing: The Power and Biology of Belief

(New York: Scribner, 1996)

Category: Self-Help
Subject(s): Spirituality; Religious Life; Health
Age range(s): Adult

Summary: Based on his work as a doctor, Herbert Benson offers a look at the connection between religious belief and overall health. *Timeless Healing* offers readers insight into the patient's role in maintaining and regaining health through various aspects of self-care, including what Benson refers to as "the faith factor." Benson notes that both positive and negative mental images and spiritual messages can be extremely influential in the outcome of medical procedures, and he suggests ways to minimize the negative while drawing on the positive to promote wellness and health of the whole person.

Other books by the same author:
Beyond the Relaxation Response: How to Harness the Healing Power of Your Personal Beliefs, 1984 (William Proctor, co-author)
The Mind/Body Effect, 1979
The Relaxation Response, 1975

Other books you might like:
William F. Haynes Jr., *Minding the Whole Person*, 1994
Dale A. Matthews, *The Faith Factor: Proof of the Healing Power of Prayer*, 1998
C. Norman Shealy, *Sacred Healing: The Curing Power of Energy and Spirituality*, 1999

43

SUSAN BERGMAN, Editor

Martyrs: Contemporary Writers on Modern Lives of Faith

(San Francisco: HarperSanFrancisco, 1996)

Category: Essays
Subject(s): Martyrs; Literature; Spirituality
Age range(s): Adult

Summary: Twentieth-century martyrs Martin Luther King, Jr. and Dietrich Bonhoeffer put their lives in danger in order to stand up for their religious, political, and social beliefs. They are among two of the famous contemporary martyrs profiled in *Martyrs* by twenty contemporary writers well-known in their own field as courageous and honest. Contributors include Carolyn Forche and Patricia Hampl; subjects include poet Osip Mandelstam, who died in a Soviet prison, and five missionaries in Ecuador, whose names are not familiar to those who never knew them.

Other books by the same author:
Anonymity, 1994

Other books you might like:
John Foxe, *The New Foxe's Book of Martyrs*, 1997
  Harold J. Chadwick, co-author
James Hefley, *By Their Blood: Christian Martyrs of the Twentieth Century*, 1996
Paul Marshall, *Their Blood Cries Out: The Untold Story of Persecution Against Christians in the Modern World*, 1997
Nina Shea, *In the Lion's Den: Persecuted Christians and What the Western Church Can Do about It*, 1997
Jon Sobrino, *Companions of Jesus: The Jesuit Martyrs of El Salvador*, 1990

44

CARDINAL JOSEPH BERNARDIN

The Gift of Peace: Personal Reflections

(Chicago: Loyola Press, 1997)

Category: Autobiography
Subject(s): Catholicism; Christianity; Death
Age range(s): Young Adult-Adult

Summary: During the last two months of his life, Cardinal Bernardin wrote *The Gift of Peace*, an account of three tumultuous years in his life. He was falsely accused of sexual misconduct, and shortly thereafter he was diagnosed with cancer. Cardinal Bernardin writes of a lifetime of learning to trust God with his anger, fear, and pain, and how in this difficult period of time he continued to learn and grow in his spirituality and faith. His honest reflections on doubt, fear, faith, and ultimate peace offer hope and encouragement.

Awards the book has won:
Christopher Award, Books for Adults, 1998

Other books by the same author:
A Moral Vision for America, 1998

Other books you might like:
Eugene Kennedy, *My Brother Joseph: The Spirit of a Cardinal and the Story of a Friendship*, 1997
Henri J.M. Nouwen, *Our Greatest Gift: A Meditation on Dying and Caring*, 1994
Tim Unsworth, *I Am Your Brother Joseph: Cardinal Bernardin of Chicago*, 1997
John H. White, *The Final Journey of Joseph Cardinal Bernardin*, 1997

45

CARL BERNSTEIN
MARCO POLITI, Co-Author

His Holiness: John Paul II and the Hidden History of Our Time

(New York: Doubleday, 1996)

Category: Biography
Subject(s): Catholicism; History; Journalism
Age range(s): Young Adult-Adult

Summary: Pulitzer Prize-winning journalist Carl Bernstein and Vatican journalist Marco Politi provide an in-depth look at the historical and political aspects of Pope John Paul II's tenure at the head of the Roman Catholic church. *His Holiness* offers a behind-the-scenes view of the Pope's involvement in global politics and world events. Bernstein and Politi note that John Paul II has had a high degree of influence on secular aspects of life in many parts of the world, including the former Soviet bloc countries.

Other books by the same author:
Loyalties: A Son's Memoirs, 1989
The Final Days, 1976
All the President's Men, 1974

Other books you might like:
Avery Robert Dulles, *The Splendor of Faith: The Theological Vision of Pope John Paul II*, 1999
Darcy O'Brien, *The Hidden Pope*, 1998
Pope John Paul II, *In My Own Words*, 1998
Tad Szulc, *Pope John Paul II: The Biography*, 1995

46

DANIEL BERRIGAN

Dark Night of Resistance

(Garden City, New York: Doubleday, 1971)

Category: Journals/Letters; Autobiography
Subject(s): Resistance Movements; Jesuits; War
Age range(s): Adult

Summary: Daniel Berrigan, Jesuit priest and prominent activist against the war in Vietnam, wrote *Dark Night of Resistance* in 1970 during four months of living underground while resisting imprisonment for the burning of draft files in 1968. This dark and brooding volume includes personal narrative, poetry, religious commentary, and philosophical discourse. Berrigan writes urgently from the heart on topics including war, injustice, love, and his personal vision of what humans must do to overcome darkness in the world.

Other books by the same author:
And the Risen Bread: Selected Poems, 1957-1997, 1998
To Dwell in Peace: An Autobiography, 1987
Uncommon Prayer: A Book of Psalms, 1978
The Raft Is Not the Shore: Conversations Toward a Buddhist/Christian Awareness, 1975
The Trial of the Catonsville Nine, 1970

Other books you might like:
Ed Griffin-Nolan, *Witness for Peace: A Story of Resistance*, 1991
Leo Tolstoy, *The Law of Love and the Law of Violence*, 1970
Jim Wallis, *The Rise of a Christian Conscience: The Emergence of a Dramatic Renewal Movement in the Church Today*, 1987

47

DANIEL BERRIGAN

Ten Commandments for the Long Haul

(Nashville: Abingdon, 1981)

Category: Devotionals
Subject(s): Christianity; Social Issues; Jesuits
Age range(s): Adult

Summary: One of the great priest activists of the late 1960s, Berrigan here offers glimpses of his journey of faith. Perhaps most famous for his involvement with Vietnam war protests, Berrigan affirms life in an uncompromising way in both the way he lives his life and in his writing. Believing that we are on the brink of permanently endangering our earth, our species, and all life, Berrigan fashions commandments that he believes will enable us to meet this crisis. His commandments range from "love your enemies, love one another" and "sell what you possess" to "do not be afraid" and "go, teach." Berrigan is one of the best at combining the desire for social justice with a deep grounding in the Gospel, and this book demonstrates it.

Other books by the same author:
Jubilee!: 1939-1989: Fifty Years a Jesuit, 1991

Other books you might like:
Robert McAfee Brown, *Is Faith Obsolete?*, 1974
Dorothy Day, *Loaves and Fishes*, 1963
Elizabeth A. Johnson, *Friends of God and Prophets: A Feminist Theological Reading of the Communion of the Saints*, 1998
Thomas Keating, *Invitation to Love: The Way of Christian Contemplation*, 1992
Jim Wallis, *The Call to Conversion: Recovering the Gospel for These Times*, 1992

48

JURJEN BEUMER

Henri Nouwen: A Restless Seeking for God

(New York: Crossroad Publishing, 1997)

Category: Biography
Subject(s): Theology; Psychology; Catholicism
Age range(s): Adult

Summary: In this volume, translated from its original Dutch by David E. Schlaver and Nancy Forest-Flier, Beumer offers a biographical portrait of the renowned pastor, professor, psychologist, and theologian Henri Nouwen. Beumer's account starts with Nouwen's early years in Holland. Then Beumer traces the ministry of a restless seeker from his ordination to the priesthood in Holland, to years of teaching at Notre Dame,

Yale Divinity School, and Harvard, and finally to his work in Canada with an organization that serves the mentally and physically disabled. Beumer characterizes Nouwen as a man whose deepening understanding of God resulted from his lifelong search for wholeness, for himself and for others.

Other books you might like:
Christopher de Vinck, *Nouwen Then: Personal Reflections on Henri*, 1999
Henri J.M. Nouwen, *Ministry and Spirituality*, 1996
Henri J.M. Nouwen, *The Wounded Healer: Ministry in Contemporary Society*, 1972

49

JIM BISHOP

The Day Christ Died
(New York: Harper, 1957)

Category: History
Subject(s): Christianity; Christian Life; Jesus
Age range(s): Adult

Summary: Not quite a novel, but a combination of fictionalization and journalism, Bishop's book suggests an hour-by-hour account of what happened on the day of Christ's death. He begins with the hour of Jesus' arrival in Jerusalem (6 p.m. on Thursday) and ends with Jesus' hour upon the cross (4 p.m. the next afternoon). Journalist Bishop writes this account as if he were a reporter present in Jerusalem to report on the events. While he adheres to the Gospel accounts, he also adds imaginative insights into the major figures involved in the event. Very popular in its time, the book retains some of its attraction for those interested in reimagining Christ's last days.

Other books by the same author:
The Day Christ Was Born: A Reverential Reconstruction, 1960

Other books you might like:
Taylor Caldwell, *Great Lion of God*, 1970
Billy Graham, *The Secret of Happiness*, 1985
Paul L. Maier, *In the Fullness of Time: A Historian Looks at Christmas, Easter, and the Early Church*, 1991
Charles M. Sheldon, *In His Steps: What Would Jesus Do?*, 1935
Philip Yancey, *The Jesus I Never Knew*, 1995

50

JIM BISHOP

The Day Christ Was Born: A Reverential Reconstruction
(New York: Harper, 1960)

Category: Biography
Subject(s): Christianity; Bible; History
Age range(s): Young Adult-Adult

Summary: Jim Bishop's *The Day Christ Was Born*, a companion to his bestseller *The Day Christ Died*, offers a novel-like, biblically sensitive account of the day Jesus Christ was born.

With the attention to detail of an investigative reporter, Bishop presents readers with a rich tapestry of cultural, political, religious, and historical context in which to examine and appreciate the 2,000-year-old story of the nativity of Christ.

Other books by the same author:
The Days of Martin Luther King, Jr., 1971
The Day Kennedy Was Shot, 1968
Go with God, 1958
The Day Christ Died, 1957
The Day Lincoln Was Shot, 1955

Other books you might like:
Gene Edwards, *The Birth*, 1991
Paul L. Maier, *A Skeleton in God's Closet: A Novel*, 1994
Fulton Oursler, *The Greatest Story Ever Told: A Tale of the Greatest Life Ever Lived*, 1949

51

PETER BISHOP, Editor
MICHAEL DARTON, Co-Editor

The Encyclopedia of World Faiths: An Illustrated Survey of the World's Living Religions
(New York: Facts on File, 1988)

Category: Religious Encyclopedias/Dictionaries
Subject(s): World Religions; History; Culture
Age range(s): Young Adult-Adult

Summary: *The Encyclopedia of World Faiths* is a single-volume reference source for information about the world's living religions. Because it covers the history, theology, religious practices, cultural aspects, and societal impact of the both famous and lesser-known religions, this is a good research resource for a variety of disciplines.

Other books by the same author:
The Christian and People of Other Faiths, 1997
World Religions: A Glossary and a Guide, 1977

Other books you might like:
Peter B. Clarke, *The World's Religions: Understanding the Living Faiths*, 1993
Robert S. Ellwood, *Many Peoples, Many Faiths: Women and Men in the World Religions*, 1999
   Barbara A. McGraw, co-author; sixth edition
Soloman A. Nigosian, *World Faiths*, 1994

52

BLACK ELK
JOHN G. NEIHARDT, Co-Author
STANDING BEAR, Illustrator

Black Elk Speaks: Being the Life Story of a Holy Man of the Ogalala Sioux
(New York: W. Morrow and Company, 1932)

Category: Autobiography; History
Subject(s): Indians of North America; Mythology; Spirituality
Age range(s): Adult
Time period(s): 19th century (1860s-1890s)

Locale(s): United States

Summary: This classic autobiography relates the life story of Black Elk, a Sioux medicine man and visionary, as related to John G. Neihardt. Born in December 1863, Black Elk realized even as a child that he was destined for something special. A vision experienced at age nine led him to begin a lifelong journey of spiritual discovery. Interspersed with his personal history are historical anecdotes, some humorous and others solemn. Neihardt has been criticized by some for skewing the words of Black Elk in order to present a more stereotypically ''Indian'' viewpoint to Caucasian readers in the 1930s, but the volume is still a valuable introduction to a culture which was even then vanishing.

Other books by the same author:
The Sacred Pipe: Black Elk's Account of the Seven Rites of the Oglala Sioux, 1953

Other books you might like:
Susan Bordeaux Bettelyoun, *With My Own Eyes: A Lakota Woman Tells Her People's History*, 1998
   Josephine Waggoner, co-author
Clyde Holler, *Black Elk's Religion: The Sun Dance and Lakota Catholicism*, 1995
Archie Fire Lame Deer, *Gift of Power: The Life and Teachings of a Lakota Medicine Man*, 1992
   Richard Erdoes, co-author
Hilda Neihardt, *Black Elk and Flaming Rainbow: Personal Memories of the Lakota Holy Man and John Neihardt*, 1995
John G. Neihardt, *The Sixth Grandfather: Black Elk's Teachings Given to John G. Neihardt*, 1984
Michael F. Steltenkamp, *Black Elk: Holy Man of the Oglala*, 1993
Mary Elizabeth Thunder, *Thunder's Grace: Walking the Road of Visions with My Lakota Grandmother*, 1995
Severt Young Bear, *Standing in the Light: A Lakota Way of Seeing*, 1994
   R.D. Theisz, co-author

53

HENRY T. BLACKABY
CLAUDE V. KING, Co-Author

Experiencing God: How to Live the Full Adventure of Knowing and Doing the Will of God

(Nashville: Broadman & Holman, 1994)

Category: Self-Help; Theology
Subject(s): Spirituality; Christianity
Age range(s): Adult

Summary: Encouraging readers to cultivate a relationship with God, Blackaby and King emphasize that Christian spiritual growth comes not from following a prescribed course of study or engaging in particular activities, but from knowing God in a personal way. *Experiencing God* offers suggestions for developing this relationship, noting that it develops in the course of everyday life, through interactions with people, problems, and privileges God makes available to us for spiri-

tual growth. A journal is also available that reinforces the principles introduced in *Experiencing God*.

Awards the book has won:
Gold Medallion Book Award, Devotional, 1998

Other books by the same author:
Experiencing God Day by Day: The Devotional and Journal, 1997

Other books you might like:
M. Lloyd Erickson, *The Embrace of God*, 1996
Jan Johnson, *Enjoying the Presence of God*, 1996
Blaine Smith, *Knowing God's Will: Finding Guidance for Personal Decisions*, 1991

54

DONALD BLOESCH

Essentials of Evangelical Theology

(San Francisco: Harper & Row, 1978-1979)

Category: Theology
Subject(s): Christianity; Protestantism; Bible
Age range(s): Adult

Summary: Donald Bloesch's *Essentials of Evangelical Theology* presents a comprehensive overview of the characteristics of modern evangelical Christianity. Bloesch addresses issues such as baptism by water and the Spirit, justification, sanctification, Biblical vs. cultural preaching, evangelism and concern for social issues, and the personal return of Jesus Christ. The two-volume work identifies the aspects that define evangelicalism in American Christianity at the end of the 20th century.

Other books by the same author:
God, the Almighty: Power, Wisdom, Holiness, Love, 1995
Theology of Word and Spirit: Authority and Method in Theology, 1992
The Future of Evangelical Christianity: A Call for Unity Amid Diversity, 1983

Other books you might like:
David S. Dockery, *Christian Scripture: An Evangelical Perspective on Inspiration, Authority and Interpretation*, 1995
James Davidson Hunter, *American Evangelicalism: Conservative Religion and the Quandary of Modernity*, 1983
Francis A. Schaeffer, *The Church at the End of the Twentieth Century*, 1970

55

CRAIG L. BLOMBERG

Jesus and the Gospels: An Introduction and Survey

(Nashville: Broadman & Holman, 1997)

Category: Religious Commentaries; Theology
Subject(s): Scripture; History
Age range(s): Adult

Summary: In this single-volume guide to the four books of the New Testament commonly called the Gospels—Matthew, Mark, Luke, and John—the author examines what is known

Non-Fiction

about Jesus from the largest source of information currently available: eyewitness accounts of people who knew him and interacted with him. Blomberg provides background information about the time period during which the texts were written, discusses critical methods of studying the works, offers an overview of the distinctive characteristics of each gospel, and summarizes current theological and historical thought about Jesus as a person.

Awards the book has won:
Gold Medallion Book Award, Theology/Doctrine, 1998

Other books by the same author:
Neither Poverty Nor Riches: A Biblical Theology of Material Possessions, 1999
How Wide the Divide?: A Mormon & an Evangelical in Conversation, 1997
Interpreting the Parables, 1990
The Historical Reliability of the Gospels, 1987

Other books you might like:
Marcus J. Borg, *Conflict, Holiness, and Politics in the Teachings of Jesus*, 1998
Joel B. Green, *Dictionary of Jesus and the Gospels*, 1992
Russell Shorto, *Gospel Truth: The New Image of Jesus Emerging From Science and History and Why It Matters*, 1997
Gerd Theissen, *The Shadow of the Galilean: The Quest of the Historical Jesus in Narrative Form*, 1987

56

HAROLD BLOOM

The American Religion: The Emergence of the Post-Christian Nation

(New York: Simon & Schuster, 1992)

Category: Doctrine; Theology
Subject(s): Religion; Culture
Age range(s): Adult
Locale(s): United States

Summary: Literary critic Harold Bloom turns his attention to the status of faith and spirituality in the United States in *The American Religion*. Arguing that the nature of Americans is to be independent and self-directed, Bloom suggests that these cultural characteristics have led to a plethora of religious groups that offer adherents the sense of direct access to God, unmediated by hierarchy or priests. One of Bloom's conclusions is that this free-form evolution of faith and spirituality is leading to the re-invention of God to fit the image of man, which contradicts the expressed theology of the Christian groups and leaders engaged in this practice. His survey of the political and social ramifications of religious practice and belief in America focuses particularly on the sects, denominations, and cults whose origins are intertwined with the birth, growth, and maturation of the United States as a country through more than two centuries.

Other books by the same author:
The Book of J, 1990 (David Rosenberg, co-author)
Ruin the Sacred Truths: Poetry and Belief From the Bible to the Present, 1989
Agon: Towards a Theory of Revisionism, 1982

Other books you might like:
Milton V. Backman Jr., *Christian Churches of America: Origins and Beliefs*, 1996
Paul Keith Conkin, *American Originals: Homemade Varieties of Christianity*, 1997
William M. Newman, *Patterns in Pluralism: A Portrait of American Religion, 1952-1971*, 1980

57

HAROLD BLOOM
DAVID ROSENBERG, Co-Author

The Book of J

(New York: Grove Weidenfeld, 1990)

Category: Theology
Subject(s): Scripture; History
Age range(s): Adult

Summary: In Old Testament scholarship, there is a belief that a first strand of several Old Testament books was written by an author known as J. In this volume, David Rosenberg provides a new translation of the document written by J, and Harold Bloom makes the controversial assertion that J was a woman.

Other books by the same author:
The Western Canon: The Books and School of the Ages, 1994
The American Religion: The Emergence of the Post-Christian Nation, 1992
Agon: Towards a Theory of Revisionism, 1982

Other books you might like:
Richard Elliott Friedman, *The Hidden Face of God*, 1997
Richard Elliott Friedman, *Who Wrote the Bible?*, 1987
Theodore Hiebert, *The Yahwist's Landscape: Nature and Religion in Early Israel*, 1996

58

HAROLD BLOOM

Ruin the Sacred Truths: Poetry and Belief From the Bible to the Present

(Cambridge, Massachusetts: Harvard University Press, 1989)

Category: Scripture
Subject(s): Literature; Poetry; Religion
Age range(s): Adult

Summary: Noted literary critic Harold Bloom goes in search of the sublime in this volume. The title is taken from poet Andrew Marvell's initial response to *Paradise Lost*, in which he feared Milton might make light of Christianity. Later, Marvell decided that Milton's work was in fact respectful of the sacred. Bloom, on the other hand, argues that the genius of Milton was in his very destruction of Christian sacrality, and its replacement with an uniquely human vision. He further theorizes that poetry and belief are "antithetical modes of knowledge." The text of *Ruin the Sacred Truths* is based on the author's 1987-1988 Charles Eliot Norton lectures at Harvard University.

Awards the book has won:
Christian Gauss Award, 1989

Other books by the same author:
The Western Canon: The Books and School of the Ages, 1994
Agon: Towards a Theory of Revisionism, 1982
The Anxiety of Influence: A Theory of Poetry, 1975

Other books you might like:
Stephen Dobyns, *Best Words, Best Order: Essays on Poetry*, 1997
Harold Fisch, *The Biblical Presence in Shakespeare, Milton, and Blake: A Comparative Study*, 1999
Stanley Fish, *Surprised by Sin: The Reader in Paradise Lost*, 1998
second edition
John Milton, *John Milton's Paradise Lost*, 1987
Harold Bloom, editor
Lois Rock, *Glimpses of Heaven: Poems and Prayers of Mystery and Wonder*, 1998

59

KENNETH D. BOA
ROBERT M. BOWMAN JR., Co-Author

An Unchanging Faith in a Changing World: Understanding and Responding to Critical Issues that Christians Face Today

(Nashville: Oliver Nelson, 1997)

Category: Self-Help
Subject(s): Christianity; Christian Life; Conduct of Life
Age range(s): Adult

Summary: How should Christians live in a world where society's values are so contradictory to those of biblical teachings? Kenneth D. Boa and Robert M. Bowman offer suggestions for Christians who want to make a difference in the world around them, from sharing their faith to standing firm in their beliefs.

Awards the book has won:
Gold Medallion Book Award, Missions/Evangelism, 1998

Other books by the same author:
Cults, World Religions, and the Occult, 1990
God, I Don't Understand, 1975

Other books you might like:
David W. Henderson, *Culture Shift: Communicating God's Truth to Our Changing World*, 1997
Catherine Marshall, *Beyond Our Selves*, 1994
Hannah Whitall Smith, *The Christian's Secret of a Happy Life*, 1883

60

RICHARD BODE

First You Have to Row a Little Boat: Reflections on Life and Living

(New York: Warner Books, 1993)

Category: Essays
Subject(s): Meditation; Boats and Boating
Age range(s): Young Adult-Adult

Summary: Speaking metaphorically, Bode teaches lessons about life through lessons learned from sailing. In the essays in this volume, the author emphasizes such concepts as mastering the simple before moving on to the complex, and learning to be open to the opportunity to learn, even when that opportunity looks suspiciously like the kind of situation you'd rather avoid entirely.

Other books by the same author:
Beachcombing at Miramar: The Quest for an Authentic Life, 1996
Blue Sloop at Dawn, 1979

Other books you might like:
Randy Deering, *The Sailor's Guide to Life*, 1999
Craig Lambert, *Mind over Water: Lessons on Life From the Art of Rowing*, 1998
Ann Linnea, *Deep Water Passage: A Spiritual Journey at Midlife*, 1995

61

DIETRICH BONHOEFFER

The Cost of Discipleship

(London: SCM Press, 1948)

Category: Theology
Subject(s): Christianity; Christian Life
Age range(s): Adult

Summary: Theologian Bonhoeffer (1906-1945), who was executed for his participation in an assassination plot against Nazi leader Adolph Hitler, offers here an extended meditation on Jesus' words: "Whoever would follow me, must take up his cross and die." Bonhoeffer argues that the church too often offers "cheap grace" to its followers, while the *Bible* teaches that being a disciple of Jesus is a costly undertaking, even unto death.

Other books by the same author:
Christ the Center, 1966
Life Together, 1954

Other books you might like:
Karl Barth, *The Humanity of God*, 1960
Robert Coles, *Dietrich Bonhoeffer*, 1998
Henri J.M. Nouwen, *Life of the Beloved: Spiritual Living in a Secular World*, 1992
Renate Wind, *Dietrich Bonhoeffer: A Spoke in the Wheel*, 1992
Philip Yancey, *What's So Amazing about Grace?*, 1997

62

DIETRICH BONHOEFFER

Letters and Papers From Prison

(London: SCM Press, 1953)

Category: Journals/Letters; Autobiography
Subject(s): Christianity; Prisoners and Prisons
Age range(s): Adult

Summary: In 1943, Lutheran pastor Bonhoeffer was imprisoned for his part in a plot against Nazi leader Adolph Hitler's life. His letters to his family, friends, and theological colleagues raise important questions about the function of Christianity in the modern world. In these stirring letters, edited by Eberhard Bethge, Bonhoeffer makes his now-famous call for a religionless Christianity.

Other books by the same author:
Ethics, 1955
The Cost of Discipleship, 1948

Other books you might like:
Karl Barth, *The Humanity of God*, 1960
John de Gruchy, *Dietrich Bonhoeffer: Witness to Jesus*, 1988
Richard J. Foster, *Celebration of Discipline: The Path to Spiritual Growth*, 1978
Reinhold Niebuhr, *Moral Man and Immoral Society: A Study in Ethics and Politics*, 1932
Ruth-Alice Von Bismarck, *Love Letters From Cell 92: The Correspondence between Dietrich Bonhoeffer and Maria von Wedemeyer, 1943-1945*, 1995

63

YVES BONNEFOY, Editor

Mythologies

(Chicago: University of Chicago Press, 1991)

Category: History
Subject(s): Mythology; Religion
Age range(s): Adult

Summary: Published in multiple volumes (two in the hardback edition, four in paperback), Yves Bonnefoy's *Mythologies* offers a wide scope of scholarly information about the origins and history of myths worldwide. The four major groupings are Greek and Egyptian mythologies; Roman and European mythologies; Asian mythologies; and American, African, and Old European mythologies. Coverage is particularly detailed for Indo-European traditions. Noticeably absent is coverage of Hebrew, Islamic, and Mesopotamian myths. The entries are arranged geographically, and the articles range in length from dictionary-like paragraphs to encyclopedia entries of more than ten pages. Geared toward scholarly use, *Mythologies* may also appeal to non-specialists who are ready to enhance their background knowledge in particular areas with more detailed and academic information.

Other books by the same author:
The Lure and the Truth of Painting: Selected Essays on Art, 1995
New and Selected Poems, 1995
Early Poems, 1947-1959, 1991 (Galway Kinnell, Richard Pevear, translators)
In the Shadow's Light, 1991 (John Naughton, translator)
The Act and the Place of Poetry: Selected Essays, 1989

Other books you might like:
Richard Cavendish, *An Illustrated Encyclopedia of Mythology*, 1980
Anita Ganeri, *Out of the Ark: Stories From the World's Religions*, 1996
  Jackie Morris, illustrator
Marilyn McFarlane, *Sacred Myths: Stories of World Religions*, 1996

64

SYLVIA BOORSTEIN

It's Easier than You Think: The Buddhist Way to Happiness

(San Francisco: HarperSanFrancisco, 1995)

Category: Self-Help
Subject(s): Meditation; Spirituality; Buddhism
Age range(s): Adult

Summary: Sylvia Boorstein's warm, down-to-earth tone conveys her practical approach to spirituality. In a collection of short meditations, Boorstein shares her perspective on what Buddhist spirituality is and is not. Her aim is to demystify spirituality as an intangible aspect of religious life and instead promote the understanding that spirituality is about gracefully managing the uncertainties of everyday life. Serving as something of a ''bridge'' between ancient wisdom and daily life, Boorstein's reflections can inspire and enlighten practitioners of many faith traditions.

Other books by the same author:
That's Funny, You Don't Look Buddhist: On Being a Faithful Jew and a Passionate Buddhist, 1997

Other books you might like:
Bhikkhu Ajahn Sumano, *Questions From the City, Answers From the Forest: Simple Lessons You Can Use From a Western Buddhist Monk*, 1999
Franz Metcalf, *What Would Buddha Do?: 101 Answers to Life's Daily Dilemmas*, 1999
Sharon Salzburg, *A Heart as Wide as the World: Living with Mindfulness, Wisdom, and Compassion*, 1997

65

SYLVIA BOORSTEIN

That's Funny, You Don't Look Buddhist: On Being a Faithful Jew and a Passionate Buddhist

(San Francisco: HarperSanFrancisco, 1997)

Category: Autobiography
Subject(s): Buddhism; Meditation; Judaism
Age range(s): Adult

Summary: Sylvia Boorstein writes, lectures, and teaches about Buddhist meditation. This is a personal account of her spiritual journey as a practitioner of two faith traditions: Judaism and Buddhism. She shares her experience and the reasons she has chosen to embrace both traditions, and provides an overview of American Buddhism as a practical application of spirituality that is inclusive of all other faith traditions.

Other books by the same author:
It's Easier than You Think: The Buddhist Way to Happiness, 1995

Other books you might like:
Christopher Ives, *The Emptying God: A Buddhist-Jewish-Christian Conversation*, 1990

Rodger Kamenetz, *The Jew in the Lotus: A Poet's Redis-
covery of Jewish Identity in Buddhist India*, 1994
Alan Lew, *One God Clapping: The Spiritual Path of a Zen
Rabbi*, 1999

66

EVANGELINE BOOTH
GRACE LIVINGSTON HILL, Co-Author

The War Romance of the Salvation Army
(Philadelphia: J.B. Lippincott, 1919)

Category: Biography
Subject(s): Volunteerism; Christianity; World War I
Age range(s): Young Adult-Adult
Time period(s): 1910s (1914-1918)
Locale(s): Europe; United States

Summary: This is one of only two nonfiction books by Grace
Livingston Hill. Co-written with Evangeline Booth, one of the
founders of the Salvation Army, it tells true stories of the
women of the Salvation Army who worked at home and
abroad during World War I to comfort the wounded soldiers
and share the story of Christian salvation with them.

Other books by the same author:
To Be or Not to Be, That Is the Question, 1937
Woman, 1930
Toward a Better World, 1928
Love Is All, 1908
Songs of Salvation, 1905

Other books you might like:
Stephen Brook, *God's Army: The Story of the Salvation Army*,
1999
Robert Collins, *The Holy War of Sally Ann: The Salvation
Army in Canada*, 1984
Lawrence Fellows, *A Gentle War: The Story of the Salvation
Army*, 1979
Jean Grant, *The Promise of the Willows*, 1994
George Bernard Shaw, *Major Barbara*, 1905

67

MARCUS J. BORG

*The God We Never Knew: Beyond
Dogmatic Religion to a More Authentic
Contemporary Faith*
(San Francisco: HarperSanFrancisco, 1997)

Category: Theology
Subject(s): God; Christianity; Faith
Age range(s): Adult

Summary: Is it possible to reconcile science, religious belief,
and critical thinking? In this volume religious scholar Marcus
J. Borg sets out to prove that it is possible, addressing issues
of faith left unanswered by other recent publications focusing
on the nature and history of God. Borg offers his own journey
of faith and intellect as a guide for others, using insights from
his personal life and professional research to demonstrate new
ways of understanding God. He suggests that those who do

not believe in the existence of God are basing their reasoning
on long-standing misinterpretations of scriptural writings. He
further concludes that belief in God only as a distant entity
contributes to one's inability to integrate faith and science in
rational and meaning ways.

Other books by the same author:
The Meaning of Jesus: Two Visions, 1999
Jesus and Buddha: The Parallel Sayings, 1997
*Meeting Jesus Again for the First Time: The Historical Jesus
and the Heart of Contemporary Faith*, 1994

Other books you might like:
John Dominic Crossan, *Jesus: A Revolutionary Biography*,
1994
John Dominic Crossan, *The Jesus Controversy: Perspectives
in Conflict*, 1999
John Polkinghorne, *Belief in God in an Age of Science*, 1998

68

JOAN BORYSENKO

*Pocketful of Miracles: Prayers,
Meditations, and Affirmations to Nurture
Your Spirit Every Day of the Year*
(New York: Warner Books, 1994)

Category: Self-Help
Subject(s): Spirituality; Prayer; Meditation
Age range(s): Adult

Summary: Joan Borysenko is the author of *Minding the Body,
Mending the Mind*, a ground-breaking work in the field of
mind-body-wellness research. In *Pocketful of Miracles*, she
presents daily practices designed to enhance spiritual
wholeness, which in turn can enhance physical wellness. The
meditations and exercises draw on the power of everyday
activities to be used as tools to bring peace and balance into
busy lives.

Other books by the same author:
The Ways of the Mystic: Seven Paths to God, 1997
The Power of the Mind to Heal, 1994 (Miroslav Borysenko,
co-author)
On Wings of Light, 1992
Minding the Body, Mending the Mind, 1987

Other books you might like:
Sarah Ban Breathnach, *Simple Abundance: A Daybook of
Comfort and Joy*, 1995
Beth Moran, *Intuitive Healing: A Woman's Guide to Finding
the Healer Within*, 1998
Caroline Myss, *The Creation of Health: The Emotional, Psy-
chological, and Spiritual Responses That Promote Health
and Healing*, 1988
Ron Roth, *Prayer and the Five Stages of Healing*, 1999

69

E.M. BOUNDS

The Complete Works of E.M. Bounds on Prayer

(Grand Rapids, Michigan: Baker Book House, 1990)

Category: Prayer
Subject(s): Christianity; Christian Life; Bible
Age range(s): Adult

Summary: E.M. Bounds (1835-1913) was a pastor and a chaplain in the Confederate Army. His best-known individual work was his devotional classic, *Power through Prayer*, but he wrote and spoke prolifically on the topic of prayer. Among evangelical Christian authors and leaders of the 19th and early 20th centuries, E.M. Bounds was considered the prime authority on prayer. *The Complete Works of E.M. Bounds on Prayer* offers the full spectrum of his writings on the subject.

Awards the book has won:
Gold Medallion Book Award, Classics, 1991

Other books by the same author:
The Necessity of Prayer, 1929
The Essentials of Prayer, 1925
Purpose in Prayer, 1920
Power through Prayer, 1912

Other books you might like:
Richard J. Foster, *Prayer: Finding the Heart's True Home*, 1992
Lawrence A. Hoffman, *The Art of Public Prayer: Not for Clergy Only*, 1988
Darrel D. King, *E.M. Bounds: The Man Whose Life of Prayer Inspired Millions*, 1998
Edith Schaeffer, *The Life of Prayer*, 1992

70

ALAN COATES BOUQUET

Everyday Life in New Testament Times

(London: B. T. Batsford, 1953)

Category: Religious Encyclopedias/Dictionaries
Subject(s): Bible; Customs; History
Age range(s): Young Adult-Adult
Locale(s): Holy Lands; Ancient Greece; Ancient Rome

Summary: *Everyday Life in New Testament Times* offers a comprehensive and compact overview of the people who inhabited the areas of the Middle East and Mediterranean that have been considered the Holy Lands for three major world faiths. Bouquet begins with an introduction to the general characteristics of life during the first centuries of the Christian era. He follows that with chapters devoted to specific aspects of life, including housing, water supply, sanitation, clothing, food, travel and roads, education and reading, business and trade, family celebrations and observations, science, and recreation, among others. More than 100 illustrations-line drawings, woodcuts, black-and-white photographs-add detail and clarity to Bouquet's easy-to-follow text.

Other books by the same author:
The Christian Faith and Non-Christian Religions, 1958
Sacred Books of the World, 1954

Other books you might like:
Joseph P. Free, *Archaeology and Bible History*, 1950
John Rogerson, *The Atlas of the Bible*, 1985

71

JOHN BOWKER, Editor

The Oxford Dictionary of World Religions

(New York: Oxford University Press, 1997)

Category: Religious Encyclopedias/Dictionaries
Subject(s): World Religions; Culture; History
Age range(s): Adult

Summary: *The Oxford Dictionary of World Religions* is a single-volume reference guide to past and present religions worldwide. Over 8,200 detailed entries and articles cover topics including movements and sects associated with all the world's religions, living and dead; sacred sites and scriptures; leaders and other individuals famous within their religious traditions; art and architecture, music, customs, and prayer; and much more. Although it is termed a dictionary for its concise approach to identifying and explaining all entry terms, *The Oxford Dictionary of World Religions* actually functions more like a concise encyclopedia.

Other books by the same author:
The Complete Bible Handbook, 1998
World Religions, 1997
Worlds of Faith: Religious Belief and Practice in Britain Today, 1983
The Religious Imagination and the Sense of God, 1978

Other books you might like:
Elizabeth Breuilly, *Religions of the World: The Illustrated Guide to Origins, Beliefs, Traditions, & Festivals*, 1997
Jeanne O'Brien, Martin Palmer, co-authors
F.L. Cross, *The Oxford Dictionary of the Christian Church*, 1977
E.A. Livingstone, co-editor
Jonathan Z. Smith, *HarperCollins Dictionary of Religion*, 1995

72

JOHN BOWKER

World Religions

(New York: DK Publishing, 1997)

Category: Religious Encyclopedias/Dictionaries
Subject(s): World Religions; Culture; History
Age range(s): Young Adult-Adult

Summary: John Bowker's *World Religions* is a graphically rich blend of text and images that surveys the wide range of religious traditions of the world. Each is represented through carefully selected artwork-icons, paintings, sculptures-that illuminate the theology or doctrine of the religion. Bowker integrates images and commentary throughout; neither is supplemental or secondary to the other. *World Religions* is accessible as an introductory volume, but its rich layers of theology, history, art, and philosophy make it an attractive and informative survey for religion specialists, as well.

Other books by the same author:
The Complete Bible Handbook, 1998
The Oxford Dictionary of World Religions, 1997
Hallowed Ground: Religions and the Poetry of Place, 1993
Is Anybody Out There? Religions and Belief in God in the Contemporary World, 1988

Other books you might like:
Elizabeth Breuilly, *Religions of the World: The Illustrated Guide to Origins, Beliefs, Traditions, & Festivals*, 1997
Jeanne O'Brien, Martin Palmer, co-authors
F.L. Cross, *The Oxford Dictionary of the Christian Church*, 1997
E.A. Livingstone, co-editor; third edition
Josh McDowell, *Handbook of Today's Religions*, 1982
Jonathan Z. Smith, *HarperCollins Dictionary of Religion*, 1995

73

MALCOLM BOYD

Are You Running with Me, Jesus?: Prayers

(New York: Holt, Rinehart and Winston, 1965)

Category: Devotionals; Prayer
Subject(s): Christian Life; Christianity; Jesus
Age range(s): Adult

Summary: Written during the chaotic 1960s, Boyd's book attempts to find the relevance of God in a secular world. Involved in issues of social justice, Boyd wondered what Jesus would say to increased U.S. involvement in Vietnam, the segregation of blacks and whites, and the growing poverty rate. Boyd found the church of his time had very little relevant to say, and he set out as a kind of maverick priest to run his own street ministry. These reflections capture many of Boyd's loneliest times and struggles with his vocation and spiritual vision.

Other books by the same author:
Am I Running with You, God?, 1977

Other books you might like:
Harvey Cox, *Seduction of the Spirit: The Use and Misuse of People's Religion*, 1973
John Howard Griffin, *The Hermitage Journals: A Diary Kept While Working on the Biography of Thomas Merton*, 1981
Sam Keen, *To a Dancing God*, 1970
Henri J.M. Nouwen, *Life of the Beloved: Spiritual Living in a Secular World*, 1992
John A.T. Robinson, *Honest to God*, 1963

74

PAUL BOYER

When Time Shall Be No More: Prophecy Belief in Modern American Culture

(Cambridge, Massachusetts: Harvard University Press, 1992)

Category: Doctrine
Subject(s): Prophecy; Scripture; End-Times
Age range(s): Adult
Locale(s): United States

Summary: When wars and natural disasters happen around the globe these days, CNN is on the spot to beam reports into American family rooms, the International Red Cross marshals support for diaster relief, and America's preachers of prophecy explain to their followers how the latest catastrophe fits into the "end-times" puzzle based on the prophetic Book of the Revelation in the New Testament. In *When Time Shall Be No More*, a study of prophecy culture in America, Paul Boyer examines the history and current landscape of biblical prophecy dating back to Jewish and Christian apocalyptic writings as found in the Bible. He describes the impact of prophecy belief on the development and interpretation of themes in popular culture, and he relects on the future of prophecy belief and the direction it may take during the late 20th century. Throughout the volume, Boyer maintains a respectful, objective stance that results in an informative guide to a relatively unstudied phenomenon in American culture.

Awards the book has won:
Banta Award, 1993

Other books by the same author:
By the Bomb's Early Light: American Thought and Culture at the Dawn of the Atomic Age, 1985
Urban Masses and Moral Order in America, 1820-1920, 1978
Purity in Print: Book Censorship in America, 1968

Other books you might like:
Richard G. Kyle, *The Last Days Are Here Again: A History of the End Times*, 1998
Thomas Robbins, *Millennium, Messiahs, and Mayhem: Contemporary Apocalyptic Movements*, 1997
Damian Thompson, *The End of Time: Faith and Fear in the Shadow of the Millennium*, 1997
Daniel Wojcik, *The End of the World as We Know It: Faith, Fatalism, and Apocalypse in America*, 1997

75

PAUL BRAND
PHILIP YANCEY, Co-Author
CHARLES SHAW, Illustrator

Fearfully and Wonderfully Made

(Grand Rapids, Michigan: Zondervan, 1980)

Category: Theology
Subject(s): Anatomy; Creation; Christianity
Age range(s): Young Adult-Adult

Summary: Paul Brand, accomplished surgeon, and Philip Yancey, prolific Christian writer, team up to offer *Fearfully and Wonderfully Made*, a unique look at the human body and mind, from a shared perspective of science and soul. In almost poetic prose, Yancey and Brand examine the intricacies of cell structure and the architectural balance of the skeletal system, referencing biblical texts and theological ideas that enhance the mood of wonder and admiration they ascribe to the Creator and the Creation.

Awards the book has won:
Gold Medallion Book Award, Inspirational, 1980

Other books by the same author:
The Forever Feast: Letting God Satisfy Your Deepest Hunger, 1993
Pain: The Gift Nobody Wants, 1993 (Philip Yancey, co-author)
In His Image, 1984 (Philip Yancey, co-author; Charles Shaw, illustrator)

Other books you might like:
Norman J. Berridge, *The Natural Basis of Spiritual Reality*, 1993
Carl Koch, *Created in God's Image*, 1991
Jane Marie Law, *Religious Reflections on the Human Body*, 1995
Dorothy Clarke Wilson, *Ten Fingers for God: The Life and Work of Dr. Paul Brand*, 1983

76

MARTIN BRAUEN
PETER NEBEL, Illustrator
DORO ROTHLISBERGER, Illustrator

The Mandala: Sacred Circle in Tibetan Buddhism
(Boston: Shambhala, 1997)

Category: Doctrine
Subject(s): Buddhism; Art; Meditation
Age range(s): Adult

Summary: The mandala is a component of Buddhism that fulfills several functions. As sacred art, it has a symbolic aspect. The mandala also exists as a tool of ritual for certain Buddhist observances and ceremonies. Martin Brauen's *The Mandala* brings this little-known aspect of Buddhist practice and culture to life in a lavishly illustrated volume that introduces to a western audience the history, symbolism, significance, and various rituals associated with the mandala.

Other books you might like:
Judith Cornell, *Mandala: Luminous Symbols for Healing*, 1996
Susanne F. Fincher, *Creating Mandalas: For Insight, Healing, and Self-Expression*, 1991
Steven M. Kossak, *Sacred Visions: Early Paintings From Central Tibet*, 1998

77

JERRY BRIDGES

The Discipline of Grace: God's Role and Our Role in the Pursuit of Holiness
(Colorado Springs, Colorado: NavPress, 1994)

Category: Devotionals
Subject(s): Christianity; Conduct of Life
Age range(s): Adult

Summary: Evangelical Bible teacher Jerry Bridges writes about the relationship between God's grace and a believer's pursuit of holiness, explaining that it is only through the grace of God that Christians can seek holiness and grow in their spiritual life in Christ. In *The Discipline of Grace*, Bridges offers guidance to Christians in matters pertaining to spiritual disciplines and spiritual growth.

Awards the book has won:
Gold Medallion Book Award, Christian Living, 1995

Other books by the same author:
The Crisis of Caring: Recovering the Meaning of True Fellowship, 1992
Transforming Grace: Living Confidently in God's Unfailing Love, 1991
The Pursuit of Holiness, 1978

Other books you might like:
J.I. Packer, *Great Grace*, 1997
R.C. Sproul, *Grace Unknown: The Heart of Reformed Theology*, 1999
Charles R. Swindoll, *The Grace Awakening*, 1990

78

DANNION BRINKLEY
PAUL PERRY, Co-Author

Saved by the Light: The True Story of a Man Who Died Twice and the Profound Revelations He Received
(New York: Villard Books, 1994)

Category: Autobiography
Subject(s): Afterlife; Death; Spirituality
Age range(s): Adult

Summary: Dannion Brinkley has twice been near death. The first time he spent nearly half an hour in a morgue, having been pronounced dead, before reviving. The story he tells after that 1975 experience is of traveling through a dark tunnel into a crystal city, and seeing thirteen angels, each of whom tells him of things which will come to pass—events that have, indeed, transpired since then. After a second, related experience, Brinkley speaks of a message from the angels that leads him to use his newly discovered psychic abilities to help the dying.

Other books by the same author:
At Peace in the Light: The Further Adventures of a Reluctant Psychic Who Reveals the Secret of Your Spiritual Powers, 1995

Other books you might like:
Morse Melvin, *Closer to the Light: Learning From Children's Near Death Experiences*, 1990
Morse Melvin, *Transformed by the Light: The Powerful Effect of Near-Death Experiences on People's Lives*, 1992
M. Scott Peck, *In Heaven as on Earth: A Vision of the Afterlife*, 1996

79

SYLVIA BROWNE

The Other Side and Back: A Psychic's Guide to Our World and Beyond

(New York: Dutton, 1999)

Category: New Age (Nonfiction)
Subject(s): Spiritualism; Afterlife; Angels
Age range(s): Adult

Summary: Psychic and successful clairvoyant Sylvia Browne writes of ways to deepen spirituality and tap psychic energy in *The Other Side and Back*. Browne draws on her personal and professional experience as a medium to answer questions about spirit guides, angels, ghosts, hauntings, communication with the dead, reincarnation, and developing psychic skills.

Other books by the same author:
Adventures of a Psychic: The Fascinating and Inspiring True-Life Story of One of America's Most Successful Clairvoyants, 1998 (Antoinette May, co-author)
My Guide, Myself: The Psychic Odyssey of Sylvia Browne, 1990 (Antoinette May, co-author)

Other books you might like:
Rosemary Altea, *Proud Spirit: Lessons, Insights & Healing From "The Voice of the Spirit World"*, 1997
Norma Kalina, *Spirit Guides: Angels in the Army of God*, 1997
James Van Praagh, *Reaching to Heaven: A Spiritual Journey through Life and Death*, 1999

80

F.F. BRUCE

Paul: Apostle of the Heart Set Free

(Grand Rapids, Michigan: Eerdmans, 1977)

Category: Biography
Subject(s): Scripture; Christianity; History
Age range(s): Adult

Summary: *Paul: Apostle of the Heart Set Free* offers a richly textured examination of the life of the apostle Paul from one of the 20th century's leading Pauline scholars. F.F. Bruce focuses on the context of Paul's life through a multi-disciplinary approach that includes the study of historical and archaeological findings and analysis of biblical texts. In addition, Bruce presents the major themes of Paul's teaching and preaching ministry, as revealed in his various letters that have become books of the New Testament.

Awards the book has won:
Gold Medallion Book Award, Biography/Autobiography, 1979

Other books by the same author:
In the Steps of the Apostle Paul, 1995
Paul and His Converts, 1985
The Real Jesus, 1985
An Expanded Paraphrase of the Epistles of Paul, 1965

Other books you might like:
Charles Ferguson Ball, *The Life and Times of the Apostle Paul*, 1996
C.K. Barrett, *Paul: An Introduction to His Thought*, 1994
Gerald F. Hawthorne, *Dictionary of Paul and His Letters*, 1993

81

FREDERIC BRUSSAT
MARY ANN BRUSSAT, Co-Author

Spiritual Literacy: Reading the Sacred in Everyday Life

(New York: Scribner, 1996)

Category: Self-Help
Subject(s): Essays; Literature; Religious Life
Age range(s): Young Adult-Adult

Summary: With a variety of prose, essays, and poems from contemporary writers, teachers, philosophers, leaders, and spiritual mentors, *Spiritual Literacy* is a treasure trove of writings on the essence of spirituality in everyday life. Frederic and Mary Ann Brussat provide exercises following each chapter—with titles such as ''Nature,'' ''Leisure,'' and ''Place''—to help readers develop an awareness that can lead to spiritual sustenance in the ordinariness of every day life.

Other books by the same author:
100 Ways to Keep Your Soul Alive: Living Deeply and Fully Every Day, 1994 (Mary Ann Brussat, co-author)

Other books you might like:
Carol L. McClelland, *Seasons of Change: Using Nature's Wisdom to Grow through Life's Inevitable Ups and Downs*, 1998
Gunilla Brodde Norris, *Being Home: A Book of Meditations*, 1991
Marianne Williamson, *Illuminata: Thoughts, Prayers, Rites of Passage*, 1994
Philip Zaleski, *The Best Spiritual Writing, 1998*, 1998
Myla Kabat-Zinn, *Everyday Blessings: The Inner Work of Mindful Parenting*, 1997
Jon Kabat-Zinn, co-author

82

MARTIN BUBER

I and Thou

(Edinburgh: 1937)

Category: Theology
Subject(s): Judaism; Mysticism

Age range(s): Adult

Summary: Buber (1878-1965) believes that mechanical relationships mark our everyday lives. By combining the insights of earlier German philosophy and Jewish mysticism, Buber shows that individuals can begin to recognize and embrace the sacred in all things.

Other books by the same author:
Ecstatic Confessions, 1985
Good and Evil: Two Interpretations, 1953

Other books you might like:
Maurice Friedman, *Encounter on the Narrow Ridge: A Life of Martin Buber*, 1991
Abraham Joshua Heschel, *Man's Quest for God: Studies in Prayer and Symbolism*, 1954
Lawrence Kushner, *Invisible Lines of Connection: Sacred Stories of the Ordinary*, 1996
Elie Wiesel, *Souls on Fire: Portraits and Legends of Hasidic Masters*, 1972
Aryeh Wineman, *Mystic Tales From the Zohar*, 1997

83

WILLIAM F. BUCKLEY JR.

Nearer, My God: An Autobiography of Faith

(New York: Doubleday, 1997)

Category: Autobiography
Subject(s): Catholicism; Religion
Age range(s): Adult

Summary: Renowned political and cultural commentator William F. Buckley, Jr. writes about his lifelong Roman Catholic faith in a volume of personal revelation and observation. While some portions of the book are truly autobiographical, Buckley also explores questions of wider societal interest, including the Vatican's traditional and unchanging stance on birth control and the ban on the ordination of women as priests. The author applies a personal perspective to discussion of a world-wide faith tradition, remaining careful to distinguish between modern-day practices of Roman Catholic adherents and the wider heritage of Catholicism.

Other books by the same author:
Buckley: The Right Word, 1998
God and Man at Yale: The Superstitions of "Academic Freedom", 1978

Other books you might like:
Patrick Glynn, *God: The Evidence*, 1997
Bernard Haring, *Free and Faithful: My Life in the Catholic Church: An Autobiography*, 1998
Ed Stivender, *Raised Catholic (Can You Tell?)*, 1994

84

ZSUZSANNA E. BUDAPEST

The Holy Book of Women's Mysteries

(Berkeley, California: Wingbow Press, 1989)

Category: Self-Help

Subject(s): Wicca; Health; Spirituality
Age range(s): Adult

Summary: First published privately in 1979, *The Holy Book of Women's Mysteries* was re-released commercially in 1989 and is now considered to be a staple of literature that addresses both pagan and feminist issues. Zsuzsanna E. Budapest has gathered wisdom for women in a variety of areas including witchcraft, nutrition, health, and celebrations of events unique to women's lives, such as conception, birth, and menopause.

Other books by the same author:
Grandmother Moon: Lunar Magic in Our Lives: Spells, Rituals, Goddesses, Legends, and Emotions under the Moon, 1991
The Grandmother of Time: A Woman's Book of Celebrations, 1989

Other books you might like:
Scott Cunningham, *The Truth about Witchcraft*, 1988
Shekhinah Mountainwater, *Ariadne's Thread: A Workbook of Goddess Magic*, 1991
Starhawk, *The Spiral Dance: A Rebirth of the Ancient Religion of the Great Goddess*, 1979

85

E.A. WALLIS BUDGE

The Gods of the Egyptians; or, Studies in Egyptian Mythology

(New York: Dover, 1969)

Category: History
Subject(s): Egyptian Religion; Customs; Religious Traditions
Age range(s): Young Adult-Adult

Summary: While the gods and goddesses of the Greek and Roman pantheons are very familiar to many readers, the Egyptians gods and goddesses are less familiar. Yet, the stories of Isis and Osiris, for example, play a major formative role in later religions like Christianity. Budge's book provides a thorough introduction to the fascinating stories of the Egyptian gods. Along the way, Budge offers examples of the wide variety of religious beliefs of the ancient Egyptians. Though the book's prose is a little dated, it remains an accessible introduction and is suitable for young adults.

Other books by the same author:
Egyptian Magic, 1971

Other books you might like:
Fritz Graf, *Magic in the Ancient World*, 1997
Dimitri Meeks, *Daily Life of the Egyptian Gods*, 1996
John F. Nunn, *Ancient Egyptian Medicine*, 1996
Geraldine Pinch, *Magic in Ancient Egypt*, 1995
Byron E. Shafer, *Religion in Ancient Egypt: Gods, Myths and Personal Practice*, 1991

86

FREDERICK BUECHNER

The Alphabet of Grace
(New York: Seabury, 1970)

Category: Essays
Subject(s): Theology; Faith; Self-Perception
Age range(s): Adult

Summary: Novelist, poet, essayist, and clergyman Frederick Buechner reflects on mysteries of life and faith. In this three-part series of essays, Buechner reveals that literary, biblical, and spiritual insights into life can be mined from the most unremarkable of circumstances or memories. He explores faith as it is both hidden and revealed in the routine thoughts and activities of ordinary days.

Other books by the same author:
The Eyes of the Heart: A Memoir of the Lost and Found, 1999
The Storm: A Novel, 1998
The Longing for Home: Recollections and Reflections, 1996
Listening to Your Life: Daily Meditations with Frederick Buechner, 1992 (George Connor, compiler)

Other books you might like:
Brennan Manning, *The Ragamuffin Gospel: Good News for the Bedraggled, Beat-Up, and Burnt Out*, 1990
Calvin Miller, *An Owner's Manual for the Unfinished Soul*, 1997
Henri J.M. Nouwen, *In Memoriam*, 1980
Barbara Brown Taylor, *Home by Another Way*, 1999
Barbara Brown Taylor, *Mixed Blessings*, 1998
second edition

87

FREDERICK BUECHNER
KATHERINE A. BUECHNER, Illustrator

Peculiar Treasures: A Biblical Who's Who
(San Francisco: Harper & Row, 1979)

Category: Biography
Subject(s): Bible; Christianity
Age range(s): Young Adult-Adult

Summary: Frederick Beuchner applies his humor and insight to profiles of more than 125 people from the Bible-from the holy to the profane-who are much like the rest of us. The less-than-perfect, the ambitious, the dreamers, the people whose names and stereotypes we recognize in the Bible turn out to be less distant from "real life" than we ever thought possible.

Other books by the same author:
The Eyes of the Heart: A Memoir of the Lost and Found, 1999
The Storm: A Novel, 1998
The Longing for Home: Recollections and Reflections, 1996
Listening to Your Life: Daily Meditations with Frederick Buechner, 1992 (George Connor, compiler)

Other books you might like:
J. Vernon McGee, *Real Characters: How God Uses Unlikely People to Accomplish Great Things*, 1995

John Phillips, *Introducing People of the Bible*, 1991-1995 three volumes
David A. Skates, *Carry On!: Help and Hope for Life's Everyday Battles*, 1996
Walter Wangerin Jr., *The Simple Truth: A Bare Bones Bible*, 1996

88

FREDERICK BUECHNER

The Sacred Journey
(San Francisco: Harper & Row, 1982)

Category: Autobiography
Subject(s): Christianity; Family; Faith
Age range(s): Adult
Time period(s): 20th century (1920s-1950s)
Locale(s): United States

Summary: In *The Sacred Journey*, Frederick Buechner reflects on memories from what he terms "the early days" of his life-the time from childhood through the point in adulthood at which he encountered God as a force and a compelling mystery in his life. That experience led him to attend seminary to explore the meaning of God and faith. In poetic prose that strikes directly at the heart and meaning of each episode he recounts, Buechner reveals aspects of life, love, history, and family that demonstrate the hand of God in a life unaware of and yet strangely in tune with the unseen. *The Sacred Journey* is the first in an autobiographical trilogy that continues with *Now and Then* and *Telling Secrets*.

Other books by the same author:
The Eyes of the Heart: A Memoir of the Lost and Found, 1999
The Longing for Home: Recollections and Reflections, 1996
Listening to Your Life: Daily Meditations with Frederick Buechner, 1992 (George Connor, compiler)
Telling Secrets, 1991
Now and Then, 1983

Other books you might like:
Brennan Manning, *The Ragamuffin Gospel: Good News for the Bedraggled, Beat-Up, and Burnt Out*, 1990
Calvin Miller, *An Owner's Manual for the Unfinished Soul*, 1997
Henri J.M. Nouwen, *In Memoriam*, 1980
Barbara Brown Taylor, *Home by Another Way*, 1999
Barbara Brown Taylor, *Mixed Blessings*, 1998
second edition

89

FREDERICK BUECHNER
KATHERINE A. BUECHNER, Illustrator

Whistling in the Dark: A Doubter's Dictionary
(San Francisco: HarperSanFrancisco, 1993)

Category: Theology
Subject(s): Christianity; Spirituality; Language
Age range(s): Adult

Summary: *Whistling in the Dark* is a journey-in-essays through the language of everyday life and modern spirituality. Frederick Buechner casts his unique observational spotlight on concepts, activities, and objects that we take for granted and yet which often have significance far beyond our conscious awareness. Among the terms that catch Buechner's contemplative fancy in this volume are money, politics, preaching, the born again, and jogging. This volume was first published as *Whistling in the Dark: An ABC Theologized* in 1988.

Other books by the same author:
The Eyes of the Heart: A Memoir of the Lost and Found, 1999
The Longing for Home: Recollections and Reflections, 1996
Wishful Thinking: A Seeker's ABC, 1993
Listening to Your Life: Daily Meditations with Frederick Buechner, 1992 (George Connor, compiler)
Peculiar Treasures: A Biblical Who's Who, 1979 (Katherine A. Buechner, illustrator)

Other books you might like:
Brennan Manning, *The Ragamuffin Gospel: Good News for the Bedraggled, Beat-Up, and Burnt Out*, 1990
Calvin Miller, *An Owner's Manual for the Unfinished Soul*, 1997
Henri J.M. Nouwen, *In Memoriam*, 1980
Barbara Brown Taylor, *Home by Another Way*, 1999
Barbara Brown Taylor, *Mixed Blessings*, 1998
second edition

90

FREDERICK BUECHNER

Wishful Thinking: A Seeker's ABC

(San Francisco: HarperSanFrancisco, 1993)

Category: Theology
Subject(s): Language; Spirituality; Faith
Age range(s): Adult

Summary: In a volume that has been expanded and revised since its initial release in 1973 as *Wishful Thinking: A Theological ABC*, Frederick Buechner explores words common to modern faith and spirituality and reflects on their multiple levels of meaning. *Wishful Thinking: A Seeker's ABC* is the first volume in Buechner's "lexical trilogy" that includes *Peculiar Treasures: A Biblical Who's Who* and *Whistling in the Dark: A Doubter's Dictionary*. With wit, irony, and his customary unique perspective, Buechner comtemplates the significance of such everyday words-and theological concepts-as love, sin, and envy.

Other books by the same author:
The Eyes of the Heart: A Memoir of the Lost and Found, 1999
The Longing for Home: Recollections and Reflections, 1996
Whistling in the Dark: A Doubter's Dictionary, 1993
Listening to Your Life: Daily Meditations with Frederick Buechner, 1992 (George Connor, compiler)
Peculiar Treasures: A Biblical Who's Who, 1979 (Katherine A. Buechner, illustrator)

Other books you might like:
Brennan Manning, *The Ragamuffin Gospel: Good News for the Bedraggled, Beat-Up, and Burnt Out*, 1990

Calvin Miller, *An Owner's Manual for the Unfinished Soul*, 1997
Henri J.M. Nouwen, *In Memoriam*, 1980
Barbara Brown Taylor, *Home by Another Way*, 1999
Barbara Brown Taylor, *Mixed Blessings*, 1998
second edition

91

SOPHY BURNHAM

A Book of Angels: Reflections on Angels Past and Present and True Stories of How They Touch Our Lives

(New York: Ballantine, 1990)

Category: Essays
Subject(s): Angels; Miracles; Religious Life
Age range(s): Young Adult-Adult

Summary: After a narrow escape from death on the ski slopes, Sophy Burnham became convinced that her life had been saved by an angel. Although she had not grown up believing that angels exist and miracles are possible, this experience changed her mind and her life. In this volume, Burnham presents stories about other people's experiences with angels, interspersed with quotations from classic and religious literature, including the Bible and the Koran. Illustrations contribute a visual component to Burnham's examination of the work of angels in modern times.

Other books by the same author:
Revelations, 1992
Angel Letters, 1991

Other books you might like:
Don Fearheiley, *Angels Among Us*, 1993
Eileen Elias Freeman, *Touched by Angels*, 1993
Billy Graham, *Angels: God's Secret Agents*, 1975
Guideposts Associates, *Angels in Our Midst*, 1993
Doreen Virtue, *Angel Therapy: Healing Messages for Every Area of Your Life*, 1997

92

LEO BUSCAGLIA

Loving Each Other: The Challenge of Human Relationships

(Thorofare, New Jersey: Slack, 1984)

Category: Self-Help
Subject(s): Love; Interpersonal Relations
Age range(s): Adult

Summary: Leo Buscaglia's non-sectarian teachings about love and interpersonal relationships have been part of the cultural landscape in America since the 1970s with the publication of *Love* (1972) and *Personhood: The Art of Being Fully Human* (1978), collections of his University of Southern California lectures and forerunners of the wholeness-in-relationships movement in publishing and popular psychology. In *Loving Each Other: The Challenge of Human Relationships*, Buscaglia turns his attention to society as a whole, noting that cynical attitudes in society toward love, compassion, and tenderness result in people who have difficulty overcoming a sense of detachment and apathy in order to forge positive relationships with others.

Other books by the same author:
Born for Love: Reflections on Loving, 1992
Profiles in Caring: Advocates for the Elderly, 1990
Living, Loving, Learning, 1982
Love, 1972

Other books you might like:
Linda V. Berens, *Understanding Yourself and Others: An Introduction to Temperament*, 1998
Conari Press, *Community of Kindness*, 1999
Larry Crabb, *Connecting: Healing for Ourselves and Our Relationships: A Radical New Vision*, 1997
David W. McMillan, *Create Your Own Love Story: The Art of Lasting Relationships*, 1997
Mark Robert Waldman, *The Art of Staying Together: Embracing Love, Intimacy and Spirit in Relationships*, 1998

93

GEORGE BUTTRICK, Editor

Interpreter's Bible
(New York: Abingdon-Cokesbury, 1951-57)

Category: Religious Commentaries
Subject(s): Bible
Age range(s): Adult

Summary: The *Interpreter's Bible* is a 12-volume classic of biblical scholarship, most importantly because it attempts to reach a broad audience of laypeople and clergy. Each volume lists side-by-side passages from the King James and the Revised Standard versions of the Bible. A second section offers a verse-by-verse analysis of each particular passage, while a third section provides a broader commentary with insights which can be folded into sermons and church school lessons. Although Buttrick gathers the best scholarship of his time, most of the contributors are from mainstream Protestant churches and there are very few women scholars in the commentary's pages. In 1994, the *New Interpreter's Bible* was published, offering many of the same features of the *Interpreter's Bible*, but gathering diverse voices and viewpoints, taking it beyond mainstream Protestant biblical scholarship. It is likely that the *New Interpreter's Bible* will eventually supersede the *Interpreter's Bible*.

Other books you might like:
Raymond E. Brown, *The Jerome Biblical Commentary*, 1968
Raymond E. Brown, *The New Jerome Biblical Commentary*, 1999
David Noel Freedman, *Anchor Bible*, 1964
James L. Mays, *Harper's Bible Commentary*, 1988
Carol A. Newsom, *The Women's Bible Commentary*, 1998

94

SUSAN CAHILL, Editor

Wise Women: Over Two Thousand Years of Spiritual Writing by Women
(New York: W.W. Norton, 1996)

Category: Prayer; Poetry
Subject(s): Essays; Women; Philosophy
Age range(s): Adult

Summary: Representing women's spiritual experiences from many faith traditions and more than two thousand years, Susan Cahill's *Wise Women* is a collection of prayers, poetry, essays, stories, journals, letters, and theological writings designed to inspire, enlighten, and embrace women at the end of the 20th century. Religious narratives from the women mystics of eastern traditions are found side by side with writings from contemporary authors such as Rita Dove and Denise Levertov. Carefully selected to celebrate the global and historical breadth and depth of women's spiritual experiences and writings, the ninety selections included in this anthology treat the universal themes of love and loss, justice and freedom, age and youth, and faith.

Other books by the same author:
Writing Women's Lives: An Anthology of Autobiographical Narratives, 1994
Growing Up Female: Stories by Women Writers From the American Mosaic, 1993
Mothers: Memories, Dreams, and Reflections by Literary Daughters, 1988

Other books you might like:
Amber Coverdale Sumrall, *Storming Heaven's Gate: An Anthology of Spiritual Writings by Women*, 1997
Carol Lee Flinders, *Enduring Grace: Living Portraits of Seven Women Mystics*, 1993
Sara Maitland, *A Big-Enough God: A Feminist's Search for a Joyful Theology*, 1995

95

PETER CALVOCORESSI

Who's Who in the Bible
(New York: Viking, 1987)

Category: Religious Encyclopedias/Dictionaries; Biography
Subject(s): Bible; Literature
Age range(s): Young Adult-Adult

Summary: Here in one volume is an overview of the life and times of the people of the Bible. The author provides an introductory essay about the Bible's origins, with timeline charts that identify when each portion was probably completed. A glossary defines the terms and categories used in the biographical descriptions, and maps are included for time periods throughout Bible history. The bulk of the book consists of alphabetically arranged biographical sketches of more than 450 people who appear in the Old and New Testaments, as well as in Apocryphal writings. Each profile discusses the context in which the person appears in biblical writings and refers readers to subsequent treatments of the person in literature, history, and the fine arts.

Other books by the same author:
World War II and the Shaping of Postwar Europe, 1997
Threading My Way, 1994

Other books you might like:
Trent C. Butler, *Concise Holman Bible Dictionary*, 1997
Paul D. Gardner, *The Complete Who's Who in the Bible*, 1995
Dietrich Gruen, *Who's Who in the Bible: An Illustrated Biographical Dictionary*, 1998

96

PAULINE CAMPANELLI
DAN CAMPANELLI, Illustrator

Ancient Ways: Reclaiming Pagan Traditions

(St. Paul, Minnesota: Llewellyn Publications, 1991)

Category: Self-Help
Subject(s): Paganism; Customs
Age range(s): Adult

Summary: With an emphasis on craft ideas and recipes, Pauline Campanelli's *Ancient Ways* is a useful resource for those who wish to incorporate the celebration of pagan holidays into their daily lives. Among the seasonal rituals addressed are Imbolc, the Vernal Equinox, and the Summer and Winter Solstices.

Other books by the same author:
Pagan Rites of Passage, 1998
Rites of Passage: The Pagan Wheel of Life, 1994
Wheel of the Year: Living the Magical Life, 1989

Other books you might like:
Jan Brodle, *Earth Dance: A Year of Pagan Rituals*, 1995
Edain McCoy, *The Sabbats: A New Approach to Living the Old Way*, 1994
Gwydion O'Hara, *Pagan Ways: Finding Your Spirituality in Nature*, 1997

97

JOSEPH CAMPBELL

The Hero with a Thousand Faces

(New York: Pantheon Books, 1949)

Category: New Age (Nonfiction)
Subject(s): Mythology; Folklore; History
Age range(s): Young Adult-Adult

Summary: Campbell examines the literary elements contained in hero myths from the world's mythologies to demonstrate the tremendous similarities in the quest myths of every culture. He notes that all such myths contain a hero whose birth is often mysterious, who undergoes some sort of special "training," who faces what seem to be insurmountable obstacles, and who receives a reward for attaining the object of his quest.

Awards the book has won:
National Institute of Arts and Letters Grant, Literature, 1947

Other books by the same author:
The Power of Myth, 1988 (Co-authored with Bill Moyers)
The Masks of God, 1959-1968

Other books you might like:
Mircea Eliade, *The Sacred and the Profane: The Nature of Religion*, 1959
James George Frazer, *The Golden Bough: A Study in Magic and Religion*, 1911-1915
Marija Gimbutas, *The Language of the Goddess: Unearthing the Hidden Symbols of Western Civilization*, 1989
Carl Jung, *Man and His Symbols*, 1964
Francis A. Yates, *The Art of Memory*, 1966

98

JOSEPH CAMPBELL

The Masks of God

(New York: Viking, 1959-1968)

Category: Theology
Subject(s): Mythology; Religion; Archaeology
Age range(s): Adult

Summary: In a work that was originally published as four individual books between 1959 and 1968, Joseph Campbell explores the roots of mythology worldwide that evolved into the religions of the world. *The Masks of God* brings together research from the disciplines of archaeology, anthropology, history, psychology, and theology to identify and compare the mythologies that form the bedrock of art, literature, and worship throughout the modern world. The four individual volumes that make up this work are *Primitive Mythology* (1959), *Oriental Mythology* (1962), *Occidental Mythology* (1964), and *Creative Mythology* (1968).

Other books by the same author:
The Mythic Imagination, 1998
Transformations of Myth through Time, 1990
The Power of Myth, 1988 (Bill Moyers, co-author)

Other books you might like:
J.F. Bierlein, *Parallel Myths*, 1994
Yves Bonnefoy, *American, African and Old European Mythologies*, 1993
Moyra Caldecott, *Mythical Journeys, Legendary Quests*, 1996
Arthur Cottrell, *A Dictionary of World Mythology*, 1990

99

WILL D. CAMPBELL

Brother to a Dragonfly

(New York: Seabury, 1977)

Category: Autobiography
Subject(s): Family Relations; Civil Rights
Age range(s): Adult
Time period(s): 20th century
Locale(s): Mississippi

Summary: Will D. Campbell's commitment to civil rights in the deep South during the 1960s cost him career opportunities in academia, but it opened other doors to him, and he has remained committed to reflective honesty in addressing issues that others shy away from. An ordained Baptist preacher, Campbell had written other books before his 1977 autobiographical *Brother to a Dragonfly*, but it was this volume, which was nominated for a National Book Award, that placed him squarely in the public eye as an outspoken and forthright advocate of civil and human rights. *Brother to a Dragonfly* addresses the author's years of growing up in Amite County, Mississippi. The two focal points of this volume are Campbell's desperate and ongoing attempts to help his brother deal with the devastation of mental illness in his life, and his personal struggle to reconcile his life-long faith with the civil rights abuses he sees all around him. Campbell's later memoir, *Forty Acres and a Goat*, deals more specifically with the years he devoted to the civil rights movement.

Awards the book has won:
Lillian Smith Book Award, 1978

Other books by the same author:
Soul Among Lions: Musings of a Bootleg Preacher, 1999
And Also with You: Duncan Gray and the American Dilemma, 1997
Forty Acres and a Goat: A Memoir, 1986
Race and the Renewal of the Church, 1962

Other books you might like:
Paul Lichterman, *The Search for Political Community: American Activists Reinventing Commitment*, 1996
David B. Mixner, *Stranger Among Friends*, 1997
Anne Moody, *Coming of Age in Mississippi*, 1997
Ida B. Wells, *Crusade for Justice: The Autobiography of Ida B. Wells*, 1994

100

TONY CAMPOLO

You Can Make A Difference: Real Commitment for Young Christians

(Waco, Texas: Word, 1994)

Category: Sermons
Subject(s): Adolescence; Christian Life; Conduct of Life
Age range(s): Young Adult-Adult

Summary: Tony Campolo's *You Can Make a Difference* is based on motivational presentations made by the author for teens. His focus is on helping young people connect their Christian faith with life in the world around them to make good things happen in their lives and in the world around them. He addresses issues including interpersonal relationships, career choices, faith development, and commitment to high ideals. Campolo, whose evangelical Christian ministry has been criticized by some conservative Christian leaders for its emphasis on social action, remains committed to promoting an active gospel of Jesus with people of all ages. The first edition of *You Can Make a Difference* was published in 1984 and won the Gold Medallion Book Award for Youth Books in 1985; the 1994 version is updated to reach a new generation of teens.

Other books by the same author:
Following Jesus Without Embarrassing God, 1997

Wake Up America!: Answering God's Radical Call While Living in the Real World, 1991
Partly Right, 1985
A Reasonable Faith: Responding to Secularism, 1983

Other books you might like:
Gary Rice Doud, *God Loves Me, So What!*, 1992
Carl Koch, *Creating a Christian Lifestyle*, 1988
Josh McDowell, *Don't Check Your Brains at the Door*, 1992
David Veerman, *Reality 101*, 1999

101

JACK CANFIELD, Editor
MARK VICTOR HANSEN, Co-Editor

A 2nd Helping of Chicken Soup for the Soul: 101 More Stories to Open the Heart and Rekindle the Spirit

(Deerfield Beach, Florida: Health Communications, 1995)

Category: Self-Help
Series: Chicken Soup for the Soul
Subject(s): Psychology; Conduct of Life
Age range(s): Young Adult-Adult

Summary: The first of many sequels and spin-offs to the original bestseller, *A 2nd Helping of Chicken Soup for the Soul* offers more of the personal narratives and anecdotes about life and love that made the first collection so popular. Some of the stories are written specifically for the series, while others are familiar, time-tested accounts of people finding meaning for life in unexpected places. Extensions of the series include volumes of literary Chicken Soup for children, teens, college students, pet lovers, golfers, mothers, and others.

Awards the book has won:
Storytelling World Book Award, 1996

Other books by the same author:
Chicken Soup for the Christian Soul: 101 Stories to Open the Heart and Rekindle the Spirit, 1997 (Mark Victor Hansen, Patty Aubery, Nancy Mitchell, co-editors)
A 3rd Serving of Chicken Soup for the Soul: 101 More Stories to Open the Heart and Rekindle the Spirit, 1996 (Mark Victor Hansen, co-editor)
Chicken Soup for the Soul: 101 Stories to Open the Heart and Rekindle the Spirit, 1993 (Mark Victor Hansen, co-editor)

Other books you might like:
H. Jackson Brown Jr., *Life's Little Instruction Book*, 1991
H. Jackson Brown Jr., *Live and Learn and Pass It On: People Ages 5 to 95 Share What They've Discovered about Life, Love, and Other Good Stuff*, 1991
Richard Carlson, *Don't Sweat the Small Stuff—and It's All Small Stuff: Simple Ways to Keep the Little Things From Taking over Your Life*, 1997
Arielle Ford, *Hot Chocolate for the Mystical Soul: 101 True Stories of Angels, Miracles, and Healings*, 1998

102

JACK CANFIELD, Editor
MARK VICTOR HANSEN, Co-Editor
PATTY AUBERY, Co-Editor
NANCY MITCHELL, Co-Editor

Chicken Soup for the Christian Soul: 101 Stories to Open the Heart and Rekindle the Spirit

(Deerfield Beach, Florida: Health Communications, 1997)

Category: Self-Help
Series: Chicken Soup for the Soul
Subject(s): Psychology; Christianity; Religious Life
Age range(s): Young Adult-Adult

Summary: In *Chicken Soup for the Christian Soul*, the inspirational writings that characterize the Chicken Soup series take on a specifically Christian flavor. With stories written by and for Christians, this entry into the Chicken Soup line addresses issues of love, friendship, and life in general from the perspective of Christianity. Anecdotes and personal narratives acknowledge the relationship with God as a central component of life, and the writings include excerpts from published works by well-known Christian writers including Corrie Ten Boom, Gary Smalley, John Trent, and Joan Wester Anderson.

Other books by the same author:
A 2nd Helping of Chicken Soup for the Soul: 101 More Stories to Open the Heart and Rekindle the Spirit, 1995 (Mark Victor Hansen, co-editor)
Chicken Soup for the Soul: 101 Stories to Open the Heart and Rekindle the Spirit, 1993 (Mark Victor Hansen, co-editor)

Other books you might like:
H. Jackson Brown Jr., *Life's Little Instruction Book*, 1991
H. Jackson Brown Jr., *Live and Learn and Pass It On: People Ages 5 to 95 Share What They've Discovered about Life, Love, and Other Good Stuff*, 1991
Neil Eskelin, *101 Promises Worth Keeping*, 1996

103

JACK CANFIELD, Editor
MARK VICTOR HANSEN, Co-Editor
MARK DONNELLY, Co-Editor
CHRISSY DONNELLY, Co-Editor
BARBARA DE ANGELIS, Co-Editor

Chicken Soup for the Couple's Soul: Inspirational Stories about Love and Relationships

(Deerfield Beach, Florida: Health Communications, 1999)

Category: Self-Help
Series: Chicken Soup for the Soul
Subject(s): Psychology; Relationships; Love
Age range(s): Adult

Summary: The focus is on love and commitment to a significant other in *Chicken Soup for the Couple's Soul*, from the editors of the perennially popular Chicken Soup books. The various stages of "couplehood" are addressed through per-

sonal narrative, anecdote, and poetry. As in other Chicken Soup volumes, the emphasis is on stories that inspire, comfort, and strengthen readers in their daily lives.

Other books by the same author:
A 2nd Helping of Chicken Soup for the Soul: 101 More Stories to Open the Heart and Rekindle the Spirit, 1995 (Mark Victor Hansen, co-editor)
Chicken Soup for the Soul: 101 Stories to Open the Heart and Rekindle the Spirit, 1993 (Mark Victor Hansen, co-editor)

Other books you might like:
Kay Allenbaugh, *Chocolate for a Lover's Heart: Soul-Soothing Stories That Celebrate the Power of Love*, 1999
H. Jackson Brown Jr., *Life's Little Treasure Book on Love*, 1995
Richard Carlson, *Handbook for the Heart: Original Writings on Love*, 1996
Deepak Chopra, *The Path to Love: Renewing the Power of Spirit in Your Life*, 1997
Eva Shaw, *365 Reflections on Love & Friendship*, 1998

104

JACK CANFIELD, Editor
MARK VICTOR HANSEN, Co-Editor
JENNIFER READ HAWTHORNE, Co-Editor
MARCI SHIMOFF, Co-Editor

Chicken Soup for the Mother's Soul: 101 Stories to Open the Hearts and Rekindle the Spirits of Mothers

(Deerfield Beach, Florida: Health Communications, 1997)

Category: Self-Help
Series: Chicken Soup for the Soul
Subject(s): Psychology; Mothers; Family Life
Age range(s): Adult

Summary: The editors of the Chicken Soup series introduce a volume written with a focus on the special concerns of mothers and grandmothers. As in other Chicken Soup collections, *Chicken Soup for the Mother's Soul* features inspirational and heart-warming personal stories, anecdotes, and poetry. From great-grandmothers looking back over three generations of parenting to women just starting their families, mothers of all ages will find something in this collection that resonates with their experience.

Other books by the same author:
Another Sip of Chicken Soup for the Soul: Heartwarming Stories of the Love Between Parents and Children, 1998 (Mark Victor Hansen, co-editor)
Chicken Soup for the Woman's Soul: 101 Stories to Open the Hearts and Rekindle the Spirits of Women, 1996 (Mark Victor Hansen, Jennifer Read Hawthorne, Marci Shimoff, co-editors)
A 2nd Helping of Chicken Soup for the Soul: 101 More Stories to Open the Heart and Rekindle the Spirit, 1995 (Mark Victor Hansen, co-editor)
Chicken Soup for the Soul: 101 Stories to Open the Heart and Rekindle the Spirit, 1993 (Mark Victor Hansen, co-editor)

Other books you might like:

H. Jackson Brown Jr., *Life's Little Instruction Book*, 1991

H. Jackson Brown Jr., *Live and Learn and Pass It On: People Ages 5 to 95 Share What They've Discovered about Life, Love, and Other Good Stuff*, 1991

Richard Carlson, *Don't Sweat the Small Stuff—and It's All Small Stuff: Simple Ways to Keep the Little Things From Taking over Your Life*, 1997

Elsa Hornfischer, *Mother Knew Best: Wit and Wisdom From the Moms of Celebrities*, 1996

Vickie LoPiccolo Jennett, *MOMStories: Instant Inspiration for Mothers*, 1998

105

JACK CANFIELD, Editor

Chicken Soup for the Soul: 101 Stories to Open the Heart and Rekindle the Spirit

(Deerfield Beach, Florida: Health Communications, 1993)

Category: Self-Help
Subject(s): Self-Confidence; Spirituality
Age range(s): Young Adult-Adult

Summary: In the midst of a fast-paced and often hectic world, people often look for little daily moments that can warm their souls and help them to regroup. Just as chicken soup is purported to have restorative powers for the body, these stories of people doing good for others, even when they haven't been asked to do so, may restore calm to the spirit and soul. This collection is so popular that the editors have compiled multiple volumes and "special flavor" *Chicken Soup* books of similar heart-warming stories targeted to children, teens, women, and people of various interest groups, including golfers.

Awards the book has won:

American Booksellers Book of the Year (ABBY) Award, 1995

American Family Institute Nonfiction Literary Award, 1996

Other books by the same author:

A 2nd Helping of Chicken Soup for the Soul: 101 More Stories to Open the Heart and Rekindle the Spirit, 1995

Other books you might like:

William J. Bennett, *The Book of Virtues: A Treasury of Great Moral Stories*, 1993

H. Jackson Brown Jr., *Life's Little Instruction Book*, 1991

H. Jackson Brown Jr., *Live and Learn and Pass It On: People Ages 5 to 95 Share What They've Discovered about Life, Love, and Other Good Stuff*, 1991

Richard Carlson, *Don't Sweat the Small Stuff—and It's All Small Stuff: Simple Ways to Keep the Little Things From Taking over Your Life*, 1997

Robert Fulghum, *All I Really Need to Know I Learned in Kindergarten: Uncommon Thoughts on Common Things*, 1988

106

JACK CANFIELD, Editor
MARK VICTOR HANSEN, Co-Editor
KIMBERLY KIRBERGER, Co-Editor

Chicken Soup for the Teenage Soul: 101 Stories of Life, Love, and Learning

(Deerfield Beach, Florida: Health Communications, 1997)

Category: Self-Help
Series: Chicken Soup for the Soul
Subject(s): Adolescence; Love; Relationships
Age range(s): Young Adult

Summary: The editors of the popular Chicken Soup series have expanded their menu with a volume of stories targeted specifically to young adults. Filled with personal narratives, poetry, and anecdotes written for and by teenagers, this first collection of *Chicken Soup for the Teenage Soul* touches on topics of concern to young adults: relationships with friends and parents, school life and self-esteem, dealing with emotional loss, and bridging the gap between childhood and the adult world.

Other books by the same author:

Chicken Soup for the College Soul: Inspiring and Humorous Stories about College, 1999 (Mark Victor Hansen, Kimberly Kirberger, Dan Clark, co-editors)

Chicken Soup for the Teenage Soul II: 101 More Stories of Life, Love, and Learning, 1997 (Mark Victor Hansen, Kimberly Kirberger, co-editors)

Chicken Soup for the Christian Soul: 101 Stories to Open the Heart and Rekindle the Spirit, 1997 (Mark Victor Hansen, Patty Aubery, Nancy Mitchell, co-editors)

A 2nd Helping of Chicken Soup for the Soul: 101 More Stories to Open the Heart and Rekindle the Spirit, 1995 (Mark Victor Hansen, co-editor)

Other books you might like:

H. Jackson Brown Jr., *Life's Little Instruction Book*, 1991

H. Jackson Brown Jr., *Live and Learn and Pass It On: People Ages 5 to 95 Share What They've Discovered about Life, Love, and Other Good Stuff*, 1991

Bettie B. Youngs, *Taste Berries for Teens: Inspirational Short Stories and Encouragement on Life, Love, Friendship and Tough Issues*, 1999

Jennifer Leigh Youngs, co-author

107

RICHARD CARLSON

Don't Sweat the Small Stuff—and It's All Small Stuff: Simple Ways to Keep the Little Things From Taking over Your Life

(New York: Hyperion, 1997)

Category: Self-Help
Subject(s): Spirituality; Conduct of Life; Self-Confidence
Age range(s): Young Adult-Adult

Summary: In life it's often the little things that stand in the way of happiness. Carlson's book urges people to look at the bigger picture rather than getting caught up in all the little daily messes or catastrophes that inconvenience us and disrupt our spiritual state of mind.

Other books you might like:

Sarah Ban Breathnach, *Simple Abundance: A Daybook of Comfort and Joy*, 1995

Jack Canfield, *Chicken Soup for the Soul: 101 Stories to Open the Heart and Rekindle the Spirit*, 1993

Deepak Chopra, *The Seven Spiritual Laws of Success: A Practical Guide to the Fulfillment of Your Dreams*, 1994

Iyanla Vanzant, *One Day My Soul Just Opened Up: 40 Days and 40 Nights Toward Spiritual Strength and Personal Growth*, 1998

Marianne Williamson, *Illuminata: Thoughts, Prayers, Rites of Passage*, 1994

108

RICHARD CARLSON, Editor
BENJAMIN SHIELD, Co-Editor

Handbook for the Soul

(Boston: Little, Brown, 1995)

Category: Essays
Subject(s): Spirituality; Pilgrims and Pilgrimages; Prayer
Age range(s): Young Adult-Adult

Summary: Richard Carlson has gathered inspirational essays from more than 30 contemporary writers in his *Handbook for the Soul*. The contributing authors, theologians, clergy, inspirational and motivational writers, physicians, philosophers, and journalists include Rabbi Harold Kushner, Dr. Bernie Siegel, Dr. Elizabeth Kubler-Ross, Dr. Wayne Dyer, Thomas Moore, and Marianne Williamson. The essays are arranged in seven groupings: soul in everyday life, the heart of soul, journey of the soul, rekindling your soul, lessons of the soul, soul communion, and a return to soul.

Other books by the same author:

Don't Sweat the Small Stuff—and It's All Small Stuff: Simple Ways to Keep the Little Things From Taking over Your Life, 1997

Slowing Down to the Speed of Life, 1997

Handbook for the Heart: Original Writings on Love, 1996

Other books you might like:

Michael Goddart, *Spiritual Revolution: A Seeker's Guide*, 1998

Keith Miller, *The Secret Life of the Soul*, 1997

Thomas Moore, *The Education of the Heart*, 1997

109

JIMMY CARTER

Living Faith

(New York: Times Books, 1996)

Category: Autobiography
Subject(s): Baptists; Christian Life; Volunteerism
Age range(s): Adult
Locale(s): Plains, Georgia

Summary: In this personal account, former President Jimmy Carter provides a look at the faith that influences his public and private life. Carter has spent his post-presidency years building homes for the poor through Habitat for Humanity, traveling to developing democracies to help monitor elections, and sharing his faith on Sunday mornings at the Maranatha Baptist Church in Plains, Georgia. Carter shares both the joys and sorrows of his life in *Living Faith*, and reveals the depth of belief that most often finds its expression in service to others and in the pursuit of peace and reconciliation.

Awards the book has won:

Christopher Award, Books for Adults, 1997

Other books by the same author:

Always a Reckoning, and Other Poems, 1995

An Outdoor Journal: Adventures and Reflections, 1988

Everything to Gain: Making the Most of the Rest of Your Life, 1987

Keeping Faith: Memoirs of a President, 1983

Other books you might like:

Catherine Marshall, *Meeting God at Every Turn*, 1980

B. McKay, *Bruised but Not Broken*, 1995

J.B. Phillips, *The Price of Success: An Autobiography*, 1984

Pat Williams, *Ahead of the Game: The Pat Williams Story*, 1999

James D. Denney, co-author

110

CARLOS CASTANEDA

Magical Passes: The Practical Wisdom of the Shamans of Ancient Mexico

(New York: HarperCollins, 1998)

Category: New Age (Nonfiction)
Subject(s): Shamanism; Religious Life; Customs
Age range(s): Adult

Summary: Carlos Castaneda introduces the visions and mystical traditions of the shaman tradition of ancient Mexico in his *Magical Passes*. The focus in this book is on using intricate and specific body movements and poses he terms ''tensegrity'' to promote energy and wellness. This practice is demonstrated in more than 450 photographs and passages detailing the series of movements.

Other books by the same author:

The Active Side of Infinity, 1998

Tensegrity: The Magical Passes of the Sorcerers of Ancient Mexico, 1997

The Art of Dreaming, 1993

A Separate Reality: Further Conversations with Don Juan, 1971

Other books you might like:

Taisha Abelar, *The Sorcerers' Crossing*, 1992

Ken Eagle Feather, *A Toltec Path: A User's Guide to the Teachings of Don Juan Matus, Carlos Castaneda, and Other Toltec Seers*, 1995

Victor Sanchez, *The Teachings of Don Carlos: Practical Applications of the Works of Carlos Castaneda*, 1995

111

CARLOS CASTANEDA

A Separate Reality: Further Conversations with Don Juan

(New York: Simon & Schuster, 1971)

Category: New Age (Nonfiction)
Subject(s): Mysticism; Shamanism; Indians of North America
Age range(s): Adult

Summary: In his 1968 book *Teachings of Don Juan*, Carlos Castaneda introduced his five-year period of study and training with Yaqui Indian sorcerer Don Juan. *A Separate Reality* is an account of his continued journey into the heart of the magic and spirituality of the Yaqui culture, during which he returned to his apprenticeship and delved more deeply into a culture that few Westerners have ever encountered.

Other books by the same author:
The Active Side of Infinity, 1998
Tensegrity: The Magical Passes of the Sorcerers of Ancient Mexico, 1997
The Art of Dreaming, 1993
The Teachings of Don Juan: A Yaqui Way of Knowledge, 1968

Other books you might like:
Taisha Abelar, *The Sorcerers' Crossing*, 1992
Ken Eagle Feather, *A Toltec Path: A User's Guide to the Teachings of Don Juan Matus, Carlos Castaneda, and Other Toltec Seers*, 1995
Victor Sanchez, *The Teachings of Don Carlos: Practical Applications of the Works of Carlos Castaneda*, 1995

112

CARLOS CASTANEDA

The Teachings of Don Juan: A Yaqui Way of Knowledge

(Berkeley: University of California, 1968)

Category: New Age (Nonfiction)
Subject(s): Indians of North America; Shamanism
Age range(s): Adult

Summary: Castaneda helped turn America's eyes to Native American spirituality. In this popular book, Castaneda records the conversations of a Native American shaman who shares his advice on spiritual matters, like the use of mind-altering drugs to achieve a spiritual state.

Other books by the same author:
A Separate Reality: Further Conversations with Don Juan, 1971

Other books you might like:
Taisha Abelar, *The Sorcerers' Crossing*, 1992
Florinda Donner, *Being-in-Dreaming*, 1991
Ken Eagle Feather, *Tracking Freedom: A Guide for Personal Evolution*, 1998
Holger Kalweit, *Dreamtime and Inner Space: The World of the Shaman*, 1988

Victor Sanchez, *Toltecs for the New Millennium*, 1996
Robert Nelson, translator

113

OWEN CHADWICK

A History of Christianity

(New York: St. Martin's Press, 1996)

Category: History
Subject(s): Christianity; Art; Music and Musicians
Age range(s): Adult

Summary: Covering nearly 2,000 years of religious traditions, this is a personal, accessible overview of the geographic and cultural spread of Christianity from ancient Hebrew lands through Europe to the American continents, and then to Africa and Asia. The author discusses the variety of church-state alliances and adversarial relationships that have existed since the origin of Christianity and the myriad forms of organized religious institutions that have their roots in Christian traditions. He is attentive throughout to the relationships between religion and the arts—visual, musical, written, and architectural—that exemplify the cultural influence Christianity has exerted on Western civilizations.

Other books by the same author:
The Christian Church in the Cold War, 1992
The Popes and European Revolution, 1981
Catholicism and History, 1977

Other books you might like:
Mircea Eliade, *A History of Religious Ideas*, 1978-1985
Paul Johnson, *A History of Christianity*, 1976
Kenneth Scott Latourette, *A History of Christianity*, 1953
John McManners, *The Oxford Illustrated History of Christianity*, 1990

114

OSWALD CHAMBERS

My Utmost for His Highest

(Old Tappan, NJ: Revell, 1935)

Category: Devotionals
Subject(s): Christian Life; Christianity; God
Age range(s): Adult

Summary: In this popular collection of devotional meditations, Chambers (1874-1917) reflects on the sovereignty and majesty of God. He also ponders the ways that Christians can render their greatest service to the glorious and magnificent God who has created them and provides for them. His meditations are arranged in the form of daily devotions, and his book is one of the most popular and timeless of its kind, having been published in some form or another by a number of different Christian publishers ever since its first appearance.

Awards the book has won:
Gold Medallion Book Award, Classics, 1996

Other books you might like:
Andrew Murray, *Daily Experience with God*, 1999
Watchman Nee, *The Normal Christian Life*, 1963

J.I. Packer, *Knowing God*, 1973
R.C. Sproul, *Almighty over All: Understanding the Sovereignty of God*, 1999
A.W. Tozer, *The Pursuit of God*, 1982

115

GARY CHAPMAN
ROSS CAMPBELL, Co-Author

The Five Love Languages of Children

(Chicago: Moody Press, 1997)

Category: Self-Help
Subject(s): Parent and Child; Communication; Psychology
Age range(s): Adult

Summary: Based on the popularity and success of Gary Chapman's *The Five Love Languages*, a guide to interpersonal communication for couples, *The Five Love Languages of Children* addresses ways for parents to improve communication with their children. The five love languages are actually modes of interaction that include physical touch, giving and receiving gifts, spending time together, performing acts of service, and using words of affirmation. The authors' premise is that every person of any age has a primary ''love language'' through which they interpret and feel the love of their parents. They describe each of the modes of communication and explain how to recognize and build stronger relationships by understanding each child's unique love language. *The Five Love Languages of Children* offers a non-sectarian guide to teaching values and developing spiritual awareness in children.

Other books by the same author:
The Other Side of Love: Handling Anger in a Godly Way, 1999
Five Signs of a Functional Family, 1997 (Derek Chapman, co-author)
The Five Love Languages, 1992

Other books you might like:
James McGinnis, *Parenting for Peace and Justice*, 1981
Dorothy Law Nolte, *Children Learn What They Live: Parenting to Inspire Values*, 1998
Fred Rogers, *Mister Rogers Talks with Parents*, 1983
Fred Rogers, *You Are Special: Words of Wisdom From America's Most Beloved Neighbor*, 1994
Randy Rolfe, *The Seven Secrets of Successful Parents*, 1997

116

MARY ELLEN CHASE

The Bible and the Common Reader

(New York: Macmillan, 1944)

Category: Theology; Religious Commentaries
Subject(s): Bible; Christianity; Criticism
Age range(s): Adult

Summary: Novelist Chase offers an elegant reading of the *Bible* as literature. Looking at the *Bible* as if she were looking at a novel, short story, or poem, Chase analyzes the forms of biblical literature and the ways that each form is used to transmit meaning. Written long before literary criticism became an accepted method of interpreting the *Bible*, Chase's book offers lyrical readings of one of the world's most important literary masterpieces.

Other books by the same author:
The Lovely Ambition: A Novel, 1960
The Life and Language in the Old Testament, 1955

Other books you might like:
Northrop Frye, *The Great Code: The Bible and Literature*, 1982
John B. Gabel, *The Bible as Literature: An Introduction*, 1986
David Lyle Jeffrey, *People of the Book: Christian Identity and Literary Culture*, 1996
Robert Alter, *The Literary Guide to the Bible*, 1987
Frank Kermode, co-editor
Leland Ryken, *A Complete Literary Guide to the Bible*, 1993

117

G.K. CHESTERTON

St. Francis of Assisi

(London: Hodder & Stoughton, 1924)

Category: Biography
Subject(s): Saints; Catholicism
Age range(s): Adult

Summary: G.K. Chesterton's portrait of St. Francis of Assisi describes a man of warmth, vigor, and commitment to his ideals. Colorfully set within the context of the High Middle Ages, this view of the beloved priest traces the influence Francis had on the culture of his day, as well as on the centuries that followed. Chesterton's biography of Francis of Assisi was first published in 1924, and remains a classic portrayal of a well-known figure in the history of Christianity.

Other books by the same author:
St. Thomas Aquinas, 1933
A Chesterton Catholic Anthology, 1928
The Catholic Church and Conversion, 1926

Other books you might like:
Chiara Frugoni, *Francis of Assisi: A Life*, 1998
Julien Green, *God's Fool: The Life and Times of Francis of Assisi*, 1985
Peter Heinegg, translator
Nikos Kazantzakis, *Saint Francis: A Novel*, 1962
P.A. Bien, translator
Patti Normile, *Following Francis of Assisi: A Spirituality for Daily Living*, 1996
Alan Paton, *Instrument of Thy Peace*, 1968

118

CHILDREN OF AMERICA

The 11th Commandment: Wisdom From Our Children

(Woodstock, Vermont: Jewish Lights, 1996)

Category: Essays
Subject(s): Conduct of Life; Children; Religious Life

Age range(s): Children-Adult

Summary: This is a full-color volume of children's writing and artwork addressing the question, "If there were an Eleventh Commandment, what would it be?" The youthful answers range from the general-"Be nice"-to the particular-"You must be nice to your mom." Responses come from city and country, church and synagogue. Amid the humor, important themes emerge about what children believe is important in their world, and how they view their relationship to God.

Other books you might like:
Robert Coles, *The Spiritual Life of Children*, 1990
Judith E. Greenberg, *Young People's Letters to the President*, 1998
David Heller, *Dear God: Children's Letters to God*, 1987
 John Alcorn, illustrator

119

PEMA CHODRON

The Wisdom of No Escape: And the Path of Loving-Kindness

(Boston: Shambhala, 1991)

Category: Self-Help
Subject(s): Buddhism; Self-Acceptance; Meditation
Age range(s): Adult

Summary: The secret to bringing order into chaotic lifestyles is shared in this volume by American Buddhist nun Pema Chodron. Her thesis is that we cannot find happiness by trying to escape suffering, but rather by embracing it and accepting pain as part of our lives. Chodron outlines basic Buddhist teachings about mindfulness, and presents her thoughts in readings that can be used as lessons or meditations for one's personal journey through pain to peace.

Other books by the same author:
When Things Fall Apart: Heart Advice for Difficult Times, 1997
Awakening Loving-Kindness, 1996
Start Where You Are: A Guide to Compassionate Living, 1994

Other books you might like:
Joseph Goldstein, *The Path of Insight Meditation*, 1995
Rob Nairn, *What Is Meditation?: Buddhism for Everyone*, 1999
Rinpoche Sogyal, *Meditation*, 1994
Diana St. Ruth, *Sitting: A Guide to Buddhist Meditation*, 1998

120

The Path to Love: Renewing the Power of Spirit in Your Life

(New York: Harmony Books, 1997)

Category: Self-Help
Subject(s): Spirituality; Love; Meditation
Age range(s): Adult

Summary: With his characteristic blend of Eastern philosophy and Western psychology, Deepak Chopra offers a roadmap for navigating seven stages of love: attraction, infatuation, courtship, intimacy, surrender, passion, and ecstasy. Drawing on ancient philosophies, personal experiences, and stories of other couples in love, he invites readers to enhance their relationships with these spiritual teachings.

Other books by the same author:
The Way of the Wizard: Twenty Spiritual Lessons in Creating the Life You Want, 1995
Ageless Body, Timeless Mind: The Quantum Alternative to Growing Old, 1993

Other books you might like:
John Bradshaw, *Creating Love: The Next Great Stage of Growth*, 1992
Jack Canfield, *Chicken Soup for the Couple's Soul: Inspirational Stories about Love and Relationships*, 1999
 Mark Victor Hansen, co-editor
Shepherd Hoodwin, *Loving From Your Soul: Creating Powerful Relationships*, 1995
Miguel Ruiz, *The Mastery of Love: A Practical Guide to the Art of Relationship*, 1999
Charlotte Sophia Kasl, *If the Buddha Dated: A Handbook for Finding Love on a Spiritual Path*, 1999

121

DEEPAK CHOPRA

The Seven Spiritual Laws of Success: A Practical Guide to the Fulfillment of Your Dreams

(San Rafael, California: New World Library, 1994)

Category: New Age (Nonfiction); Self-Help
Subject(s): Self-Confidence; Spirituality; Self-Esteem
Age range(s): Adult

Summary: Chopra's books have a large and devoted following. In most of his books he encourages readers to seek spiritual peace with both body and soul. Indeed, he says, if you are living well spiritually, you will also be living well materially. In this book, Chopra combines the teachings of Hinduism, psychology, and Western religions to offer seven laws he believes are crucial to spiritual success. He also provides meditation exercises that can be used to enact these laws in one's life.

Other books by the same author:
The Way of the Wizard: Twenty Spiritual Lessons in Creating the Life You Want, 1995
Ageless Body, Timeless Mind: The Quantum Alternative to Growing Old, 1993

Other books you might like:
Wayne W. Dyer, *Wisdom of the Ages: A Modern Master Brings Eternal Truths into Everyday Life*, 1998
Maharishi Mahesh Yogi, *Science of Being and Art of Living: Transcendental Meditation*, 1994
Thomas Moore, *Care of the Soul: A Guide for Cultivating Depth and Sacredness in Everyday Life*, 1992
Amadea Morningstar, *The Ayurvedic Cookbook: A Personalized Guide to Good Nutrition and Health*, 1990
M. Scott Peck, *The Road Less Traveled: A New Psychology of Love, Traditional Values, and Spiritual Growth*, 1978

122

CAROL P. CHRIST, Editor
JUDITH PLASKOW, Co-Editor

Womanspirit Rising: A Feminist Reader in Religion

(San Francisco: Harper and Row, 1982)

Category: Theology
Subject(s): Religion; Women
Age range(s): Adult

Summary: This valuable anthology includes writings from the early years of feminist theology. Each of the essays provides a feminist reading of traditional theological doctrines like sin, salvation, and creation. The anthology is a helpful introductory source of primary writings for anyone interested in the roots of feminist theology.

Other books by the same author:
Weaving the Visions: New Patterns in Feminist Spirituality, 1989 (Co-authored with Judith Plaskow)
Diving Deep and Surfacing: Women Writers on a Spiritual Quest, 1980

Other books you might like:
Elizabeth Clark, *Women and Religion: A Feminist Source-book of Christian Thought*, 1977
Mary Daly, *Beyond God the Father: Toward a Philosophy of Women's Liberation*, 1973
Anne Carolyn Klein, *Meeting the Great Bliss Queen: Buddhists, Feminists, and the Art of the Self*, 1995
Rosemary Radford Ruether, *Sexism and God-Talk: Toward a Feminist Theology*, 1983

123

F. FORRESTER CHURCH

Life Lines: Holding On (And Letting Go)

(Boston: Beacon Press, 1996)

Category: Self-Help
Subject(s): God; Spirituality; Faith
Age range(s): Adult
Time period(s): 1990s

Summary: In the early 1990s, the Rev. F. Forrester Church, senior minister at the Unitarian Church of All Souls in New York City, received an anonymous letter from a parishioner asking in part, ''What is the meaning of adversity?. I am very tired of this stupid life. If you can tell me the reason for suffering or pain or adversity, please tell me.'' Because the letter contained veiled suicidal language, the reverend at first sought to find the letter-writer. When this proved to be impossible, he went back to the letter and realized that virtually anyone could have written these thoughts. To address the universal questions about the nature of God, the purpose of suffering and the meaning of adversity, Church began an exploration of these themes in personal study and essays. These essays are collected in *Life Lines*, a non-sectarian exploration of love and death, guilt and forgiveness, compassion and humility, and the lifelines that faith offers to those in circumstances of adversity. Church turns to the Old Testa-

ment book of Ecclesiastes for wisdom and insight, drawing on contemporary thought and personal experience, as well.

Other books by the same author:
God and Other Famous Liberals: Recapturing Bible, Flag, and Family From the Far Right, 1996
Everyday Miracles: Stories From Life, 1988
The Seven Deadly Virtues: A Guide to Purgatory for Atheists and True Believers, 1988
Father and Son: A Personal Biography of Senator Frank Church of Idaho by His Son, 1985

Other books you might like:
V. Gilbert Beers, *Finding Purpose in Your Pain*, 1998
Roy H. Clarke, *Beside Still Waters: Words of Comfort for the Soul*, 1999
Reynolds Price, *Letter to a Man in the Fire: Does God Exist and Does He Care?*, 1999
Terry Wardle, *Draw Close to the Fire: Finding God in the Darkness*, 1998

124

F. FORRESTER CHURCH, Editor
TERRENCE J. MULRY, Co-Editor

The Macmillan Book of Earliest Christian Prayers

(New York: Macmillan, 1988)

Category: Prayer
Subject(s): Christianity; History; Literature
Age range(s): Young Adult-Adult

Summary: This is a collection of translated prayers that demonstrate the evolution of prayer in Christianity. The book is divided into sections starting with the first appearance of prayer in the teachings of Jesus in the New Testament. Prayers from the first and second centuries of the church are culled from scriptural and other writings. Prayers from the early fathers of the church, including Origen and Clement of Alexandria are followed by the earliest-known liturgical prayers of formal worship. After Constantine declared Christianity the official state religion, persecution of Christians was replaced by widespread growth of formal Christian worship; this stage is represented by post-Nicene prayers from Greek, Syriac, Coptic, and Latin sources. A significant portion of the book is devoted to the prayer works of St. Augustine (354-430), because so many of his prayers and teachings can be traced to their original sources.

Other books by the same author:
The Macmillan Book of Earliest Christian Meditations, 1998 (Terrence J. Mulry, co-editor)
Everyday Miracles: Stories From Life, 1988
The Macmillan Book of Earliest Christian Hymns, 1988 (Terrence J. Mulry, co-editor)
The Seven Deadly Virtues: A Guide to Purgatory for Atheists and True Believers, 1988
Entertaining Angels: A Guide to Heaven for Atheists and True Believers, 1987

Other books you might like:
Duane W.H. Arnold, *Prayers of the Martyrs*, 1991

Nikolaos S. Natziniklolaou, *Voices in the Wilderness: An Anthology of Patristic Prayers*, 1988

Eugene H. Peterson, *Praying with the Early Christians: A Year of Daily Prayers and Reflections on the Words of the Early Christians*, 1994

125

CHURCH OF JESUS CHRIST OF LATTER-DAY STS

The Book of Mormon

(Salt Lake City: G. Q. Cannon & Sons Co., 1891)

Category: Doctrine; Theology
Subject(s): History; Mormons
Age range(s): Young Adult-Adult

Summary: Serving as a source of both history and doctrine for Mormon practitioners, *The Book of Mormon* is one of several sacred writings for followers of the Mormon faith, which was established in the mid-1800s by Joseph Smith. The text was said to have been found written on golden plates; Smith translated the plates into English and the first *Book of Mormon* was published in 1830. The volume was later divided into chapters and verses. *The Book of Mormon* emphasizes America as a chosen land connected to the Holy Lands of the Judeo-Christian faiths through immigrants from Jerusalem who traveled to the North American continent in 600 B.C., as well as through the appearance of Jesus Christ, after his resurrection, to inhabitants of North America.

Other books you might like:
Robert D. Anderson, *Inside the Mind of Joseph Smith: Psychobiography and the Book of Mormon*, 1999
Joseph H. Anway, *Adventures in a New Land: An Overview of the Book of Mormon*, 1987
Lynn F. Price, *Every Person in the Book of Mormon*, 1995

126

HENRY CLOUD
JOHN TOWNSEND, Co-Author

Boundaries: When to Say Yes, When to Say No to Take Control of Your Life

(Grand Rapids, Michigan: Zondervan, 1992)

Category: Self-Help
Subject(s): Self-Confidence; Family Relations; Psychology
Age range(s): Young Adult-Adult

Summary: The author offers biblical guidelines for setting personal boundaries in order to ensure healthy relationships with others. His principles and practices for handling manipulative or excessively restrictive relationships provide a Christian approach to assertiveness. *Boundaries* addresses the concerns readers may have about appearing selfish, feeling guilty, or increasing tension in relationships by establishing personal boundaries for their time, energy, money, and emotions.

Awards the book has won:
Gold Medallion Book Award, Christian Living, 1993

Other books by the same author:
Boundaries in Marriage, 1999

Boundaries with Kids, 1998
Changes That Heal, 1992
When Your World Makes No Sense, 1990

Other books you might like:
Les Parrott, *Relationships 101*, 1998
Greg M. Sumii, *The Christian's Handbook on Conflict Resolution*, 1998
H. Norman Wright, *Relationships That Work (And Those That Don't)*, 1998

127

ABRAHAM COHEN

Everyman's Talmud: The Major Teachings of the Rabbinic Sages

(New York: Schocken Books, 1995)

Category: Religious Commentaries
Subject(s): Judaism; Scripture
Age range(s): Adult

Summary: Originally published in London in 1932 and in America in 1949, this guide to the Talmud has been updated to reflect generational changes to the Jewish book of wisdom. It is still considered a premier "handbook" to the ever-growing doctrinal writings of Judaism. The book is arranged in chapters that together describe all the major doctrines of Judaism as found in the Talmud. A comprehensive table of contents will help readers easily find answers to their questions.

Other books by the same author:
Ancient Jewish Proverbs, 1980
The Teachings of Maimonides, 1968

Other books you might like:
Michael Katz, *Swimming in the Sea of the Talmud: Lessons for Everyday Living*, 1998
    Gershon Schwartz, co-author
Judah Nadich, *The Legends of the Rabbis*, 1994
Jacob Neusner, *The Book of Jewish Wisdom: The Talmud of the Well-Considered Life*, 1996
    Noam M. M. Neusner, co-editor
Marc-Alain Ouaknin, *The Burnt Book: Reading the Talmud*, 1995

128

ROBERT COLES

The Spiritual Life of Children

(Boston: Houghton Mifflin, 1990)

Category: Journals/Letters
Subject(s): Children; Spirituality; Psychology
Age range(s): Adult

Summary: Child psychiatrist Robert Coles interviewed more than 500 children between the ages of eight and twelve from many spiritual backgrounds (including Christian, Islamic, Jewish, and agnostic) and in a variety of places around the world (including the Americas, Europe, Africa, and the Middle East). In their talks, the children reveal their personal imagination, skepticism, questioning, and reflective thinking about what God is and how their idea of God fits into what they know of the world. This best-selling book is the final component of a trilogy of works by Cole that focus on the inner lives of children.

Awards the book has won:
Christopher Award, Books for Adults, 1997

Other books by the same author:
The Ongoing Journey: Awakening Spiritual Life in At-Risk Youth, 1996
The Moral Life of Children, 1986
The Political Life of Children, 1986

Other books you might like:
David Heller, *Dear God: Children's Letters to God*, 1987
Peggy J. Jenkins, *Nurturing Spirituality in Children: Simple Hands-on Activities*, 1995
Rami Vissell, *Rami's Book: The Inner Life of a Child*, 1989
Mimi Walch Doe, *10 Principles for Spiritual Parenting: Nurturing Your Child's Soul*, 1998

129

MICHAEL COLLOPY

Works of Love Are Works of Peace: Mother Teresa of Calcutta and the Missionaries of Charity: A Photographic Record

(San Francisco: Ignatius Press, 1996)

Category: Essays; Prayer
Subject(s): Catholicism; Poverty; Charity
Age range(s): Young Adult-Adult

Summary: This volume offers a comprehensive visual introduction to the work of Mother Teresa and her order of Missionaries of Charity. Included are photos of the sisters at work, in worship, and in prayer, along with letters, comments, and spiritual guidance from Mother Teresa, and the text of the daily prayers of the Missionaries of Charity. Collopy collected his material during a four-year period, capturing images of Mother Teresa and her work in all parts of the world.

Other books you might like:
Mother Teresa, *In the Heart of the World: Thoughts, Stories, & Prayers*, 1997
Raghu Rai, *Faith and Compassion: The Life and Work of Mother Teresa*, 1996
    Navin Chawla, co-author
Kathryn Spink, *Mother Teresa: A Complete Authorized Biography*, 1997
Sam Wellman, *Mother Teresa: Missionary of Charity*, 1996

130

CHARLES COLSON

Born Again

(Old Tappan, New Jersey: Chosen Books, 1976)

Category: Autobiography
Subject(s): Christianity; Prisoners and Prisons; Politics

Age range(s): Adult
Time period(s): 1970s
Locale(s): United States

Summary: This is the first book written by Charles Colson following his conviction for crimes committed during the Watergate scandal of the 1970s that resulted in the resignation of President Richard Nixon. Once a formidable Nixon lawyer and staff member, Colson experienced a Christian conversion during his imprisonment and found a new life in ministry to others who are incarcerated. In this volume, he describes his role in the events that led to the end of the Nixon presidency and also, paradoxically, to his own spiritual and professional rebirth.

Awards the book has won:
Eternity Outstanding Evangelical Book, 1976

Other books by the same author:
Convicted: New Hope for Ending America's Crime Crisis, 1989
Kingdoms in Conflict: An Insider's Challenging View of Politics, Power, and the Pulpit, 1987
Who Speaks for God?: Confronting the World with Real Christianity, 1985
Loving God, 1983
Life Sentence, 1979

Other books you might like:
G. Gordon Liddy, *Will: The Autobiography of G. Gordon Liddy*, 1980
Jerry McClain, *Happy Days: And Dark Nights*, 1996
    Susanne McClain, co-author
William J. Murray, *My Life Without God*, 1982

131

CHARLES COLSON

Life Sentence

(Lincoln, Virginia: Chosen Books, 1979)

Category: Autobiography
Subject(s): Christianity; Prisoners and Prisons; Ministry
Age range(s): Adult

Summary: In this sequel to Colson's autobiographical *Born Again*, the author talks about how he put his life back together again after his imprisonment for Watergate crimes. Colson experienced a Christian conversion through the events connected to the Watergate investigation and subsequent trials, and in this volume he reveals the ways God used his life experiences—good and bad alike—to help him find new purpose and direction. *Life Sentence* has remained popular and in print since its first appearance in 1979.

Awards the book has won:
Gold Medallion Book Award, Contemporary Issues, 1981

Other books by the same author:
Convicted: New Hope for Ending America's Crime Crisis, 1989
Kingdoms in Conflict: An Insider's Challenging View of Politics, Power, and the Pulpit, 1987
Who Speaks for God?: Confronting the World with Real Christianity, 1985

Loving God, 1983
Born Again, 1976

Other books you might like:
Terry Whalin, *Chuck Colson*, 1994
Stella Wiseman, *Charles Colson*, 1995
Vaughan Booker, *From Prison to Pulpit: My Road to Redemption*, 1994
    David Phillips, co-author

132

CHARLES COLSON

Loving God

(Grand Rapids, Michigan: Zondervan, 1983)

Category: Devotionals
Subject(s): Christian Life; Conduct of Life; Spirituality
Age range(s): Young Adult-Adult

Summary: In this book, Charles Colson tells the stories of both famous and unfamiliar people whose decision to love God changed their lives and influenced the world around them. From stories of martyrdom in the Roman Coliseum to modern-day tales of politicians affected by the faith of others, Colson's collection covers topics including obedience to God, reading the Bible, sin and forgiveness, and what it means to be a holy nation.

Awards the book has won:
Gold Medallion Book Award, Devotional/Christian Living, 1984

Other books by the same author:
Convicted: New Hope for Ending America's Crime Crisis, 1989
Kingdoms in Conflict: An Insider's Challenging View of Politics, Power, and the Pulpit, 1987
Who Speaks for God?: Confronting the World with Real Christianity, 1985
Life Sentence, 1979
Born Again, 1976

Other books you might like:
Catherine Marshall, *Beyond Our Selves*, 1961
Hannah Whitall Smith, *The Christian's Secret of a Happy Life*, 1883
Corrie ten Boom, *Anywhere He Leads Me*, 1997
    Judith Couchman, compiler

133

JAMES H. CONE

A Black Theology of Liberation

(Maryknoll, New York: Orbis Books, 1990)

Category: Theology
Subject(s): African Americans; Civil Rights Movement; Christianity
Age range(s): Adult

Summary: In the late 1960s, when the civil rights movement in America was at its zenith, James Cone began formulating a revolutionary theology rooted in black identity and oppression. First published in 1970, *A Black Theology of Liberation* puts forth the idea that theology evolves from the experience of a people, and therefore a black theology should reflect the centuries-old struggle to cast off oppression by non-black peoples. At the heart of Cone's theology is the image of a black God whose might and power are directed toward freedom and justice for his people. In 1990, Cone reissued a 20th anniversary edition of his original treatise, remaining committed to the overarching themes of his theology, but expanding it by incorporating inclusive language, recognizing the relationship between black liberation and feminist theology, and integrating a more global perspective on liberation theology—focusing less on the experience of black Americans, and more on the experiences of oppressed races worldwide.

Other books by the same author:
Risks of Faith, 1999
Speaking the Truth: Ecumenism, Liberation, and Black Theology, 1986
My Soul Looks Back, 1982
Black Theology: A Documentary History, 1966-1979, 1979
    (Gayraud S. Wilmore, co-editor)
God of the Oppressed, 1975

Other books you might like:
Rufus Burrow Jr., *James H. Cone and Black Liberation Theology*, 1994
George C.L. Cummings, *A Common Journey: Black Theology*, 1993
Diana L. Hayes, *And Still We Rise: An Introduction to Black Liberation Theology*, 1996

134

JAMES H. CONE

God of the Oppressed

(New York: Seabury, 1975)

Category: Theology
Subject(s): Christianity; African Americans; Social Issues
Age range(s): Adult

Summary: Cone contends that for too long white Christianity has marginalized black Christians. The white God reflects the love of material comfort and assurance of salvation central to white Christianity. The God of the oppressed, though, is one who takes sides with the marginalized, as He did with Moses and the Israelite slaves in Egypt. The God of the oppressed will be a warrior for His people and help them overcome their oppression foisted upon them by white Christians. Cone's is a truly revolutionary theology that changes the ways people think about race, society, and religion.

Other books by the same author:
Black Theology and Black Power, 1969

Other books you might like:
Albert B. Cleage, *The Black Messiah*, 1968
Paulo Friere, *Pedagogy of the Oppressed*, 1970
Diana L. Hayes, *And Still We Rise: An Introduction to Black Liberation Theology*, 1996
Dwight N. Hopkins, *Cut Loose Your Stammering Tongue: Black Theology in Slave Narratives*, 1991

William R. Jones, *Is God a White Racist?: A Preamble to Black Theology*, 1973

135
CONFUCIUS

Analects
(c. 500 BC)

Category: Scripture
Subject(s): Relationships; Religion; Government
Age range(s): Young Adult-Adult

Summary: In this classic of Chinese literature, Confucius (551-479 BC) teaches the perfectibility of humanity. Confucius believes that there are rules of propriety that govern everyday relationships between family members and between citizens and the state. In order for these relationships to be harmonious, they must reflect reciprocity. Confucius' version of the Golden Rule is: "What you do not want done to yourself, do not do to others."

Other books you might like:
Elizabeth Breuilly, *Religions of the World: The Illustrated Guide to Origins, Beliefs, Traditions, & Festivals*, 1997
Wing-tsit Chan, *A Source Book in Chinese Philosophy*, 1963
Lao Tzu, *Tao-te Ching*, c. 650 BC
Yutang Lin, *The Importance of Living*, 1937
Ninian Smart, *The World's Religions*, 1989

136
CONFUCIUS

I Ching
(c. 1,000 BC)

Category: Scripture
Subject(s): Future; Religion
Age range(s): Young Adult-Adult

Summary: The *I Ching* is also called the *Book of Changes*. It is a book concerned primarily with the ancient Chinese art of divination. Each section of the book is numbered. People who wish to know something about their future can shake a bundle of 100 sticks until one stick falls out. The number on the stick corresponds to a number in the book and provides the person with a fortune. Although the *I Ching* was first compiled by shamans and dates to around 1,000 BC, many people give Confucius credit for editing or compiling it. English translations were published beginning in the 19th century.

Other books you might like:
Thomas Cleary, *Practical Taoism*, 1996
Lao Tzu, *Tao-te Ching*, c. 650 BC
Tung-Pin Lu, *Secret of the Golden Flower: A Chinese Book of Life*, 1975
Hellmut Wilhelm, *Understanding the I Ching*, 1995
Eva Wong, *Harmonizing Yin and Yang: The Dragon-Tiger Classic*, 1997

137
RUSSELL H. CONWELL

Acres of Diamonds: All Good Things Are Possible, Right Where You Are, and Now!
(Joshua Tree, California: Tree of Life Publications, 1993)

Category: Self-Help
Subject(s): Faith; Success; Business
Age range(s): Young Adult-Adult

Summary: Russell H. Conwell, a lawyer, pastor, and writer who lived from 1843 to 1925, was the founder of Philadelphia's Temple University. In 1870 he took a trip to Mesopotamia, where he heard a tour guide tell a story. According to this story, a man died far from his home, which he had left long before in search of a diamond mine. Shortly after his death, his own land was found to be hiding acres of diamonds. Conwell was so impressed by the notion that one's treasure can be easily found if one will but seek it in the small, everyday things of life, that when he returned to the United States, he began sharing it publicly. His ideas became a popular inspirational lecture, which he delivered more than 6,000 times during his lifetime. The founding of Temple College to provide ministry education to interested young men was Conwell's way of mining the diamonds in his own backyard, and the fledgling college was financed during its early years of growth through the proceeds of his *Acres of Diamonds* lectures across the country. With its message of optimism and practical advice, Conwell's uplifting essay, which was first published in 1890, has found appreciative audiences throughout the 20th century among generations of entrepreneurs and business leaders.

Other books by the same author:
How to Live the Christ Life, 1912
He Goeth Before You, 1909
Gleams of Grace, 1887

Other books you might like:
James Allen, *As a Man Thinketh*, 1910
Joyce Proctor Beaman, *Bloom Where You Are Planted*, 1975
Norman Vincent Peale, *The Power of Positive Thinking*, 1952

138
DAVID A. COOPER

Entering the Sacred Mountain: A Mystical Odyssey
(New York: Bell Tower, 1994)

Category: Autobiography
Subject(s): Meditation; Judaism; Buddhism
Age range(s): Adult

Summary: In this autobiographical account of his own spiritual journey, the author explores mysticism and meditation in Judaism, Buddhism, and Sufism. In particular, Cooper writes about how the practice of spiritual meditation has enriched his marriage through retreats in many places, including New Mexico, Massachusetts, and Israel. His thoughtful approach to understanding the spiritual quest offers an introduction that can be meaningful to adherents of various faith traditions.

Other books by the same author:
God Is a Verb: Kabbalah and the Practice of Mystical Judaism, 1997
Renewing Your Soul: A Guided Retreat for the Sabbath and Other Days of Rest, 1995
The Heart of Stillness: The Elements of Spiritual Practice, 1992
Silence, Simplicity, and Solitude: A Guide for Spiritual Retreat, 1992

Other books you might like:
Donald H. Bishop, *Mysticism and the Mystical Experience: East and West*, 1995
James P. Carse, *Breakfast at the Victory: The Mysticism of Ordinary Experience*, 1994
Wolfgang Kopp, *Free Yourself of Everything: Radical Guidance in the Spirit of Zen and Christian Mysticism*, 1994
Betsy Serafin, *The Rose of Five Petals: A Path for the Christian Mystic*, 1997

139

PATRICIA CORNWELL

Ruth, a Portrait: The Story of Ruth Bell Graham

(New York: Doubleday, 1997)

Category: Biography
Subject(s): Christian Life; Ministry; Family Life
Age range(s): Young Adult-Adult
Time period(s): 20th century (1920s-1980s)

Summary: In this volume, Edgar Award-winning mystery novelist Patricia Cornwell updates her original biographical portrait of Ruth Bell Graham. From her childhood in China to looking back on her child-rearing years, the woman who has shared her life with Christian evangelist Billy Graham is portrayed as a strong and loving wife and mother whose personal faith has buoyed her through good times and bad. The young girl who dreamed of becoming a missionary found herself called to a life of ministry at home that still touched millions around the world.

Other books by the same author:
Life's Little Fable, 1999
Southern Cross, 1999
Scarpetta's Winter Table, 1998
All That Remains, 1992
A Time for Remembering: The Story of Ruth Bell Graham, 1983

Other books you might like:
Billy Graham, *Just as I Am: The Autobiography of Billy Graham*, 1997
Ruth Bell Graham, *Sitting by My Laughing Fire*, 1977
Linda McGinn, *The Strength of a Woman: Activating the 12 Dynamic Qualities Every Woman Possesses*, 1993
Gigi Graham Tchividjian, *Passing It On*, 1992

140

PATRICIA CORNWELL

A Time for Remembering: The Story of Ruth Bell Graham

(San Francisco: Harper & Row, 1983)

Category: Biography
Subject(s): Christian Life; Ministry; Family Life
Age range(s): Young Adult-Adult
Time period(s): 20th century (1920s-1980s)
Locale(s): China; United States

Summary: Ruth Bell Graham was the daughter of medical missionaries in China during the 1920s and 1930s. She herself had hoped to become a missionary to Tibet, but her plans changed in 1940 when she crossed paths with young Billy Graham at Wheaton College in the United States. Ruth married Graham, who would become one of the world's best-known and most respected Christian evangelists of the 20th century. Cornwell presents the portrait of a woman whose heart is always open to those in need of spiritual guidance or comfort, a woman who found fulfillment in her faith and her family.

Awards the book has won:
Gold Medallion Book Award, Biography/Autobiography, 1985

Other books by the same author:
Life's Little Fable, 1999 (a picture book for children; Barbara Leonard Gibson, illustrator)
Southern Cross, 1999
Scarpetta's Winter Table, 1998
Ruth, a Portrait: The Story of Ruth Bell Graham, 1997
All That Remains, 1992

Other books you might like:
Billy Graham, *Just as I Am: The Autobiography of Billy Graham*, 1997
Ruth Bell Graham, *Sitting by My Laughing Fire*, 1977
Linda McGinn, *The Strength of a Woman: Activating the 12 Dynamic Qualities Every Woman Possesses*, 1993
Gigi Graham Tchividjian, *Passing It On*, 1992

141

PHIL COUSINEAU

The Art of Pilgrimage: The Seeker's Guide to Making Travel Sacred

(Berkeley: Conari Press, 1998)

Category: Essays
Subject(s): Travel; Pilgrims and Pilgrimages; Spirituality
Age range(s): Adult

Summary: Although we travel further and more often than ever before in search of rest, entertainment, or adventure, our experiences are frequently disappointing. In the midst of traffic jams and crowded airports, we wonder why our vacation travels leave us feeling exhausted instead of refreshed. Phil Cousineau's reflections on the spiritual aspects of travel suggest that finding and understanding our purpose for traveling is more important than where we go or how much we spend while we're there. This volume offers a collection of personal stories about how to make travel a personal pilgrimage, whether the destination is a ball park or a religious shrine.

Other books by the same author:
Soul Moments: Marvelous Stories of Synchronicity— Meaning Coincidences From a Seemingly Random World, 1997
The Soul of the World: A Modern Book of Hours, 1993

Other books you might like:
Mitch Albom, Tuesdays with Morrie: An Old Man, a Young Man, and Life's Greatest Lesson, 1997
Sir Richard Francis Burton, Personal Narrative of a Pilgrimage to El-Medinah and Meccah, 1855
Paulo Coelho, The Pilgrimage: A Contemporary Quest for Ancient Wisdom, 1995
    Alan Clarke, translator
Simon Coleman, Pilgrimage: Past and Present in the World Religions, 1995
    John Elsner, co-author
Jennifer Westwood, Sacred Journeys: An Illustrated Guide to Pilgrimages around the World, 1997
Michael Hood, Cranberry Smoke, 1989

142

NORMAN COUSINS, Editor

The Words of Albert Schweitzer
(New York: Newmarket Press, 1984)

Category: Essays
Subject(s): Ethics; Music and Musicians; Peace
Age range(s): Adult

Summary: This collection of the words and thoughts of Albert Schweitzer was edited and prepared by Norman Cousins. Topics include Schweitzer's signature thoughts on reverence for life, plus essays on music, peace, and other characteristic topics associated with the life and work of Schweitzer. This is a good introduction to the philosophies of life espoused by Schweitzer.

Other books by the same author:
Albert Schweitzer's Mission: Healing and Peace, 1985
The Celebration of Life: A Dialogue on Immortality and Infinity, 1974
Dr. Schweitzer of Lambarene, 1960

Other books you might like:
Paul Helm, Faith and Reason, 1999
Peter Joseph, Freedom, Truth, and Hope, 1987
Margaret Knight, Humanist Anthology: From Confucius to Attenborough, 1995
Thomas V. Morris, God and the Philosophers: The Reconciliation of Faith and Reason, 1996

143

DENNIS COVINGTON

Salvation on Sand Mountain: Snake Handling and Redemption in Southern Appalachia
(New York: Addison-Wesley, 1995)

Category: History
Subject(s): Christianity; Snake-handling; Appalachia
Age range(s): Adult
Time period(s): 1990s (1991)
Locale(s): Sand Mountain, Alabama

Summary: In 1991 in Sand Mountain, Alabama, preacher Glendel Buford Summerford tries to kill his wife by forcing her to stick her hand in a box of rattlesnakes. Journalist Covington, whose family had once lived on Sand Mountain, covers the trial for the New York Times. During his stay, he discovers an Old South full of poverty and faith. As he questions residents about the Summerford case, he becomes involved in a sectarian movement that exhibits its faith by handling serpents, drinking strychnine, speaking in tongues, and exorcising demons. In a stirring narrative, Covington describes his own search for his snake-handling relatives, and he even handles serpents himself.

Awards the book has won:
Rea Nonfiction Prize, 1996
Reference and User Service Association (RUSA) Award, Nonfiction, 1996

Other books by the same author:
Cleaving: The Story of a Marriage, 1999
Lasso the Moon, 1995
Lizard, 1991

Other books you might like:
James Agee, A Death in the Family, 1957
    Although Agee did not complete his novel before his death, he had left enough written material for editors to complete it posthumously.
Harry Crews, A Feast of Snakes, 1976
Sinclair Lewis, Elmer Gantry, 1927
Carson McCullers, The Ballad of the Sad Cafe and Other Stories, 1951
Flannery O'Connor, Wise Blood, 1952

144

HARVEY COX

The Secular City: Secularization and Urbanization in Theological Perspective
(New York: Macmillan, 1965)

Category: Theology
Subject(s): Christianity; History; City Life
Age range(s): Adult

Summary: What happens to religion when the city becomes more industrialized and more secular, leaving religion behind? In his famous little book, Cox uses sociological analysis to paint a portrait of the new urban environment in which traditional Christianity has little influence. He contends that secularization and urbanization has fostered anonymity and alienation. He notes that we are so separated from one another that traditional forms of religious worship that focus on community are no longer possible. His book can spark a remarkable rethinking of the role of religion, especially Christianity, in the modern world. Cox's book is a classic in the field of contemporary ministry.

Other books by the same author:
Religion in the Secular City: Toward a Postmodern Theology, 1984
Seduction of the Spirit: The Use and Misuse of People's Religion, 1973

Other books you might like:
Peter L. Berger, *The Sacred Canopy: Elements of a Sociological Theory of Religion*, 1967
Robert S. Ellwood, *The Sixties Spiritual Awakening: American Religion Moving From Modern to Postmodern*, 1994
Michael Harrington, *The Politics at God's Funeral: The Spiritual Crisis of Western Civilization*, 1983
A.N. Wilson, *God's Funeral*, 1999
Robert Wuthnow, *After Heaven: Spirituality in America Since the 1950s*, 1998

145

MALLY COX-CHAPMAN

The Case for Heaven: Near-Death Experiences as Evidence of the Afterlife
(New York: G.P. Putnam's Sons, 1995)

Category: Self-Help
Subject(s): Afterlife; Death; Faith
Age range(s): Young Adult-Adult

Summary: Journalist Mally Cox-Chapman explores the phenomenon of near-death experiences that seem to provide a glimpse of a heavenly hereafter. Herself a near-death survivor, Cox-Chapman interviewed more than 50 others who have had similar experiences. In this volume, she provides a record of these interviews, noting that most people who have had the experience of being clinically dead and revived once again share a firm belief that there is an afterlife and that they themselves have seen a preview of it.

Other books you might like:
Richard Abanes, *Journey Into the Light: Exploring Near-Death Experiences*, 1996
P.M.H. Atwater, *Beyond the Light: What Isn't Being Said about Near-Death Experience*, 1994
P.B.C. Fenwick, *The Truth in the Light: An Investigation of over 300 Near-Death Experiences*, 1997
Elizabeth Fenwick, co-author
Karlis Osis, *What They Saw—At the Hour of Death*, 1977
Erlendur Haraldsson, co-author
Maurice Rawlings, *To Hell and Back: Life After Death—Startling New Evidence*, 1993

146

F.L. CROSS, Editor
E.A. LIVINGSTONE, Co-Editor

The Oxford Dictionary of the Christian Church
(New York: Oxford University Press, 1997)

Category: Religious Encyclopedias/Dictionaries
Subject(s): Christianity; History
Age range(s): Adult

Summary: Since it was first published in 1957, *The Oxford Dictionary of the Christian Church* has earned a reputation as one of the most important general references on Christianity. Now in its third edition, the one-volume reference source has been extensively updated to cover contemporary academic, moral, and social issues. More than 6,000 entries offer a comprehensive examination of the history, theology, beliefs, and practices of Christianity in a format that is useful for general readers as well as specialists in the field of religion.

Other books you might like:
J.C. Cooper, *Cassell Dictionary of Christianity*, 1996
J.D. Dixon, *The Concise Dictionary of the Christian Tradition: Doctrine, Liturgy, History*, 1989
Cecil B. Murphey, *The Dictionary of Biblical Literacy*, 1989
Daniel G. Reid, *Dictionary of Christianity in America*, 1990
Alan Richardson, *The Westminster Dictionary of Christian Theology*, 1983
John S. Bowden, co-editor

147

JOHN DOMINIC CROSSAN

The Birth of Christianity: Discovering What Happened in the Years Immediately After the Execution of Jesus
(San Francisco: HarperSanFrancisco, 1998)

Category: Theology; History
Subject(s): Christianity; Ancient History; Jesus
Age range(s): Adult

Summary: Integrating study principles from history, anthropology, and archaeology, Crossan examines current beliefs about Christianity. One of his more controversial suggestions is that Western Christianity is more reflective of the Greek and Roman heritage of the Apostle Paul than it is of the Palestinian world and religion of Jesus himself. Crossan demonstrates a high level of intelligent scholarship with this volume. His style of writing, however, keeps the book accessible and interesting to those who do not have a theological background but are interested in the work of religious historians who study the roots of Western religious expressions and beliefs.

Other books by the same author:
Who Is Jesus?: Answers to Your Questions about the Historical Jesus, 1996
Jesus: A Revolutionary Biography, 1994

The Historical Jesus: The Life of a Mediterranean Jewish Peasant, 1991

Other books you might like:

Marcus J. Borg, *The God We Never Knew: Beyond Dogmatic Religion to a More Authentic Contemporary Faith*, 1997

Wayne A. Meeks, *The First Urban Christians: The Social World of the Apostle Paul*, 1983

John P. Meier, *A Marginal Jew: Rethinking the Historical Jesus*, 1991-1994

148

JOHN DOMINIC CROSSAN

Jesus: A Revolutionary Biography

(San Francisco: HarperSanFrancisco, 1994)

Category: Theology
Subject(s): Christianity; History; Jesus
Age range(s): Adult

Summary: A leading scholar in the field of historical research about Jesus, Crossan here provides one of his most definitive statements about the nature and mission of Jesus in history. He describes Jesus as a social philosopher and activist who challenged the hierarchies of Jewish society with courage and a Socratic method of teaching. According to Crossan's biography, Jesus was the first person ever to invite all to participate in the rule and worship of God, regardless of gender, class, or ethnic heritage-making him a revolutionary in the truest sense of the word.

Other books by the same author:

The Jesus Controversy: Perspectives in Conflict, 1999
The Birth of Christianity: Discovering What Happened in the Years Immediately After the Execution of Jesus, 1998
Who Is Jesus?: Answers to Your Questions about the Historical Jesus, 1996
The Historical Jesus: The Life of a Mediterranean Jewish Peasant, 1991

Other books you might like:

Jeffrey Daniel Carlson, *Jesus and Faith: A Conversation on the Work of John Dominic Crossan*, 1994
William Lane Craig, *Will the Real Jesus Please Stand Up?*, 1998
John P. Meier, *A Marginal Jew: Rethinking the Historical Jesus*, 1991-1994

149

ALEXANDER CRUDEN

Cruden's Complete Concordance to the Old and New Testaments

(Grand Rapids, Michigan: Zondervan, 1968)

Category: Religious Encyclopedias/Dictionaries
Subject(s): Bible
Age range(s): Young Adult-Adult

Summary: First published more than 250 years ago, the life's work of Alexander Cruden (1701-1770) remains a standard reference tool for biblical students and scholars. It contains more than 220,000 references to *Bible* verses, plus word definitions as warranted, and a list of all the names that appear in the Old and New Testaments, along with their meanings. Many editions of Cruden's original work have been published in the past two centuries. This latest version offers both complete coverage of the original at a language level appropriate for contemporary readers.

Other books you might like:

Charles P. Pfeiffer, *The Wycliffe Bible Commentary*, 1962
    Everett F. Harrison, co-editor
James Strong, *The New Strong's Exhaustive Concordance of the Bible*, 1996
Merrill F. Unger, *New Unger's Bible Handbook*, 1984

150

NICKY CRUZ

Run, Baby, Run

(Plainfield, New Jersey: Logos International, 1968)

Category: Autobiography
Subject(s): Gangs; Crime and Criminals; Evangelism
Age range(s): Young Adult-Adult
Time period(s): 1950s; 1960s
Locale(s): New York, New York

Summary: A popular classic in evangelical Christian writings, this is the story of a young man who escaped the gang life he led during the 1950s and 1960s on the streets of Brooklyn in New York City. Nicky Cruz was involved in drugs, alcohol, and street violence as a young man until he met a street pastor, David Wilkerson, whose message of Christ's love broke through the walls Cruz had constructed around his heart. Cruz is still active in Christian outreach efforts toward America's urban youth. An updated version of his story was published in 1992.

Other books by the same author:

Code Blue: Urgent Care for the American Youth Emergency, 1995
Where Were You When I Was Hurting?, 1986
Lonely, but Never Alone, 1981
Satan on the Loose, 1973

Other books you might like:

Brother Andrew, *God's Smuggler*, 1967
Jackie Pullinger, *Chasing the Dragon*, 1980
David Wilkerson, *The Cross and the Switchblade*, 1962
Don Wilkerson, *The Cross Is Still Mightier than the Switchblade*, 1996

151

DALAI LAMA
HOWARD C. CUTLER, Co-Author

The Art of Happiness: A Handbook for Living

(New York: Riverhead, 1998)

Category: Devotionals
Subject(s): Spirituality; Buddhism; Ethics
Age range(s): Adult

Summary: Journalist Howard C. Cutler asks the Dalai Lama a number of questions about the relationship between spirituality and everyday life. The Dalai Lama discusses topics ranging from marriage and sex to friendship and finances. As he talks about each topic, he says that it is indeed possible for people to be happy in all areas of their lives. However, the happiness he talks about is not a superficial happiness that is tied to mere pleasure. The Dalai Lama says that spiritual awareness brings true happiness to all that we do.

Other books by the same author:
The Good Heart: A Buddhist Perspective on the Teachings of Jesus, 1996

Other books you might like:
Marilyn M. Rhie, *Worlds of Transformation: Tibetan Art of Wisdom and Compassion*, 1999
Rinpoche Sogyal, *The Tibetan Book of Living and Dying*, 1992
Clark Strand, *The Wooden Bowl: Simple Meditation for Everyday Life*, 1998
Swami Rama, *Living with the Himalayan Masters*, 1999
Robert Thurman, *Circling the Sacred Mountain: A Spiritual Adventure through the Himalayas*, 1999

152

DALAI LAMA

Freedom in Exile: The Autobiography of the Dalai Lama

(New York: HarperCollins, 1990)

Category: Autobiography
Subject(s): Buddhism; Communism; Human Rights
Age range(s): Young Adult-Adult
Time period(s): 20th century
Locale(s): Tibet; Dharamsala, India

Summary: Tenzin Gyatso, better known as the 14th Dalai Lama, writes of his life as the current spiritual leader of Tibet, most of which has taken place outside the land of his birth. He describes the years of his childhood in Tibet, followed by the brutal invasion of Chinese Communism, which precipitated his escape to India. In personally revealing stories, anecdotes, and observations, Gyatso sheds light on his culture as well as his own life, and demonstrates the quiet, down-to-earth spirituality and commitment to peace for which he is known all over the world.

Other books by the same author:
Cultivating a Daily Meditation: Selections From a Discourse on Buddhist View, Meditation, and Action, 1991
My Tibet, 1990
Oceans of Wisdom: Guidelines for Living, 1989
The Dalai Lama at Harvard: Lectures on the Buddhist Path to Peace, 1988

Other books you might like:
Gill Farrer-Halls, *The World of the Dalai Lama: An Inside Look at His Life, His People, and His Vision*, 1998
Heinrich Harrer, *Seven Years in Tibet*, 1953
Mary Craig Kundun, *A Biography of the Family of the Dalai Lama*, 1997

Sidney Piburn, *The Dalai Lama, a Policy of Kindness: An Anthology of Writings by and about the Dalai Lama*, 1990

153

DALAI LAMA

The Way to Freedom

(San Francisco: HarperSanFrancisco, 1994)

Category: Doctrine
Subject(s): Buddhism; Scripture; Religious Life
Age range(s): Adult

Summary: *The Way to Freedom* is a collection of Buddhist teachings from the 14th century that are available to a general English-language readership for the first time with this publication. The volume contains over 1,000 years of teachings that form the core of Tibetan Buddhist practice. The Dalai Lama has arranged these writings to provide an organized approach to learning and living by the tenets and principles of Tibetan Buddhism. *The Way to Freedom* may be used as an introduction for the novice or as a continuing guide for the experienced practitioner.

Other books by the same author:
The World of Tibetan Buddhism: An Overview of its Philosophy and Practice, 1995 (Geshe Thupten Jinpa, translator)
Cultivating a Daily Meditation: Selections From a Discourse on Buddhist View, Meditation, and Action, 1991
My Tibet, 1990
Oceans of Wisdom: Guidelines for Living, 1989
The Dalai Lama at Harvard: Lectures on the Buddhist Path to Peace, 1988

Other books you might like:
Rinpoche Akong Tulku, *Taming the Tiger: Tibetan Teachings on Right Conduct, Mindfulness, and Universal Compassion*, 1995
Padma Sambhava, *The Tibetan Book of the Dead: The Great Book of Natural Liberation through Understanding in the Between*, 1993
Robert A.F. Thurman, translator
Padma Sambhava, *Advice From the Lotus-Born*, 1994
Erik Pema Kunsang, translator
Tulku Thondup, *Hidden Teachings of Tibet: An Explanation of the Terma Tradition of the Nyingma School of Buddhism*, 1986
Thupten Wangyal, *The Door of Liberation: Essential Teachings of the Tibetan Buddhist Tradition*, 1995
Robert Thurman, *Essential Tibetan Buddhism*, 1995
B. Alan Wallace, *Tibetan Buddhism From the Ground Up: A Practical Approach for Modern Life*, 1993
Steven Wilhelm, co-author

154

MARY DALY

Beyond God the Father: Toward a Philosophy of Women's Liberation

(Boston: Beacon Press, 1973)

Category: Theology

Subject(s): Christianity; Women; History
Age range(s): Adult
Summary: Daly's revolutionary book challenges the notion that God is male. For too long, she contends, Christianity has oppressed women by subjecting them to the image of a male God. Moreover, the Church itself, particularly the Catholic Church, has perpetuated this subjection of women by the establishment of a patriarchal hierarchy that regulates the ways in which women participate in the life of the Church. Daly calls for the death of God the Father and attempts to offer some ways that women can be religious beings after this death occurs.

Other books by the same author:
Gyn/Ecology: The Metaethics of Radical Feminism, 1978

Other books you might like:
Carol P. Christ, *Rebirth of the Goddess: Finding Meaning in Feminist Spirituality*, 1997
Elinor W. Gadon, *The Once and Future Goddess: A Symbol for Our Time*, 1989
Rosemary Radford Ruether, *Sexism and God-Talk: Toward a Feminist Theology*, 1983
Elisabeth Schussler Fiorenza, *In Memory of Her: A Feminist Theological Reconstruction of Christian Origins*, 1983
Phyllis Trible, *God and the Rhetoric of Sexuality*, 1978

155

ALMA DANIEL
TIMOTHY WYLLIE, Co-Author
ANDREW RAMER, Co-Author

Ask Your Angels

(New York: Ballantine Books, 1992)

Category: New Age (Nonfiction); Self-Help
Subject(s): Angels; Spirituality; Healing
Age range(s): Adult

Summary: How do angels help people in modern times? *Ask Your Angels* offers a guide for readers to follow to learn to tap the spiritual power of angels to help us achieve success in every aspect of life. Personal accounts and self-help suggestions advise on how to turn to the angels for help with health and healing, personal relationships, and spiritual growth.

Other books you might like:
Janice T. Connell, *Angel Power*, 1995
Linda Georgian, *Your Guardian Angels: Use the Power of Angelic Messengers to Enrich and Empower Your Life*, 1994
John Randolph Price, *The Angels Within Us*, 1993

156

LAMA SURYA DAS

Awakening the Buddha Within: Eight Steps to Enlightenment: Tibetan Wisdom for the Western World

(New York: Broadway Books, 1997)

Category: Self-Help

Subject(s): Buddhism; Meditation; Spirituality
Age range(s): Adult

Summary: Spiritual guidance in Western Buddhism from the Tibetan tradition is what readers will find in this volume. Lama Surya Das offers a complete yet easily understandable overview of the Buddhist teachings of the Eight-Fold Path and the Three Enlightenment Trainings-wisdom, ethics, and meditation. Surya Das has spent nearly three decades learning from the great Asian Buddhist masters and is one of the leading voices in Western Buddhism. His writing makes difficult concepts accessible to novices and provides practical new perspectives for those more experienced in the ways of Western Buddhism.

Other books by the same author:
Awakening to the Sacred: Creating a Spiritual Life From Scratch, 1999
Natural Great Perfection: Dzogchen Teachings and Vajra Songs, 1995 (Nyoshul Khenpo Rinpoche, co-author)
The Snow Lion's Turquoise Mane: Wisdom Tales From Tibet, 1992

Other books you might like:
Stephen Batchelor, *Buddhism Without Beliefs: A Contemporary Guide to Awakening*, 1997
Charlotte Joko Beck, *Everyday Zen: Love and Work*, 1989
Gavin Harrison, *In the Lap of the Buddha*, 1994
Thich Nhat Hanh, *Peace Is Every Step: The Path of Mindfulness in Everyday Life*, 1991
Claude Whitmyer, *Mindfulness and Meaningful Work: Explorations in Right Livelihood*, 1994

157

ALEXANDRA DAVID-NEEL

My Journey to Lhasa: The Personal Story of the Only White Woman Who Succeeded in Entering the Forbidden City

(New York: Harper and Brothers, 1927)

Category: Autobiography
Subject(s): Buddhism; Women; Adventure and Adventurers
Age range(s): Adult

Summary: First published in 1927 but reprinted to meet popular interest since then, *My Journey to Lhasa* is the account of Alexandra David-Neel's adventure as the first white woman to enter the Forbidden City of Lhasa in 1923. At age 55, David-Neel trekked through treacherous mountain passes for four months disguised as a man in order to reach Lhasa. She remained in Tibet for many years, becoming fluent in the language of the lamas and living a Buddhist life. Her travel writings are valued for their portrayal of Tibetan culture and the Tibetan Buddhist tradition as they were prior to 1950 when Tibet fell under Chinese control.

Other books by the same author:
The Secret Oral Teachings in Tibetan Buddhist Sects, 1967
Magic and Mystery in Tibet, 1932

Other books you might like:
Wade Brackenbury, *Yak Butter and Black Tea: A Journey into Forbidden China*, 1997

Heinrich Harrer, *Seven Years in Tibet*, 1953
Robert Thurman, *Circling the Sacred Mountain: A Spiritual Adventure through the Himalayas*, 1999

158

SARA SHENDELMAN
AVRAM DAVIS, Co-Author

Traditions: The Complete Book of Prayers, Rituals, and Blessings for Every Jewish Home

(New York: Hyperion, 1998)

Category: Self-Help
Subject(s): Holidays, Jewish; Judaism; Religious Life
Age range(s): Adult

Summary: In this volume, the editors have compiled a treasury of prayers-ancient, traditional, and modern-and more, all designed to inspire non-Orthodox individuals and families to incorporate the rich heritage of Judaism into their daily lives. With blessings and prayers for every day, as well as for special occasions, the work also offers practical guidance for building traditions into holiday celebrations. Included are Passover recipes and directions for building a sukkah.

Other books by the same author:
Judaic Mysticism, 1997
Meditation From the Heart of Judaism: Today's Teachers Share Their Practices, Techniques, and Faith, 1997

Other books you might like:
Anita Diamant, *Living a Jewish Life: A Guide for Starting, Learning, Celebrating, and Parenting*, 1991
   Howard Cooper, co-author
Alfred J. Kolatch, *The Jewish Book of Why*, 1981
Harold S. Kushner, *To Life!: A Celebration of Jewish Being and Thinking*, 1993
Joseph Telushkin, *Jewish Literacy: The Most Important Things to Know about the Jewish Religion, Its People, and Its History*, 1991

159

KEN DAVIS

I Don't Remember Dropping the Skunk, but I Do Remember Trying to Breathe: A Survival Guide for Teenagers

(Grand Rapids, Michigan: Zondervan, 1990)

Category: Self-Help
Subject(s): Christianity; Adolescence; Conduct of Life
Age range(s): Young Adult

Summary: Acknowledging the reality that kids often do things they probably shouldn't have done, and that oftentimes kids aren't consciously aware that their actions will have consequences, Ken Davis offers advice and guidance to kids about surviving their teen years. Without being preachy, Davis uses quirky humor and provides Christian standards for decision-making and maturing spiritually and emotionally.

Awards the book has won:
Gold Medallion Book Award, Youth, 1991

Other books by the same author:
Jumper Fables: Strange-but-True Devotions to Jump-Start Your Day, 1994 (David Lambert, co-author)

Other books you might like:
Gary Egeberg, *My Feelings Are Like Wild Animals! How Do I Tame Them?: A Practical Guide to Help Teens (and Former Teens) Feel and Deal with Painful Emotions*, 1998
Matthew J. Pinto, *Did Adam and Eve Have Belly Buttons?: And 199 Other Questions From Catholic Teenagers*, 1998
Ron Wheeler, *Jeremiah: I Wouldn't Be Tempted If Temptation Wasn't So Tempting*, 1995

160

KEN DAVIS
DAVID LAMBERT, Co-Author

Jumper Fables: Strange-but-True Devotions to Jump-Start Your Day

(Grand Rapids, Michigan: Zondervan, 1994)

Category: Devotionals
Subject(s): Conduct of Life; Christian Life; Prayer
Age range(s): Young Adult

Summary: Author Ken Davis helps teens tackle daily lifestyle decisions with an effective blend of contemporary humor and Christian values. The daily devotionals in this volume are designed to appeal to young adults who want practical spiritual guidance with a twist of comedy.

Awards the book has won:
Gold Medallion Book Award, Youth, 1995

Other books by the same author:
How to Live with Your Kids When You've Already Lost Your Mind, 1992
I Don't Remember Dropping the Skunk, but I Do Remember Trying to Breathe: A Survival Guide for Teenagers, 1990
How to Live with Your Parents Without Losing Your Mind, 1988

Other books you might like:
William Coleman, *Life in a Teenage Jungle*, 1994
Josh McDowell, *Thirteen Things You Gotta Know to Make It as a Christian*, 1992
Lorraine Peterson, *Anybody Can Be Cool—But Awesome Takes Practice*, 1988

161

DOROTHY DAY

The Long Loneliness: The Autobiography of Dorothy Day

(New York: Harper, 1952)

Category: Autobiography
Subject(s): Catholicism; Pacifism; Poverty
Age range(s): Adult

Summary: Dorothy Day combined radical social activism and orthodox Catholicism in her work and writings during most of the 20th century. She was the cofounder of the Catholic Worker movement and editor of a monthly newspaper by the same name. In this volume, she reflects on her life and work in what has become a spiritual classic on activist Catholicism.

Other books by the same author:
On Pilgrimage: The Sixties, 1972
Loaves and Fishes, 1963
House of Hospitality, 1939
From Union Square to Rome, 1938

Other books you might like:
William F. Buckley Jr., *Nearer, My God: An Autobiography of Faith*, 1997
Elizabeth O'Connor, *Letters to Scattered Pilgrims*, 1979

162

BARBARA DE ANGELIS

Real Moments
(New York: Delacorte Press, 1994)

Category: Self-Help
Subject(s): Love; Relationships
Age range(s): Adult

Summary: Barbara De Angelis offers non-religious spiritual guidance to readers seeking happiness and contentment. She demonstrates how to let go of past disappointments or expectations and learn to recognize and enjoy real moments of joy in life.

Other books by the same author:
Secrets about Life Every Woman Should Know: Ten Principles for Total Emotional and Spiritual Fulfillment, 1999
Secrets about Men Every Woman Should Know, 1990

Other books you might like:
Neil Bezaire, *First Empty Your Cup*, 1999
Dan Millman, *No Ordinary Moments: A Peaceful Warrior's Guide to Daily Life*, 1992
Carol Orsborn, *The Art of Resilience: 100 Paths to Wisdom and Strength in an Uncertain World*, 1997

163

EDITH DEEN

All the Women of the Bible
(New York: Harper and Row, 1955)

Category: History
Subject(s): Bible; Women
Age range(s): Young Adult-Adult

Summary: Deen's book is a helpful reference aid for students completing research papers and for Sunday School teachers looking for material about the *Bible*'s women. Deen includes character sketches of familiar women like Bathsheba, Jezebel, Ruth, and Mary as well as sketches of lesser-known women like Jephthah's daughter from the book of Judges, the deaconess Phoebe from 1 Timothy, and the woman with the hemorrhage from Matthew's Gospel. Deen provides both a literal

look at these women and a plethora of spiritual insights about these individuals.

Other books by the same author:
Family Living in the Bible, 1963
Great Women of the Christian Faith, 1959

Other books you might like:
Carolyn Nabors Baker, *Caught in a Higher Love: Inspiring Stories of Women in the Bible*, 1998
Joan Comay, *Who's Who in the Bible?: Two Volumes in One*, 1993
Herbert Lockyer, *All the Men of the Bible; All the Women of the Bible*, 1996
Virginia Stem Owens, *Daughters of Eve: Women of the Bible Speak to Women of Today*, 1995
Helen Bruch Pearson, *Do What You Have the Power to Do: Studies of Six New Testament Women*, 1992

164

DEMI, Author/Illustrator

Buddha Stories
(New York: Henry Holt, 1997)

Category: Morality Tales
Subject(s): Buddhism; Folklore
Age range(s): Children-Adult

Summary: Demi presents ten of the 550 known stories of the Buddha in this beautifully illustrated collection of fables with universally recognizable morals. Stories include "Tortoise and Two Geese," "The Black Bull," and "The Little Gray Donkey." The tales have morals such as "Pride leads to a fall, but humility is rewarded in the end."

Other books by the same author:
The Dalai Lama: A Biography of the Tibetan Spiritual and Political Leader, 1998
The Dragon's Tale and Other Animal Fables of the Chinese Zodiac, 1996

Other books you might like:
Judith Ernst, *The Golden Goose King*, 1995
Pamlyn Grider, *The Buddha's Question*, 1994
Jeanne M. Lee, *I Once Was a Monkey: Stories Buddha Told*, 1999

165

ALAN M. DERSHOWITZ

Chutzpah
(Boston: Little, Brown, 1991)

Category: Autobiography
Subject(s): Anti-Semitism; Jews; Law
Age range(s): Adult

Summary: In this autobiography, famed trial lawyer Dershowitz examines his life not only in the courtroom, but also as an American Jew. The book traces his rise from childhood on the streets of Brooklyn to adulthood as a powerful and outspoken lawyer with a roster of famous clients. Along the way he faces discrimination in law school and various law firms. He also examines the plight of Jews through history from his own unique perspective.

Other books by the same author:
Just Revenge: A Novel, 1999
Reasonable Doubts: The Criminal Justice System and the O.J. Simpson Case, 1996
The Story of My Life, 1996
The Advocate's Devil, 1995
The Best Defense, 1983

Other books you might like:
David Klinghoffer, *The Lord Will Gather Me In: My Journey to Jewish Orthodoxy*, 1999
Arthur L. Liman, *Lawyer: A Life of Counsel and Controversy*, 1998
Gerry Spence, *The Making of a Country Lawyer*, 1996
Israel Zamir, *Journey to My Father, Isaac Bashevis Singer*, 1995

166

ANITA DIAMANT

Choosing a Jewish Life: A Handbook for People Converting to Judaism and for Their Family and Friends
(New York: Schocken Books, 1997)

Category: Self-Help
Subject(s): Judaism; Religious Life; Customs
Age range(s): Adult

Summary: The choice to convert to Judaism entails many changes in one's life. Anita Diamant, contemporary expert on Jewish celebrations, observances, and practices, drew on her own experience of being married to a convert to write *Choosing a Jewish Life*. Her handbook offers guidance to new converts on everything from choosing a synagogue and a Hebrew name to how to build relationships with your new faith community and maintain relationships with the family of your heritage. Diamant's advice is practical, comprehensive, and designed to help one shape a newly-chosen Jewish life.

Other books by the same author:
Saying Kaddish: How to Comfort the Dying, Bury the Dead, and Mourn as a Jew, 1998
The New Jewish Baby Book: Names, Ceremonies, Customs, a Guide for Today's Families, 1994
Living a Jewish Life: A Guide for Starting, Learning, Celebrating, and Parenting, 1991 (Howard Cooper, co-author)
The New Jewish Wedding, 1985

Other books you might like:
Allan L. Berkowitz, *Embracing the Covenant: Converts to Judaism Talk about Why & How*, 1996
   Patti Moskovitz, co-editor
Lydia Kukoff, *Choosing Judaism*, 1981
Adin Steinsaltz, *Teshuvah: A Guide for the Newly Observant Jew*, 1987
   Michael Swirsky, translator

167

ANITA DIAMANT
HOWARD COOPER, Co-Author

Living a Jewish Life: A Guide for Starting, Learning, Celebrating, and Parenting
(New York: HarperCollins, 1991)

Category: Self-Help
Subject(s): Judaism; Family Life; Religious Life
Age range(s): Adult

Summary: Anita Diamant presents a guide to incorporating one's Jewish heritage into daily living, regardless of past or current faith practices. In addition to practical suggestions for everything from lighting Sabbath candles to celebrating a wedding, she offers stories, historical background, prayers, quotations, and more to bring the traditions of Judaism into contemporary life.

Other books by the same author:
Choosing a Jewish Life: A Handbook for People Converting to Judaism and for Their Family and Friends, 1997
What to Name Your Jewish Baby, 1989
The New Jewish Wedding, 1985

Other books you might like:
Morris N. Kertzer, *What Is a Jew?*, 1953
Alfred J. Kolatch, *The Concise Family Seder*, 1989
Alfred Kolatch, *The Jewish Book of Why*, 1981
Joseph Telushkin, *Jewish Literacy: The Most Important Things to Know about the Jewish Religion, Its People, and Its History*, 1991

168

ANNIE DILLARD

Holy the Firm
(New York: Harper and Row, 1977)

Category: Essays
Subject(s): Nature; Creation; Violence
Age range(s): Adult

Summary: The author of *Pilgrim at Tinker Creek* turns her attention to the problem of faith in the face of an often violent and painful world. In rich, poetic language, Annie Dillard contemplates the respective fates of a moth consumed by the flame of a candle and a child burned in an accident. She seeks to find a message of hope in the natural order of the world.

Other books by the same author:
Mornings Like These: Found Poems, 1995
The Living, 1992
The Writing Life, 1989
An American Childhood, 1987
Pilgrim at Tinker Creek, 1974

Other books you might like:
Amy Blackmarr, *Going to Ground: Simple Life on a Georgia Pond*, 1997
Frederick Buechner, *The Sacred Journey*, 1982
Anne Lamott, *Traveling Mercies: Some Thoughts on Faith*, 1999

Kathleen Norris, *Dakota: A Spiritual Geography*, 1993

169

ANNIE DILLARD

Pilgrim at Tinker Creek

(New York: Harper and Row, 1974)

Category: Autobiography
Subject(s): Nature; Religion; God
Age range(s): Young Adult-Adult

Summary: Dillard won a Pulitzer Prize for this book, her first, in 1974. A kind of spiritual autobiography, like a modern-day Thoreau, Dillard's book uses the natural world as a context for meditating on spiritual things. Dillard records the ordinary happenings in the world around her at Tinker Creek. For example, she uses the death of a frog as a starting point for reflecting on the nature of God and the creation of the universe. Dillard's book is a little treasure trove that can be mined over and over again for precious gems.

Awards the book has won:
Pulitzer Prize, Nonfiction, 1974

Other books by the same author:
Teaching a Stone to Talk, 1982
Holy the Firm, 1977

Other books you might like:
Amy Blackmarr, *Going to Ground: Simple Life on a Georgia Pond*, 1997
Frederick Buechner, *The Sacred Journey*, 1982
Loren Eiseley, *The Night Country*, 1971
Anne Lamott, *Traveling Mercies: Some Thoughts on Faith*, 1999
Kathleen Norris, *Dakota: A Spiritual Geography*, 1993

170

JAMES C. DOBSON

Life on the Edge

(Dallas, Texas: Word, 1995)

Category: Self-Help
Subject(s): Money; Love; Self-Perception
Age range(s): Young Adult-Adult

Summary: Between the ages of 16 and 26, according to Dr. James C. Dobson, young people are faced with some of the biggest decisions of their lives. These choices concern relationships, education, career, and purpose in life. In *Life on the Edge*, Dr. Dobson offers guidance to young people who are in what he terms the "critical decade," focusing on principles of Christian behavior and spirituality as standards that will assist them in making choices they will be able to live with in the long run.

Awards the book has won:
Gold Medallion Book Award, Christian Living, 1996

Other books by the same author:
Help for Home and Family, 1990
Parenting Isn't for Cowards: Dealing Confidently with the Frustrations of Child-Rearing, 1987

Emotions, Can You Trust Them?, 1980

Other books you might like:
Josh McDowell, *Don't Check Your Brains at the Door*, 1992
Josh McDowell, *The Teenage Q & A Book*, 1990

171

JAMES C. DOBSON

Love Must Be Tough: New Hope for Families in Crisis

(Waco, Texas: Word, 1983)

Category: Self-Help
Subject(s): Psychology; Christianity; Family Problems
Age range(s): Adult

Summary: In *Love Must Be Tough*, which has become a classic in the field of self-help literature about family problems, James C. Dobson identifies disrespect as the underlying cause of most conflict in marriages. Whether the visible problem is alcoholism, physical or emotional abuse, infidelity or some other break in a relationship, Dobson recommends addressing the issue of respect as a first-line course of action and change. Dobson is the founder of the Focus on the Family ministry, and his writings are directed toward the development of strong marriages and healthy family lives.

Awards the book has won:
Gold Medallion Book Award, Marriage and Family, 1984

Other books by the same author:
Emotions, Can You Trust Them?, 1980
Help for Home and Family, 1990
Parenting Isn't for Cowards: Dealing Confidently with the Frustrations of Child-Rearing, 1987

Other books you might like:
Bill Bright, *Building a Home in a Pull-Apart World: Powerful Principles for a Happier Marriage: 4 Steps That Work*, 1995
    Vonette Bright, co-author
Henry Cloud, *Boundaries in Marriage*, 1992
Gary R. Collins, *Baby Boomer Blues*, 1992
H. Norman Wright, *The Secrets of a Lasting Marriage*, 1995

172

JAMES C. DOBSON

When God Doesn't Make Sense

(Wheaton, Illinois: Tyndale House, 1993)

Category: Self-Help
Subject(s): Death; Diseases; Christianity
Age range(s): Young Adult-Adult

Summary: Based on his experience as a Christian counselor and psychologist, Dr. James C. Dobson addresses the question, "Why?" in connection with the hard times of life. In a volume directed toward Christian believers, Dobson shares his thoughts and observations about how to find hope in the midst of despair and regain one's sense of faith in God in the face of earthly trials.

Awards the book has won:
Gold Medallion Book Award, Christian Living, 1994

Other books by the same author:
Help for Home and Family, 1990
Parenting Isn't for Cowards: Dealing Confidently with the Frustrations of Child-Rearing, 1987
Emotions, Can You Trust Them?, 1980

Other books you might like:
Billy Graham, *Hope for the Troubled Heart*, 1991
Harold S. Kushner, *When Bad Things Happen to Good People*, 1981
Charles R. Swindoll, *For Those Who Hurt*, 1994

173

JAY P. DOLAN

The American Catholic Experience: A History from Colonial Times to the Present
(Garden City, New York: Doubleday, 1985)

Category: History
Subject(s): Catholicism; Customs; Culture
Age range(s): Adult

Summary: From the time that Christopher Columbus arrived on the shores of what would be called the New World, through almost five hundred years of religious growth and change, Jay P. Dolan traces the advent and evolution of Catholicism on the North American continent. With each new wave of immigrants from Eastern and Western Europe, new urban ethnic communities were formed across the United States, many of them rooted in Catholicism. How these settlers and their descendants transformed the face of American Catholicism over several centuries is the major theme of *The American Catholic Experience*. In the latter portion of the book, Dolan addresses the impact of contemporary social upheaval on the Catholic church, and vice versa. He highlights such issues as abortion, pacifism, social justice, the ordination of women, and the presence of married clergy-albeit converts from other ordained traditions-within American Catholicism in the late 20th century.

Other books by the same author:
Transforming Parish Ministry: The Changing Roles of Catholic Clergy, Laity, and Women Religious, 1989
The American Catholic Parish: A History From 1850 to the Present, 1987
The American Catholic Tradition, 1978
Catholic Revivalism: The American Experience, 1830-1900, 1978

Other books you might like:
John Tracy Ellis, *American Catholicism*, 1969
Thomas J. Ferraro, *Catholic Lives, Contemporary America*, 1997
Mark Stephen Massa, *Catholics and American Culture*, 1999
Charles R. Morris, *American Catholic: The Saints and Sinners Who Built America's Most Powerful Church*, 1997

174

HAYIM HALEVY DONIN

To Be a Jew: A Guide to Jewish Observance in Contemporary Life
(New York: Basic Books, 1972)

Category: Doctrine
Subject(s): Judaism; Religious Life; Customs
Age range(s): Adult

Summary: *To Be a Jew*, Donin's treasury of inspiration and information, has become a classic guide to Jewish laws and traditions from a modern Orthodox position. Covering topics from daily prayer to Jewish law and philosophy, Donin offers spiritual and practical guidance on the Jewish approach to aspects of everyday modern life.

Other books by the same author:
To Pray as a Jew: A Guide to the Prayer Book and the Synagogue Service, 1980
To Raise a Jewish Child: A Guide for Parents, 1977

Other books you might like:
Wayne D. Dosick, *Living Judaism: The Complete Guide to Jewish Belief, Tradition, and Practice*, 1995
Alfred J. Kolatch, *The Jewish Book of Why*, 1981
Joseph Telushkin, *Jewish Literacy: The Most Important Things to Know about the Jewish Religion, Its People, and Its History*, 1991

175

JOHN DONNE

Poetical Works
(London: Oxford, 1912)

Category: Poetry
Subject(s): Christianity; Christian Life
Age range(s): Adult

Summary: Although John Donne (1572-1631) did not write religious poetry all his life, in his later years he worked as a bishop in the Anglican Church. Donne's religious poetry contains much of the wit, irony, ambiguity, and paradox as does his earlier love poetry. In one of his Holy Sonnets, he asks the "three-personed God" to "batter his heart" and to "ravish him." His fear of death and his love of Christ are twin themes of his religious poetry. In his prose works and sermons of the same period, Donne utters some of his most well-known ideas: "No man is an island, entire of itself . any man's death diminishes me, because I am involved in mankind, and therefore do not send to know for whom the bell tolls; it tolls for you."

Other books by the same author:
Devotions upon Emergent Occasions, 1624

Other books you might like:
William Blake, *The Complete Poetry and Prose of William Blake*, 1982
Complete collection of works by William Blake (1757-1827)

Emily Dickinson, *Complete Poems of Emily Dickinson*, 1976
   Complete collection of poetry by Emily Dickinson (1830-1886)
Gerard Hopkins, *Poems and Prose of Gerard Manley Hopkins*, 1990
   An edition of works by Gerard Manley Hopkins (1844-1889)
Francois Mauriac, *Flesh and Blood*, 1955
John Milton, *Paradise Lost*, 1667

176

WAYNE D. DOSICK

Living Judaism: The Complete Guide to Jewish Belief, Tradition, and Practice

(San Francisco: HarperSanFrancisco, 1995)

Category: Self-Help
Subject(s): Judaism; Religious Life; Customs
Age range(s): Adult

Summary: Whether you know very little about Jewish history and customs, or you've practiced Judaism all your life, Wayne D. Dosick's *Living Judaism* can enhance your knowledge of Jewish ways. Rabbi Dosick explains complex ideas and traditions in language that is direct and understandable, blending knowledge and spirit to provide an overview of Judaism and the Jewish faith.

Other books by the same author:
Soul Judaism: Dancing with God into a New Era, 1999
When Life Hurts: A Book of Hope, 1998
Golden Rules: The Ten Ethical Values Parents Need to Teach Their Children, 1995

Other books you might like:
Anita Diamant, *Choosing a Jewish Life: A Handbook for People Converting to Judaism and for Their Family and Friends*, 1997
Anita Diamant, *Living a Jewish Life: A Guide for Starting, Learning, Celebrating, and Parenting*, 1991
   Howard Cooper, co-author
Alfred J. Kolatch, *The Jewish Book of Why*, 1981
Milton Steinberg, *Basic Judaism*, 1947
Joseph Telushkin, *Jewish Literacy: The Most Important Things to Know about the Jewish Religion, Its People, and Its History*, 1991

177

LARRY DOSSEY

Recovering the Soul: A Scientific and Spiritual Search

(New York: Bantam Books, 1989)

Category: Self-Help
Subject(s): Psychology; Science; Spirituality
Age range(s): Adult

Summary: Scientist and physician Larry Dossey explores the evidence from medical, scientific, and spiritual study to identify new understandings about the mind and universal consciousness. Called a link between New Age "soul" philosophers and the scientific community that has virtually ignored the immeasurable aspects of spirituality, Dr. Dossey offers new perspectives on medicine, healing, faith, and spirituality.

Other books by the same author:
Scientific and Pastoral Perspectives on Intercessory Prayer, 1998
Be Careful What You Pray For—You Just Might Get It: What We Can Do about the Unintentional Effects of Our Thoughts, Prayers, and Wishes, 1997
The Power of Meditation and Prayer, 1997
Prayer Is Good Medicine: How to Reap the Healing Benefits of Prayer, 1996

Other books you might like:
John Hargreaves, *As "I" See It: The Scientifically Spiritual Perspective*, 1995
John Polkinghorne, *Belief in God in an Age of Science*, 1998

178

MARY DRAHOS

Angels of God, Our Guardians Dear: Today's Catholics Rediscover Angels

(Ann Arbor, Michigan: Charis Books, 1995)

Category: History
Subject(s): Angels; Miracles; Catholicism
Age range(s): Young Adult-Adult

Summary: With a look to the past to see how angels worked in the lives of the saints, Mary Drahos re-introduces today's Catholics to angels and their work on earth. In *Angels of God, Our Guardians Dear*, she has collected inspiring and sometimes dramatic contemporary stories of angels intervening in the daily lives of Catholics. Past or present, Drahos offers accounts that suggest that God's plan for people includes protection by angels.

Other books by the same author:
The Healing Power of Hope: Down-to-Earth Alternatives to Euthanasia and Assisted Suicide, 1997
To Touch the Hem of His Garment: A True Story of Healing, 1983

Other books you might like:
Charlene Altemose, *What You Should Know about Angels*, 1996
Bernard Cooke, *Why Angels?: Are they Real—Really Needed?*, 1996
Jean Danielou, *Angels and Their Mission: According to the Fathers of the Church*, 1957

179

DAVE DRAVECKY

Comeback

(Grand Rapids, Michigan: Zondervan, 1990)

Category: Autobiography
Subject(s): Cancer; Christianity; Sports/Baseball

Age range(s): Young Adult-Adult

Summary: Former San Francisco Giants pitcher Dave Dravecky found out in the fall of 1988 that he had a tumor in his pitching arm. This is the story of how his belief in God helped him deal with that discovery, as well as the subsequent treatment and recurrences of the cancer. This is the first book Dravecky wrote about his experience; additional titles focus on the reality that cancer can change one's life (*When You Can't Come Back*) and on ways to encourage people facing challenges (*Do Not Lose Heart* and *Stand By Me*).

Awards the book has won:
Gold Medallion Book Award, Biography/Autobiography, 1991

Other books by the same author:
Glimpses of Heaven: Reflections on Your Eternal Hope, 1998
Portraits in Courage: Extraordinary Lessons From Everyday Heroes, 1998
Stand by Me: A Guidebook of Practical Ways to Encourage a Hurting Friend, 1998
When You Can't Come Back: A Story of Courage and Grace, 1992

Other books you might like:
Joni Eareckson Tada, *Joni*, 1976
    written as Joni Eareckson; Joe Musser, co-author
Mark H. Gerner, *Climbing Back*, 1997
Julia Sweeney, *God Said, "Ha!"*, 1997

180

WAYNE W. DYER

Manifest Your Destiny: The Nine Spiritual Principles for Getting Everything You Want

(New York: HarperCollins, 1997)

Category: Self-Help
Subject(s): Success; Spirituality; Meditation
Age range(s): Adult

Summary: Through meditation, people find the spiritual resources to reveal what it is they truly want in life, writes Dr. Wayne W. Dyer in *Manifest Your Destiny*. According to Dyer, the dream-like state we achieve through meditation allows goals and desires that they keep locked up in their subconscious to emerge, only to be met with the conscious response of "I can't do that!" Part of Dyer's teaching in this volume focuses on using nine spiritual principles to pinpoint one's desires and overcome one's resistance to pursuing them.

Other books by the same author:
Your Sacred Self: Making the Decision to Be Free, 1995
Real Magic: Creating Miracles in Everyday Life, 1992
What Do You Really Want for Your Children?, 1985
Your Erroneous Zones, 1976

Other books you might like:
Deepak Chopra, *The Path to Love: Renewing the Power of Spirit in Your Life*, 1997
Deepak Chopra, *The Seven Spiritual Laws of Success: A Practical Guide to the Fulfillment of Your Dreams*, 1994

Barbara De Angelis, *Real Moments*, 1994
Dan Millman, *The Life You Were Born to Live: A Guide to Finding Your Life Purpose*, 1993

181

WAYNE W. DYER

Real Magic: Creating Miracles in Everyday Life

(New York: HarperCollins, 1992)

Category: Self-Help
Subject(s): Success; Psychology; Self-Perception
Age range(s): Adult

Summary: In *Real Magic*, Dr. Wayne W. Dyer notes that waiting around for miracles to happen in our lives is not as satisfying as making them happen. His advice in this book focuses on imagining what would make one happy, and applying specific actions and strategies for making these goals become reality. Whether it's in the arena of personal relationships, health, economic security, or a sense of self, Dyer offers a step-by-step approach to making magic happen in anyone's life.

Other books by the same author:
Manifest Your Destiny: The Nine Spiritual Principles for Getting Everything You Want, 1997
Your Sacred Self: Making the Decision to Be Free, 1995
What Do You Really Want for Your Children?, 1985
Your Erroneous Zones, 1976

Other books you might like:
Deepak Chopra, *The Path to Love: Renewing the Power of Spirit in Your Life*, 1997
Deepak Chopra, *The Seven Spiritual Laws of Success: A Practical Guide to the Fulfillment of Your Dreams*, 1994
Barbara De Angelis, *Real Moments*, 1994
Dan Millman, *The Life You Were Born to Live: A Guide to Finding Your Life Purpose*, 1993

182

WAYNE W. DYER

Your Sacred Self: Making the Decision to Be Free

(New York: HarperCollins, 1995)

Category: Self-Help
Subject(s): Psychology; Spirituality
Age range(s): Adult

Summary: Finding one's place in the world leads to satisfaction, according to Dr. Wayne W. Dyer. The road to achieving this state involves becoming spiritually oriented rather than ego-oriented, according to Dyer in *Your Sacred Self*. Dr. Dyer presents a three-step program to help readers move from self-awareness to spiritual development, thereby finding more freedom in their everyday lives, no matter what their external circumstances may be.

Other books by the same author:
Manifest Your Destiny: The Nine Spiritual Principles for Getting Everything You Want, 1997
Real Magic: Creating Miracles in Everyday Life, 1992
What Do You Really Want for Your Children?, 1985
Your Erroneous Zones, 1976

Other books you might like:
Deepak Chopra, *The Path to Love: Renewing the Power of Spirit in Your Life*, 1997
Deepak Chopra, *The Seven Spiritual Laws of Success: A Practical Guide to the Fulfillment of Your Dreams*, 1994
Barbara De Angelis, *Real Moments*, 1994
Dan Millman, *The Life You Were Born to Live: A Guide to Finding Your Life Purpose*, 1993

183

BETTY J. EADIE
CURTIS TAYLOR, Co-Author

Embraced by the Light

(Placerville, California: Gold Leaf Press, 1992)

Category: New Age (Nonfiction)
Subject(s): Angels; Afterlife; Death
Age range(s): Adult

Summary: In a story similar in detail to that of other near-death survivors, Betty J. Eadie shares her memories of what happened while she was declared clinically dead following surgery. Her account includes what she was told by angels and other spirit beings about the nature of the universe and the laws of nature, including answers to the questions, "Why are we here?" and "Why is there sin in the world?" Eadie's portrayal of what happens after death involves the dark tunnel and bright light common in other such testimonials, as well as the message that death is not an end, but a transition to a new existence.

Other books by the same author:
The Awakening Heart: My Continuing Journey to Love, 1996

Other books you might like:
Mally Cox-Chapman, *The Case for Heaven: Near-Death Experiences as Evidence of the Afterlife*, 1995
P.B.C. Fenwick, *The Truth in the Light: An Investigation of over 300 Near-Death Experiences*, 1997
Elizabeth Fenwick, co-author
Karlis Osis, *What They Saw—At the Hour of Death*, 1977
Erlendur Haraldsson, co-author
Maurice Rawlings, *To Hell and Back: Life After Death—Startling New Evidence*, 1993

184

JONI EARECKSON
JOE MUSSER, Co-Author

Joni

(Grand Rapids, Michigan: Zondervan, 1976)

Category: Autobiography
Subject(s): Physically Handicapped; Faith; Christian Life
Age range(s): Young Adult-Adult

Time period(s): 1960s; 1970s (1967-1975)
Locale(s): United States

Summary: When she was just in her teens, Joni Eareckson lost control of her body as the result of a diving accident. Suddenly a quadriplegic, the once-athletic young woman now faced a life of total dependence on others. In her first book, Joni describes the emotional, psychological, and spiritual struggle that led her to find meaning for her life through faith in God. Joni also writes under her married name, Joni Eareckson Tada.

Other books by the same author:
A Step Further, 1978 (Steve Estes, co-author)

Other books you might like:
Christopher Reeve, *Still Me*, 1998
Evans G. Valens, *A Long Way Up: The Story of Jill Kinmont*, 1966
Heidi Von Beltz, *My Soul Purpose: Living, Learning, and Healing*, 1996
Peter Copeland, co-author

185

JONI EARECKSON
STEVE ESTES, Co-Author

A Step Further

(Grand Rapids, Michigan: Zondervan, 1978)

Category: Autobiography
Subject(s): Physically Handicapped; Faith; Christian Life
Age range(s): Young Adult-Adult
Locale(s): United States

Summary: In her second autobiographical story, Joni Eareckson Tada shares more of her experiences following the diving accident that left her paralyzed. She writes from her own perspective about how the difficulties of life can help individuals draw closer to God. Joni and Friends, an organization that ministers to the disabled and their families, recommends this book as a resource to those who are beginning to come to grips with their loss following a traumatic injury. Joni has also written works as Joni Eareckson.

Awards the book has won:
Gold Medallion Book Award, Inspirational, 1979

Other books by the same author:
Joni, 1976 (Joe Musser, co-author)

Other books you might like:
Heidi Von Beltz, *My Soul Purpose: Living, Learning, and Healing*, 1996
Peter Copeland, co-author
Christopher Reeve, *Still Me*, 1998
Evans G. Valens, *A Long Way Up: The Story of Jill Kinmont*, 1966

186

H. BYRON EARHART

Religions of Japan: Many Traditions Within One Sacred Way

(San Francisco: Harper & Row, 1984)

Category: Theology
Subject(s): Religious Life; Buddhism; Culture
Age range(s): Adult

Summary: From rural community traditions to modern urban practices, Earhart describes the rich diversity of Japanese religious life. He provides an overview of the major Japanese religious traditions within a historical context, and explains the role of ancestors, Buddhas, holy people, and gods in everyday worship practices. He also explores the impact of diverse Japanese religious practices on the modern culture of Japanese society.

Other books by the same author:
Religion in the Japanese Experience: Sources and Interpretations, 1997
Religious Traditions of the World, 1993
Japanese Religion, Unity and Diversity, 1982

Other books you might like:
Winston Bradley Davis, *Japanese Religion and Society: Paradigms of Structure and Change*, 1992
Robert S. Ellwood, *Japanese Religion: A Cultural Perspective*, 1985
    Richard B. Pilgrim, co-author
Joseph Mitsuo Kitagawa, *On Understanding Japanese Religion*, 1987
Minoru Kiyota, *Japanese Buddhism: Its Tradition, New Religions, and Interaction with Christianity*, 1987
David Reid, *New Wine: The Cultural Shaping of Japanese Christianity*, 1991
Floyd Hiatt Ross, *Shinto, the Way of Japan*, 1965
Noriyoshi Tamaru, *Religion in Japanese Culture: Where Living Traditions Meet a Changing World*, 1996
    David Reid, co-editor

187

MARY BAKER EDDY

Science and Health: With Key to the Scriptures

(Boston: First Church of Christ, Scientist, 1994)

Category: Doctrine
Subject(s): Christian Science; Health; Religious Life
Age range(s): Young Adult-Adult

Summary: This famous treatise on health, science, and religion was first published in 1875. Author Mary Baker Eddy rejected the notion that pain and suffering comes from God, and instead believed that choosing to live with spirituality at the center of one's life would lead to better health. This volume, which has been in print since its earliest appearance, contains the basic tenets upon which Christian Science is

based. In 1908, Eddy founded the *Christian Science Monitor*, a newspaper which is still published daily.

Other books by the same author:
Pond and Purpose, 1892
Christian Healing, 1881

Other books you might like:
Georgine Milmine, *The Life of Mary Baker G. Eddy and the History of Christian Science*, 1909
Gillian Gill, *Mary Baker Eddy*, 1998
Bliss Knapp, *The Destiny of the Mother Church*, 1947
Louise A. Smith, *Mary Baker Eddy: Discoverer and Founder of Christian Science*, 1991

188

JONATHAN EDWARDS

A Treatise Concerning Religious Affections

(Boston: Kneeland & Green, 1746)

Category: Sermons
Subject(s): Christianity; Religious Life; Conduct of Life
Age range(s): Adult

Summary: In this document, which began as a series of sermons in 1742 and 1743, Jonathan Edwards sets out a clear description of the evidence one can use to identify those who have been truly converted through religious revival efforts. He argues that neither emotion nor visions nor particular actions are indicative of a conversion, but that the true ''regenerate'' will display a consistency of thought, action, and emotion that can only be the work of God.

Other books by the same author:
The Great Christian Doctrine of Original Sin Defended, 1758
Some Thoughts Concerning the Present Revival of Religion in New-England, 1742
Sinners in the Hands of an Angry God, 1741

Other books you might like:
Millard J. Erickson, *Christian Theology*, 1983
John Piper, *God's Passion for His Glory: Living the Vision of Jonathan Edwards, with the Complete Text of the End for Which God Created the World*, 1998
David F. Wells, *God in the Wasteland: The Reality of Truth in a World of Fading Dreams*, 1994

189

MIRCEA ELIADE, Editor

The Encyclopedia of Religion

(New York: Macmillan, 1987)

Category: Religious Encyclopedias/Dictionaries
Subject(s): History; Culture; Religion
Age range(s): Adult

Summary: In a sixteen volume publication considered to be one of the most comprehensive ever compiled, Eliade surveys the wide horizons of world religions. The editor's own diverse background-born in Bucharest, he was a student in Calcutta, and later a professor in both France and the United States-may contribute to the cultural sensitivity for which his

Encyclopedia of Religion has been lauded. His treatment of the least known religious practices and philosophies is regarded as as comprehensive and carefully documented as that of the more familiar religious traditions.

Other books by the same author:
The Eliade Guide to World Religions, 1991
The Quest: History and Meaning in Religion, 1969
A History of Religious Ideas, 1978-1985 (three volumes)

Other books you might like:
R. Pierce Beaver, *Eerdmans' Handbook to the World's Religions*, 1982
Peter Bishop, *The Encyclopedia of World Faiths: An Illustrated Survey of the World's Living Religions*, 1988
   Michael Darton, co-editor
John Bowker, *The Oxford Dictionary of World Religions*, 1997
Chris Richards, *The Illustrated Encyclopedia of World Religions*, 1997

190

MIRCEA ELIADE

A History of Religious Ideas

(Chicago: University of Chicago Press, 1978-1985)

Category: Theology
Subject(s): Christianity; Judaism; Islam
Age range(s): Adult

Summary: A three-volume work, Eliade's *A History of Religious Ideas* offers a chronological, parallel perspective on a wide range of religious beliefs, expressions, and experiences. All the world's major religious traditions are represented here, as are lesser-known practices and philosophies. Of particular interest to Eliade is the evolutionary interplay of religion and popular culture throughout human history, including the influence of popular culture on religious thought and action.

Other books by the same author:
The Eliade Guide to World Religions, 1991
The Encyclopedia of Religion, 1987
The Quest: History and Meaning in Religion, 1969

Other books you might like:
Owen Chadwick, *A History of Christianity*, 1996
John R. Mason, *Reading and Responding to Mircea Eliade's History of Religious Ideas*, 1993
Jaroslav Pelikan, *The World Treasury of Modern Religious Thought*, 1990

191

MIRCEA ELIADE

The Sacred and the Profane: The Nature of Religion

(New York: Harcourt, Brace and Jovanovich, 1959)

Category: Theology
Subject(s): World Religions; History; Customs
Age range(s): Adult

Summary: Eliade contends that modern times lack the sense of the sacred that marked so deeply many ancient cultures. However, he notes, that even in the profane world there remain traces of the sacred and its significance in the ways that people arrange their space and time. Translated from the French by Willard R. Trask.

Other books by the same author:
The Myth of the Eternal Return; Or, Cosmos and History, 1954 (Translated from the French by Willard R. Trask.)

Other books you might like:
William James, *The Varieties of Religious Experience: A Study in Human Nature*, 1902
Rudolf Otto, *The Idea of the Holy: An Inquiry into the Non-Rational Factor in the Idea of the Divine and Its Relation to the Rational*, 1923
Wilfred Cantwell Smith, *The Meaning and End of Religion: A New Approach to the Religious Traditions of Mankind*, 1963
Paul Tillich, *Christianity and the Encounter of the World Religions*, 1963
Alfred North Whitehead, *Religion in the Making: Lowell Lectures 1926*, 1926

192

T.S. ELIOT

Murder in the Cathedral

(New York: Harcourt, Brace and Company, 1935)

Category: Plays; Historical Fiction
Subject(s): Martyrs; Politics; Christianity
Age range(s): Adult
Time period(s): 12th century (December 1170)
Locale(s): Canterbury, England (Canterbury Cathedral)

Summary: In this play written in both prose and verse, Nobel Laureate T.S. Eliot portrays the last month of Thomas Becket's life. The historical archbishop Becket argued with the British King Henry II over the extent to which the church should influence the state. As the play opens, Becket is returning to Canterbury after having been away in France for seven years, a virtual exile. Becket is visited by four tempters, the most powerful of whom paints a glorious picture of life after death through martyrdom. The greater part of the play details the archbishop's inner struggle to understand his destiny, and also explores the nature of martyrdom.

Other books by the same author:
Sweeney Agonistes: Fragments of an Aristophanic Melodrama, 1932
The Rock, 1934
The Cocktail Party, 1950
The Confidential Clerk, 1954
The Elder Statesman, 1959

Other books you might like:
Jean Anouilh, *Becket: Or, the Honor of God*, 1960
   Lucienne Hill, translator
Aubrey De Vere, *St. Thomas of Canterbury: A Dramatic Poem*, 1876
Christopher Fry, *Curtmantle, a Play*, 1961

Robert Gittings, *Conflict at Canterbury: An Entertainment in Sound and Light*, 1970

Alfred Tennyson, *Becket*, 1884

193

ELISABETH ELLIOT

Love Has a Price Tag

(Chappaqua, New York: Christian Herald Books, 1979)

Category: Essays
Subject(s): Christian Life; Conduct of Life; Love
Age range(s): Adult

Summary: Popular conservative Christian commentator Elisabeth Elliot has seen many aspects of Christian life and practice since her days growing up in a inner-city Philadelphia neighborhood. She and her first husband were missionaries in South America, where her husband was killed for his beliefs and commitment to Christ. Elliot's writings often focus on the depth of grace offered to Christians through the death and resurrection of Jesus and the corresponding depth of responsibility—Christians have to respond to this grace in ways that are worthy of the sacrifice of Christ. In *Love Has a Price Tag*, Elliot offers thought-provoking and inspirational essays on the nature of life and the response of Christians to life's challenges.

Awards the book has won:
Gold Medallion Book Award, Inspirational, 1980

Other books by the same author:
Taking Flight: Wisdom for Your Journey, 1999
Quest for Love, 1996
Keep a Quiet Heart, 1995

Other books you might like:
Madeleine L'Engle, *A Circle of Quiet*, 1972
Edith Schaeffer, *The Art of Life*, 1987
Edith Schaeffer, *L'Abri*, 1969
Ruth Holinger Senter, *Beyond Safe Places: Trusting God through Life's Risks*, 1992

194

EPISCOPAL CHURCH

Book of Common Prayer

(Greenwich, Connecticut: Seabury Press, 1979)

Category: Doctrine
Subject(s): Anglicans; Episcopalians; Prayer
Age range(s): Young Adult-Adult

Summary: The *Book of Common Prayer and Administration of the Sacraments and Other Rites and Ceremonies of the Church* is the official prayer book of the Church of England, used by Anglican churches worldwide, including the Episcopal church in the United States. The first edition of a Protestant *Book of Common Prayer* was published in 1549 and revised several times during the 1500s and 1600s. In 1783, it was revised for use in America. Additional substantive revisions were made in 1892, 1928, and 1979. Originally written to provide a Protestant equivalent to the liturgical books used

to govern Roman Catholic worship, it contains prayers and worship liturgies that follow the ecclesiastical calendar.

Other books by the same author:
Praying with the Family of God: Selections for Children From the Book of Common Prayer, 1979

Other books you might like:
Church of England, *The Collects of Thomas Cranmer*, 1998
   C. Frederick Barbee, Paul F.M. Zahl, compilers
Presbyterian Chuch (U.S.A), *Book of Common Worship*, 1993
Thaddaus A. Schnitker, *The Church's Worship: The 1979 American Book of Common Prayer in a Historical Perspective*, 1989

195

MARK EPSTEIN

Going to Pieces Without Falling Apart: A Buddhist Perspective on Wholeness

(New York: Broadway Books, 1998)

Category: Self-Help
Subject(s): Buddhism; Psychology; Self-Perception
Age range(s): Adult

Summary: Drawing on his expertise as a psychiatrist and his experience as a Buddhist, Mark Epstein offers guidance for discovering happiness in life. Epstein asserts that the self-help movement in America has done people a disservice by focusing on the development of self-esteem rather than the pursuit of true self-awareness. He suggests instead that happiness results from the letting-go of self. This volume presents a guide for discovering, rather than creating, one's spiritual self.

Other books by the same author:
Thoughts Without a Thinker: Psychotherapy From a Buddhist Perspective, 1995

Other books you might like:
Khema Ayya, *Be an Island: The Buddhist Practice of Inner Peace*, 1999
David Brazier, *Zen Therapy: Transcending the Sorrows of the Human Mind*, 1996
Harry M. Buck, *Spiritual Discipline in Hinduism, Buddhism, and the West*, 1981
John Tarrant, *The Light Inside the Dark: Zen, Soul and the Spiritual Life*, 1998

196

ERIK H. ERIKSON

Gandhi's Truth: On the Origins of Militant Nonviolence

(New York: Norton, 1969)

Category: Biography
Subject(s): Psychology; Resistance Movements; History
Age range(s): Adult

Summary: In this volume, Erik H. Erikson takes a psychoanalytic approach to telling the life story of Mohandas Gandhi, the great teacher of nonviolent protest. The biography is notable for its treatment of the inner life of its subject, set within the context of historical events and circumstances. *Gandhi's Truth* won the Pulitzer Prize in 1970.

Awards the book has won:
Pulitzer Prize, Nonfiction, 1970
National Book Award, Science, Philosophy, and Religion, 1970

Other books by the same author:
A Way of Looking at Things, 1987
Identity: Youth and Crisis, 1968
Identity and the Life Cycle, 1959
Young Man Luther: A Study in Psychoanalysis and History, 1958

Other books you might like:
A.L. Basham, *The Father of the Nation: Life and Message of Mahatma Gandhi*, 1988
    Arun Bhattacharjee, co-author
Yogesh Chadha, *Gandhi: A Life*, 1997
Mohandas K. Gandhi, *An Autobiography: The Story of My Experiments with Truth*, 1949
Homer A. Jack, *The Gandhi Reader: A Sourcebook of His Life and Writings*, 1956

197

ERIK H. ERIKSON

Young Man Luther: A Study in Psychoanalysis and History
(New York: Norton, 1958)

Category: Biography
Subject(s): History; Christianity; Psychology
Age range(s): Young Adult-Adult

Summary: Erikson applies his theory of developmental psychology to the early years of Martin Luther's life. The author plumbs Luther's psyche in an attempt to discover the reasons for the German churchman's religious inclinations and motivations. The book offers speculation about why Luther chose a religious vocation, although the author bases many of his conclusions on secondary evidence rather than on Luther's own writings. This volume is one of the earliest attempts at "psycho-biography," the endeavor to tell a person's life story purely from the perspective of psychology.

Other books by the same author:
Identity and the Life Cycle, 1959
Childhood and Society, 1950

Other books you might like:
Roland H. Bainton, *Here I Stand: A Life of Martin Luther*, 1950
Heinrich Boehmer, *Road to Reformation*, 1946
Richard Marius, *Martin Luther: The Christian between God and Death*, 1999
Heiko A. Oberman, *Luther: Man between God and the Devil*, 1989
Ian Siggins, *Luther and His Mother*, 1981

198

CARL W. ERNST

The Shambhala Guide to Sufism
(Boston: Shambhala, 1997)

Category: Doctrine
Subject(s): Sufism; Religious Life; History
Age range(s): Adult

Summary: Carl W. Ernst provides a comprehensive overview of Sufism, the mystical tradition of Islam, from its earliest roots at the time of Mohammad to the development of contemporary Western Sufi practices. The author outlines the personal and political aspects of Sufism, noting its rocky relationship with modern fundamentalist Islam. Also included is an introduction to the poetry, music, and dance of Sufism.

Other books by the same author:
Teachings of Sufism, 1999
Manifestations of Sainthood in Islam, 1993
Words of Ecstasy in Sufism, 1985

Other books you might like:
Omar Ali-Shah, *Sufism for Today*, 1991
James Fadiman, *Essential Sufism*, 1997
    Robert Frager, co-author
Robert Frager, *Heart, Self & Soul; The Sufi Psychology of Growth, Balance, and Harmony*, 1999
Martin Lings, *What Is Sufism?*, 1975
J. Spencer Trimingham, *The Sufi Orders in Islam*, 1998

199

JOHN L. ESPOSITO

Islam: The Straight Path
(New York: Oxford University Press, 1988)

Category: Doctrine
Subject(s): Islam; History; Religious Life
Age range(s): Adult

Summary: In *Islam: The Straight Path*, John L. Esposito offers a comprehensive overview of the Islamic faith. Tracing the origins and development of Islam, the author highlights the evolving relationships between religious belief and personal practice, noting that Muslims worldwide continue to struggle to define what it means to be Islamic and to live an Islamic lifestyle. The volume offers a historical context for understanding the diversity and global impact of Islam today.

Other books by the same author:
The Oxford History of Islam, 1999
Islam, Gender, and Social Change, 1998
Islam and Democracy, 1996
Islam in Transition: Muslim Perspectives, 1982

Other books you might like:
Thomas Patrick Hughes, *Dictionary of Islam*, 1994
Shireen T. Hunter, *The Future of Islam and the West: Clash of Civilizations or Peaceful Coexistence?*, 1998
I.A. Ibrahim, *A Brief Illustrated Guide to Understanding Islam*, 1997

Francis Robinson, *The Cambridge Illustrated History of the Islamic World*, 1996

200

JAMES FADIMAN, Editor
ROBERT FRAGER, Co-Editor

Essential Sufism

(San Francisco: HarperSanFrancisco, 1997)

Category: Doctrine
Subject(s): Sufism; Islam; Literature
Age range(s): Adult

Summary: This is a collection of prayers, poetry, and other literature from many traditions of Sufism spanning fifteen centuries. The editors have compiled the first comprehensive anthology of Sufic literary works in English, gathering more than 300 writings and placing them within a historical context, with biographical and critical background on the Sufi philosophers and artists who created them. The volume provides an introduction to basic Sufi beliefs, as well as the history and current status of Sufism, through the exploration of representative writings.

Other books by the same author:
Health for the Whole Person: The Complete Guide to Holistic Medicine, 1980
Personality and Personal Growth, 1976

Other books you might like:
B.M. Dervish, *Journeys with a Sufi Master*, 1982
Carl W. Ernst, *The Shambhala Guide to Sufism*, 1997
Fadhlalla Haeri, *Sufism*, 1997
Idries Shah, *Learning How to Learn: Psychology and Spirituality in the Sufi Way*, 1978

201

MARCIA FALK

The Book of Blessings: New Jewish Prayers for Daily Life, the Sabbath, and the New Moon Festival

(San Francisco: HarperSanFrancisco, 1996)

Category: Prayer
Subject(s): Judaism; Feminism; Meditation
Age range(s): Young Adult-Adult

Summary: In this volume, poet, translator and professor Marcia Falk blends traditional and contemporary themes of Judaism in prayers, blessings, poems, and meditations for liturgical use in personal and congregational worship. Writing in both Hebrew and English, Falk combines the intellect of a scholar and the sensitivity of a poet to breathe new life into ancient blessings and to recast the old to reflect the evolution of the Jewish faith.

Other books by the same author:
This Year in Jerusalem, 1986
The Song of Songs: Love Poems From the Bible, 1977 (Barry Moser, illustrator)

Other books you might like:
Joseph H. Hertz, *A Book of Jewish Thoughts: Selected and Arranged by the Very Reverend J.H. Hertz*, 1917
Debra Orenstein, *Lifecycles: Jewish Women on Biblical Themes in Contemporary Life*, 1994
Jane Rachel Litman, co-editor
Sara Shandelman, *Traditions: The Complete Book of Prayers, Rituals, and Blessings for Every Jewish Home*, 1998
Avram Davis, co-author
Chaim Stern, *On the Doorposts of Your House*, 1994
Neil Waldman, illustrator

202

GILL FARRER-HALLS

The World of the Dalai Lama: An Inside Look at His Life, His People, and His Vision

(Wheaton, Illinois: Theosophical Publishing House, 1998)

Category: Biography
Subject(s): Buddhism; Photography; Religious Life
Age range(s): Young Adult-Adult
Locale(s): Tibet; Dharamsala, India

Summary: Blending text and photography, Buddhist practitioner Gill Farrer-Halls presents a glimpse into the life and times of the fourteenth Dalai Lama, a much-loved spiritual figure of the 20th century. From his precarious childhood in Tibet to his receipt of the Nobel Prize while in exile, the Dalai Lama is portrayed through word and image in a volume that includes excerpts from his own writings and the transcript of an interview conducted for this publication. In addition to presenting a biographical sketch of the Dalai Lama, the author offers an introduction to the troubled history and current status of Tibetan Buddhism.

Other books you might like:
P.N. Chopra, *The Ocean of Wisdom: The Life of Dalai Lama XIV*, 1986
Demi, *The Dalai Lama: A Biography of the Tibetan Spiritual and Political Leader*, 1998
Dalai Lama, *Freedom in Exile: The Autobiography of the Dalai Lama*, 1990
Ram Rahul, *The Dalai Lama: The Institution*, 1995
Whitney Stewart, *The 14th Dalai Lama: Spiritual Leader of Tibet*, 1996

203

GEORG FEUERSTEIN

Living Yoga: A Comprehensive Guide for Daily Life

(New York: J.P. Tarcher, 1993)

Category: New Age (Nonfiction)
Subject(s): Meditation; Yoga; Spirituality
Age range(s): Young Adult-Adult

Summary: One hundred years after yoga was introduced to Americans, this volume celebrates the diverse disciplines and practices of yoga. The author addresses a spectrum of health and lifestyle topics from the perspective of a yoga master, including nutrition and diet, stress, and interpersonal relationships.

Other books by the same author:

The Yoga Tradition: Its History, Literature, Philosophy, and Practice, 1998
The Essence of Yoga: Essays on the Development of Yogic Philosophy From the Vedas to Modern Times, 1997
Teachings of Yoga, 1997
The Shambhala Guide to Yoga, 1996

Other books you might like:

T.R. Anantharaman, *Ancient Yoga and Modern Science*, 1996
Stephen Cope, *Yoga and the Quest for the True Self*, 1999
Trevor Leggett, *Yoga and the Discovery of the Universal Self: A Practical Guide to Changing Individual Consciousness*, 1998

204

RICK FIELDS
PEGGY TAYLOR, Co-Author
REX WEYLER, Co-Author
RICK INGRASSI, Co-Author

Chop Wood Carry Water: A Guide to Finding Spiritual Fulfillment in Everyday Life

(New York: J.P. Tarcher, 1984)

Category: Self-Help
Subject(s): Spirituality; Conduct of Life; Meditation
Age range(s): Adult

Summary: Looking at all aspects of life, from personal issues such as relationships, work, and money to wider concerns including technology, the environment, and social justice, *Chop Wood Carry Water* offers practical suggestions for integrating mindful living into daily activities. The reflections, observations, and advice are drawn from personal experience, the teachings of religious traditions such as Christianity and Buddhism, and New Age writings including *A Course in Miracles*.

Other books by the same author:

The Awakened Warrior: Living with Courage, Compassion, and Discipline, 1994
The Code of the Warrior: In History, Myth and Everyday Life, 1991
How the Swans Came to the Lake: A Narrative of Buddhism in America, 1981

Other books you might like:

Richard J. Foster, *Freedom of Simplicity*, 1981
Janet Luhrs, *The Simple Living Guide: A Sourcebook for Less Stressful, More Joyful Living*, 1997
Ronald S. Miller, *As Above, So Below: Paths to Spiritual Renewal in Daily Life*, 1992

205

FINDHORN COMMUNITY

The Findhorn Garden

(New York: Harper and Row, 1975)

Category: Essays
Subject(s): Gardens and Gardening; Communal Living; Relationships
Age range(s): Adult
Time period(s): 1960s
Locale(s): Findhorn Bay, Scotland

Summary: In 1962, Peter and Eileen Caddy and their family moved from a comfortable middle-class home to a "caravan" park at Findhorn Bay, Scotland. In their caravan—a mobile home—they embarked on a spiritual journey that would become a world-famous community of harmony with nature and many forms of spirituality. *The Findhorn Garden* tells the story of the early days of the community's development through the words of its residents, including Peter and Eileen, Dorothy MacLean, R. Ogilvie Crombie, David Spangler, and others. The book combines essays, diary entries, photographs, and spiritual journey records that portray a community whose communication with "nature intelligences" resulted in exceptionally beautiful and unusual gardens and human relationships.

Other books by the same author:

The Findhorn Family Cook Book: A Vegetarian Cookbook Which Celebrates the Wholeness of Life, 1981

Other books you might like:

Eileen Caddy, *The Spirit of Findhorn*, 1976
Peter Caddy, *In Perfect Timing: Memoirs of a Man for the New Millennium*, 1996
Paul Hawken, *The Magic of Findhorn*, 1975
Carol Riddell, *The Findhorn Community: Creating a Human Identity for the 21st Century*, 1991
David Spangler, *Vision of Findhorn: Anthology*, 1976

206

ARIELLE FORD, Editor

Hot Chocolate for the Mystical Soul: 101 True Stories of Angels, Miracles, and Healings

(New York: Plume, 1998)

Category: Self-Help
Subject(s): Angels; Mysticism; Healing
Age range(s): Young Adult-Adult

Summary: In much the same way as the *Chicken Soup for the Soul* titles, Arielle Ford has collected inspirational tales of mystery and miracles, near-death experiences, angelic interventions, and personal healings. Stories come from well-known and unknown writers, all of whom are convinced that something miraculous has happened in their lives, courtesy of an unseen being or force for good.

Other books by the same author:
More Hot Chocolate for the Mystical Soul: 101 True Stories of Angels, Miracles, and Healings, 1999

Other books you might like:
Joan Wester Anderson, *Where Miracles Happen: True Stories of Heavenly Encounters*, 1994
Jack Canfield, *Chicken Soup for the Christian Soul: 101 Stories to Open the Heart and Rekindle the Spirit*, 1997
Mark Victor Hansen, Patty Aubery, Nancy Mitchell, co-editors
Jack Canfield, *Chicken Soup for the Soul: 101 Stories to Open the Heart and Rekindle the Spirit*, 1993
Mark Victor Hansen, co-editor
Jack Canfield, *A 3rd Serving of Chicken Soup for the Soul: 101 More Stories to Open the Heart and Rekindle the Spirit*, 1996
Mark Victor Hansen, co-editor
Nathalie Ladner-Bischoff, *An Angel's Touch: True Stories about Angels, Miracles, and Answers to Prayers*, 1998

207

NELSON FOSTER, Editor
JACK SHOEMAKER, Co-Editor

The Roaring Stream: A New Zen Reader
(Hopewell, New Jersey: Ecco Press, 1996)

Category: Doctrine
Subject(s): Buddhism; History; Literature
Age range(s): Adult

Summary: Spanning 1500 years, the great masterpieces of Zen Buddhist literature are gathered in this volume, accompanied by brief introductory essays. Taken together, the writings compiled by the editors provide a comprehensive overview of the teachings of Zen Buddhism, which developed in Japan out of Chinese Ch'an Buddhism. Included are poetry, essays, and teachings from leading figures in Zen Buddhism, including Bodhidharma, Dogen, and Basho.

Other books by the same author:
The Ground We Share: Everyday Practice, Buddhist and Christian, 1994 (David Steindl-Rast, co-author)

Other books you might like:
Trevor Leggett, *The Tiger's Cave and Translations of Other Zen Writings*, 1994
originally published in London in 1977
Paul Reps, *Zen Flesh, Zen Bones: A Collection of Zen and Pre-Zen Writings*, 1957
Ryokan, *Great Fool: Zen Master Ryokan: Poems, Letters, and Other Writings*, 1996
Ryuichi Abe, Peter Haskel, translators
Marian Ury, *Poems of the Five Mountains: An Introduction to the Literature of the Zen Monasteries*, 1977
Amy Zerner, *Zen ABC*, 1993
Jessie Spicer Zerner, co-author

208

RICHARD J. FOSTER

Celebration of Discipline: The Path to Spiritual Growth
(New York: Harper, 1978)

Category: Self-Help
Subject(s): Spirituality; Religious Life; Conduct of Life
Age range(s): Adult

Summary: Foster's premise in this volume is that spiritual growth is impossible without overcoming the superficiality of American experience. He proposes a solution that involves examining and applying twelve disciplines: the inward disciplines of meditation, prayer, fasting, and study; the outwardly visible yet still individual disciplines of simplicity, solitude, submission, and service; and the corporate or congregational disciplines of confession, worship, guidance, and celebration. First published in 1978, *Celebration of Discipline* continues to provide readers with timeless spiritual guidance and support.

Awards the book has won:
Writer of the Year, Warner Pacific College, 1978

Other books by the same author:
Prayer: Finding the Heart's True Home, 1992
The Challenge of the Disciplined Life, 1985
Freedom of Simplicity, 1981

Other books you might like:
Deborah Dedford, *Seeking a Simpler Spirit: An 8-Week Guide Toward a Lifelong Relationship with God*, 1999
John Ortberg, *The Life You've Always Wanted: Spiritual Disciplines for Ordinary People*, 1997
Dallas Willard, *The Spirit of the Disciplines: Understanding How God Changes Lives*, 1988

209

RICHARD J. FOSTER

Freedom of Simplicity
(San Francisco: Harper & Row, 1981)

Category: Self-Help
Subject(s): Christianity; Spirituality; Conduct of Life
Age range(s): Adult

Summary: Richard J. Foster applies scriptural knowledge, wisdom, and compassion to the problem of achieving simplicity in modern life. Rather than simply fleeing from the complexities of life, Foster promotes learning to live in harmony with the world and influencing our surroundings through prayer, listening, and acting compassionately.

Awards the book has won:
Gold Medallion Book Award, Contemporary Issues, 1982
Christy Award, 1982

Other books by the same author:
Prayer: Finding the Heart's True Home, 1992
The Challenge of the Disciplined Life, 1985
Celebration of Discipline: The Path to Spiritual Growth, 1978

Other books you might like:
Rick Fields, *Chop Wood Carry Water: A Guide to Finding Spiritual Fulfillment in Everyday Life*, 1984
Delia Halverson, *Living Simply*, 1996
Victoria Moran, *Shelter for the Spirit*, 1997
Kim Thomas, *Simplicity: Finding Peace by Uncluttering Your Life*, 1999
David Yount, *Spiritual Simplicity: Simplify Your Life and Enrich Your Soul*, 1997

210

RICHARD J. FOSTER

Prayer: Finding the Heart's True Home

(San Francisco: HarperSanFrancisco, 1992)

Category: Prayer
Subject(s): Christianity; Religious Life
Age range(s): Adult

Summary: The great mysteries of prayer are addressed in Richard J. Foster's introduction to Christian prayer. He covers 21 forms of prayer with wisdom from a wide spectrum of Christian thinkers and theologians, including E.M. Bounds, C.S. Lewis, Brother Lawrence, Thomas Merton, and Henri Nouwen, among others. Foster groups prayers into three general categories: inward, upward, and outward. He demonstrates how these three categories correspond to human needs for personal renewal, connection with God, and outreach to others.

Awards the book has won:
Gold Medallion Book Award, Inspirational, 1993

Other books by the same author:
The Challenge of the Disciplined Life, 1985
Freedom of Simplicity, 1981
Celebration of Discipline: The Path to Spiritual Growth, 1978

Other books you might like:
E.M. Bounds, *The Best of E.M. Bounds on Prayer*, 1987
Romano Guardini, *The Art of Praying: The Principles and Methods of Christian Prayer*, 1994
C.S. Lewis, *Letters to Malcolm: Chiefly on Prayer*, 1964
Catherine Marshall, *Adventures in Prayer*, 1975

211

JAMES W. FOWLER

Stages of Faith: The Psychology of Human Development and the Quest for Meaning

(New York: Harper, 1981)

Category: Self-Help
Subject(s): Psychology; Spirituality

Summary: James W. Fowler conducted a study in which he asked a set of questions concerning faith, meaning, and values in life to nearly 600 people ranging in age from four to eighty-nine and of all faith persuasions. The responses form a consistent picture of development through six stages from the intuitive faith of childhood to a fully mature faith that transcends

self. Foster's conclusions are drawn not only from personal studies but also from the ground-breaking work of such thinkers as Piaget and Erikson, acknowledged leaders in the field of tracking and understanding human development.

Other books by the same author:
Faithful Change: The Personal and Public Challenges of Postmodern Life, 1996
Weaving the New Creation: Stages of Faith and the Public Church, 1991
Becoming Adult, Becoming Christian: Adult Development and Christian Faith, 1984
Toward Moral and Religious Maturity, 1980 (Antoine Vergote, co-author)
Life Maps: Conversations on the Journey of Faith, 1978 (Sam Keen, co-author)

Other books you might like:
Janet O. Hagberg, *The Critical Journey: Stages in the Life of Faith*, 1989
Robert A. Guelich, co-author
Robert Kegan, *The Evolving Self: Problems and Process in Human Development*, 1982
Paul Tillich, *Dynamics of Faith*, 1956

212

EMMET FOX

The Sermon on the Mount: A General Introduction to Scientific Christianity in the Form of a Spiritual Key to Matthew V, VI, and VII

(New York: Church of the Healing Christ, 1934)

Category: Scripture
Subject(s): Conduct of Life; Science; History
Age range(s): Adult

Summary: Emmet Fox (1886-1951) was a scientist and philosopher who lectured and wrote on his theories about finding strength for earthly life through the power of the unseen and infinite. This work has become a classic in spiritual literature as a straightforward guide to achieving happiness through faith in Jesus. Fox applies the principles of Jesus' teachings without dogma or doctrinal bias.

Other books by the same author:
Make Your Life Worthwhile, 1946
Power through Constructive Thinking, 1940

Other books you might like:
Stuart Briscoe, *The Sermon on the Mount: Daring to be Different*, 1995
John R.W. Stott, *The Message of the Sermon on the Mount: Christian Counter-Culture*, 1978
Ed Townley, *Meditations on the Mount: A Daily Guide to Spiritual Living*, 1998
Michael Warden, *Why Be Normal?: A Creative Study of the Sermon on the Mount*, 1998
Scott Angle, illustrator

213

MATTHEW FOX

The Coming of the Cosmic Christ: The Healing of Mother Earth and the Birth of a Global Renaissance
(San Francisco: Harper & Row, 1988)

Category: Theology
Subject(s): Christianity; Mysticism
Age range(s): Adult

Summary: In *The Coming of the Cosmic Christ*, Matthew Fox presents a vision of a Christian spirituality that returns believers to a faith rooted in a relationship with God that transcends modern divisions of sacred and secular. Fox rejects both the political schisms and secular liberalism that define American Christianity, and suggests that a spiritual renaissance is imminent if Christians can leave behind their differences and unite in a faith that exemplifies itself in divine mysticism, rather than human roles and rules.

Other books by the same author:
Sins of the Spirit, Blessings of the Flesh: Lessons for Transforming Evil in Soul and Society, 1999
Confessions: The Making of a Post-Denominational Priest, 1997
Natural Grace: Dialogues on Creation, Darkness, and the Soul in Spirituality and Science, 1997
The Reinvention of Work: A New Vision of Livelihood for Our Time, 1995

Other books you might like:
Harvey Egan, *An Anthology of Christian Mysticism*, 1991
Ursula King, *Christian Mystics: The Spiritual Heart of the Christian Tradition*, 1998
Manuela Dunn Mascetti, *Christian Mysticism*, 1998

214

MATTHEW FOX

Creation Spirituality: Liberating Gifts for the Peoples of the Earth
(San Francisco: HarperSanFrancisco, 1991)

Category: Theology
Subject(s): Ecology; Creation; Spirituality
Age range(s): Adult

Summary: Controversial religious figure Matthew Fox presents yet another aspect of his modern Christian theology based in Christian mysticism in *Creation Spirituality*. He addresses global concerns about the well-being of the physical world and connects the precarious health of the planet with the unbalanced state of souls and spirituality worldwide. Fox promotes an awe-inspired mystical response to God and the creation, suggesting that liberation for women, ethnic minorities, and dispossessed of all walks of life is best sought through a mystical approach to faith and action that seeks as its highest ideal what is good for all of creation.

Other books by the same author:
Sins of the Spirit, Blessings of the Flesh: Lessons for Transforming Evil in Soul and Society, 1999
Confessions: The Making of a Post-Denominational Priest, 1997
Natural Grace: Dialogues on Creation, Darkness, and the Soul in Spirituality and Science, 1997
The Reinvention of Work: A New Vision of Livelihood for Our Time, 1995

Other books you might like:
Johann Baptist Metz, *A Passion for God: The Mystical-Political Dimension of Christianity*, 1998
William Reiser, *To Hear God's Word, Listen to the World: The Liberation of Spirituality*, 1997
Jon Sobrino, *Spirituality of Liberation: Toward Political Holiness*, 1990

215

MATTHEW FOX

On Becoming a Musical, Mystical Bear: Spirituality American Style
(New York: Harper & Row, 1972)

Category: Theology
Subject(s): Culture; Prayer; Mysticism
Age range(s): Adult

Summary: In one of his earliest treatments of mysticism in Christianity, Matthew Fox explores aspects of the personal and social responses to prayer in American culture. Fox focuses specifically on what prayer is and is not, noting that above all, prayer is a radical response to life and a demonstration of spiritual maturity, not a ''parroting'' of words and structures defined by childhood faith. He espouses the ideal of a mature faith that finds its sustenance in mysticism and not in the repetition of ideas and words learned during childhood and held forevermore in the same esteem. He urges a comtemplative approach to prayer and faith that breaks out of the boundaries of structure and organization to a new level of awareness of self and purpose in the universe.

Other books by the same author:
Sins of the Spirit, Blessings of the Flesh: Lessons for Transforming Evil in Soul and Society, 1999
Confessions: The Making of a Post-Denominational Priest, 1997
Natural Grace: Dialogues on Creation, Darkness, and the Soul in Spirituality and Science, 1997
The Reinvention of Work: A New Vision of Livelihood for Our Time, 1995

Other books you might like:
Malcolm Boyd, *Am I Running with You, God?*, 1977
Malcolm Boyd, *Are You Running with Me, Jesus?: Prayers*, 1965
Joseph Campbell, *Myths to Live By*, 1972

216

MATTHEW FOX

Original Blessing

(Santa Fe, New Mexico: Bear, 1983)

Category: Theology
Subject(s): Spirituality; Creation
Age range(s): Adult

Summary: Contemporary theologian and de-frocked Catholic priest Matthew Fox espouses a controversial theology of spiritual liberation that reduces the traditional Christian focus on original sin and instead raises the possibility that Christians should think of God's relationship to humans in terms of God's original blessing of life and spirituality. Noting that Christianity once celebrated the beauty and goodness of life, Fox suggests that a return to such a creation-based spirituality would address concerns about environmental stewardship, gender equity, and social justice.

Other books by the same author:

Sins of the Spirit, Blessings of the Flesh: Lessons for Transforming Evil in Soul and Society, 1999
Confessions: The Making of a Post-Denominational Priest, 1997
Natural Grace: Dialogues on Creation, Darkness, and the Soul in Spirituality and Science, 1997
The Reinvention of Work: A New Vision of Livelihood for Our Time, 1995
The Coming of the Cosmic Christ: The Healing of Mother Earth and the Birth of a Global Renaissance, 1988

Other books you might like:

Joseph Campbell, *Myths to Live By*, 1972
Diane K. Osborn, *A Joseph Campbell Companion: Reflections on the Art of Living*, 1992
Charlene Spretnak, *States of Grace: The Recovery of Meaning in the Postmodern Age*, 1991
Robert M. Torrance, *The Spiritual Quest: Transcendence in Myth, Religion, and Science*, 1994

217

JOHN FOXE

Foxe's Book of Martyrs and How They Found Christ: In Their Own Words

(Springfield, Missouri: World Press Library, 1998)

Category: History
Subject(s): Saints; Martyrs; Christianity
Age range(s): Young Adult-Adult

Summary: John Foxe (1516-1587), a professor at Oxford University and a protestant minister, wrote his original *Book of Martyrs* while exiled from England during the reign of Queen Mary. When Queen Elizabeth I's reign began, he returned to England and published the first edition of the book. His purpose in collecting the stories of early Christian and Protestant martyrs was to bring attention to the long-and ongoing-history of believers who faced death for espousing their faith. Numerous editions of this title have been published during the last two centuries, and it has been updated and expanded

several times to accommodate changes in language and the addition of stories about contemporary martyrs.

Other books you might like:

James Hefley, *By Their Blood: Christian Martyrs of the Twentieth Century*, 1996
  Marti Hefley, co-author; second edition
Robert J. Morgan, *On This Day: 365 Amazing and Inspiring Stories about Saints, Martyrs, and Heroes*, 1997
Nina Shea, *In the Lion's Den: Persecuted Christians and What the Western Church Can Do about It*, 1997

218

FELICIAN A. FOY, Editor

Our Sunday Visitor's Catholic Almanac 2000: The Most Complete One-Volume Source of Facts and Information on the Catholic Church

(Huntington, Indiana: Our Sunday Visitor, 1999)

Category: Religious Encyclopedias/Dictionaries
Subject(s): Catholicism; Religious Life; History
Age range(s): Young Adult-Adult

Summary: *Our Sunday Visitor's Catholic Almanac* is published annually by *Our Sunday Visitor*, a weekly Catholic newspaper. Curious about Catholic church statistics? Do you know who's who in Catholic history? The almanac—a one-volume, mini-encyclopedia of information about contemporary Catholic life—is the place to look for names, numbers, and more. The *Catholic Almanac 2000* features a special section about the Year of Jubilee declared by Pope John Paul II, newly revised material about church doctrine, and new information about the Catholic Church in Mexico.

Other books you might like:

John Deedy, *The Book of Catholic Anecdotes*, 1997
John O'Connor, *The Essential Catholic Handbook: A Summary of Beliefs, Practices, and Prayers*, 1997
Paul Wilkes, *The Good Enough Catholic: A Guide for the Perplexed*, 1996

219

ANNE FRANK

Anne Frank: The Diary of a Young Girl

(Garden City, New York: Doubleday, 1952)

Category: Journals/Letters
Subject(s): Adolescence; Holocaust; Survival
Age range(s): Young Adult-Adult
Time period(s): 1940s (World War II)
Locale(s): Netherlands

Summary: This classic story of the Holocaust is told through the now famous diaries of Anne Frank, a Jewish girl who hid with her family from the Germans in an attic in Holland. Through her eyes, details of two years spent in cramped quarters in close contact with eight people emerge, and she illustrates the feelings of fear, frustration and courage that this situation caused. Despite Frank's death over 50 years ago at the early age of sixteen, her story still affects readers today. This original American edition is translated from the Dutch by B.M. Mooyart-Doubleday.

Other books by the same author:

The Diary of a Young Girl: The Definitive Edition, 1995
The Diary of Anne Frank: The Critical Edition, 1989
Anne Frank's Tales From the Secret Annex, 1983
Tales From the House Behind, 1966
The Works of Anne Frank, 1959

Other books you might like:

Alicia Appleman-Jurman, *Alicia: My Story*, 1988
Zlata Filipovic, *Zlata's Diary: A Child's Life in Sarajevo*, 1994
Miep Gies, *Anne Frank Remembered: The Story of the Woman Who Helped to Hide the Frank Family*, 1988
Olga Lengyel, *Five Chimneys: A Woman's True Story of Auschwitz*, 1947
Johanna Hurwitz, *Anne Frank: Life in Hiding*, 1989
Melissa Muller, *Anne Frank: The Biography*, 1998
Ruud van der Rol, *Anne Frank, Beyond the Diary: A Photographic Remembrance*, 1993
    Rian Verhoeven, co-author
Jacqueline van Maarsen, *My Friend Anne Frank*, 1997

220

VIKTOR E. FRANKL

Man's Search for Ultimate Meaning

(New York: Insight Books, 1997)

Category: Theology
Subject(s): Psychology
Age range(s): Adult

Summary: In nine essays, Frankl expands on the concept of ''logotherapy'' that he presented in *Man's Search for Meaning*, a revised and expanded edition of *From Death-Camp to Existentialism: A Psychiatrist's Path to a New Therapy*. In *Man's Search for Ultimate Meaning*, Frankl explores the relationship between religion and psychology, sugggesting that human beings possess a natural inclination toward religiosity which must be accounted for in psychological terms in order for true psychological wholeness to be present or possible. He also discusses the nature of faith and belief, stating his position that faith and doubt cannot co-exist in the same mind.

Other books by the same author:

Viktor Frankl, Recollections: An Autobiography, 1997
The Unheard Cry for Meaning, 1978
The Unconscious God: Psychotherapy and Theology, 1975
Man's Search for Meaning: An Introduction to Logo Therapy, 1963
From Death-Camp to Existentialism: A Psychiatrist's Path to a New Therapy, 1959 (Ilse Lasch, translator)

Other books you might like:

Joseph B. Fabry, *Finding Meaning in Life: Logotherapy*, 1995
    Reuven P. Bulka, William S. Sahakian, co-editors
William Blair Gould, *Viktor E. Frankl: Life with Meaning*, 1993

David Guttmann, *Logotherapy for the Helping Professional: Meaningful Social Work*, 1996
Elisabeth S. Lukas, *Meaning in Suffering: Comfort in Crisis through Logotherapy*, 1986

221

JAMES GEORGE FRAZER

The Golden Bough: A Study in Magic and Religion

(London: Macmillan, 1911-1915)

Category: History
Subject(s): Mythology; World Religions; Magic
Age range(s): Young Adult-Adult

Summary: Frazer's learned and exhaustive study explores the form and content of religious worship, religious language, and religious mythology in a number of ancient cultures. He also shows the similarities in magic, religion, and mythology through his detailed study. Frazer's book greatly influenced T.S. Eliot's epic poem ''The Wasteland.'' This massive tome was initially published in 1890, expanded in 1900, and finally was revised into this twelve-volume third edition.

Other books you might like:

Joseph Campbell, *The Hero with a Thousand Faces*, 1949
Mircea Eliade, *The Sacred and the Profane: The Nature of Religion*, 1959
Robert Graves, *The White Goddess: A Historical Grammar of Poetic Myth*, 1948
Claude Levi-Strauss, *Myth and Meaning*, 1978
Jessie L. Weston, *From Ritual to Romance*, 1941

222

DAVID NOEL FREEDMAN, Editor

Anchor Bible

(New York: Doubleday, 1964)

Category: Religious Commentaries
Subject(s): Bible; Catholicism; Protestantism
Age range(s): Adult

Summary: The *Anchor Bible* is a multi-volume *Bible* commentary set. The commentaries offer some of the finest biblical scholarship available at the end of the 20th century. Its authors represent Catholicism and Protestantism. Each volume contains a fresh translation of the biblical book under consideration. Notes and commentary follow each chapter of the translation. Users of the *Anchor Bible* will gain a deeper understanding of the *Bible*'s language, of a particular book's historical context, and of the relevant questions that have motivated scholarly study of the particular book. As with any multi-volume commentary, some volumes are stronger than others. E.A. Speiser's volume on Genesis, Marvin Pope's on Job, P. Kyle McCarter's on 1 and 2 Samuel, and Raymond E. Brown's volumes on John are particularly strong.

Other books you might like:

Raymond E. Brown, *The New Jerome Biblical Commentary*, 1999
George Buttrick, *Interpreter's Bible*, 1951-1957

Leander Keck, *New Interpreter's Bible*, 1994
James L. Mays, *Harper's Bible Commentary*, 1988

223

DAVID NOEL FREEDMAN, Editor

The Anchor Bible Dictionary

(New York: Doubleday, 1992)

Category: Religious Encyclopedias/Dictionaries
Subject(s): Bible; Archaeology
Age range(s): Adult

Summary: This six-volume *Bible* dictionary represents the finest in modern biblical scholarship. The entries are arranged alphabetically and provide definitions for archaeological terms, biblical names, and biblical places. A unique feature of this dictionary is its extensive analysis of biblical books. Each entry on a biblical book contains an outline of the chapters, an in-depth examination of its contents, and a lengthy discussion of various critical approaches to the book. Atlases and illustrations add to the dictionary's usefulness. The exhaustive quality of *The Anchor Bible Dictionary* makes it extremely helpful to both the novice and the professional. The six volumes are also available on CD-ROM.

Other books you might like:
Paul J. Achtemeier, *HarperCollins Bible Dictionary*, 1996
W.R.F. Browning, *A Dictionary of the Bible*, 1997
George Buttrick, *The Interpreter's Dictionary of the Bible*, 1976
Watson E. Mills, *Mercer Dictionary of the Bible*, 1990
Allen C. Myers, *The Eerdmans Bible Dictionary*, 1987

224

EILEEN ELIAS FREEMAN

Angelic Healing: Working with Your Angels to Heal Your Life

(New York: Warner Books, 1994)

Category: Self-Help
Subject(s): Angels; Self-Confidence; Health
Age range(s): Young Adult-Adult

Summary: Combining scholarship and inspiration, Eileen Elias Freeman's *Angelic Healing* offers guidance to readers seeking emotional, spiritual, or physical healing through the work of angels. This volume follows the author's introductory work on the topic, *Touched by Angels* (1993), and it covers a wide range of ways that people report having received or witnessed healing as a result of an encounter with angelic forces or beings. Chapters focus on categories of healing such as spiritual, physiological, and relational, and an annotated bibliography and resource list provides interested readers with avenues for further study.

Other books by the same author:
Mary's Little Instruction Book: Learning From the Wisdom of the Blessed Mother, 1995
The Angels' Little Instruction Book, 1994
Touched by Angels, 1993

Other books you might like:
William A. Burt, *Embraced by Angels: How to Get in Touch with Your Own Guardian Angel*, 1997
LaUna Huffines, *Healing Yourself with Light: How to Connect with the Angelic Healers*, 1995
Kim O'Neill, *How to Talk with Your Angels*, 1995
Ninon Prevost, *Wings of Light: The Art of Angelic Healing*, 1998
Ambika Wauters, *Angel Oracle: Working with the Angels for Guidance, Inspiration and Love*, 1995

225

EILEEN ELIAS FREEMAN

Touched by Angels

(New York: Warner Books, 1993)

Category: Self-Help
Subject(s): Angels; Theology
Age range(s): Young Adult-Adult

Summary: Eileen Elias Freeman remembers an encounter she had as a young child with an angel who assured her that her beloved grandmother was at peace after her death, and not abandoned in an underground grave, which was a distressing image in the granddaughter's mind. From that point, Freeman has been convinced that guardian angels exist, and she has made it a major part of her life's work to study the phenomenon of angels and share the message that they are at work in the world. In *Touched by Angels*, Freeman shares her own encounters as well as those of others. She uses anecdotal research, her own intuition, and theological and scriptural resources to explain the nature of angels in the modern world.

Other books by the same author:
Mary's Little Instruction Book: Learning From the Wisdom of the Blessed Mother, 1995
Angelic Healing: Working with Your Angels to Heal Your Life, 1994
The Angels' Little Instruction Book, 1994

Other books you might like:
Sophy Burnham, *A Book of Angels: Reflections on Angels Past and Present and True Stories of How They Touch Our Lives*, 1990
William A. Burt, *Embraced by Angels: How to Get in Touch with Your Own Guardian Angel*, 1997
James Van Praagh, *Talking to Heaven: A Medium's Message of Life After Death*, 1997

226

RICHARD ELLIOTT FRIEDMAN

The Disappearance of God: A Divine Mystery

(Boston: Little, Brown and Co., 1995)

Category: Theology
Subject(s): Nature of God; Scripture
Age range(s): Adult

Summary: Richard Elliott Friedman examines the nature of God's interaction with humankind in *The Disappearance of*

God, a theological journey along the timeline from God's earliest appearances to people, as recorded in the Old Testament, through Friedrich Nietzsche's "God is Dead" statement in the 20th century, and beyond. He draws on insights from history, theology, physics, and world literature to trace the gradual and consistent disappearance of God's face from the earth's people throughout the Scriptural record of Old and New Testaments, and suggests that the current general lack of spirituality in modern society is due to the invisibility of God.

Other books by the same author:
The Hidden Book in the Bible, 1998
The Hidden Face of God, 1997
Who Wrote the Bible?, 1987
The Poet and the Historian: Essays in Literary and Historical Biblical Criticism, 1983

Other books you might like:
Samuel E. Balentine, *The Hidden God: The Hiding of the Face of God in the Old Testament*, 1993
J.L. Schellenberg, *Divine Hiddenness and Human Reason*, 1993

227

RICHARD ELLIOTT FRIEDMAN

Who Wrote the Bible?
(New York: Summit Books, 1987)

Category: Theology; Religious Commentaries
Subject(s): Bible; Criticism; History
Age range(s): Adult

Summary: Friedman uses modern literary criticism to challenge long-held theories about the *Bible*'s authorship. He argues, as did earlier biblical critics, that the *Bible* is written by several hands and many of the writings are edited by several hands. Friedman does not approach the *Bible* as a document delivered from the hand of God. Rather, he asserts that various authors wrote individual biblical books, or portions of them, in a particular place at a particular time for a particular audience. Friedman's book is an excellent introduction to the *Bible*.

Other books by the same author:
The Hidden Book in the Bible, 1998

Other books you might like:
Harold Bloom, *The Book of J*, 1990
David Rosenberg, translator
James L. Kugel, *The Bible as It Was*, 1997
Burton L. Mack, *Who Wrote the New Testament?: The Making of the Christian Myth*, 1995
Jack Miles, *God: A Biography*, 1995
John Shelby Spong, *Liberating the Gospels: Reading the Bible with Jewish Eyes: Freeing Jesus From 2,000 Years of Misunderstanding*, 1996

228

ROBERT FULGHUM

All I Really Need to Know I Learned in Kindergarten: Uncommon Thoughts on Common Things
(New York: Villard Books, 1988)

Category: Essays
Subject(s): Conduct of Life; Essays
Age range(s): Young Adult-Adult

Summary: Robert Fulghum's well-known essay, "All I Really Need to Know I Learned in Kindergarten" is the title essay in this collection of thoughts and insights on everyday life. Fulghum's perspectives on the ordinary moments of life-opening and using a box of crayons, walking into a spider web, doing something the way you've always done it even though it has never worked for you that way-are expressed in folksy, homespun essays that connect with readers on an emotional and experiential level. His insight-filled observations and life-lesson narratives serve up non-sectarian inspirational reading in short, easy-to-read portions.

Other books by the same author:
Words I Wish I Wrote: A Collection of Writing That Inspired My Ideas, 1997
From Beginning to End: The Rituals of Our Lives, 1995
Maybe (Maybe Not): Second Thoughts From a Secret Life, 1993
Uh-Oh, 1991
It Was on Fire When I Lay Down on It, 1989

Other books you might like:
Jack Canfield, *Chicken Soup for the Soul: 101 Stories to Open the Heart and Rekindle the Spirit*, 1993
Mark Victor Hansen, co-author
Richard Carlson, *Don't Sweat the Small Stuff—and It's All Small Stuff: Simple Ways to Keep the Little Things From Taking over Your Life*, 1997
Richard Carlson, *Shortcut through Therapy: Ten Principles of Growth-Oriented, Contented Living*, 1995
Deepak Chopra, *The Seven Spiritual Laws of Success: A Practical Guide to the Fulfillment of Your Dreams*, 1994
Wayne W. Dyer, *Manifest Your Destiny: The Nine Spiritual Principles for Getting Everything You Want*, 1997

229

WINIFRED GALLAGHER

Working on God
(New York: Random House, 1999)

Category: Autobiography
Subject(s): Theology; Religious Life
Age range(s): Adult

Summary: In *Working on God*, Winifred Gallagher relates her quest to figure out where religion should fit into her life by participating in numerous traditions, interviewing practitioners of a variety of faiths, and reflecting on the nature and purpose of religion in the lives of human beings. She asks such questions as "What is real?" and "What are the choices?" She focuses mainly on Judaism, Christianity, and Buddhism, all of which are part of her life, and she offers insightful though light-hearted assessments of what motivates modern skeptics to continue searching for religious grounding, working on God in their lives, as it were.

Other books by the same author:
Just the Way You Are: How Heredity and Experience Create the Individual, 1997
The Power of Place: How Our Surroundings Shape Our Thoughts, Emotions, and Actions, 1993

Other books you might like:
Richard P. Cimino, *Shopping for Faith: American Religion in the New Millennium,* 1998
Reynolds Price, *Letter to a Man in the Fire: Does God Exist and Does He Care?,* 1999
James Thornton, *Field Guide to the Soul: A Down-to-Earth Handbook of Spiritual Practice,* 1999
Dan Wakefield, *Returning: A Spiritual Journey,* 1997

230

MAUREEN GARTH

Starbright: Meditations for Children

(San Francisco: HarperSanFrancisco, 1991)

Category: New Age (Nonfiction)
Subject(s): Meditation; Spirituality; Children
Age range(s): Children

Summary: Motivated by a mother's concern for her child, Maureen Garth created meditations for her young daughter to help her end the day peacefully before sleep. As the child grew older, a collection of visualizations for children evolved that became *Starbright: Meditations for Children.* Garth describes the benefits of visualization and meditation for young children and guides parents through the process of teaching their children to use these tools to help them develop creativity, focus their learning energy, calm themselves, and sleep soundly.

Other books by the same author:
Earthlight: New Meditations for Children, 1997
Sunshine: More Meditations for Children, 1994
Moonbeam: A Book of Meditations for Children, 1993

Other books you might like:
Peggy J. Jenkins, *Nurturing Spirituality in Children: Simple Hands-on Activities,* 1995
James McGinnis, *Parenting for Peace and Justice,* 1981
Deborah A. Rozman, *Meditation for Children: Pathways to Happiness, Harmony, Creativity and Fun for the Family,* 1989

231

INA GASKIN

Spiritual Midwifery

(Summertown, Tennessee: Book Publishing Co., 1990)

Category: Self-Help
Subject(s): Spirituality; Pregnancy; Birth

Age range(s): Adult

Summary: This classic handbook for non-traditional birthing was first published in 1975. It includes general information about the birthing experience for parents and their friends and family as well as specific technical information for midwives and other birth attendants. The emphasis throughout is on the spiritual nature of pregnancy, labor, and birth. This edition is updated for the 1990s.

Other books by the same author:
Babies, Breastfeeding, and Bonding, 1987

Other books you might like:
Penny Armstrong, *A Midwife's Story,* 1986
Elizabeth Davis, *Heart and Hands: A Midwife's Guide to Pregnancy and Birth,* 1987
Robbie E. Davis-Floyd, *Birth as an American Rite of Passage,* 1992

232

KAHLIL GIBRAN

The Prophet

(New York: A.A. Knopf, 1923)

Category: Poetry
Subject(s): Spirituality; Religion; Conduct of Life
Age range(s): Young Adult-Adult

Summary: First published in 1923, *The Prophet* offers Kahlil Gibran's philosophy on aspects of daily life including friendship, love, marriage, joy, sorrow, pain, and the passing of time. The work is poetic and fictional in nature, set in a distant place and time as a prophet walks the earth until his time to leave has come. Possessing nothing but wishing to leave gifts to those around him, he offers answers of wisdom to their questions of the heart. The words of Gibran's unnamed prophet have been popular with readers of all ages for generations, and the work has become a classic of inspirational literature for people of many faith traditions.

Other books by the same author:
The Beloved: Reflections on the Path of the Heart, 1994
The Vision: Reflections on the Way of the Soul, 1994
The Garden of the Prophet, 1933
Jesus, the Son of Man, 1928

Other books you might like:
Robert Bly, *What Have I Ever Lost by Dying?,* 1992
Jeannette Caruth, *Song of My Life: A Journey to the Feet of Sathya Sai Baba,* 1996
Walt Whitman, *Leaves of Grass,* 1855
    was revised by Whitman many times until his death in 1892

233

MARIJA GIMBUTAS

The Language of the Goddess: Unearthing the Hidden Symbols of Western Civilization

(San Francisco: Harper & Row, 1989)

Category: New Age (Nonfiction)

Subject(s): Women; History

Age range(s): Adult

Summary: In the West, the worship of the goddess has been largely lost, supplanted very early by a patriarchal society. Gimbutas engages in a thorough study of the history of goddess worship, the ways it continues to be practiced, and the tremendous influence it has had on western religion.

Other books by the same author:

Goddesses and Gods of Old Europe, 6500-3500 BC: Myths and Cult Images, 1982

Other books you might like:

Jean Shinoda Bolen, *Goddesses in Everywoman: A New Psychology of Women*, 1984

Joseph Campbell, *Transformations of Myth through Time*, 1990

Riane Eisler, *The Chalice and the Blade: Our History, Our Future*, 1987

Joan Marler, *From the Realm of the Ancestors: An Anthology in Honor of Marija Gimbutas*, 1997

Merlin Stone, *When God Was a Woman*, 1976

234

JOSEPH F. GIRZONE

Never Alone: A Personal Way to God

(New York: Doubleday, 1994)

Category: Self-Help

Subject(s): Spirituality; Faith

Age range(s): Young Adult-Adult

Summary: Retired priest and best-selling novelist Joseph F. Girzone writes in an autobiographical vein in this volume of spiritual guidance and encouragement. Girzone's message is that while organized religion often fails to alleviate loneliness and insecurity in human beings, the living message of God's love can touch the hearts of people, transcending the bounds of religious institutions and doctrine. He especially notes that each person's spirituality is unique, and that no one should be forced to shape a spiritual life on anyone else's experience.

Other books by the same author:

Joshua in the Holy Land, 1992

The Shepherd, 1990

Joshua, 1987

Other books you might like:

Sarah Ban Breathnach, *Simple Abundance: A Daybook of Comfort and Joy*, 1995

William F. Buckley Jr., *Nearer, My God: An Autobiography of Faith*, 1997

235

NATHAN GLAZER

American Judaism

(Chicago: University of Chicago Press, 1989)

Category: History; Theology

Subject(s): Judaism; Jews; American History

Time period(s): 20th century

Locale(s): United States

Summary: *American Judaism* was first published in 1957 and it quickly became a definitive work on the nature of Judaism in post-World War II America. In its current edition, the author offers a new introduction that covers a major shift since the 1970s: American Judaism has gradually drifted away from the liberalism with which it had been synonymous for decades, as new interest in Orthodoxy has grown stronger. Glazer suggests that this may lead to divisiveness among Orthodox, Conservative, and Reform Jews in America. He also considers the effect this phenomenon may have on relations between American and Israeli Jews.

Other books by the same author:

We Are All Multiculturalists Now, 1997

The Limits of Social Policy, 1988

Ethnic Dilemmas, 1964-1982, 1984

The Charcteristics of American Jews, 1965

Other books you might like:

Elliott Abrams, *Faith or Fear: How Jews Can Survive in a Christian America*, 1997

Bill Adler, *Growing Up Jewish: An Anthology*, 1997

Abraham J. Karp, *A History of Jews in America*, 1997

Tina Levitan, *First Facts in American Jewish History: From 1492 to the Present*, 1996

Mark A. Raider, *The Emergence of American Zionism*, 1998

Stephen J. Whitfield, *In Search of American Jewish Culture*, 1999

236

NORMAN GOLB

Who Wrote the Dead Sea Scrolls?: The Search for the Secret of Qumran

(New York: Scribner, 1995)

Category: History

Subject(s): Archaeology; Judaism; Christianity

Age range(s): Adult

Summary: Based on more than three decades of research and study, scholar Norman Golb disagrees with the past assessment that the Dead Sea Scrolls, the archaeological find of the 1940s, represents works written by the Essenes during the first century A.D. Instead, Golb asserts that they were written by many different groups and were moved to a spot in the Judean wilds to preserve them during the Roman siege of Jerusalem in 70 A.D. *Who Wrote the Dead Sea Scrolls?* presents his findings and his assessment of the significance of the writings in terms of the development of Judaism and Christianity.

Other books by the same author:

The Jews in Medieval Normandy: A Social and Intellectual History, 1998

Jewish Proselytism: A Phenomenon in the Religious History of Early Medieval Europe, 1988

Khazarian Hebrew Documents of the Tenth Century, 1982 (Omeljan Pritsak, co-author)

Other books you might like:

James H. Charlesworth, *Jesus and the Dead Sea Scrolls*, 1992

Robert H. Eisenman, *The Dead Sea Scrolls Uncovered: The First Complete Translation and Interpretation of 50 Key Documents Withheld for over 35 Years*, 1992

Richard Elliott Friedman, *The Hidden Book in the Bible*, 1998

Lawrence H. Schiffman, *Reclaiming the Dead Sea Scrolls: The History of Judaism, the Background of Christianity, and the Lost Library of Qumran*, 1994

Hershel Shanks, *The Mystery and Meaning of the Dead Sea Scrolls*, 1998

Hershel Shanks, *Understanding the Dead Sea Scrolls*, 1992

237

KAREN GOLDMAN
ANTHONY D'AGOSTINO, Illustrator

The Angel Book: A Handbook for Aspiring Angels

(New York: Simon & Schuster, 1992)

Category: Self-Help
Subject(s): Meditation; Angels; Spirituality
Age range(s): Adult

Summary: Karen Goldman's *Angel Book* offers readers an inspirational collection of text and images celebrating the ephemeral nature of angelic beings, the best in human and divine ideals. Heavenly places and the rewards of transcending earthly cares are reflected in full-color illustrations and Goodman's simple prose.

Other books by the same author:
Angel Voices: The Advanced Handbook for Aspiring Angels, 1993

Other books you might like:
Alma Daniel, *Ask Your Angels*, 1992
Barbara Mark, *Angelspeake: How to Talk with Your Angels: A Guide*, 1995
Ambika Wauters, *Angel Oracle: Working with the Angels for Guidance, Inspiration and Love*, 1995

238

KAREN GOLDMAN
ANTHONY D'AGOSTINO, Illustrator

Angel Voices: The Advanced Handbook for Aspiring Angels

(New York: Simon & Schuster, 1993)

Category: Self-Help
Subject(s): Angels; Spirituality; Meditation
Age range(s): Adult

Summary: Karen Goldman's *The Angel Book* introduced her approach to angel culture in America during the late 20th century. In *Angel Voices*, Goldman expands on her introductory images in text and illustrations, using both poetry and prose to explore earthly relationships with the beings of heaven.

Other books by the same author:
Angel Encounters: True Stories of Divine Intervention, 1995 (Patricia Languedoc, illustrator)

The Angel Book: A Handbook for Aspiring Angels, 1992 (Anthony D'Agostino, illustrator)

Other books you might like:
Alma Daniel, *Ask Your Angels*, 1992
Barbara Mark, *Angelspeake: How to Talk with Your Angels: A Guide*, 1995
Ambika Wauters, *Angel Oracle: Working with the Angels for Guidance, Inspiration and Love*, 1995

239

PETER J. GOMES

The Good Book: Reading the Bible with Mind and Heart

(New York: Morrow, 1996)

Category: Religious Commentaries
Subject(s): Criticism; Bible
Age range(s): Adult

Summary: In this volume, renowned Harvard preacher Peter J. Gomes provides a fresh perspective on one of the world's oldest books, the *Bible*. First he sets the context, discussing the world within which the various parts of the Judeo-Christian scriptures were composed and combined into a holy canon. Then he presents twelve social issues—including wealth, the role of women, homosexuality, and race relations-about which biblical writings have historically been used to def-ine cultural and religious policies and practices. Finally, in a section called ''The True and Lively Word,'' Gomes engages readers in thoughtful consideration of how to interpret Bible writings in a secular world.

Awards the book has won:
Lambda Literary Award, Spirituality, 1997

Other books by the same author:
Sermons: Biblical Wisdom for Daily Living, 1998
History of Harvard Divinity School, 1992
The Books of the Pilgrims, 1975

Other books you might like:
Mortimer J. Adler, *How to Think about God: A Guide for the 20th-Century Pagan*, 1980
Karen Armstrong, *In the Beginning: A New Interpretation of Genesis*, 1996
Richard Elliott Friedman, *Who Wrote the Bible?*, 1987
Joseph Telushkin, *Biblical Literacy: The Most Important People, Events, and Ideas of the Hebrew Bible*, 1997

240

LINDA GOODMAN

Linda Goodman's Star Signs: The Secret Codes of the Universe

(New York: St. Martin's Press, 1987)

Category: New Age (Nonfiction)
Subject(s): Astrology; Spirituality
Age range(s): Young Adult-Adult

Summary: In this volume, Linda Goodman focuses on aspects of new age spirituality including numerology and astrology.

Goodman offers astrological guidance on such matters as money, diet, work-life, and one's perspective on life and death.

Other books by the same author:
Linda Goodman's Love Poems, 1980
Linda Goodman's Love Signs, 1978
Linda Goodman's Sun Signs, 1968

Other books you might like:
Ronald C. Davison, *Astrology: The Classic Guide to Understanding Your Horoscope*, 1963
Sasha Fenton, *Rising Signs: The Astrological Guide to the Image We Project*, 1989
Sydney Omarr, *My World of Astrology*, 1965

241

LINDA GOODMAN

Linda Goodman's Sun Signs

(New York: Taplinger, 1968)

Category: New Age (Nonfiction)
Subject(s): Astrology; Spirituality

Summary: Linda Goodman's guide to astrological characteristics helped popularize astrology and horoscopes among Americans of all ages during the late 1960s and early 1970s. Offering popular guidance for people who seek to understand their loved ones and co-workers better by analyzing their horoscopes, her volume remains a classic and basic introduction to the field of astrological self-help writings.

Other books by the same author:
Linda Goodman's Star Signs: The Secret Codes of the Universe, 1987
Linda Goodman's Love Poems, 1980
Linda Goodman's Love Signs, 1978

Other books you might like:
Ronald C. Davison, *Astrology: The Classic Guide to Understanding Your Horoscope*, 1963
Sasha Fenton, *Rising Signs: The Astrological Guide to the Image We Project*, 1989
Sydney Omarr, *My World of Astrology*, 1965

242

DANIEL GORDIS

God Was Not in the Fire: The Search for a Spiritual Judaism

(New York: Scribner, 1995)

Category: Doctrine
Subject(s): Judaism; Religious Life
Age range(s): Adult

Summary: Concerned about the future vitality and growth of American Judaism, Rabbi Daniel Gordis explores the answers to why many American Jews are willing or eager leave their faith. Among his conclusions: traditional Jewish religious expression is without the spirituality that many Jews are seeking when they abandon their religious heritage, and there is not enough emphasis on the value and significance of a

spiritually rich Judaism in contemporary life. As personal ties to the traditions of Judaism weaken, the customs and practices of the Jewish life become ever less familiar and eventually meaningless. Rabbi Gordis seeks to remedy this with a new look at the relevance of prayers, rituals, teachings, observances, and celebrations in modern Jewish life.

Other books by the same author:
Raising Jewish Children: How to Add Wonder and Spirituality to Your Child's Everyday Life, 1999
Does the World Need the Jews?: Rethinking Chosenness and American Jewish Identity, 1997

Other books you might like:
Neil Gillman, *Conservative Judaism: The New Century*, 1993
Lawrence Kushner, *God Was in This Place and I, I Did Not Know: Finding Self, Spirituality, and Ultimate Meaning*, 1991
David J. Wolpe, *Teaching Your Children about God: A Modern Jewish Approach*, 1995
David J. Wolpe, *Why Be Jewish?*,

243

BILLY GRAHAM

The 7 Deadly Sins

(Grand Rapids, Michigan: Zondervan, 1955)

Category: Doctrine
Subject(s): Christian Life; Conduct of Life; Sin
Age range(s): Adult

Summary: One of Billy Graham's earliest books focuses on the transgressions known as the seven deadly sins-pride, greed, envy, anger, lust, gluttony, and sloth. In *The 7 Deadly Sins*, Graham discusses the meaning and manifestations of each form of sin in mid-20th-century American life, and outlines biblical principles for breaking the cycle of thought and action that keeps people in bondage to these negative aspects of life. *The 7 Deadly Sins* has been out of print for many years and is difficult to find.

Other books by the same author:
Just as I Am: The Autobiography of Billy Graham, 1997
Hope for the Troubled Heart, 1991
Unto the Hills, 1984
How to Be Born Again, 1977
My Answer, 1960

Other books you might like:
Bernard Bangley, *If I'm Forgiven, Why Do I Still Feel Guilty?*, 1992
Henry Fairlie, *The Seven Deadly Sins Today*, 1978
Robert C. Solomon, *The Seven Deadly Sins: Jewish, Christian, and Classical Reflections on Human Psychology*, 1992
Robert C. Solomon, *Wicked Pleasures: Meditations on the Seven "Deadly" Sins*, 1999

244

BILLY GRAHAM

Angels: God's Secret Agents

(Garden City, New York: Doubleday, 1975)

Category: Theology
Subject(s): Christianity; Angels; God
Age range(s): Adult

Summary: Long before the angel craze of the early 1990s, evangelist Graham wrote and spoke about angels and their activities. Angels are considered to be God's messengers, but Graham suggests that they also carry out God's wishes for people. Graham weaves together a number of personal stories and accounts from the *Bible* as he demonstrates that angels exist and that they are part of God's plan for people's lives. They are also carriers of God's goodness, and if people are attentive, they can receive this goodness.

Other books by the same author:
Hope for the Troubled Heart, 1991
World Aflame, 1965

Other books you might like:
Sophy Burnham, *Angel Letters*, 1991
Donna Gates, *The ABCs of Angels*, 1992
Dale Evans Rogers, *Angel Unaware*, 1953
Ann Spangler, *An Angel a Day: Stories of Angelic Encounters*, 1994
Nancy Willard, *An Alphabet of Angels*, 1994

245

BILLY GRAHAM

Approaching Hoofbeats: The Four Horsemen of the Apocalypse

(Waco, Texas: Word Books, 1983)

Category: Doctrine
Subject(s): Scripture; End-Times; Christianity
Age range(s): Adult

Summary: Addressing the visions described in the Book of Revelation, the final chapters of the New Testament, Billy Graham explores contemporary global problems-war, economic crisis, disease, poverty-in the light of biblical prophecy. He equates certain symbols and imagery with modern circumstances, sounding a warning that all is not well in contemporary civilization, and outlining ways in which Christians can respond to the ills of society.

Awards the book has won:
Gold Medallion Book Award, Christianity and Society, 1984

Other books by the same author:
Till Armageddon, 1981
How to Be Born Again, 1977
Peace with God, 1953

Other books you might like:
Hal Lindsey, *The Late Great Planet Earth*, 1970
Richard E. Madsen, *The Sealed Book: An Interpretation of the Book of Revelation*, 1998

George T. Montague, *The Apocalypse and the Third Millennium: Today's Guide to the Book of Revelation*, 1998

246

BILLY GRAHAM

The Holy Spirit

(Waco, Texas: Word Books, 1988)

Category: Doctrine
Subject(s): Christianity; Nature of God
Age range(s): Young Adult-Adult

Summary: In a conversational manner, framed by references to Bible verses and peppered with metaphorical anecdotes, renowned Christian evangelist Billy Graham shares his theological and spiritual insight in *The Holy Spirit*. Acknowledging that this is one of the most misunderstood aspects of Christianity, Graham begins with New Testament writings and addresses many reader questions about the nature and purpose of the Holy Spirit. As the study progresses, he shares historical information about the various ways the church has interpreted and responded to the Holy Spirit since the early days of Christianity.

Other books by the same author:
Just as I Am: The Autobiography of Billy Graham, 1997
Answers to Life's Problems, 1988
Angels: God's Secret Agents, 1975

Other books you might like:
Catherine Marshall, *The Helper*, 1978
J.I. Packer, *Life in the Spirit*, 1996
Charles Caldwell Ryrie, *The Holy Spirit*, 1997
R.C. Sproul, *The Mystery of the Holy Spirit*, 1990

247

BILLY GRAHAM

How to Be Born Again

(Waco, Texas: Word Books, 1977)

Category: Doctrine
Subject(s): Christianity; Religious Life; Christian Life
Age range(s): Young Adult-Adult

Summary: *How to Be Born Again* is a classic of contemporary, evangelical Christian literature. Billy Graham, world-famous evangelist, describes in simple terminology what the phrase ''born again'' means-and what it doesn't. He disputes the misconception that the religious experience of ''being born again'' must be an emotional or public event, and he offers guidance to those who wish to pursue further study on the topics of Christianity and conversion.

Other books by the same author:
The Holy Spirit, 1988
Just as I Am: The Autobiography of Billy Graham, 1997
Angels: God's Secret Agents, 1975

Other books you might like:
Jon Alexander, *American Personal Religious Accounts, 1600-1980: Toward an Inner History of America's Faiths*, 1983
Larry Crabb, *Finding God*, 1993

Terry L. Terrell, *Born Again and Growing*, 1998

248

BILLY GRAHAM

Just as I Am: The Autobiography of Billy Graham

(San Francisco: Harper SanFrancisco, 1997)

Category: Autobiography
Subject(s): Christianity; Evangelism; Presidents
Age range(s): Young Adult-Adult

Summary: One of the world's most famous Christian preachers, Billy Graham tells the story of his life, from his dairy farm roots to his international career as evangelist and minister to United States presidents. In addition to his high profile as a conservative Christian teacher and preacher, Graham is well-known as a man of integrity whose ministry has been characterized not only by large-scale ''crusades'' in stadiums and arenas worldwide, but by relationships that transcend politics and ideology with political powerbrokers around the globe. In his autobiography, Graham shares stories about the people, principles, and events that have shaped his mission and fueled his desire to reach the world with his message of salvation through Christ.

Awards the book has won:
Gold Medallion Book Award, Biography/Autobiography, 1998

Other books by the same author:
Hope for the Troubled Heart, 1991
Unto the Hills, 1986
How to Be Born Again, 1977
My Answer, 1960

Other books you might like:
Patricia Cornwell, *Ruth, a Portrait: The Story of Ruth Bell Graham*, 1997
Franklin Graham, *Rebel with a Cause*, 1995
Ruth Bell Graham, *It's My Turn*, 1982
William Martin, *A Prophet with Honor: The Billy Graham Story*, 1991
Sherwood Eliot Wirt, *Billy: A Personal Look at Billy Graham, the World's Best-Loved Evangelist*, 1997

249

BILLY GRAHAM

My Answer

(Garden City, New York: Doubleday, 1960)

Category: Journals/Letters
Subject(s): Christianity; Christian Life; Conduct of Life
Age range(s): Adult
Time period(s): 1950s; 1960s (1954-1960)

Summary: *My Answer* is a collection of questions submitted to Billy Graham's syndicated newspaper column from 1954 to 1960. It is one of Graham's early publications, and a number of the questions and answers reflect American culture preceding the turbulence and social upheaval of the 1960s. In 1988,

Graham published *Answers to Life's Problems*, a similar volume based on thirty years' worth of questions.

Other books by the same author:
Just as I Am: The Autobiography of Billy Graham, 1997
Answers to Life's Problems, 1988

Other books you might like:
Jeb Gaub, *Answers to Questions You Always Wanted to Ask*, 1991
Josh McDowell, *Answers to Tough Questions Skeptics Ask about the Christian Faith*, 1980
Ronald F. Thiemann, *Why Are We Here?*, 1988

250

BILLY GRAHAM

World Aflame

(Garden City, New York: Doubleday, 1965)

Category: Doctrine
Subject(s): Christianity; Ethics; Christian Life
Age range(s): Adult
Time period(s): 1960s

Summary: *World Aflame* is one of Billy Graham's earlier writings. First published in 1965, it addresses the ills of mid-20th century Western society and what was perceived at the time as the imminent threat of Communism worldwide. Graham draws parallels between American society in the 1960s and biblical societies of the Old and New Testaments, noting that while many aspects of life have changed since then, the nature of human beings has not. He cautions Christians to keep their eyes simultaneously on two worlds, the human world in which they live and the heavenly world in which they will one day abide, so as to avoid pitfalls in the first that may pose obstacles to attaining the second.

Other books by the same author:
Storm Warning: Deceptive Evil Looms on the Horizon, 1992
Hope for the Troubled Heart, 1991
Death and the Life After, 1988

Other books you might like:
John Lawrence, *The Hammer and the Cross: Christianity in the Communist World*, 1986
Charles Joseph McFadden, *Christianity Confronts Communism*, 1982
Desmond O'Grady, *The Turned Card: Christianity before and After the Wall*, 1995

251

FRANKLIN GRAHAM

Rebel with a Cause

(Nashville: Thomas Nelson, 1995)

Category: Autobiography
Subject(s): Evangelism; Christianity
Age range(s): Young Adult-Adult

Summary: For Franklin Graham, the difficulties of growing up as the son of a famous person were compounded by the fact that his much-loved father was Billy Graham, perhaps the most recognizable Christian preacher of the mid-twentieth century. Much was expected, publicly and privately, of the eldest son, and in this autobiography he describes his youthful attempts to thumb his nose at the constant public scrutiny by smoking, drinking, and getting into scrapes with the law. He also writes about his eventual decision to make peace with God, which led to his finding positive ways to channel his restless and adventurous spirit. He recounts his war victim assistance work in Rwanda and Croatia, and discusses the worldwide ministry of The Samaritan's Purse, a Christian evangelism and relief organization.

Awards the book has won:
Gold Medallion Book Award, Biography/Autobiography, 1996

Other books by the same author:
Living Beyond the Limits, 1998
Miracle in a Shoe Box, 1995

Other books you might like:
Billy Graham, *Just as I Am: The Autobiography of Billy Graham*, 1997
Ruth Bell Graham, *It's My Turn*, 1982
Gigi Graham Tchividjian, *Passing It On*, 1992

252

RUTH BELL GRAHAM

It's My Turn

(Old Tappan, New Jersey: F.H. Revell, 1982)

Category: Autobiography
Subject(s): Family Life; Christian Life
Age range(s): Young Adult-Adult
Time period(s): 20th century
Locale(s): China; United States

Summary: The wife of world-famous evangelist Billy Graham tells her story, from her early years as the daughter of missionaries in China to life as the mother of five, often holding down the home front while her husband traveled the world. She reveals that the faith built during her youth provided strength and wisdom for the circumstances of her adult life. In a warm and loving style, she provides a glimpse into the relatively normal family life she and her husband tried to create for their children, and shares insight and encouragement for all families.

Awards the book has won:
Gold Medallion Book Award, Biography/Autobiography, 1983

Other books by the same author:
Sitting by My Laughing Fire, 1977

Other books you might like:
Patricia Cornwell, *Ruth, a Portrait: The Story of Ruth Bell Graham*, 1977
Patricia Cornwell, *A Time for Remembering: The Story of Ruth Bell Graham*, 1983
Billy Graham, *Just as I Am: The Autobiography of Billy Graham*, 1997

253

JOEL B. GREEN, Editor
SCOT MCKNIGHT, Co-Editor

Dictionary of Jesus and the Gospels

(Downer's Grove, Illinois: InterVarsity Press, 1992)

Category: Religious Encyclopedias/Dictionaries
Subject(s): Bible
Age range(s): Young Adult-Adult

Summary: The *Dictionary of Jesus and the Gospels* provides a one-volume reference guide to words and concepts related to the study of Jesus and the Gospels of the New Testament. The concise entries contain enough depth to be useful to pastors and scholars but are written simply and directly enough to appeal to students and laity.

Other books you might like:
William Barclay, *New Testament Words*, 1977
Ronald Brownrigg, *Who's Who in the New Testament*, 1964
Gerald F. Hawthorne, *Dictionary of Paul and His Letters*, 1993
Gerhard Kittel, *Theological Dictionary of the New Testament*, 1964
Ralph P. Martin, *Dictionary of the Later New Testament and Its Developments*, 1997

254

PAUL GREEN

In Abraham's Bosom

(London: G. Allen & Unwin, 1929)

Category: Plays
Subject(s): Race Relations; Racial Conflict; Family Relations
Age range(s): Adult
Major character(s): Abraham, Bastard Son (of Colonel Mc-Cranie); Colonel McCranie, Landowner, Father (of Abraham and Lonnie); Lonnie McCranie, Son (of Colonel Mc-Cranie)
Time period(s): 20th century (early)
Locale(s): Harnett County, North Carolina

Summary: *In Abraham's Bosom* tells the life story of Abraham, the illegitimate black son of white landowner Colonel McCranie, who has never publicly admitted to being Abraham's father. A self-educated man, Abraham becomes a teacher, marries, and has a son, at which time the Colonel acknowledges the relationship and gives Abraham the gift of a house and 25 acres of land as a christening present for the baby. Abraham fulfills his dream of opening a school for black children of the county, but the tensions between black and white neighbors and interpersonal difficulties with Abraham himself doom the school. Abraham and his wife become low-paid laborers, and life continues in a downward spiral. Ultimately, he must turn to Lonnie, his white half-brother, to keep his family together. Racial uneasiness once again arises in the community and in the relationship of the brothers, and a killing takes place. Playwright Paul Green's exploration of racial tensions in the American South during the 1920s was awarded the Pulitzer Prize for Drama in 1927. The play was first produced in Provincetown, Massachusetts, at Provincetown Playhouse on December 30, 1926; this print edition is its first publication as an individual play.

Awards the book has won:
Pulitzer Prize, Drama, 1927

Other books by the same author:
Trumpet in the Land, 1972
Plough and Furrow, 1963
The Stephen Foster Story, 1960
Salvation on a String and Other Tales of the South, 1946

Other books you might like:
Ann Fairbairn, *Five Smooth Stones: A Novel*, 1966
Hatcher Hughes, *Hell-Bent fer Heaven: A Play in Three Acts*, 1924
play
Walker Percy, *Love in the Ruins: The Adventures of a Bad Catholic at a Time Near the End of the World*, 1971
novel

255

BLU GREENBERG

How to Run a Traditional Jewish Household

(New York: Simon and Schuster, 1983)

Category: Self-Help
Subject(s): Judaism; Women; Religious Traditions
Age range(s): Adult

Summary: Greenberg's now-classic little book describes from a woman's point of view how to incorporate Jewish domestic religious practices into everyday life. Her book is a milestone because it is the first to discuss the tremendous importance of women's roles in organizing and transmitting the religious atmosphere of the home.

Other books by the same author:
On Women and Judaism: A View From Tradition, 1981

Other books you might like:
Trudy Garfunkel, *The Kosher Companion: A Guide to Food, Cooking, Shopping, and Services*, 1997
Susannah Heschel, *On Being a Jewish Feminist*, 1983
Maurice Lamm, *The Jewish Way in Love and Marriage*, 1980
Michael Strassfeld, *Jewish Catalog: A Do-It-Yourself Kit*, 1973
Arthur Waskow, *Down-to-Earth Judaism: Food, Money, Sex, and the Rest of Life*, 1995

256

IRVING GREENBERG

The Jewish Way: Living the Holidays

(New York: Summit Books, 1998)

Category: Doctrine
Subject(s): Judaism; Holidays, Jewish; Religious Life
Age range(s): Young Adult-Adult

Summary: In *The Jewish Way*, Rabbi Irving Greenberg offers practical information about all the Jewish holidays, explain-

ing their origins and significance, introducing their rituals and customs, and guiding viewers toward resources for food, music, prayers, and artifacts useful in their celebration. From Passover and Yom Kippur to Israeli Independence Day and Holocaust Remembrance Day, the holy days of Jewish life are identified and described for Jews and non-Jews alike. According to Rabbi Greenberg, the honoring of holy days helps people connect their everyday lives with the basic tenets of their faith.

Other books by the same author:
Living in the Image of God: Jewish Teachings to Perfect the World: Conversations with Rabbi Irving Greenberg, 1998
Confronting the Holocaust: The Impact of Elie Wiesel, 1978

Other books you might like:
Isaac Klein, *A Guide to Jewish Religious Practice*, 1979
Nicolas D. Mandelkern, *The Jewish Holiday Home Companion*, 1994
Ron Wolfson, *The Art of Jewish Living: The Passover Seder*, 1996
Joel Lurie Grishaver, co-author
Ron Wolfson, *Hanukkah*, 1996

257

MELISSA FAY GREENE

The Temple Bombing

(Reading, Massachusetts: Addison-Wesley, 1996)

Category: History
Subject(s): Anti-Semitism; Racism; Civil Rights Movement
Age range(s): Young Adult-Adult
Time period(s): 1950s (1958)
Locale(s): Atlanta, Georgia

Summary: Racism in the American South during the 1950s extended past divisions between the white and black communities. In *The Temple Bombing*, Melissa Fay Greene vividly documents an attack on Atlanta's wealthiest synagogue, the Temple, in October of 1958, and traces the events that preceded and followed the devastation of both the building and a city's self-deception. Greene captures the mood of Atlanta—a sophisticated, urbane metropolis under the illusion that it was immune to the raucous violence of the civil rights movement that was gathering steam elsewhere.

Other books by the same author:
Praying for Sheetrock: A Work of Nonfiction, 1991

Other books you might like:
James Carroll, *An American Requiem: God, My Father, and the War That Came Between Us*, 1996
Eli N. Evans, *The Provincials: A Personal History of Jews in the South*, 1997
Gary M. Pomerantz, *Where Peachtree Meets Sweet Auburn: A Saga of Race and Family*, 1996
Gregory Howard Williams, *Life on the Color Line: The True Story of a White Boy Who Discovered He Was Black*, 1995

258

M. CAMERON GREY, Editor
WARREN CHAPPELL, Illustrator

Angels and Awakenings: Stories of the Miraculous by Great Modern Writers

(Garden City, New York: Doubleday, 1980)

Category: Essays
Subject(s): Angels; Miracles; Literature
Age range(s): Adult

Summary: *Angels and Awakenings* serves as evidence that angels have long been part of the fabric of the Western literary imagination. This collection of literary accounts of angelic and miraculous intervention in human affairs includes works by Mark Twain, Leo Tolstoy, Isaac Asimov, O. Henry, Flannery O'Connor, Ray Bradbury, and many others.

Other books you might like:
Susan Bergman, *Martyrs: Contemporary Writers on Modern Lives of Faith*, 1996
C. Michael Curtis, *God: Stories*, 1998
Jane Hamilton, *The Guardian*, 1994
Sara Maitland, *Angel & Me*, 1997
Katherine Paterson, *A Midnight Clear: Stories for the Christmas Season*, 1998

259

JOHN HOWARD GRIFFIN

The Hermitage Journals: A Diary Kept While Working on the Biography of Thomas Merton

(Kansas City: Andrews and McMeel, 1981)

Category: Journals/Letters
Subject(s): Meditation; Writing; Catholicism
Age range(s): Adult
Time period(s): 20th century
Locale(s): Kentucky (Gethsemani Abbey)

Summary: John Howard Griffin's career as a journalist led him to transform himself physically in order to explore what life was really like for a black man in America in the late 1950s. The written account of his experience was his landmark book *Black Like Me*. Griffin's Roman Catholic faith and interest in the contemplative life of Thomas Merton similarly led him to an extended stay at Gethsemani Abbey in Kentucky to conduct research for a biography of Merton's last three years of life there within the monastery grounds. The record of this chapter of Griffin's work and life is found in *The Hermitage Journals*, which was compiled from the personal diary he kept during his work at the Abbey. Griffin's biography of Merton and the journal reflecting on the creation of that work were both published after his death in 1980.

Other books by the same author:
Follow the Ecstasy: Thomas Merton, the Hermitage Years, 1965-1968, 1983
A Time to Be Human, 1977

A Hidden Wholeness: The Visual World of Thomas Merton, 1970
The Church and the Black Man, 1969
Black Like Me, 1961

Other books you might like:
Robert Bonazzi, *Man in the Mirror: John Howard Griffin and the Story of Black Like Me*, 1997
John Dear, *The Sound of Listening: A Retreat From Thomas Merton's Hermitage*, 1999
Jim Forest, *Living with Wisdom: A Life of Thomas Merton*, 1991
Thomas Merton, *The Courage for Truth: The Letters of Thomas Merton to Writers*, 1993
Christine M. Bochen, editor
Matt Murray, *The Father and the Son: My Father's Journey into the Monastic Life*, 1999

260

ROSEMARY ELLEN GUILEY, Editor

The Encyclopedia of Ghosts and Spirits

(New York: Facts on File, 1992)

Category: Religious Encyclopedias/Dictionaries
Subject(s): Ghosts; Spiritualism; Unexplained Phenomena
Age range(s): Young Adult-Adult

Summary: A wide range of ghost lore is described in 400 entries. Alphabetically arranged, the articles cover both sympathetic and skeptical perspectives on the existence of ghosts, highlighting beliefs, first-hand accounts, and unexplained phenomena. References, cross-references, and a comprehensive index add utility and depth to this resource, which manages to entertain while it informs.

Other books by the same author:
The Encyclopedia of Witches and Witchcraft, 1999
Harper's Encyclopedia of Mystical and Paranormal Experience, 1991

Other books you might like:
W. Haden Blackman, *The Field Guide to North American Hauntings: Everything You Need to Know about Encountering over 100 Ghosts, Phantoms, and Spectral Entities*, 1998
Matthew Bunson, *The Vampire Encyclopedia*, 1993
J. Aelwyn Roberts, *Holy Ghostbuster: A Parson's Encounters with the Paranormal*, 1996

261

ROSEMARY ELLEN GUILEY, Editor

The Encyclopedia of Witches and Witchcraft

(New York: Facts on File, 1999)

Category: Religious Encyclopedias/Dictionaries
Subject(s): Witches and Witchcraft; Wicca; Occult
Age range(s): Young Adult-Adult

Summary: A well-researched reference work covering both history and current developments, *The Encyclopedia of*

Witches and Witchcraft is a useful resource for facts about many aspects of witchcraft and Wiccan philosophy. Much information is featured about the period of history during which practitioners of folk magic and spiritual healing were persecuted in Europe and North America. More than 500 entries and 100 photographs are included on Wiccan beliefs and practices and the philosophies of pagan and neo-pagan organizations worldwide. Well-known twentieth century witches, including Starhawk, Zsussanah Budapest, and Morning Glory Zell, are profiled in biographical essays in this second edition of the work, which was originally published in 1989.

Other books by the same author:
The Encyclopedia of Ghosts and Spirits, 1992
Harper's Encyclopedia of Mystical and Paranormal Experience, 1991

Other books you might like:
Phyllis Curott, *Book of Shadows: A Modern Woman's Journey into the Wisdom of Witchcraft and the Magic of the Goddess*, 1998
Gerina Dunwich, *The Wicca Book of Days: Legend and Lore for Every Day of the Year*, 1995
Gerina Dunwich, *The Wicca Spellbook*, 1994
Sarah Lyddon Morrison, *The Modern Witch's Book of Symbols*, 1997
David Pickering, *Cassell Dictionary of Witchcraft*, 1996

262

ROSEMARY ELLEN GUILEY

Harper's Encyclopedia of Mystical and Paranormal Experience

(San Francisco: HarperSanFrancisco, 1991)

Category: Religious Encyclopedias/Dictionaries
Subject(s): Religion; Extrasensory Perception; Mysticism
Age range(s): Young Adult-Adult

Summary: This volume offers an alphabetical arrangement of theories, explanations, and personal stories about mystical experiences, metaphysical phenomena, and religious techniques that cross faith traditions. Concise and clearly written, the entries provide detailed information about spirituality and mysticism. References for each subject entry add depth to topics that range from angels and Native American religious practices to zombies.

Other books by the same author:
The Encyclopedia of Witches and Witchcraft, 1999
The Encyclopedia of Ghosts and Spirits, 1992

Other books you might like:
James R. Lewis, *The Astrology Encyclopedia*, 1994
Lewis Spence, *An Encyclopedia of Occultism*, 1920
Gordon Stein, *The Encyclopedia of the Paranormal*, 1996

263

G.I. GURDJIEFF

Meetings with Remarkable Men

(New York: Dutton, 1963)

Category: New Age (Nonfiction); Autobiography
Subject(s): Spirituality; World Religions
Age range(s): Adult

Summary: A guru for the modern age, Gurdjieff records his meetings and conversations with ordinary people and world leaders as he searches for inner truth on his many travels. This book was published after Gurdjieff's death in 1949.

Other books by the same author:
All and Everything: Beelzebub's Tales to His Grandson, 1950

Other books you might like:
John G. Bennett, *Creative Thinking*, 1989
Rodney Collin Smith, *The Theory of Celestial Influence: Man, the Universe and Cosmic Mystery*, 1954
P.D. Uspenskii, *In Search of the Miraculous: Fragments of an Unknown Teaching*, 1949
Ken Wilber, *A Brief History of Everything*, 1996

264

PALDEN GYATSO

The Autobiography of a Tibetan Monk

(New York: Grove Press, 1997)

Category: Autobiography
Subject(s): Prisoners and Prisons; Buddhism; Religious Life
Age range(s): Young Adult-Adult
Time period(s): 20th century (1950-1992)
Locale(s): Tibet

Summary: Palden Gyatso decided at the age of 10 to become a Buddhist monk. By the time he was in his mid-20s, however, his intended path of meditation and contemplation turned into a life of torture and imprisonment at the hands of the Chinese, who invaded Tibet in 1950 and considered native monks to be enemies of the state. In 1992, after having spent more than three decades in labor camps and prisons, Gyatso was released. His escape from Tibet, carrying not only his horror stories but also examples of Chinese instruments of torture, led to this account of his experience, written at the urging of the exiled Dalai Lama. Gyatso credits his early Buddhist training and environment with giving him the ability to endure his suffering, and takes seriously this opportunity to reveal the horrors of life in Tibet under the communist Chinese regime.

Other books you might like:
John F. Avedon, *In Exile From the Land of Snows: The Definitive Account of the Dalai Lama and Tibet Since the Chinese Conquest*, 1984
Joy Blakeslee, *Ama Adhe, The Voice That Remembers: The Heroic Story of a Woman's Fight to Free Tibet*, 1997
He-ru-ka Gtsan-smyon, *The Life of Milarepa*, 1977
Lobsang P. Chalungpa, translator
Herbert V. Guenther, *The Life and Teaching of Naropa*, 1986
originally published in England in 1963

Blake Kerr, *Sky Burial: An Eyewitness Account of China's Brutal Crackdown in Tibet*, 1993
Tashi Khedrup, *Adventures of a Tibetan Fighting Monk*, 1986
Tsering Shakya, *The Dragon in the Land of the Snows: A History of Modern Tibet*, 1999

265

STEVE HAGEN

Buddhism Plain and Simple

(Boston: Charles E. Tuttle, 1997)

Category: Doctrine
Subject(s): Buddhism; Religious Life
Age range(s): Adult

Summary: With stories from Buddhist masters and examples from life, Steve Hagen outlines the philosophy of Buddhism in simple language. He presents the original teachings of the Buddha through practical observations and straightforward stories.

Other books by the same author:
How the World Can Be the Way It Is, 1995

Other books you might like:
Stephen Batchelor, *Buddhism Without Beliefs: A Contemporary Guide to Awakening*, 1997
Clive Ericker, *Buddhism*, 1995
Lama Surya Das, *Awakening the Buddha Within: Eight Steps to Enlightenment: Tibetan Wisdom for the Western World*, 1997
Kogen Mizuno, *Basic Buddhist Concepts*, 1987
Walpola Rahula, *What the Buddha Taught*, 1959

266

HENRY H. HALLEY

Halley's Bible Handbook: An Abbreviated Bible Commentary

(Grand Rapids, Michigan: Zondervan, 1965)

Category: Religious Commentaries
Subject(s): Bible; Christianity; Archaeology
Age range(s): Young Adult-Adult

Summary: This reference tool for non-scholars was written to provide guidance for everyday readers of the *Bible*. It provides background about each book of the *Bible*, including who the writer was, when it was written and why, and a general summary of the book itself. Features include church history information, maps, illustrations, archaeological updates, and biographies of Christian leaders. Its 24th edition was published in 1993.

Other books you might like:
Trent C. Butler, *Holman Bible Dictionary*, 1991
Henry M. Morris, *The Bible Has the Answer: Practical Biblical Discussions of 100 Frequent Questions*, 1971
Charles F. Pfeiffer, *The Wycliffe Bible Commentary*, 1962
     Everett F. Harrison, co-editor
Merrill F. Unger, *The New Unger's Bible Dictionary*, 1988

267

REUVEN HAMMER

Entering Jewish Prayer: A Guide to Personal Devotion and the Worship Service

(New York: Schocken Books, 1994)

Category: Prayer
Subject(s): Judaism; Spirituality; Religious Life
Age range(s): Young Adult-Adult

Summary: Rabbi Hammer presents an accessible guide to prayer in the Jewish tradition. Ideal for people who are new or returning to Judaism, *Entering Jewish Prayer* offers an introduction to personal and congregational prayers, explaining the significance of each prayer and providing guidance for making prayer part of one's everyday experience. While the history of prayer in Judaism is explored, the emphasis is on how prayer can be part of contemporary Jewish life and spirituality.

Other books by the same author:
Entering the High Holy Days: A Guide to the Origins, Themes, and Prayers, 1998

Other books you might like:
Hayim Halevy Donin, *To Pray as a Jew: A Guide to the Prayer Book and the Synagogue Service*, 1980
Arnold S. Rosenberg, *Jewish Liturgy as a Spiritual System: A Prayer-by-Prayer Explanation of the Nature and Meaning of Jewish Worship*, 1997
Jordan Lee Wagner, *The Synagogue Survival Kit*, 1997

268

HANK HANEGRAAFF

Christianity in Crisis

(Eugene, Oregon: Harvest House, 1993)

Category: Doctrine
Subject(s): Christianity; Evangelism
Age range(s): Young Adult-Adult

Summary: Hank Hanegraaff is president of the Christian Research Institute, a conservative, Protestant parachurch organization and is also "The Bible Answer Man," host of a syndicated Christian radio program. In *Christianity in Crisis*, he examines the "Faith" messages preached by contemporary charismatic evangelists Kenneth Copeland and Kenneth M. Hagin, among others, and outlines the doctrinal points on which he argues the "Faith" ministries depart from historic biblical teachings.

Awards the book has won:
Gold Medallion Book Award, Theology/Doctrine, 1994

Other books by the same author:
The Face That Demonstrates the Farce of Evolution, 1998
Counterfeit Revival, 1997

Other books you might like:
John Ankerberg, *The Facts on the Faith Movement*, 1993
Dave Hunt, *Seduction of Christianity: Spiritual Discernment in the Last Days*, 1985

D.R. McConnell, *A Different Gospel: A Historical and Biblical Analysis of the Modern Faith Movement*, 1988
John F. MacArthur Jr., *Charismatic Chaos*, 1993

269

JOHN A. HARDON, Editor

The Treasury of Catholic Wisdom

(New York: Doubleday, 1987)

Category: Doctrine; Theology
Subject(s): Catholicism; Religion

Summary: *The Treasury of Catholic Wisdom* provides a comprehensive collection of writings from the greatest theologians, writers, and philosophers of the Catholic tradition. Works by the early saints are followed by those of Catholic reformers, including Catherine of Siena and Teresa of Avila, as well as the writings of 20th century Catholic leaders. Writings are included because they are the most representative of an author's work and care was taken not to select only the most familiar works of an author.

Other books by the same author:
The Faith: A Popular Guide Based on the Catechism of the Catholic Church, 1995
The Catholic Lifetime Reading Plan, 1989
Christianity in the Twentieth Century, 1971

Other books you might like:
Hugh Feiss, *Essential Monastic Wisdom: Writings on the Contemplative Life*, 1999
Theodore E. James, *Classics of Catholicism: The Greatest Writings From the Gospels to the Vatican II*, 1990
John Henry Newman, *Roman Catholic Writings on Doctrinal Development*, 1997
George Tyrrell, *Tradition and the Critical Spirit: Catholic Modernist Writings*, 1991

270

HEINRICH HARRER

Seven Years in Tibet

(New York: Putnam, 1997)

Category: Autobiography
Subject(s): Refugees; Mountain Life; Buddhism
Age range(s): Young Adult-Adult
Time period(s): 1940s; 1950s (1943-1950)
Locale(s): Tibet

Summary: An account of an adventurer's experience in Tibet during the 1940s, *Seven Years in Tibet* tells the story of Heinrich Harrer's escape from a British internment camp in India and his subsequent sojourn in the Forbidden City of Lhasa, where he became the tutor of the young Dalai Lama. Harrer describes Tibet as it existed before the Chinese occupancy, which many believe has effectively destroyed the people and culture of Tibet. In 1950, when the Chinese invaded Tibet and began persecuting Tibetan Buddhists, Harrer and the Dalai Lama escaped. Harrer's story was originally published in 1953; this 1997 edition includes an epilogue

describing the devastating effects of Chinese rule on the culture of Tibet during the latter half of the 20th century.

Other books by the same author:
Return to Tibet, 1984

Other books you might like:
Wade Brackenbury, *Yak Butter and Black Tea: A Journey into Forbidden China*, 1997
Alexandra David-Neel, *Magic and Mystery in Tibet*, 1932
Alexandra David-Neel, *My Journey to Lhasa: The Personal Story of the Only White Woman Who Succeeded in Entering the Forbidden City*, 1927
Inge Sargent, *Twilight over Burma: My Life as a Shan Princess*, 1994
Vikram Seth, *From Heaven Lake: Travels through Sinkiang and Tibet*, 1987
Robert Thurman, *Circling the Sacred Mountain: A Spiritual Adventure through the Himalayas*, 1999
Tad Wise, co-author

271

HERMANN HARTFELD

Faith Despite the KGB

(Chappaqua, New York: Christian Herald Books, 1980)

Category: Autobiography
Subject(s): Christianity; Communism; Politics
Age range(s): Adult
Time period(s): 1960s
Locale(s): Union of Soviet Socialist Republics

Summary: Between 1962, when he was first indicted as a leader of a Christian church in the Soviet Union, and 1970, when he was released from a labor camp for the last time, Hermann Hartfeld was persecuted and imprisoned several times for promoting Christianity in what was then the U.S.S.R. In *Faith Despite the KGB*, Hartfeld describes the nearly seven years he spent in hard labor and solitary confinement, accused of religious propaganda. His testimony sheds light on the dangers that existed for Christians behind the Iron Curtain during the middle of the 20th century.

Awards the book has won:
Gold Medallion Book Award, Biography/Autobiography, 1981

Other books by the same author:
Irina's Story, 1983
Irina, a Love Stronger than Terror, 1981 (Henry Wagner, translator)

Other books you might like:
Anita Deyneka, *Christians in the Shadow of the Kremlin*, 1974
L. Merlin, *Courage for a Cross: Six Stories about Growing Up Christian in the U.S.S.R.*, 1987
Georgi Vins, *Let the Waters Roar: Evangelists in the Gulag*, 1989

272

SUSAN HASKINS

Mary Magdalen: Myth and Metaphor

(New York: Harcourt, Brace & Co., 1994)

Category: History; Theology
Subject(s): Scripture; Literature
Age range(s): Adult

Summary: Who was Mary Magdalen? A disciple of Jesus? A friend to the apostles? A prostitute? The sister of Lazarus? The gospel records reveal only four facts about this woman-she was part of the group that followed Jesus, she was a witness to the crucifixion, she was a witness to the resurrection, and she was the first person instructed to proclaim the news of the resurrection-yet liturgical and literary depictions of Mary Magdalen focus on her status as a repentant prostitute. Susan Haskins traces the historical evolution of the identity of Mary Magdalen through early Christian writings, medieval sermons and liturgies, and the art, devotional writings, and literature of the past two thousand years. Her goal is to unravel the identity of a historical and spiritual figure whose persona and identity have been shaped, says Haskins, by the forces of church doctrine and ecclesiastical politics.

Other books you might like:

Mary Ellen Ashcroft, *The Magdalene Gospel*, 1995
   novel
Esther de Boer, *Mary Magdalene: Beyond the Myth*, 1997
Mary R. Thompson, *Mary of Magdala: Apostle and Leader*, 1995
Anne Williman, *Mary of Magdala: A Novel*, 1990

273

GERALD F. HAWTHORNE, Editor
RALPH P. MARTIN, Co-Editor

Dictionary of Paul and His Letters

(Downers Grove, Illinois: InterVarsity Press, 1993)

Category: Religious Encyclopedias/Dictionaries; Theology
Subject(s): Christianity; Bible
Age range(s): Adult

Summary: In one volume, editor Gerald F. Hawthorne has assembled an exhaustive guide to Pauline theology, commentary, and ideology, for use by laity, clergy, and scholars. A primary focus is on indexing all the main issues addressed in the letters of Paul, along with the prominent commentaries on each, from all perspectives, summarized and annotated with bibliographic references.

Awards the book has won:

Gold Medallion Book Award, Biography/Autobiography, 1994

Other books by the same author:

The Presence & the Power, 1991
Tradition and Interpretation in the New Testament: Essays in Honor of E. Earle Ellis for His 60th Birthday, 1987 (Otto Betz, co-editor)
Philippians, 1983

Current Issues in Biblical and Patristic Interpretation: Studies in Honor of Merrill C. Tenney Presented by His Former Students, 1975

Other books you might like:

Joel B. Green, *Dictionary of Jesus and the Gospels*, 1992
Ralph P. Martin, *Dictionary of the Later New Testament and Its Developments*, 1997
Douglas J. Moo, *An Introduction to the New Testament*, 1992
Calvin J. Roetzel, *The Letters of Paul: Conversations in Context*, 1975

274

JOYCE LANDORF HEATHERLEY (Pseudonym of Joyce Landorf)

Special Words: Notes for When You Don't Know What to Say

(Nashville: Moorings, 1996)

Category: Self-Help
Subject(s): Communication; Letters
Age range(s): Young Adult-Adult

Summary: In *Special Words*, Joyce Landorf Heatherley offers guidance for expressing thoughts in a personal letter on the occasion of any circumstance, special or ordinary. She presents more than two hundred letters as models, and inspiration appropriate for occasions including Christmas, birthdays, and Mother's or Father's Day. Less structured occasions, such as a note of congratulations, thanks, sympathy, or apology, also have representative letters in the volume. Although the book is written from a Christian perspective-the author expresses her passion for reviving the art of personally written communication by noting that letter-writing as a tradition brought about many of the books of the New Testament-there is value in its guidance that transcends religious boundaries.

Other books you might like:

Florence Isaacs, *Just a Note to Say.: The Perfect Words for Every Occasion*, 1996
Florence Littauer, *The Gift of Encouraging Words*, 1995
Rosalie Maggio, *How to Say It: Choice Words, Phrases, Sentences, and Paragraphs for Every Situation*, 1990
Robyn Freedman Spizman, *When Words Matter Most*, 1996

275

JAMES HEFLEY
MARTI HEFLEY, Co-Author

By Their Blood: Christian Martyrs of the Twentieth Century

(Grand Rapids, Michigan: Baker Books, 1996)

Subject(s): Martyrs; Christianity; Jesus
Age range(s): Young Adult-Adult

Summary: *By Their Blood* is a collection of stories of Christian martyrs who were killed for their faith in Christ. Some stories are well-known, others are not. The authors' purpose in presenting these biographical accounts of sacrifice for the cause of Christianity is to remind people that martyrdom did not end hundreds of years ago. An earlier edition of this title, published in 1978, won the Gold Medallion Book Award for Biography/Autobiography in 1980.

Other books by the same author:
Human Cloning: Playing God or Scientific Progress?, 1998
Way Back When, 1992
The Truth in Crisis: The Controversy in the Southern Baptist Convention, 1986

Other books you might like:
M. Bernall, *She Said Yes: The Unlikely Martyrdom of Cassie Bernall*, 1999
Andrew Chandler, *The Terrible Alternative: Christian Martyrdom in the Twentieth Century*, 1998
Eileen Fraser Crossman, *Mountain Rain: A Biography of James O. Fraser, Pioneer Missionary of China*, 1994
Paul Marshall, *Their Blood Cries Out: The Untold Story of Persecution Against Christians in the Modern World*, 1997
Nina Shea, *In the Lion's Den: Persecuted Christians and What the Western Church Can Do about It*, 1997

276

DAVID HELLER

Talking to Your Child about God

(New York: Bantam Books, 1988)

Category: Self-Help
Subject(s): Parenthood; Parent and Child; Spirituality
Age range(s): Adult

Summary: *Talking to Your Child about God* offers parents suggestions for providing spiritual guidance to their children. Author David Heller discusses such issues as the nature of religion and its purpose, and children's natural curiosity about God. The book focuses on spiritual and value development for children between four and twelve.

Other books by the same author:
Just Build the Ark and the Animals Will Come: Children on Bible Stories, 1994
Fathers Are Like Elephants Because They're the Biggest Ones Around: (But They Still Are Pretty Gentle Underneath), 1993
My Mother Is the Best Gift I Ever Got: Children on Mothers, 1993
Dear God: Children's Letters to God, 1987 (John Alcorn, illustrator)
The Children's God, 1986

Other books you might like:
John M. Drescher, *Parents Passing the Torch of Faith*, 1997
Joanne Loecher, *Taking Time Together: Faith Experiences for Teens and Parents*, 1996
Doris Sanford, *How to Answer Tough Questions Kids Ask*, 1995
Catherine Stonehouse, *Joining Children on the Spiritual Journey*, 1998

277

THOMAS E. HELM

The Christian Religion: An Introduction

(Englewood Cliffs, New Jersey: Prentice Hall, 1991)

Category: Doctrine; History
Subject(s): Christianity; Theology; Customs

Summary: Thomas E. Helm provides a cultural and historical introduction to Christianity, focusing on its historical development, religious foundation, and forms of worship and practice. Various forms of Christianity are analyzed and compared. The basic tenets and practices of other world religions are also compared with those of Christianity.

Other books you might like:
E.O. James, *Christianity and Other Religions*, 1968
C.S. Lewis, *Mere Christianity*, 1952
Francis A. Schaeffer, *A Christian Manifesto*, 1981

278

KABIR HELMINSKI

Living Presence: A Sufi Way to Mindfulness and the Essential Self

(New York: Jeremy P. Tarcher/Perigee, 1992)

Category: Self-Help
Subject(s): Mysticism; Religious Life; Meditation
Age range(s): Adult

Summary: *Living Presence* uses spiritual principles drawn from Sufi poetry and wisdom writings to integrate mystical practice into everyday contemporary living. In straightforward language, Kabir Helminski offers practical guidance for making mystical spirituality a foundational part of a modern lifestyle.

Other books by the same author:
Knowing Heart: A Sufi Path of Transformation, 1999
The Rumi Collection: An Anthology of Translations of Mevlana Jalaluddin Rumi, 1998
Jewels of Remembrance: A Daybook of Spiritual Guidance, 1996 (Camille Helminski, co-author)

Other books you might like:
Javad Nurbakhsh, *Discourses on the Sufi Path*, 1996
John O'Toole, *The Wisdom of Islam*, 1996
Avideh Shashaani, *Promised Paradise*, 1993

279

A.L. HERMAN

A Brief Introduction to Hinduism: Religion, Philosophy, and Ways of Liberation

(Boulder, Colorado: Westview Press, 1991)

Category: Doctrine
Subject(s): Hinduism; Philosophy; Freedom
Age range(s): Adult

Summary: A general overview of one of the world's oldest living religions, Herman's *A Brief Introduction to Hinduism* suggests that to understand Hinduism, one must identify the human problems the religion purports to address and the ways in which it does so. Herman profiles three famous Hindu leaders: Ramana Maharshi, the great Hindu sage and spiritual teacher; Mohandas Gandhi, whose path of *satyagraha*, or non-violent resistance, led to the end of British rule in India; and A.C. Bhaktivedanta, the founder of the Hare Krishna sect. Herman argues that each of these three figures is demonstrative of a different branch of Hindu thought.

Other books by the same author:

The Ways of Philosophy: Searching for a Worthwhile Life, 1990
An Introduction to Buddhist Thought: A Philosophic History of Indian Buddhism, 1983
The Problem of Evil and Indian Thought, 1976
An Introduction to Indian Thought, 1976

Other books you might like:

Alain Danielou, *The Myths and Gods of India: The Classic Work on Hindu Polytheism From the Princeton Bollingen Series*, 1991
Ainslie T. Embree, *The Hindu Tradition*, 1966
Swami Kriyananda, *The Hindu Way of Awakening: Its Revelation, Its Symbol, an Essential View of Religion*, 1998

280

JAMES HERRIOT

The James Herriot Series

(1972-1992)

Category: Autobiography; Gentle Reads
Series: James Herriot
Subject(s): Veterinarians; Rural Life; Animals
Age range(s): Young Adult-Adult
Time period(s): 20th century
Locale(s): Yorkshire, England

Summary: This autobiographical series of books by country veterinarian James Herriot relates his life and career from his initial job in the field to his service in the RAF during World War II to parenthood. The animals and people Herriot deals with on the job are both described in gentle yet honest detail, as are the ups and downs of everyday life in rural England. This eternally popular series (which, while classified as non-fiction, reads like fiction) consists of five books: *All Creatures Great and Small* (1972), *All Things Bright and Beautiful* (1973), *All Things Wise and Wonderful* (1977), *The Lord God Made Them All* (1981), and *Every Living Thing* (1992).

Other books by the same author:

Vets Might Fly, 1976 (Larry, illustrator)
Vet in Harness, 1974 (Larry, illustrator)
Let Sleeping Vets Lie, 1973 (Larry, illustrator)
It Shouldn't Happen to a Vet, 1972
If Only They Could Talk, 1970

Other books you might like:

Jan Karon, *The Mitford Series*, 1994-

Grant Kendall, *The Animals in My Life: Stories of a Country Vet*, 1996
  Jane Thissen, illustrator
Grant Kendall, *More Animals in My Life: Stories of a Country Vet*, 1998
  Jane Thissen, illustrator
Graham Lord, *James Herriot: The Life of a Country Vet*, 1997

281

ABRAHAM JOSHUA HESCHEL

God in Search of Man: A Philosophy of Judaism

(New York: Farrar, Straus and Cudahy, 1955)

Category: Theology
Subject(s): Judaism; Philosophy
Age range(s): Adult

Summary: In this book and its companion volume, *Man Is Not Alone*, the sagacious Heschel ponders the key meaning of the *Bible*: God reveals himself to man through history and covenant. Heschel explores the role of Israel's prophets, the meaning of *Torah*, the God of Abraham, and the paradox of Sinai.

Other books by the same author:

The Prophets, 1962
The Sabbath: Its Meaning for Modern Man, 1951

Other books you might like:

Arthur A. Cohen, *Contemporary Jewish Religious Thought: Original Essays on Critical Concepts, Movements, and Beliefs*, 1987
Neil Gillman, *Sacred Fragments: Recovering Theology for the Modern Jew*, 1990
Barry Holtz, *Back to the Sources: Reading the Classic Jewish Texts*, 1984
Isaac Klein, *A Guide to Jewish Religious Practice*, 1979
Rifat Sonsino, *Finding God: Ten Jewish Responses*, 1986

282

HUGH HEWITT

Searching for God in America

(Dallas: Word, 1996)

Category: Biography; History
Subject(s): Judaism; Christianity; Islam
Age range(s): Adult
Locale(s): United States

Summary: Hugh Hewitt sets out to create a living portrait of religion in America at the end of the 20th century in *Searching for God in America* and the television series of the same name. He traces the development of religion in the United States from the days of the Pilgrims and the Mayflower Compact to the 1990s. Eight interviews with people whose lives are characterized by the author as ''faith-filled'' plus essays and other writings make up the largest portion of the book. Interviewees include Rabbi Harold Kushner, Charles Colson (of the Prison Ministry), and the Dalai Lama.

Awards the book has won:
Gold Medallion Book Award, Christianity and Society, 1997

Other books by the same author:
Embarrassed Believer: Reviving Christian Witness in an Age of Unbelief, 1998
First Principles: A Primer of Ideas for the College-Bound Student, 1987

Other books you might like:
George Barna, *The Second Coming of the Church*, 1998
David Chichester, *American Sacred Space*, 1995
Peter W. Williams, *America's Religions: Traditions and Cultures*, 1998
Robert Wuthnow, *After Heaven: Spirituality in America Since the 1950s*, 1998

283

CHRISTINE LEIGH HEYRMAN

Southern Cross: The Beginnings of the Bible Belt

(New York: A.A. Knopf, 1997)

Category: History; Theology
Subject(s): Christianity; Small Town Life
Age range(s): Adult
Locale(s): South

Summary: Christine Leigh Heyrman explores the roots of evangelical Protestantism in the United States and demonstrates how its center of influence gradually shifted from northeastern Protestant traditions to the heart of southern Conservative worship and belief, taking on the political and cultural aspects of the south as well. During the late 18th century, Southerners were offended by a number of philosophical tenets of evangelical Christianity, including the rejection of slavery and the acceptance of women in public roles in the church. Over the course of a century, the denominations that moved from the east to the south-particularly the Methodists and the Baptists-shed some of their more progressive social characteristics and began to defend the status quo of the deep South, including its dependence on slavery and its insistence on patriarchal authority in the church and in the home.

Awards the book has won:
Bancroft Prize, 1998

Other books by the same author:
Commerce and Culture: The Maritime Communities of Colonial Massachusetts, 1690-1750, 1984

Other books you might like:
Marion D. Aldridge, *The Changing Shape of Protestantism in the South*, 1996
    Kevin Lewis, co-editor
Erskine Caldwell, *Deep South: Memory and Observation*, 1968
Joel A. Carpenter, *Revive Us Again: The Reawakening of American Fundamentalism*, 1997
Edwin S. Gaustad, *A Religious History of America*, 1990
R. Marie Griffith, *God's Daughters: Evangelical Women and the Power of Submission*, 1997
Samuel S. Hill, *Encyclopedia of Religion in the South*, 1997

Harry S. Stout, *New Directions in American Religious History*, 1997

284

MARJORIE HOLMES
BETTY FRASER, Illustrator

How Can I Find You, God?

(Garden City, New York: Doubleday, 1975)

Category: Essays
Subject(s): Christianity; Women; Prayer
Age range(s): Adult

Summary: In timeless essays and prayers, Marjorie Holmes shares her personal search for a faith that answers the need in her life for God. *How Can I Find You, God?* addresses the search for God in chapters that focus on people, birth, death, reading, work, nature, the church, prayer, the arts, pain, the Holy Spirit, and loving. With a conversational style of writing that personalizes every subject, the author invites readers into a lifelong journey of faith and discovery.

Other books by the same author:
Hold Me Up a Little Longer, Lord, 1977 (Patricia Mighell, illustrator)
Nobody Else Will Listen: A Girl's Conversations with God, 1973
Who Am I, God?, 1971 (Betty Fraser, illustrator)
I've Got to Talk to Somebody, God: A Woman's Conversations with God, 1969

Other books you might like:
Ann Kiemel Anderson, *I Love the Word Impossible*, 1976
Ann Kiemel Anderson, *I'm out to Change My World*, 1974
Emilie Barnes, *Fill My Cup, Lord: A Teatime Devotional*, 1996
Susan Classen, *Dewdrops on Spiderwebs: Connections Made Visible*, 1997
John Albert Taylor, *Notes on an Unhurried Journey*, 1991
Iyanla Vanzant, *One Day My Soul Just Opened Up: 40 Days and 40 Nights Toward Spiritual Strength and Personal Growth*, 1998

285

MARJORIE HOLMES

I've Got to Talk to Somebody, God: A Woman's Conversations with God

(Garden City, New York: Doubleday, 1969)

Category: Prayer
Subject(s): Christianity; Faith; Women
Age range(s): Adult

Summary: Marjorie Holmes shares her personal prayers in *I've Got to Talk to Somebody, God*. Focusing on the everyday aspects of life as a mother, wife, worker, and nurturer, this collection of conversational chats offers thoughts on everything from disciplining a child to being too tired at the end of a long day to think about much of anything. The concerns of the author will resonate with women readers, in particular, and the essence of the prayers is timeless.

Other books by the same author:
Hold Me Up a Little Longer, Lord, 1977 (Patricia Mighell, illustrator)
How Can I Find You, God?, 1975 (Betty Fraser, illustrator)
Nobody Else Will Listen: A Girl's Conversations with God, 1973
Who Am I, God?, 1971 (Betty Fraser, illustrator)
I've Got to Talk to Somebody, God: A Woman's Conversations with God, 1969

Other books you might like:
Ann Kiemel Anderson, *I'm out to Change My World*, 1974
Ann Kiemel Anderson, *I Love the Word Impossible*, 1976
Emilie Barnes, *Fill My Cup, Lord: A Teatime Devotional*, 1996
Susan Classen, *Dewdrops on Spiderwebs: Connections Made Visible*, 1997
John Albert Taylor, *Notes on an Unhurried Journey*, 1991
Iyanla Vanzant, *One Day My Soul Just Opened Up: 40 Days and 40 Nights Toward Spiritual Strength and Personal Growth*, 1998

286

WALTER HOOPER

C.S. Lewis: A Companion and Guide
(San Francisco: HarperSanFrancisco, 1996)

Category: Biography
Subject(s): Essays; Religion; Literature
Age range(s): Adult

Summary: Walter Hooper, well-known critic and interpreter of the works of C.S. Lewis, offers a biographical portrait of the legendary author and an examination of his works. Hooper provides an overview of Lewis's life from his Irish childhood through his years in academia, his religious conversion, and his late-in-life marriage. The key themes and ideas of Lewis's works are discussed, and Hooper provides a ''Who's Who'' guide to the people in Lewis's life and a ''What's What'' list of places, terminology, concepts and items significant to Lewis and relevant in understanding his life and work.

Awards the book has won:
Gold Medallion Book Award, Biography/Autobiography, 1997

Other books by the same author:
The C.S. Lewis Handbook, 1994
Through Joy and Beyond: A Pictorial Biography of C.S. Lewis, 1982
Past Watchful Dragons: The Narnian Chronicles of C.S. Lewis, 1979

Other books you might like:
Janine Goffar, *The C.S. Lewis Index: A Comprehensive Guide to Lewis's Writings and Ideas*, 1998
Roger Lancelyn Green, *C.S. Lewis: A Biography*, 1994
   Walter Hooper, co-author; revised edition
Douglas H. Gresham, *Lenten Lands*, 1988
Thomas C. Peters, *Simply C.S. Lewis: A Beginner's Guide to the Life and Works of C.S. Lewis*, 1997
George Sayer, *Jack: A Life of C.S. Lewis*, 1994

Jeffrey D. Schultz, *The C.S. Lewis Readers' Encyclopedia*, 1998

287

JOHN A. HOSTETLER

Amish Society
(Baltimore: Johns Hopkins University Press, 1993)

Category: History
Subject(s): Amish; Culture; Religion
Age range(s): Young Adult-Adult
Locale(s): United States

Summary: Although the plain dress and traditional habits of the Amish make them quite recognizable, there is far more to Amish culture and society than somber clothes and old-fashioned ways. John A. Hostetler's *Amish Society*, first published in 1968, is considered one of the most complete and authoritative sources of information about the Amish in America. This fourth edition contains updated information on subjects including population trends in Amish communities, farming practices, and legal issues. *Amish Society* provides a view into the community life of the Amish, who are concentrated in Indiana, Ohio, and Pennsylvania. Religious beliefs, practices, education, and ceremonies are described and discussed, as are a variety of community life issues, including the tension between traditional ways and the values of the world outside the Amish enclave.

Other books by the same author:
The Amish, 1995 (revised edition)
Amish Children: Education in the Family, School, and Community, 1992 (Gertrude Enders Huntington, co-author; second edition)
Amish Roots: A Treasury of History, Wisdom, and Lore, 1989
Mennonite Life, 1954
Amish Life, 1952

Other books you might like:
Jan Folsom, *The Amish: Images of a Tradition*, 1995
Beverly Lewis, *The Heritage of Lancaster County: The Shunning, the Confession, the Reckoning*, 1998
   novels
Donald B. Kraybill, *The Riddle of Amish Culture*, 1989
Louise Stoltzfus, *Amish Women: Lives and Stories*, 1994

288

L. RON HUBBARD

Scientology: The Fundamentals of Thought
(London: Hubbard, 1956)

Category: New Age (Nonfiction)
Subject(s): Religion; Scientology
Age range(s): Adult

Summary: L. Ron Hubbard outlines the principles and fundamentals of Scientology, a controversial religion he founded in 1954 based on ''Dianetics,'' a psychotherapy method also devised by Hubbard. *Scientology: The Fundamentals of Thought* offers guidance for improving communication with loved ones, overcoming life's problems, and achieving a higher level of personal peace. Among the principles outlined are Hubbard's Eight Dynamics, or subdivisions, of life.

Other books by the same author:
The Way to Happiness, 1984
Scientology Abridged Dictionary, 1965
Dianetics: The Original Thesis, 1951
Introduction to Scientology Ethics, 1951
Self Analysis, 1951

Other books you might like:
Jon Atack, *A Piece of Blue Sky: Scientology, Dianetics and L. Ron Hubbard Exposed*, 1990
Church of Scientology of California, *What Is Scientology?: Based on the Works of L. Ron Hubbard*, 1978
Robert Kaufman, *Inside Scientology*, 1972
Roy Wallis, *The Road to Total Freedom: A Sociological Analysis of Scientology*, 1977

289

WINTHROP S. HUDSON
JOHN CORRIGAN, Co-Author

Religion in America: An Historical Account of the Development of American Religious Life

(Upper Saddle River, New Jersey: Prentice-Hall, 1998)

Category: Religious Encyclopedias/Dictionaries; History
Subject(s): Culture; Religion
Age range(s): Adult
Locale(s): United States

Summary: Winthrop S. Hudson's *Religion in America* traces the development and history of religion in the United States from earliest colonial days in 1607 through the late 20th century. Highlighting the historical and sociological relationships between religion and society, Hudson addresses topics including the origins of American religious thought in the European and Puritan traditions, the influences of the ''Great Awakening'' on American culture, and the development of religious diversity and plurality in the 19th and 20th centuries. The title was first published in 1965; this sixth updated edition was published in 1998.

Other books by the same author:
Nationalism and Religion in America: Concepts of American Identity and Mission, 1970
American Protestantism, 1961
Understanding Roman Catholicism: A Guide to Papal Teaching for Protestants, 1959
The Story of the Christian Church, 1958

Other books you might like:
Edwin S. Gaustad, *A Documentary History of Religion in America*, 1993
2 volumes
William R. Hutchinson, *Between the Times: The Travail of the Protestant Establishment in America, 1900-1960*, 1989
Martin E. Marty, *Pilgrims in Their Own Land: 500 Years of Religion in America*, 1984

Theophus H. Smith, *Conjuring Culture: Biblical Formations of Black America*, 1995

290

HATCHER HUGHES

Hell-Bent fer Heaven: A Play in Three Acts

(New York: Harper & Brothers, 1924)

Category: Plays
Subject(s): Folklore; Religion; Mountain Life
Age range(s): Adult
Time period(s): 20th century (early)
Locale(s): North Carolina

Summary: *Hell-Bent fer Heaven* won the Pulitzer Prize for Drama in 1924. Seldom performed anywhere in the United States since the early 1950s, *Hell-Bent fer Heaven* is a folk play about life and religion in the rural reaches of the Carolina Mountains.

Awards the book has won:
Pulitzer Prize, Drama, 1924

Other books by the same author:
Wake up, Jonathan: A Comedy in a Prologue and Three Acts, 1928 (Elmer L. Rice, co-author)
Ruint: A Folk Comedy in Four Acts, 1925

Other books you might like:
Marc Connelly, *The Green Pastures: A Fable Suggested by Roark Bradford's Southern Sketches, ''Ol' Man Adam an' His Chillun''*, 1929
Donald Davis, *Barking at a Fox-Fur Coat*, 1991
North Carolina stories
Paul Green, *In Abraham's Bosom*, 1929
Mary Wright Toynbee, *Lonesome Children*, 1996

291

THOMAS PATRICK HUGHES

Dictionary of Islam

(Chicago: KAZI Publications, 1994)

Category: Religious Encyclopedias/Dictionaries
Subject(s): Islam; Customs; Culture
Age range(s): Young Adult-Adult

Summary: Thomas Patrick Hughes's *Dictionary of Islam* was first compiled and published in the 19th century. It remains one of the most comprehensive, single-volume, illustrated reference sources of information about the origins of the customs, ceremonies, doctrines, and rituals of Islam. Terms and concepts are defined, and articles provide information about 19th-century Muslim lifestyles and practices dealing with life occasions such as birth, death, and other transitions.

Other books you might like:
H.A.R. Gibb, *Shorter Encyclopaedia of Islam*, 1997
J.H. Kramers, co-editor
Thomas W. Lippman, *Understanding Islam: An Introduction to the Muslim World*, 1995
Ian Richard Netton, *A Popular Dictionary of Islam*, 1992

E. Van Donzel, *Islamic Desk Reference: Compiled From the Encyclopedia of Islam*, 1994

292

AKE HULTKRANTZ

The Religions of the American Indians

(Berkeley: University of California Press, 1979)

Category: History
Series: Hermeneutics Studies in the History of Religions
Subject(s): Religion; Indians of North America; Indians of South America
Locale(s): North America; South America; Central America

Summary: Ake Hultkrantz is a Swedish scholar and author of *The Religions of the American Indians*, an ambitious survey of Amerindian religious traditions and practices, translated by Monica Setterwall. This book has become a standard introduction to the study of North and South American Indian cultures for its broad approach, seeking patterns and similarities among widely separated groups of tribes and traditions.

Other books by the same author:

The Attraction of Peyote: An Inquiry into the Basic Conditions of the Diffusion of the Peyote Religion in North America, 1997
Shamanic Healing and Ritual Drama: Health and Medicine in Native North American Religious Traditions, 1992
Native Religions of North America: The Power of Visions and Fertility, 1987
Study of American Indian Religions, 1983
Belief and Worship in Native North America, 1981

Other books you might like:

John Bierhorst, *The Sacred Path: Spells, Prayers, & Power Songs of the American Indians*, 1983
David L. Carmichael, *Sacred Sites, Sacred Places*, 1994
    Jane Hubert, Brian Reeves, Audhild Schanche, co-editors
Robert M. Torrance, *The Spiritual Quest: Transcendence in Myth, Religion, and Science*, 1994

293

HANNAH HURNARD

Hind's Feet on High Places

(New York: Walker, 1977)

Category: Devotionals
Subject(s): Christianity; Christian Life; God
Age range(s): Young Adult-Adult

Summary: Taking her title from the book of Psalms, Hurnard likens the Christian to a deer (hind) who pants after God. This daily devotional book emphasizes God's majesty and omnipotence. The meditations also remind readers of the heart within them that will not rest until it finds its rest in God. Hurnard's devotional continues in popularity among young adults and college students.

Other books by the same author:
Mountains of Spices, 1976

Other books you might like:
John Bunyan, *Grace Abounding to the Chief of Sinners*, 1666
Phillip Keller, *A Shepherd Looks at Psalm 23*, 1970
Keith Miller, *The Taste of New Wine*, 1965
Watchman Nee, *The Normal Christian Life*, 1963
Philip Yancey, *What's So Amazing about Grace?*, 1997

294

ALDOUS HUXLEY

The Devils of Loudon

(New York: Harper, 1952)

Category: History
Subject(s): Demons; Superstition; Religion
Age range(s): Adult
Time period(s): 17th century
Locale(s): Loudun, France

Summary: *The Devils of Loudun* is a non-fiction account of superstition and hysteria in 17th century France. Priest Urbanus Grandier was accused of being a magician and Satanist whose ties to the Devil led to the demon possession of the Ursuline nuns at the convent in Loudun. Huxley's treatment of these historical events highlights the danger of mass hysteria when political interests, extreme self-righteousness, and unchecked superstition combine to "demonize" a person or organization that stands at political cross purposes with those who are in power.

Other books by the same author:
Heaven and Hell, 1956
The Doors of Perception, 1954
Brave New World, 1932
Point Counter Point, 1928

Other books you might like:
C. Fred Dickason, *Demon Possession & the Christian*, 1987
Gerald Messadie, *A History of the Devil*, 1996
    Marc Romano, translator
Jeffrey Burton Russell, *Lucifer, the Devil in the Middle Ages*, 1984
Lester Sumrall, *Bitten by Devils*, 1987
Merrill F. Unger, *What Demons Can Do to Saints*, 1977

295

BILL HYBELS

Honest to God?: Becoming an Authentic Christian

(Grand Rapids, Michigan: Zondervan, 1990)

Category: Self-Help
Subject(s): Christian Life; Relationships; Conduct of Life
Age range(s): Adult

Summary: Bill Hybels, pastor, writer, and church consultant, asks Christians if their beliefs have made a real and noticeable difference in their lifestyles. He notes that many Christians are in what he terms a state of "pseudocommunity" with God and their fellow Christians, going through the motions of a Christian life, but not really living consistently and authentically in ways that demonstrate the difference Christian faith can make in a person's life. He also suggests ways to overcome obstacles to authentic Christian living, and shares examples from his own spiritual journey to honesty in his Christianity.

Awards the book has won:
Gold Medallion Book Award, Inspirational, 1991

Other books by the same author:
Making Life Work: Putting God's Wisdom into Action: With Questions for Reflection and Discussion, 1998 (Lynne Hybels, co-author)
The God You're Looking For, 1997
Seven Wonders of the Spiritual World, 1988
Who You Are When No One's Looking: Choosing Consistency, Resisting Compromise, 1987
Caution: Christians under Construction: A Nuts and Bolts Look at Living a Not-So-Perfect Christian Life, 1978 (Jay Caress, co-author)

Other books you might like:
Melinda Fish, *I'm So Tired of Acting Spiritual: Peeling Back the Mask*, 1996
Catherine Marshall, *Beyond Our Selves*, 1961
Elizabeth Cody Newenhuyse, *God, I Know You're Here Somewhere*, 1996
John Ortberg, *The Life You've Always Wanted: Spiritual Disciplines for Ordinary People*, 1997

296

SAINT IGNATIUS OF LOYOLA

The Spiritual Exercises of St. Ignatius
(c. 1522)

Category: Devotionals
Subject(s): Christianity; Mysticism; Jesuits
Age range(s): Adult

Summary: Ignatius of Loyola (1491-1556) is most famous for founding the Jesuit order. This 16th-century monastic leader also offers a set of ascetic practices and meditations that lead the soul to conquer its worldly self and unite with God. Ignatius' exercises are still very popular with a broad range of people seeking a method of liberating their souls from the cares of the world.

Other books you might like:
Saint Benedict of Nursia, *The Rule of St. Benedict*, c. 520
John Cassian, *Conferences*, 1985
    Colm Luibheid, translator
John Howard Griffin, *The Hermitage Journals: A Diary Kept While Working on the Biography of Thomas Merton*, 1981
John A. Hardon, *Retreat with the Lord: A Popular Guide to the Spiritual Exercises of Ignatius of Loyola*, 1993
Saint Teresa of Avila, *The Way of Perfection, and Conceptions of Divine Love*, 1852
    John Dalton, translator

297

RONALD H. ISAACS

Sacred Seasons: A Sourcebook for the Jewish Holidays
(Northvale, New Jersey: Jason Aronson, 1997)

Category: Self-Help
Subject(s): Judaism; Holidays, Jewish; Folklore
Age range(s): Young Adult-Adult

Summary: The folk stories and scriptural roots of Jewish feast and fast days are collected by Rabbi Ronald H. Isaacs in this volume. Rabbi Isaacs explores the background and significance of the major and lesser Jewish holidays, and provides stories that illuminate the meaning of each. From Sabbath observances to Passover, Shavuot, and Sukkot, the occasions that help bind Jews to each other and to God are explained in folktale, legend, and rabbinic writings.

Other books by the same author:
Every Person's Guide to Holiness: The Jewish Perspective, 1999
Every Person's Guide to Jewish Blessings, 1999
Every Person's Guide to the High Holy Days, 1998
The Jewish Book of Etiquette, 1998
Critical Jewish Issues: A Book for Teenagers, 1996

Other books you might like:
S.Y. Agnon, *Days of Awe: A Treasury of Jewish Wisdom for Reflection, Repentance, and Renewal on the High Holy Days*, 1995
Lesli Koppelman Ross, *Celebrate!: The Complete Jewish Holidays Handbook*, 1994
Ron Wolfson, *The Art of Jewish Living: The Passover Seder*, 1996
    Joel Laurie Grishaver, co-author

298

PHIL JACKSON
HUGH DELEHANTY, Co-Author

Sacred Hoops: Spiritual Lessons of a Hardwood Warrior
(New York: Hyperion, 1995)

Category: Autobiography
Subject(s): Sports/Basketball; Buddhism; Sports
Age range(s): Young Adult-Adult
Time period(s): 1990s
Locale(s): Chicago, Illinois

Summary: Phil Jackson, head coach of the Chicago Bulls, shares his philosophy of "mindful basketball" and describes how he creates team unity through the tenets of Zen Buddhism and the influence of Lakota Sioux spiritual traditions. Jackson calls himself a Zen Christian, and in this volume he reveals the roots of his leadership style, which rejects the Western model of winning through intimidation. Basketball fans will be particularly interested in the stories about Bulls stars, including Michael Jordan, Scottie Pippen, and Dennis Rodman.

Other books by the same author:
Fifty Years of Cheers and Jeers, 1997

Other books you might like:
Bill Bradley, *Values of the Game*, 1998
David Whitaker, *The Gospel According to Phil: The Words and Wisdom of Chicago Bulls Coach Phil Jackson: An Unauthorized Collection*, 1997
Pat Williams, *Ahead of the Game: The Pat Williams Story*, 1999
  James D. Denney, co-author

299

DAVID JEREMIAH

Prayer: The Great Adventure

(Sisters, Oregon: Multnomah, 1997)

Category: Prayer; Journals/Letters
Subject(s): Christianity; Bible; Prayer
Age range(s): Young Adult-Adult

Summary: Radio host and pastor David Jeremiah's teachings about prayer became more significant when he was diagnosed with cancer. In *Prayer: The Great Adventure*, Jeremiah invites readers to discover what he has learned about prayer as a result of his personal trials and challenges. The first part of the book focuses on general teachings about prayer from the Bible and addresses frequently asked questions. The second part, called "Digging for Gold," highlights the Lord's Prayer as a model for personal petitions. The third section uses the New Testament chapter of John 17 as a foundation for learning about prayer. Examples of the author's prayer journal are included, and guidelines are offered to readers for keeping prayer diaries of their own.

Awards the book has won:
Gold Medallion Book Award, Christian Living, 1998

Other books by the same author:
Gifts From God: Encouragement and Hope for Today's Parents, 1999
Jesus' Final Warning, 1999
God in You: Releasing the Power of the Holy Spirit in Your Life, 1998

Other books you might like:
Ronald Dunn, *Don't Just Stand There, Pray Something*, 1991
Richard J. Foster, *Prayer: Finding the Heart's True Home*, 1992
Robert Schuller, *Prayer: My Soul's Adventure with God: A Spiritual Autobiography*, 1995

300

SAINT JOHN OF THE CROSS

Dark Night of the Soul

(Barcelona, Spain: 1619)

Category: Devotionals
Subject(s): Christianity; Mysticism
Age range(s): Adult

Summary: Along with Teresa of Avila (1515-1582), John of the Cross (1542-1591) traced the development of the pure soul as it undergoes various cleansings. This book describes the various ways that the soul is purified and transformed through suffering, preparing it for unification with God. The 1990 edition of this book is translated and edited by E. Allison Peers.

Other books by the same author:
The Poems of St. John of the Cross, 1968 (The volume is introduced by Willis Barnstone.)

Other books you might like:
Anonymous, *The Cloud of Unknowing*, c. 1300
William Johnston, *The Inner Eye of Love: Mysticism and Religion*, 1978
Ramon Lull, *Romancing God: Contemplating the Beloved*, 1999
  Henry L. Carrigan Jr., editor
Mechthild of Magdeburg, *Meditations From Mechthild of Magdeburg*, 1999
  Henry L. Carrigan Jr., editor
Saint Teresa of Avila, *The Way of Perfection, and Conceptions of Divine Love*, 1852
  John Dalton, translator

301

POPE JOHN PAUL II

Crossing the Threshold of Hope

(New York: Knopf, 1994)

Category: Theology
Subject(s): Christianity; Catholicism; Meditation

Summary: Pope John Paul II departs from making an official pronouncement—an encyclical—to offer some of his thoughts on the present and future state of the Catholic Church. In these meditations he ruminates on the ways the Church can be a vital institution in the new millennium. He advocates a return to some of the traditions the Church lost after Vatican II, but above all he calls for a renewed respect for life, a position seen especially in his stance toward abortion. He also calls for the world to think of itself as a community working together toward the common goal of peace.

Other books you might like:
Carl Bernstein, *His Holiness: John Paul II and the Hidden History of Our Time*, 1996
Charla H. Honea, *A Reader's Companion to Crossing the Threshold of Hope*, 1996
Karl Keating, *What Catholics Really Believe—Setting the Record Straight: 52 Answers to Common Misconceptions about the Catholic Faith*, 1992
Jonathan Kwitny, *Man of the Century: The Life and Times of Pope John Paul II*, 1997
Tad Szulc, *Pope John Paul II: The Biography*, 1995

302

JAMES WELDON JOHNSON

God's Trombones: Seven Negro Sermons in Verse

(New York: Viking Press, 1927)

Category: Sermons
Subject(s): Poetry; African Americans; Bible
Age range(s): Young Adult-Adult

Summary: Drawing on the inspirational cadences of 19th century southern preaching, James Weldon Johnson has used poetry to convey the deep emotions of sermons from the African American tradition. A prolific writer, lawyer, and diplomat, Johnson here preserves the essence of seven sermons and contributes to a new generation of the oral tradition, albeit in print. A classic within just years of its original publication, this collection of spiritual and inspirational poetry is still enjoyed by readers and listeners of all ages.

Other books by the same author:
Fifty Years and Other Poems, 1975
Along This Way, 1933
The Book of American Negro Poetry, 1931
The Autobiography of an Ex-Coloured Man, 1927

Other books you might like:
Arna Wendell Bontemps, *American Negro Poetry*, 1963
Peter J. Gomes, *Sermons: Biblical Wisdom for Daily Living*, 1998
Iyanla Vanzant, *Acts of Faith: Daily Meditations for People of Color*, 1993

303

KEVIN ORLIN JOHNSON

Why Do Catholics Do That?: A Guide to the Teachings and Practices of the Catholic Church

(New York: Ballantine Books, 1994)

Category: Doctrine
Subject(s): Catholicism; History; Customs
Age range(s): Young Adult-Adult

Summary: Without making light the sacred, Johnson interjects humor into his comprehensive and wide-ranging *Why Do Catholics Do That?*. He explains and defines many aspects of Catholic worship and observance, including the Mass, the rosary, and the pope. The art and culture of Catholicism are also included in this enlightening reference volume that can help non-Catholics understand unfamiliar traditions and encourage Catholics to better understand the rituals, symbols, and history of their faith.

Other books by the same author:
Apparitions: Mystic Phenomena and What They Mean, 1996
Expressions of the Catholic Faith: A Guide to the Teachings and Practices of the Catholic Church, 1994

Other books you might like:
Greg Dues, *Catholic Customs and Traditions: A Popular Guide*, 1992
John O'Connor, *The Essential Catholic Handbook: A Summary of Beliefs, Practices, and Prayers*, 1997
Sean O'Reilly, *Our Name Is Peter: An Anthology of Key Teachings of Pope Paul VI*, 1977

304

LUKE TIMOTHY JOHNSON

The Real Jesus: The Misguided Quest for the Historical Jesus and the Truth of the Traditional Gospels

(San Francisco: HarperSanFrancisco, 1996)

Category: Theology
Subject(s): History; Christianity; Bible
Age range(s): Adult

Summary: In response to publications by members of the Jesus Seminar, an interdisciplinary scholarly effort devoted to reconstructing historical evidence of the life of Jesus, Luke Timothy Johnson contends that the Christian faith is not built upon a historical Christ, but upon a resurrected Jesus who supersedes historical artifact. One of Johnson's objections to the Jesus Seminar approach is that the work of seeking information about Jesus is not being done by religious scholars under the protective wing of the church, but by historians, anthropologists, and archaeologists-as well as biblical scholars-in the glare of public attention and media coverage.

Other books by the same author:
The Writings of the New Testament: An Interpretation, 1986
Decision Making in the Church: A Biblical Model, 1983
Some Hard Blessings: Meditations on the Beatitudes in Matthew, 1981

Other books you might like:
Charlotte Allen, *The Human Christ: The Search for the Historical Jesus*, 1998
Gary R. Habermas, *The Historical Jesus: Ancient Evidence for the Life of Christ*, 1996
Raymond Martin, *The Elusive Messiah: A Philosophical Overview of the Quest for the Historical Jesus*, 1999
Stephen J. Patterson, *The God of Jesus: The Historical Jesus and the Search for Meaning*, 1998

305

SANDY JOHNSON

The Book of Tibetan Elders: Life Stories and Wisdom From the Great Spiritual Masters of Tibet

(New York: Riverhead Books, 1996)

Category: Biography
Subject(s): Buddhism; Spirituality
Age range(s): Adult
Time period(s): 1990s (1994)
Locale(s): India

Summary: In a volume that can be likened to a spiritual travelogue, Sandy Johnson reveals some of the wisdom of Tibetan Buddhist elders living in exile in India. She also reveals her own path of spiritual discovery and learning. From conversations with Tibetan Buddhists in several parts of India, Johnson records teachings that share each elder's interpretation of the meaning of Buddhism.

Other books by the same author:

The Book of Elders: The Life Stories of Great American Indians, 1994

Other books you might like:

Dalai Lama, *Buddhism in the West: Spiritual Wisdom for the 21st Century*, 1998

Dalai Lama, *The Joy of Living and Dying in Peace: Core Teachings of Tibetan Buddhism*, 1997

He-ru-ka Gtsan-smyon, *The Life of Milarepa*, 1977
   Lobsang P. Lhalungpa, translator

Herbert V. Guenther, *The Life and Teaching of Naropa*, 1986
   originally published in England in 1963

Palden Gyatso, *The Autobiography of a Tibetan Monk*, 1997

Tulku Thondup, *Masters of Meditation and Miracles*, 1995

306

SPENCER JOHNSON

The Precious Present

(Millbrae, California: Celestial Arts, 1981)

Category: Self-Help
Subject(s): Self-Acceptance; Conduct of Life
Age range(s): Adult

Summary: Before he co-authored *The One Minute Manager*, Spencer Johnson wrote this essay on the value of time and contentment. *The Precious Present* offers gentle guidance in finding personal happiness through self-awareness and an appreciation of what life has to offer now, and not just in the future.

Other books by the same author:

Who Moved My Cheese?: An Amazing Way to Deal with Change in Your Work and in Your Life, 1998

One Minute for Yourself, 1998

The One Minute Manager, 1982 (Kenneth Blanchard, co-author)

Other books you might like:

H. Jackson Brown Jr., *The Complete Life's Little Instruction Book*, 1997

Og Mandino, *The Greatest Miracle in the World*, 1975

Lee J. Painter Each D, *Each Day Is a Gift: That's Why It's Called the Present*, 1996

307

JOLANDE JACOBI, Editor

Paracelsus: Selected Writings

(New York: Pantheon, 1951)

Category: New Age (Nonfiction)
Subject(s): Alchemy; Medicine; God
Age range(s): Adult

Summary: Paracelsus is the name used by the 16th-century Swiss physician Theophrastus Bombastus von Hohenheim. In addition to his medical studies, Paracelsus was one of the first secretly to practice bringing life to inorganic matter. He also believed that people know God only as much as they are God. These selected writings provide a glimpse at the astonishing range of Paracelsus' writing.

Other books you might like:

Marty P. Hall, *Paracelsus: His Mystical and Medical Philosophy*, 1999

Carl Jung, *Alchemical Studies*, 1983

John Maxson Stillman, *Paracelsus: His Personality and Influence as a Physician, Chemist and Reformer*, 1997

Arthur E. Waite, *Three Famous Alchemists: Raymond Lolley, Cornelius Agrippa, Theophrastus Paracelsus*, 1997

Francis A. Yates, *The Art of Memory*, 1966

308

E. STANLEY JONES

The Christ of Every Road: A Study in Pentecost

(New York: Abingdon Press, 1930)

Category: Doctrine
Subject(s): Missionaries; Christianity; Culture
Age range(s): Adult
Time period(s): 1910s; 1920s
Locale(s): India; South America

Summary: E. Stanley Jones was an innovative Methodist missionary who began his ministry in India in 1907. During a lifetime of mission work, Jones developed the approach of sharing Christ within the culture of a country, rather than by imposing Western religious practices or denominational structures on those who responded to the message of Christ. He was a leader in encouraging the people of a given culture to determine the expression of Christianity that might emerge. He was a personal friend of Mohandas K. Gandhi and he established a Christian version of the Hindu ashram, or religious community, that has grown into an international fellowship organization. In *The Christ of Every Road*, Jones shares his work in missions in South America and India, which led him to personal revelations and his own brand of ministry.

Other books by the same author:

A Song of Ascents: A Spiritual Autobiography, 1968

Christian Maturity, 1957

Mahatma Gandhi: An Interpretation, 1948

The Christ of the American Road, 1944

Along the Indian Road, 1939

Other books you might like:

Levi Keidel, *Conflict or Connection: Interpersonal Relationships in Cross-Cultural Settings*, 1996

C.J. McNaspy, *Conquistador Without Sword: The Life of Roque Gonzalez, S.J.*, 1984

Bruce Olson, *Bruchko*, 1978

Stephen E. Savage, *Rejoicing in Christ: The Biography of Robert Carlton Savage*, 1990

309

LAURIE BETH JONES

Jesus in Blue Jeans: A Practical Guide to Everyday Spirituality

(New York: Hyperion, 1997)

Category: Essays
Subject(s): Spirituality; Christianity; Meditation
Age range(s): Adult

Summary: In the final entry of a trilogy of works applying Biblical wisdom to contemporary life, Laurie Beth Jones examines the central figure in Christianity through four ''prisms'': poise, perspective, passion, and power. Each mini-essay addresses an aspect of character or personality ascribed to Jesus, and offers questions, personal reflections, or anecdotes to help readers develop these traits in their own spiritual lives.

Other books by the same author:
Jesus, CEO: Using Ancient Wisdom for Visionary Leadership, 1996
The Path: Creating Your Mission Statement for Work and for Life, 1996

Other books you might like:
Russell H. Conwell, *Acres of Diamonds: All Good Things Are Possible, Right Where You Are, and Now!*, 1993
new edition
Kent Crockett, *The 911 Handbook: Biblical Solutions to Everyday Problems*, 1997
Edith Schaeffer, *The Art of Life*, 1987
Floyd E. Hosmer, illustrator
Neale Donald Walsch, *Conversations with God: An Uncommon Dialogue*, 1996

310

TIMOTHY JONES

The Art of Prayer: A Simple Guide

(New York: Ballantine Books, 1997)

Category: Prayer
Subject(s): Christianity; Religious Life
Age range(s): Adult

Summary: Exploring commonly-asked questions about how and why to pray, author Timothy Jones offers a guide to the quiet art of prayer. In reflective prose that reveals a wide range of prayer forms and perspectives on prayer, this volume provides guidance to the novice and insight for the veteran. Each chapter ends with prayers written by notable people of faith. Although the author writes from a Christian point of view, his thoughts are applicable to people of other faith traditions.

Other books by the same author:
21 Days to a Better Quiet Time with God: A Proven Plan for Beginning New Habits, 1998
Celebration of Angels, 1994

Other books you might like:
Richard J. Foster, *Prayer: Finding the Heart's True Home*, 1992
Thomas A. Green, *Opening to God: A Guide to Prayer*, 1977
Thomas Merton, *Contemplative Prayer*, 1969

311

CLARENCE L. JORDAN

The Cotton Patch Version of Luke and Acts: Jesus' Doings and the Happenings

(New York: Association Press, 1969)

Category: Scripture
Subject(s): Popular Culture; Civil Rights; Baptists
Age range(s): Young Adult-Adult

Summary: Southern Baptist minister Clarence L. Jordan uses the colloquial accents of the Deep South to paraphrase the New Testament gospel of Luke and the book of the Acts of the Apostles in this addition to his Cotton Patch collection of biblical writings. Pulling no punches, Jordan uses real-life language and experiences to convey the timeless message of the New Testament and apply it to the social concerns of the mid-twentieth century American South. Earthy, humorous, and direct, the Cotton Patch writings address issues of peace, spirituality, and civil rights.

Other books by the same author:
The Cotton Patch Version of Hebrews and the General Epistles, 1973
The Substance of Faith and Other Cotton Patch Sermons, 1972
The Cotton Patch Version of Matthew and John, 1970
The Cotton Patch Version of Paul's Epistles, 1968

Other books you might like:
Al Fasol, *With a Bible in Their Hands: Southern Baptist Preaching, 1679-1979*, 1997
Tom Key, *Cotton Patch Gospel: A Toe-Tapping Full-Length Musical*, 1982
Russell Treyz, co-author
Edward L. Queen, *In the South the Baptists Are the Center of Gravity: Southern Baptists and Social Change, 1930-1980*, 1991
P. Joel Snider, *The ''Cotton Patch'' Gospel: The Proclamation of Clarence Jordan*, 1985

312

CARL JUNG

Answer to Job

(New York: Meridian Books, 1960)

Category: Theology
Subject(s): Religion; Psychology
Age range(s): Adult

Summary: The famous psychologist of the unconscious applies his theory of the collective unconscious and dreams to the biblical book of Job. He seeks to offer answers to the age-old questions of suffering and evil raised by the account of Job's tribulations. The work was translated by R.F.C. Hull.

Other books by the same author:
Memories, Dreams, Reflections, 1963
Dreams, 1905

Other books you might like:
J. Allen Blair, *Living Patiently: When God Seems Far Away: A Devotional Study of Job*, 1994
Harold S. Kushner, *When Bad Things Happen to Good People*, 1981
Raymond Scheindlin, *Book of Job*, 1998
Bill Thomason, *God on Trial: The Book of Job and Human Suffering*, 1997
John Thornton, *Book of Job*, 1998
This edition is part of the series of Vintage Spiritual Classics.

313

MYLA KABAT-ZINN
JON KABAT-ZINN, Co-Author

Everyday Blessings: The Inner Work of Mindful Parenting

(New York: Hyperion, 1997)

Category: Self-Help
Subject(s): Meditation; Parenthood; Parent and Child
Age range(s): Adult

Summary: Myla and Jon Kabat-Zinn offer practical suggestions for incorporating the wisdom of Zen Buddhist mindfulness into the everyday world of family life. In a world where family life is driven by calendars full of commitments, work schedules, and sports activities, *Everyday Blessings* offers a whiff of silence and support for just spending quiet time together as parent and child. The authors assert that deliberately making time for spirituality and mindfulness in family life is enriching for all generations and allows natural creativity to blossom.

Other books you might like:
Phil Catalfo, *Raising Spiritual Children in a Material World*, 1997
Harville Hendrix, *The Parenting Companion*, 1999
Vimala McClure, *The Tao of Motherhood*, 1997
James McGinnis, *Parenting for Peace and Justice*, 1981

314

KALIDASA

The Loom of Time: A Selection of His Plays and Poems

(New York: Viking Penguin, 1989)

Category: Poetry; Plays
Subject(s): Nature; Literature; Hinduism
Age range(s): Adult

Summary: Kalidasa was an Indian poet and dramatist whose works date back to between 375 and 415. He is noted for writing during a period of time when Sanskrit literature was evolving from Vedic hymns composed by unknown authors to secular poetry and drama attributable to specific literary

figures. Kalidasa is particularly remembered for his verse dramas celebrating romantic love and his lyric poems describing nature. Few of Kalidasa's works are currently available in English, and *The Loom of Time*, which offers a selection of Kalidasa's poetry and drama, is difficult to find.

Other books by the same author:
Kumarasambhava, 1986
Theater of Memory: Three Plays of Kalidasa, 1984
The Cloud Messenger: An Indian Love Lyric, 1930

Other books you might like:
Buddhadeva Bose, *Modern Poetry and Sanskrit Kavya*, 1997
  Sujit Mukherjee, translator
Ainslie T. Embree, *The Hindu Tradition*, 1966
Ainslie T. Embree, *Sources of Indian Tradition: From the Beginning to 1800*, 1988
Umasankara Josi, *Kalidasa's Poetic Voice*, 1988

315

RODGER KAMENETZ

The Jew in the Lotus: A Poet's Rediscovery of Jewish Identity in Buddhist India

(San Francisco: HarperSanFrancisco, 1994)

Category: Autobiography
Subject(s): Judaism; Buddhism; Mysticism
Age range(s): Adult
Locale(s): India

Summary: As a young man, Kamenetz is raised in a fairly orthodox Jewish home. He becomes disinterested in Judaism, though, and leaves religion behind for a while. During his travels to India and his study with various Buddhist teachers, including conversations with the Dalai Lama, he begins to rediscover his Jewish religious identity through the eyes of Buddhism.

Other books by the same author:
Stalking Elijah: Adventures with Today's Jewish Mystical Masters, 1997

Other books you might like:
Sylvia Boorstein, *That's Funny, You Don't Look Buddhist: On Being a Faithful Jew and a Passionate Buddhist*, 1997
Avram Davis, *Meditation From the Heart of Judaism: Today's Teachers Share Their Practices, Techniques, and Faith*, 1997
Aryeh Kaplan, *Jewish Meditation: A Practical Guide*, 1985
Michael Lerner, *Jewish Renewal: A Path to Healing and Transformation*, 1994
Rami M. Shapiro, *Minyan: Ten Principles for Living a Life of Integrity*, 1997

316

RODGER KAMENETZ

Stalking Elijah: Adventures with Today's Jewish Mystical Masters

(San Francisco: HarperSanFrancisco, 1997)

Category: Autobiography
Subject(s): Judaism; Mysticism; Religious Life
Age range(s): Adult

Summary: A celebration of Judaism and Jewish life in the 1990s, *Stalking Elijah* is the story of Rodger Kamenetz's physical and spiritual journey to meet the mystical masters of his time. In one adventure, Kamenetz, a poet and essayist, mixes with Tibetan Buddhists in Baton Rouge, Louisiana. In another, he celebrates a Passover Seder for Tibetan freedom with none other than the exiled Dalai Lama. A blend of quirky and humorous reporting and personal revelation, this account of one man's quest for spiritual meaning offers something for readers of all faith traditions.

Awards the book has won:
National Jewish Book Award, Jewish Thought, 1997

Other books by the same author:
The Jew in the Lotus: A Poet's Rediscovery of Jewish Identity in Buddhist India, 1994
The Missing Jew: New and Selected Poems, 1992
Terra Infirma, 1985

Other books you might like:
David S. Ariel, *The Mystic Quest: An Introduction to Jewish Mysticism*, 1998
David A. Cooper, *Entering the Sacred Mountain: A Mystical Odyssey*, 1994
Lawrence Kushner, *The River of Light: Spirituality, Judaism, Consciousness*, 1981
Gershom Scholem, *Major Trends in Jewish Mysticism: Based on the Hilda Strook Lectures Delivered at the Jewish Institute of Religion, New York*, 1995
revised edition

317

ARYEH KAPLAN

Jewish Meditation: A Practical Guide

(New York: Schocken Books, 1985)

Category: Self-Help
Subject(s): Meditation; Judaism
Age range(s): Adult

Summary: Written for the general reader in non-scholarly language, *Jewish Meditation* is an introduction to the world of spiritual meditation. Although part of the book focuses specifically on meditation within the boundaries of Judaism, orthodox rabbi Aryeh Kaplan provides a comprehensive overview of meditative techniques that can be used by anyone, and he also demonstrates how meditation can be integrated into traditional Jewish practice.

Other books by the same author:
Meditation and Kabbalah, 1995

The Light Beyond: Adventures in Hassidic Thought, 1981
The Handbook of Jewish Thought, 1979
Meditation and the Bible, 1978

Other books you might like:
Avram Davis, *Meditation From the Heart of Judaism: Today's Teachers Share Their Practices, Techniques, and Faith*, 1997
Avram Davis, *The Way of Flame: A Guide to the Forgotten Mystical Tradition of Jewish Meditation*, 1996
Taram Frankiel, *Minding the Temple of the Soul: Balancing Body, Mind and Spirit through Traditional Jewish Prayer, Movement and Meditation*, 1997
Judy Greenfeld, co-author

318

PHILIP KAPLEAU, Editor

The Three Pillars of Zen: Teaching, Practice, and Enlightenment

(New York: Harper & Row, 1965)

Category: Doctrine
Subject(s): Buddhism; Meditation; Religious Life
Age range(s): Adult

Summary: Philip Kapleau offers an introduction to the foundations of Zen Buddhism in a volume that has become a classic in Western Buddhist literature. The author and teacher explores the three key aspects of Zen-teaching, practice, and enlightenment-providing information that will be useful to both novices and experienced disciples of Zen.

Other books by the same author:
The Zen of Living and Dying: A Practical and Spiritual Guide, 1998
Zen: Merging of East and West, 1989
Zen: Dawn in the West, 1979
The Wheel of Death, 1971

Other books you might like:
Charlotte Joko Beck, *Nothing Special: Living Zen*, 1993
David Scott, *The Elements of Zen*, 1992
Soyen Shaku, *Zen for Americans*, 1906

319

CAROL F. KARLSEN

The Devil in the Shape of a Woman: Witchcraft in Colonial New England

(New York: Norton, 1987)

Category: History
Subject(s): Christianity; Witches and Witchcraft; American History
Age range(s): Adult

Summary: How did the American colonial authorities define witchcraft, and what perceived dangers did they associate with witchcraft? Karlsen presents case studies of women who were tried and convicted of witchcraft by their various colonial governments. He uses these stories to demonstrate how the governing parties manipulated people's fear of outsiders to bolster their own power.

Other books you might like:

Paul Boyer, *Salem Possessed: The Social Origins of Witch-craft*, 1974

John Putnam Demos, *Entertaining Satan: Witchcraft and the Culture of Early New England*, 1982

Chadwick Hansen, *Witchcraft at Salem*, 1969

Frances Hill, *A Delusion of Satan: The Full Story of the Salem Witch Trials*, 1995

Elizabeth Reis, *Damned Women: Sinners and Witches in Puritan New England*, 1997

320

JUDITH A. KATES, Editor
GAIL TWERSKY REIMER, Co-Editor

Reading Ruth: Contemporary Women Reclaim a Sacred Story

(New York: Ballantine Books, 1994)

Category: Religious Commentaries
Subject(s): Bible; Judaism; Women
Age range(s): Adult

Summary: The voices of thirty contemporary Jewish women (among them rabbis, scholars, psychologists, poets, novelists, and essayists) are collected in this volume of commentary on the Old Testament tale of Ruth, the Moabite woman who made a life as the daughter of her mother-in-law after the death of her husband. In poetry, personal stories, essays, and fiction, women in the late 20th century discuss how the story of Ruth is relevant today. The figure of Ruth is considered in her roles as a widow, a daughter-in-law, a friend, and a woman at a crossroads in her life.

Other books by the same author:
Tasso and Milton: The Problem of Christian Epic, 1983

Other books you might like:

Regina Coll, *Christianity and Feminism in Conversation*, 1994

Merle Feld, *A Spiritual Life: A Jewish Feminist Journey*, 1999

Ellen Jaffe-Gill, *The Jewish Woman's Book of Wisdom*, 1998

Miki Raver, *Listen to Her Voice: Women of the Hebrew Bible*, 1998

321

STEPHANIE KAZA
DAVIS TE SELLE, Illustrator

The Attentive Heart: Conversations with Trees

(New York: Fawcett Columbine, 1993)

Category: Essays
Subject(s): Buddhism; Environment; Meditation
Age range(s): Young Adult-Adult

Summary: A collection of essays and lithographs, *Conversations with Trees* blends an environmentalist fervor with Buddhist contemplation. Stephanie Kaza offers twenty-seven reflective, lyrical discourses on her personal connection with the natural world through the textures and personalities of trees. Her writing suggests insightful new ways to observe and participate in the world around us.

Other books by the same author:
Dharma Rain: Sources of Buddhist Environmentalism, 1999

Other books you might like:

Allan Hunt Badiner, *Dharma Gaia: A Harvest of Essays in Buddhism and Ecology*, 1990

Anne Morrow Lindbergh, *Gift From the Sea*, 1955

W. Scott Olsen, *The Sacred Place: Witnessing the Holy in the Physical World*, 1996
    Scott Cairns, co-editor

Chet Raymo, *Honey From Stone: A Naturalist's Search for God*, 1987
    Bob O'Cathail, illustrator

Michael J. Roads, *Talking with Nature: Sharing the Energies and Spirit of Trees, Plants, Birds, and Earth*, 1987

Henry David Thoreau, *Walden*, 1854

322

HOWARD CLARK KEE, Editor
ERIC M. MEYERS, Co-Editor
JOHN ROGERSON, Co-Editor
ANTHONY J. SALDARIN, Co-Editor

The Cambridge Companion to the Bible

(New York: Cambridge University Press, 1997)

Category: Religious Commentaries
Subject(s): Bible; History; Culture
Age range(s): Adult

Summary: In a single volume *The Cambridge Companion to the Bible* offers a comprehensive background on the various contexts-historical, cultural, social-in which biblical texts were written and compiled. The articles are arranged in four categories: an introduction to biblical writings, a focus on the world of the Old Testament, reflection on Jewish interaction with the Greek and Roman culture of the day, and views on the development of the Christian world as seen in the New Testament. Old and New Testament writings are treated equally, and the apocryphal writings are addressed as well.

Other books by the same author:
Who Are the People of God?, 1995
Christianity: A Social and Cultural History, 1991

Other books you might like:

Raymond E. Brown, *The New Jerome Biblical Commentary*, 1999
    Joseph A. Fitzmyer, Roland E. Murphy, co-editors

David S. Dockery, *The Holman Concise Bible Commentary*, 1998

Bruce M. Metzger, *The Oxford Companion to the Bible*, 1993

323

SAM KEEN

To a Dancing God

(New York: Harper and Row, 1970)

Category: Theology
Subject(s): Christianity; Christian Life; God
Age range(s): Adult

Summary: Keen's joyous book celebrates the body and the ways it can be used to worship God. Too often, he notes, religious worship is an uptight exercise in which people try to separate their spirit from their bodies. Keen is one of the first to celebrate in a significant way the idea of embodied theology, promoting the idea that people can worship God with the rhythms of their bodies. He also asserts that people can worship God with the music of their souls. Keen offers numerous suggestions for incorporating body theology into worship.

Other books by the same author:
Learning to Fly: Trapeze-Reflections on Fear, Trust, and the Joy of Letting Go, 1999
What to Do When You're Bored and Blue, 1980

Other books you might like:
Harvey Cox, *Seduction of the Spirit: The Use and Misuse of People's Religion*, 1973
Tom F. Driver, *Patterns of Grace: Human Experience as Word of God*, 1977
John Y. Fenton, *Theology and Body*, 1974
Wes Seeliger, *Western Theology*, 1973
Robert L. Short, *Something to Believe In: Is Kurt Vonnegut the Exorcist of Jesus Christ Superstar?*, 1978

324

HELEN KELLER

The Story of My Life

(New York: Doubleday, Page & Company, 1903)

Category: Autobiography
Subject(s): Blind; Deafness; Physically Handicapped
Age range(s): Young Adult-Adult
Time period(s): 19th century; 20th century (1880-1902)
Locale(s): United States

Summary: *The Story of My Life* is an inspirational, autobiographical account of Helen Keller's first two decades of life, written during her college years at Radcliffe. The author recounts the childhood terror of being locked in a soundless, sightless world without the ability to communicate with others or articulate thoughts, needs, or desires. She retells the now-familiar story of how her tireless teacher, Annie Sullivan, finally found a way to break through the darkness and silence of Helen's world and opened the doors to education and spiritual growth. Helen Keller writes of the beginnings of her spiritual journey-which she expands on in a later volume, *My Religion* (1962).

Other books by the same author:
Helen Keller's Journal, 1936-1937, 1938
Mid Stream: My Later Life, 1929
The World I Live In, 1908

Other books you might like:
Richard Harrity, *Three Lives of Helen Keller*, 1962
Dorothy Herrmann, *Helen Keller: A Life*, 1998
Johanna Hurwitz, *Helen Keller: Courage in the Dark*, 1997
Joseph P. Lash, *Helen and Teacher: The Story of Helen Keller and Anne Sullivan Macy*, 1980

325

PHILLIP KELLER

A Layman Looks at the Lord's Prayer

(Chicago: Moody Press, 1976)

Category: Devotionals
Subject(s): Nature; Christian Life; Prayer
Age range(s): Adult

Summary: In *A Shepherd Looks at Psalm 23*, Phillip Keller examined "the shepherd's psalm" from the perspective of a sheep rancher. In *A Layman Looks at the Lord's Prayer*, Keller applies his down-to-earth ways of reading and thinking about Scripture to an exploration of one of the most recognizable passages of the words of Jesus-the prayer he taught his disciples. In numerous volumes, Keller offers readers new ways to think about familiar scriptures.

Other books by the same author:
Sky Edge, 1987
God Is My Delight, 1991
Lessons From a Sheep Dog, 1983
A Shepherd Looks at Psalm 23, 1970

Other books you might like:
Arthur Paul Boers, *Lord, Teach Us to Pray: A New Look at the Lord's Prayer*, 1992
Emmet Fox, *The Sermon on the Mount: The Key to Success in Life; and, the Lord's Prayer, an Interpretation*, 1938
Pierre Raphael, *God Behind Bars: A Prison Chaplain Reflects on the Lord's Prayer*, 1999
Ron Sebring, *Inner Peace: Using the Lord's Prayer in Contemplation*, 1990
Robert G. Tuttle, *The Key to Life: Reflections on the Lord's Prayer*, 1998

326

PHILLIP KELLER

A Shepherd Looks at Psalm 23

(Grand Rapids, Michigan: Zondervan, 1970)

Category: Devotionals
Subject(s): Bible; Meditation; Nature
Age range(s): Young Adult-Adult

Summary: What does it mean in the 20th century to say, "The Lord is my shepherd.?" This is the question addressed by modern-day sheep-herder Phillip Keller in *A Shepherd Looks at Psalm 23*. With the insight of someone who understands the relationship between sheep and shepherd, between green pastures and still waters, Keller offers a new perspective on an old and much-loved passage of Old Testament literature.

Other books by the same author:
Outdoor Moments with God, 1994

A Layman Looks at the Lord's Prayer, 1976

Other books you might like:
James D. Capozzi, *Beside Quiet Waters: Reflections on the Psalms in Our Everyday Lives*, 1999
C.S. Lewis, *Reflections on the Psalms*, 1958
Nan C. Merrill, *Psalms for Praying: An Invitation to Wholeness*, 1996
F.B. Meyer, *The Shepherd Psalm*, 1979

327

SEAN KELLY
ROSEMARY ROGERS, Co-Author

Saints Preserve Us!: Everything You Need to Know about Every Saint You'll Ever Need

(New York: Random House, 1993)

Category: Doctrine
Subject(s): Saints; Religion; Catholicism
Age range(s): Young Adult-Adult

Summary: What do you get when you combine two humor writers and the stories of most of the saints ever named? The answer is *Saints Preserve Us!*, a light-hearted but fact-filled book of information describing more than 575 saints and the aspects of life associated with them, from dog bites and hemorrhoids to parties and oversleeping. Entertaining while educational, this volume is comprehensive, cross-referenced, and a lot of fun.

Other books by the same author:
How to Be Irish (Even If You Already Are), 1999

Other books you might like:
Wendy Beckett, *Sister Wendy's Book of Saints*, 1998
Elizabeth Hallam, *Saints: Who They Are and How They Help You*, 1994
Annette Sandoval, *The Directory of Saints: A Concise Guide to Patron Saints*, 1996

328

EUGENE KENNEDY

My Brother Joseph: The Spirit of a Cardinal and the Story of a Friendship

(New York: St. Martin's Press, 1997)

Category: Biography
Subject(s): Catholicism; Religious Life; Friendship
Age range(s): Adult
Time period(s): 20th century
Locale(s): United States

Summary: Two men of the same age became priests and friends, but one left the priesthood and married, while the other became a Cardinal in the Roman Catholic church. Their friendship survived their choice of divergent paths, and in this book, Eugene Kennedy writes of his friend, who would become widely known as Cardinal Joseph Bernardin. The story begins when the two meet in 1967, coworkers on a joint project. Kennedy traces the growth of their friendship through

the changes in each of their lives, including Bernardin's appointment as archbishop of Chicago, to Bernardin's death in 1996.

Other books by the same author:
Bernardin: Life to the Full, 1997
Tomorrow's Catholics, Yesterday's Church, 1995
Cardinal Bernardin: Easing Conflicts-and Battling for the Soul of American Catholicism, 1989

Other books you might like:
Cardinal Joseph Bernardin, *The Gift of Peace: Personal Reflections*, 1997
A.E.P. Wall, *The Spirit of Cardinal Bernardin*, 1983
John H. White, *The Final Journey of Joseph Cardinal Bernardin*, 1997

329

ANDREA KING

If I'm Jewish and You're Christian, What Are the Kids?: A Parenting Guide for Interfaith Families

(New York: UAHC Press, 1993)

Category: Self-Help
Subject(s): Judaism; Christianity; Family Life
Age range(s): Adult

Summary: In many interfaith marriages, conflict over individual religious practices doesn't arise until there are children. What then? Andrea King offers practical and proven ways to deal with this sensitive issue that affects parents, children, and extended family members.

Other books you might like:
Lee F. Gruzen, *Raising Your Jewish-Christian Child: Wise Choices for Interfaith Parents*, 1987
Judy Petsonk, *The Intermarriage Handbook: A Guide for Jews and Christians*, 1988
Iris M. Yob, *Keys to Interfaith Parenting*, 1998

330

DR. MARTIN LUTHER KING JR.

Strength to Love

(New York: Harper and Row, 1963)

Category: Autobiography
Subject(s): Christianity; Prejudice; Civil Rights Movement
Age range(s): Young Adult-Adult

Summary: In this eloquent plea for nonviolence, King uses examples from the New Testament and from the life of Indian leader Mahatma Gandhi to contend that love can overcome hate. Written during King's rise to prominence as the leader of the Civil Rights Movement, this book examines the great difficulty of using nonviolence to confront violence. King argues that loving one's enemies can bring about tremendous change in personal and social relationships. The popular preacher and activist shares his own struggles in this passionate book.

Other books by the same author:

Testament of Hope: The Essential Writings of Martin Luther King, Jr., 1986

Why We Can't Wait, 1964

Other books you might like:

James H. Cone, *Martin and Malcolm and America: A Dream or a Nightmare?*, 1991

Mohandas K. Gandhi, *Anasaktiyoga: The Gospel of Selfless Action: The Gita According to Gandhi*, 1993

C. Eric Lincoln, *Martin Luther King, Jr.: A Profile*, 1970

Thomas Merton, *The Nonviolent Alternative*, 1980

James Melvin Washington, *I Have a Dream: Writings and Speeches That Changed the World*, 1992

331

ALFRED J. KOLATCH

The Concise Family Seder

(New York: Jonathan David Publishers, 1989)

Category: Doctrine
Subject(s): Judaism; Holidays, Jewish; Family Life
Age range(s): Adult

Summary: Lack of knowledge of Hebrew need not be an obstacle to celebrating the traditional Passover Haggadah. Alfred Kolatch's *Concise Family Seder* bridges the gap for those whose wish to observe the traditions of their heritage is not matched by expertise in the Hebrew language of the ceremonies.

Other books by the same author:

What Jews Say about God, 1999

Great Jewish Quotations, 1996

The Jewish Home Advisor, 1990

The Jewish Book of Why, 1981

Other books you might like:

Ziporah Hildebrandt, *This Is Our Seder*, 1999

Lynne Sharon Schwartz, *The Four Questions*, 1994

Ron Wolfson, *The Art of Jewish Living: The Passover Seder*, 1996

Joel Lurie Grishaver, co-author

Ron Wolfson, *The Art of Jewish Living: The Shabbat Seder*, 1985

332

ALFRED J. KOLATCH

The Jewish Book of Why

(New York: Jonathan David, 1981)

Category: Doctrine
Subject(s): Judaism; Customs; Religious Life
Age range(s): Young Adult-Adult

Summary: What are the roots of modern Jewish practice? How do traditions begin? In *The Jewish Book of Why*, Alfred Kolatch explains various aspects of Jewish life, including marriage, dietary laws, holidays, synagogue practices, and more, drawing on the long history of the Talmud, the Old Testament, and the evolution of rabbinical writings. The di-

versity of practice among Orthodox, Conservative, and Reformed Jews is also addressed.

Other books by the same author:

The Jewish Mourner's Book of Why, 1993

The Jewish Child's First Book of Why, 1992 (Harry Araten, illustrator)

The Jewish Home Advisor, 1990

The Concise Family Seder, 1989

The Second Jewish Book of Why, 1985

Other books you might like:

Anita Diamant, *Living a Jewish Life: A Guide for Starting, Learning, Celebrating, and Parenting*, 1991

Lucien Gubbay, *The Jewish Book of Why and What: A Guide to Jewish Tradition, Custom, Practice, and Belief*, 1989

Abraham Levy, co-author

Morris N. Kertzer, *What Is a Jew?*, 1953

Joseph Telushkin, *Jewish Literacy: The Most Important Things to Know about the Jewish Religion, Its People, and Its History*, 1991

333

KATHRYN KOOB

Guest of the Revolution

(Nashville: Thomas Nelson, 1982)

Category: Autobiography
Subject(s): Hostages; Christianity; Prisoners and Prisons
Age range(s): Young Adult-Adult
Time period(s): 1970s; 1980s (1979-1981)
Locale(s): Teheran, Iran

Summary: From November 1979 until January 1981, Kathryn Koob was among a group of American hostages held prisoner in Iran. Of the 66 men and women captured, only 13 were released within a short period of time. The remainder, including the author of *Guest of the Revolution*, were held for 444 days. This is the story of one woman's experience and the faith that helped her maintain hope for more than a year away from her loved ones and homeland.

Awards the book has won:

Gold Medallion Book Award, Biography/Autobiography, 1984

Other books you might like:

Terry A. Anderson, *Den of Lions: Memoirs of Seven Years*, 1993

Moorhead Kennedy, *The Ayatollah in the Cathedral*, 1986

Peggy Say, *Forgotten: A Sister's Struggle to Save Terry Anderson, America's Longest-Held Hostage*, 1991

Charles W. Scott, *Pieces of the Game: The Human Drama of Americans Held Hostage in Iran*, 1984

Tim Wells, *444 Days: The Hostages Remember*, 1985

334

JACK KORNFIELD

A Path with Heart: A Guide through the Perils and Promises of Spiritual Life

(New York: Bantam Books, 1993)

Category: Self-Help
Subject(s): Spirituality; Buddhism; Meditation
Age range(s): Young Adult-Adult

Summary: Theravada Buddhism is the focus of Jack Kornfield's *Path with Heart*. Based on 25 years as a practitioner and teacher of this tradition of Buddhist thought, Kornfield offers practical, specific steps for incorporating peace and serenity into daily life. With simple and often humorous anecdotes, Kornfield leads the way in a journey toward spiritual awareness and reduced stress.

Other books by the same author:
Living Dharma: Teachings of Twelve Buddhist Masters, 1996
Soul Food: Stories to Nourish the Spirit and the Heart, 1996
Teachings of the Buddha, 1993
Buddha's Little Instruction Book, 1994
Stories of the Spirit, Stories of the Heart, 1991

Other books you might like:
Mark Epstein, *Going to Pieces Without Falling Apart: A Buddhist Perspective on Wholeness*, 1998
Dinty W. Moore, *The Accidental Buddhist: Mindfulness, Enlightenment, and Sitting Still*, 1997
C. Alexander Simpkins, *Simple Zen: A Guide to Living Moment by Moment*, 1999

335

JACK KORNFIELD, Editor
GIL FRONSDAL, Co-Editor

Teachings of the Buddha

(Boston: Shambhala, 1993)

Category: Doctrine
Subject(s): Buddhism; Literature; Meditation
Age range(s): Young Adult-Adult

Summary: This treasury of Buddha's teachings is compiled from the most popular and widely studied Indian, Chinese, Japanese, Zen, and Tibetan Buddhist writings. Instruction in the traditional Buddhist practice of meditation is included, as are the earliest known sayings of the Buddha and contemporary guidance for living compassionately. The collection captures the essence of Buddhism from past to present.

Other books by the same author:
Living Buddhist Masters, 1977

Other books you might like:
Marc de Smedt, *The Wisdom of the Buddha*, 1996
Geoffrey Parrinder, *The Sayings of the Buddha*, 1998
Walpola Rahula, *What the Buddha Taught*, 1959
Paul Carus, *The Teachings of Buddha*, 1998

336

DONALD B. KRAYBILL

The Riddle of Amish Culture

(Baltimore: Johns Hopkins University Press, 1989)

Category: History
Subject(s): Amish; Culture; Conduct of Life
Age range(s): Young Adult-Adult

Summary: Why don't the Amish drive cars? How do they live without modern technology? Many questions are asked about the Amish way of life, which hasn't changed substantially for hundreds of years. Donald B. Kraybill has lived and worked in the Amish community in Lancaster County, Pennsylvania, and in this volume he poses questions to Amish men and women and records their responses.

Other books by the same author:
Amish Enterprise: From Plows to Profits, 1995
The Amish Struggle with Modernity, 1994
The Amish and the State, 1993

Other books you might like:
John A. Hostetler, *Amish Life*, 1952
John A. Hostetler, *Amish Society*, 1993
    fourth edition
Louise Stoltzfus, *Amish Women: Lives and Stories*, 1994

337

HANS KUNG

Great Christian Thinkers

(New York: Continuum, 1994)

Category: Theology
Subject(s): Christianity; History
Age range(s): Adult

Summary: Many of the great Christian philosophers and theologians of the last two thousand years are represented in this collection of essays and explorations of the ideas and concepts of Christianity. Hans Kung analyzes and comments on the relevance of each figure, including Thomas Aquinas, Karl Barth, Martin Luther, and the apostle Saint Paul. More than just a summary of theology, the work addresses the question, ''What does this mean for readers and thinkers today?''

Other books by the same author:
Christianity and World Religions: Paths of Dialogue with Islam, Hinduism, and Buddhism, 1993 (Peter Heinegg, translator)
Does God Exist?: An Answer for Today, 1980 (Edward Quinn, translator)

Other books you might like:
James Bacik, *Contemporary Theologians*, 1989
John Bowden, *Who's Who in Theology: From the First Century to the Present*, 1992
Ted M. Dorman, *A Faith for All Seasons: Historic Christian Belief in its Classical Expression*, 1995
Gareth Jones, *Christian Theology: A Brief Introduction*, 1999

Mark G. Toulouse, *Makers of Christian Theology in America*, 1997
James O. Duke, co-editor

338

HANS KUNG

On Being a Christian

(Garden City, New York: Doubleday, 1976)

Category: Theology
Subject(s): Christianity; Apologetics; History
Age range(s): Adult

Summary: In his *On Being a Christian*, Hans Kung traces Christianity back to the historical Christ, affirming that the evidence of Jesus' life supports, and is supported by, the uniqueness of the Christian faith. Kung is a former Roman Catholic priest and professor whose commission to teach was revoked by the Vatican in 1979 in response to his unorthodox and controversial writings. This work is a comprehensive statement of his theology of Christianity.

Other books by the same author:
Great Christian Thinkers, 1994
Christianity Among World Religions, 1986
Why I Am Still a Christian, 1986

Other books you might like:
Schuyler Brown, *The Origins of Christianity: A Historical Introduction to the New Testament*, 1993
revised edition
John Dominic Crossan, *The Birth of Christianity: Discovering What Happened in the Years Immediately After the Execution of Jesus*, 1998
Bart D. Ehrman, *After the New Testament: A Reader in Early Christianity*, 1999
Walter H. Wagner, *After the Apostles: Christianity in the Second Century*, 1994

339

HAROLD S. KUSHNER

How Good Do We Have to Be?: A New Understanding of Guilt and Forgiveness

(Boston: Little, Brown, 1996)

Category: Self-Help
Subject(s): Faith; Guilt; Self-Respect
Age range(s): Adult

Summary: Rabbi Kushner addresses the issue of guilt and shame and reveals that acceptance and forgiveness are life-changing choices that we can make for ourselves. Collecting wisdom from scripture, theology, psychology, literature, and his own personal experience, Kushner encourages readers to explore the benefits of self-acceptance and forgiveness.

Other books by the same author:
When All You've Ever Wanted Isn't Enough, 1986
When Bad Things Happen to Good People, 1981

Other books you might like:
Linda H. Hollies, *Taking Back My Yesterdays: Lessons in Forgiving and Moving Forward with Your Life*, 1997
Greg Laurie, *The God of Second Chance: Experiencing Forgiveness*, 1997
Harlan J. Wechsler, *What's So Bad About Guilt?: Learning to Live with It Since We Can't Live Without It*, 1990

340

HAROLD S. KUSHNER

To Life!: A Celebration of Jewish Being and Thinking

(Boston: Little, Brown, 1993)

Category: Self-Help
Subject(s): Judaism; Religious Traditions; Religious Life
Age range(s): Adult

Summary: Emphasizing community over theology, Rabbi Kushner celebrates what it is to be Jewish in the late 20th century. He explains what it is to keep a kosher home and why it is desirable. He promotes Judaism as the primary religious force that shapes how the world perceives God, and he encourages practicing Jews to find joy in observing the laws of their faith.

Other books by the same author:
When All You've Ever Wanted Isn't Enough, 1986
When Bad Things Happen to Good People, 1981

Other books you might like:
Bradley Shavit Artson, *It's a Mitzvah!: Step-by-Step to Jewish Living*, 1995
Anita Diamant, *Living a Jewish Life: A Guide for Starting, Learning, Celebrating, and Parenting*, 1991
Howard Cooper, co-author
Daniel Gordis, *God Was Not in the Fire: The Search for a Spiritual Judaism*, 1995
Steven Z. Leder, *The Extraordinary Nature of Ordinary Things*, 1999

341

HAROLD S. KUSHNER

When Bad Things Happen to Good People

(New York: Schocken Books, 1981)

Category: Self-Help
Subject(s): Religion; Psychology; Death
Age range(s): Adult

Summary: Why do innocent children suffer? Why does the blameless and upright man like Job lose his health, his wealth, and his family? How can one explain the reasons that suffering and misfortune sometimes strike the people who least deserve them? Kushner offers his own explanations in this popular attempt to justify the ways of God to humankind. He examines the traditional reasons many people give for the presence of suffering in the world and goes on to propose some of his own theories. Eighteen years after its publication, the book remains the most popular book on the topic.

Other books by the same author:
Who Needs God?, 1989

Other books you might like:
John Claypool, *Tracks of a Fellow Struggler: Living and Growing through Grief*, 1995
James C. Dobson, *When God Doesn't Make Sense*, 1993
John Hick, *Evil and the God of Love*, 1966
Robert A. Schuller, *What Happens to Good People When Bad Things Happen?*, 1995
Ann Kaiser Stearns, *Living Through Personal Crisis*, 1984

342

HAROLD S. KUSHNER

When Children Ask about God

(New York: Schocken Books, 1989)

Category: Self-Help; Theology
Subject(s): Children; Faith
Age range(s): Adult

Summary: In a volume originally published in 1971, Rabbi Kushner draws on his years of experience in congregational ministry to help parents and others learn to answer children's questions about God and religious beliefs and practices. Among the topics Kushner covers are questions about death and illness and advice about the kinds of spiritual questions children generally have at certain stages of their young lives.

Other books by the same author:
When All You've Ever Wanted Isn't Enough, 1986
When Bad Things Happen to Good People, 1981

Other books you might like:
John M. Hull, *God-Talk with Young Children: Notes for Parents and Teachers*, 1991
Larry Libby, *Someone Awesome: Children's Questions about God*, 1995
Tim Jonke, illustrator
Christine Yount, *Helping Children Know God*, 1995

343

HAROLD S. KUSHNER

Who Needs God?

(New York: Summit Books: 1989)

Category: Theology
Subject(s): Faith; Spirituality; Judaism
Age range(s): Adult

Summary: In this volume, Rabbi Kushner defends faith in God, offering reasons why personal faith in God can enrich our lives. Although Kushner writes from the perspective of Judaism, his principles transcend the boundaries of sectarianism. He asserts that love, compassion, and personal strength can be replenished and preserved only through a personal faith in God that leads us into connection with others.

Other books by the same author:
When All You've Ever Wanted Isn't Enough, 1986
When Bad Things Happen to Good People, 1981

Other books you might like:
Daniel Gordis, *God Was Not in the Fire: The Search for a Spiritual Judaism*, 1995
Steven L. Jacobs, *Rethinking Jewish Faith: The Child of a Survivor Responds*, 1994
William E. Kaufman, *The Case for God*, 1991
Michael Levin, *What Every Jew Needs to Know about God*, 1997

344

LAWRENCE KUSHNER

The Book of Letters: A Mystical Alef-Bait

(New York: Harper & Row, 1975)

Category: Religious Encyclopedias/Dictionaries
Subject(s): Judaism; Literacy; Folklore
Age range(s): Children-Adult

Summary: Kushner's *Book of Letters* brings to life the history and folklore of the Hebrew alphabet in a prayerbook-like format filled with the author's calligraphy. Each letter is treated to an exploration of form, origin, and mystical meaning that celebrates the culture and heritage of Judaism and the written language that is at the heart of that religious tradition.

Other books by the same author:
The River of Light: Spirituality, Judaism, Consciousness, 1981
Honey From the Rock: An Easy Introduction to Jewish Mysticism, 1977

Other books you might like:
Penina V. Adelman, *The Bible From Alef to Tav*, 1998
Matityahu Glazerson, *Building Blocks of the Soul: Studies on the Letters and Words of the Hebrew Language*, 1997
Edward Hoffmann, *The Hebrew Alphabet: A Mystical Journey*, 1998
Mark Podwal, *A Book of Hebrew Letters*, 1978

345

TONY KUSHNER

Angels in America: A Gay Fantasia on National Themes

(London: Nick Hern Books, 1992)

Category: Plays
Subject(s): AIDS (Disease); Homosexuality/Lesbianism; Angels
Age range(s): Adult
Major character(s): Roy Cohn, Lawyer
Time period(s): 1980s; 1990s
Locale(s): United States

Summary: Tony Kushner's seven-hour play *Angels in America: A Gay Fantasia on National Themes* is actually comprised of two separate units: *Millennium Approaches* and *Perestroika*. The drama is an exploration of what it is to be gay and affected by AIDS in the United States during the last two decades of the 20th century. The action centers on men dealing with identity and discrimination issues, their interaction with a hostile culture, and an eventual recognition that life with AIDS requires community, not isolation. An angel visitor at the end of the first play grants one AIDS patient a reprieve from death to go out into the world and serve as a prophet to others. In the second part—which is itself also an independent play—the man realizes that the angelic being is not what he had at first understood it to be. The character of lawyer Roy Cohn is based on the historical figure of the same name and occupation who assisted in the McCarthy-era persecution of suspected communists and homosexuals in the 1950s.

Awards the book has won:
Pulitzer Prize, Drama, 1993
Antoinette Perry (Tony) Award, 1993

Other books by the same author:
Thinking about the Longstanding Problems of Virtue and Happiness, 1995
A Bright Room Called Day, 1994

Other books you might like:
Brian Bouldrey, *Wrestling with the Angel*, 1996
Mary Fisher, *Sleep with the Angels: A Mother Challenges AIDS*, 1994
Deborah R. Geis, *Approaching the Millennium: Essays on Angels in America*, 1997
Steven F. Kruger, co-editor
David Rabe, *A Question of Mercy*, 1998

346

JONATHAN KWITNY

Man of the Century: The Life and Times of Pope John Paul II

(New York: Henry Holt, 1997)

Category: Biography
Subject(s): Catholicism; Politics; Religious Life
Age range(s): Adult
Time period(s): 20th century
Locale(s): Europe

Summary: Journalist Jonathan Kwitny traces the life and times of Polish priest, bishop, and archbishop Karol Wojtyla, who became Pope John Paul II in 1978. Kwitny offers an in-depth look at the history of the man who would become the first Polish pope, noting that his long-standing commitment to nonviolence and freedom pre-dated Martin Luther King Jr.'s civil rights movement in America and helped bring down the Iron Curtain of Communism in Eastern Europe. He asserts that throughout more than two decades as the leader of the Roman Catholic church in the world, Pope John Paul II's natural charisma has won the hearts of people of many faiths worldwide, and that the Pope has contributed immeasurably to political evolution and revolution.

Other books you might like:
Carl Bernstein, *His Holiness: John Paul II and the Hidden History of Our Time*, 1996
Marco Politi, co-author
Rocco Buttiglione, *Karol Wojtyla: The Thought of the Man Who Became Pope John Paul II*, 1997
Paolo Guietti and Francesca Murphy, translators

Pope John Paul II, *Crossing the Threshold of Hope*, 1994
Vittorio Messori, editor; Jenny McPhee and Martha McPhee, translators
Pope John Paul II, *In My Own Words*, 1998
Anthony F. Chiffolo, compiler and editor
Tad Szulc, *Pope John Paul II: The Biography*, 1995

347

ANNE LAMOTT

Traveling Mercies: Some Thoughts on Faith

(New York: Pantheon Books, 1999)

Category: Autobiography
Subject(s): Spirituality; Catholicism; Christian Science
Age range(s): Adult

Summary: Anne Lamott traces the development of faith in her life through troubled times and good ones. In spite of the chaos of her hippie-like upbringing and a lack of spiritual teaching from her family, Lamott became familiar with religious beliefs through interaction with friends who practiced Catholicism and Christian Science. Her story is interspersed with scriptural passages and anecdotes that are alternately funny and poignant.

Other books by the same author:
Bird by Bird: Some Instructions on Writing and Life, 1994
Operating Instructions: A Journal of My Son's First Year, 1993

Other books you might like:
Madeleine L'Engle, *A Circle of Quiet*, 1972
Madeleine L'Engle, *Glimpses of Grace: Daily Thoughts and Reflections*, 1996
Carol F. Chase, co-author
Madeleine L'Engle, *A Stone for a Pillow*, 1986
Irene Mahony, *A Company of Women: Journeys through the Feminine Experience of Faith*, 1996
Nancy Mairs, *Ordinary Time: Cycles in Marriage, Faith, and Renewal*, 1993

348

ROBIN LANE FOX

Pagans and Christians

(New York: Knopf, 1987)

Category: History
Subject(s): Christianity
Age range(s): Adult
Time period(s): Multiple Time Periods (2nd-4th centuries)
Locale(s): Roman Empire

Summary: Robin Lane Fox illuminates the world of early Christianity after its first one hundred years. Focusing her attention on the growth of Christianity until Constantine's conversion, which resulted in Christianity becoming the sanctioned religion of the Mediterranean world, she explores the period from the second to the fourth century A.D., a period when the Greek and Roman gods first flourished, then lost their supremacy to the God of the Judeo-Christian tradition.

Other books by the same author:
The Unauthorized Version: Truth and Fiction in the Bible, 1992
The Search for Alexander, 1980

Other books you might like:
Douglas R. Edwards, *Religion and Power: Pagans, Jews, and Christians in the Greek East*, 1996
M.J. Edwards, *Apologetics in the Roman Empire: Pagans, Jews, and Christians*, 1999
Judith Lieu, *The Jews Among Pagans and Christians: In the Roman Empire*, 1992
    John North, Tessa Rajak, co-editors

349

LAO TZU

Tao-te Ching

(c. 650 BC)

Category: Scripture
Subject(s): Philosophy; Chinese; Politics
Age range(s): Adult

Summary: The great Chinese philosopher Lao Tzu, who lived during the 7th-6th centuries BC, teaches in his book that the Tao, or the Way, is one and eternal. He encourages individuals and governments to conform themselves to the Tao, for people cannot force the Tao to change. The *Tao-te Ching*'s poetry provides not only a theory of creation but also a theory of government and politics.

Other books you might like:
Wing-tsit Chan, *A Source Book in Chinese Philosophy*, 1963
Chuang Tzu, *The Complete Works*, 1968
    Original texts are more than 2,000 years old.
Confucius, *Analects*, c. 500 BC
Mencius, *Mencius*, 1970
    Original texts are more than 2,000 years old.
D. Howard Smith, *Confucius*, 1973

350

EDWARD J. LARSON

Summer for the Gods: The Scopes Trial and America's Continuing Debate over Science and Religion

(New York: Basic Books, 1997)

Category: History
Subject(s): Christianity; Evolution; Creationism
Age range(s): Adult

Summary: In 1925, the so-called monkey trial of school teacher John Scopes, who was teaching evolution, captured the nation's attention, and began a new conversation about the relationship between science and religion. Larson takes a fresh look at the trial and its consequences. He argues that this signal event in American culture created a battleground on which the proponents and opponents of evolution and creationism continue to challenge each other.

Other books you might like:
Philip D. Clayton, *God and Contemporary Science*, 1997
Jared Diamond, *Guns, Germs and Steel: The Fates of Human Societies*, 1997
Langdon Gilkey, *Creationism on Trial: Evolution and God at Little Rock*, 1985
Henry M. Morris, *The Long War Against God: The History and Impact of the Creation/Evolution Conflict*, 1989
Ted Peters, *Science and Theology: The New Consonance*, 1998

351

DAVID LASKIN, Editor

An Angel a Week

(New York: Ballantine Books, 1992)

Category: Devotionals
Subject(s): Angels; Literature; Religious Life
Age range(s): Young Adult-Adult

Summary: Literature lovers who also appreciate angel lore will find this volume tailored to their interests. The author combines reproductions of great artworks with quotations from such literary giants as John Milton, John Donne, and William Shakespeare. The weekly journal format provides space for a reader's own reflection and thoughts. The text and graphics celebrate the miracle of angels and their offerings of guidance, consolation, and renewal.

Other books you might like:
Eileen Elias Freeman, *Touched by Angels*, 1993
Karen Goldman, *The Angel Book: A Handbook for Aspiring Angels*, 1992
Karen Goldman, *Angel Voices: The Advanced Handbook for Aspiring Angels*, 1993
Barbara Mark, *The Angelspeake Book of Prayer and Healing: How to Work with Your Angels*, 1997

352

KENNETH SCOTT LATOURETTE

A History of Christianity

(New York: Harper, 1953)

Category: History
Subject(s): Christianity; History
Age range(s): Adult

Summary: In two volumes, Kenneth Scott Latourette offers a comprehensive history of the development of Christianity through 1975. Volume I covers the years through 1500; Volume II covers the history from the Reformation through 1975. Latourette's work is notable for its attention to the development of the Eastern church and the role of Christianity as a force throughout the history of nearly 2000 years.

Other books by the same author:
The Gospel, the Church and the World, 1946
A History of the Expansion of Christianity, 1937

Other books you might like:
Owen Chadwick, *A History of Christianity*, 1996

Elizabeth Isichei, *A History of Christianity in Africa: From Antiquity to the Present*, 1995

Clyde Leonard Manschreck, *A History of Christianity in the World*, 1985

Samuel Hugh Moffett, *A History of Christianity in Asia*, 1992

353

BROTHER LAWRENCE
CONRAD DE MEESTER, Co-Author

Writings and Conversations on the Practice of the Presence of God

(Washington, D.C.: ICS Publications, 1994)

Category: Journals/Letters
Subject(s): Spirituality; God; Catholicism
Age range(s): Young Adult-Adult

Summary: *Writings and Conversations on the Practice of the Presence of God* is a spiritual classic that dates back to the 1600s. Brother Lawrence of the Resurrection was a monastery cook who lived from 1611 to 1691. His peace and serenity were notable even when he was busy performing daily kitchen tasks. When asked, he explained to friends and colleagues how he managed to live on earth as though in the Kingdom of God. His life was humble, but his legacy lives on more than 300 years after his death through his conversations, letters, and essays. There are many translations and editions of *The Practice of the Presence of God*; the volume listed here is a critical edition by Conrad DeMeester, translated by Salvatore Sciurba.

Other books you might like:
Thomas a Kempis, *The Imitation of Christ*, 1932
John J. Kirvan, *Living in the Presence of God: The Everyday Spirituality of Brother Lawrence*, c. 1572
Saint Teresa of Avila, *Interior Castle*, c. 1572

354

BENTLEY LAYTON

The Gnostic Scriptures: A New Translation with Annotations and Introductions

(Garden City, New York: Doubleday, 1987)

Category: Scripture
Subject(s): Gnosticism; Jesus
Age range(s): Adult

Summary: The archaeological discoveries of ancient texts at Nag Hammadi in Egypt in 1945 provided new information about the world that Jesus and his followers lived in. In many cases, these recently discovered texts record Jesus' words and many accounts about his life that cannot be found in the New Testament. Layton's anthology offers new translations of many of these writings.

Other books you might like:
Hans Jonas, *The Gnostic Religion: The Message of the Alien God and the Beginnings of Christianity*, 1958
Marvin Meyer, *The Gospel of Thomas: The Hidden Sayings of Jesus*, 1992

Elaine Pagels, *The Gnostic Gospels*, 1979
Pheme Perkins, *Gnosticism and the New Testament*, 1993
James M. Robinson, *The Nag Hammadi Library in English*, 1988

355

MADELEINE L'ENGLE

A Circle of Quiet

(New York: Farrar, Straus & Giroux, 1972)

Category: Autobiography
Series: Crosswicks Journal
Subject(s): Writing; Family Life; Christian Life
Age range(s): Young Adult-Adult
Time period(s): 1970s
Locale(s): Connecticut

Summary: The first of Madeleine L'Engle's autobiographical works that make up the Crosswicks Journal collection, *A Circle of Quiet* introduces the author's personal life in the rambling Connecticut home called Crosswicks. A place of life, family fun and learning, and personal reflection, Crosswicks could house four generations at one time, each learning from the other. From this vantage, L'Engle reflects on writing, living and loving and shares her perspective on spirituality and its relationship to work and family life.

Other books by the same author:
Two-Part Invention: The Story of a Marriage, 1988
The Irrational Season, 1977
The Summer of the Great-Grandmother, 1974

Other books you might like:
Sarah Ban Breathnach, *Simple Abundance: A Daybook of Comfort and Joy*, 1995
Edith Schaeffer, *L'Abri*, 1969
Edith Schaeffer, *What Is a Family?*, 1975
Luci Shaw, *The Swiftly Tilting Worlds of Madeleine L'Engle*, 1998
Luci Shaw, *Water My Soul: Cultivating the Interior Life*, 1998

356

MADELEINE L'ENGLE

Walking on Water: Reflections on Faith and Art

(New York: North Point Press, 1995)

Category: Essays; Journals/Letters
Subject(s): Christianity; Art; Writing
Age range(s): Adult
Time period(s): 20th century

Summary: In a series of essays and journal-like writings, novelist Madeleine L'Engle offers reflections on tragedy, joy, the unexplainable, and the relationship between Christianity and art in her life and profession. She writes in *Walking on Water* that faith, like the creation of art or literature, "is always a becoming," a process, not an end result. L'Engle is best known for her award-winning novel *A Wrinkle in Time*, but her works include numerous other novels for young people as well as journals and nonfiction essays that reveal the essence of her spirituality and its connection to her writing.

Other books by the same author:
Penguins and Golden Calves: Icons and Idols, 1996
The Glorious Impossible, 1990
Trailing Clouds of Glory: Spiritual Values in Children's Literature, 1985
And It Was Good: Reflections on Beginnings, 1983

Other books you might like:
Sarah Anderson, *Heaven's Face Thinly Veiled: A Book of Spiritual Writing by Women*, 1998
Chuck Fager, *Wisdom and Your Spiritual Journey: Wisdom in the Biblical and Quaker Tradition*, 1993
Leland Ryken, *The Liberated Imagination: Thinking Christianly about the Arts*, 1989
Steve Scott, *Like a House on Fire: Renewal of the Arts in a Postmodern Culture*, 1997
Luci Shaw, *Water My Soul: Cultivating the Interior Life*, 1998

357

CARLO LEVI

Christ Stopped at Eboli: The Story of a Year
(New York: Farrar, Strauss and Company, 1947)

Category: Journals/Letters
Subject(s): Politics; Superstition; Folklore
Age range(s): Adult
Time period(s): 1930s (1935-1936)
Locale(s): Gagliano, Italy

Summary: In 1935, Carlo Levi, an Italian physician, writer and artist, was exiled to a tiny rural village in southern Italy for engaging in anti-Fascist activities. During one year, he lived among the peasants in this poorest region of his country. *Christ Stopped at Eboli* is his record of that time, complete with observations of the lives of the poorest of the poor and his own commentary. More than a diary or journal, his account has an almost novel-like atmosphere as it introduces a varied cast of inhabitants, all of whom accepted Levi, despite his outsider status, because he was able to treat their medical needs. The title of the book comes from a saying by the peasants of Gagliano that their lives will always be difficult because Christ never reached their part of the world, having stopped in the neighboring region of Eboli.

Other books by the same author:
The Watch, 1951

Other books you might like:
Forrest C. Eggleston, *Where Is God Not?: An American Surgeon in India*, 1999
Albert Schweitzer, *On the Edge of the Primeval Forest*, 1923
Ignazio Silone, *Bread and Wine*, 1937
    Gwenda David, Eric Mosbacher, translators

358

C.S. LEWIS

Mere Christianity
(New York: Macmillan, 1952)

Category: Theology
Subject(s): Christianity; Apologetics; Atheism
Age range(s): Adult

Summary: In what is perhaps his most significant apologetic work, Lewis offers his prime defense of the Christian faith. With his characteristically sober and logical prose, Lewis attacks the philosophical foundations of agnosticism and atheism, demonstrating what he perceives as the untenable nature of each position. He then outlines his own logical proofs for the value and meaning of the Christian faith.

Other books by the same author:
The Screwtape Letters, 1944

Other books you might like:
C. Stephen Evans, *Why Believe?: Reason and Mystery as Pointers to God*, 1996
Walter Hooper, *C.S. Lewis: A Companion and Guide*, 1996
Kathryn Lindskoog, *C.S. Lewis: Mere Christian*, 1981
J.B. Phillips, *Your God Is Too Small*, 1953
Philip Yancey, *What's So Amazing about Grace?*, 1997

359

C.S. LEWIS

Miracles: A Preliminary Study
(New York: Macmillan, 1947)

Category: Theology
Subject(s): Christianity; History; Apologetics
Age range(s): Adult

Summary: Lewis makes a sustained argument for the existence of miracles in the modern world. He contends that the power of the miraculous is woven into the natural world, despite the claim of science that the natural world is closed to supernatural intervention. Lewis divides miracles into two categories: those that occurred prior to Jesus' birth, and those that occurred afterward. He argues that the incarnation of God in Jesus constitutes the greatest miracle of all time.

Other books by the same author:
Mere Christianity, 1952

Other books you might like:
Walter Hooper, *C.S. Lewis: A Companion and Guide*, 1996
Marjorie L. Kimbrough, *Everyday Miracles: Realizing God's Presence in Ordinary Life*, 1997
Carolyn Godschild Miller, *Creating Miracles: Understanding the Experience of Divine Intervention*, 1995
J.B. Phillips, *Your God Is Too Small*, 1953

360

C.S. LEWIS

The Screwtape Letters

(New York: Macmillan, 1944)

Category: Theology
Subject(s): Christianity; Devil; Apologetics
Age range(s): Young Adult-Adult

Summary: What would it be like to talk to the Devil? How would the Devil try to dissuade a Christian from practicing his or her faith? How should the Christian respond? In this humorous yet insightful volume, Lewis writes the Devil (Screwtape) a series of letters in which he defends the Christian faith on a point by point basis. First published in 1942, shortly after Lewis' own conversion from skeptical unbeliever to Christian believer, *The Screwtape Letters* is the author's own witty contribution to apologetics.

Other books by the same author:
Miracles: A Preliminary Study, 1947

Other books you might like:
Dante Alighieri, *The Divine Comedy*, c. 1310
John Bunyan, *The Pilgrim's Progress*, 1678-1684
Walter Hooper, *C.S. Lewis: A Companion and Guide*, 1996
Madeleine L'Engle, *Glimpses of Grace: Daily Thoughts and Reflections*, 1996
Kathryn Lindskoog, *C.S. Lewis: Mere Christian*, 1981

361

ANNE MORROW LINDBERGH

Gift From the Sea

(New York: Pantheon, 1955)

Category: Self-Help
Subject(s): Conduct of Life; Family Relations; Women
Age range(s): Adult
Time period(s): 20th century

Summary: Anne Morrow Lindbergh, who married famous aviator Charles Lindbergh, uses the metaphor of sea shells to reflect on the lifelong need for personal and spiritual growth in women's lives. In a journal-like essay, Lindbergh explores themes of self-fulfillment, creativity, relationships, and the balance between solitude and the traditional nurturing activities in which women often find themselves involved. Written during the mid-1950s, Lindbergh's essay on self-awareness was an unintentional precursor to the Women's Liberation movement of the 1960s and 1970s. Still in print and popular more than four decades after it was first published, Lindbergh's best-known work speaks to issues universal to women who find themselves balancing traditional and contemporary roles and seeking a spiritual life, as well.

Other books by the same author:
Bring Me a Unicorn: Diaries and Letters of Anne Morrow Lindbergh, 1972
The Unicorn and Other Poems, 1956
The Wave of the Future: A Confession of Faith, 1940

Other books you might like:
Dorothy Hermann, *Anne Morrow Lindbergh: A Gift for Life*, 1993
Anne M. Johnson, *Return to the Sea: Reflections on Anne Morrow Lindbergh's Gift From the Sea*, 1998
Reeve Lindbergh, *Under a Wing: A Memoir*, 1998

362

REEVE LINDBERGH
CATHIE FELSTEAD, Illustrator

The Circle of Days

(Cambridge, Massachusetts: Candlewick Press, 1997)

Category: Prayer
Subject(s): Creation; Nature
Age range(s): Children-Adult

Summary: Reeve Lindbergh blends poetic language with richly colored illustrations by Cathie Felstead in an adaptaion of ''The Canticle of the Sun,'' a prayer by St. Francis of Assisi. *The Circle of Days* offers thankfulness for the wonder of nature and the universe in an ecumenical way that focuses on the creation, rather than on the creator.

Other books by the same author:
Under a Wing: A Memoir, 1998
If I'd Known Then What I Know Now, 1994
The Names of the Mountain: A Novel, 1992

Other books you might like:
Cecil Francis Alexander, *All Things Bright and Beautiful*, 1987
Paul Goble, *I Sing for the Animals*, 1991
Jake Swamp, *Giving Thanks: A Native American Good Morning Message*, 1995

363

HAL LINDSEY
C.C. CARLSON, Co-Author

The Late Great Planet Earth

(Grand Rapids, Michigan: Zondervan, 1970)

Category: Theology
Subject(s): End-Times; Christianity; Bible
Age range(s): Adult
Time period(s): 20th century; Indeterminate Future

Summary: *The Late Great Planet Earth* is Hal Lindsey's original prophetic description of the latter years of the 20th century. He opens by discussing the nature of interest in the future, noting that fortune-tellers and psychic celebrities are popular in American culture, and explaining how his predictions differ from those of the party-and-media entertainment predictions because his are based on biblical prophecy. He then goes on to interpret events of the 20th century, including the independence of Israel and the horrors of the Holocaust, through the lens of biblical prophecy. Finally, he outlines the geopolitical scenario of the end times, with an emphasis on Middle East tensions as the catalyst to a major world war and the identification of Russia and China as the two primary forces involved in starting and escalating this conflict.

Other books by the same author:

Vanished into Thin Air: The Hope of Every Believer, 1999

Facing Millennial Midnight: The Y2K Crisis Confronting America and the World, 1999

Planet Earth: The Final Chapter, 1998

The 1980's, Countdown to Armageddon, 1980

Satan Is Alive and Well on Planet Earth, 1972 (C.C. Carlson, co-author)

Other books you might like:

Charles Capps, *End Time Events: Journey to the End of the Age*, 1997

Stanley A. Ellisen, *Three Worlds in Conflict: God, Satan, Man: The High Drama of Bible Prophecy*, 1998

John Hagee, *From Daniel to Doomsday: The Countdown Has Begun*, 1999

Randal Ross, *The Next Seven Great Events of the Future: And What They Mean to You*, 1997

Jack Van Impe, *11:59 and Counting*, 1992

364

HAL LINDSEY

Planet Earth: The Final Chapter

(Beverly Hills, California: Western Front, 1998)

Category: Theology
Subject(s): End-Times; Christianity; Bible
Age range(s): Adult
Time period(s): 20th century

Summary: *Planet Earth: The Final Chapter* is another in Hal Lindsey's growing line of Bible prophecy interpretation. At the end of the 1990s, Lindsey looks back on a half-century of Israeli statehood and the ongoing unrest in the region. He ties these events to applicable prophecies found in the Book of the Revelation in the New Testament of the *Bible*. He then examines such factors in American and world culture as personal violence, economics, military firepower and strength, and societal morality, again linking current conditions with ancient writings. Finally, Lindsey discusses the cultural and political signs that may signal the imminent return of Jesus.

Other books by the same author:

Vanished into Thin Air: The Hope of Every Believer, 1999

Facing Millennial Midnight: The Y2K Crisis Confronting America and the World, 1999

The 1980's, Countdown to Armageddon, 1980

Satan Is Alive and Well on Planet Earth, 1972 (C.C. Carlson, co-author)

The Late Great Planet Earth, 1970 (C.C. Carlson, co-author)

Other books you might like:

Charles Capps, *End Time Events: Journey to the End of the Age*, 1997

Stanley A. Ellisen, *Three Worlds in Conflict: God, Satan, Man: The High Drama of Bible Prophecy*, 1998

John Hagee, *From Daniel to Doomsday: The Countdown Has Begun*, 1999

Randal Ross, *The Next Seven Great Events of the Future: And What They Mean to You*, 1997

Jack Van Impe, *11:59 and Counting*, 1992

365

HAL LINDSEY

A Prophetical Walk through the Holy Land

(Eugene, Oregon: Harvest House, 1983)

Category: History
Subject(s): Bible; Christianity; Prophecy
Age range(s): Adult
Locale(s): Israel; Egypt; Jordan

Summary: Hal Lindsey, whose reputation as an interpreter of biblical prophecy originated with his book, *The Late Great Planet Earth* (1970) takes readers on a journey through the lands of biblical times to discover Old Testaments prophecies that have come to pass. *A Prophetical Walk through the Holy Land* is a guidebook to the Middle East areas where Lindsey says there is proof that prophecies once made are now prophecies fulfilled.

Other books by the same author:

Vanished into Thin Air: The Hope of Every Believer, 1999

Facing Millennial Midnight: The Y2K Crisis Confronting America and the World, 1999

The 1980's, Countdown to Armageddon, 1980

Satan Is Alive and Well on Planet Earth, 1972 (C.C. Carlson, co-author)

The Late Great Planet Earth, 1970 (C.C. Carlson, co-author)

Other books you might like:

Charles Capps, *End Time Events: Journey to the End of the Age*, 1997

Stanley A. Ellisen, *Three Worlds in Conflict: God, Satan, Man: The High Drama of Bible Prophecy*, 1998

John Hagee, *From Daniel to Doomsday: The Countdown Has Begun*, 1999

Randal Ross, *The Next Seven Great Events of the Future: And What They Mean to You*, 1997

Jack Van Impe, *11:59 and Counting*, 1992

366

DENISE LINN
MEADOW LINN, Co-Author

Quest: A Guide for Creating Your Own Vision Quest

(New York: Random House, 1998)

Category: Self-Help
Subject(s): Meditation; Spirituality
Age range(s): Young Adult-Adult

Summary: Drawing on the Native American traditions of her heritage and the practices and philosophies of other cultures as well, Denise Linn offers guidance to seekers of spiritual retreat from the day-to-day distractions of life. She presents profiles of various types of personal retreat, ranging from a personal day of silence to wilderness group quests, and explains how each can enhance one's spirituality. Designed to help readers focus their personal faith and vision with techniques that span many cultures, this handbook includes both practical and philosophical assistance to help readers select the right tools for their spiritual journey.

Other books by the same author:

Altars: Bringing Sacred Shrines into Your Everyday Life, 1999

Sacred Legacies: Healing Your Past and Creating a Positive Future, 1999

The Hidden Power of Dreams: How to Use Dreams on Your Spiritual Journey, 1997

Sacred Space: Clearing and Enhancing the Energy of Your Home, 1995

Other books you might like:

Steven Foster, *The Book of the Vision Quest: Personal Transformation in the Wilderness*, 1980
  Meredith Little, co-author

Marie Herbert, *Healing Quest: In the Sacred Space of the Medicine Wheel*, 1997

Daniel Quinn, *Providence: The Story of a Fifty-Year Vision Quest*, 1995

367

ANN LINNEA

Deep Water Passage: A Spiritual Journey at Midlife

(Boston: Little, Brown, 1995)

Category: Autobiography
Subject(s): Spirituality; Adventure and Adventurers; Sports/ Kayaking
Age range(s): Adult

Summary: At age 43, Ann Linnea braved the waters of Lake Superior in a kayak in search of challenge and triumph in the face of danger. For 65 days she traveled the world's largest lake, becoming the first woman ever to circumnavigate its brutal waters in a kayak. In this account of her physical and spiritual journey, Linnea shares what she learned about herself, her values, and her future through this very personal venture.

Other books you might like:

Linda Lewis, *Water's Edge: Women Who Push the Limits in Rowing, Kayaking and Canoeing*, 1992

Michael J. Roads, *Journey into Nature: A Spiritual Adventure*, 1990

Mark Zelinski, *Outward Bound: The Inward Odyssey*, 1991
  Gary Shaeffer, text editor

368

CHARLES H. LIPPY, Editor
PETER W. WILLIAMS, Co-Editor

Encyclopedia of the American Religious Experience: Studies of Traditions and Movements

(New York: Scribner, 1998)

Category: Religious Encyclopedias/Dictionaries
Subject(s): Religious Life; History; American History
Age range(s): Adult

Summary: In three volumes, the editors have compiled a general look at religion throughout American history. Covering such subjects as denominational differences and backgrounds, the influence of religion on American culture, and the spread of religion in America, the *Encyclopedia of the American Religious Experience* provides a comprehensive overview in the form of articles written by authoritative scholars. Both Christian and non-Christian religious traditions are highlighted, as are relevant socio-political issues. Researchers will find extensive bibliographic and cross-referenced information.

Other books by the same author:

Modern American Popular Religion: A Critical Assessment and Annotated Bibliography, 1996

Being Religious, American Style: A History of Popular Religiosity in the United States, 1994

Christianity Comes to the Americas, 1492-1776, 1992 (Robert Choquette, Stafford Poole, co-authors)

Twentieth-Century Shapers of American Popular Religion, 1989

Bibliography of Religion in the South, 1985

Other books you might like:

Mircea Eliade, *The Encyclopedia of Religion*, 1987
  Charles J. Adams and others, co-editors

Arlene Hirschfelder, *The Encyclopedia of Native American Religions: An Introduction*, 1992
  Paulette Molin, co-author

William H. Swatos Jr., *Encyclopedia of Religion and Society*, 1998
  Peter Kivisto, Barbara J. Denison, and James McClenon, co-editors

---

369

BARRY LOPEZ

Arctic Dreams: Imagination and Desire in a Northern Landscape

(New York: Scribner, 1986)

Category: Essays
Subject(s): Travel; Discovery and Exploration; Nature
Age range(s): Adult
Time period(s): 1980s
Locale(s): Canada

Summary: While chronicling the author's adventures in northern Canada, the award-winning *Arctic Dreams* offers Lopez's unique views on the land, its people and animals, and the state of the environment in this beautiful region. His passion for the natural world is conveyed in his vivid descriptions of his travels, which included braving dangers as well as witnessing storms, mirages, and the aurora borealis. Acknowledging a spiritual connection between people and the earth, he inspires others to experience the beauty and joy of nature first-hand.

Awards the book has won:

Christopher Award, Books for Adults, 1987
National Book Award, Nonfiction, 1986

Other books by the same author:

About This Life: Journeys on the Threshold of Memory, 1998
Field Notes: The Grace Note of the Canyon Wren, 1994

Crossing Open Ground, 1989
Winter Count, 1981
River Notes: The Dance of Herons, 1979
Of Wolves and Men, 1978
Desert Notes: Reflections in the Eye of a Raven, 1976

Other books you might like:
Annie Dillard, *Pilgrim at Tinker Creek*, 1974
Peter Matthiessen, *The Snow Leopard*, 1978
David Suzuki, *Wisdom of the Elders: Honoring Sacred Native Visions of Nature*, 1992
    Peter Knudtson, co-author
Paul Theroux, *The Happy Isles of Oceania: Paddling the Pacific*, 1992

370

PETER LORIE, Editor
MANUELA DUNN MASCETTI, Co-Editor

The Quotable Spirit: A Treasury of Religious and Spiritual Quotations From Ancient Times to the Twentieth Century

(New York: Macmillan USA, 1996)

Category: Religious Encyclopedias/Dictionaries
Subject(s): Religion; Scripture; Spirituality
Age range(s): Adult

Summary: Drawn from many centuries and cultures, this is a collection of inspirational, religious, and philosophical quotations arranged in fifty sections by theme and chronology. More than 5000 quotations are included, each with an annotation describing its origin. From Jesus, Buddha, and Muhammad to Black Elk, Mother Teresa, and Emily Dickinson, wisdom and inspiration spanning thousands of years and many faith traditions are indexed and categorized for easy access.

Other books by the same author:
The Buddhist Directory: United States of America & Canada, 1997 (Julie Foakes, co-author)
Millennium Planner: Your Personal Guide to the Year 2000, 1997
Superstitions, 1992
History of the Future: A Chronology, 1989 (Sidd Murray-Clark, co-author)
Wonder Child: Rediscovering the Magical World of Innocence and Joy Within Ourselves and Our Children, 1989

Other books you might like:
Rebecca Davis, *The Treasury of Religious and Spiritual Quotations*, 1994
William Neil, *Concise Dictionary of Religious Quotations*, 1975
Geoffrey Parrinder, *Dictionary of Religious and Spiritual Quotations*, 1989
F.B. Proctor, *Treasury of Quotations on Religious Subjects From the Great Writers and Preachers of All Ages*, 1977
Gerald Tomlinson, *Treasury of Religious Quotations*, 1991

371

ANNE GRAHAM LOTZ

Glorious Dawn of God's Story: Finding Meaning for Your Life in Genesis

(Dallas, Texas: Word, 1997)

Category: Devotionals
Subject(s): Bible; Christianity; Creation
Age range(s): Adult

Summary: Anne Graham Lotz, daughter of Billy Graham and an accomplished bible teacher, explores the lessons of Genesis and their application to life today. In this book, which covers the first eleven books of Genesis, Lotz provides a *Bible* study guide to Old Testament teachings that can help believers find meaning in their lives.

Awards the book has won:
Gold Medallion Book Award, Bible Study, 1998

Other books by the same author:
The Vision of His Glory: Finding Hope through the Revelation of Jesus Christ, 1996

Other books you might like:
Allen P. Ross, *Creation and Blessing: A Guide to the Study and Exposition of Genesis*, 1998
Francis A. Schaeffer, *Genesis in Space and Time: The How of Biblical History*, 1972

372

ANNE GRAHAM LOTZ

The Vision of His Glory: Finding Hope through the Revelation of Jesus Christ

(Dallas, Texas: Word, 1996)

Category: Devotionals
Subject(s): Bible; Christianity; Scripture
Age range(s): Adult

Summary: Anne Graham Lotz is an accomplished bible teacher and the daughter of evangelist Billy Graham. In *The Vision of His Glory*, she explores the last book of the New Testament of the *Bible*—the book of the Revelation. In an approach to the Scriptures that seeks hope for those in pain, Lotz shares insights of encouragement and blessing from one of the most-studied portions of Christian scripture.

Awards the book has won:
Gold Medallion Book Award, Bible Study, 1997

Other books by the same author:
Glorious Dawn of God's Story: Finding Meaning for Your Life in Genesis, 1997

Other books you might like:
Mary K. Baxter, *A Divine Revelation of Heaven*, 1998
Richard H. Lowery, *Revelation: Hope for the World in Troubled Times*, 1994

373

MAX LUCADO

The Applause of Heaven

(Dallas: Word, 1990)

Category: Religious Commentaries
Subject(s): Bible; Christian Life
Age range(s): Adult

Summary: Storyteller and Bible teacher Max Lucado turns his attention to the Beatitudes. He reveals for readers the secrets of finding the joy and peace of God in all things.

Other books by the same author:
The Gift for All People, 1999
Let the Journey Begin, 1998
No Wonder They Call Him the Savior, 1996
God Came Near: Chronicles of Christ, 1987

Other books you might like:
Bill Dodds, *Happily Ever After Begins Here and Now: Living the Beatitudes Today*, 1997
   Michael J. Dodds, co-author
Ronald S. Lello, *The Beatitudes: Living with Blessing, Meditation and Prayer*, 1997
Rudolf Schnackenburg, *All Things Are Possible to Believers: Reflections on the Lord's Prayer and the Sermon on the Mount*, 1995

374

MAX LUCADO

He Still Moves Stones

(Dallas: Word, 1993)

Category: Self-Help
Subject(s): Christianity; Miracles; Faith
Age range(s): Adult

Summary: In his unique way, Bible teacher and storyteller Max Lucado shares stories of hope rewarded and miracles performed by God in this collection of real-life experiences shared by ordinary Christians. Lucado encourages readers confronted with problems that just seem unsolvable to remember that the God who moved the stone covering the tomb of Jesus still performs miracles in the lives of believers.

Other books by the same author:
The Gift for All People, 1999
Let the Journey Begin, 1998
No Wonder They Call Him the Savior, 1996
A Gentle Thunder: Hearing God through the Storm, 1995

Other books you might like:
Arthur Gordon, *A Light in the Darkness: Stories about God's Mysterious Ways From Guideposts*, 1996
C.S. Lewis, *Miracles: A Preliminary Study*, 1947
Catherine Marshall, *Beyond Our Selves*, 1961
Quin Sherrer, *Miracles Happen When You Pray*, 1997

375

MAX LUCADO

Just Like Jesus

(Nashville, Tennessee: Word, 1998)

Category: Theology
Subject(s): Christianity; Jesus; Discipleship
Age range(s): Adult

Summary: Popular author Lucado offers an inspirational look at Christian discipleship. Combining stories from the Bible and his own life, Lucado uses his humorous style to ask what Jesus would do in particular situations. He begins the book by imagining what Jesus would do if he woke up in our beds and had to live our lives for 24 hours. Taking their cues from Jesus' experience, readers can begin to see how they might live more like Jesus.

Awards the book has won:
Charles "Kip" Jordan Christian Book of the Year, 1999

Other books by the same author:
The Great House of God: A Home for Your Heart, 1997

Other books you might like:
Angela Elwell Hunt, *The Tale of Three Trees: A Traditional Folktale*, 1989
Tim LaHaye, *Jesus: Who Is He?*, 1996
Charles R. Swindoll, *The Family of God: Understanding Your Role in the Body of Christ*, 1997
Walter Wangerin Jr., *Reliving the Passion: Meditations on the Suffering, Death and Resurrection of Jesus as Recorded in Mark*, 1992
Philip Yancey, *The Jesus I Never Knew*, 1995

376

MAX LUCADO

Six Hours, One Friday: Anchoring to the Power of the Cross

(Portland, Oregon: Multnomah, 1989)

Category: Self-Help
Subject(s): Christian Life; Faith; Scripture
Age range(s): Adult

Summary: The day that Jesus Christ was crucified is commemorated every year in Good Friday observances. Using this occasion as his focus in *Six Hours, One Friday*, Max Lucado offers readers hope for daily living through three lessons tied to this event. Lucado writes that a study of the day of crucifixion and its significance in history reveals that life has purpose, forgiveness is available, and death is not the end of life.

Awards the book has won:
Gold Medallion Book Award, Inspirational, 1990

Other books by the same author:
And the Angels Were Silent: The Final Week of Jesus, 1992
God Came Near: Chronicles of Christ, 1987
No Wonder They Call Him the Savior, 1986

Other books you might like:
Don M. Aycock, *Eight Days That Changed the World*, 1990

Francis X. Gaeta, *What He Did for Love: A Companion for the Forty Days of Lent*, 1998
Paul L. Maier, *In the Fullness of Time: A Historian Looks at Christmas, Easter, and the Early Church*, 1991
Tricia McCary Rhodes, *A Pilgrimage of Prayer*, 1998

377

MAX LUCADO

When God Whispers Your Name

(Dallas: Word, 1994)

Category: Essays
Subject(s): Allegories; Christian Life; Storytelling
Age range(s): Young Adult-Adult

Summary: Through allegory, personal anecdote, and paraphrased and retold stories from the Bible, Christian storyteller Max Lucado shares the good news of God's grace. Lucado uses ordinary circumstances to convey extraordinary messages. In one tale, Moses is not an imaginary figure on an ancient mountain conversing with a burning bush, he's a modern-day maintenance worker, and God speaks to him through a bucket of water while he's mopping a floor. These short reads are intended for those who are Christians as well as those who are not.

Other books by the same author:
The Gift for All People, 1999
Let the Journey Begin, 1998
No Wonder They Call Him the Savior, 1996
God Came Near: Chronicles of Christ, 1987

Other books you might like:
Jack Canfield, *Chicken Soup for the Christian Soul: 101 Stories to Open the Heart and Rekindle the Spirit*, 1997
   Mark Victor Hansen, Patty Aubery, Nancy Mitchell, co-authors
Chris Fabry, *At the Corner of Mundane and Grace: Finding Glimpses of Glory in Ordinary Days*, 1999
Billy Graham, *Answers to Life's Problems*, 1988
Pam W. Vredevelt, *Angel Behind the Rocker: Stories of Hope in Unexpected Places*, 1997

378

ALLAN LUKS
PEGGY PAYNE, Co-Author

The Healing Power of Doing Good: The Health and Spiritual Benefits of Helping Others

(New York: Fawcett Columbine, 1992)

Category: Self-Help
Subject(s): Human Behavior; Health; Volunteerism
Age range(s): Adult

Summary: The people who volunteer to help others have known this for generations, but now there is medical evidence to support their beliefs: volunteering to do things for other people is good for a person. Researchers are inreasingly interested in studying people who volunteer to find out how and

why this happens. In the meantime, however, Allan Luks offers evidence in *The Healing Power of Doing Good* that those who freely donate time to others, whether through a community or church program or on an individual basis, are healthier-physically, spiritually and emotionally-and more likely to live longer than non-volunteers are.

Other books by the same author:
You Are What You Drink, 1989
Will America Sober Up?, 1983
Having Been There., 1979

Other books you might like:
Douglas M. Lawson, *Volunteering: 101 Ways You Can Improve the World and Your Life*, 1998
John Raynolds, *The Halo Effect*, 1998
Robert Wuthnow, *Acts of Compassion: Caring for Others and Helping Ourselves*, 1991

379

MARTIN LUTHER

Conversations with Luther, Selections From Recently Published Sources of the Table Talk

(Boston: Pilgrim Press, 1915)

Category: Doctrine
Subject(s): Lutherans; Christianity; Protestantism
Age range(s): Adult

Summary: Some of the most personal ideals, passions, and observations of Martin Luther (1483-1546), catalyst for the Reformation and the founder of the Protestant branch of Christianity, are found in this volume, which was first published in German two decades after Luther's death, in 1566. The book consists of notes compiled by Luther's close associates during private conversations and group discussions over meals, and during Luther's day-to-day activities. Pope Gregory XIII, who headed the Vatican from 1572 to 1585 and strove to reclaim Europe for the Roman Catholic Church, ordered all 4000 copies of the book confiscated and burned; the penalty for retaining possession of the book was death. However, at least one copy was preserved, covered with cloth, sealed in wax, and buried under the foundation stones of a home. That volume resurfaced in 1626 when the grandson of the man who had buried it smuggled it out of Germany and into the hands of Englishman Captain Henry Bell, with the urgent request that he translate and distribute the volume. *Conversations with Luther* reveals the humor, wit, and personality of the Christian reformer, whose own prolific writings are more scholarly. This edition is edited and translated by Preserved Smith and Herbert Percival Gallinger.

Other books by the same author:
Basic Luther, 1995
Luther's Prayers, 1994
Martin Luther: Selections From His Writings, 1972

Other books you might like:
Roland H. Bainton, *Here I Stand: A Life of Martin Luther*, 1950

Erik H. Erikson, *Young Man Luther: A Study in Psychoanalysis and History*, 1958

Timothy F. Lull, *My Conversations with Martin Luther*, 1999

380

SUSAN SCHAEFFER MACAULAY
SLUG SIGNORINO, Illustrator

How To Be Your Own Selfish Pig

(Elgin, Illinois: Chariot Books, 1982)

Category: Theology
Subject(s): Apologetics; Adolescence; Christianity
Age range(s): Young Adult-Adult

Summary: Susan Schaeffer Macaulay presents the evangelical world view of Francis A. Schaeffer-her father-in a study geared toward teens and young adults. With humor, directness, and appealing cartoons, Macaulay introduces the origins of her own Christian beliefs and emulates her father's interactive method of teaching through questions, exploration, and logical argument. Workbook materials are available for teachers and students to use Macaulay's approach in group settings; it is equally useful by individual readers, with or without workbook supplements.

Awards the book has won:
Gold Medallion Book Award, Youth, 1983

Other books by the same author:
For the Family's Sake: The Value of Home in Everyone's Life, 1999
For the Children's Sake: Foundations of Education for Home and School, 1984
Something Beautiful From God, 1980

Other books you might like:
Karen Andreola, *A Charlotte Mason Companion: Personal Reflections on the Gentle Art of Learning*, 1998
David A. Noebel, *Understanding the Times: The Story of the Biblical Christian, Marxist/Leninist, and Secular Humanist Worldviews*, 1991
Edith Schaeffer, *L'Abri*, 1969
Francis A. Schaeffer, *The God Who Is There: Speaking Historic Christianity into the Twentieth Century*, 1968
Francis A. Schaeffer, *How Should We Then Live?: The Rise and Decline of Western Thought and Culture*, 1976

381

SHIRLEY MACLAINE

Going Within

(New York: Bantam, 1989)

Category: New Age (Nonfiction); Self-Help
Subject(s): Spiritualism; Meditation
Age range(s): Adult

Summary: In *Going Within*, Shirley MacLaine answers many of the questions she has received about her spiritual journey and the New Age practices she embraces. She shares the philosophies and techniques that have brought her inner peace. She explains the way she uses crystals, visualization, and meditation to increase love and reduce disharmony in her life, and offers guidance to those who wish to follow her program of spirituality.

Other books by the same author:
Dancing in the Light, 1987
Out on a Limb, 1983
You Can Get There From Here, 1975
Don't Fall Off the Mountain, 1970

Other books you might like:
Pam Cameron, *Bridge into Light*, 1994
Joy Gardner Gordon, *Color and Crystals: A Journey through the Chakras*, 1988
Robert B. Leichtman, *Active Meditation: The Western Tradition*, 1990
Elizabeth Clare Prophet, *Access the Power of Your Higher Self*, 1998

382

ARTHUR J. MAGIDA, Editor

How to Be a Perfect Stranger: A Guide to Etiquette in Other People's Religious Ceremonies

(Woodstock, Vermont: Jewish Lights, 1996)

Category: Self-Help
Subject(s): Religious Traditions; Culture; Customs
Age range(s): Young Adult-Adult

Summary: This two-volume set offers a guide to the practices and beliefs of the world's major religions and sects. The books are intended to make "strangers" comfortable as they participate in religious ceremonies other than their own. For each religion, Magida describes its holidays, its sacred texts, and its worship liturgies. The books are rich deposits of information about various religions and are important guidebooks to the often perplexing modern religious landscape.

Other books by the same author:
Prophet of Rage: A Life of Louis Farrakhan and His Nation, 1996

Other books you might like:
Dean Halverson, *The Compact Guide to World Religions*, 1996
Lawrence A. Hoffman, *The Art of Public Prayer: Not for Clergy Only*, 1988
Meryl Hyman, *Who Is a Jew?: Conversations, Not Conclusions*, 1998
Kay Lynn Isca, *Catholic Etiquette: What You Need to Know about Catholic Rites and Wrongs*, 1997
Gayle Colquitt White, *Believers and Beliefs: A Practical Guide to Religious Etiquette for Business and Social Occasions*, 1997

383

MOSES MAIMONIDES

Guide for the Perplexed: A 15th Century Spanish Translation by Pedro de Toledo

(Culver City, California: Labyrinthos, 1989)

Category: Theology
Subject(s): Philosophy; Judaism; Mysticism

Summary: Jewish philosopher, rabbi, and physician Maimonides (1135-1204) was born in Spain, but emigrated from his homeland when Islam became the official state religion in 1148. Eventually, he settled in Cairo, Egypt, where he became chief rabbi. Maimonides' thought and writings were influential not only in Jewish mysticism, but also on Christian philosophers including St. Thomas Aquinas. In *Guide for the Perplexed*, written around 1190, he addresses philosophical issues of religion including the nature of God, the problem of good and evil, and the nature of creation and free will. In this work he brought together the faith of rabbinic Judaism with the rational philosophy of Aristotle. For his contributions to Judaism through this work, his *Mishneh Torah*, and the Thirteen Articles of Faith, a creed still embraced by Orthodox Jews, Maimonides has been called "the second Moses."

Other books by the same author:
Ethical Writings of Maimonides, 1975
A Maimonides Reader, 1972
The Book of Holiness, 1965
The Book of Offerings, 1950

Other books you might like:
Martin Buber, *The Way of Man, According to the Teachings of Hasidism*, 1950
Memachem Mendel Schneerson, *Toward a Meaningful Life: The Wisdom of the Rebbe*, 1995
Adin Steinsaltz, *The Candle of God: Discourses on Chasidic Thought*, 1998

384

KAREN BURTON MAINS

With My Whole Heart: Disciplines for Strengthening the Inner Life

(Portland, Oregon: Multnomah, 1987)

Category: Self-Help
Subject(s): Christian Life; Conduct of Life; Bible
Age range(s): Adult

Summary: Karen Burton Mains offers guidance for women, in particular, in developing the spiritual disciplines that are part of living a Christian life. With stories from personal experience and direction from the Bible, the author discusses the daily disciplines of life, including prayer, that strengthen faith and build spirituality.

Awards the book has won:
Gold Medallion Book Award, Devotional, 1988

Other books by the same author:
Comforting One Another: In Life's Sorrows, 1997

Lonely No More: A Woman's Journey to Personal, Marital, and Spiritual Healing, 1993
Friends and Strangers: Divine Enounters in Lonely Places, 1990
The Key to a Loving Heart, 1979
Open Heart, Open Home, 1976

Other books you might like:
Ruth Bell Graham, *Sitting by My Laughing Fire*, 1977
Anne Ortlund, *Disciplines of the Heart: Tuning Your Inner Life to God*, 1987
Edith Schaeffer, *The Life of Prayer*, 1992

385

BETTY MALZ

Angels Watching over Me

(Old Tappan, New Jersey: Chosen Books, 1986)

Category: Theology
Subject(s): Angels; Christian Life; Bible
Age range(s): Young Adult-Adult

Summary: In *Angels Watching over Me*, Betty Malz shares profiles of people, including herself, who have had encounters with angels. Through stories and biblical descriptions of the work and role of angels, she considers what God's purpose is for angels on earth.

Other books by the same author:
Touching the Unseen World, 1991
Heaven, 1989
Super Natural Living, 1982
Prayers That Are Answered, 1980
My Glimpse of Eternity, 1977

Other books you might like:
Joan Wester Anderson, *Where Wonders Prevail: True Accounts That Bear Witness to the Existence of Heaven*, 1996
Billy Graham, *Angels: God's Secret Agents*, 1975
Sarah Hornsby, *Angels All around Me*, 1995

386

BRENNAN MANNING

The Ragamuffin Gospel: Good News for the Bedraggled, Beat-Up, and Burnt Out

(Portland, Oregon: Multnomah, 1990)

Category: Self-Help
Subject(s): Faith; Christian Life
Age range(s): Adult

Summary: The author of *The Ragamuffin Gospel* notes that when Jesus was engaged in his ministry, he did not seek out the rich and powerful-instead, he sought out the ragamuffins, the folks whose lives were frayed around the edges, the ones without power over others, the ones who struggled with every step or worried about where their next meal would come from. Brennan Manning shares his own "ragamuffin" story and reminds readers that the ragamuffin gospel is the good news of God's grace for everyone who recognizes a need for healing and encouragement.

Other books by the same author:
Reflections for Ragamuffins: Daily Devotionals From the Writings of Brennan Manning, 1998
The Boy Who Cried Abba: A Parable of Trust and Acceptance, 1997
Abba's Child: The Cry of the Heart for Intimate Belonging, 1994
The Signature of Jesus, 1988
Lion and Lamb, 1986

Other books you might like:
Leanne Payne, *Restoring the Christian Soul*, 1991
Sandra Wilson, *Into Abba's Arms: Finding the Acceptance You've Always Wanted*, 1998
Philip Yancey, *What's So Amazing about Grace?*, 1997

387

PETE MARAVICH
DARREL CAMPBELL, Co-Author
FRANK SCHROEDER, Co-Author

Heir to a Dream

(Nashville: T. Nelson, 1987)

Category: Autobiography
Subject(s): Sports/Basketball; Fathers and Sons; Christian Life
Age range(s): Young Adult-Adult

Summary: In an autobiography published only a short time before his death, popular basketball star Pete Maravich wrote of the sport that had dominated so much of his life and the God he ultimately dedicated his life to. Called "Pistol Pete" for his scoring prowess, Maravich retired from the NBA in 1980. In *Heir to a Dream*, he writes of the special relationship he had with his father and the dramatic changes that Christian faith brought into his life.

Awards the book has won:
Gold Medallion Book Award, Biography/Autobiography, 1988

Other books you might like:
Bill Bradley, *Values of the Game*, 1998
Phil Jackson, *Sacred Hoops: Spiritual Lessons of a Hardwood Warrior*, 1995
Pat Williams, *Ahead of the Game: The Pat Williams Story*, 1999
James D. Denney, co-author

388

BARBARA MARK
TRUDY GRISWOLD, Co-Author

The Angelspeake Book of Prayer and Healing: How to Work with Your Angels

(New York: Simon & Schuster, 1997)

Category: Self-Help
Subject(s): Angels; Health; Prayer
Age range(s): Adult

Summary: In a follow up to *Angelspeake: How to Talk with Your Angels*, Barbara Mark and Trudy Griswold take angel communication guidance a step further. *The Angelspeake Book of Prayer and Healing* offers guidance in requesting angelic help to heal body, soul, and mind.

Other books by the same author:
Angelspeake: How to Talk with Your Angels: A Guide, 1995 (Trudy Griswold, co-author)

Other books you might like:
Alma Daniel, *Ask Your Angels*, 1992
Eileen Elias Freeman, *Angelic Healing: Working with Your Angels to Heal Your Life*, 1994
Ambika Wauters, *Angel Oracle: Working with the Angels for Guidance, Inspiration and Love*, 1995

389

CATHERINE MARSHALL

Beyond Our Selves

(New York: McGraw-Hill, 1961)

Category: Autobiography
Subject(s): Christianity; Faith
Age range(s): Adult

Summary: *Beyond Our Selves* is a very personal record of Catherine Marshall's spiritual journey from a vaguely empty feeling to a life of faith and wholeness. Sharing her own stories and those of others, the author reveals some of the ways that faith grows through adversity as well as blessing.

Other books by the same author:
A Closer Walk, 1986
The Helper, 1978
Something More, 1974
A Man Called Peter: The Story of Peter Marshall, 1951

Other books you might like:
Brenda Poinsett, *Not My Will but Thine: Coming to Terms with Things You Can't Change*, 1998
Hannah Whitall Smith, *The Christian's Secret of a Happy Life*, 1883
Joni Eareckson Tada, *Glorious Intruder: God's Presence in Life's Chaos*, 1989

390

CATHERINE MARSHALL

A Closer Walk

(Old Tappan, New Jersey: Chosen Books, 1986)

Category: Autobiography
Subject(s): Spirituality; Christian Life; Prayer
Age range(s): Young Adult-Adult
Time period(s): 20th century (1959-1983)
Locale(s): United States

Summary: Catherine Marshall was a life-long journal-writer. Her daily records of prayers answered and "on hold," of questions she had, and of insights revealed were the foundation of her published writing projects. *A Closer Walk* was edited by Marshall's husband, Leonard LeSourd, after her death in 1983. These writings depict a woman always growing in her faith, always moving closer to the God she loved. This spiritual autobiography offers an intimate and inspirational glimpse into the personal and prayer life of Catherine Marshall from her marriage to LeSourd in 1959, to the days immediately preceding her death in 1983.

Awards the book has won:
Gold Medallion Book Award, Devotional/Christian Living, 1987

Other books by the same author:
The Helper, 1978
Something More, 1974
Beyond Our Selves, 1961
A Man Called Peter: The Story of Peter Marshall, 1951

Other books you might like:
Richard J. Foster, *Celebration of Discipline: The Path to Spiritual Growth*, 1978
Morton T. Kelsey, *Adventure Inward: Christian Growth through Personal Journal Writing*, 1980
Edith Schaeffer, *Affliction*, 1978
Edith Schaeffer, *The Life of Prayer*, 1992

391

CATHERINE MARSHALL

A Man Called Peter: The Story of Peter Marshall
(New York: McGraw-Hill, 1951)

Category: Biography
Subject(s): Love; Christianity; Marriage
Age range(s): Young Adult-Adult

Summary: In the late 1940s, Peter Marshall was the chaplain of the United States Senate. A well-known Presbyterian preacher and pastor, he had come a long way from his beginnings as a poor immigrant from Scotland who dug ditches to make a living before attending seminary. Catherine Marshall's *A Man Called Peter* is the story of this man, her husband, who died young following a heart attack, but not without leaving a legacy of faith and spirituality. *A Man Called Peter* remained on bestseller lists for three years. Not just the story of a young man called to share his faith, it is also the story of a happy marriage and an earthly love cut short.

Other books by the same author:
A Closer Walk, 1986
The Helper, 1978
Something More, 1974
Beyond Our Selves, 1961

Other books you might like:
Billy Graham, *Just as I Am: The Autobiography of Billy Graham*, 1997
Edith Schaeffer, *The Tapestry: The Life and Times of Francis and Edith Schaeffer*, 1981
Jurjen Beumer, *Henri Nouwen: A Restless Seeking for God*, 1997
David E. Schlaver, Nancy Forest-Flier, translators

392

PAUL MARSHALL
LELA GILBERT, Co-Author

Their Blood Cries Out: The Untold Story of Persecution Against Christians in the Modern World
(Dallas: Word, 1997)

Category: Biography
Subject(s): Christianity; Martyrs
Age range(s): Young Adult-Adult
Time period(s): 20th century

Summary: Paul Marshall and Lela Gilbert address the issue of religious persecution of Christians worldwide. For most contemporary American Christians, the issue of true religious persecution is generally nonexistent. The authors point out that although persecution and death are very real concerns for Christians in other places in the world during the 1990s, this issue remains invisible in both religious and mainstream media in the United States. They detail where the greatest persecutions are taking place and challenge all Christians, Protestant and Catholic, to become aware of these circumstances and to take a stand against it.

Awards the book has won:
Gold Medallion Book Award, Christianity and Society, 1998

Other books by the same author:
Heaven Is Not My Home: Learning to Live in God's Creation, 1998 (Lela Gilbert, co-author)
A Kind of Life Imposed on Man: Vocation and Social Order From Tyndale to Locke, 1996
Stained Glass: Worldviews and Social Science, 1989 (Sander Griffioen, Richard J. Mouw, co-editors)
Social Science in Christian Perspective, 1988 (Robert E. VanderVennen, co-editor)
Thine Is the Kingdom: A Biblical Perspective on the Nature of Government and Politics Today, 1984

Other books you might like:
M. Bernall, *She Said Yes: The Unlikely Martyrdom of Cassie Bernall*, 1999
Andrew Chandler, *The Terrible Alternative: Christian Martyrdom in the Twentieth Century*, 1998
James Hefley, *By Their Blood: Christian Martyrs of the Twentieth Century*, 1996
William Purcell, *Martyrs of Our Time*, 1985
Nina Shea, *In the Lion's Den: Persecuted Christians and What the Western Church Can Do about It*, 1997

393

PETER MARSHALL

Mr. Jones, Meet the Master: Sermons and Prayers
(New York: F.H. Revell, 1949)

Category: Sermons; Prayer
Subject(s): Christianity; Presbyterians
Age range(s): Adult

Summary: This volume of Peter Marshall's works was edited by his widow, Catherine Marshall, after his death. *Mr. Jones, Meet the Master* is a collection of sermons and prayers that reflect the personality and mission of the chaplain and pastor memorialized in the book (and later movie), *A Man Called Peter*.

Other books by the same author:
His Hand on Your Shoulder, 1990
John Doe, Disciple: Sermons for the Young in Spirit, 1963
The First Easter, 1959
The Prayers of Peter Marshall, 1954
Let's Keep Christmas, 1953

Other books you might like:
David Frost, *Billy Graham: Personal Thoughts of a Public Man*, 1997
Eugene L. Lowry, *How to Preach a Parable: Designs for Narrative Sermons*, 1989
Catherine Marshall, *A Man Called Peter: The Story of Peter Marshall*, 1951
George H. Morrison, *The Wings of the Morning: Addresses From a Glasgow Pulpit*, 1994

394

RALPH P. MARTIN, Editor
PETER H. DAVIDS, Co-Editor

Dictionary of the Later New Testament and Its Developments

(Downers Grove, Illinois: InterVarsity Press, 1997)

Category: Religious Encyclopedias/Dictionaries
Subject(s): Bible; History; Culture
Age range(s): Young Adult-Adult

Summary: The *Dictionary of the Later New Testament and Its Developments* is the third such New Testament reference source from InterVarsity Press, following *Dictionary of Paul and His Letters* and *Dictionary of Jesus and the Gospels*. This volume covers the books of Acts, Hebrews, and the Revelation, as well as the letters of Peter, James, Jude, and John.

Awards the book has won:
Gold Medallion Book Award, Reference Works/Commentaries, 1998

Other books by the same author:
The Worship of God: Some Theological, Pastoral, and Practical Reflections, 1982
Reconciliation: A Study of Paul's Theology, 1981
The Family and the Fellowship: New Testament Images of the Church, 1979
Worship in the Early Church, 1964

Other books you might like:
Joel B. Green, *Dictionary of Jesus and the Gospels*, 1992
Gerald F. Hawthorne, *Dictionary of Paul and His Letters*, 1993
    Ralph P. Martin, co-editor
Arthur G. Patzia, *The Making of the New Testament: Origin, Collection, Text and Canon*, 1995
Leland Ryken, *Dictionary of Biblical Imagery*, 1998

395

WILLIAM MARTIN

A Prophet with Honor: The Billy Graham Story

(New York: W. Morrow and Co., 1991)

Category: Biography
Subject(s): Christianity; Ministry; Evangelism
Age range(s): Young Adult-Adult
Time period(s): 20th century

Summary: *A Prophet with Honor* offers an even-handed portrayal of Billy Graham, the most influential evangelist during the latter half of the 20th century. The man who started out selling Fuller Brushes in North and South Carolina has preached the gospel of Christian salvation to more people worldwide than any other evangelist. Biographer William Martin examines the Billy Graham Evangelical Association, headed by Graham, and documents its marketing and ministry efforts, but his primary focus is on Graham himself, "..ulcers.tumors.high blood pressure.spider bites," broken ribs, and all.

Other books by the same author:
Sociological Concepts, 1979
Christians in Conflict, 1972

Other books you might like:
Billy Graham, *Just as I Am: The Autobiography of Billy Graham*, 1997
John Pollock, *To All the Nations: The Billy Graham Story*, 1985
Jay Walker, *Billy Graham: A Life in Word and Deed*, 1998
Sherwood Eliot Wirt, *Billy: A Personal Look at Billy Graham, the World's Best-Loved Evangelist*, 1997

396

MARTIN E. MARTY

Modern American Religion

(Chicago: University of Chicago Press, 1986-1996)

Category: History
Subject(s): Religion; Culture; American History
Age range(s): Adult
Time period(s): 20th century
Locale(s): United States

Summary: A distinguished religion professor and ordained Lutheran minister, Martin E. Marty is considered one of the foremost authorities on the 20th century culture and context of religion in America. *Modern American Religion* is an exhaustive multi-volume series covering the history, influence, and eras of religious belief and practice in the United States. Three volumes have been released since 1986; the series is projected to include five volumes covering the entire 20th century. Volume I, "The Irony of it All," covers 1893 to 1919. "The Noise of Conflict," Volume II, covers the end of World War I through 1941. Volume III, "Under God, Indivisible," focuses on 1941 through 1960.

Other books by the same author:

The One and the Many: America's Struggle for the Common Good, 1997

A Short History of American Catholicism, 1995

Religion and Republic: The American Circumstance, 1987

Pilgrims in Their Own Land: 500 Years of Religion in America, 1984

Other books you might like:

Paul E. Johnson, *African-American Christianity: Essays in History*, 1994

Mark A. Noll, *A History of Christianity in the United States and Canada*, 1992

Peter W. Williams, *America's Religions: Traditions and Cultures*, 1998

James P. Wind, *American Congregations*, 1995

Robert Wuthnow, *The Restructuring of American Religion*, 1988

397

MARTIN E. MARTY

Pilgrims in Their Own Land: 500 Years of Religion in America

(Boston: Little, Brown, 1984)

Category: History
Subject(s): Christianity; Judaism; American History
Age range(s): Adult

Summary: Marty, considered by many to be the dean of American church historians, provides a comprehensive, single-volume history of American religion. First, he examines the social and political forces that contributed to the development of religion in the American colonies. Second, he explores the ways that individual religious groups like the Quakers and the Catholics developed from the colonial period to the 20th century. Third, he discusses significant religious personalities, including William Bradford, the first governor of the colony at Plymouth, Massachusetts, and Dr. Martin Luther King, Jr., civil rights activist and preacher. Finally, Marty presents this material in a manner that is accessible and engaging to readers without any background in church history.

Awards the book has won:

Christopher Award, Books for Adults, 1985

Other books by the same author:

Modern American Religion, 1986-1996

Other books you might like:

Sydney Ahlstrom, *A Religious History of the American People*, 1972

Jon Butler, *Awash in a Sea of Faith: Christianizing the American People*, 1990

Edwin S. Gaustad, *A Religious History of America*, 1990

Winthrop S. Hudson, *Religion in America: An Historical Account of the Development of American Religious Life*, 1998

Robert Wuthnow, *After Heaven: Spirituality in America Since the 1950s*, 1998

398

JUAN MASCARO, Editor

The Upanishads

(Baltimore: Penguin Books, 1965)

Category: Scripture
Subject(s): Hinduism; Philosophy; Meditation
Age range(s): Adult

Summary: *The Upanishads* are mystical prose and poetic writings that provide part of the foundation of Hindu philosophy. Between 100 and 150 Upanishads exist, and they date back to between 1500 and 200 B.C. The main theme of the Upanishads is the nature of the universal soul, Brahman, and the primary doctrine that has to do with the identity of each person's individual soul with that of Brahman. The Upanishads also cover topics including nature, purpose of existence, meditation and worship, and the destiny of souls. This 1965 edition, translated by Juan Mascaro, has become an English-language classic.

Other books you might like:

Eknath Easwaran, *Classics of Indian Spirituality Series: The Bhagavad Gita, The Dhammapada, and the Upanishads*, 1989

Wendy Doniger O'Flaherty, *Hindu Myths: A Sourcebook*, 1975

Geoffrey Parrinder, *Upanishads, Gita, and Bible: A Comparative Study of Hindu and Christian Scriptures*, 1963

399

FREDERICA MATHEWES-GREEN

Facing East: A Pilgrim's Journey into the Mysteries of Orthodoxy

(San Francisco: HarperSanFrancisco, 1997)

Category: Journals/Letters
Subject(s): Pilgrims and Pilgrimages; Christianity; Eastern Orthodoxy
Age range(s): Adult
Time period(s): 20th century
Locale(s): Maryland

Summary: When her Episcopal priest husband became disillusioned with the Western church and found his way into the Eastern Orthodox Church, radio commentator and newspaper columnist Frederica Mathewes-Green went along for the journey, and then chose for herself the ancient liturgical religious tradition. In *Facing East*, Mathewes-Green employs a journal format to take readers through a year in the life of her family and its connections within an Eastern Orthodox congregation. The journal is both an insightful, personal revelation and an accessible, fresh look at the world of Christian Orthodoxy, which is enjoying unprecedented growth in North America as the 20th century draws to a close.

Other books by the same author:

At the Corner of East and Now: A Modern Life in Ancient Christian Orthodoxy, 1999

Real Choices: Offering Practical Life-Affirming Alternatives to Abortion, 1994

Other books you might like:

Daniel B. Clendenin, *Eastern Orthodox Theology: A Contemporary Reader*, 1995

Peter E. Gillquist, *Becoming Orthodox: A Journey to the Ancient Christian Faith*, 1989

Peter E. Gillquist, *Coming Home: Why Protestant Clergy Are Becoming Orthodox*, 1992

Virginia Nieuwsma, *Our Hearts' True Home: Fourteen Warm, Inspiring Stories of Women Discovering the Ancient Christian Faith*, 1996

400

PETER MATTHIESSEN

Nine-Headed Dragon River: Zen Journals, 1969-1985

(Boston: Shambhala, 1985)

Category: Journals/Letters
Subject(s): Travel; Spirituality; Buddhism
Age range(s): Adult
Time period(s): 20th century (1969-1985)

Summary: Novelist Peter Matthiessen shares his experience with the practice of Zen in its Western form in *Nine-Headed Dragon River*, which features his journal writings from 1969 to 1982. The journals describe his spiritual quest for meaning in life and his deep connection with the natural world.

Other books by the same author:

African Silences, 1991
Indian Country, 1984
The Snow Leopard, 1978
The Cloud Forest: A Chronicle of the South American Wilderness, 1961

Other books you might like:

Dogen, *Moon in a Dewdrop: Writings of Zen Master Dogen*, 1985
    Kazuaki Tanahashi, editor; Robert Aitken, translator
Dainin Katagiri, *Returning to Silence: Zen Practice in Daily Life*, 1988
Stephanie Kaza, *The Attentive Heart: Conversations with Trees*, 1993

401

RICHARD P. MCBRIEN

Catholicism

(Minneapolis, Minnesota: Winston Press, 1980)

Category: History; Theology
Subject(s): Catholicism; Christianity; Religious Traditions
Age range(s): Adult

Summary: McBrien's book offers a classic study of Catholicism. The author combines solid historical analysis with elegant and engaging prose as he traces the development of Catholicism from its roots in the earliest Christian communities. He also provides a panoramic look at the personalities, politics and practices of the Catholic Church.

Other books by the same author:

Lives of the Popes: The Pontiffs From St. Peter to John Paul II, 1997
The HarperCollins Encyclopedia of Catholicism, 1995

Other books you might like:

Greg Dues, *Catholic Customs and Traditions: A Popular Guide*, 1992
Mitch Finley, *The Seeker's Guide to Being Catholic*, 1997
Charles R. Morris, *American Catholic: The Saints and Sinners Who Built America's Most Powerful Church*, 1997
John O'Connor, *The Essential Catholic Handbook: A Summary of Beliefs, Practices, and Prayers*, 1997
Kenneth L. Woodward, *Making Saints: How the Catholic Church Determines Who Becomes a Saint, Who Doesn't, and Why*, 1990

402

DAVID MCCASLAND

Oswald Chambers: Abandoned to God

(Grand Rapids, Michigan: Discovery House, 1993)

Category: Biography
Subject(s): Christianity; Evangelism
Age range(s): Adult
Time period(s): 19th century; 20th century (1874-1917)

Summary: Oswald Chambers (1874-1917), whose *My Utmost for His Highest* has become a classic of Christian literature, didn't live to see this famous work in print. After his death at the age of 42, his wife, Gertrude, transcribed the shorthand notes she had made of all his talks and lectures as a chaplain and a Bible College teacher, and she began compiling them into more than thirty different books. In *Oswald Chambers: Abandoned to God*, David McCasland illuminates the life of this Scotsman whose ministry took him all over the world, and whose bestselling devotional book has been in print continuously since its posthumous publication in 1935.

Awards the book has won:

Gold Medallion Book Award, Biography/Autobiography, 1994

Other books by the same author:

Pinstripe Parables: Searching Stories about Things That Matter Most to a Man, 1995
Free to Choose, 1983
Open to Change, 1981

Other books you might like:

Oswald Chambers, *The Best From All His Books*, 1987
David Lambert, *Oswald Chambers*, 1997
William Martin, *A Prophet with Honor: The Billy Graham Story*, 1991
Rolland Hein, *Harmony Within: The Spiritual Vision of George MacDonald*, 1989

403

COLLEEN MCDANNELL
BERNHARD LANG, Co-Author

Heaven: A History

(New Haven: Yale University Press, 1988)

Category: Theology
Subject(s): Heaven; Scripture; Religion
Age range(s): Adult

Summary: Colleen McDannell presents a comprehensive view of heaven as seen through biblical sources and the teachings of religious thinkers throughout time. McDannell identifies a variety of religious messages about heaven, and discusses the ways in which art, history, literature, and a wide range of religious traditions have all influenced popular Western interpretations of heaven, inside the church and beyond.

Other books by the same author:
Material Christianity: Religion and Popular Culture in America, 1995
The Christian Home in Victorian America, 1840-1900, 1986

Other books you might like:
Timothy Freke, *Heaven: An Illustrated History of the Higher Realms*, 1996
Jeffrey Burton Russell, *A History of Heaven: The Singing Silence*, 1997
J. Edward Wright, *The Early History of Heaven*, 1999

404

JOSH MCDOWELL

Evidence That Demands a Verdict: Historical Evidences for the Christian Faith

(Nashville: T. Nelson, 1993)

Category: Theology
Subject(s): Apologetics; Christianity; Scripture
Age range(s): Adult

Summary: Josh McDowell's *Evidence That Demands a Verdict* offers a detailed defense of the Christian faith in the form of answers to the most-often asked questions about the validity of Christianity. Written in an outline format with references to many sources, biblical and other, the book contains carefully constructed arguments in support of Christianity. *Evidence That Demands a Verdict* has been expanded, revised, and in print continuously since the publication of its first edition in 1979.

Other books by the same author:
Right From Wrong, 1994
He Walked Among Us, 1988 (Bill Wilson, co-author)
The Secret of Loving, 1987
Answers to Tough Questions Skeptics Ask about the Christian Faith, 1980
Daniel in the Critics' Den: Historical Evidence for the Authenticity of the Book of Daniel, 1979

Other books you might like:
Ronald B. Mayers, *Balanced Apologetics: Using Evidences and Presuppositions in Defense of the Faith*, 1996
Francis A. Schaeffer, *The God Who Is There: Speaking Historic Christianity into the Twentieth Century*, 1968
Lee Strobel, *The Case for Christ: A Journalist's Personal Investigation of the Evidence for Jesus*, 1998

405

BERNARD MCGINN

Antichrist: Two Thousand Years of the Human Fascination with Evil

(San Francisco: HarperSanFrancisco, 1994)

Category: Theology
Subject(s): Good and Evil; Judaism; Christianity
Age range(s): Adult

Summary: Bernard McGinn traces the various ways that the Judeo-Christian concept of the Antichrist has been interpreted in teaching, theology, and religious practice. One of McGinn's conclusions is that the way people interpret the existence of the Antichrist-whether it is seen as an external entity, such as a political leader, or it is seen as a manifestation of inner evil-is reflected in how they perceive themselves and evil in the world around them. McGinn notes that there are American religious and social groups suspicious of things such as credit card systems and the United Nations because their interpretation of the rise of the Antichrist sees signs and portents in the political and economic changes of the last decades of the 20th century.

Other books by the same author:
The Doctors of the Church: Thirty-Three Men and Women Who Shaped Christianity, 1999
Apocalypticism in the Western Tradition, 1994
The Foundations of Mysticism, 1991
Christian Spirituality: Origins to the Twelfth Century, 1985
Visions of the End: Apocalyptic Traditions in the Middle Ages, 1979

Other books you might like:
Richard Kenneth Emmerson, *Antichrist in the Middle Ages*, 1981
Robert C. Fuller, *Naming the Antichrist: The History of an American Obsession*, 1995
John Edward Christopher Hill, *Antichrist in Seventeenth-Century England*, 1971
Gregory C. Jenks, *The Origins and Early Development of the Antichrist Myth*, 1990

406

JAMES MCGINNIS
KATHLEEN MCGINNIS, Co-Author

Parenting for Peace and Justice

(Maryknoll, New York: Orbis Books, 1981)

Category: Self-Help
Subject(s): Ethics; Parent and Child; Spirituality
Age range(s): Adult

Summary: In *Parenting for Peace and Justice*, Kathleen and James McGinnis note that child-raising takes place in a social or societal context, rather than just within individual households. With this in mind, the authors discuss what it means to promote peace and justice through family life, and they outline a wide variety of ways to bring up children who care for each other and the world, rather than focus exclusively on their personal needs and wants. The insights and experiences of a dozen culturally diverse families are incorporated in narratives throughout the book. Topics covered include stewardship of time and resources, simplicity of lifestyle, nonviolence in the home, overcoming sex-role and racial stereotyping, engaging in social action as a family, and integrating prayer and action in the process of parenting for peace and justice.

Other books by the same author:
Helping Teens Care, 1991
Parenting for Peace and Justice: Ten Years Later, 1990 (Kathleen McGinnis, co-author)
Journey into Compassion: A Spirituality for the Long Haul, 1989
Partners in Peacemaking: Family Workshop Models Guidebook for Leaders, 1984
Education for Peace and Justice, 1981 (Kathleen McGinnis, co-author)

Other books you might like:
Doris Janzen Longacre, *Living More with Less*, 1980
Dorothy Law Nolte, *Children Learn What They Live: Parenting to Inspire Values*, 1998
Fred Rogers, *Mister Rogers Talks with Parents*, 1983
David Veerman, *103 Questions Children Ask about Right From Wrong*, 1995

407

JOHN MCMANNERS, Editor

The Oxford Illustrated History of Christianity

(New York: Oxford University Press, 1990)

Category: History
Subject(s): Christianity; Culture; Politics
Age range(s): Adult

Summary: Spanning 2,000 years of history, culture, religion, and politics, *The Oxford Illustrated History of Christianity* is one of the most complete single volume publications ever intended to capture the development and impact of Christianity for a general audience. Nineteen scholars contribute their knowledge and expertise in essays and articles that illuminate the origins, variations, and cultural influence of Christianity worldwide. The book features more than 350 graphic elements, including full-color photographs, line drawings, and other artwork. Maps, a chronology of events during the history of Christianity, and an annotated further reference guide are also included.

Other books by the same author:
Church and Society in Eighteenth-Century France, 1998
Abbes and Actresses: The Church and the Theatrical Profession in Eighteenth-Century France, 1986

Death and the Enlightenment: Changing Attitudes to Death Among Christians and Unbelievers in Eighteenth-Century France, 1981
Church and State in France, 1870-1914, 1972
The French Revolution and the Church, 1969

Other books you might like:
Kenneth Cain Kinghorn, *The Illustrated Book of Christian Literature: The First Two Millennia*, 1998
Alister McGrath, *The Blackwell Encyclopedia of Modern Christian Thought*, 1993
Daniel G. Reid, *Dictionary of Christianity in America*, 1990

408

FRANK S. MEAD

Handbook of Denominations in the United States

(Nashville: Abingdon, 1995)

Category: Religious Encyclopedias/Dictionaries
Subject(s): Christianity; Religion; Directories
Age range(s): Adult

Summary: This 10th edition of Frank Spencer Mead's *Handbook of Denominations in the United States* provides information on more than two hundred American religious groups. Descriptions of each denomination and its subdivisions cover topics including denominational history, doctrine and practices, and organizational governance and structure. Membership statistics and information about schools, churches, and affiliated institutions are also provided.

Other books by the same author:
Talking with God: Prayers for Today, 1976
The Encyclopedia of Religious Quotations, 1965
What the Bible Says, 1958
Who's Who in the Bible: 250 Bible Biographies, 1938
Ten Decisive Battles of Christianity, 1937

Other books you might like:
Eileen W. Lindner, *Yearbook of American and Canadian Chuches*, 1999
Leo Calvin Rosten, *Religions of America: Ferment and Faith in an Age of Crisis*, 1975
Shelly Steig, *Finding the Right Church: A Guide to Denominational Beliefs*, 1997

409

MICHAEL MEDVED

Hollywood Vs. America: Popular Culture and the War on Traditional Values

(New York: HarperCollins, 1992)

Category: Essays
Subject(s): Movie Industry; Television; Ethics
Age range(s): Young Adult-Adult

Summary: Michael Medved's *Hollywood Vs. America* is a traditional values-based critique of the entertainment industry. Medved takes issue with the violence, sex, and profanity so prevalent in the films and television programming of the late 20th century, and with what he terms the industry's "assault" on the values of family, marriage, and religion. *Hollywood Vs. America* has served as a lightning rod for opposing responses: Religious and politically conservative groups find support for their concerns in Medved's work, while representatives of the movie and television industry point to his comments as a warning shot against first amendment rights and creative freedom. Medved bases his assessment on studies, interviews with industry leaders, and his long professional association with the entertainment industry as a popular movie critic.

Awards the book has won:

Gold Medallion Book Award, Christianity and Society, 1993

Other books by the same author:

Saving Childhood: Protecting Our Children From the National Assault on Innocence, 1998 (Diane Medved, co-author)

Hospital, the Hidden Lives of a Medical Center Staff, 1982

The Shadow Presidents: The Secret History of the Chief Executives and Their Top Aides, 1979

What Really Happened to the Class of '65, 1976 (David Wallechinsky, co-author)

Other books you might like:

Daniel Lapin, *America's Real War*, 1999

Dana Mack, *The Assault on Parenthood: How Our Culture Undermines the Family*, 1997

Newton N. Minow, *Abandoned in the Wasteland: Children, Television, and the First Amendment*, 1995

410

JOHN P. MEIER

A Marginal Jew: Rethinking the Historical Jesus

(New York: Doubleday, 1991-1994)

Category: History
Subject(s): Religion; Scripture; Miracles
Age range(s): Adult

Summary: In a two-volume effort, John P. Meier attempts to create a new picture of Jesus of Nazareth, as if, in his words, ".a Catholic, a Protestant, a Jew, and an agnostic.hammered out a consensus document" about the historical reality of Jesus. In trying to undertake such a task, Meier relies on meticulous examination of all the documents, scriptural and other, in order to reveal information about Jesus not rooted in the basic tenets of any religious tradition. He notes that the very marginality of Jesus in written accounts from his own time period-not including the gospel writings of the New Testament-is an ironic counterpoint to the centrality he has achieved in Western society in the nearly 2,000 years since his death. The first volume focuses on the origins of Jesus and the processes used to study the historical aspects of his life. The second volume focuses on the adult life of Jesus: the years during which he performed miracles and spoke the words that have become his legacy.

Other books by the same author:

The Mission of Christ and His Church: Studies on Christology and Ecclesiology, 1990

The Gospel According to Matthew, 1983

The Vision of Matthew: Christ, Church, and Morality in the First Gospel, 1979

Law and History in Matthew's Gospel: A Redactional Study of Mt. 5:17-48, 1976

Other books you might like:

Philip J. Cunningham, *A Believer's Search for the Jesus of History*, 1999

Scott McCormick Jr., *Behold the Man: Re-Reading the Gospels, Re-Humanizing Jesus*,

E.P. Sanders, *Jesus and Judaism*, 1985

411

J. GORDON MELTON

Encyclopedic Handbook of Cults in America

(New York: Garland, 1992)

Category: Religious Encyclopedias/Dictionaries
Subject(s): Cults; Religion; Culture
Age range(s): Young Adult-Adult
Locale(s): United States

Summary: The *Encyclopedic Handbook of Cults in America* was first published in 1984 but has been updated to reflect widespread changes following the initial edition. The reference volume provides comprehensive, balanced information on more than 500 non-conventional religious groups and belief systems, including Neo-Paganism, Scientology, Hare Krishna, Vajradhatu, and the Identity Movement. Coverage includes the origin and development of each group, along with its founders, leaders, beliefs, doctrines, literature, and practices.

Other books by the same author:

Vampire Book: The Encyclopedia of the Undead, 1999

New Age Almanac, 1991

Biographical Dictionary of American Cult and Sect Leaders, 1986

Encyclopedia of American Religions, 1996

The Cult Experience: Responding to the New Religious Pluralism, 1982 (Robert L. Moore, co-author)

Other books you might like:

James R. Lewis, *Cults in America: A Reference Handbook*, 1998

James R. Lewis, *The Encyclopedia of Cults, Sects, and New Religions*, 1998

George A. Mather, *Dictionary of Cults, Sects, Religions, and the Occult*, 1993

Timothy Miller, *America's Alternative Religions*, 1995

412

J. GORDON MELTON
JEROME CLARK, Co-Author
AIDAN A. KELLY, Co-Author

New Age Almanac

(Detroit: Visible Ink, 1991)

Category: New Age (Nonfiction); Religious Encyclopedias/
Dictionaries
Subject(s): Religion; Customs; Culture
Age range(s): Young Adult-Adult

Summary: The authors provide balanced, comprehensive
overviews of New Age philosophies, practices, organizations,
and leaders. A chronology of the development of New Age
thought is a valuable feature, as are the resource lists leading
readers to publications and institutions devoted to New Age
thought.

Other books by the same author:
Encyclopedia of American Religions, 1996 (fifth edition)
Encyclopedia of Occultism & Parapsychology, 1996 (fouth
edition)
*Magic, Witchcraft, and Paganism in America: A Bibliogra-
phy*, 1992 (Isotta Poggi, co-author)
Perspectives on the New Age, 1992 (James R. Lewis, co-
editor)

Other books you might like:
Eileen Campbell, *Body, Mind & Spirit: A Dictionary of New
Age Ideas, People, Places, and Terms*, 1994
J.H. Brennan, co-author
Alex Jack, *The New Age Dictionary*, 1990
Timothy Miller, *America's Alternative Religions*, 1995

413

J. GORDON MELTON

Religious Bodies in the United States: A Directory

(New York: Garland, 1992)

Category: Religious Encyclopedias/Dictionaries
Subject(s): Directories; Religious Life
Age range(s): Adult
Locale(s): United States

Summary: This volume provides a comprehensive alphabetical directory of religious organizations operating in the
United States. Available information includes names, addresses, phone numbers, and descriptions of each organization. The entries are arranged in three sections: interfaith and
ecumenical entities, denominations, and publications.

Other books by the same author:
Encyclopedia of American Religions, 1996
*National Directory of Churches, Synagogues, and Other
Houses of Worship*, 1994
Encyclopedia of African American Religions, 1993
Religious Information Sources: A Worldwide Guide, 1992

Other books you might like:
American Baptist Churches in the U.S.A., *Directory of the
American Baptist Churches in the United States of Amer-
ica*, 1994
Anonymous, *The Official Catholic Directory: Anno Domini
1999*, 1999
James V. Geisendorfer, *Religion in America: A Directory*,
1983
Peter Lorie, *The Buddhist Directory: United States of Amer-
ica & Canada*, 1997
Julie Foakes, co-editor
Wardell J. Payne, *Directory of African American Religious
Bodies: A Compendium by the Howard University School
of Divinity*, 1995

414

THOMAS MERTON

Conjectures of a Guilty Bystander

(Garden City, New York: Doubleday, 1966)

Category: Journals/Letters
Subject(s): Essays; Ethics; Religion
Age range(s): Adult
Locale(s): United States

Summary: Thomas Merton is one of the most widely read
spiritual writers of the 20th century, in part because of publications such as *Conjectures of a Guilty Bystander*, a journal of
writings dating back to 1956 and first published a decade
later. In these essays, notes, and reflective thoughts, Merton
considers modern problems such as racial unrest and inequal-
ity, changes in social values, political dilemmas, and the lack
of God-awareness in the world. Although the notes in this
journal were recorded during the mid-century years, the insights are timeless and the topics and concerns addressed by
Merton in the 1950s and 1960s seem remarkably-and perhaps
regrettably-familiar at the end of the century.

Other books by the same author:
Seasons of Celebration, 1965
New Seeds of Contemplation, 1962
Thoughts in Solitude, 1958
The Seven Storey Mountain, 1948

Other books you might like:
Esther De Waal, *Living with Contradiction: An Introduction
to Benedictine Spirituality*, 1997
Thomas Keating, *Finding Grace at the Center*, 1978
Bernard McGinn, *The Growth of Mysticism*, 1994

415

THOMAS MERTON

New Seeds of Contemplation

(Norfolk, Connecticut: New Directions, 1961)

Category: Essays
Subject(s): Meditation; Mysticism
Age range(s): Adult

Summary: Thomas Merton was an American Trappist monk,
writer, and poet who possessed a unique ability to share with

Western audiences the relatively unfamiliar practices of contemplation, meditation, and other aspects of Christian mysticism. *New Seeds of Contemplation* is a collection of thoughts about what it is to be contemplative and meditative in one's spiritual life.

Other books by the same author:
Mystics and Zen Masters, 1967
Seasons of Celebration, 1965
The Silent Life, 1957

Other books you might like:
Esther De Waal, *A Seven Day Journey with Thomas Merton*, 1993
Tilden Edwards, *Living Simply through the Day: Spiritual Survival in a Complex Age*, 1998
Brother Lawrence, *Writings and Conversations on the Practice of the Presence of God*, 1994
    Conrad De Meester, co-author

416

THOMAS MERTON

The Seven Storey Mountain
(New York: Farrar, Straus and Giroux, 1948)

Category: Autobiography
Subject(s): Monasticism; Christianity
Age range(s): Young Adult-Adult

Summary: Merton's beautifully written book gives the account of his transformation from a lover of the world's pleasures to a deeply committed monk obedient to his vows of silence and poverty. Merton's bright intelligence shines through on every page, and his descriptions of the search to hold head and heart together remains one of the finest religious autobiographies of the modern age.

Other books by the same author:
Zen and the Birds of Appetite, 1968
Conjectures of a Guilty Bystander, 1966
New Seeds of Contemplation, 1962

Other books you might like:
Augustine, *Confessions*, c. 400
John Howard Griffin, *The Hermitage Journals: A Diary Kept While Working on the Biography of Thomas Merton*, 1981
Kathleen Norris, *The Cloister Walk*, 1996
Henri J.M. Nouwen, *The Return of a Prodigal Son: A Story of Homecoming*, 1993
William H. Shannon, *Silent Lamp: The Thomas Merton Story*, 1992

417

THOMAS MERTON

Zen and the Birds of Appetite
(New York: New Directions, 1968)

Category: Essays
Subject(s): Buddhism; Meditation; Mysticism
Age range(s): Adult

Summary: Thomas Merton recorded clear, compelling thoughts on the nature of Zen and the relationships that could be developed between Western religion and Eastern philosophy in *Zen and the Birds of Appetite*. This is considered one of his most accessible collections of thoughts on Zen for Western audiences.

Other books by the same author:
Mystics and Zen Masters, 1967
Thoughts in Solitude, 1958
The Silent Life, 1957

Other books you might like:
Christmas Humphreys, *Zen Comes West: The Present and Future of Zen Buddhism in Western Society*, 1977
Philip Kapleau, *Zen: Dawn in the West*, 1979
D.T. Suzuki, *Essays in Zen Buddhism, First Series*, 1927
Alan Watts, *Uncarved Block, Unbleached Silk: The Mystery of Life*, 1978

418

JACK MILES

God: A Biography
(New York: Knopf, 1995)

Category: Biography; History
Subject(s): Literature; Bible; God
Age range(s): Adult

Summary: In this irreverent yet compelling book, Pulitzer Prize-winning journalist Miles sets out to tell the life story of God. His primary source of information about God's life is found in the record of events in the *Bible* in which God was involved. Miles contends that God is simply a character in the *Bible*, and he begins his investigation of God in that way. Using literary analysis, he shows how God develops as a character in the many narratives in the *Bible*. Thus, readers see God variously as a nurturing figure and as a condemning, authoritarian figure. Miles' fun-to-read book challenges conventional portraits of God.

Awards the book has won:
Pulitzer Prize, Biography or Autobiography, 1996

Other books you might like:
Karen Armstrong, *A History of God: The 4000-Year Quest of Judaism, Christianity, and Islam*, 1993
John Dominic Crossan, *Jesus: A Revolutionary Biography*, 1994
C. Michael Curtis, *God: Stories*, 1998
Richard Elliott Friedman, *The Disappearance of God: A Divine Mystery*, 1995
Elaine Pagels, *The Origin of Satan*, 1995

419

KEITH MILLER

The Taste of New Wine
(Waco, Texas: Word, 1965)

Category: Self-Help
Subject(s): Christianity; Spirituality
Age range(s): Adult

Summary: *The Taste of New Wine* is Keith Miller's invitation to Christians to break out of self-centered patterns of indifference and see what Christian living can and should be all about. Miller's message that renewal and adventure can take the place of routine is presented without a lot of ''church'' talk, and it was quite revolutionary in evangelical Christian literature when it was first published in the mid-1960s. *The Taste of New Wine* has become a classic title used by individuals and church groups seeking spiritual growth and renewal through Bible study.

Other books by the same author:
The Secret Life of the Soul, 1997
Hope in the Fast Lane: A New Look at Faith in a Compulsive World, 1990
The Passionate People: Carriers of the Spirit, 1979
Living the Adventure: Faith and ''Hidden'' Difficulties, 1975
The Edge of Adventure: An Experiment in Faith, 1974 (Bruce Larson, co-author)

Other books you might like:
Dietrich Bonhoeffer, *The Cost of Discipleship*, 1948
Bill Hybels, *Honest to God?: Becoming an Authentic Christian*, 1990
Henry Morgan, *Approaches to Prayer: A Resource Book for Groups and Individuals*, 1993
Charles R. Swindoll, *The Grace Awakening*, 1990

420

DAN MILLMAN

The Life You Were Born to Live: A Guide to Finding Your Life Purpose

(Tiburon, California: H.J. Kramer, 1993)

Category: Self-Help
Subject(s): Success; Self-Acceptance; Spirituality
Age range(s): Adult

Summary: *The Life You Were Born to Live* offers an introduction to the author's ''Life Purpose'' system, a method of self-discovery based on ancient wisdom. The author describes what he calls the thirty-seven ''paths of life,'' and provides techniques for readers to identify which of these paths are theirs. He also presents background information on the relationship between the paths of life and certain core talents and personality aspects, and explains how readers should use this information to improve their interpersonal relationships and career development. Throughout the book, Millman focuses on the necessity of discovering one's life purpose as a prelude to spiritual awareness and growth.

Other books by the same author:
Divine Interventions: True Stories of Mystery and Miracles That Change Lives, 1999 (Doug Childers, co-author)
Everyday Enlightenment: The Twelve Gateways to Personal Growth, 1998
The Laws of Spirit: Simple, Powerful Truths for Making Life Work, 1995
No Ordinary Moments: A Peaceful Warrior's Guide to Daily Life, 1992
Way of the Peaceful Warrior: A Basically True Story, 1980

Other books you might like:
Deepak Chopra, *The Seven Spiritual Laws of Success: A Practical Guide to the Fulfillment of Your Dreams*, 1994
Barbara De Angelis, *Real Moments*, 1994
Joel S. Goldsmith, *Practicing the Presence: The Inspirational Guide to Regaining Meaning and a Sense of Purpose in Your Life*, 1991

421

JOHN MILTON

Paradise Lost

(1667)

Category: Poetry
Subject(s): Christianity; Bible
Age range(s): Young Adult-Adult

Summary: Milton's epic poem is a retelling of the stories of Adam and Eve in Genesis 2-4. Milton's imaginative epic opens with Satan and other rebellious angels discussing whether they will try to regain their place in heaven, after having been kicked out for attempting to take God's place. They decide not to challenge God directly. When Satan learns that God is creating a new world, he decides that the best way to avenge himself is to corrupt this new world. He enters the new world and sneaks into the Garden of Eden where both Adam and Eve reside. He then disguises himself as one of their fellow creatures, a serpent, and has a long conversation with Eve, eventually encouraging her to disobey God. God punishes Adam, Eve, and Satan for their crimes. Milton's poem is responsible for the Christian association of Satan with the serpent in Genesis 3, and he also introduces the idea of Satan as a fallen angel.

Other books by the same author:
Samson Agonistes, 1671
Areopagitica, 1644

Other books you might like:
Dante Alighieri, *The Divine Comedy*, c. 1310
Geoffrey Chaucer, *The Canterbury Tales*, c. 1386
John Donne, *Poetical Works*, 1912
A selection of works by John Donne (1572-1631)
C.S. Lewis, *The Screwtape Letters*, 1944
Francis Thompson, *The Hound of Heaven*, 1890

422

STEPHEN MITCHELL

The Gospel According to Jesus: A New Translation and Guide to His Essential Teachings for Believers and Unbelievers

(New York: HarperCollins, 1991)

Category: Religious Commentaries
Subject(s): Scripture; Buddhism; Bible
Age range(s): Adult

Summary: *The Gospel According to Jesus* is a three-part study of the gospel teachings of the New Testament that consists of Mitchell's introduction to the work, Mitchell's rewriting of the gospel account of Jesus, and Mitchell's commentary on this rewritten gospel. The Jesus of Mitchell's interpretation is human, rather than divine, and his essential teachings reflect those of the Eastern traditions of Hinduism and Buddhism. Mitchell challenges and dismisses the doctrinal leanings of the writers of the New Testament. He explains that his interpretation of the person and message of Christ is more accurately based on what Jesus actually did and said than on an institutionalized need to shape the life of Christ to fit a prescribed religious agenda or institutional need for holy writings.

Other books by the same author:
Meetings with the Archangel, 1998
An Enlightened Heart: An Anthology of Sacred Poetry, 1993
The Book of Job, 1992
Parables and Portraits, 1990

Other books you might like:
Thomas Jefferson, *The Jefferson Bible: The Life and Morals of Jesus of Nazareth*, 1989
Reynolds Price, *The Three Gospels*, 1996
Walter Wangerin Jr., *The Book of God: The Bible as a Novel*, 1996

423

RAYMOND A. MOODY JR.
PAUL PERRY, Co-Author

The Light Beyond
(New York: Bantam Books, 1988)

Category: Self-Help
Subject(s): Death; Afterlife
Age range(s): Adult

Summary: Dr. Raymond A. Moody, Jr. intrigued Americans with stories of afterlife experiences in his 1970s bestseller *Life After Life*. In *The Light Beyond*, he presents new material based on the study of more than 1000 people of all ages who have returned from the point of clinical death. He explains some of the ways that medical and psychiatric professionals are working to understand the mystery of what happens to human beings after death, and discusses the directions that future scientific exploration might take. From both a spiritual and a scientific mindset, Moody offers inspiration and comfort to people with questions and fears about death and what is beyond death.

Other books by the same author:
Reunions: Visionary Encounters with Departed Loved Ones, 1993 (Paul Perry, co-author)
Coming Back: A Psychiatrist Explores Past Life Journeys, 1991 (Paul Perry, co-author)
Life Before Life: Regression into Past Lives, 1990 (Paul Perry, co-author)
Reflections on Life After Life, 1977
Life After Life: The Investigation of a Phenomenon-Survival of Bodily Death, 1975

Other books you might like:
P.M.H. Atwater, *Beyond the Light: What Isn't Being Said about Near-Death Experience*, 1997
Mally Cox-Chapman, *The Case for Heaven: Near-Death Experiences as Evidence of the Afterlife*, 1995
Betty J. Eadie, *Embraced by the Light*, 1992
Maurice Rawlings, *Beyond Death's Door*, 1978

424

RAYMOND A. MOODY JR.
PAUL PERRY, Co-Author

Reunions: Visionary Encounters with Departed Loved Ones
(New York: Villard Books, 1993)

Category: Self-Help
Subject(s): Death; Afterlife; Communication
Age range(s): Adult

Summary: Moody's *Life after Life* brought common aspects of near-death experiences to the cultural forefront with images of bright light, the sensation of traveling through a tunnel, and the appearance of deceased relatives and friends. *Reunions* suggests that it is possible to facilitate the last of these phenomena without the physical trauma of the near-death experience. Moody profiles cases in which people who consider themselves non-psychic have used his techniques, explained in the book, to make contact with dead loved ones. The afterlife implications of Moody's work and his use of certain tools and methods have brought him criticism from some secular and religious media commentators.

Other books by the same author:
Coming Back: A Psychiatrist Explores Past Life Journeys, 1991 (Paul Perry, co-author)
Life Before Life: Regression into Past Lives, 1990 (Paul Perry, co-author)
The Light Beyond, 1988
Reflections on Life After Life, 1977
Life After Life: The Investigation of a Phenomenon—Survival of Bodily Death, 1975

Other books you might like:
Bill Guggenheim, *Hello From Heaven!: A New Field of Research Confirms That Life and Love Are Eternal*, 1995
Louis E. Legrand, *After-Death Communication: Final Farewells*, 1997
James Van Praagh, *Talking to Heaven: A Medium's Message of Life After Death*, 1997

425

DINTY W. MOORE

The Accidental Buddhist: Mindfulness, Enlightenment, and Sitting Still
(Chapel Hill: Algonquin Books, 1997)

Category: Autobiography
Subject(s): Buddhism; Travel; Spirituality
Age range(s): Adult

Summary: Dinty W. Moore wants to know why Buddhism's popularity has increased dramatically in the United States at the end of the 20th century, so he sets out on a quest to find out. He visits Eastern spiritual events across the country, talks with people of all walks of life, and seeks out the Dalai Lama for a personal interview. In the course of conducting his research, Moore finds himself drawn to particular practices of Buddhism that help him relax during ''downtime'' and focus on work during other times. As a result, his research becomes a blend of examination and personal experience. In the end, he demonstrates exactly how Buddhist practices have become part of the fabric of America's culture—through the typical American habit of adopting only those religious or spiritual practices of a belief system that meet a particular need.

Other books by the same author:
The Emperor's Virtual Clothes: The Naked Truth about Internet Culture, 1995

Other books you might like:
Stephen Batchelor, *Buddhism Without Beliefs: A Contemporary Guide to Awakening*, 1997
Sylvia Boorstein, *It's Easier than You Think: The Buddhist Way to Happiness*, 1995
Lama Surya Das, *Awakening the Buddha Within: Eight Steps to Enlightenment: Tibetan Wisdom for the Western World*, 1997

426

THOMAS MOORE

Care of the Soul: A Guide for Cultivating Depth and Sacredness in Everyday Life

(New York: HarperCollins, 1992)

Category: Self-Help
Subject(s): Christianity; Mysticism; Spirituality
Age range(s): Adult

Summary: Taking care of the soul and enabling its growth through study and meditation is a key aspect of spiritual life. Too often, former monk Moore says, spiritual seekers don't know how to nurture their souls. Combining the wisdom of the cloistered life with the sagacious teachings of Eastern religions, Moore recommends ways to cultivate depth of soul. Foremost among his suggestions is to incorporate the rituals of prayer and meditation into everyday life.

Other books by the same author:
The Soul of Sex: Cultivating Life as an Act of Love, 1998

Other books you might like:
Wayne W. Dyer, *Real Magic: Creating Miracles in Everyday Life*, 1992
Matthew Fox, *Original Blessing*, 1983
Sam Keen, *To a Dancing God*, 1970
M. Scott Peck, *The Road Less Traveled: A New Psychology of Love, Traditional Values, and Spiritual Growth*, 1978
Robert J. Wicks, *Living a Gentle, Passionate Life*, 1998

427

PATRICK M. MORLEY

The Man in the Mirror: Solving the 24 Problems Men Face

(Brentwood, Tennessee: Wolgemuth & Hyatt, 1989)

Category: Self-Help
Subject(s): Conduct of Life; Christian Life
Age range(s): Adult

Summary: Patrick M. Morley examines the challenges of life for men and offers suggestions for making the most of life. From a Christian perspective, Morley outlines 24 problems faced by men in relationships, money, time management, sense of identity, personality, and commitment to change and growth. Drawing on biblical principles as well as personal experience, Morley provides practical approaches to achieve focus and a sense of purpose in life, offering support for men who want to add a dimension of spirituality to their daily lives.

Awards the book has won:
Gold Medallion Book Award, Christian Living, 1990

Other books by the same author:
Second Wind for the Second Half: Twenty Ideas to Help You Reinvent Yourself for the Rest of the Journey, 1999
The Ten Secrets of a Happy Man, 1999
What Husbands Wish Their Wives Knew about Men, 1998
The Seven Seasons of a Man's Life: Examining the Unique Challenges Men Face, 1995
Getting to Know the Man in the Mirror: An Interactive Guide for Men, 1994

Other books you might like:
Ken R. Canfield, *The Seven Secrets of Effective Fathers*, 1992
Robert C. Crosby, *Living Life From the Soul*, 1997
Frederick G. Grosse, *The Eight Masks of Men*, 1998
Charles R. Swindoll, *Man to Man: Chuck Swindoll Selects His Most Significant Writings for Men*, 1996

428

CHARLES R. MORRIS

American Catholic: The Saints and Sinners Who Built America's Most Powerful Church

(New York: Times Books, 1997)

Category: History
Subject(s): Christianity; Catholicism; History
Age range(s): Adult

Summary: Morris' book traces the development of Catholicism in America. He examines the 19th-century American Catholic Church as an immigrant church that reached its nadir in the 1950s. Morris explores the lives and work of such Catholic personalities as Fulton Sheen and Father Coughlin, the radio personality remembered by many for anti-Semitic remarks broadcast nationwide. Morris contends that following Vatican II (1963), the Church became more fragmented and that the resulting challenges can be addressed only by a revitalized and unified Church.

Other books you might like:

Clyde F. Crews, *American and Catholic: A Popular History of Catholicism in the United States*, 1994

Michael W. Cuneo, *The Smoke of Satan: Conservative and Traditionalist Dissent in Contemporary American Catholicism*, 1997

John Tracy Ellis, *American Catholicism*, 1969

Brian Murphy, *The New Men: Inside the Vatican's Elite School for American Priests*, 1997

Thomas J. Reese, *Inside the Vatican: The Politics and Organization of the Catholic Church*, 1996

429

BILL MOYERS

Genesis: A Living Conversation

(New York: Doubleday, 1996)

Category: Religious Commentaries
Subject(s): Theology; Scripture; Bible
Age range(s): Adult

Summary: *Genesis: A Living Conversation* is the companion book to the PBS series of the same name. Moyers brings together Old Testament scholars and contemporary writers for a lively discussion of the relevance of Genesis to the world today. Among the four dozen contributors are scholars Karen Armstrong and Elaine Pagels and novelists Oscar Hijuelos and Stephen Mitchell. Roundtable conversations take place on topics such as what it means to be "in the image of God," a major theme of Genesis. The text is organized by biblical tale, with a half dozen participants focusing on each, exploring the stories for moral, literary, and personal insight. The volume is useful as a collection of thoughts on the Old Testament book of Genesis from great contemporary minds, but it is also valuable as a glimpse into the relationships between text and interpreter, which can be applied to individual reader experiences.

Awards the book has won:

Audie Award, Nonfiction, Unabridged, 1997

Other books by the same author:

The Language of Life: A Festival of Poets, 1995
Healing and the Mind, 1993
A World of Ideas II: Public Opinions From Private Citizens, 1990
A World of Ideas: Conversations with Thoughtful Men and Women about American Life Today and the Ideas Shaping Our Future, 1989
Listening to America: A Traveler Rediscovers His Country, 1971

Other books you might like:

Thomas J.J. Altizer, *Genesis and Apocalypse: A Theological Voyage Toward Authentic Christianity*, 1990

Karen Armstrong, *In the Beginning: A New Interpretation of Genesis*, 1996

Anne Graham Lotz, *Glorious Dawn of God's Story: Finding Meaning for Your Life in Genesis*, 1997

David Rosenberg, *Genesis as It Is Written: Contemporary Writers on Our First Stories*, 1996

Naomi H. Rosenblatt, *Wrestling with Angels: What the First Family of Genesis Teaches Us about Our Spiritual Identity, Sexuality, and Personal Relationships*, 1995

Francis A. Schaeffer, *Genesis in Space and Time: The How of Biblical History*, 1972

430

MALCOLM MUGGERIDGE

Jesus: The Man Who Lives

(New York: Harper, 1975)

Category: Biography
Subject(s): Christianity; History; Jesus
Age range(s): Young Adult-Adult

Summary: Malcolm Muggeridge was a journalist, novelist, academic, and British television commentator. Once a socialist and an avowed athiest, Muggeridge converted to Christianity in the late 1960s, ultimately joining the Roman Catholic Church. In his *Jesus Rediscovered* (1969), Muggeridge recounted his journey to spirituality. In *Jesus: The Man Who Lives*, the author offers an illustrated biographical portrait of Jesus, not simply as a historically significant figure, but as a man whose influence on individuals and societies remains alive and life-changing, nearly 2000 years after he lived on earth.

Other books by the same author:

Confessions of a Twentieth-Century Pilgrim, 1988
Conversion: A Spiritual Journey, 1988
Something Beautiful for God: Mother Teresa of Calcutta, 1971
Jesus Rediscovered, 1969

Other books you might like:

Richard I. Abrams, *An Illustrated Life of Jesus: From the National Gallery of Art Collection*, 1982

Marjorie Holmes, *The Messiah*, 1987

George M. Lamsa, *The Man From Galilee: A Life of Jesus*, 1970

John Pollock, *The Master: A Life of Jesus*, 1984

431

MULTIPLE AUTHORS

The Bible

(c. 3rd century B.C. - 4th century A.D.)

Category: Scripture
Subject(s): Christianity; Judaism; History
Age range(s): Children-Adult

Summary: *The Bible* contains writings that are sacred to both Judaism and Christianity. The Old Testament narrates the history and religion of Israel from its beginnings in the 10th century BC. The New Testament describes the establishment and development of Christianity against the backdrop of the Roman Empire in the 1st century AD. The so-called apocryphal books record the evolution of Judaism in the years between 587 BC and AD 63. *The Bible* is a mini-library of legal texts, poetry, songs, parables, and history. Written originally in Hebrew and Greek, *The Bible* has been translated into hundreds of languages and dialects. The most enduring English translation is the *King James Version* (1611), and many popular modern translations, like the *New International Version* (1973), continue to be published. Portions of *The Bible* are read for both personal enrichment and inspiration as well as for community instruction in churches and temples.

Other books you might like:

John Bowker, *The Complete Bible Handbook*, 1998
George Buttrick, *The Interpreter's Dictionary of the Bible*, 1962
Mary Ellen Chase, *The Bible and the Common Reader*, 1944
Richard Elliott Friedman, *Who Wrote the Bible?*, 1987
Samuel Sandmel, *The Enjoyment of Scripture: The Law, the Prophets, and the Writings*, 1972

432

MULTIPLE AUTHORS

Koran
(c. 600)

Category: Scripture
Subject(s): Islam; History; Allah
Age range(s): Children-Adult

Summary: In 610, the prophet Muhammad received a command from the angel Gabriel to recite the words of Allah. For the next 22 years, the prophet continued to receive these revelations and to record Allah's words. After Muhammad's death, his writings were compiled into a single volume, the *Koran*, that Muslims believe contains the foundation of all knowledge. Written in a beautiful poetic style, the *Koran* is full of teachings about social justice, God, and daily life.

Other books you might like:

Shabbir Akhtar, *A Faith for All Seasons: Islam and the Challenge of the Modern World*, 1990
Annie Besant, *Beauties of Islam*, 1990
V.S. Naipaul, *Beyond Belief: Islamic Excursions Among the Converted Peoples*, 1998
F.E. Peters, *Mecca: A Literary History of the Muslim Holy Land*, 1994
Frithjof Schuon, *Understanding Islam*, 1963

433

MULTIPLE AUTHORS

Talmud
(c. 550)

Category: Scripture
Subject(s): Judaism; Torah
Age range(s): Young Adult-Adult

Summary: Compiled in the 6th century AD, the *Talmud* is a collection of rabbinical interpretations of the *Torah*, the central text of Judaism. The rabbis believed that the laws and teachings of the *Torah* had been delivered so many thousands of years ago that they had to be reinterpreted for a new world. The *Talmud* records the many ways that various rabbis

through the years have interpreted various portions of the *Torah*. Rabbis today use the *Talmud* as an aid in applying the Jewish laws in particular situations. For Orthodox Judaism, the *Torah* and the *Talmud* are both authoritative for faith and practice, and the *Talmud* offers an excellent example of Judaism's belief in the living character of the law.

Other books you might like:

Scot A. Berman, *Learning Talmud: A Guide to Talmudic Terminology and Rashi Commentary*, 1997
Abraham Cohen, *Everyman's Talmud: The Major Teachings of the Rabbinic Sages*, 1995
Abraham Joshua Heschel, *God in Search of Man: A Philosophy of Judaism*, 1955
Adin Steinsaltz, *The Essential Talmud*, 1976
Joseph Telushkin, *Jewish Wisdom: Ethical, Spiritual, and Historical Lessons From the Great Works and Thinkers*, 1994

434

MULTIPLE AUTHORS

TANAKH
(c. 92)

Category: Scripture; History
Subject(s): Judaism; Literature; Torah
Age range(s): Young Adult-Adult

Summary: TANAKH (TNK) is the acronym for the three divisions of the Jewish Bible. Each group of books was canonized at a different period in history, but TANAKH assumed its final canonical form in the year 92. The first division of TANAKH is *Torah*. This section contains the teachings or laws of Israel, and the five books of *Torah* are Genesis, Exodus, Leviticus, Numbers, and Deuteronomy. The second section is the Nebiim, or the Prophets. In the Hebrew Bible this section includes historical books like 1 and 2 Kings and 1 and 2 Chronicles. The Nebiim also contains the books in which the words and deeds of Israel's and Juday's many prophets are recorded. Some of the prophets, like Isaiah and Jeremiah, may have written their own books, while others, like Jonah, may have had their words collected and recorded by later editors. The third section, Kethubim, or writings, contains "Wisdom" literature like Psalms, Proverbs, and Song of Solomon as well as literature, like Ruth, Esther, Ecclesiastes, and Job that was used in various religious festivals in Israel. The order of the TANAKH differs from the order of the Old Testaments of Protestant and Catholic Christian Bibles. The Hebrew Bible opens with Genesis and concludes with 2 Chronicles and the Exile, while the Old Testament of Christian Bibles opens with Genesis closes with the prophet Malachi. There are several English translations of TANAKH, the most recent of which reproduces the Hebrew and English on facing pages.

Other books you might like:

Arthur A. Cohen, *Contemporary Jewish Religious Thought: Original Essays on Critical Concepts, Movements, and Beliefs*, 1987
Neil Gillman, *Sacred Fragments: Recovering Theology for the Modern Jew*, 1990
Abraham Joshua Heschel, *The Prophets*, 1962

Barry Holtz, *Back to the Sources: Reading the Classic Jewish Texts*, 1984

Rifat Sonsino, *Finding God: Ten Jewish Responses*, 1986

435

V.S. NAIPAUL

Among the Believers: An Islamic Journey

(New York: Knopf, 1981)

Category: History
Subject(s): Islam; Travel; Culture
Age range(s): Young Adult-Adult
Locale(s): Indonesia; Iran; Malaysia

Summary: Essayist and novelist V.S. Naipaul offers an account of his travels in the Islamic countries of Indonesia, Iran, Malaysia, and Pakistan. A British resident of Indian descent born in Trinidad, Naipaul writes from a sociopolitical and sometimes controversial perspective. Here his travel observations are geographical, political, social, and religious in nature.

Other books by the same author:
Beyond Belief: Islamic Excursions Among the Converted Peoples, 1998
India: A Wounded Civilization, 1977

Other books you might like:
Titus Burckhardt, *Fez, City of Islam*, 1992
Isabelle Eberhardt, *In the Shadow of Islam*, 1982
Nitza Rosovsky, *City of the Great King*, 1996

436

SEYYED HOSSEIN NASR, Editor

Islamic Spirituality: Foundations

(New York: Crossroad, 1987)

Category: Devotionals; Poetry
Subject(s): Islam; Spirituality; Allah
Age range(s): Adult

Summary: The great diversity of Islam's spiritual tradition is represented in this anthology. From the poems of Rumi to the earliest writings of the *Koran*, this anthology offers a wealth of insights into Islam's deep spiritual aspects. Nasr's commentary and introductions make this a valuable basic guidebook to Islamic spirituality.

Other books by the same author:
Islamic Art and Spirituality, 1987
Sufi Essays, 1972

Other books you might like:
Akbar S. Ahmed, *Islam Today: A Short Introduction to the Muslim World*, 1999
Molana Shah Maghsoud Sadegh Angha, *Al-Salat: The Reality of Prayer in Islam*, 1998
William C. Chittick, *The Sufi Path of Love: The Spiritual Teachings of Rumi*, 1983
John L. Esposito, *Islam: The Straight Path*, 1988
Annemarie Schimmel, *Mystical Dimensions of Islam*, 1975

437

WATCHMAN NEE

Spiritual Authority

(New York: Christian Fellowship Publications, 1972)

Category: Doctrine
Subject(s): Conduct of Life; Faith; Spirituality
Age range(s): Adult

Summary: Watchman Nee was a famous Chinese Christian whose "house church" ministry in his homeland led to his imprisonment in 1956 and death in 1972. Nee's works have been translated into English in various editions both during his lifetime and after his death. *Spiritual Authority* comes from a series of teachings he presented during a 1948 training program for potential leaders within his ministry in China. Although numerous denominations consider Nee's works and doctrine controversial, there are many other Christian groups worldwide that find the teachings of Watchman Nee fundamental to their beliefs and practices.

Other books by the same author:
Come, Lord Jesus: A Study of the Book of Revelation, 1976
Spiritual Man, 1968
Sit, Walk, Stand, 1963
The Normal Christian Life, 1963

Other books you might like:
Frank Damazio, *Seasons of Revival*, 1996
Frank Damazio, *The Vanguard Leader*, 1994
Gene Edwards, *A Tale of Three Kings*, 1992

438

WATCHMAN NEE

Spiritual Man

(New York: Christian Fellowship Publications, 1968)

Category: Doctrine
Subject(s): Conduct of Life; Faith; Spirituality
Age range(s): Adult

Summary: In the early 1920s, Watchman Nee, a famous Chinese Christian, began the writings that eventually became *Spiritual Man*. Nee's focus in this work is spiritual warfare as a component of spiritual life. Nee's "house church" ministry in his homeland led to his imprisonment in 1956 and death in 1972. His works, considered controversial by some Christian denominations, have been translated into English in various editions both during his lifetime and after his death, and they remain popular among many groups of Christians in the United States as well as around the world.

Other books by the same author:
Come, Lord Jesus: A Study of the Book of Revelation, 1976
Spiritual Authority, 1972
Sit, Walk, Stand, 1963
The Normal Christian Life, 1963

Other books you might like:
Frank Damazio, *Seasons of Revival*, 1996
Frank Damazio, *The Vanguard Leader*, 1994
Gene Edwards, *A Tale of Three Kings*, 1992

439

THICH NHAT HANH

Being Peace

(Berkeley: Parallax Press, 1987)

Category: Sermons
Subject(s): Buddhism; Meditation; Self-Perception
Age range(s): Adult

Summary: Thich Nhat Hanh is a poet, modern Buddhist master, and native of Vietnam whose writings have become classics in Western Buddhism. In *Being Peace*, Nhat Hanh teaches that one's state of mind and body has an impact on environmental and global peace. The writings in this volume are collected from a series of talks presented in the United States during the fall of 1985.

Other books by the same author:
The Long Road Turns to Joy: A Guide to Walking Meditation, 1996
Living Buddha, Living Christ, 1995
Peace Is Every Step: The Path of Mindfulness in Everyday Life, 1991
Zen Keys, 1974

Other books you might like:
Stephen Batchelor, *Buddhism Without Beliefs: A Contemporary Guide to Awakening*, 1997
Samuel Bercholz, *Entering the Stream: An Introduction to the Buddha and His Teachings*, 1993
Sherab Chodzin Kohn, co-author
Pema Chodron, *Start Where You Are: A Guide to Compassionate Living*, 1994
Rinpoche Sogyal, *The Tibetan Book of Living and Dying*, 1992

440

THICH NHAT HANH

Living Buddha, Living Christ

(New York: Riverhead Books, 1995)

Category: Doctrine
Subject(s): Christianity; Buddhism; Religion
Age range(s): Adult

Summary: Buddhist master Thich Nhat Hanh compares Buddhism and Christianity, noting points of both philosophical similarity and theological difference that exist between the two faith traditions. Nhat Hahn draws on the teachings and doctrinal writings of each system and stories of personal experience to explore what he sees as unity beyond diversity. Respect and open-mindedness are the hallmarks of this comparative overview of two worldwide religious traditions.

Other books by the same author:
The Long Road Turns to Joy: A Guide to Walking Meditation, 1996
Peace Is Every Step: The Path of Mindfulness in Everyday Life, 1991
Being Peace, 1987
Zen Keys, 1974

Other books you might like:
Robert Aitken, *The Ground We Share: Everyday Practice, Buddhist and Christian*, 1994
Antony Fernando, *Buddhism Made Plain: An Introduction for Christians and Jews*, 1985
Leonard Swidler, co-author
Paul Ingram, *Buddhist-Christian Dialogue: Mutual Renewal and Transformation*, 1986
Frederick J. Streng, co-editor
Leo D. Lefebure, *The Buddha and the Christ: Explorations in Buddhist and Christian Dialogue*, 1993
Ninian Smart, *Buddhism and Christianity: Rivals and Allies*, 1993
Seiichi Yagi, *A Bridge to Buddhist-Christian Dialogue*, 1990
Leonard Swidler, co-author

441

THICH NHAT HANH

The Long Road Turns to Joy: A Guide to Walking Meditation

(Berkeley: Parallax Press, 1996)

Category: Self-Help
Subject(s): Meditation; Buddhism
Age range(s): Adult

Summary: This volume is a pocket-sized guide to walking meditation by Thich Nhat Hanh, a contemporary Buddhist teacher and poet. Focusing on the author's method of walking as a way to maintain serenity and mindfulness, *The Long Road Turns to Joy* offers practical as well as philosophical perspectives on a simple, accessible meditative practice that transcends religious beliefs.

Other books by the same author:
Living Buddha, Living Christ, 1995
Peace Is Every Step: The Path of Mindfulness in Everyday Life, 1991
Being Peace, 1987
Zen Keys, 1974

Other books you might like:
Michael Gilman, *108 Insights into Tai Chi Chuan: A String of Pearls*, 1998
Dick Harding, *Walking through Stress: Meditation in Motion*, 1989
Linus Mundy, *Prayer Walking: A Simple Path to Body and Soul Fitness*, 1994

442

THICH NHAT HANH

Peace Is Every Step: The Path of Mindfulness in Everyday Life

(New York: Bantam, 1991)

Category: Devotionals
Subject(s): Buddhism; Zen Buddhism; Peace
Age range(s): Adult

Summary: Vietnamese Buddhist monk Thich Nhat Hanh is a very popular purveyor of Zen Buddhism. In this book, he contends that true peace comes only from a deep mindfulness. In order to gain peace, one must be completely attentive and focused on the numerous steps one takes throughout the day. Contrary to many other teachings, he argues, peace does not come simply by sitting down and engaging in contemplative meditation. Rather, every step we take should be mindful, and thus we can achieve peace and harmony as we walk through our daily lives.

Other books by the same author:

The Miracle of Mindfulness: A Manual on Meditation, 1987

Other books you might like:

Pema Chodron, *When Things Fall Apart: Heart Advice for Difficult Times*, 1997

Dalai Lama, *The Art of Happiness: A Handbook for Living*, 1998

Sheng-Yen, *Getting the Buddha Mind: On the Practice of Ch'an Retreat*, 1982

D.T. Suzuki, *Buddha of Infinite Light*, 1997

Chogyam Trungpa, *Cutting through Spiritual Materialism*, 1973

443

THICH NHAT HANH

Zen Keys

(Garden City, New York: Anchor Press, 1974)

Category: Doctrine
Subject(s): Buddhism; Meditation; Religious Life
Age range(s): Adult

Summary: Vietnamese Buddhist master Thich Nhat Hanh has become a major voice introducing Zen Buddhism to Western practitioners. In *Zen Keys*, one of his early writings (originally published in 1974) available again by popular demand, he explains central elements of Zen Buddhist practice and thought. Starting with a look at life in a Zen monastery, the author explicates and demonstrates key concepts, including awareness, impermanence, and mindfulness. He also addresses contemporary issues of spirituality, such as the tension between technology and Zen practice and philosophy. The book includes a set of 43 koans, or stories used by Buddhist masters to convey truths; these, by Tran Thai Tong, 13th century Vietnamese Buddhist monk, are translated into English for the first time in this volume.

Other books by the same author:

The Long Road Turns to Joy: A Guide to Walking Meditation, 1996

Living Buddha, Living Christ, 1995

Peace Is Every Step: The Path of Mindfulness in Everyday Life, 1991

Being Peace, 1987

Other books you might like:

Alexander Holstein, *Pointing at the Moon: 100 Zen Koans From Chinese Masters*, 1994

Manuela Dunn Mascetti, *Koans: The Lessons of Zen*, 1998

Richard McLean, *Zen Fables for Today: Stories Inspired by the Zen Masters*, 1998

Janwillem Van de Wetering, *A Glimpse of Nothingness: Experiences in an American Zen Community*, 1975

444

H. RICHARD NIEBUHR

Christ and Culture

(New York: Harper and Row, 1951)

Category: Theology
Subject(s): Christianity; Culture; Jesus
Age range(s): Adult

Summary: Niebuhr's classic little volume explores five models that can be used to understand the various ways that Christianity and culture relate to each other. This work promotes the concept of transforming modern society following the spirit of Christ.

Other books by the same author:

Radical Monotheism and Western Culture, 1960

The Kingdom of God in America, 1937

Other books you might like:

Robert N. Bellah, *Habits of the Heart: Individualism and Commitment in American Life*, 1985

Peter L. Berger, *The Sacred Canopy: Elements of a Sociological Theory of Religion*, 1967

Will Herberg, *Protestant, Catholic, Jew: An Essay in American Religious Sociology*, 1960

Reinhold Niebuhr, *Love and Justice: Selections From the Shorter Writings of Reinhold Niebuhr*, 1957

John Howard Yoder, *Authentic Transformation: A New Vision of Christ and Culture*, 1996

445

H. RICHARD NIEBUHR

The Social Sources of Denominationalism

(New York: Holt, 1929)

Category: Theology
Subject(s): Protestantism; Christianity
Age range(s): Adult

Summary: Niebuhr was a well-known theologian and religion scholar during the first half of the 20th century. Throughout his teachings and writings, he focused on the theme of the transcendence and sovereignty of God over all finite phenomena. In this volume, Niebuhr examines the societal roots of denominationalism within the Western Christian tradition.

Other books by the same author:

Christian Ethics, 1973

The Responsible Self, 1963

Radical Monotheism and Western Culture, 1960

Other books you might like:

Samuel G. Dawson, *Denominational Doctrines*, 1990

Frank S. Mead, *Handbook of Denominations in the United States*, 1995

Russell E. Richey, *Reimagining Denominationalism: Interpretive Essays*, 1994

446

REINHOLD NIEBUHR

Beyond Tragedy: Essays on the Christian Interpretation of History

(New York: Scribner, 1937)

Category: Essays
Subject(s): Apologetics; Christianity; History
Age range(s): Adult

Summary: Reinhold Niebuhr was one of America's foremost 20th century theologians. His *Beyond Tragedy* is characteristic of his lifelong effort to apply the principles and tenets of Christianity to social, economic, and political issues. In theological terms, he argues that it is the responsibility of Christian believers and organizations to promote social justice and create a social, political, and spiritual environment in which the wrongs of the past can not be repeated.

Other books by the same author:
Faith and Politics, 1968
Children of Light and Children of Darkness, 1944
Christian Realism in Contemporary American Theology, 1940
Europe's Catastrophe and the Christian Faith, 1940

Other books you might like:
Douglas John Hall, *God and the Nations*, 1995
   Rosemary Radford Ruether, co-author
Richard L. Rubenstein, *Approaches to Auschwitz: The Holocaust and Its Legacy*, 1987
   John K. Roth, co-author
David Toole, *Waiting for Godot in Sarajevo: Theological Reflections on Nihilism, Tragedy, and Apocalypse*, 1998

447

REINHOLD NIEBUHR

Leaves From the Notebook of a Tamed Cynic

(New York: Willett, Clark, and Colby, 1929)

Category: Theology; Autobiography
Subject(s): Christianity; Christian Life; Faith
Age range(s): Adult

Summary: Written toward the end of Niebuhr's parish ministry at an inner-city church, this classic little journal raises significant questions about the role of the church in society. During the years covered by this book, Niebuhr was a young pastor working at his first assignment. As he confronted various parish problems, he raised poignant questions about the nature of faith and his own effectiveness as a minister. At the center of his entries are his probing, ethical questions about the church's role in making a better society.

Other books by the same author:
The Irony of American History, 1952
The Nature and Destiny of Man: A Christian Interpretation, 1941-1943 (Two volumes.)

Other books you might like:
Karl Barth, *The Humanity of God*, 1960

Will D. Campbell, *Soul Among Lions: Musings of a Bootleg Preacher*, 1999
John Howard Griffin, *The Hermitage Journals: A Diary Kept While Working on the Biography of Thomas Merton*, 1981
Joseph A. Sittler, *Grace Notes and Other Fragments*, 1981
Paul Tillich, *The Courage to Be*, 1952

448

KATHLEEN NORRIS

The Cloister Walk

(New York: Riverhead, 1996)

Category: Autobiography
Subject(s): Christianity; Monasticism; Christian Life
Age range(s): Adult

Summary: As a teenager Norris rejected many of the religious teachings of her youth. She spent almost 10 years outside of any religious faith. In 1994, though, she went to a Benedictine monastery for a retreat. The simplicity of the rules of the monastery and the rhythms of life in the cloister deeply penetrated her life. As a result, she became an oblate—someone who lives by the rules of the order but who cannot live in the cloister—in the monastery. As a result, Norris began to weave the rhythms of Benedictine spirituality into her everyday life. Norris' account of her months in the cloister provides a riveting spiritual autobiography.

Other books by the same author:
Amazing Grace: A Vocabulary of Faith, 1998

Other books you might like:
Saint Benedict of Nursia, *The Rule of St. Benedict*, c. 520
Esther De Waal, *Seeking God: The Way of St. Benedict*, 1984
Thomas Merton, *The Seven Storey Mountain*, 1948
Clayton Sullivan, *Jesus and the Sweet Pilgrim Baptist Church: A Fable*, 1992
Judith Sutera, *The Work of God: Benedictine Prayer*, 1997

449

OLIVER NORTH
WILLIAM NOVAK, Co-Author

Under Fire: An American Story

(New York: HarperCollins, 1992)

Category: Autobiography
Subject(s): Politics; Military Life; Christian Life
Age range(s): Adult

Summary: In the mid-1980s, Lieutenant Colonel Oliver North was involved in a covert military plan to support rebels fighting against the government of Nicaragua through funds garnered from the sale of weapons to Iran. This was done in violation of U.S. laws prohibiting trade with Iran. In 1989, North was tried and convicted of charges relating to this episode in U.S. history, but his conviction was overturned. In his autobiography, *Under Fire*, North tells the story of his role in what came to be known as the Iran-Contra scandal. He also shares memories from his childhood and writes of his other years in military service, including his term in Vietnam.

Awards the book has won:
Gold Medallion Book Award, Biography/Autobiography, 1992

Other books by the same author:
One More Mission: Oliver North Returns to Vietnam, 1993

Other books you might like:
Gary T. Amos, *Attainted: The Political Branding of Oliver North*, 1994
Amy Fried, *Muffled Echoes: Oliver North and the Politics of Public Opinion*, 1997
Gavin Hewitt, *Terry Waite and Ollie North: The Untold Story of the Kidnapping and the Release*, 1991

450

NOSTRADAMUS

The Complete Prophecies of Nostradamus
(New York: Three Rivers Press, 1998)

Category: New Age (Nonfiction)
Subject(s): Prophecy; Astrology
Age range(s): Young Adult-Adult

Summary: Nostradamus, born Michel de Nostredame, was a French astrologer in the sixteenth century. In 1555 his collection of prophecies titled *Centuries* was published, completely written in verse. Without providing details, these prophecies vaguely described events that would come to pass over several centuries, culminating with the end of the world in 3737 A.D. For centuries, philosophers and others have interpreted the prophecies of Nostradamus, finding in his vague predictions parallels to catastrophic and momentous events in history and current times. This edition of his prophecies contains a chronological list of the prophecies, background material about Nostradamus, and an overview of the practice of prophecy. Although the words of Nostradamus are more than four centuries old, the prophecies are considered central to certain New Age religious philosophies and practices.

Other books you might like:
C. Marvin Pate, *Doomsday Delusions: What's Wrong with Predictions about the End of the World*, 1995
   Calvin B. Haines, Jr., co-author
Gordon-Michael Scallion, *Notes From the Cosmos: A Futurist's Insight into the World of Dream Prophecy and Intuition*, 1997
Mark A. Thurston, *Millennium Prophecies: Predictions for the Coming Century From Edgar Cayce*, 1997

451

HENRI J.M. NOUWEN

The Wounded Healer: Ministry in Contemporary Society
(Garden City, New York: Doubleday, 1972)

Category: Devotionals
Subject(s): Christianity; Spirituality; Clergy
Age range(s): Adult

Summary: How best can a minister perform his task? In order to feel the pain of his parishioners, the minister must also acknowledge his own pain. Nouwen's now-classic book introduces his sparkling prose and lucid insights to the world. He contends that ministers cannot separate themselves from their congregations the way that so many are taught to do. Instead, ministers and parishioners should become priests to each other, ministering to each other's pain. This is a radical book, both for the time in which it was written and for now.

Other books by the same author:
Sabbatical Journey: The Diary of His Final Year, 1998
The Road to Daybreak: A Spiritual Journey, 1988
Reaching Out: The Three Movements of the Spiritual Life, 1975

Other books you might like:
Michael Ford, *Wounded Prophet: A Portrait of Henri J.M. Nouwen*, 1999
Timothy Jones, *Awake, My Soul: Practical Spirituality for Busy People*, 1999
Carlyle Marney, *Priests to Each Other*, 1974
Donald P. McNeill, *Compassion: A Reflection on the Christian Life*, 1982
Thomas Merton, *New Seeds of Contemplation*, 1962

452

MICHAEL NOVAK

Ascent of the Mountain, Flight of the Dove: An Invitation to Religious Studies
(New York: Harper, 1971)

Category: Theology
Subject(s): Philosophy; Religion; Popular Culture
Age range(s): Adult

Summary: Social philosopher Michael Novak's approach to studying American culture is to view experience through the prism of a theological perspective. A key theme throughout his works is the relationship between Judeo-Christian teachings and the principles of democratic capitalism. In this volume, Novak invites readers to explore social and historical issues through the lens of theology.

Other books by the same author:
Business as a Calling: Work and the Examined Life, 1996
Confession of a Catholic, 1983
Capitalism and Socialism: A Theological Inquiry, 1979
Choosing Our King: Powerful Symbols in Presidential Politics, 1974

Other books you might like:
Tim Cooney, *Connections and Disconnections: Between Linguistics, Morality, Religion and Democracy*, 1999
Nathan O. Hatch, *The Democratization of American Christianity*, 1991
Ronald F. Thiemann, *Religion in Public Life: A Dilemma for Democracy*, 1996

453

ELIZABETH O'CONNOR

Letters to Scattered Pilgrims

(San Francisco: Harper and Row, 1979)

Category: Journals/Letters
Subject(s): Christianity; Ministry; Social Issues
Age range(s): Adult

Summary: O'Connor is one of the founders of the Potter's House at the Church of the Savior in Washington, D.C. For many years, the Church of the Savior has offered a model of a Christian community engaging in social justice. This urban church is one of the first to erase the boundaries between clergy and laity, encouraging all members to think of themselves as ministers of the Gospel. This book is both a portrait of the work that the Church does and a call to other Christian communities to stop looking inward and to start looking around them to help to practice social justice.

Other books by the same author:
Journey Inward, Journey Outward, 1968

Other books you might like:
Dorothy Day, *Loaves and Fishes*, 1963
Henri J.M. Nouwen, *The Road to Daybreak: A Spiritual Journey*, 1988
Jim Wallis, *Agenda for Biblical People*, 1976

454

FLANNERY O'CONNOR

The Habit of Being: Letters

(New York: Farrar, Straus, Giroux, 1979)

Category: Journals/Letters
Subject(s): Catholicism; Human Behavior
Age range(s): Adult

Summary: This is a collection of letters written by Flannery O'Connor, who was well-known for the Catholic underpinnings of her short and long fiction and essays. Edited by Sally Fitzgerald, the letters reveal their author's personality and sense of humor, strength, and spiritual sensitivity. A picture emerges of a lively, artistic individual whose creative expression had its roots in a well-centered, honest life.

Awards the book has won:
National Book Critics Circle ''Board'' Award, 1980
Library Journal Notable Book Citation, 1980

Other books by the same author:
The Correspondence of Flannery O'Connor and the Brainard Cheneys, 1986
The Presence of Grace, and Other Book Reviews, 1983
Everything That Rises Must Converge, 1965
A Good Man Is Hard to Find, 1955

Other books you might like:
Caroline Gordon, *A Literary Friendship: Correspondence between Caroline Gordon and Ford Madox Ford*, 1999
Ford Madox Ford, co-author
May Sarton, *Selected Letters*, 1997
Susan Sherman, editor

Anne Morrow Lindbergh, *War Within and Without: Diaries and Letters of Anne Morrow Lindbergh*, 1980
Dorothy Thompson, *Dorothy Thompson and Rose Wilder Lane: Forty Years of Friendship: Letters, 1921-1960*, 1991
William Holtz, editor

455

J.I. PACKER

Knowing God

(Downers Grove, Illinois: InterVarsity Press, 1973)

Category: Theology
Subject(s): Christianity; Bible; Faith
Age range(s): Adult

Summary: In *Knowing God*, J. I. Packer sets forth the principle that God is knowable. Packer asserts that God is revealed to believers through the words of the *Bible*.

Other books by the same author:
Grief Sanctified: Passing through Grief to Peace and Joy, 1997
Quest for Godliness: The Puritan Vision of the Christian Life, 1990
Your Father Loves You: Daily Insights for Knowing God, 1986 (Jean Watson, editor)
Daily Life in Bible Times, 1982
God's Words: Studies of Key Bible Themes, 1981

Other books you might like:
Millard J. Erickson, *Does It Matter If God Exists?*, 1996
J. Vernon McGee, *Who Is God? Bringing the Infinite into Focus*, 1999
Charles F. Stanley, *A Touch of His Love: Meditations on Knowing and Receiving the Love of God*, 1994
A.W. Tozer, *The Knowledge of the Holy: The Attributes of God*, 1961

456

PADMA SAMBHAVA

The Tibetan Book of the Dead: The Great Book of Natural Liberation through Understanding in the Between

(New York: Bantam Doubleday Dell, 1993)

Category: Scripture
Subject(s): Buddhism; Poetry; Death
Age range(s): Young Adult-Adult

Summary: *The Tibetan Book of the Dead* is an essential set of writings in Tibetan Buddhism. Originally written in the late eighth century, it describes the various stages of transition after death and provides a guide for prayers to be said in the presence of the dead. This edition is translated by Robert A.F. Thurman, a prominent leader in the Tibetan Buddhist movement in the West, and has been approved and blessed by the Dalai Lama.

Other books by the same author:
Natural Liberation: Padmasambhava's Teachings on the Six Bardos, 1998 (B. Alan Wallace, translator)
Dakini Teachings: Padmasambhava's Oral Instructions to Lady Tsogyal, 1990 (Erik Pema Kunsang, translator)

Other books you might like:
Dalai Lama, *Awakening the Mind, Lightening the Heart: Core Teachings of Tibetan Buddhism*, 1995
Raymond O. Faulkner, *The Egyptian Book of the Dead: The Book of Going Forth Day by Day*, 1994
Dwight Goddard, *A Buddhist Bible*, 1938
Anton Grosz, *Letters to a Dying Friend: Helping Those You Love Make a Conscious Transition*, 1997
Rinpoche Sogyal, *Glimpse After Glimpse: Daily Reflections on Living and Dying*, 1995
Rinpoche Sogyal, *The Tibetan Book of Living and Dying*, 1992
Robert Thurman, *Essential Tibetan Buddhism*, 1995
Jean-Claude Van Itallie, *The Tibetan Book of the Dead for Reading Aloud*, 1998

457

ELAINE PAGELS

The Gnostic Gospels

(New York: Random House, 1979)

Category: Theology; History
Subject(s): Gnosticism; Christianity; Jesus
Age range(s): Adult

Summary: Pagels is one of the first popularizers of the Nag Hammadi writings that were discovered in Egypt in 1945. Here she summarizes the major themes of the various writings and traces the evolution of the texts and the communities that produced them. Pagels' book is a fine introduction to the Gnostic gospels and their implications for Christianity.

Awards the book has won:
National Book Award, Religion and Inspiration, 1980
National Book Critics Circle Award, Criticism, 1979

Other books by the same author:
Adam, Eve, and the Serpent, 1988

Other books you might like:
Gerd Ludemann, *Heretics: The Other Side of Early Christianity*, 1996
Marvin Meyer, *The Secret Teachings of Jesus: Four Gnostic Gospels*, 1984
Pheme Perkins, *Gnosticism and the New Testament*, 1993
James M. Robinson, *The Nag Hammadi Library in English*, 1988
Kurt Rudolph, *Gnosis: The Nature and History of Gnosticism*, 1983

458

ELAINE PAGELS

The Origin of Satan

(New York: Random House, 1995)

Category: Theology

Subject(s): Prejudice; Religious Conflict; Bible
Age range(s): Adult

Summary: In this in-depth but accessible work based on extensive theological scholarship, Pagels traces the evolution of Satan in Christian thought, writing, and doctrine. From scripture accounts and contemporaneous evidence of the evolving nature and character of the Devil, Pagels identifies a common denominator among Christians whose shared defense against the invisible enemy of darkness and evil reinforced their unity and identity as believers in Christ. In its early days as a minority faith, Christianity was strengthened by the resolve that came from fighting a common and unseen enemy. As flesh-and-blood adversaries threatened the freedom and well-being of believers, it bacame common to associate the forces of the hidden enemy—Satan—with the actions and demeanor of those human adversaries. Following this basic thesis, Pagels outlines the progressive development of the character of Satan and highlights the historical and contemporary conflicts that have risen from the personification of Good and Evil.

Other books by the same author:
Adam, Eve, and the Serpent, 1988
The Gnostic Jesus and Early Christian Politics, 1981
The Gnostic Gospels, 1979

Other books you might like:
Peggy L. Day, *An Adversary in Heaven: Satan in the Hebrew Bible*, 1988
Neil Forsyth, *The Old Enemy: Satan and the Combat Myth*, 1987

459

PAT PALMER

Teen Esteem: A Self-Direction Manual for Young Adults

(San Luis Obispo, California: Impact Publishers, 1989)

Category: Self-Help
Subject(s): Adolescence; Conduct of Life; Self-Acceptance
Age range(s): Young Adult

Summary: Pat Palmer's *Teen Esteem* is a handbook to help young adults develop skills and thought processes that will help them recognize their worth, in turn helping them stand up to peer pressure and reject self-destructive behaviors. Social workers, school counselors, and youth pastors know that ''risky behavior,'' including substance abuse and sexual activity, are starting earlier in each generation. *Teen Esteem* is a non-sectarian approach to building positive coping skills to help teens make wise life choices.

Other books by the same author:
Liking Myself, 1977 (Betty L. Shondeck, illustrator)
The Mouse, the Monster, and Me, 1977

Other books you might like:
Jack Canfield, *Chicken Soup for the Teenage Soul: 101 Stories of Life, Love, and Learning*, 1997
Mark Victor Hansen, Kimberly Kirberger, co-authors
Sean Covey, *The 7 Habits of Highly Effective Teens: The Ultimate Teenage Success Guide*, 1998

Joey O'Connor, *Breaking Your Comfort Zones: And 49 Other Extremely Radical Ways to Live for God*, 1996

Bonnie M. Parsley, *The Choice Is Yours: A Teenager's Guide to Self-Discovery, Relationship, Values, and Spiritual Growth*, 1992

Michael Smith, *Between Fathers & Sons: A Program for Sharing Faith, Strengthening Bonds, and Growing into Manhood*, 1997

460

CHARLES PANATI

Sacred Origins of Profound Things

(New York: Penguin Arcana, 1996)

Category: History
Subject(s): Customs; Legends; Religion
Age range(s): Adult

Summary: Why do we do what we do when we worship? Who first named and talked about Heaven? Hell? In this volume, Charles Panati uncovers the beginnings of practices and customs associated with Western religious beliefs, explaining why certain holidays are celebrated, how the patron saints were named, and much more. Line drawings accompany the text which entertains while it informs.

Other books by the same author:
Panati's Extraordinary Origins of Everyday Things, 1987
The Browser's Book of Beginnings, 1984

Other books you might like:
Ronda De Sola Chervin, *The Book of Catholic Customs and Traditions*, 1994
    Carla Conley, co-author
Judy Fraser, *Did You Know.?: Hidden Treasures From Church History*, 1996
Alfred J. Kolatch, *The Jewish Book of Why*, 1981
John McCollister, *The Christian Book of Why*, 1983

461

GEOFFREY PARRINDER

Dictionary of Religious and Spiritual Quotations

(New York: Simon & Schuster, 1989)

Category: Religious Encyclopedias/Dictionaries
Subject(s): Religion; Literature; Language
Age range(s): Adult

Summary: *Dictionary of Religious and Spiritual Quotations* is a collection of pithy sayings, maxims both famous and lesser known, and generally useful inspirational quotations representing multiple religious traditions. The quotations were compiled by Geoffrey Parrinder, Professor of the Comparative Study of Religions at the University of London.

Other books you might like:
Tony Castle, *The New Book of Christian Quotations*, 1982
Ronda De Sola Chervin, *Quotable Saints*, 1992
Frank S. Mead, *The Encyclopedia of Religious Quotations*, 1965

Shelley Tucker, *Openings: Quotations on Spirituality in Everyday Life*, 1997

462

RAPHAEL PATAI

The Hebrew Goddess

(Detroit: Wayne State University, 1990)

Category: History
Subject(s): Judaism; Women
Age range(s): Adult
Locale(s): Israel

Summary: When the Hebrews moved back into the land of Canaan, they adopted many of the practices of Canaanite religion, including goddess worship. Very quickly, though, under the monotheism of David's kingdom, goddess worship began to disappear. Patai's engaging history of the goddess in Israel traces this disappearance and the importance of goddess worship in early Israel.

Other books you might like:
Enid Dame, *Which Lilith?: Feminist Writers Re-Create the World's First Woman*, 1998
Merle Feld, *A Spiritual Life: A Jewish Feminist Journey*, 1999
Ellen Frankel, *The Five Books of Miriam: A Woman's Commentary on the Torah*, 1996
Naomi M. Hyman, *Biblical Women in the Midrash: A Sourcebook*, 1997
Barbara Black Koltuv, *The Book of Lilith*, 1987

463

NORMAN VINCENT PEALE

The Power of Positive Living

(New York: Doubleday, 1990)

Category: Self-Help
Subject(s): Conduct of Life; Self-Confidence; Success
Age range(s): Young Adult-Adult

Summary: Nearly forty years after penning his bestselling book *The Power of Positive Thinking*, Norman Vincent Peale, one of the "fathers" of the personal success literature genre, provides another guide to happiness. Here he presents stories of men and women of all ages who have adopted his principles of positive living and created success in their lives. Peale emphasizes that believing in oneself and having faith in God are two of the key components to success and happiness for everyone.

Other books by the same author:
Positive Imaging, 1996
The American Character, 1988
The True Joy of Positive Living, 1984
The Positive Principle Today: How to Renew and Sustain the Power of Positive Thinking, 1976
The Power of Positive Thinking, 1952

Other books you might like:
Florence Littauer, *Personality Plus*, 1983
John C. Maxwell, *The Winning Attitude*, 1991

Robert Schuller, *Tough Times Never Last, but Tough People Do!*, 1983

464

NORMAN VINCENT PEALE

The Power of Positive Thinking
(New York: Prentice-Hall, 1952)

Category: Self-Help
Subject(s): Conduct of Life; Self-Confidence; Success
Age range(s): Young Adult-Adult

Summary: *The Power of Positive Thinking* has been translated into fifteen languages and has remained in print since it first appeared. Peale's message of self-help in this volume is designed to help readers overcome self-doubt, worry, stress, and anger by eliminating negativity of thought, which Peale argues will always result in unhappiness and a lack of self-confidence. Peale's work as a pastor experimenting with principles of psychology in his ministry led to the writing of this book to share with others what he was learning as a counselor. The themes of this book (the primary one being, if you think you can, you can) have been well-received for more than four decades.

Other books by the same author:
Positive Imaging, 1996
The Power of Positive Living, 1990
The American Character, 1988
The True Joy of Positive Living, 1984
The Positive Principle Today: How to Renew and Sustain the Power of Positive Thinking, 1976

Other books you might like:
Florence Littauer, *Personality Plus*, 1983
John C. Maxwell, *The Winning Attitude*, 1991
Robert Schuller, *Tough Times Never Last, but Tough People Do!*, 1983

465

F. DAVID PEAT

Synchronicity: The Bridge between Matter and Mind
(New York: Bantam, 1987)

Category: New Age (Nonfiction)
Subject(s): Philosophy; Physics; Psychology
Age range(s): Adult

Summary: Physicist F. David Peat brings together science, ancient philosophy, and contemporary theory to give readers a new perspective on why things happen the way they do. Applying principles of physics to the question of coincidence and chaos in the universe, Peat sets forth a context for spiritual guidance and growth that he suggests will work from a scientific point of view. He offers both anecdote and analysis in his thesis that science and intuition, or faith, must be combined for the greatest understanding of the universe and our place in it.

Other books by the same author:
Lighting the Seventh Fire: The Spiritual Ways, Healing, and Science of the Native American, 1994
Superstrings and the Search for the Theory of Everything, 1989

Other books you might like:
Phil Cousineau, *Soul Moments: Marvelous Stories of Synchronicity—Meaning Coincidences From a Seemingly Random World*, 1997
Robert H. Hopke, *There Are No Accidents: Synchronicity and the Stories of Our Lives*, 1997
Carl Jung, *Synchronicity: An Acausal Connecting Principle*, 1955
Mark A. Thurston, *Synchronicity as Spiritual Guidance*, 1997

466

M. SCOTT PECK

Further Along the Road Less Traveled: The Unending Journey Toward Spiritual Growth
(New York: Simon & Schuster, 1993)

Category: Self-Help
Series: Road Trilogy
Subject(s): Mental Health; Psychology; Religion
Age range(s): Adult

Summary: Three stages of spiritual development-mature self-awareness, self-examination, and an individual search for God in one's life-are described by Christian psychiatrist M. Scott Peck as universal steps in personal and spiritual growth. Issues dealt with in this sequel to Peck's best-selling *The Road Less Traveled* include blame and forgiveness, the relationships between physical health and psychospiritual well-being, and the author's belief that the exploration of the mystery of death can add meaning to one's life.

Other books by the same author:
The Road Less Traveled and Beyond: Spiritual Growth in an Age of Anxiety, 1997
People of the Lie: The Hope for Healing Human Evil, 1983
The Road Less Traveled: A New Psychology of Love, Traditional Values, and Spiritual Growth, 1978

Other books you might like:
Leo Buscaglia, *Love*, 1972
Wayne W. Dyer, *Wisdom of the Ages: A Modern Master Brings Eternal Truths into Everyday Life*, 1998
Sam Keen, *To Love and Be Loved*, 1997
Jacob Needleman, *A Little Book on Love*, 1996
Mark Robert Waldman, *The Art of Staying Together: Embracing Love, Intimacy and Spirit in Relationships*, 1998

467

M. SCOTT PECK

The Road Less Traveled and Beyond: Spiritual Growth in an Age of Anxiety

(New York: Simon & Schuster, 1997)

Category: Self-Help
Series: Road Trilogy
Subject(s): Psychology; Religion; Human Behavior
Age range(s): Adult

Summary: Although the title sounds familiar, this book from M. Scott Peck is not just an update of his 1978 bestseller, *The Road Less Traveled*. Spirituality and mental health are still central themes of his writing, but his focus is specifically on issues relevant to the 1990s. Peck contends that in the face of more complex lifestyle choices, Americans are in danger of oversimplifying their thought processes and relying on stereotyped and programmed responses to life's challenges. Peck encourages readers to work through problems, rather than try to escape them, and to consider the pursuit of spiritual growth an essential component to mental and physical health. This is the third book in what Peck calls the Road Trilogy.

Other books by the same author:
Further Along the Road Less Traveled: The Unending Journey Toward Spiritual Growth, 1993
People of the Lie: The Hope for Healing Human Evil, 1983
The Road Less Traveled: A New Psychology of Love, Traditional Values, and Spiritual Growth, 1978

Other books you might like:
Leo Buscaglia, *Love*, 1972
Wayne W. Dyer, *Wisdom of the Ages: A Modern Master Brings Eternal Truths into Everyday Life*, 1998
Sam Keen, *To Love and Be Loved*, 1997
Jacob Needleman, *A Little Book on Love*, 1996
Mark Robert Waldman, *The Art of Staying Together: Embracing Love, Intimacy and Spirit in Relationships*, 1998

468

M. SCOTT PECK

The Road Less Traveled: A New Psychology of Love, Traditional Values, and Spiritual Growth

(New York: Simon & Schuster, 1978)

Category: Self-Help
Subject(s): Psychology; Self-Respect
Age range(s): Adult

Summary: A ground-breaking book in the renewal of attention to things spiritual, Peck's study explores the ways that traditional values can be integrated into the journey of the spirit through religion, love, and science. Peck's approach to spiritual psychology acknowledges that personal growth is a lifelong process, not a short-term activity.

Other books by the same author:
Further Along the Road Less Traveled: The Unending Journey Toward Spiritual Growth, 1993

People of the Lie: The Hope for Healing Human Evil, 1983

Other books you might like:
Leo Buscaglia, *Love*, 1972
Wayne W. Dyer, *Wisdom of the Ages: A Modern Master Brings Eternal Truths into Everyday Life*, 1998
Sam Keen, *To Love and Be Loved*, 1997
Jacob Needleman, *A Little Book on Love*, 1996
Mark Robert Waldman, *The Art of Staying Together: Embracing Love, Intimacy and Spirit in Relationships*, 1998

469

JAROSLAV PELIKAN

Jesus through the Centuries: His Place in the History of Culture

(New Haven, Connecticut: Yale University Press, 1985)

Category: History
Subject(s): Christianity; Culture; Religion
Age range(s): Adult

Summary: Suitable for both general and academic readers, this is a study of Jesus as portrayed throughout history. Historian Jaroslav Pelikan draws on art, music, literature, history, theology, and scripture to explore the many ways human beings have interpreted the person and life of Jesus.

Other books by the same author:
Mary through the Centuries: Her Place in the History of Culture, 1996
Christianity and Classical Culture, 1993
The Mystery of Continuity: Time and History, Memory, and Eternity, 1986

Other books you might like:
George Gallup Jr., *Who Do Americans Think That I Am?*, 1986
George O'Connell, co-author
D. James Kennedy, *What If Jesus Had Never Been Born?*, 1994
Jerry Newcombe, co-author
J.R. Porter, *Jesus Christ: The Jesus of History, the Christ of Faith*, 1999

470

JAROSLAV PELIKAN

Mary through the Centuries: Her Place in the History of Culture

(New Haven, Connecticut: Yale University Press, 1996)

Category: History
Subject(s): Christianity; Culture; Religion
Age range(s): Adult

Summary: In the history of Christianity, no woman has received more acclaim than Mary, mother of Jesus. In this study, Christian historian Jaroslav Pelikan has gathered together images and lore about Mary created since the early days of the Christian faith. From folk traditions to fine arts and literature, in Christian scriptures and canonical writings of multiple faiths, Pelikan explores the ways in which generations of people have honored, adored, and interpreted the person and life of Mary.

Other books by the same author:
The Illustrated Jesus through the Centuries, 1997
Christianity and Classical Culture, 1993
Imago Dei, 1990
Jesus through the Centuries: His Place in the History of Culture, 1985

Other books you might like:
Kathleen Coyle, *Mary in the Christian Tradition: From a Contemporary Perspective*, 1996
Sally Cunneen, *In Search of Mary: The Woman and the Symbol*, 1996
Herbert Haag, *Mary: Art, Culture, and Religion through the Ages*, 1998
    Caroline Ebertshauser, Joe H. Kirchberger, co-editors; Peter Heinegg, translator

471

JAROSLAV PELIKAN, Editor

The World Treasury of Modern Religious Thought

(Boston: Little, Brown, 1990)

Category: Theology
Subject(s): Religion; Philosophy
Age range(s): Adult

Summary: Modern writings from a variety of belief systems are represented in this collection that explores faith and its meanings from diverse perspectives—atheism, Judaism, Christianity, Buddhism, Islam, and more. Included are contemplative essays, inspirational thought, and religious treatises by scientists, philosophers, political leaders, and literary figures.

Other books by the same author:
Faust the Theologian, 1995
Christians of the East, 1994
Christianity and Classical Culture, 1993
The Excellent Empire: The Fall of Rome and the Triumph of the Church, 1987

Other books you might like:
Heiko A. Oberman, *The Dawn of the Reformation: Essays in Late Medieval and Early Reformation Thought*, 1992
Mary Pope Osborn, *One World, Many Religions: The Way We Worship*, 1996
Bernard M.G. Reardon, *Religious Thought in the Victorian Age: A Survey From Coleridge to Gore*, 1980
Philip Zaleski, *The Best Spiritual Writing, 1998*, 1998

472

CHARLES PELLEGRINO

Return to Sodom and Gomorrah: Bible Stories From Archaeologists

(New York: Random House, 1994)

Category: History

Subject(s): Archaeology; Bible; Mythology
Age range(s): Young Adult-Adult

Summary: What can archaeology tell us about faith and religion today? Plenty, according to Charles Pellegrino, whose *Return to Sodom and Gomorrah* is a journey through the past with relevance to modern religious beliefs. Blending theology, history, archaeological science, and adventure, Pellegrino links Old Testament stories with their physical locations, revealing through archaeological digs what really happened and how. It's history brought to life, exotic travel, and mysteries uncovered, all in one lively format.

Other books by the same author:
Unearthing Atlantis: An Archaeological Odyssey, 1991
Darwin's Universe: Origins and Crises in the History of Life, 1983

Other books you might like:
Alfred J. Hoerth, *Archaeology and the Old Testament*, 1998
H. Darrell Lance, *The Old Testament and the Archaeologist*, 1981
Amihi Mazar, *Archaeology of the Land of the Bible: 10,000-586 B.C.E.*, 1992

473

NIGEL PENNICK

The Pagan Book of Days: A Guide to the Festivals, Traditions, and Sacred Days of the Year

(Rochester, Vermont: Destiny Books, 1992)

Category: New Age (Nonfiction)
Subject(s): Holidays; Culture; Paganism
Age range(s): Young Adult-Adult

Summary: From lunar phases and their significance to traditional rituals of Celtic and Anglo-Saxon origins, Nigel Pennick's *Pagan Book of Days* is a source of day-by-day information about holidays and cultural traditions that date back many centuries. The practices of Wicca, celebratory occasions marked by the ancient Greeks, and the dates and meaning of the solstices and equinoxes are just some of the topics covered in this day book.

Other books by the same author:
Runic Astrology, 1990
Practical Magic in the Northern Tradition, 1989
Earth Harmony, 1987
Labyrinths: Their Geomancy and Symbolism, 1984

Other books you might like:
Jan Brodle, *Earth Dance: A Year of Pagan Rituals*, 1995
Laurie Cabot, *Celebrate the Earth: A Year of Holidays in the Pagan Tradition*, 1994
Pauline Campanelli, *Ancient Ways: Reclaiming Pagan Traditions*, 1991

474

EUGENE H. PETERSON

Leap over a Wall: Earthy Spirituality for Everyday Christians

(New York: HarperCollins, 1997)

Category: Religious Commentaries
Subject(s): Conduct of Life; Bible; Storytelling
Age range(s): Young Adult-Adult
Major character(s): King David, Biblical Figure, Historical Figure, Royalty (king of Israel)
Locale(s): Israel

Summary: By examining and telling stories from the life of Old Testament figure David, who was a boy shepherd, psalm writer, and king of Israel, Eugene H. Peterson shares insights for contemporary living. The poetry of the Psalms, the energy of David's life, the good and bad decisions he made—all provide lessons in love, worship, friendship, grief, and suffering. Peterson frames these lessons in a story that is about the spirituality of all humankind as much as it is about David and his personal faith journey.

Other books by the same author:
Where Your Treasure Is, 1993
The Contemplative Pastor: Returning to the Art of Spiritual Direction, 1989

Other books you might like:
Woodrow Kroll, *Lessons on Living From David*, 1999
David Rosenberg, *The Book of David: A New Story of the Spiritual Warrior and Leader Who Shaped Our Inner Consciousness*, 1997
Charles P. Schmitt, *A Heart for God: A Journey with David From Brokenness to Wholeness*, 1995

475

LORRAINE PETERSON

Why Isn't God Giving Cash Prizes?

(Minneapolis: Bethany House, 1982)

Category: Devotionals
Subject(s): Adolescence; Christian Life
Age range(s): Young Adult

Summary: *Why Isn't God Giving Cash Prizes?* is a devotional and Bible study guide for teens. The author, Lorraine Peterson, is a teacher who began writing inspirational materials when young people came to her looking for resources to help them learn about their Christian faith. When she couldn't find high-interest material to meet their needs, she created it herself. The questions and concerns addressed in this and other devotional and study guides by Peterson come directly from teens.

Other books by the same author:
Lord, I Haven't Talked to You Since the Last Crisis, But., 1994
If You Really Trust Me, Why Can't I Stay out Later?, 1991
If God Loves Me, Why Can't I Get My Locker Open?, 1980

Other books you might like:
Thomas F. Catucci, *Time with Jesus: Twenty Guided Meditations for Youth*, 1993
William Coleman, *God Doesn't Play Favorites: Gutsy Devotions for Teens*, 1992
Ken Davis, *I Don't Remember Dropping the Skunk, but I Do Remember Trying to Breathe: A Survival Guide for Teenagers*, 1990
Brian Shipman, *WWJD Today?: Daily Time with Jesus: A Devotional*, 1998

476

J.B. PHILLIPS

Your God Is Too Small

(New York: Macmillans, 1953)

Category: Theology
Subject(s): Christianity
Age range(s): Adult

Summary: In a very slim volume that has become a Christian nonfiction classic, J.B. Phillips addresses the limits of the human imagination in visualizing and comprehending God. He points out that most of us are likely to reduce our mind's picture of God to something like ''Grand Old Man,'' or ''Resident Policeman.'' To counteract this, Phillips suggests ways to move beyond these limits that can result in a more mature and meaningful faith, and a more realistic portrayal of an infinite entity that cannot be physically seen.

Other books by the same author:
The Price of Success: An Autobiography, 1984
The New Testament in Modern English, 1972

Other books you might like:
Mortimer J. Adler, *How to Think about God: A Guide for the 20th-Century Pagan*, 1980
Tom Harpur, *The Thinking Person's Guide to God: Overcoming the Obstacles to Belief*, 1996
J.I. Packer, *Knowing God*, 1973
Francis A. Schaeffer, *The God Who Is There: Speaking Historic Christianity into the Twentieth Century*, 1968

477

ROBERT M. PIRSIG

Zen and the Art of Motorcycle Maintenance: An Inquiry into Values

(New York: Morrow, 1974)

Category: Autobiography
Subject(s): Buddhism; Self-Awareness; Ethics
Age range(s): Adult

Summary: Pirsig's book tuned an entire generation on to the powers of the mind. He sets off on his motorcycle with his 11-year-old son on a coast-to-coast journey, searching to find himself. As he makes his way, he becomes more and more at one with his machine. Thus, he discovers that taking care of himself is analogous to maintaining his cycle, and he begins describing his literal journey in figurative flights of fancy that end with his gaining self-awareness. While the book now has a dated feel, it still remains popular.

Other books by the same author:
Lila: An Inquiry into Morals, 1991

Other books you might like:
Richard Bach, *Illusions: The Adventures of a Reluctant Messiah*, 1977
Ram Dass, *Be Here Now*, 1971
Eugen Herrigel, *Zen in the Art of Archery*, 1953
Jack Kerouac, *On the Road*, 1957
Shunryu Suzuki, *Zen Mind, Beginner's Mind*, 1970

478

JOHN POLKINGHORNE

Belief in God in an Age of Science
(New Haven, Connecticut: Yale University Press, 1998)

Category: Theology
Subject(s): Religion; Science
Age range(s): Adult

Summary: Author John Polkinghorne draws upon his knowledge as both a theoretical physicist and an ordained Anglican priest in this exploration of the common ground between science and theology. Polkinghorne's thesis is that each discipline has evolved from an ongoing search for truth, however that may be found, and that the mysteries and discoveries of each side should enlighten and enrich the inquiry of the other.

Other books by the same author:
Science and Theology: An Introduction, 1998
The Faith of a Physicist, 1994
Quarks, Chaos and Christianity: Questions to Science and Religion, 1995
Serious Talk: Science and Religion in Dialogue, 1995

Other books you might like:
Robert H. Eisenman, *The Dead Sea Scrolls Uncovered: The First Complete Translation and Interpretation of 50 Key Documents Withheld for over 35 Years*, 1992
Chet Raymo, *Skeptics and True Believers: The Exhilarating Connection between Science and Religion*, 1998
Russell Shorto, *Gospel Truth: The New Image of Jesus Emerging From Science and History and Why It Matters*, 1997
Richard Swinburne, *Is There a God?*, 1996
Edward O. Wilson, *Consilience: The Unity of Knowledge*, 1998

479

JOHN POLLOCK

Billy Graham, Evangelist to the World: An Authorized Biography of the Decisive Years
(New York: Harper, 1979)

Category: Biography
Subject(s): Christianity; Evangelism; Ministry
Age range(s): Adult

Summary: *Billy Graham, Evangelist to the World* is one of numerous biographies written about Billy Graham during his long and successful career as a world-renowned Christian evangelist. This authorized biography, written with cooperation from Billy Graham and the Billy Graham Evangelistic Association, focuses particularly on the late 1960s and early 1970s in Billy Graham's life and ministry. The emphasis is on the behind-the-scenes preacher and the team that worked with him to expand the Billy Graham Crusades throughout the world. A few years after this volume appeared, Pollock's biographical study of Billy Graham was expanded with the publication of *To All the Nations: The Billy Graham Story*.

Other books by the same author:
On Fire for God: Great Missionary Pioneers, 1990
A Fistful of Heroes: Great Reformers and Evangelists, 1988
To All the Nations: The Billy Graham Story, 1985

Other books you might like:
Billy Graham, *Just as I Am: The Autobiography of Billy Graham*, 1997
William Martin, *A Prophet with Honor: The Billy Graham Story*, 1991
Gerald S. Strober, *Graham: A Day in Billy's Life*, 1976
Sherwood Eliot Wirt, *Billy: A Personal Look at Billy Graham, the World's Best-Loved Evangelist*, 1997

480

DENNIS PRAGER
JOSEPH TELUSHKIN, Co-Author

The Nine Questions People Ask about Judaism
(New York: Simon and Schuster, 1981)

Category: Doctrine; Theology
Subject(s): Judaism; Religion
Age range(s): Adult

Summary: A revised edition of *Eight Questions People Ask about Judaism* (1975), *The Nine Questions People Ask about Judaism* has become a well-read introduction to the Jewish faith. Prager offers answers to basic theological and doctrinal questions that help Jews and non-Jews alike, presenting Judaism as a logical, morally sound religious tradition that has much to offer in a well-educated, sophisticated, contemporary society.

Other books by the same author:
Happiness Is a Serious Problem, 1998
Think a Second Time, 1995
Why the Jews?: The Reason for Antisemitism, 1983

Other books you might like:
Alfred J. Kolatch, *The Jewish Book of Why*, 1995 revised edition
Maurice Lamm, *Living Torah in America*, 1993
Norman Lamm, *Faith and Doubt: Studies in Traditional Jewish Thought*, 1971

481

ELIZABETH PRENTISS

Stepping Heavenward: A Tale of Home Life

(London: T. Nelson and Sons, 1876)

Category: Journals/Letters
Subject(s): Adolescence; Christian Life
Age range(s): Young Adult-Adult
Time period(s): 19th century (1834-1878)

Summary: From her sixteenth birthday on, Elizabeth Prentiss, an eighteenth-century writer of stories for children, recorded her personal and spiritual journey. Quite popular during the years following her death in 1878, her words, still in print, have found new audiences more than a century after she lived and died. Elizabeth Prentiss's journal opens a door to finding true happiness in the routines and tasks of one's daily life through love of Christ.

Other books by the same author:
The Life and Letters of Elizabeth Prentiss, 1987
Little Suzy's Little Servants, 1869

Other books you might like:
Elisabeth Elliot, *Love Has a Price Tag*, 1979
Susan Hunt, *The True Woman: The Beauty and Strength of a Godly Woman*, 1997
Anne Ortlund, *Disciplines of the Beautiful Woman*, 1977
Edith Schaeffer, *Hidden Art*, 1971

482

JOHN RANDOLPH PRICE

The Angels Within Us

(New York: Fawcett Columbine, 1993)

Category: Self-Help
Subject(s): Angels; Spirituality
Age range(s): Adult

Summary: Do you know how to meet your angels? John Randolph Price introduces twenty-two angel archetypes, such as the Angel of Unconditional Love and Freedom, that live in the hearts and souls of those who believe. Price offers guidance, in the form of exercises and meditations, for identifying which angel is needed for a particular problem, finding that angel within, and asking it for help and direction.

Other books by the same author:
Living a Life of Joy, 1997
The Superbeings: They Are with Us Now, Demonstrating What We All Can Become, 1997
Angel Energy: How to Harness the Power of Angels in Your Everyday Life, 1995

Other books you might like:
Sophy Burnham, *A Book of Angels: Reflections on Angels Past and Present and True Stories of How They Touch Our Lives*, 1990
Karen Goldman, *Angel Voices: The Advanced Handbook for Aspiring Angels*, 1993
Anthony D'Agostino, illustrator

David Laskin, *An Angel a Week*, 1992

483

REYNOLDS PRICE

The Three Gospels

(New York: Scribner, 1996)

Category: Scripture; Religious Commentaries
Subject(s): Bible; Spirituality
Age range(s): Adult

Summary: Acclaimed novelist, poet, essayist, literary critic and playwright Reynolds Price presents the life of Jesus from a literary and intimately spiritual perspective, faithful to the renderings of the New Testament, as seen through the prism of his faith and personal experience. In *The Three Gospels*, Price offers his translations of the writings of the apostles Mark and John, accompanied by prefatory essays that provide commentary and background on the original Greek texts and the context in which they were written. The third gospel of the collection consists of apocryphal writings by Price himself, in which he blends gospel accounts from the four Biblical books, Matthew, Mark, Luke, and John, and events from unorthodox sources.

Other books by the same author:
Letter to a Man in the Fire: Does God Exist and Does He Care?, 1999
Learning a Trade: A Craftsman's Notebook, 1998
A Whole New Life: An Illness and a Healing, 1994

Other books you might like:
Robert Alter, *The Literary Guide to the Bible*, 1987
Frank Kermode, co-editor
Francis J. Moloney, *Beginning the Good News: A Narrative Approach*, 1995
Walter Wangerin Jr., *The Book of God: The Bible as a Novel*, 1996

484

MICHEL QUOIST

Prayers

(New York: Sheed and Ward, 1963)

Category: Prayer
Subject(s): Spirituality; Christianity
Age range(s): Adult

Summary: This volume, translated from Michel Quoist's original French in 1963 by Agnes M. Forsyth and Anne Marie de Commaille, reveals a wide spectrum of prayerful spirituality within the Christian tradition. Here, prayer is not just words, petitions, or recitations. Prayer is living and breathing action, from the act of offering help in the name of Jesus to the complete submission of oneself to God in mystical prayer and worship.

Other books by the same author:
New Prayers, 1989
With Open Heart, 1983
The Secret to Success, 1963

Other books you might like:
Duane W.H. Arnold, *Prayers of the Martyrs*, 1991
James P. Carse, *The Silence of God: Meditations on Prayer*, 1985
Edith Schaeffer, *The Life of Prayer*, 1992

485

MAHARSHI RAMANA

Be as You Are: The Teachings of Sri Ramana Maharshi

(New York: Viking Penguin, 1991)

Category: Biography
Subject(s): Hinduism; Spirituality; Religious Life
Age range(s): Adult

Summary: This collection and examination of the teachings of Sri Ramana Maharshi offers an introduction to a contemporary master of Indian thought. A charismatic teacher and spiritual leader, Sri Ramana Maharshi encourages followers to use self-inquiry and silence in the pursuit of self-awareness and spiritual identity. Godman provides valuable background and context for new and veteran readers of the master's works.

Other books by the same author:
The Spiritual Teaching of Ramana Maharshi, 1972
The Teachings of Bhagavan Sri Ramana Maharshi in His Own Words, 1962
The Collected Works of Ramana Maharshi, 1959 (Arthur Osborne, editor)

Other books you might like:
T.S. Anantha Murthy, *The Life and Teachings of Sri Ramana Maharshi*, 1990
T.M.P. Mahadevan, *Ramana Maharshi: The Sage of Aruncala*, 1977
Arthur Osborne, *Ramana Maharshi and the Path of Self-Knowledge: A Biography*, 1954

486

WILLIAM M. RAMSAY

The Westminster Guide to the Books of the Bible

(Louisville: Westminster John Knox Press, 1994)

Category: Religious Commentaries
Subject(s): Bible; History; Culture
Age range(s): Adult

Summary: *The Westminster Guide to the Books of the Bible* is a compact, one-volume reference work suitable for use by students, ministers, and lay study groups. William Ramsay presents current biblical knowledge in an accessible, ecumenical format, providing an introduction to each book of the Bible, including the Apocryphal writings. The guide is based on the New Revised Standard Version of the Bible.

Other books by the same author:
The Layman's Guide to the New Testament, 1981
The Meaning of Jesus Christ, 1964

The Christ of the Earliest Christians, 1959

Other books you might like:
John Bowker, *The Complete Bible Handbook*, 1998
Carl Lofmark, *What Is the Bible?*, 1992
Bruce M. Metzger, *The Oxford Companion to the Bible*, 1993
  Michael D. Coogan, co-editor
Richard G. Walsh, *Reading the Bible: An Introduction*, 1997

487

CHAIM RAPHAEL

Festival Days: A History of Jewish Celebrations

(New York: Grove Weidenfeld, 1991)

Category: History
Subject(s): Culture; Holidays, Jewish
Age range(s): Adult

Summary: Chaim Raphael's *Festival Days* provides a solid resource for information about Jewish holidays, festivals, celebrations, and observances. With a focus on the history and origins of events central to Jewish experience, this volume offers background information for those who want to know more about how certain customs and traditions came to be a part of the Jewish heritage.

Other books by the same author:
The Bible Heritage, 1998
A Jewish Book of Common Prayer, 1986
The Springs of Jewish Life, 1983
Encounters with the Jewish People, 1979

Other books you might like:
Hyman E. Goldin, *Treasury of Jewish Holidays: History, Legends, Traditions*, 1953
Alfred J. Kolatch, *The Jewish Book of Why*, 1995 revised edition
Hayyim Schauss, *The Jewish Festivals: From Their Beginnings to Our Own Day*, 1938
  Samuel Jaffe, translator

488

SILVER RAVENWOLF

To Ride a Silver Broomstick: New Generation Witchcraft

(St. Paul: Llewellyn, 1993)

Category: Self-Help
Subject(s): Wicca; Witches and Witchcraft
Age range(s): Young Adult-Adult

Summary: Silver RavenWolf is an accomplished author of handbooks and guides to Wicca and witchcraft targeted at beginners. Written with humor, *To Ride a Silver Broomstick* offers a step-by-step approach to learning the basics of witchcraft. The book includes progressive lessons, personal anecdotes and journal suggestions for people of all ages and backgrounds who are interested in knowing more about fundamental aspects of witchcraft.

Other books by the same author:
To Light a Sacred Flame, 1999
Silver's Spells for Prosperity, 1999
Teen Witch: Wicca for a New Generation, 1998
To Stir a Magick Cauldron, 1995

Other books you might like:
Laurie Cabot, *Power of the Witch*, 1989
  Tom Cowan, co-author
Scott Cunningham, *Wicca: A Guide for the Solitary Practitioner*, 1988
Starhawk, *The Spiral Dance: A Rebirth of the Ancient Religion of the Great Goddess*, 1979

489

JAMES REDFIELD

The Celestine Vision: Living the New Spiritual Awareness
(New York: Warner Books, 1997)

Category: New Age (Nonfiction); Self-Help
Subject(s): Success; Spirituality
Age range(s): Adult

Summary: James Redfield turns to psychology and physics to demonstrate the blending of philosophies from East and West that is taking place in the world. Basing his work on research about reader response to his bestselling novel *The Celestine Prophecy*, Redfield guides readers of *The Celestine Vision* through the process of finding and claiming their own vision for life.

Other books by the same author:
The Song of Celestine, 1998
The Tenth Insight: Holding the Vision, 1996
The Celestine Prophecy: An Adventure, 1993

Other books you might like:
Sarah Ban Breathnach, *Simple Abundance: A Daybook of Comfort and Joy*, 1995
Deepak Chopra, *The Way of the Wizard: Twenty Spiritual Lessons in Creating the Life You Want*, 1995
Gregg Levoy, *Callings: Finding and Following an Authentic Life*, 1997
Marianne Williamson, *Illuminata: Thoughts, Prayers, Rites of Passage*, 1994

490

CHRISTOPHER REEVE

Still Me
(New York: Random House, 1998)

Category: Autobiography
Subject(s): Accidents; Family; Physically Handicapped
Age range(s): Young Adult-Adult
Time period(s): 20th century
Locale(s): United States

Summary: In *Still Me*, ''Superman'' Christopher Reeve describes his life before and after the accident that paralyzed him. He recounts his early childhood, his schooling, and his

budding acting career. Reeve writes about the riding accident that resulted in quadraplegia, and he discusses his recovery, his family life and support, and his dreams and plans for the future.

Other books you might like:
Adrian Havill, *Man of Steel: The Career and Courage of Christopher Reeve*, 1996
Jane Kelly Kosek, *Learning about Courage From the Life of Christopher Reeve*, 1999
Chris Nickson, *Superhero: A Biography of Christopher Reeve*, 1998
Joni Eareckson, *Joni*, 1976
Evans G. Valens, *A Long Way Up: The Story of Jill Kinmont*, 1966

491

GAIL TWERSKY REIMER, Editor
JUDITH A. KATES, Co-Editor

Beginning Anew: A Woman's Companion to the High Holy Days
(New York: Simon & Schuster, 1997)

Category: Devotionals; Theology
Subject(s): Religious Life; Women
Age range(s): Adult

Summary: *Beginning Anew* is a collection of essays and articles written by contemporary feminist writers, philosophers, scholars, and theologians. The focus is on women's relationships with other women and with God throughout Jewish history, and the writings are centered on the biblical texts read in observance of Rosh Hashanah and Yom Kippur. Themes throughout the essays include sacrifice, repentance, forgiveness, and love. The anthology provides thought-provoking commentary and new perspectives on women in Judaism.

Other books you might like:
Ellen Frankel, *The Five Books of Miriam: A Woman's Commentary on the Torah*, 1996
Judith Hauptman, *Rereading the Rabbis: A Woman's Voice*, 1998
Judith Plaskow, *Standing Again at Sinai: Judaism From a Feminist Perspective*, 1990

492

PAUL REPS, Editor

Zen Flesh, Zen Bones: A Collection of Zen and Pre-Zen Writings
(Rutland, Vermont: Tuttle, 1957)

Category: Scripture
Subject(s): Buddhism; Storytelling; Literature
Age range(s): Adult

Summary: This classic collection of works from the Zen canon was first published in the United States in 1957, and it remains a valued resource. Paul Reps has gathered four important works that provide the basis for Zen as it is understood today. ''101 Zen Stories'' relates stories from five centuries of Chinese and Japanese Zen teachers. "The Gateless Gate" dates back to the 13th century, and shares mind problems (koans) used in Zen practice. Fundamental teachings about awareness and enlightenment are found in "The Ten Bulls," a manuscript from the 12th century. Finally, from India, there is "Centering," a 4000-year-old collection of thoughts that is thought to be the origin of Zen.

Other books by the same author:
Ten Ways to Meditate, 1969
Zen Telegrams, 1962 (poems)
Unknot the World in You, 1955

Other books you might like:
Philip Kapleau, *The Three Pillars of Zen: Teaching, Practice, and Enlightenment*, 1965
Nelson Foster, *The Roaring Stream: A New Zen Reader*, 1996 Jack Shoemaker, co-editor
Alan Watts, *The Way of Zen*, 1957

493

HELEN STEINER RICE

A Book of Prayer

(Grand Rapids, Michigan: F.H. Revell, 1995)

Category: Prayer
Subject(s): Christianity; Religious Life
Age range(s): Adult

Summary: From one of America's best-loved inspirational poets comes this compilation of prayers. Helen Steiner Rice (1900-1981) wrote poetry for the Gibson Greeting Card company for many years, starting in 1931. Her books of verse and prayers have remained popular, and many of her works have been recombined into new collections, such as this one compiled by Virginia J. Ruehlmann. The focus of these verse prayers is on the fact that God is always present and listening to our prayers.

Other books by the same author:
Helen Steiner Rice's Poems of Faith, 1981
Somebody Loves You, 1976
Life Is Forever, 1974
Someone Cares: The Collected Poems of Helen Steiner Rice, 1972

Other books you might like:
Joy Morgan Davis, *I'm Ready for My Rainbow, Lord*, 1998
Catherine De Vinck, *A Basket of Bread: An Anthology of Selected Poems*, 1997
Peggy L. Shriver, *Pinches of Salt: Spiritual Seasonings*, 1990

494

HELEN STEINER RICE

Somebody Loves You

(Old Tappan, New Jersey: F.H. Revell, 1976)

Category: Poetry
Subject(s): Christianity; Love; Friendship
Age range(s): Adult

Summary: This collection of poems by Helen Steiner Rice is a reminder in verse of God's love and the gift of friendship. Rice's poetry still appears on a line of greeting cards, and her works continue to be popular in new collections. This is one of Rice's original gift books of Christian poetry.

Other books by the same author:
A Book of Prayer, 1995
Helen Steiner Rice's Poems of Faith, 1981
Life Is Forever, 1974
Someone Cares: The Collected Poems of Helen Steiner Rice, 1972

Other books you might like:
Ruth Bell Graham, *Ruth Bell Graham's Collected Poems*, 1997
Linda Dini Jenkins, *Journey of a Returning Christian: Writing into God*, 1994
Anne Porter, *An Altogether Different Language: Poems 1934-1994*, 1994

495

ANTHONY ROBBINS

Awaken the Giant Within: How to Take Immediate Control of Your Mental, Emotional, Physical, & Financial Destiny

(New York: Summit Books, 1991)

Category: Self-Help
Subject(s): Success; Money
Age range(s): Adult

Summary: Motivational speaker and seminar "guru" Anthony Robbins shares step-by-step plans and strategies for overcoming emotional obstacles to material success. Anecdotes from people's experiences with Robbins' "Date with Destiny" seminars are featured. Robbins explains how subconscious beliefs can sabotage conscious efforts to change behaviors, and he offers ways to remedy the problem.

Other books by the same author:
Ebony Power Thoughts: Inspirational Thoughts From Outstanding African-Americans, 1997 (Joseph McClendon III, co-author)
Unlimited Power: A Black Choice, 1997 (Joseph McClendon III, co-author)
Notes From a Friend: A Quick and Simple Guide to Taking Charge of Your Life, 1995
Giant Steps: Small Changes to Make a Big Difference: Daily Lessons in Self-Mastery, 1994
Unlimited Power: The New Science of Personal Achievement, 1986

Other books you might like:
Deepak Chopra, *The Way of the Wizard: Twenty Spiritual Lessons in Creating the Life You Want*, 1995
Stephen R. Covey, *The 7 Habits of Highly Effective People*, 1989
Stephen R. Covey, *First Things First*, 1994
Zig Ziglar, *Over the Top*, 1994
Zig Ziglar, *See You at the Top*, 1979

496

PAT ROBERTSON
JAMIE BUCKINGHAM, Co-Author

The Autobiography of Pat Robertson: Shout It From the Housetops!

(South Plainfield, New Jersey: Bridge, 1995)

Category: Autobiography
Subject(s): Christian Life; Television; Politics
Age range(s): Adult

Summary: Pat Robertson, long-time host of ''The 700 Club'' on television and a well-known Christian conservative and political candidate, tells the story of his life in an autobiography first published in 1972 but revised in 1995. Robertson shares the story of his faith journey and the call to ministry that resulted in his becoming a public figure, first through television ministry and then through involvement in presidential politics.

Other books by the same author:
The End of the Age: A Novel, 1995
Beyond Reason: How Miracles Can Change Your Life, 1985
The Secret Kingdom, 1982

Other books you might like:
John B. Donovan, *Pat Robertson: The Authorized Biography*, 1988
Billy Graham, *Just as I Am: The Autobiography of Billy Graham*, 1997
Oral Roberts, *Expect a Miracle: My Life and Ministry*, 1995
Gerard Thomas Straub, *Salvation for Sale: An Insider's View of Pat Robertson*, 1988

497

JAMES M. ROBINSON, Editor

The Nag Hammadi Library in English

(San Francisco: Harper and Row, 1988)

Category: Scripture; History
Subject(s): Gnosticism; Jesus; Christianity
Age range(s): Adult

Summary: In 1945, workers discovered a wealth of writings that shed light on the practices of Egyptian Christianity. These writings developed a particular form of Christianity, called Gnosticism, that often focused on the evil of the material world and the good of the spiritual world. This collection represents the first translation of many of these texts into English. Many of the Gospels in the collection contain the sayings of Jesus as recorded by this particular community.

Other books by the same author:
Trajectories through Early Christianity, 1971

Other books you might like:
Ron Cameron, *The Other Gospels: Non-Canonical Gospel Texts*, 1982
Burton L. Mack, *The Lost Gospel: The Book of Q and Christian Origins*, 1993
Marvin Meyer, *The Gospel of Thomas: The Hidden Sayings of Jesus*, 1992

Elaine Pagels, *The Gnostic Paul: Gnostic Exegesis of the Pauline Letters*, 1975
Birger A. Pearson, *The Roots of Egyptian Christianity*, 1986

498

JOHN A.T. ROBINSON

Honest to God

(Philadelphia: Westminster Press, 1963)

Category: Theology
Subject(s): Christianity; God; Jesus
Age range(s): Adult

Summary: What does it mean to be honest to God? For Robinson, it means nothing less than the overthrowing of the conventional image of God. In order for us to be citizens of the modern world, he notes, we must do away with the image of God as ''up there'' or ''out there.'' He also contends that Christians cannot continue to think of Christ in the purely mythical or supernatural terms of Christian doctrine. Robinson challenges every aspect of Christian doctrine in his revolutionary book.

Other books by the same author:
Truth Is Two-Eyed, 1979

Other books you might like:
Thomas J.J. Altizer, *The Descent into Hell: A Study of the Radical Reversal of the Christian Consciousness*, 1970
Harvey Cox, *The Secular City: Secularization and Urbanization in Theological Perspective*, 1965
Robert W. Funk, *Honest to Jesus: Jesus for a New Millennium*, 1996
Michael Goulder, *Incarnation and Myth: The Debate Continued*, 1979
John Hick, *The Myth of God Incarnate*, 1977

499

DALE EVANS ROGERS

Angel Unaware

(Westwood, New Jersey: Revell, 1953)

Category: Devotionals; Journals/Letters
Subject(s): Christianity; Down Syndrome; Death
Age range(s): Young Adult-Adult

Summary: Born with Down Syndrome in a time when the condition was little understood, Robin Elizabeth Rogers, daughter of celebrities Dale Evans and Roy Rogers, died when she was two years old. This endearing book takes the form of letters to her mother from heaven. Robin offers comfort and love to her mother as well as a portrait of God's love and His heavenly realm. Though saddened by the death of her child, Dale Evans Rogers learns the wonders of God's unswerving mercy and grace from the pen of her own little angel, Robin.

Other books you might like:
Deborah L. Davis, *Empty Cradle, Broken Heart: Surviving the Death of Your Baby*, 1991

Jack Hayford, *I'll Hold You in Heaven: Healing and Hope for the Parent Who Has Lost a Child through Miscarriage, Stillbirth, Abortion, or Early Infant Death*, 1990

Larry Jansen, *My Sister Is Special*, 1998

Lee Klein, *Are There Stripes in Heaven?*, 1994

Pam W. Vredevelt, *Angel Behind the Rocker: Stories of Hope in Unexpected Places*, 1997

500

FRED ROGERS

You Are Special: Words of Wisdom From America's Most Beloved Neighbor

(New York: Viking, 1994)

Category: Self-Help
Subject(s): Parent and Child; Childhood; Relationships
Age range(s): Adult

Summary: Mister Rogers steps out of his neighborhood to visit with adults in *You Are Special*. Fred Rogers is an ordained Presbyterian clergyman whose specialized ministry for more than 25 years has been to families, especially young children, through the work of Family Communications and his eponymous television program, "Mister Rogers' Neighborhood." In this volume, Rogers shares his insights and encouragement on topics from parent-child relationships to seeking and maintaining friendships throughout a lifetime. The thoughtful attention to diversity and respect that characterizes his work with children is evident in Rogers' messages to adults, as well.

Other books by the same author:
Dear Mister Rogers, Does It Ever Rain in Your Neighborhood?: Letters to Mr. Rogers, 1996
Mister Rogers Talks with Families about Divorce, 1988
Mister Rogers' Playbook: Insights and Activities for Parents and Children, 1986
Mister Rogers Talks with Parents, 1983

Other books you might like:
Vicki Lansky, *101 Ways to Make Your Child Feel Special*, 1991
    Kaye Pomaranc White, illustrator
Vicki Lansky, *101 Ways to Tell Your Child "I Love You"*, 1988
    Kaye Pomaranc White, illustrator
Clifton L. Taulbert, *Eight Habits of the Heart: Embracing the Values That Build Strong Families and Communities*, 1999

501

RICHARD ROHR
ANDREAS EBERT, Co-Author

Discovering the Enneagram: An Ancient Tool for a New Spiritual Journey

(New York: Crossroad, 1990)

Category: New Age (Nonfiction); Self-Help
Subject(s): Spirituality; Psychology
Age range(s): Adult

Summary: Richard Rohr and Andreas Ebert explain how to use the enneagram to promote self-awareness and spiritual growth. The enneagram is a structured approach to knowing oneself that blends contemporary psychology and ancient philosophy in a system for identifying one's strengths, tendencies, and ideals. Applying this tool to one's personal life and relationships is the focus of this book, translated by Peter Heinegg.

Other books by the same author:
Enneagram II: Advancing Spiritual Discernment, 1995
The Wild Man's Journey: Reflections on Male Spirituality, 1992 (Joseph Martos, co-author)
Simplicity: The Art of Living, 1991 (Peter Heinegg, translator)

Other books you might like:
Renee Baron, *Are You My Type, Am I Yours?: Relationships Made Easy through the Enneagram*, 1995
    Elizabeth Wagele, co-author
Kathleen V. Hurley, *My Best Self: Using the Enneagram to Free the Soul*, 1993
    Theodora E. Dobson, co-author
Helen Palmer, *The Enneagram in Love and Work: Understanding Your Intimate and Business Relationships*, 1995
Elizabeth Wagele, *The Enneagram of Parenting: The 9 Types of Children and How to Raise Them Successfully*, 1997

502

DAVID ROSENBERG, Editor

Communion: Contemporary Writers Reveal the Bible in Their Lives

(New York: Anchor Books, 1996)

Category: Essays
Subject(s): Bible; Religious Life; Spirituality
Age range(s): Adult

Summary: What effect has the Bible had on the lives of famous writers? More than thirty authors from a wide background of cultures and religious traditions share their thoughts about the influence of biblical writings on their personal and professional lives in this collection of essays. Some reflect on their childhood memories of hearing Bible stories and poetry read aloud. Some recognize patterns in their work that have their roots in the themes or cadences of Old Testament chronicles. Their essays are personal, profound, funny, reflective, and revealing. Authors who have contributed to this collection include Joyce Carol Oates, Bharati Mukherjee, Denise Levertov, Robert Coles, John Barth, Michael Dorris, and David Bradley.

Other books by the same author:
The Lost Book of Paradise: Adam and Eve in the Garden of Eden, 1993
The Movie That Changed My Life, 1991
A Poet's Bible: Rediscovering the Voices of the Original Text, 1991

Other books you might like:
Kathy Keay, *Dancing on Mountains: An Anthology of Women's Spiritual Writings*, 1996

Amy Mandelker, *Pilgrim Souls: An Anthology of Spiritual Autobiographies*, 1999
Elizabeth Powers, co-editor
Lucinda Vardey, *God in All Worlds: An Anthology of Contemporary Spiritual Writing*, 1995
Philip Zaleski, *The Best Spiritual Writing, 1998*, 1998

503

DAVID ROSENBERG, Editor

Genesis as It Is Written: Contemporary Writers on Our First Stories

(San Francisco: HarperSanFrancisco, 1996)

Category: Religious Commentaries
Subject(s): Bible; Creation; Faith
Age range(s): Adult

Summary: In *Genesis as It Is Written*, editor David Rosenberg brings together a wide community of contemporary writers to reflect the diversity of the authors of the Old Testament book of Genesis. Representing three major world religious traditions-Judaism, Catholicism, and Protestantism-the authors also represent a spectrum of genres, including poetry, drama, stories, novels, and essays. In this collection of literary writings on Genesis, the emphasis is on returning to the original stories, stripping away generations of contemporary commentary and theological explication, and hearing the stories anew, from the perspective of the storyteller. Writings collected here include Arthur Miller on the story of Adam and Eve; Ron Hansen on the story of Cain; Kathleen Norris on the story of Rebekah as a mother; Edward Hirsch on the story of Jacob's encounter with an angel; and Norma Rosen on the story of Sarah's late-in-life pregnancy.

Other books by the same author:
Communion: Contemporary Writers Reveal the Bible in Their Lives, 1996
A Poet's Bible: Rediscovering the Voices of the Original Text, 1991
Testimony: Contemporary Writers Make the Holocaust Personal, 1989
Job Speaks: Interpreted From the Original Hebrew Book of Job, 1977

Other books you might like:
Karen Armstrong, *In the Beginning: A New Interpretation of Genesis*, 1996
Norman J. Cohen, *Voices From Genesis: Guiding Us through the Stages of Life*, 1998
Bill Moyers, *Genesis: A Living Conversation*, 1996
Burton L. Visotzky, *Reading the Book: Making the Bible a Timeless Text*, 1991
Avivah Gottlieb Zornberg, *The Beginning of Desire: Reflections on Genesis*, 1996

504

NAOMI H. ROSENBLATT
JOSHUA HORWITZ, Co-Author

Wrestling with Angels: What the First Family of Genesis Teaches Us about Our Spiritual Identity, Sexuality, and Personal Relationships

(New York: Delacorte, 1995)

Category: Religious Commentaries
Subject(s): Bible; Psychology; Spirituality
Age range(s): Adult

Summary: What can we learn from the first recorded accounts of interpersonal relationships in the Old Testament of the Bible? Naomi Rosenblatt, psychotherapist and long-time Bible study teacher, explores this question in *Wrestling with Angels*, an examination of the book of Genesis. She organizes her thoughts into four themes: the formation of spiritual identity, the family as a covenant with God, managing the challenge of relationships, and family reconciliation as a natural outcome of a faith journey. The problems within the families of the Old Testament mirror those that exist today, says Rosenblatt, noting that sibling rivalry, greed, and infidelity are still causing problems thousands of years later. This title is appropriate for both Jews and Christians as a vehicle for discovering how the teachings of their heritage can be applied to life today.

Other books by the same author:
In God's Image: Enduring Wisdom From the Old Testament, 1998

Other books you might like:
Karen Armstrong, *In the Beginning: A New Interpretation of Genesis*, 1996
Norman J. Cohen, *Voices From Genesis: Guiding Us through the Stages of Life*, 1998
Avivah Gottlieb Zornberg, *The Beginning of Desire: Reflections on Genesis*, 1996

505

CHRISTINA ROSSETTI

Poems and Prose

(New York: Everyman Paperback Classics, 1997)

Category: Poetry; Essays
Subject(s): Essays; Fiction; Poetry
Age range(s): Young Adult-Adult

Summary: One of Britain's most memorable poets, Christina Rossetti (1830-1894) is still read by poetry enthusiasts of all ages. Rossetti also wrote fiction and essays. This volume offers poems and prose that represent the best and most characteristic works of Rossetti. Themes of religion and spirituality are common in her work. This edition, edited by Jan Marsh, provides background material about the poet, including an introduction to the text, a biography, and a chronology of her life and times.

Other books you might like:
Diane D'Amico, *Christina Rossetti: Faith, Gender, and Time*, 1999
Emily Dickinson, *Selected Poems and Letters of Emily Dickinson*, 1959
  Robert N. Linscott, editor
Debi Gliori, *What Can I Give Him?*, 1998
  based on a Rossetti poem
C.S. Lewis, *Spirits in Bondage: A Cycle of Lyrics*, 1984
Jan Marsh, *Christina Rossetti: A Writer's Life*, 1995

506

JELALUDDIN RUMI

The Essential Rumi

(San Francisco: HarperSanFrancisco, 1995)

Category: Poetry
Subject(s): Mysticism; Islam
Age range(s): Adult

Summary: Coleman Barks has translated major works by thirteenth-century Persian mystic poet Rumi for this volume. Rumi (1207-1273), whose full name was Jalal al-Din Muhammad, was notable as a Sufi devotee and poet whose thousands of works were inspired by spiritual mentors and friends. Themes in Rumi's poetry include love, sadness, loneliness, sexuality, beauty, and human friendship.

Other books by the same author:
Love Is a Stranger: Selected Lyric Poetry of Jelaluddin Rumi, 1993
Delicious Laughter: Rambunctious Teaching Stories From the Mathnawi of Jelaluddin Rumi, 1990

Other books you might like:
Coleman Barks, *The Hand of Poetry: Five Mystic Poets of Persia*, 1993
Kahlil Gibran, *The Prophet*, 1923
Hafiz, *The Gift: Poems by the Great Sufi Master*, 1999
  Daniel James Ladinsky, translator
Omar Khayyam, *Rubayait of Omar Khayyam, the Astronomer-Poet of Persia*, 1859
Anuradha Mahapatra, *Another Spring, Darkness*, 1996
  Carolyn Wright, Paramita Banerjee, Datta Jvotirmoy, translators

507

JELALUDDIN RUMI

Love Is a Stranger: Selected Lyric Poetry of Jelaluddin Rumi

(Putney, Vermont: Threshold Books, 1993)

Category: Poetry
Subject(s): Islam; Sufism; Allah
Age range(s): Adult

Summary: Jelaluddin Rumi (1207-1273) is the best known of the great Sufi poets. His beautiful lyrics that contemplate Allah and the love between lover and beloved have become tremendously popular among groups of spiritual seekers of all faiths. This collection provides a nice introduction to Rumi's

soaring contemplative flights. The 1993 edition was translated by Kabir Edmund Helminski.

Other books by the same author:
Rumi: In the Arms of the Beloved, 1997 (Jonathan Star, translator)

Other books you might like:
Denise Breton, *Love, Soul, and Freedom: Dancing with Rumi on the Mystic Path*, 1998
Andrew Harvey, *Perfume of the Desert: Inspirations From the Sufi Wisdom*, 1999
Daniel Ladinsky, *I Heard God Laughing: Renderings of Hafiz*, 1996
Seyyed Hossein Nasr, *Sufi Essays*, 1972
Annemarie Schimmel, *Mystical Dimensions of Islam*, 1975

508

BERTRAND RUSSELL

Why I Am Not a Christian

(London: Watts, 1927)

Category: Theology
Subject(s): Philosophy; Atheism
Age range(s): Adult

Summary: In a classic of 20th century philosophical thought, Bertrand Russell outlines his arguments against all religion. Russell's rational approach to religion was an extension of his point of view on matters of social and scientific significance. The explication of his beliefs in *Why I Am Not a Christian* and *What I Believe* (1925) created professional obstacles for him during the years he lived and worked in the United States, but the volume has become a foundational work for those who espouse a rationalist or atheist perspective on religion.

Other books by the same author:
A History of Western Philosophy, 1945
Religion and Science, 1935
The Scientific Outlook, 1931
What I Believe, 1925

Other books you might like:
Peter A. Angeles, *Critiques of God: Making the Case Against Belief in God*, 1997
Jim Herrick, *Against the Faith: Essays on Deists, Skeptics, and Atheists*, 1985
Gordon Stein, *An Anthology of Atheism and Rationalism*, 1980

509

PENELOPE RYAN

Practicing Catholic: The Search for a Livable Catholicism

(New York: H. Holt, 1998)

Category: Doctrine
Subject(s): Catholicism; Culture; Religious Life
Age range(s): Young Adult-Adult
Locale(s): United States

Summary: American Catholicism is characterized by disenchantment with church teachings on social issues, writes Penelope Ryan in this volume. A teacher and Catholic scholar, Ryan is concerned that the teachings of the Vatican on such subjects as birth control, ordination of women, and homosexuality is weakening the strength and vitality of Catholicism in the United States and elsewhere. She examines the background of dialogue on these and other issues, and calls for changes that will enhance the growth of Catholicism by reconciling alienated believers with the church and its teachings.

Other books you might like:

Andrew M. Greeley, *The Catholic Myth: The Behavior and Beliefs of American Catholics*, 1990

Bernard Haring, *Free and Faithful: My Life in the Catholic Church: An Autobiography*, 1998

James Killgallon, *Becoming Catholic Even If You Happen to Be One*, 1980

Paul Wilkes, *The Good Enough Catholic: A Guide for the Perplexed*, 1996

510

CHARLES CALDWELL RYRIE

The Miracles of Our Lord

(Nashville: T. Nelson, 1984)

Category: Religious Commentaries
Subject(s): Bible; Miracles
Age range(s): Adult

Summary: The miracles of Jesus are a focal point of Christianity and of the New Testament books called the gospels. In his *The Miracles of Our Lord*, biblical scholar Charles Caldwell Ryrie applies research and personal experience to his examination of each of the thirty-five miracles that are recorded in the Bible by the apostles Matthew, Mark, Luke and John.

Awards the book has won:
Gold Medallion Book Award, Gift Book/Poetry, 1985

Other books by the same author:
Transformed by His Glory, 1989
Basic Theology, 1986
You Mean the Bible Teaches That?, 1974
A Survey of Bible Doctrine, 1972

Other books you might like:

William Barclay, *And He Had Compassion*, 1975

Dwight J. Pentecost, *The Words and Work of Jesus Christ*, 1981

Warren W. Wiersbe, *Classic Sermons on the Miracles of Jesus*, 1995

511

JEFFREY K. SALKIN

Putting God on the Guest List: How to Reclaim the Spiritual Meaning of Your Child's Bar or Bat Mitzvah

(Woodstock, Vermont: Jewish Light, 1992)

Category: Self-Help
Subject(s): Judaism; Culture; Coming of Age
Age range(s): Young Adult

Summary: What is the significance of bar and bat mitzvah? Can even non-observant Jewish families find spiritual meaning in this special event? Rabbi Salkin answers these and many more questions in a contemporary, upbeat manner. He covers the historical, religious, and social aspects of the bar mitzvah ritual, and guides parents and young people in planning an occasion that serves not only as a rite of passage, but also as a connection to their heritage.

Other books by the same author:
Searching for My Brothers: Jewish Men in a Gentile World, 1999
For Kids—Putting God on Your Guest List, 1998
Being God's Partner: How to Find the Hidden Link Between Spirituality and Your Work, 1994

Other books you might like:

Judith Davis, *Whose Bar/Bat Mitzvah Is This Anyway?: A Guide for Parents through a Family Rite of Passage*, 1998

Helen Leneman, *Bar/Bat Mitzvah Basics: A Practical Family Guide to Coming of Age Together*, 1996

Linda Seifer Sage, *The Complete Bar-Bat Mitzvah Planner*, 1993

512

E.P. SANDERS

The Historical Figure of Jesus

(London: Penguin Press, 1993)

Category: History
Subject(s): Judaism
Age range(s): Adult
Time period(s): 1st century
Locale(s): Palestine

Summary: Using an analytical and historical approach, Sanders presents a picture of Jesus that emphasizes his role as a historical, rather than a religious, figure. Careful to distinguish between what can be assessed with certainty and what can only be suggested from the evidence, Sanders notes that it is possible to know when Jesus lived, where he traveled, and what the main themes of his teachings were. However, he asserts that it is not possible to draw conclusions, from a historical perspective, about his personality, his motivations, and the subtle meanings of his teachings. The author provides an overview of the context in which Jesus lived his life, including an account of the religious and political climate during the first century after the birth of Jesus. He also discusses the source material and analytical methods used for this study.

Other books by the same author:
Judaism: Practice and Belief, 1992
Jesus and Judaism, 1985
Studying the Synoptic Gospels, 1989

Other books you might like:
John Dominic Crossan, *Jesus: A Revolutionary Biography*, 1994
Mircea Eliade, *A History of Religious Ideas*, 1978-1985
Linwood Urban, *A Short History of Christian Thought*, 1995

513

DOROTHY L. SAYERS

The Mind of the Maker
(San Francisco: Harper & Row, 1941)

Category: Theology
Subject(s): Christianity; Nature of God; Creation
Age range(s): Adult

Summary: Dorothy L. Sayers is remembered as one of the 20th century's greatest mystery writers, but she is also recognized as a Christian scholar. In this volume, which has become a classic of Christian spiritual literature, she examines the connection between a Creator God and the creative instincts and capabilities of the human intellect. Using the analogy of the trinitarian deity—Father, Son, Holy Spirit—she explains the human creative process in triune terms as well—Idea, Energy (which translates into action), and Power (which results in interpretation of the idea).

Other books by the same author:
The Whimsical Christian: Eighteen Essays, 1978
Creed or Chaos?: And Other Essays in Popular Theology, 1949

Other books you might like:
Alan Donagan, *Reflections on Philosophy and Religion*, 1999
Thomas V. Morris, *Philosophy and the Christian Faith*, 1988
Edith Schaeffer, *A Way of Seeing*, 1977
James J. Thompson Jr., *Christian Classics Revisited*, 1983

514

DOROTHY L. SAYERS

The Whimsical Christian: Eighteen Essays
(New York: Macmillan, 1978)

Category: Theology
Subject(s): Christianity; Essays; Religion
Age range(s): Adult

Summary: Published posthumously in 1969 as *Christian Letters to a Post-Christian World*, this collection of eighteen essays demonstrates Dorothy L. Sayers' rigor in theological thinking. At the center of her writing is the belief that the creative human mind is a reflection of the Creator God. She particularly addresses the issue of doctrine and faith, taking to task those who would ignore the structure of doctrine in the living out of one's beliefs.

Other books by the same author:
Spiritual Writings, 1993 (Ann Loades, editor)
A Matter of Eternity: Selections From the Writings of Dorothy L. Sayers, 1973 (Rosamond Kent Sprague, editor)
Creed or Chaos?: And Other Essays in Popular Theology, 1949
The Mind of the Maker, 1941

Other books you might like:
Alan Donagan, *Reflections on Philosophy and Religion*, 1999
C.S. Lewis, *Surprised by Joy: The Shape of My Early Life*, 1955
Roger Lundin, *Emily Dickinson and the Art of Belief*, 1998
Thomas V. Morris, *Philosophy and the Christian Faith*, 1988

515

EDITH SCHAEFFER

Affliction
(Old Tappan, New Jersey: F.H. Revell, 1978)

Category: Essays
Subject(s): Faith; Spirituality; Christianity
Age range(s): Adult

Summary: Edith Schaeffer and her theologian husband, Francis A. Schaeffer, spent decades ministering to seekers and travelers of all ages at their home, L'Abri, in Switzerland. Based on those years of listening, counseling, biblical study, and personal experience, she shares some of the ways God reveals himself in the lives of believers. Schaeffer doesn't provide instant answers to questions about pain and suffering, but she offers a thoughtful approach for personal study and discovery.

Awards the book has won:
Gold Medallion Book Award, Bible Study/Theology, 1979

Other books by the same author:
The Life of Prayer, 1992
Common Sense Christian Living, 1983
What Is a Family?, 1975
Hidden Art, 1971
L'Abri, 1969

Other books you might like:
Kay Arthur, *As Silver Refined: Learning to Embrace Life's Disappointments*, 1998
Luis Palau, *Where Is God When Bad Things Happen?*, 1999
Joyce Rupp, *Little Pieces of Light*, 1994
Charles F. Stanley, *The Blessings of Brokenness*, 1997

516

EDITH SCHAEFFER

The Tapestry: The Life and Times of Francis and Edith Schaeffer
(Waco, Texas: Word Books, 1981)

Category: Autobiography
Subject(s): Ministry; Family Life; Christianity
Age range(s): Young Adult-Adult

Summary: This autobiographical account of a marriage weaves together the facts of a lifetime—the jobs undertaken, homes lived in, children raised—and the feelings that accompanied the day-to-day events in the lives of Edith and Francis Schaeffer. From their individual backgrounds (hers as the daughter of missionaries, his as a young atheist) to their shared ministry at L'Abri in Switzerland, Edith Schaeffer offers a personal glimpse into a marriage of loving partners whose mutual Christian faith influenced the direction of their lives together.

Awards the book has won:
Gold Medallion Book Award, Biography/Autobiography, 1982

Other books by the same author:
The Life of Prayer, 1992
Common Sense Christian Living, 1983
What Is a Family?, 1975
Everybody Can Know, 1973 (Francis A. Schaeffer, co-author)
Hidden Art, 1971

Other books you might like:
Lyle W. Dorsett, *A Love Observed: Joy Davidman's Life and Marriage to C.S. Lewis*, 1998
Madeleine L'Engle, *Two-Part Invention: The Story of a Marriage*, 1988
a journal about her marriage to Hugh Franklin
William J. Petersen, *25 Surprising Marriages: Faith-Building Stories From the Lives of Famous Christians*, 1997

517

FRANCIS A. SCHAEFFER

A Christian Manifesto

(Westchester, Illinois: Crossway Books, 1981)

Category: Theology
Subject(s): Apologetics; Christianity; History
Age range(s): Adult

Summary: In *A Christian Manifesto*, Schaeffer asserts that Christian beliefs provided the original foundation for the establishment of America's government, and that in the late 20th century, a return to those foundations is needed. Schaeffer warns of the dangers of humanism, predicting that a collapse in civility and basic regard for fellow human beings is the logical consequence of what he identifies as America's systematic dismantling of a God-centered society. Although Schaeffer's passionate belief in his point of view could lead him to write emotionally about this subject, he instead takes a thoughtful, logical approach, offering Biblical, theological, and social evidence to support his thesis.

Other books by the same author:
Whatever Happened to the Human Race?, 1979
How Should We Then Live?: The Rise and Decline of Western Thought and Culture, 1976
Back to Freedom and Dignity, 1972
The Church at the End of the Twentieth Century, 1970
The God Who Is There: Speaking Historic Christianity into the Twentieth Century, 1968

Other books you might like:
Walter C. Kaiser, *Quest for Renewal*, 1986

Arthur Michael Ramsey, *The Future of Christianity*, 1970
Paul Tillich, *The Future of Religions*, 1966

518

FRANCIS A. SCHAEFFER

Complete Works of Francis A. Schaeffer

(Westchester, Illinois: Crossway Books, 1982)

Category: Theology
Subject(s): Apologetics; Christianity; History
Age range(s): Adult

Summary: The philosophical and spiritual writings of Francis A. Schaeffer, recognized as influential within evangelical Christianity during the latter decades of the 20th century, are collected here in full. Included are his early works, in which he rigorously analyzed various world views and compared them to an equally rigorous analysis of the Christian perspective, as well as the later works that examined culture, politics, and such controversial issues as abortion and euthanasia. His first major publication, *The God Who is There*, attracted the attention of young people seeking answers to life's great questions. His later works, including *How Should We Then Live?* and *Whatever Happened to the Human Race?*, served as touchstones for evangelical Christians concerned about eroding social and civic values during the 1970s and 1980s.

Awards the book has won:
Gold Medallion Book Award, Special Judges Award, 1983

Other books by the same author:
A Christian Manifesto, 1981
He Is There and He Is Not Silent, 1972
Escape From Reason, 1968

Other books you might like:
Lane T. Dennis, *Letters of Francis A. Schaeffer: Spiritual Reality in the Personal Christian Life*, 1985
Lane T. Dennis, *Francis A. Schaeffer: Portraits of the Man and His Work*, 1986
Ronald W. Ruegsegger, *Reflections on Francis Schaeffer*, 1986

519

FRANCIS A. SCHAEFFER
C. EVERETT KOOP, Co-Author

Whatever Happened to the Human Race?

(Old Tappan, New Jersey: F.H Revell, 1979)

Category: Theology
Subject(s): Christianity; Ethics; Conduct of Life
Age range(s): Adult

Summary: *Whatever Happened to the Human Race?* was written by Francis A. Schaeffer with Dr. C. Everett Koop, who later became Surgeon General of the United States. Together, Schaeffer and Koop examine the ethics and human rights issues of controversial medical practices, including abortion. Their position is that the protection of human rights and personal security is at risk if Americans view abortion and euthanasia as nothing more than individual quality-of-life issues.

Awards the book has won:
Gold Medallion Book Award, Contemporary Issues, 1980

Other books by the same author:
A Christian Manifesto, 1981
How Should We Then Live?: The Rise and Decline of Western Thought and Culture, 1976
The God Who Is There: Speaking Historic Christianity into the Twentieth Century, 1968

Other books you might like:
Geoffrey G. Drutchas, *Is Life Sacred?*, 1998
Cynthia Gorney, *Articles of Faith: A Frontline History of the Abortion Wars*, 1998
William F. Maestri, *What the Church Teaches: A Guide for the Study of Evanglium Vitae, the Gospel of Life*, 1996

520

ULRICH SCHAFFER, Author/Illustrator

Surprised by Light

(San Francisco: Harper & Row, 1980)

Category: Poetry
Subject(s): Photography
Age range(s): Young Adult-Adult

Summary: The prayerful Christian poetry of Ulrich Schaffer is paired with his photography in this collection of poems. His work illuminates the relationship between faith and the everyday aspects of living. Other works by the author include *Greater Than Our Hearts: Prayers and Reflections*, and *A Growing Light*, a collection of meditations illustrated with Schaffer's photography and calligraphy.

Awards the book has won:
Gold Medallion Book Award, Poetry, 1982

Other books by the same author:
Growing into the Blue, 1984
With Open Eyes, 1982
Into Your Light, 1980
Searching for You, 1978

Other books you might like:
Kate Farrell, *Art and Wonder: An Illustrated Anthology of Visionary Poetry*, 1996
Douglas Lochhead, *All Things Do Continue: Poems of Celebration*, 1997
Anna Belle Pallen, *Our Day and Age: A Poetic Narration*, 1976

521

HAYYIM SCHAUSS

The Jewish Festivals: A Guide to Their History and Observance

(New York: Schocken Books, 1996)

Category: History
Subject(s): Judaism; Holidays, Jewish; Religious Traditions
Age range(s): Young Adult-Adult

Summary: In this now-classic book, first issued in 1938, Schauss offers an in-depth guide to the history of Jewish Holy Days. He provides detailed profiles of the numerous customs, rituals, and recipes that Jews use to observe these special days. The work is translated by Samuel Jaffe.

Other books by the same author:
The Lifetime of a Jew Throughout the Ages of Jewish History, 1950

Other books you might like:
Hayim Halevy Donin, *To Be a Jew: A Guide to Jewish Observance in Contemporary Life*, 1972
Reuven Hammer, *Entering the High Holy Days: A Guide to the Origins, Themes, and Prayers*, 1998
Harold S. Kushner, *To Life!: A Celebration of Jewish Being and Thinking*, 1993
Milton Steinberg, *Basic Judaism*, 1947
Jordan Lee Wagner, *The Synagogue Survival Kit*, 1997

522

ANNEMARIE SCHIMMEL

My Soul Is a Woman: The Feminine in Islam

(New York: Continuum, 1997)

Category: Theology
Subject(s): Islam; Women; Religious Life
Age range(s): Adult

Summary: In *My Soul Is a Woman*, Schimmel examines the place of women in Islamic spirituality, theology, and practice. She outlines the presence of women and the feminine nature in the roots of Islam, the teachings of the Prophet Muhammad, the language of the Islamic mystics, and the Koran. She discusses women in Sufism and as brides of God, and sheds light on the role of women as "manifestations of God."

Other books by the same author:
As through a Veil: Mystical Poetry in Islam, 1982
Islam in the Indian Subcontinent, 1980
The Triumphal Sun: A Study of the Works of Jaloloddin Rumi, 1978

Other books you might like:
Leila Ahmed, *Women and Gender in Islam: Historical Roots of a Modern Debate*, 1992
Elizabeth Warnock Fernea, *In Search of Islamic Feminism*, 1998
Anwar Hekmat, *Women and the Koran: The Status of Women in Islam*, 1997

523

LAURA SCHLESSINGER
STEWART VOGEL, Co-Author

The Ten Commandments: The Significance of God's Laws in Everyday Life

(New York: Cliff Street Books, 1998)

Category: Doctrine
Subject(s): Bible; Ethics; Conduct of Life
Age range(s): Young Adult-Adult

Summary: With co-author Stewart Vogel, renowned talk-radio host Dr. Laura Schlessinger examines the Ten Commandments, the foundation of Western ethics. She discusses how to make them the basis of everyday decisions.

Other books by the same author:

Ten Stupid Things Men Do to Mess Up Their Lives, 1997

How Could You Do That?!: The Abdication of Character, Courage, and Conscience, 1996

Ten Stupid Things Women Do to Mess Up Their Lives, 1994

Other books you might like:

Hillel Litwack, *Honor Your Father and Mother*, 1978

Michael G. Moriarty, *The Perfect 10: The Blessings of Following God's Commandments in a Postmodern World*, 1999

Larry L. Thompson, *Take Two Tablets: A Prescription for Today's Family*, 1999

John H. Timmerman, *Do We Still Need the Ten Commandments? A Fresh Look at God's Laws of Love*, 1997

524

MENACHEM MENDEL SCHNEERSON

Toward a Meaningful Life: The Wisdom of the Rebbe

(New York: William Morrow, 1995)

Category: Doctrine; Self-Help
Subject(s): Judaism; Religious Life
Age range(s): Young Adult-Adult

Summary: In a volume translated and compiled by Simon Jacobson, the teachings of Rebbe Menachem Mendel Schneerson are available in English for the first time. Until his death in 1994, Schneerson was the leader of the Lubavitcher Hasidim, one of the most widely recognized Hasidic groups in the world. In nonsectarian language that can speak to non-Jews as meaningfully as to Jews, Schneerson reflects on issues ranging from the nature of God and the problem of good and evil, to the day-to-day questions people ask about God, love, work, personal relationships, and other issues that arise at various stages throughout the human life cycle.

Other books you might like:

Reuven Alpert, *God's Middlemen: A Habbad Retrospective: Stories of Mystical Rabbis*, 1998

Martin Buber, *The Way of Man, According to the Teachings of Hasidism*, 1950

Chaim X. Dalfin, *Conversations with the Rabbi: Encouragement, Wisdom and Advice*, 1996

Chaim X. Dalfin, *The Seven Chabad-Lubavitch Rebbes*, 1998

525

GERSHOM SCHOLEM

Kabbalah

(New York: Quadrangle/New York Times Book Co., 1974)

Category: History
Subject(s): Judaism; Mysticism
Age range(s): Adult

Summary: The *Kabbalah* is the great mystical text of Judaism. For hundreds of years, rabbis and others specially trained in Kabbalistic study have been pondering the secrets contained in its words and letters. Scholem's timeless work provides an introduction to the history of *Kabbalah* and the development of the tradition of Kabbalistic study.

Other books by the same author:

On the Mystical Shape of the Godhead: Basic Concepts in the Kabbalah, 1997

Other books you might like:

David A. Cooper, *God Is a Verb: Kabbalah and the Practice of Mystical Judaism*, 1997

Moshe Idel, *Messianic Mystics*, 1998

Aryeh Kaplan, *Jewish Meditation: A Practical Guide*, 1985

Daniel C. Matt, *God and the Big Bang: Discovering Harmony between Science and Spirituality*, 1996

Burton L. Visotzky, *Reading the Book: Making the Bible a Timeless Text*, 1991

526

ROBERT SCHULLER

The Be-Happy Attitudes

(Waco, Texas: Word, 1985)

Category: Self-Help
Subject(s): Psychology; Christian Life; Conduct of Life
Age range(s): Young Adult-Adult

Summary: Robert Schuller, renowned pastor of the Crystal Cathedral and author of many inspirational books, outlines eight positive mental attitudes designed to improve one's outlook on life. Schuller draws his material from the Beatitudes, part of the Sermon on the Mount, one of the most famous teachings of Jesus as recorded in the New Testament of the Christian Bible. Writing with his characteristic humor and using examples taken from the lives of ordinary people, Schuller proposes that one can find true happiness only through a change of heart and mind, not in a change of external circumstances.

Other books by the same author:

Life's Not Fair, but God Is Good, 1991

Success is Never Ending, Failure is Never Final, 1988

Tough Times Never Last, but Tough People Do!, 1983

Move Ahead with Possibility Thinking, 1967

Other books you might like:

Ronald S. Lello, *The Beatitudes: Living with Blessing, Meditation and Prayer*, 1997

Norman Vincent Peale, *The Power of Positive Thinking*, 1952

Rudolf Schnackenburg, *All Things Are Possible to Believers: Reflections on the Lord's Prayer and the Sermon on the Mount*, 1995

Ed Townley, *Meditations on the Mount: A Daily Guide to Spiritual Living*, 1998

Rick Warren, *The Purpose-Driven Life: 7 Steps for Discovering and Fulfilling Your Life Mission*, 1999

527

FRITHJOF SCHUON

The Essential Writings of Frithjof Schuon
(Amity, New York: Amity House, 1986)

Category: New Age (Nonfiction)
Subject(s): Philosophy; Science; World Religions
Age range(s): Adult

Summary: Schuon's writings seek to discover the wisdom that lies behind all of the world's religions. This collection offers in one handy place Schuon's reflections on the genius of great religious figures, the ''soul'' of wisdom, and gnosis.

Other books by the same author:
To Have a Center, 1990

Other books you might like:
Ananda K. Coomaraswamy, *Time and Eternity*, 1989
James S. Cutsinger, *Advice to the Serious Seeker: Meditations on the Teaching of Frithjof Schuon*, 1997
Aldous Huxley, *The Perennial Philosophy*, 1945
Michael A. Sells, *Mystical Languages of Unsaying*, 1994
Rudolf Steiner, *An Outline of Esoteric Science*, 1997

528

TONY SCHWARTZ

What Really Matters: Searching for Wisdom in America
(New York: Bantam Books, 1995)

Category: Autobiography
Subject(s): Spirituality; Journalism; Travel
Age range(s): Adult
Locale(s): United States

Summary: In the late 1980s, *New York Times* journalist Tony Schwartz wondered why his life felt empty despite professional achievement, a happy marriage, and the fulfillment of his dreams. This led him on a five-year search for true meaning in life. The journalist traveled around the United States interviewing philosophers, physicians, scientists, and mystics, exploring and challenging their ideas, and ultimately discovering what he presents as a uniquely American ''wisdom tradition.'' This volume is a record of his journey and the conclusions drawn from his intense search for what really matters.

Other books by the same author:
Media, the Second God, 1981

Other books you might like:
Bill Moyers, *Healing and the Mind*, 1993
Bill Moyers, *A World of Ideas: Conversations with Thoughtful Men and Women about American Life Today and the Ideas Shaping Our Future*, 1989
Ken Wilber, *The Marriage of Sense and Soul: Integrating Science and Religion*, 1998
Ken Wilber, *One Taste: The Journals of Ken Wilber*, 1999

529

ALBERT SCHWEITZER

The Quest of the Historical Jesus: A Critical Study of Its Progress from Reimarus to Wrede
(New York: Macmillan, 1910)

Category: Theology; History
Subject(s): Christianity; Bible; Jesus
Age range(s): Adult

Summary: Since the 18th century, numerous scholars have engaged in the quest to discover the historical identity of Jesus of Nazareth, the central figure of the Gospels. Schweitzer's survey of this scholarship provides glimpses of ways that contemporary writers have fashioned Jesus in their own images. After surveying and analyzing the work of theologians like William Wrede, who claims that Jesus keeps his messianic identity a secret from his followers, and David Friedrich Strauss, who claims that the Gospels are simply myths, Schweitzer says that Jesus is an eschatological prophet who proclaims the coming Kingdom of God. Schweitzer's book remains an excellent introduction to the history of interpreting the figure of Jesus.

Other books by the same author:
Reverence for Life: An Anthology of Selected Writings, 1965 (Thomas Kiernan, editor)
Paul and His Interpreters, 1912

Other books you might like:
John Dominic Crossan, *Jesus: A Revolutionary Biography*, 1994
Paula Fredriksen, *From Jesus to Christ: The Origins of the New Testament Images of Jesus*, 1988
Robert W. Funk, *Honest to Jesus: Jesus for a New Millennium*, 1996
James M. Robinson, *A New Quest of the Historical Jesus*, 1959
E.P. Sanders, *The Historical Figure of Jesus*, 1993
Ben Witherington III, *The Jesus Quest: The Third Search for the Jew of Nazareth*, 1995

530

ALBERT SCHWEITZER

Reverence for Life
(New York: Harper & Row, 1969)

Category: Journals/Letters; Biography
Subject(s): Conduct of Life; Ethics; Essays
Age range(s): Adult

Summary: Albert Schweitzer's deep respect for all living beings is articulated in this edition of his *Reverence for Life*, a collection that includes essays and excerpts from letters Schweitzer (1875-1965) wrote to people including John F. Kennedy. Schweitzer believed that Western civilization needed to cultivate an ethic built on respect for others and the highest expectations of stewardship in using one's resources for good in the world. This edition of *Reverence for Life*, translated by Reginald H. Fuller, includes an overview of Schweitzer's life and a foreword written by his daughter, Rhena Schweitzer Miller.

Other books by the same author:
The Light Within Us, 1956
Out of My Life and Thought, 1949
The Spiritual Life, 1947
The Mysticism of Paul the Apostle, 1931

Other books you might like:
Paul Helm, *Faith and Reason*, 1999
Peter Joseph, *Freedom, Truth, and Hope*, 1987
Margaret Knight, *Humanist Anthology: From Confucius to Attenborough*, 1995
Thomas V. Morris, *God and the Philosophers: The Reconciliation of Faith and Reason*, 1996

531

IDRIES SHAH

The Sufis
(London: Cape, 1969)

Category: History; Doctrine
Subject(s): Islam; Mysticism; Sufism
Age range(s): Adult

Summary: Shah offers a splendid survey of Islam's mystical sect, Sufism. He traces Sufism's history and development, examines its teachings and practices, and offers biographical glimpses of its leaders.

Other books by the same author:
Tales of the Dervishes: Teaching Stories of the Sufi Masters over the Past Thousand Years, 1967

Other books you might like:
Muhyidden Ibn Arabi, *Journey to the Lord of Power: A Sufi Manual on Retreat*, 1981
William C. Chittick, *Faith and Practice of Islam: Three 13th-Century Sufi Texts*, 1992
Henry Corbin, *History of Islamic Philosophy*, 1993
Kabir Helminski, *Living Presence: A Sufi Way to Mindfulness and the Essential Self*, 1992
Llewellyn Vaughan-Lee, *The Face Before I Was Born: A Spiritual Biography*, 1998

532

HERSHEL SHANKS, Editor

Understanding the Dead Sea Scrolls
(New York: Random House, 1992)

Category: History
Subject(s): Scripture; Christianity; Judaism
Age range(s): Adult

Summary: The Dead Sea Scrolls were discovered in 1947. For more than 35 years, they were guarded by an exclusive group of scholars who controlled access to the texts. Once this monopoly was broken by the Biblical Archaeology Review, study and analysis of the ancient texts exploded worldwide. This anthology provides a first comprehensive examination of the texts by a variety of scholars whose perspectives on the history and content of the Dead Sea Scrolls shed new light on understanding both rabbinic Judaism and early Christianity.

Other books by the same author:
Jerusalem: An Archaeological Biography, 1995
Christianity and Rabbinic Judaism, 1992
Judaism in Stone: The Archaeology of Ancient Synagogues, 1979
The City of David: A Guide to Biblical Jerusalem, 1973

Other books you might like:
Michael Wise, *The Dead Sea Scrolls: A New Translation*, 1996
    Martin Abegg, Jr., Edward Cook, co-authors
Peter W. Flint, *The Dead Sea Scrolls After Fifty Years: A Comprehensive Assessment*, 1998
Norman Golb, *Who Wrote the Dead Sea Scrolls?: The Search for the Secret of Qumran*, 1995
Eugene Charles Ulrich, *The Dead Sea Scrolls and the Origins of the Bible*, 1999

533

RAMI M. SHAPIRO

Minyan: Ten Principles for Living a Life of Integrity
(New York: Bell Tower, 1997)

Category: Self-Help
Subject(s): Judaism; Conduct of Life
Age range(s): Adult

Summary: Rabbi Rami M. Shapiro proposes and explores ten spiritual principles, or practices, for those who wish to live a life of integrity and peace. These include meditation, inspirational reading, dream interpretation, generosity, kindness, ethical consumption, and observing a weekly Sabbath. Although the focus is on Jewish spirituality, the rabbi's teachings are applicable to practitioners of other faiths, as well. The title of the book is taken from the rabbinic law that identifies "minyan" as a quorum of 10 Jews, the minimum number required for a religious service.

Other books by the same author:
The Way of Solomon: Finding Joy and Contentment in the Wisdom of Ecclesiastes, 1999
Wisdom of Jewish Sages, 1995

Other books you might like:
Avram Davis, *The Way of Flame: A Guide to the Forgotten Mystical Tradition of Jewish Meditation*, 1996
Rodger Kamenetz, *Stalking Elijah: Adventures with Today's Jewish Mystical Masters*, 1997
Kerry M. Olitzky, *Sacred Intentions: Daily Inspiration to Strengthen the Spirit, Based on Jewish Wisdom*, 1999

534

ROBIN S. SHARMA

The Monk Who Sold His Ferrari: A Fable about Fulfilling Your Dreams and Reaching Your Destiny

(San Francisco: HarperSanFrancisco, 1998)

Category: Self-Help
Subject(s): Psychology; Self-Perception; Spirituality
Age range(s): Adult
Major character(s): Julian Mantle, Lawyer

Summary: A typical high-profile lawyer lives a high pressure life with all the luxuries he believes he deserves to enjoy. A heart attack stops him in his tracks and when he examines his life, he finds it lacking in meaning. Selling all his expensive belongings, he set out on a journey to find significance in life. Along the way, he is given insight into "the seven virtues" that will help him discover purpose and direction in life. The author uses this fable to suggest spiritual yet practical ways to change your way of thinking, find and follow your personal mission, develop self-discipline, take action, protect personal relationships, and get the most from daily life.

Other books you might like:

D. Richard Bellamy, *Twelve Secrets for Manifesting Your Vision, Inspiration and Purpose*, 1998
Sophy Burnham, *The Ecstatic Journey: The Transforming Power of Mystical Experience*, 1997
Deepak Chopra, *The Seven Spiritual Laws of Success: A Practical Guide to the Fulfillment of Your Dreams*, 1994

535

RUPERT SHELDRAKE

The Rebirth of Nature: The Greening of Science and God

(New York: Bantam, 1990)

Category: Theology
Subject(s): Nature; Science; God
Age range(s): Adult

Summary: Biologist Rupert Sheldrake offers a revolutionary and spiritual way of thinking about nature in this volume. He asserts that the traditional scientific view of the world as inanimate and without purpose is no longer supported by biological and other physical evidence. Instead, he envisions the universe as a living, evolving entity with memory and habits that we must learn to recognize and understand.

Other books by the same author:

Seven Experiments That Could Change the World, 1995
The Presence of the Past: Morphic Resonance and the Habits of Nature, 1988
A New Science of Life: The Hypothesis of Formative Causation, 1981

Other books you might like:

Charles Cummings, *Eco-Spirituality: Toward a Reverent Life*, 1991

Michael W. Fox, *The Boundless Circle: Caring for Creatures and Creation*, 1996
Stephanie Kaza, *The Attentive Heart: Conversations with Trees*, 1993
Janice E. Kirk, *Cherish the Earth: The Environment and Scripture*, 1993
Brown Gilkey Langdon, *Nature, Reality, and the Sacred: The Nexus of Science and Religion*, 1993
Shirley Nicholson, *Gaia's Hidden Life: The Unseen Intelligence of Nature*, 1992

536

ROBERT L. SHORT

The Gospel According to Peanuts

(Richmond, Virginia: John Knox Press, 1965)

Category: Theology
Subject(s): Christianity; Humor; Culture
Age range(s): Adult
Locale(s): United States

Summary: Theologian Robert L. Short noticed something more in the newspaper comic strip "Peanuts," created by Charles Schulz, than cute children, a funny dog, and humorous situations—he saw Christian theology. In the mid-1960s, as Charles Schulz's pen and imagination were becoming more and more popular, Short began to examine the underlying values and symbolism in this group of children who lived in a world in which grown-ups were unseen entities. In *The Gospel According to Peanuts*, Short shares his observations and insights, punctuated by plenty of "Peanuts" illustrations, quotes from the characters, relevant *Bible* passages, and comments from Schulz himself, who discusses some of the theological roots of his own philosophies.

Other books by the same author:
Short Meditations on the Bible and Peanuts, 1991

Other books you might like:
Rheta Grimsley Johnson, *Good Grief: The Story of Charles M. Schulz*, 1989
Bil Keane, *Behold the Family Circus*, 1989
Charles M. Schulz, *And the Beagles and the Bunnies Shall Lie Down Together: The Theology in Peanuts*, 1984

537

RUSSELL SHORTO

Gospel Truth: The New Image of Jesus Emerging From Science and History and Why It Matters

(New York: Riverhead Books, 1997)

Category: History
Subject(s): Christianity; Science; History
Age range(s): Adult

Summary: Journalist Russell Shorto sorts through the media hype about-and the conservative backlash against-the Jesus Seminar, a multi-disciplinary approach to using science to study the roots of Christianity. He begins by describing the

Jesus Seminar and its work, highlighting the academic and intellectual foundations of the effort that transcend its portrayal in the popular media. He then traces the New Testament account of the life of Jesus and shows that the evidence produced by the Jesus Seminar, in some cases, sheds new light on our perceptions and interpretation of the culture in which Jesus lived. Shorto discusses the findings and their potential significance from multiple points of view and suggests that historical evidence about Jesus need not diminish the spiritual essence of the the Christian faith.

Other books by the same author:
Saints and Madmen: Breaking Down the Barriers between Psychiatry and Spirituality, 1999

Other books you might like:
Charlotte Allen, *The Human Christ: The Search for the Historical Jesus*, 1997
John Dominic Crossan, *Jesus: A Revolutionary Biography*, 1994
Gary R. Habermas, *The Historical Jesus: Ancient Evidence for the Life of Christ*, 1996
Luke Timothy Johnson, *The Real Jesus: The Misguided Quest for the Historical Jesus and the Truth of the Traditional Gospels*, 1996
Raymond Martin, *The Elusive Messiah: A Philosophical Overview of the Quest for the Historical Jesus*, 1999
Stephen J. Patterson, *The God of Jesus: The Historical Jesus and the Search for Meaning*, 1998
A.N. Wilson, *How Can We Know?*, 1985
A.N. Wilson, *Jesus*, 1992
N.T. Wright, *Who Was Jesus?*, 1993

538

BRIAN SIBLEY

C.S. Lewis: Through the Shadowlands

(Old Tappan, New Jersey: F.H. Revell, 1985)

Category: Biography
Subject(s): Marriage; Love; Grief
Age range(s): Young Adult-Adult
Time period(s): 19th century; 20th century (1898-1963)
Locale(s): England

Summary: Brian Sibley's *C.S. Lewis: Through the Shadowlands* is a carefully drawn portrait of the brief but deeply loving marriage of Joy Davidman and C.S. Lewis. Sibley notes that although the marriage is the focus of his study, the union itself lasted less than four years, due to Joy's death of cancer in 1960. So, he begins the story by tracing the pre-marriage years of each partner, demonstrating how their separate lives prepared them so well for their life together, and describing how many ways their paths crossed before they accepted one another as life partners. Sibley's portrayal of the famous author and scholar continues through the day of Lewis's death in 1963, not much more than three years after the passing of his beloved Joy.

Awards the book has won:
Gold Medallion Book Award, Biography/Autobiography, 1987

Other books by the same author:
A Christmas Carol: The Unsung Story, 1994
The Land of Narnia: Brian Sibley Explores the World of C.S. Lewis, 1990 (Pauline Baynes, illustrator)
A.A. Milne, a Handlist of His Writings for Children, 1976

Other books you might like:
Janine Goffar, *The C.S. Lewis Index: A Comprehensive Guide to Lewis's Writings and Ideas*, 1998
Douglas H. Gresham, *Lenten Lands*, 1988
Walter Hooper, *C.S. Lewis: A Companion and Guide*, 1996
C.S. Lewis, *Surprised by Joy: The Shape of My Early Life*, 1955
Thomas C. Peters, *Simply C.S. Lewis: A Beginner's Guide to the Life and Works of C.S. Lewis*, 1997

539

UMA SIBLEY

The Complete Crystal Guidebook: A Practical Path to Self Development, Empowerment, and Healing

(New York: Bantam, 1986)

Category: New Age (Nonfiction)
Subject(s): Healing; Mysticism; Crystals
Age range(s): Young Adult-Adult

Summary: Sibley's book provides a comprehensive introduction to crystals and their use in connecting with the spiritual world. Sibley offers explanations of the various spiritual powers associated with particular crystals.

Other books you might like:
Scott Cunningham, *Cunningham's Encyclopedia of Crystal, Gem and Metal Magic*, 1988
Dolfyn, *Crystal Wisdom: Spiritual Properties of Crystals and Gemstones*, 1989
Simon Lilly, *Crystals and Crystal Healing: Placements and Techniques for Restoring Balance and Health*, 1998
Katrina Raphaell, *Crystal Healing: Applying the Therapeutic Properties of Crystals and Stones*, 1987
Kevin Sullivan, *The Crystal Handbook*, 1996

540

TOM SINE

The Mustard Seed Conspiracy: You Can Make a Difference in Tomorrow's Troubled World

(Waco, Texas: Word, 1981)

Category: Self-Help
Subject(s): Faith; Christianity
Age range(s): Adult

Summary: Tom Sine encourages Christians who want to make a difference in the world to let go of a commercial-influenced, consumer-oriented faith and instead embrace a ''mustard seed'' faith. The mustard seed is a reference to the parable of Jesus in which faith the size of a tiny mustard seed is more than enough faith needed to move mountains. In *The Mustard Seed Conspiracy*, Sine suggests that a mustard seed lifestyle that is more focused on giving than on acquiring ultimately nourishes one's soul and one's neighbors, and so is better for the world as a whole. Sine's message of downsizing and simplifying is accompanied by specific, practical suggestions and study questions for use in personal devotions or in group study.

Awards the book has won:
Gold Medallion Book Award, Christianity and Society, 1983

Other books by the same author:
Mustard Seed vs. McWorld: Reinventing Life and Faith for the Future, 1999
Cease Fire: Searching for Sanity in America's Culture Wars, 1995
Live It Up!: How to Create a Life You Can Love, 1993
Wild Hope, 1991
Why Settle for More and Miss the Best?: Linking Your Life to the Purposes of God, 1987

Other books you might like:
Adam Daniel Corson-Finnerty, *No More Plastic Jesus: Global Justice and Christian Lifestyle*, 1977
Doris Janzen Longacre, *Living More with Less*, 1980
John Michael Talbot, *Simplicity*, 1989
Kim Thomas, *Simplicity: Finding Peace by Uncluttering Your Life*, 1999

541

JOSEPH A. SITTLER

Grace Notes and Other Fragments
(Philadelphia: Fortress Press, 1981)

Category: Theology
Subject(s): Ecology; Ethics; Faith
Age range(s): Adult

Summary: Lutheran pastor and theologian Joseph A. Sittler (1904-1987) believed that Christians are called to go beyond their perception of God as a source of private solace and salvation to seeing God as an entity who cares about societal and global pain. Sittler's theology of grace and justice encompasses much more than religious salvation; in his view, God's grace must be understood to embrace the healing of the earth and social injustice just as much as it is seen to embrace the healing of individual souls. Sittler addresses these issues of grace, justice, and what has been termed ''eco-theology'' in *Grace Notes and Other Fragments*.

Other books by the same author:
The Structure of Christian Ethics, 1958
Gravity & Grace: Reflections and Provocations, 1986
Essays on Nature and Grace, 1972
The Ecology of Faith, 1961
The Structure of Christian Ethics, 1958

Other books you might like:
Charles Cummings, *Eco-Spirituality: Toward a Reverent Life*, 1991
Brennan Hill, *Christian Faith and the Environment: Making Vital Connections*, 1998
Doris Janzen Longacre, *Living More with Less*, 1980

Sallie McFague, *The Body of God: An Ecological Theology*, 1993
Martin Palmer, *Living Christianity*, 1993

542

GARY SMALLEY
JOHN TRENT, Co-Author

The Blessing
(Nashville: T. Nelson, 1986)

Category: Self-Help
Subject(s): Psychology; Love; Self-Acceptance
Age range(s): Adult

Summary: Based on their work as family counselors, Gary Smalley and John Trent offer practical advice from a Christian perspective for individuals dealing with the current or past pain of family strife and division. Their suggestions and principles are valuable for those whose lives have been negatively influenced by any kind of dysfunctional relationship, whether as a consequence of parental alcoholism or abuse, or because of some other tear in the fabric of family life.

Awards the book has won:
Gold Medallion Book Award, Marriage and Family, 1987

Other books by the same author:
Celebrate the Family, 1999
Making Love Last Forever, 1996
Leaving the Light On: Building the Memories That Will Draw Your Kids Home, 1994
The Blessing Workbook, 1993
The Language of Love, 1988

Other books you might like:
Henry Cloud, *Boundaries: When to Say Yes, When to Say No to Take Control of Your Life*, 1992
James C. Dobson, *In the Arms of God*, 1997
Frank B. Minirth, *Happiness Is a Choice*, 1978

543

HANNAH WHITALL SMITH

The Christian's Secret of a Happy Life
(Chicago: F. H. Revell, 1883)

Category: Devotionals
Subject(s): Christianity; Christian Life; Faith
Age range(s): Adult

Summary: In this timeless classic of the Christian faith, Smith (1832-1911) offers a variety of devotional meditations on ways that Christians may live and maintain a happy life. The major way for Christians to be happy, according to Smith, is to follow God's will. Smith provides reflections on prayer, Bible reading, and the Christian community as ways of achieving God's direction in life. Republished by T. Nelson Publishers in 1999.

Other books by the same author:
The God of All Comfort, 1984

Other books you might like:
Brother Lawrence, *The Practice of the Presence of God*, 1945

Francois Fenelon, *Fenelon: Meditations on the Heart of God*, 1997

Jeanne Guyon, *Union with God*, 1999

Hannah Hurnard, *Hind's Feet on High Places*, 1977

Catherine Marshall, *Beyond Our Selves*, 1961

544

HUSTON SMITH

The World's Religions: Our Great Wisdom Traditions

(San Francisco: HarperSanFrancisco, 1991)

Category: History
Subject(s): World Religions; Customs; Religious Traditions
Age range(s): Young Adult-Adult

Summary: Written in engaging and accessible language, Smith's book offers an outstanding introduction to the world's religions. His book is filled with fascinating details about the history and practices of various religions, including the ways that those religions interact with their cultures. Smith's book remains one of the best introductory guide to Buddhism, Hinduism, Islam, Judaism and Christianity. His fluid prose and his in-depth explorations of these religions and their social settings are engaging and lively.

Other books by the same author:
Illustrated World's Religions: A Guide to Our Wisdom Traditions, 1994
The Religions of Man, 1958

Other books you might like:
R. Pierce Beaver, *Eerdmans' Handbook to the World's Religions*, 1982
Robert S. Ellwood, *The Encyclopedia of World Religions*, 1998
Robert S. Ellwood, *Many Peoples, Many Faiths: Women and Men in the World Religions*, 1999
   Barbara A. McGraw, co-author; sixth edition
Lewis M. Hopfe, *Religions of the World*, 1998
Ninian Smart, *The World's Religions*, 1989

545

MORTON SMITH

Jesus the Magician

(San Francisco: Harper and Row, 1978)

Category: Theology; History
Subject(s): Christianity; Jesus; Miracles
Age range(s): Adult

Summary: In this controversial book, Smith paints a portrait of Jesus far different than the one painted by traditional Christianity. He claims that most people living during Jesus' time would have seen Jesus as a magician or a trickster, someone who manipulated nature to perform his so-called miracles. Smith examines the descriptions of miracles in the Gospels, but he also examines the accounts of Jesus and his work written by "outsiders," those who did not follow or believe in Jesus. This systematic analysis of the evidence leads Smith to

conclude that Jesus is more magician than messiah. Smith's book contributes to the study of the historical Jesus.

Other books by the same author:
The Secret Gospel, 1973

Other books you might like:
John Dominic Crossan, *Jesus: A Revolutionary Biography*, 1994
James D.G. Dunn, *Jesus and the Spirit: A Study of the Religious and Charismatic Experience of Jesus and the First Christians as Reflected in the New Testament*, 1975
Bruce J. Malina, *Calling Jesus Names: The Social Value of Labels in Matthew*, 1988
James M. Robinson, *Trajectories through Early Christianity*, 1971
David Lenz Tiede, *The Charismatic Figure as Miracle Worker*, 1972

546

RINPOCHE SOGYAL

The Tibetan Book of Living and Dying

(San Francisco: HarperSanFrancisco, 1992)

Category: Doctrine
Subject(s): Buddhism; Death; Conduct of Life
Age range(s): Adult

Summary: Meditation master Sogyal Rinpoche spent the early years of his life in Tibet before its annexation by the Chinese. He was educated in Delhi and at Cambridge, and is thus something of a philosophical bridge between East and West in Tibetan Buddhism. In *The Tibetan Book of Living and Dying*, Rinpoche seeks to apply Tibetan Buddhist principles and philosophies about death and its connections to life in ways that Western minds can understand and embrace. With a background that includes education in traditional Tibetan Buddhism, Western religious thought, and modern science, Rinpoche tries to bring together disparate systems of thinking and belief to synthesize a new, cross-cultural view of life and death.

Other books by the same author:
Glimpse After Glimpse: Daily Reflections on Living and Dying, 1995
Meditation, 1994

Other books you might like:
Sushila Blackman, *Graceful Exits: How Great Beings Die*, 1997
Padma Sambhava, *The Tibetan Book of the Dead: The Great Book of Natural Liberation through Understanding in the Between*, 1993
   Robert A.F. Thurman, translator
Glenn H. Mullin, *Death and Dying: The Tibetan Tradition*, 1986
Glenn H. Mullin, *Living in the Face of Death: Advice From Tibetan Masters*, 1998

547

MALIDOMA PATRICE SOME

Of Water and the Spirit: Ritual, Magic, and Initiation in the Life of an African Shaman

(New York: Putnam, 1994)

Category: Autobiography
Subject(s): Shamanism; Culture; Customs
Age range(s): Adult
Time period(s): 20th century
Locale(s): Africa; United States

Summary: Malidoma Patrice Some was born in West Africa during the 1950s. At the age of four, he was kidnapped by a Jesuit missionary and taken to be raised in a seminary of young men being trained as native Catholic priests. Fifteen years later, Malidoma had not forgotten where he had come from. When the opportunity arose, he escaped from the seminary and found his way back ''home.'' He had been away so long, however, that he was no longer accepted as a member of his tribal people. In order to regain standing in the tribe, he underwent a month-long initiation ritual, which he describes in this book. His purpose in life, however, as determined by his elders, was to return to the world outside the Dagara tribe to ensure that the ancestral tribal ways would not succumb to extinction. Now Some, who has received two doctoral degrees from Western universities, one in France and the other in the United States, travels between his two worlds, enlightening each about the other. *Of Water and the Spirit* offers a detailed and personal introduction to the world of African black magic, healing, and spiritual ritual.

Other books by the same author:
The Healing Wisdom of Africa: Finding Life Purpose through Nature, Ritual, and Community, 1999
Ritual, Power, Healing, and Community, 1993

Other books you might like:
Tela Starhawk Lake, *Hawk Woman Dancing with the Moon: The Last Female Shaman*, 1996
Sobonfu Some, *Welcoming Spirit Home: Ancient African Teachings to Celebrate Children and Community*, 1999
Edith Turner, *Experiencing Ritual: A New Interpretation of African Healing*, 1992

548

G. SCOTT SPARROW

I Am with You Always: True Stories of Encounters with Jesus

(New York: Bantam Books, 1995)

Category: Biography
Subject(s): Spirituality; Christianity
Age range(s): Young Adult-Adult

Summary: *I Am With You Always* is a collection of personal encounters with Jesus during the 20th century. Dr. G. Scott Sparrow presents the accounts, which range from dramatic near-death experiences to unexpected encouragement for one's spiritual journey, and discusses the spiritual meaning and ramifications of such encounters. He explores differences between the experiences, but notes that there is a common thread of hope and guidance that runs through all the stories.

Other books by the same author:
Blessed Among Women: Encounters with Mary and Her Message, 1997
Witness to His Return: Personal Encounters with Christ, 1991

Other books you might like:
Nicole Gausseron, *The Little Notebook: The Journal of a Contemporary Woman's Encounters with Jesus*, 1995
William Skudlarek, Hilary Thimmesh, translators and editors
David Sereda, *Face to Face with Jesus Christ*, 1999
Philip H. Wiebe Vision, *Visions of Jesus: Direct Encounters from the New Testament to Today*, 1997

549

CHARLES H. SPURGEON

Morning and Evening: An Updated Edition of the Classic Devotional in Today's Language

(Nashville: T. Nelson, 1994)

Category: Devotionals
Subject(s): Bible; Christian Life
Age range(s): Adult

Summary: More than 100 years ago, Charles H. Spurgeon wrote his classic devotional *Morning and Evening*. Offering thoughts of God and Christian love to start and end the day, Spurgeon sought to help Christians know and experience the love of God on a daily basis, rather than just during weekly church services. This classic, edited by Roy H. Clarke, is now updated for readers at the dawn of the 21st century.

Awards the book has won:
Gold Medallion Book Award, Classics, 1995

Other books by the same author:
Evening by Evening, 1984
Morning by Morning: Meditations for Daily Living, 1984

Other books you might like:
Donald F. Ackland, *Day by Day with the Master*, 1985
Amy Bolding, *Day by Day with Amy Bolding*, 1968
W.A. Criswell, *Abiding Hope: A Daily Devotional Guide*, 1981
Warren W. Wiersbe, *A Time to Be Renewed*, 1986

550

STARHAWK

The Spiral Dance: A Rebirth of the Ancient Religion of the Great Goddess

(San Francisco: HarperSanFrancisco, 1979)

Category: New Age (Nonfiction)
Subject(s): Wicca; Witches and Witchcraft

Age range(s): Adult

Summary: For anyone interested in Wicca and earth-based goddess religions, Starhawk's book is the place to start. Her engaging portrait of Wiccan practices and the rituals associated with goddess worship provides one of the first accounts, by a practitioner of these religions, of their transformative powers.

Other books by the same author:
The Pagan Book of Living and Dying: Practical Rituals, Prayers, Blessings and Meditations on Crossing Over, 1997
Truth or Dare: Encounters with Power, Authority, and Mystery, 1987
Dreaming the Dark: Magic, Sex, and Politics, 1982

Other books you might like:
Margot Adler, *Drawing Down the Moon: Witches, Druids, Goddess-Worshippers and Other Pagans in America Today*, 1979
Raymond Buckland, *Buckland's Complete Book of Witchcraft*, 1986
Zsuzsanna E. Budapest, *The Holy Book of Women's Mysteries*, 1989
Scott Cunningham, *Wicca: A Guide for the Solitary Practitioner*, 1988
Silver RavenWolf, *To Ride a Silver Broomstick: New Generation Witchcraft*, 1993

551

BRAD STEIGER
SHERRY HANSEN STEIGER, Co-Author

Angels over Their Shoulders: Children's Encounters with Heavenly Beings
(New York: Fawcett Columbine, 1995)

Category: Self-Help
Subject(s): Angels; Children; Miracles
Age range(s): Young Adult-Adult

Summary: Years of research and many interviews with children and adults have resulted in this collection of stories about children and their encounters with angels. From near-death experiences and dramatic rescues to inspirational accounts of light and music, dozens of personal accounts are collected here, with commentary from the authors about understanding these encounters in the lives of children and protecting children from encounters with dark angels.

Other books by the same author:
Animal Miracles: Inspirational and Heroic Stories of God's Wonderful Creatures, 1999
Angels around the World, 1996
Guardian Angels and Spirit Guides, 1995

Other books you might like:
Thomas J. Donaghy, *My Guardian Angel: Helper and Friend*, 1994
Marilynn Carlson Webber, *A Rustle of Angels: Stories about Angels in Real-Life and Scripture*, 1994
William D. Webber, co-author

Richard Webster, *Spirit Guides and Angel Guardians: Contact Your Invisible Helpers*, 1998

552

MILTON STEINBERG

Basic Judaism
(New York: Harcourt, Brace, 1947)

Category: Doctrine
Subject(s): Judaism; Customs; Religious Life
Age range(s): Adult

Summary: First published in 1947 and still available today, Milton Steinberg's *Basic Judaism* is a guide to the Jewish faith. Steinberg explains the laws and Scriptural writings that provide the foundation for Judaism, and describes the customs, traditions, and beliefs that are built upon that foundation. His focus is specifically on the Jewish religion, rather than the wider context of Jewish culture. *Basic Judaism* offers a concise overview of the history of Jewish worship, prayer, and belief.

Other books by the same author:
Anatomy of Faith, 1960
A Believing Jew: The Selected Writings of Milton Steinberg, 1951
As a Driven Leaf, 1939
The Making of the Modern Jew, 1934

Other books you might like:
David S. Ariel, *What Do Jews Believe?: The Spiritual Foundations of Judaism*, 1995
Morris N. Kertzer, *What Is a Jew?*, 1953
Alfred J. Kolatch, *The Jewish Book of Why*, 1981
Joseph Telushkin, *Jewish Literacy: The Most Important Things to Know about the Jewish Religion, Its People, and Its History*, 1991

553

RUDOLF STEINER

An Outline of Esoteric Science
(Hudson, New York: Anthroposophic Press, 1997)

Category: New Age (Nonfiction)
Subject(s): Psychology; Philosophy; Science
Age range(s): Adult

Summary: Steiner (1861-1925) combined the insights of psychology, science, and spirituality to demonstrate the universality and unity of the spiritual teachings that lie beneath the diverse religions of the world. Steiner's far-reaching insights into the spiritual unity of all things anticipated the New Age tendency to want to find such unity behind all material things. Because this book provides an overview of his thoughts, it is more accessible than many of his other works. Steiner's ability to draw on all facets of science and literature is very similar to Samuel Taylor Coleridge's attempts to transmit the unity of all the natural and the supernatural in his poetry.

Other books by the same author:
How to Know Higher Worlds: A Modern Path of Initiation, 1994

Other books you might like:

Angeles Arrien, *Signs of Life: The Five Universal Shapes and How to Use Them*, 1992

Julia Cameron, *The Artist's Way: A Spiritual Path to Higher Creativity*, 1995

Natalie Goldberg, *Long Quiet Highway: Waking Up in America*, 1993

Jamie Sams, *Dancing the Dream: The Seven Sacred Paths of Human Transformation*, 1998

Frithjof Schuon, *To Have a Center*, 1990

554

IRA STEINGROOT

Keeping Passover: Everything You Need to Know to Bring the Ancient Tradition to Life and Create Your Own Passover Celebration

(San Francisco: HarperSanFrancisco, 1995)

Category: Self-Help
Subject(s): Judaism; Customs; Holidays, Jewish
Age range(s): Adult

Summary: Ira Steingroot's *Keeping Passover* provides inspiration and guidance to families and individuals who want to bring more of their Jewish heritage into their home life through the observance of Passover. Steingroot explains the history and symbolism of the traditional seder and suggests contemporary alternatives for those who wish to incorporate them. Steingroot's suggestions are practical as well as spiritual: he recommends menus and cookbooks, offers ideas for arranging the table, and lists a variety of ways to add music to the celebration and enhance children's involvement. His focus is on presenting many possible ways to enhance the Passover experience, rather than on prescribing one formula for everyone to copy, in order to keep the Passover experience meaningful from year to year for all members of the household.

Other books you might like:

Jeffrey M. Cohen, *1001 Questions and Answers on Pesach*, 1996

Toby Knobel Fluek, *Passover as I Remember It*, 1994
Lilian Fleuk Finkler, co-author

Ron Wolfson, *The Art of Jewish Living: The Passover Seder*, 1996

555

ADIN STEINSALTZ

Teshuvah: A Guide for the Newly Observant Jew

(New York: Free Press, 1987)

Category: Doctrine; Self-Help
Subject(s): Judaism; Religious Life
Age range(s): Adult

Summary: In *Teshuvah*, Adin Steinsaltz provides a concise outline of what it means to return to Orthodox Judaism. The title of the book is a Hebrew term for repentance and return. Steinsaltz explains the three steps of Teshuvah, and then discusses the relationships and activities through which Teshuvah is demonstrated in one's life. The manual establishes guidelines concerning family and social relationships, past and present sin, prayer, observance of festivals and holy days, home life, and appearance, and answers questions about Teshuvah.

Other books by the same author:

The Candle of God: Discourses on Chasidic Thought, 1998
The Essential Talmud, 1976
The Thirteen Petalled Rose, 1980

Other books you might like:

Mordechai Becher, *After the Return: Maintaining Good Family Relations and Adjusting to Your New Lifestyle—A Practical Halachic Guide for the Newly Observant*, 1994
Moshe Newman, co-author

M. Herbert Danzger, *Returning to Tradition: The Contemporary Revival of Orthodox Judaism*, 1989

Anita Diamant, *Choosing a Jewish Life: A Handbook for People Converting to Judaism and for Their Family and Friends*, 1997

556

ADIN STEINSALTZ

The Thirteen Petalled Rose

(New York: Basic Books, 1980)

Category: Devotionals
Subject(s): Judaism; Mysticism; God
Age range(s): Adult

Summary: The renowned Rabbi Steinsaltz instructs spiritual seekers in the mysteries of the *Talmud* and Jewish mystical writings. He shows how these writings provide guidance in the search to find answers to the perennial questions about the nature of God and human existence. Steinsaltz guides readers through the mysteries of these texts as he instructs them about how to read and find meaning in them.

Other books by the same author:
The Essential Talmud, 1976

Other books you might like:

Judith Z. Abrams, *A Beginner's Guide to the Steinsaltz Talmud*, 1999

Perle Besserman, *Teachings of the Jewish Mystics*, 1998

Aryeh Kaplan, *Meditation and Kabbalah*, 1995

Gershom Scholem, *Major Trends in Jewish Mysticism: Based on the Hilda Strook Lectures Delivered at the Jewish Institute of Religion, New York*, 1995

Rivkah Slonim, *Total Immersion: A Mikvah Anthology*, 1996

557

JOHN R.W. STOTT

The Cross of Christ

(Downers Grove, Illinois: InterVarsity Press, 1986)

Category: Doctrine
Subject(s): Christianity; Nature of God; Apologetics

Age range(s): Adult

Summary: In a focused and scripturally-documented volume, John R.W. Stott explains why the cross of Jesus' death is at the core of Christianity. *The Cross of Christ* sets forth arguments about Christ's divinity and the necessity of the crucifixion and subsequent resurrection in God's plan of redemption for humankind.

Awards the book has won:
Gold Medallion Book Award, Theology/Doctrine, 1988

Other books by the same author:
The Authentic Jesus, 1985
Between Two Worlds, 1982
The Message of the Sermon on the Mount: Christian Counter-Culture, 1978
Christian Mission in the Modern World, 1975

Other books you might like:
Leon Morris, *The Atonement: Its Meaning and Significance*, 1983
Leon Morris, *The Cross of Jesus*, 1988
J.I. Packer, *Concise Theology: A Guide to Historic Christian Beliefs*, 1993
J.I. Packer, *Knowing God*, 1973

558

CLARK STRAND

Seeds From a Birch Tree: Writing Haiku and the Spiritual Journey

(New York: Hyperion, 1997)

Category: Poetry
Subject(s): Meditation; Buddhism; Spirituality
Age range(s): Young Adult-Adult

Summary: Growing spiritually through the discipline of haiku is the focus of Clark Strand's *Seeds From a Birch Tree*. Strand is a former Zen Buddhist monk who promotes haiku as a valuable meditation tool. In this book, he discusses the history, philosophy, and structure of haiku, and guides the reader through the experience of reading and writing haiku for personal expression and spiritual benefit.

Other books by the same author:
The Wooden Bowl: Simple Meditation for Everyday Life, 1998

Other books you might like:
William J. Higginson, *The Haiku Handbook: How to Write, Share, and Teach Haiku*, 1985
Penny Harter, co-author
Toshimi Horiuchi, *Oasis in the Heart: Haiku with Exposition*, 1995
Yuzuru Miura, *Classic Haiku: A Master's Selection*, 1991
Lucien Stryk, *Zen Poetry: Let the Spring Breeze Enter*, 1995
Takashi Ikemoto, co-editor

559

CLARK STRAND

The Wooden Bowl: Simple Meditation for Everyday Life

(New York: Hyperion, 1998)

Category: Self-Help
Subject(s): Meditation; Spirituality
Age range(s): Young Adult-Adult

Summary: Clark Strand is a former Zen Buddhist monk who wrote *The Wooden Bowl* for people who want to incorporate meditation into their everyday lives without adopting a set of religious beliefs or structured practices. Strand's focus is on the simplicity of meditation as a natural state of being, not a series of steps, techniques, or doctrines to be followed and mastered.

Other books by the same author:
Seeds From a Birch Tree: Writing Haiku and the Spiritual Journey, 1997

Other books you might like:
Sylvia Boorstein, *It's Easier than You Think: The Buddhist Way to Happiness*, 1995
Swami Chinmayananda, *Meditation and Life*, 1992
William Johnston, *Christian Zen*, 1997
third edition
Aryeh Kaplan, *Jewish Meditation: A Practical Guide*, 1985
Patricia Monaghan, *Meditation: The Complete Guide*, 1999
Eleanor G. Viereck, co-author

560

WHITLEY STRIEBER

Communion: A True Story

(New York: Beech Tree Books, 1987)

Category: New Age (Nonfiction)
Subject(s): Aliens; UFOs; Philosophy
Age range(s): Adult
Time period(s): 1980s

Summary: In *Communion*, Whitley Strieber, author of such novels as *The Wolfen* and *The Hunger*, recounts his family's true experiences with extraterrestrials. His unbelievable stories are supported with statements from psychiatrists and the results of a lie detector test. Strieber's story begins with an account of the night in 1985 when he was transported from his bedroom to some kind of unfamiliar vehicle. The memory was suppressed for a few days, but when it surfaced, so did memories of previous similar abductions. He describes the long psychoanalytical sessions he underwent during 1986, many of which involved hypnosis. These sessions unearthed further details: descriptions of the aliens as small-bodied creatures with large, bald heads and dark, slanted eyes; abductions when Strieber was a child, for years disguised as dreams or hidden behind ''screen memories''; even an instance when the aliens informed Strieber, ''You are our chosen one.'' Strieber, a self-described skeptic of the paranormal, reportedly became suicidal over these revelations. Only when he decided to publish his story did Strieber begin to feel a sense of relief. Critics remain divided about the intent and veracity of Strieber's accounts, many noting that as a science fiction novelist, it is his job to make the unbelievable believable.

Other books by the same author:
Confirmation: The Hard Evidence of Aliens Among Us, 1998
Communion Letters, 1997
Secret School: Preparation for Contact, 1997
Transformation: The Breakthrough, 1988

Other books you might like:
Paul Christopher, *Alien Intervention: The Spiritual Mission of UFOs*, 1998
Chuck Missler, *Alien Encounters*, 1997
Barry R. Parker, *Alien Life: The Search for Extraterrestrials and Beyond*, 1998
Jenny Randles, *Alien Contact: The First Fifty Years*, 1997

561

GERALD S. STROBER

Graham: A Day in Billy's Life

(Garden City, New York: Doubleday, 1976)

Category: Biography
Subject(s): Christianity; Evangelism; Ministry
Age range(s): Adult

Summary: Author Gerald S. Strober offers readers a composite day in the life of Billy Graham, focusing on three major categories of activity common to Graham's work life. The first is the work at "home base": planning upcoming Crusades, scheduling time to spend on writing and radio projects, and carving out some family time. The second is the day of a Crusade, this one in Jackson, Mississippi. The third is world travel not necessarily connected with a Crusade or other speaking engagement; in this case, the trip is to Israel. Strober writes from a firmly evangelical viewpoint and provides extensive detail on every aspect of the evangelist's typical daily activities.

Other books by the same author:
Aflame for God: The Jerry Falwell Story, 1979
American Jews: Community in Crisis, 1974

Other books you might like:
Billy Graham, *Just as I Am: The Autobiography of Billy Graham*, 1997
William Martin, *A Prophet with Honor: The Billy Graham Story*, 1991
John Pollock, *To All the Nations: The Billy Graham Story*, 1985
Sherwood Eliot Wirt, *Billy: A Personal Look at Billy Graham, the World's Best-Loved Evangelist*, 1997

562

JAMES STRONG

The New Strong's Exhaustive Concordance of the Bible

(Nashville: T. Nelson, 1996)

Category: Religious Encyclopedias/Dictionaries

Subject(s): Bible; History
Age range(s): Young Adult-Adult

Summary: Since the late 1800s, *Strong's Exhaustive Concordance of the Bible* has been considered the standard reference volume for students, clergy, and Bible readers. The new edition maintains the standard set by James Strong in his original editions, referencing every verse in the King James Version of the Bible and providing a cross-reference format that makes it useful with other translations, as well. An index of Bible topics and dictionaries for the Hebrew and Greek testaments are also included.

Other books by the same author:
The New Strong's Complete Dictionary of Bible Words, 1996
Cyclopaedia of Biblical, Theological, and Ecclesiastical Literature, 1869 (John McClintock, co-author)

Other books you might like:
Alexander Cruden, *Cruden's Complete Concordance to the Old and New Testaments*, 1968
Edward W. Goodrick, *New International Bible Concordance*, 1999
John R. Kohlenberger III, co-editor
John R. Kohlenberger III, *The Concise Concordance to the New Revised Standard Version*, 1993
John R. Kohlenberger III, *New Living Translation Complete Concordance*, 1996
James A. Swanson, co-author
Charles F. Pfeiffer, *The New Combined Bible Dictionary and Concordance*, 1961

563

MARY STRONG, Editor

Letters of the Scattered Brotherhood

(San Francisco: HarperSanFrancisco, 1991)

Category: Journals/Letters; Devotionals
Subject(s): Christianity; Christian Life
Age range(s): Adult

Summary: Strong gathers a series of letters from numerous Christian leaders offering timeless advice on leading a Christian life. Sprinkled through the letters are little gems of inspiration from Christian sages throughout history. Originally written just after World War II, these letters have changed the lives of many readers. They offer something of a cross between the positive thinking of Norman Vincent Peale and the reflective, contemplative Christianity of Thomas Merton. These letters can be read and re-read as devotional and inspirational writings.

Other books you might like:
Lauren Artress, *Walking a Sacred Path: Rediscovering the Labyrinth as a Spiritual Tool*, 1995
Kathleen Noris, *Amazing Grace: A Vocabulary of Faith*, 1998
Joyce Rupp, *The Cup of Our Life: A Guide for Spiritual Growth*, 1997
Macrina Wiederkehr, *Gold in Your Memories: Sacred Moments, Glimpses of God*, 1998

564

MARY SUMMER RAIN, Author/Illustrator

Mountains, Meadows and Moonbeams: A Child's Spiritual Reader
(Norfolk, Virginia: Hampton Roads, 1992)

Category: New Age (Nonfiction)
Subject(s): Spirituality; Childhood
Age range(s): Children

Summary: *Mountains, Meadows and Moonbeams* is a collection of spiritual writings from a metaphysical point of view written especially for children and their parents to read together. Author Mary Summer Rain provides illustrations that children may color to their liking. The first part of the book provides a foundation of the author's principles of spirituality, outlined in language and pictures for young children; the second part is a collection of short spiritual writings that can be read at random.

Other books by the same author:
Fireside, 1998
Star Babies, 1997
Soul Sounds: Mourning the Tears of Truth, 1992
Whispered Wisdom: Portraits of Grandmother Earth, 1992

Other books you might like:
Barbara Berger, *Grandfather Twilight*, 1984
Cait Johnson, *Celebrating the Great Mother: A Handbook of Earth-Honoring Activities for Parents and Children*, 1995
  Maura D. Shaw, co-author
Reeve Lindbergh, *The Circle of Days*, 1997
  Cathie Felstead, illustrator

565

AMBER COVERDALE SUMRALL, Editor
PATRICE VECCHIONE, Co-Editor

Storming Heaven's Gate: An Anthology of Spiritual Writings by Women
(New York: Plume, 1997)

Category: Essays
Subject(s): Poetry; Women; Spirituality
Age range(s): Young Adult-Adult

Summary: The thoughts and perspectives of more than 60 women are collected in this spiritual anthology. *Storming Heaven's Gate* expresses the joy, pain, anger, and ambivalence of the spiritual lives and journeys of women including Madeleine L'Engle, Maya Angelou, and Barbara Kingsolver, among many other contemporary women writers. The essays speak to a range of religious traditions, old and new, and come from voices young and old.

Other books by the same author:
Bless Me, Father: Stories of Catholic Childhood, 1994 (Patrice Vecchione, co-editor)
Catholic Girls: Stories, Poems, and Memoirs, 1992 (Patrice Vecchione, co-editor)

Other books you might like:
Susan Cahill, *Wise Women: Over Two Thousand Years of Spiritual Writing by Women*, 1996
Carol Lee Flinders, *At the Root of This Longing: Reconciling a Spiritual Hunger and a Feminist Thirst*, 1998
Philip Zaleski, *The Best Spiritual Writing, 1998*, 1998

566

D.T. SUZUKI

Essays in Zen Buddhism, First Series
(London: Luzac and Company, 1927)

Category: Doctrine
Subject(s): Buddhism; Religious Life
Age range(s): Adult

Summary: Japanese scholar D.T. Suzuki's first series of essays introduced Zen to many Western readers in 1927. Two additional volumes of *Essays in Zen Buddhism* followed in 1933 and 1934. Instead of describing what Zen is, Suzuki's essays offer readers an opportunity to come to understand it experientially. The publication of Suzuki's essays marked the beginning of popular Western interest in Zen Buddhist thought.

Other books by the same author:
Mysticism: Christian and Buddhist, 1957
The Zen Doctrine of No Mind, 1950
A Manual of Zen Buddhism, 1935

Other books you might like:
Robert Aitken, *Taking the Path of Zen*, 1982
Sylvia Boorstein, *It's Easier than You Think: The Buddhist Way to Happiness*, 1995
Alan Watts, *The Way of Zen*, 1957

567

D.T. SUZUKI

An Introduction to Zen Buddhism
(Kyoto: Eastern Buddhist Society, 1934)

Category: Doctrine
Subject(s): Buddhism; Religious Life
Age range(s): Adult

Summary: This volume has become a classic introduction to Zen Buddhism for Western readers since it was first published in 1934. It has been reprinted in various editions since then, including a 1964 version featuring a foreword by psychologist C.G. Jung.

Other books by the same author:
Mysticism: Christian and Buddhist, 1957
The Zen Doctrine of No Mind, 1950
A Manual of Zen Buddhism, 1935

Other books you might like:
Robert Aitken, *Taking the Path of Zen*, 1982
Sylvia Boorstein, *It's Easier than You Think: The Buddhist Way to Happiness*, 1995
Alan Watts, *The Way of Zen*, 1957

568

D.T. SUZUKI

A Manual of Zen Buddhism

(Kyoto: Eastern Buddhist Society, 1935)

Category: Doctrine
Subject(s): Buddhism; Religious Life
Age range(s): Adult

Summary: Suzuki's *A Manual of Zen Buddhism* was published originally by the Eastern Buddhist Society in 1935. It has remained available in the decades since as a standard guidebook for practitioners of Zen Buddhism in the West. The early 20th-century publication of Japanese scholar D.T. Suzuki's writings on Zen Buddhism marked the beginning of popular Western interest in Eastern philosophy, which soon manifested itself in art, music, architecture, philosophy, and psychology.

Other books by the same author:
Mysticism: Christian and Buddhist, 1957
The Zen Doctrine of No Mind, 1950
An Introduction to Zen Buddhism, 1934

Other books you might like:
Robert Aitken, *Taking the Path of Zen*, 1982
Sylvia Boorstein, *It's Easier than You Think: The Buddhist Way to Happiness*, 1995
Alan Watts, *The Way of Zen*, 1957

569

D.T. SUZUKI

Zen Buddhism: Selected Writings of D.T. Suzuki

(New York: Doubleday, 1996)

Category: Doctrine
Subject(s): Buddhism; Religious Life
Age range(s): Adult

Summary: This is a 40th anniversary edition of the 1956 collection *Zen Buddhism: Selected Writings of D.T. Suzuki*. The volume, which gathers the best of Suzuki's teachings on Zen Buddhism, offers an explanation of the vocabulary and concepts of Zen Buddhism, an overview of the history of Zen Buddhism, and an introduction to the techniques of Zen practice. D.T. Suzuki's influential writings in the 1920s and 1930s popularized Zen Buddhism in the Western world.

Other books by the same author:
Mysticism: Christian and Buddhist, 1957
The Zen Doctrine of No Mind, 1950
A Manual of Zen Buddhism, 1935

Other books you might like:
Robert Aitken, *Taking the Path of Zen*, 1982
Sylvia Boorstein, *It's Easier than You Think: The Buddhist Way to Happiness*, 1995
Robert Linssen, *Living Zen*, 1958
   Diana Abrahams-Curiel, translator
Alan Watts, *The Way of Zen*, 1957

570

SHUNRYU SUZUKI

Zen Mind, Beginner's Mind

(New York: Walker/Weatherhill, 1970)

Category: Doctrine
Subject(s): Buddhism; Religious Life; Meditation
Age range(s): Young Adult-Adult

Summary: *Zen Mind, Beginner's Mind* is a collection of excerpts from lectures given by Zen master Shunryu Suzuki, founder of the San Francisco Zen Center. Suzuki's teachings answer questions about meditation, enlightenment, and other aspects of Zen Buddhism. His focus for developing Zen spirituality is to always be at the beginning, starting fresh day by day, learning with experience as one does without experience.

Other books by the same author:
Branching Streams Flow in the Darkness: Zen Talks on the Sandokai, 1999

Other books you might like:
David Chadwick, *Crooked Cucumber: The Life and Zen Teaching of Shunryu Suzuki*, 1999
Pema Chodron, *The Wisdom of No Escape: And the Path of Loving-Kindness*, 1991
Philip Kapleau, *The Three Pillars of Zen: Teaching, Practice, and Enlightenment*, 1965
Phillip Olson, *The Discipline of Freedom: A Kantian View of the Role of Moral Precepts in Zen Practice*, 1992

571

EMANUEL SWEDENBORG

Heaven and Hell

(New York: Pillar Books, 1976)

Category: New Age (Nonfiction)
Subject(s): Heaven; Philosophy; Hell
Age range(s): Adult

Summary: In this volume, mystical teacher Swedenborg (1688-1772) offers his own views of heaven and hell. Swedenborg develops an in-depth discussion of the nature of heaven and hell, rather than simply an attempt to paint the portraits of these two places. He draws upon a wide range of sources from literature and art contemporary to his time as he discusses the literal and the spiritual meanings of heaven and hell. This book is as good an introduction as any to Swedenborg's ideas. Translated by George F. Dole.

Other books you might like:
Richard Maurice Bucke, *Cosmic Consciousness: A Study in the Evolution of the Human Mind*, 1901
Andrew Cohen, *Autobiography of an Awakening*, 1992
Adi Da, *The Knee of Listening: The Early-Life Ordeal and the Radical Spiritual Realization of the Divine World-Teacher*, 1995
Joel S. Goldsmith, *Collected Essays of Joel S. Goldsmith*, 1986
Abraham H. Maslow, *Religions, Values, and Peak Experiences*, 1964

572

CHARLES R. SWINDOLL

The Grace Awakening

(Dallas: Word, 1990)

Category: Self-Help
Subject(s): Christianity; Christian Life
Age range(s): Adult

Summary: Should practicing Christianity consist of grimly fulfilling an endless array of obligations and restrictions? Not according to Charles R. Swindoll. In *The Grace Awakening*, Swindoll calls Christians to contemplate and accept the grace of God in their lives, finding hope in God's love rather than frustration in trying to live according to other people's expectations.

Awards the book has won:
Gold Medallion Book Award, Theology/Doctrine, 1991

Other books by the same author:
Simple Faith, 1991
Living on the Ragged Edge, 1985

Other books you might like:
Jerry Bridges, *The Discipline of Grace: God's Role and Our Role in the Pursuit of Holiness*, 1994
Max Lucado, *In the Grip of Grace*, 1996
Mark Rutland, *Streams of Mercy: Receiving and Reflecting God's Grace*, 1999
Philip Yancey, *What's So Amazing about Grace?*, 1997

573

CHARLES R. SWINDOLL

Growing Strong in the Seasons of Life

(Portland, Oregon: Multnomah, 1983)

Category: Devotionals
Subject(s): Christianity; Christian Life; Conduct of Life
Age range(s): Adult

Summary: Life's activities and priorities change, writes Charles R. Swindoll, but the call to faith and spiritual growth follows us throughout the seasons of life. In *Growing Strong in the Seasons of Life*, Swindoll offers a devotional guide with 144 entries designed to help readers stay close to God and maintain balance throughout life's changes. The readings include verses of Bible scripture and suggestions for applying biblical principles to every day life.

Other books by the same author:
The Bible: Applying God's Word to Your Life, 1993
Growing Deep in the Christian Life, 1986

Other books you might like:
Leroy Brownlow, *Give Us This Day: A Devotional Guide for Daily Living*, 1995
Stephen D. Eyre, *Drawing Close to God: The Essentials of a Dynamic Quiet Time*, 1995
Alister McGrath, *Beyond the Quiet Time: Practical Evangelical Spirituality*, 1996
Charles H. Spurgeon, *Morning and Evening: An Updated Edition of the Classic Devotional in Today's Language*,

1994
Roy H. Clarke, editor

574

CHARLES R. SWINDOLL

Improving Your Serve: The Art of Unselfish Living

(Waco, Texas: Word, 1981)

Category: Self-Help
Subject(s): Christianity; Christian Life; Conduct of Life
Age range(s): Adult

Summary: In a world where "looking out for number one" has become the order of the day, what are Christians to do? Preacher and author Charles R. Swindoll offers suggestions for integrating principles of generosity and unselfishness into daily life, noting that this approach to others can make a difference in the people around you. Swindoll's counsel is based on biblical principles of servanthood.

Other books by the same author:
The Quest for Character, 1993
Living Above the Level of Mediocrity, 1987
Strengthening Your Grip: Essentials in an Aimless World, 1982

Other books you might like:
Robert K. Greenleaf, *The Power of Servant-Leadership: Essays*, 1998
Larry C. Spears, editor
Julie Ruth Harley, *Soul Calling: Breathing Spirit into a Life of Service*, 1998
Stacy T. Rinehart, *Upside Down: The Paradox of Servant Leadership*, 1998
Warren W. Wiersbe, *Classic Sermons on Christian Service*, 1990

575

CHARLES R. SWINDOLL

Strengthening Your Grip: Essentials in an Aimless World

(Waco, Texas: Word, 1982)

Category: Self-Help
Subject(s): Christianity; Christian Life; Conduct of Life
Age range(s): Adult

Summary: Living a Christian life is more about character and values than it is about following rules, says Charles R. Swindoll. In *Strengthening Your Grip*, Swindoll examines the issues involved in developing a godly character and applying Christian values to daily decisions. With Bible passages and personal anecdotes, Swindoll offers guidance for those who want to find and maintain a Christ-centered direction in life.

Awards the book has won:
Gold Medallion Book Award, Insp./Devotional/Christian Living, 1983

Other books by the same author:
The Quest for Character, 1993

Living Above the Level of Mediocrity, 1987
Improving Your Serve: The Art of Unselfish Living, 1981

Other books you might like:
J.I. Packer, *Growing in Christ*, 1994
Charles F. Stanley, *Developing Inner Strength*, 1998
Richard S. Taylor, *The Disciplined Life*, 1962

576

CHARLES R. SWINDOLL

Strike the Original Match

(Portland, Oregon: Multnomah, 1980)

Category: Self-Help
Subject(s): Christianity; Christian Life; Marriage
Age range(s): Adult

Summary: With the dual perspectives of 35 years of marriage and the teachings of the Bible on love, commitment, and fidelity, Charles R. Swindoll offers guidance for rekindling the spark in marriage. *Strike the Original Match* outlines principles that will strengthen the bond between husband and wife and help them rediscover the love that first led them to exchange wedding vows.

Other books by the same author:
Start Where You Are: Catch a Fresh Vision for Your Life, 1999
Man to Man: Chuck Swindoll Selects His Most Significant Writings for Men, 1996

Other books you might like:
James C. Dobson, *Love for a Lifetime: Building a Marriage That Will Go the Distance*, 1987
Judy Petsonk, *The Intermarriage Handbook: A Guide for Jews and Christians*, 1988
    Jim Remsen, co-author
Gary Smalley, *Hidden Keys of a Loving, Lasting Marriage: A Valuable Guide to Knowing, Understanding, and Loving Each Other*, 1993
Susan Wales, *A Match Made In Heaven: A Collection of Inspirational Love Stories*, 1999
    Ann Platz, co-compiler

577

JONI EARECKSON TADA
STEVE JENSEN, Co-Author
RON DICIANNI, Illustrator

Tell Me The Promises: A Family Covenant for Eternity

(Wheaton, Illinois: Crossway Books, 1996)

Category: Devotionals
Subject(s): Children; Faith; Christianity
Age range(s): Children-Adult

Summary: This collection of devotional stories is designed for parents and children to read together. With gentle text and illustrations, the stories demonstrate seven special ways that parents and children make and keep commitments to each other, in accordance with God's plan for families.

Awards the book has won:
Gold Medallion Book Award, Gift Book/Poetry, 1997

Other books by the same author:
Tell Me The Truth: God's Eternal Truths for Families, 1997
    (Steve Jensen, co-author; Ron DiCianni, illustrator)

Other books you might like:
Debby Boone, *Nightlights: More Bedtime Hugs for Little Ones*, 1997
    Gabriel Ferrer, illustrator
Mack Thomas, *God's Best Promises for Kids*, 1999
    Dennas Davis, illustrator
John Trent, *I'd Choose You*, 1994
    Judy Love, illustrator

578

JONI EARECKSON TADA
STEVE JENSEN, Co-Author
RON DICIANNI, Illustrator

Tell Me The Truth: God's Eternal Truths for Families

(Wheaton, Illinois: Crossway Books, 1997)

Category: Devotionals
Subject(s): Trust; Faith; Family Life
Age range(s): Children-Adult

Summary: Seven biblical truths about a Christ-centered life are presented with text and illustrations in this volume by Joni Eareckson Tada and Ron DiCianni. The stories in the collection are designed to help parents reinforce Christian values in their home-life by reading with their children tales that share the truths of their faith and enhance the spiritual life of the family. Joni has also written under the name Joni Eareckson.

Awards the book has won:
Gold Medallion Book Award, Gift Book/Poetry, 1998

Other books by the same author:
Tell Me The Promises: A Family Covenant for Eternity, 1996
    (Steve Jensen, co-author; Ron DiCianni, illustrator)

Other books you might like:
Lawrence Castagnola, *More Parables for Little People*, 1987
    Nancy LaBerge Muren, illustrator
Lawrence Castagnola, *Parables for Little People*, 1982
Mack Thomas, *God's Best Promises for Kids*, 1999
    Dennas Davis, illustrator

579

KAZUAKI TANAHASHI, Editor
TENSHO DAVID SCHNEIDER, Co-Editor

Essential Zen

(San Francisco: HarperSanFrancisco, 1994)

Category: Doctrine
Subject(s): Buddhism; Spirituality
Age range(s): Adult

Summary: *Essential Zen*, called a contradiction in terms by its editors, is nonetheless a collection of writings that capture the essence of Zen Buddhist thought and practice. The works include classical wisdom from ancient Chinese and Japanese Buddhist masters and contemporary perspectives from students of Western Zen Buddhist centers in the United States and Europe. The combination of traditional and contemporary writings makes this an accessible introduction to a wide range of Zen Buddhist thought.

Other books by the same author:
Brush Mind: Text, Art, and Design, 1990
Moon in a Dewdrop: Writings of Zen Master Dogen, 1985 (Robert Aitken, translator)
Penetrating Laughter, Hakuin's Zen & Art, 1982

Other books you might like:
Dogen, *Enlightenment Unfolds: The Essential Teachings of Zen Master Dogen*, 1999
Nelson Foster, *The Roaring Stream: A New Zen Reader*, 1996
Andrew Harvey, *The Essential Mystics: The Soul's Journey into Truth*, 1996

580

GIGI GRAHAM TCHIVIDJIAN

Passing It On

(Wheaton, Illinois: Crossway Books, 1992)

Category: Autobiography
Subject(s): Family Life; Christianity; Customs
Age range(s): Young Adult-Adult

Summary: *Passing It On* was designed to be a 50th wedding anniversary tribute from a daughter to her parents. In this case, the parents are famous—Ruth and Billy Graham—and the gift-giver is their eldest daughter, Gigi Graham Tchividjian, herself an accomplished lecturer and author. Spanning four generations of memories, traditions, and photographs, this memoir celebrates the life of a family whose roots in Christianity provide the foundation from which each new generation learns of faith and love.

Other books by the same author:
Mothers Together, 1998 (Ruth Bell Graham, co-author)
Currents of the Heart: Glimpses of God in the Stream of Life, 1996
Weather of the Heart: Glimpses of God in Sunlight and Storm, 1991
Diapers & Dishes or Pinstripes & Pumps: Christian Women in a Changing World, 1987

Other books you might like:
Emilie Barnes, *My Cup Overflows*, 1998
Edith Schaeffer, *What Is a Family?*, 1975
Mary Caswell Walsh, *The Art of Tradition: A Christian Guide to Building a Family*, 1998

581

PIERRE TEILHARD DE CHARDIN

The Phenomenon of Man

(New York: Harper, 1959)

Category: Theology
Subject(s): Christianity; Evolution; Jesuits
Age range(s): Adult

Summary: Jesuit paleontologist Teilhard de Chardin offers here a reading of human nature that integrates the deep insights of science and spirituality. One of the few religious thinkers who suggests that Christianity can benefit enormously from the evolutionary model, Teilhard (as he is known) contends that humankind flows and develops between an Alpha point and an Omega point. The Omega point is pure, undifferentiated energy, and Teilhard asserts that humankind is moving toward this point. His writings are lyrical, even though his use of scientific jargon and neologisms can make for dense reading.

Other books by the same author:
Christianity and Evolution, 1971
The Divine Milieu: An Essay on the Interior Life, 1960

Other books you might like:
Annie Dillard, *Pilgrim at Tinker Creek*, 1974
Matthew Fox, *Original Blessing*, 1983
Ursula King, *Spirit of Fire: The Life and Vision of Teilhard de Chardin*, 1996
William Johnston, *The Wounded Stag*, 1998
Bernard McGinn, *Meister Eckhart and the Beguine Mystics: Hadewijch of Brabant, Mechthild of Magdeburg, and Marguerite Porte*, 1994

582

LUISAH TEISH

Jambalaya: The Natural Woman's Book of Personal Charms and Practical Rituals

(San Francisco: Harper and Row, 1985)

Category: New Age (Nonfiction)
Subject(s): Voodoo; Religious Traditions; Santeria
Age range(s): Adult

Summary: Teish, a practitioner of Voodoo and Santeria, offers an overview of the religious practices associated with both religions. She provides insights into the rituals of each religious tradition, and gives her own personal advice on the performance of the rituals. Although there are several books on these religions written by outsiders, Teish's accessible book provides one of the few explorations of these religions by a practitioner.

Other books you might like:
Migene Gonzalez-Wippler, *Santeria: The Religion, Faith, Rites, Magic*, 1994
Thomas Healki, *Creative Ritual: Combining Yoruba, Santeria, and Western Magic Traditions*, 1996
Philip John Neimark, *The Way of the Orisa: Empowering Your Life through the Ancient African Religion of Ifa*, 1993
Milo Rigaud, *Secrets of Voodoo*, 1985
Robert Tallant, *The Voodoo Queen*, 1956

583

PATRICIA TELESCO

The Urban Pagan: Magical Living in a 9-to-5 World

(St. Paul, Minnesota: Llewellyn, 1993)

Category: Self-Help
Subject(s): Paganism; Customs; City Life
Age range(s): Adult

Summary: In *The Urban Pagan*, Patricia Telesco offers ideas for incorporating the nature-inspired aspects of neopaganism into busy everyday life, particularly for those living a city lifestyle. Telesco emphasizes practicality and the evolutionary nature of changing habits. She presents suggestions for integrating magic into contemporary life through ritual, herbalism, and divination exercises and meditations.

Other books by the same author:
Magickal Places: A Wiccan Guide to Sacred Sites and Spiritual Centers, 1999

Other books you might like:
Gerina Dunwich, *The Wicca Source Book: A Complete Guide for the Modern Witch*, 1998
Janet Farrar, *The Pagan Path*, 1995
Annette Hinshaw, *Earthtime, Moontime: Rediscovering the Sacred Lunar Year*, 1999
Edain McCoy, *The Sabbats: A New Approach to Living the Old Way*, 1994
Janet Thompson, *Magical Hearth: Home for the Modern Pagan*, 1995

584

JOSEPH TELUSHKIN

Biblical Literacy: The Most Important People, Events, and Ideas of the Hebrew Bible

(New York: William Morrow, 1997)

Category: Religious Commentaries
Subject(s): Bible; Culture; History
Age range(s): Adult

Summary: Rabbi Joseph Telushkin focuses his attention on the ideas, events, people, and stories of the Jewish scriptures in *Biblical Literacy*, a companion volume to *Jewish Literacy* (1991). Telushkin provides background and context information for all the books in the Hebrew Bible, highlighting the laws and ideas of Judaism that have their roots in these teachings. He presents an annotated list of all the laws introduced in the Torah, which number more than 600. Although it is written from the perspective of Judaism, Telushkin's outline of biblical literacy lends a valuable perspective to the reading of the Old Testament of the Christian Bible, as well.

Other books by the same author:
Words That Hurt, Words That Heal: How to Choose Words Wisely and Well, 1996
Jewish Wisdom: Ethical, Spiritual, and Historical Lessons From the Great Works and Thinkers, 1994

Jewish Literacy: The Most Important Things to Know about the Jewish Religion, Its People, and Its History, 1991

Other books you might like:
Barry L. Bandstra, *Reading the Old Testament: An Introduction to the Hebrew Bible*, 1995
Alex J. Goldman, *The Eternal Books Retold: A Rabbi Summarizes the 39 Books of the Bible*, 1999
Dane R. Gordon, *Old Testament in its Cultural, Historical, and Religious Context*, 1994

585

JOSEPH TELUSHKIN

Jewish Literacy: The Most Important Things to Know about the Jewish Religion, Its People, and Its History

(New York: William Morrow, 1991)

Category: Self-Help
Subject(s): Judaism; History; Religious Life
Age range(s): Adult

Summary: *Jewish Literacy* offers encyclopedia-like information about Judaism in an elegant account of history, people, practices, ethics, and literature through thousands of years. Rabbi Joseph Telushkin takes readers on a well-planned journey through the religious and cultural heritage of Judaism, highlighting the aspects that are most important for modern Jews to know and understand. Short essays cover more than 340 facts and topics of interest to Jews and non-Jews alike.

Other books by the same author:
Biblical Literacy: The Most Important People, Events, and Ideas of the Hebrew Bible, 1997
Words That Hurt, Words That Heal: How to Choose Words Wisely and Well, 1996
Jewish Wisdom: Ethical, Spiritual, and Historical Lessons From the Great Works and Thinkers, 1994

Other books you might like:
Anita Diamant, *Living a Jewish Life: A Guide for Starting, Learning, Celebrating, and Parenting*, 1991
Dennis Prager, *The Nine Questions People Ask about Judaism*, 1981
Michael Strassfeld, *The Jewish Holidays: A Guide & Commentary*, 1985

586

JOSEPH TELUSHKIN, Editor

Jewish Wisdom: Ethical, Spiritual, and Historical Lessons From the Great Works and Thinkers

(New York: William Morrow, 1994)

Category: Religious Commentaries
Subject(s): Scripture; History; Judaism
Age range(s): Adult

Summary: Rabbi Joseph Telushkin addresses philosophical and ethical aspects of Jewish life including the quest for meaning, the search to understand God's will, and relationships with others in *Jewish Wisdom*, a collection of teachings drawn from secular and religious writings, both traditional and contemporary. Telushkin provides commentary on the relevance and meaning of each essay or quotation, which is notably useful in the case of anti-Semitic writings and the many portions of the Talmud that are included in the anthology. Among the luminaries whose ideas and thoughts are collected in *Jewish Wisdom* are Bruno Bettelheim, Hayim Bialek, Albert Einstein, Elie Wiesel, and Emile Zola.

Other books by the same author:
Biblical Literacy: The Most Important People, Events, and Ideas of the Hebrew Bible, 1997
Words That Hurt, Words That Heal: How to Choose Words Wisely and Well, 1996
Jewish Humor: What the Best Jewish Jokes Say about the Jews, 1992
Jewish Literacy: The Most Important Things to Know about the Jewish Religion, its People, and its History, 1991

Other books you might like:
Jessica Gribetz, *Wise Words: Jewish Thoughts and Stories through the Ages*, 1997
David C. Gross, *Jewish Wisdom: A Treasury of Proverbs, Maxims, Aphorisms, Wise Sayings, and Memorable Quotations*, 1992
Esther R. Gross, co-compiler
Lawrence Kushner, *The Book of Words: Talking Spiritual Life, Living Spiritual Talk*, 1993
Dennis Prager, *The Nine Questions People Ask about Judaism*, 1981
Adin Steinsaltz, *Teshuvah: A Guide for the Newly Observant Jew*, 1987

587

CORRIE TEN BOOM

The Hiding Place

(Washington Depot, Connecticut: Chosen Books, 1971)

Category: History; Autobiography
Subject(s): Christianity; Holocaust; Jews
Age range(s): Young Adult-Adult

Summary: When she was a young woman, ten Boom and her family hid families of Jews from the Nazis in their home in the Netherlands. She and her family were arrested by the Nazis and placed in concentration camps where they were separated. Ten Boom's Christian faith provided her strength for enduring the horrors of the camps. Ten Boom tells her life story and the story of God's providence in this gripping book, also the subject of a film by the Billy Graham Evangelistic Association.

Other books by the same author:
Tramp for the Lord, 1974

Other books you might like:
Brother Andrew, *God's Smuggler*, 1967
Nicky Cruz, *Run, Baby, Run*, 1968
Kathryn Kuhlman, *Nothing Is Impossible with God*, 1974
Frank E. Peretti, *This Present Darkness*, 1986
David Wilkerson, *The Cross and the Switchblade*, 1962

588

MOTHER TERESA

Heart of Joy

(Ann Arbor, Michigan: Servant Books, 1987)

Category: Sermons; Journals/Letters
Subject(s): Prayer; Essays; Jesus
Age range(s): Adult
Locale(s): India; United States; England

Summary: *Heart of Joy* is a collection of Mother Teresa's teachings taken from occasions when she spoke in public during the 1970s and 1980s and from talks and letters prepared for the sisters of the Missionaries of Charity. She covers topics including what she terms "the generosity of the poor," the call of Christ, the meaning of the work being done in the name of the poor, and how to remain joyful in the most extreme circumstances of life.

Other books by the same author:
In the Heart of the World: Thoughts, Stories, & Prayers, 1997
The Best Gift Is Love: Meditations by Mother Teresa, 1993
Words to Love By, 1989
The Love of Christ: Spiritual Counsels, 1982

Other books you might like:
Michael Collopy, *Works of Love Are Works of Peace: Mother Teresa of Calcutta and the Missionaries of Charity: A Photographic Record*, 1996
Jose Luis Gonzalez-Balado, *Mother Teresa: Her Life, Her Work, Her Message: A Memoir*, 1997
Malcolm Muggeridge, *Something Beautiful for God: Mother Teresa of Calcutta*, 1971
LaVonne Neff, *Life for God: The Mother Teresa Reader*, 1995

589

MOTHER TERESA

A Simple Path

(New York: Random House, 1995)

Category: Autobiography
Subject(s): Catholicism; Poverty; Religion
Age range(s): Young Adult-Adult

Summary: This is Mother Teresa, in her own words and in the words of those who have worked with her. Together with the Sisters of Charity, she brought light and hope to lives that might have ended without either. In this book, she shares both the philosophy and the practices that kept her working for a more loving world, one person at a time.

Other books by the same author:
Everything Starts From Prayer: Mother Teresa's Meditations on Spiritual Life for People of All Faiths, 1998 (Anthony Stern, compiler)
In the Heart of the World: Thoughts, Stories, & Prayers, 1997 (Becky Benenate, editor)
No Greater Love, 1997 (Becky Benenate, Joseph Durepos, editors)
In My Own Words, 1996 (Jose Luis Gonzalez-Baldo, compiler)

Mother Teresa, Contemplative in the Heart of the World, 1985

Other books you might like:
Eileen Egan, *At Prayer with Mother Teresa*, 1999
Malcolm Muggeridge, *Something Beautiful for God: Mother Teresa of Calcutta*, 1971
Raghu Rai, *Faith and Compassion: The Life and Work of Mother Teresa*, 1997
Kathryn Spink, *Mother Teresa: A Complete Authorized Biography*, 1997

590

SAINT TERESA OF AVILA

Interior Castle
(c. 1572)

Category: Devotionals
Subject(s): Christianity; Mysticism; God
Age range(s): Adult

Summary: In her spiritual masterpiece, Teresa of Avila discusses the steps involved in the ascent from rational thought to the "mystic marriage" between God and the soul. Along with John of the Cross, Teresa is recognized as one of the "authorities" on the perfection of the soul. Teresa describes in sensuous prose her intense desire to be married to God, and her autobiographical ascent to God remains one of the liveliest of all spiritual classics.

Other books by the same author:
The Way of Perfection, and Conceptions of Divine Love, 1852 (John Dalton, translator)

Other books you might like:
Saint Catherine of Sienna, *The Dialogue*, c. 1350
Saint John of the Cross, *Dark Night of the Soul*, 1619
Julian of Norwich, *Revelations of Divine Love*, c. 1393
Margery Kempe, *The Book of Margery Kempe*, c. 1435
Thomas Merton, *The Seven Storey Mountain*, 1948

591

KIM THOMAS

Simplicity: Finding Peace by Uncluttering Your Life
(Nashville: Broadman & Holman, 1999)

Category: Self-Help
Subject(s): Spirituality; Self-Confidence
Age range(s): Adult

Summary: Kim Thomas offers a mix of practical advice for "de-cluttering" one's physical environment and spiritual life in one of many titles during the late 1990s to focus on the relationship between lifestyle simplification and spiritual wholeness. *Simplicity: Finding Peace by Uncluttering Your Life* recommends one set of actions to address physical, emotional, and spiritual confusion in life: reduce the clutter, "persevere in the everyday," and keep an eye on the goal. Thomas further suggests several "habits of holiness" to help keep

spiritual clutter at bay, including meditation, prayer, fasting, and worship.

Other books you might like:
Sarah Ban Breathnach, *Simple Abundance: A Daybook of Comfort and Joy*, 1995
Tilden Edwards, *Living Simply through the Day: Spiritual Survival in a Complex Age*, 1998
Doris Janzen Longacre, *Living More with Less*, 1980
Jann Mitchell, *Home Sweeter Home: Creating a Haven of Simplicity and Spirit*, 1996

592

THOMAS A KEMPIS

The Imitation of Christ
(New York: E.P. Dutton, 1932)

Category: Devotionals
Subject(s): Catholicism; Saints; Christian Life
Age range(s): Adult

Summary: *The Imitation of Christ* is a classic of Christian literature that dates back to the 15th century. Its author, a monk who lived from 1380 to 1471, wrote many small devotional teachings about the conduct of Christians as that of the conduct of Christ. His writings celebrate the love, devotion, and holiness of Jesus and offer guidance for followers of Christ to live truly in the manner of their Lord. *The Imitation of Christ* has been translated into more languages than any other book except the *Bible*, and it has remained a favorite devotional guide for centuries. Since the publication of this 1932 version, many English-language editions have been published.

Other books you might like:
Brother Lawrence, *Writings and Conversations on the Practice of the Presence of God*, 1994
    Conrad DeMeester, editor; Salvatore Sciurba, translator
Saint Francis de Sales, *Introduction to the Devout Life*, 1966
    John K. Ryan, translator
Thomas a Kempis, *Come Lord Jesus: Devotional Readings from the Imitation of Christ*, 1995
    David Hazard, editor
William A. Meninger, *Bringing the Imitation of Christ into the Twenty-First Century*, 1998

593

ROBERT THURMAN

Inner Revolution: Life, Liberty, and the Pursuit of Real Happiness
(New York: Riverhead Books, 1998)

Category: Doctrine
Subject(s): Buddhism; Politics; Culture
Age range(s): Adult

Summary: Robert Thurman, professor, author, and the first Westerner to become a Tibetan Buddhist monk, writes in *Inner Revolution* of blending the technology-based society of the West with the spirituality of the East to create an enlightened world. After studying with the Dalai Lama in India in the

1960s, Thurman was unable to continue to be a monk in the United States, because there was no Tibetan Buddhist community in his homeland. Instead, he became a Buddhist scholar, and he has had a significant impact on Western acceptance of Buddhist practice and philosophy. In this volume, he describes his vision for an enlightened society that unites the "outer" life of Western material things and the "inner" life of Eastern spirituality. He offers specific political steps and philosophies for those interested in applying his ideas about inner revolution.

Other books by the same author:
Circling the Sacred Mountain: A Spiritual Adventure through the Himalayas, 1999
Essential Tibetan Buddhism, 1995
Inside Tibetan Buddhism: Rituals and Symbols Revealed, 1995

Other books you might like:
Alexander Berzin, *Developing Balanced Sensitivity: Practical Buddhist Exercises for Daily Life*, 1998
Lama Surya Das, *Awakening the Buddha Within: Eight Steps to Enlightenment: Tibetan Wisdom for the Western World*, 1997
John Tarrant, *The Light Inside the Dark: Zen, Soul and the Spiritual Life*, 1998

594

PAUL TILLICH

The Courage to Be

(New Haven, Connecticut: Yale University Press, 1952)

Category: Theology
Subject(s): Christianity; Philosophy; God
Age range(s): Adult

Summary: Tillich combines the insights of existentialist philosophy and systematic theology in order to explore the ways that contemporary individuals can summon the courage to face their anxiety and despair.

Other books by the same author:
Dynamics of Faith, 1956
Biblical Religion and the Search for Ultimate Reality, 1955

Other books you might like:
Karl Barth, *The Humanity of God*, 1960
Christoph Blumhardt, *Action in Waiting*, 1998
   Selections from the writings of Christoph Blumhardt (1842-1919).
Viktor E. Frankl, *Man's Search for Meaning: An Introduction to Logo Therapy*, 1963
Soren Kierkegaard, *Fear and Trembling*, 1985
Rollo May, *The Courage to Create*, 1975

595

PAUL TILLICH

The Eternal Now

(New York: Scribner, 1963)

Category: Sermons; Theology
Subject(s): Religion; Christianity

Age range(s): Adult

Summary: *The Eternal Now* is a collection of sermons that provide a comprehensive, yet accessible, introduction to the theology of Paul Tillich (1886-1965). Tillich, a German-American Protestant theologian, took the position that psychology, existential philosophy, and the arts could all inform the development of modern theology. Fundamental to Tillich's theology is the principle that God is the ground of all being, and that the alienation of individuals in modern society has its roots in separation from God.

Other books by the same author:
A History of Christian Thought, 1972
Systematic Theology, 1952-1963
Dynamics of Faith, 1956
The Courage to Be, 1952

Other books you might like:
Karl Barth, *The Holy Ghost and the Christian Life*, 1938
Dietrich Bonhoeffer, *Ethics*, 1955
Reinhold Niebuhr, *The Nature and Destiny of Man: A Christian Interpretation*, 1941-1943
Mark Kline Taylor, *Paul Tillich: Theologian of the Boundaries*, 1987

596

PAUL TILLICH

The Shaking of the Foundations

(New York: C. Scribner's Sons, 1948)

Category: Sermons; Theology
Subject(s): Protestantism; Christianity
Age range(s): Adult

Summary: Paul Tillich was one of America's best-known Protestant theologians from 1933 until his death in 1965. He was one of the first non-Jewish scholars to be expelled from Nazi Germany for publicly opposing Hitler. During his years at the Union Theological Seminary in New York, he was a prolific writer of books, lectures, and sermons. *The Shaking of the Foundations* is a collection of sermons that reflect Tillich's position that the social, political, and philosophical aspects of modern society are integral components of modern theology.

Other books by the same author:
My Travel Diary, 1936: Between Two Worlds, 1970
The Future of Religions, 1966
The Eternal Now, 1963
The Courage to Be, 1952

Other books you might like:
Karl Barth, *The Holy Ghost and the Christian Life*, 1938
Dietrich Bonhoeffer, *Ethics*, 1955
N. Gordon Cosby, *By Grace Transformed: Christianity for a New Millennium*, 1998
Reinhold Niebuhr, *The Nature and Destiny of Man: A Christian Interpretation*, 1941-1943
Reinhold Niebuhr, *Moral Man and Immoral Society: A Study in Ethics and Politics*, 1932
Mark Kline Taylor, *Paul Tillich: Theologian of the Boundaries*, 1987

597

PAUL TILLICH

Theology of Culture

(New York: Oxford University Press, 1959)

Category: Theology
Subject(s): Christianity; Philosophy
Age range(s): Adult

Summary: In his penetrating way, theologian Tillich examines art, morality, science, and psychoanalysis to demonstrate that religion is the ground of them all. In this book he offers his famous definition of religion: ''Religion is the substance of culture; culture the form of religion.''

Other books by the same author:
A History of Christian Thought, 1972

Other books you might like:
Thomas J.J. Altizer, *Genesis and Apocalypse: A Theological Voyage Toward Authentic Christianity*, 1990
Dietrich Bonhoeffer, *Ethics*, 1955
    Originally written in German, this work by Bonhoeffer (1906-1945) was edited by Eberhard Bethge and translated by Neville Horton Smith.
H. Richard Niebuhr, *Christ and Culture*, 1951
John Shelby Spong, *Why Christianity Must Change or Die: A Bishop Speaks to Believers in Exile: A New Reformation of the Church's Faith and Practice*, 1998
Mark Kline Taylor, *Paul Tillich: Theologian of the Boundaries*, 1987

598

TIME-LIFE BOOKS, Editor

Eastern Mysteries

(Alexandria, Virginia: Time-Life Books, 1991)

Category: Religious Encyclopedias/Dictionaries
Series: Mysteries of the Unknown
Subject(s): Religious Life; Hinduism; Buddhism
Age range(s): Young Adult-Adult

Summary: *Eastern Mysteries* is part of the Time-Life series Mysteries of the Unknown. The volume is a lavishly illustrated introduction to some of the visually unique aspects of Buddhism and Hinduism. Produced for a Western audience, the emphasis of the book's photography is on practices, rituals, and modes of dress that are unfamiliar to Western culture. *Eastern Mysteries* begins the journey into Asian religious cultures by highlighting the aura of the unknown that surrounded these cultures until the mid-nineteenth century. With the arrival of European trade in China in the 1840s, and again with the success of a British expedition to Tibet in the early 1900s, photographic and journalistic accounts began opening the mysteries of the East to the rest of the world. Many of these early records are included in this volume.

Other books by the same author:
Mysterious Lands and Peoples, 1991 (Mysteries of the Unknown)
Ancient Wisdom and Secret Sects, 1989 (Mysteries of the Unknown)

Search for the Soul, 1989 (Mysteries of the Unknown)
Cosmic Connections, 1988 (Mysteries of the Unknown)
Mystic Places, 1987 (Mysteries of the Unknown)

Other books you might like:
Robert S. Ellwood, *The Encyclopedia of World Religions*, 1998
John Y. Fenton, *Religions of Asia*, 1988
    second edition
Edward Rice, *Eastern Definitions: A Short Encyclopedia of Religions of the Orient*, 1978
Chris Richards, *The Illustrated Encyclopedia of World Religions*, 1997

599

TIME-LIFE BOOKS, Editor

Psychic Voyages

(Alexandria, Virginia: Time-Life Books, 1987)

Category: Religious Encyclopedias/Dictionaries
Series: Mysteries of the Unknown
Subject(s): Reincarnation; Spiritualism; Afterlife
Age range(s): Young Adult-Adult

Summary: Part of the Time-Life series Mysteries of the Unknown, *Psychic Voyages* focuses on the paranormal and afterlife experiential phenomena. This volume explores death and near-death experiences, journeys of the spirit, out-of-body experiences, questions and observations about reincarnation, and ritual associated with the transition from one life to the next. As with all Time-Life books, the text is well-balanced with graphic illustrations and photographs.

Other books by the same author:
The Psychics, 1992 (Mysteries of the Unknown)
The Mind and Beyond, 1991 (Mysteries of the Unknown)
Mind over Matter, 1988 (Mysteries of the Unknown)
Visions and Prophecies, 1988 (Mysteries of the Unknown)
Psychic Powers, 1987 (Mysteries of the Unknown)

Other books you might like:
Hans Holzer, *Life Beyond: Compelling Evidence for Past Lives and Existence After Death*, 1994
Raymond A. Moody Jr., *The Light Beyond*, 1988
Ian Wilson, *The After Death Experience*, 1987

600

TIME-LIFE BOOKS, Editor

The Spirit World

(Alexandria, Virginia: Time-Life Books, 1992)

Category: Religious Encyclopedias/Dictionaries
Series: American Indians
Subject(s): Indians of North America; Religious Life; Customs
Age range(s): Young Adult-Adult

Summary: This entry into the American Indians series of Time-Life Books focuses on the spirituality of Native American peoples, past and present. *The Spirit World* looks at the beliefs and practices of various tribes, tracing the roots of creation myths and the expression of spirituality through music, dance, and art. Ceremonies, rituals, holy sites, and spirit visions are depicted in photographs, line drawings, and full-color artwork.

Other books you might like:
Robert L. Hall, *An Archaeology of the Soul: North American Indian Belief and Ritual*, 1997
Paula Hartz, *Native American Religions*, 1997
Arlene Hirschfelder, *The Encyclopedia of Native American Religions: An Introduction*, 1992
Bobby Lake-Thorn, *Spirits of the Earth: A Guide to Native American Nature Symbols, Stories, and Ceremonies*, 1997

601

TIME-LIFE BOOKS, Editor

Visions and Prophecies

(Alexandria, Virginia: Time-Life Books, 1988)

Category: Religious Encyclopedias/Dictionaries
Series: Mysteries of the Unknown
Subject(s): Parapsychology; Magic; Occult
Age range(s): Young Adult-Adult

Summary: Focusing on Western fascination with predictions about the future, *Visions and Prophecies* explores the world of psychics and fortune-telling, from the ancient past to the practices of modern seers. With graphic illustration and explanatory text, the editors discuss the interpretation of signs and omens, and the use of numerology, handwriting analysis, and Tarot cards to discern aspects of personality and to conjure revelations about future circumstances.

Other books by the same author:
The Psychics, 1992 (Mysteries of the Unknown)
Dreams and Dreaming, 1990 (Mysteries of the Unknown)
Cosmic Connections, 1988 (Mysteries of the Unknown)
Psychic Powers, 1987 (Mysteries of the Unknown)
Psychic Voyages, 1987 (Mysteries of the Unknown)

Other books you might like:
Nathaniel Altman, *The Little Giant Encyclopedia of Palmistry*, 1999
Omar V. Garrison, *The Encyclopedia of Prophecy*, 1978
Rosemary Ellen Guiley, *Encyclopedia of Dreams: Symbols and Interpretations*, 1995
Stuart R. Kaplan, *The Encyclopedia of Tarot*, 1989

602

TIME-LIFE BOOKS, Editor

Witches and Witchcraft

(Alexandria, Virginia: Time-Life Books, 1990)

Category: Religious Encyclopedias/Dictionaries
Series: Mysteries of the Unknown
Subject(s): Witches and Witchcraft; Occult; Customs
Age range(s): Young Adult-Adult

Summary: Part of the Mysteries of the Unknown subscription series by Time-Life Books, *Witches and Witchcraft* focuses on visually fascinating images and customs of witchcraft, past and present. The series is well-illustrated with photographs, line drawings, and full-color artwork. The editors trace the

history of witchcraft worldwide and provide an overview of 20th century interest in the crafts of Wicca, magick, and the black and white arts of witchcraft.

Other books by the same author:
Magical Arts, 1990 (Mysteries of the Unknown)
Ancient Wisdom and Secret Sects, 1989 (Mysteries of the Unknown)
Spirit Summonings, 1989 (Mysteries of the Unknown)
Transformations, 1989 (Mysteries of the Unknown)
Visions and Prophecies, 1988 (Mysteries of the Unknown)

Other books you might like:
Gerina Dunwich, *Wicca A to Z: A Modern Witch's Encyclopedia*, 1997
Rosemary Ellen Guiley, *The Encyclopedia of Witches and Witchcraft*, 1999
James R. Lewis, *Witchcraft Today: An Encyclopedia of Wiccan and Neopagan Traditions*, 1999

603

FRANK J. TIPLER

The Physics of Immortality: Modern Cosmology, God, and the Resurrection of the Dead

(New York: Doubleday, 1994)

Category: Theology
Subject(s): Physics; Fantasy
Age range(s): Adult

Summary: Mathematician, physicist, and philosopher Frank J. Tipler explains his conclusions about the existence and nature of God and proposes that humankind is not far from developing the kind of artificial intelligence that could evolve into the equivalent of God. In *The Physics of Immortality*, Tipler reveals how a mathematical model of the universe can affirm that God exists, and he speculates about the connection between a someday resurrection of the earth-bound dead and and the development of computer intelligence powerful enough to manage the simultanous interactions of all those souls.

Other books by the same author:
The Anthropic Cosmological Principle, 1986 (John D. Barrow, co-author)
Essays in General Relativity: A Festschrift for Abraham Taub, 1980

Other books you might like:
John D. Barrow, *Theories of Everything: The Quest for Ultimate Explanation*, 1991
Paul Davies, *The Mind of God: The Scientific Basis for a Rational World*, 1992
David Deutsch, *The Fabric of Reality: The Science of Parallel Universes—and Its Implications*, 1997
John Polkinghorne, *The Faith of a Physicist*, 1994

604

LEO TOLSTOY

The Gospel in Brief

(New York: T.Y. Crowell and Company, 1896)

Category: Theology
Subject(s): Christianity; Bible
Age range(s): Adult

Summary: Leo Tolstoy's *The Gospel in Brief* is an unusual interpretive study of the four biblical Gospels. Tolstoy's study of the original Greek texts led him to create this fusion of ancient documents and his own religious philosophies. Instead of concerning himself with the divinity of Jesus and the circumstances surrounding his birth, Tolstoy focuses strictly on the teachings and actions of Jesus, noting that he wants to separate them consciously from the dogma of the Church so that the emphasis is on spirituality, and not religiosity. Tolstoy's study of the gospels has also been published as *The Gospel According to Tolstoy*, translated by David Patterson (1991).

Other books by the same author:
Anna Karenina, 1889
The Kingdom of God Is Within You: Christianity Not as a Mystic Religion but as a New Theory of Life, 1894
Confession, 1882
War and Peace: A Historical Novel, 1864-1869

Other books you might like:
Stephen Mitchell, *The Gospel According to Jesus: A New Translation and Guide to His Essential Teachings for Believers and Unbelievers*, 1991
Francis J. Moloney, *Beginning the Good News: A Narrative Approach*, 1995
Reynolds Price, *The Three Gospels*, 1996
Walter Wangerin Jr., *The Book of God: The Bible as a Novel*, 1996

605

LEO TOLSTOY

The Kingdom of God Is Within You: Christianity Not as a Mystic Religion but as a New Theory of Life

(New York: Cassell, 1894)

Category: Theology
Subject(s): Christianity; Pacifism; Christian Life
Age range(s): Adult
Time period(s): 19th century
Locale(s): Russia

Summary: A Russian novelist and short story writer, Leo Tolstoy is best remembered in literature for his classic novels *War and Peace* and *Anna Karenina*. In theological or philosophical terms, however, Tolstoy's great works include his *Confession* (1882) and *The Kingdom of God Is Within You*. In the latter, Tolstoy details his thoughts and teachings on two basic tenets of biblical Christianity: love for all fellow humans and nonresistance in the face of evil.

Other books by the same author:
Anna Karenina, 1889
What Men Live by, and Where Love Is, There God Is Also, 1887
Confession, 1882
War and Peace: A Historical Novel, 1864-1869

Other books you might like:
Peter Brock, *The Roots of War Resistance: Pacifism From the Early Church to Tolstoy*, 1981
Joseph T. Culliton, *Non-Violence: Central to Christian Spirituality: Perspectives From Scripture to the Present*, 1982
Mohandas K. Gandhi, *An Autobiography: The Story of My Experiments with Truth*, 1949
A.L. Herman, *Community, Violence, and Peace: Aldo Leopold, Mohandas K. Gandhi, Martin Luther King, Jr., and Gautama the Buddha in the Twenty-First Century*, 1999
A.N. Wilson, *The Lion and the Honeycomb: The Religious Writings of Tolstoy*, 1987

606

PAUL TOURNIER

The Meaning of Persons

(New York: Harper, 1957)

Category: Self-Help
Subject(s): Psychology; World Religions; Spirituality
Age range(s): Adult

Summary: French psychiatrist Tournier combines psychology and religion as he seeks the spiritual meaning of personal identity. He notes that people are constantly searching to find meaning in life and that people do not have a ready-made identity that gives them meaning. For Tournier, this constant search is an adventure in living. Tournier fashioned these insights into psychology and spirituality long before M. Scott Peck popularized these approaches in his works.

Other books by the same author:
The Adventure of Living, 1989
A Place for You: Psychology and Religion, 1968

Other books you might like:
Robert Hemfelt, *Love Is a Choice*, 1989
Henri J.M. Nouwen, *The Inner Voice of Love: A Journey through Anguish to Freedom*, 1996
M. Scott Peck, *The Road Less Traveled: A New Psychology of Love, Traditional Values, and Spiritual Growth*, 1978
Eugene H. Peterson, *The Wisdom of Each Other: A Conversation between Spiritual Friends*, 1998
Dallas Willard, *The Divine Conspiracy: Rediscovering Our Hidden Life in God*, 1998

607

D. ELTON TRUEBLOOD

The People Called Quakers

(New York: Harper & Row, 1966)

Category: History
Subject(s): Quakers; Religious Life; Christianity
Age range(s): Young Adult-Adult

Summary: D. Elton Trueblood traces the roots and development of the Quaker, or Society of Friends, movement of Christian thought and practice in the United States. Quaker influence on American history and religious culture extends back into the colonial days in the mid-to-late 17th century when significant numbers of Quakers emigrated from England to the New World colony of Pennsylvania. Although the denomination has undergone many changes in more than 300 years, Trueblood's portrayal of the early Quakers demonstrates that the essence of the philosophy of the Society of Friends can be seen in contemporary Quaker philosophy and practice.

Other books by the same author:
While It Is Day, 1974
Abraham Lincoln: Theologian of American Anguish, 1973
The Validity of the Christian Mission, 1972
The Future of the Christian, 1971

Other books you might like:
Mary Garman, *Hidden in Plain Sight: Quaker Women's Writings*, 1995
Robert Lawrence Smith, *A Quaker Book of Wisdom: Life Lessons in Simplicity, Service, and Common Sense*, 1998
Jessamyn West, *A Quaker Reader*, 1992
Carolyn Wilhelm, *A Certain Kind of Perfection*, 1997
Jean Kinney Williams, *The Quakers*, 1998

608

CHOGYAM TRUNGPA

The Heart of the Buddha

(Boston: Shambhala, 1991)

Category: Sermons
Subject(s): Buddhism; Religious Life; Meditation
Age range(s): Adult

Summary: Prolific writer and translator of Buddhist texts Chogyam Trungpa presents a collection of his lectures and teachings that relate the basic philosophies of Buddhism to every day life. The writings in *The Heart of the Buddha* address the individual in "Personal Journey," the journey itself in "Stages on the Path," and the relationship between individuals in "Working with Others."

Other books by the same author:
Orderly Chaos: The Mandala Principle, 1991
Shambhala: The Sacred Path of the Warrior, 1984
The Myth of Freedom and the Way of Meditation, 1976
Meditation in Action, 1969

Other books you might like:
Samuel Berholz, *An Introduction to the Buddha and His Teachings*, 1997
Thich Nhat Hanh, *The Heart of the Buddha's Teaching*, 1996
Kelsang Gyatso, *Heart of Wisdom: The Essential Wisdom Teachings of Buddha*, 1996
Jack Kornfield, *Teachings of the Buddha*, 1993

609

RUTH A. TUCKER

Private Lives of Pastors' Wives

(Grand Rapids, Michigan: Zondervan, 1992)

Category: History
Subject(s): Women; Ministry; Religious Life
Age range(s): Adult

Summary: In *Private Lives of Pastors' Wives*, Ruth A. Tucker profiles more than a dozen women throughout Protestant history who were married to influential church or evangelistic leaders of their day. Noting that the stereotype of pastors' wives is that of a "behind-the-scenes" figure, the author demonstrates that each of these women made valuable contributions to ministry in ways that were not necessarily hidden or behind the scenes. This title was previously published as *First Ladies of the Parish: Historical Portraits of Pastors' Wives*, a Gold Medallion Book Award title in 1989.

Other books by the same author:
Multiple Choices: Making Wise Decisions in a Complicated World, 1992
Sacred Stories: Devotions From the Family of God, 1989
Daughters of the Church: A History of Women and Ministry From New Testament Times to the Present, 1987
Women and the Church: A History of Changing Perspectives, 1986

Other books you might like:
Jill Briscoe, *There's a Snake in My Garden*, 1975
Patricia Cornwell, *Ruth, a Portrait: The Story of Ruth Bell Graham*, 1997
Vikki Knoche, *Me, a Minister's Wife?: Parish the Thought!*, 1984
James Schaffer, *Christian Wives: Women Behind the Evangelists Reveal Their Faith in Modern Marriage*, 1987
Denise Turner, *Home Sweet Fishbowl: Confessions of a Minister's Wife*, 1982

610

ALICE K. TURNER

The History of Hell

(New York: Harcourt Brace, 1993)

Category: History; Theology
Subject(s): Hell
Age range(s): Adult

Summary: Alice K. Turner traces more than 4,000 years of religious and societal thought and philosophy about the essence and existence of hell in *The History of Hell*. She begins by examining the significance and evidence of the concept of hell in Middle Eastern and Mediterranean cultures, and goes on to explore its development in the Christian church through text, art, music, and drama.

Other books by the same author:
Yoga for Beginners, 1973

Other books you might like:

Alan E. Bernstein, *The Formation of Hell: Death and Retribution in the Ancient and Early Christian Worlds*, 1993

Richard Craze, *Hell: An Illustrated History of the Nether World*, 1996

Tom Morgan, *The Devil: A Visual Guide to the Demonic, Evil, Scurrilous, and Bad*, 1996

Miriam Van Scott, *Encyclopedia of Hell*, 1998

611

DESMOND TUTU, Editor

An African Prayer Book

(New York: Doubleday, 1995)

Category: Prayer
Subject(s): Africans; Religious Life; Spirituality
Age range(s): Young Adult-Adult

Summary: In this volume, South African archbishop Desmond Tutu gathers prayers representing various cultures of continental Africa, as well as the African diaspora worldwide. From the mystery of the Egyptian Coptic faith to the simplicity found in a Bushman's prayer, the Nobel Laureate provides a uniquely African perspective on prayer and scripture throughout history. Archbishop Tutu offers spiritual guidance in his own prose and prayers, as well.

Other books by the same author:
The Rainbow People of God, 1994

Other books you might like:
Church of the Province of New Zealand, *A New Zealand Prayer Book: He Karakia Mihinare O Aotearoa*, 1989

612

U.S. CATHOLIC CHURCH

The Catechism of the Catholic Church

(New York: Doubleday, 1995)

Category: Doctrine
Subject(s): Catholicism; Religious Life; History
Age range(s): Children-Adult

Summary: *The Catechism of the Catholic Church* is a document of Christian doctrine written in the form of questions and answers. Used for religious instruction, the Catechism provides a structure for learning about the Catholic faith for those who wish to become communicant members of the Church. The most recent edition of the Catechism, published more than 400 years after the last major revision in 1566, appeared in 1995. It reflects the latest statement of teachings as compiled by the key leadership of the Roman Catholic Church in 1994.

Other books you might like:

Kevin Orlin Johnson, *Why Do Catholics Do That?: A Guide to the Teachings and Practices of the Catholic Church*, 1994

Karl Keating, *What Catholics Really Believe—Setting the Record Straight: 52 Answers to Common Misconceptions about the Catholic Faith*, 1992

John O'Connor, *The Essential Catholic Handbook: A Summary of Beliefs, Practices, and Prayers*, 1997

Alan Schreck, *Catholic and Christian: An Explanation of Commonly Misunderstood Catholic Beliefs*, 1984

613

URANTIA FOUNDATION

The Urantia Book

(Chicago: Urantia Foundation, 1955)

Category: New Age (Nonfiction)
Subject(s): Scripture; Philosophy
Age range(s): Adult

Summary: Billed by the Urantia Foundation as "the Fifth Revelation of God to Man," this volume consists of teachings designed to enhance spiritual growth outside the structure of traditional religious practices. Urantia teachings hold that the parables and other ministry words of Jesus were the Fourth Revelation, and that a later revelation is needed to procure whole spiritual growth for all. The book is divided into four sections: "The Central and Superuniverses," "The Local Universe," "The History of Urantia," and "The Life and Teachings of Jesus."

Other books by the same author:
The Urantia Book Concordance, 1993

Other books you might like:

Clyde Bedell, *Clyde Bedell's Concordex of the Urantia Book*, 1971

Mary Ebben, *The Urantia Book Basics*, 1994

Kelly Elstrott, *The Fifth Revelation: A Collection of Key Passages from the Urantia Book*, 1998

Duane L. Faw, *Duane L. Faw's Paramony: A Parallel and History of the Urantia Book and the Bible*, 1986

Fred Harris, *The Center Within: Lessons From the Heart of the Urantia Revelation*, 1998

William Samuel Sadler, *A Study of the Master Universe: A Development of Concepts of the Urantia Book*, 1968

614

P.D. USPENSKII

In Search of the Miraculous: Fragments of an Unknown Teaching

(New York: Harcourt, Brace and Jovanovich, 1949)

Category: New Age (Nonfiction); Autobiography
Subject(s): Psychology; Spirituality; Art
Age range(s): Adult

Summary: Ouspensky studied with guru G.I. Gurdjieff for eight years during the first half of the 20th century. In his autobiography, Ouspensky recalls his years with Gurdjieff as well as his own search for spiritual truth. He combines psychology, art, and literature as he makes his claim that very few people know what to do with the knowledge that is given to them.

Other books by the same author:
The Fourth Way: A Record of Talks and Answers to Questions Based on the Teaching of G.I. Gurdjieff, 1957

Other books you might like:
A.H. Almaas, *Essence: With the Elixir of Enlightenment*, 1998
Robert Earl Burton, *Self-Remembering*, 1991
Andrew Cohen, *My Master Is My Self*, 1989
G.I. Gurdjieff, *Meetings with Remarkable Men*, 1963
Ken Wilber, *The Eye of Spirit: An Integral Vision for a World Gone Slightly Mad*, 1997

615

ROBERT VAN DE WEYER, Editor

The HarperCollins Book of Prayers: A Treasury of Prayers through the Ages
(San Francisco: HarperSanFrancisco, 1993)

Category: Prayer
Subject(s): Spirituality; Meditation; Christianity
Age range(s): Young Adult-Adult

Summary: *The HarperCollins Book of Prayers* is an anthology of devotional, personal, and liturgical prayers gathered from a wide range of Christian sources, with a few from Islam, Judaism, and other monotheistic religious traditions. Robert Van de Weyer draws upon the early church leaders and mystics for some prayers, and from contemporary and poetic sources for others, collecting several hundred prayers in all, with something for virtually every occasion included. In addition, Van de Weyer has provided biographical overviews about each source, personalizing the works with a connection to the human beings who originally used these prayers in their private devotional lives. Indeed, the collection itself is quite personal in nature, because Van de Weyer, an Anglican priest, originally collected these prayers for personal use in his own spiritual journey.

Other books by the same author:
Roots of Faith: An Anthology of Early Christian Spirituality to Contemplate and Treasure, 1997
A Celtic Resurrection: The Diary of a Split From the Church, 1996
The Shepherd's Son, 1993
Celtic Fire: The Passionate Religious Vision of Ancient Britain and Ireland, 1991

Other books you might like:
Kenneth Cragg, *Common Prayer: A Muslim-Christian Spiritual Anthology*, 1999
Richard J. Foster, *Streams of Living Water: Celebrating the Great Traditions of Christian Faith*, 1998
Mohandas K. Gandhi, *Book of Prayers*, 1999
John Strohmeier, editor
Desmond Tutu, *An African Prayer Book*, 1995
John Uboldi, *A Book of Prayers*, 1981

616

JAMES VAN PRAAGH

Talking to Heaven: A Medium's Message of Life After Death
(New York: Dutton, 1997)

Category: New Age (Nonfiction)
Subject(s): Death; Grief; Parapsychology
Age range(s): Adult

Summary: In *Talking to Heaven* , James Van Praagh writes about communicating with the spirits of those who have died. As a medium, he works with families who have lost loved ones to death, and in this book, he shares some of the messages he has brought back on behalf of those beyond earthly life. Describing the unseen world of the afterlife, he addresses the questions people most often ask about what may be beyond death's seeming finality.

Other books by the same author:
Reaching to Heaven: A Spiritual Journey through Life and Death, 1999

Other books you might like:
Sylvia Browne, *The Other Side and Back: A Psychic's Guide to Our World and Beyond*, 1999
Lindsay Harrison, co-author
Bill Guggenheim, *Hello From Heaven!: A New Field of Research Confirms That Life and Love Are Eternal*, 1995
Louis E. Lagrand, *After-Death Communication: Final Farewells*, 1997

617

SHELDON VANAUKEN

A Severe Mercy: C.S. Lewis and a Pagan Love Invaded by Christ, Told by One of the Lovers
(London: Hodder and Stoughton, 1977)

Category: Autobiography
Subject(s): Poetry; Marriage; Death
Age range(s): Adult

Summary: Themes of human and spiritual love, God's mysterious ways, and the universality of death are woven into a moving account of the author's marriage and the untimely death of his beloved wife. Sheldon Vanauken and his wife, Jean Palmer Davis, were good friends of C.S. Lewis and his wife. *A Severe Mercy* is Vanauken's perspective on a life and love that had at its core a shared spiritual quest and strength that ultimately helped him deal with the tremendous personal loss he felt when the earthly marriage was cut short by death.

Awards the book has won:
Gold Medallion Book Award, Biography/Autobiography, 1978
National Book Award, Religion and Inspiration, 1980

Other books by the same author:
Mercies: Collected Poems, 1988
Under the Mercy, 1985 (essays)

Gateway to Heaven, 1980 (novel)

Other books you might like:

Madeleine L'Engle, *Two-Part Invention: The Story of a Marriage*, 1988

C.S. Lewis, *A Grief Observed*, 1961

Edith Schaeffer, *The Tapestry: The Life and Times of Francis and Edith Schaeffer*, 1981

Brian Sibley, *C.S. Lewis: Through the Shadowlands*, 1985

618

IYANLA VANZANT

One Day My Soul Just Opened Up: 40 Days and 40 Nights Toward Spiritual Strength and Personal Growth

(New York: Fireside, 1998)

Category: Self-Help
Subject(s): Self-Respect; Spirituality; God
Age range(s): Adult

Summary: Vanzant records the experience of opening her soul to God. Through short poems, inspirational quotations, and meditation exercises she shares ways to help readers open themselves up to the divine. Vanzant encourages readers to look for numerous ways of allowing the divine into their ordinary lives.

Other books by the same author:

In the Meantime: Finding Yourself and the Love You Want, 1998

Other books you might like:

Debrena Jackson Gandy, *Sacred Pampering Principles: An African-American Woman's Guide to Self-Care and Inner Renewal*, 1997

John Gray, *How to Get What You Want and Want What You Have: A Practical and Spiritual Guide to Personal Success*, 1999

Linda H. Hollies, *Jesus and Those Bodacious Women: Life Lessons From One Sister to Another*, 1998

T.D. Jakes, *Lay Aside the Weight: Taking Control of It Before It Takes Control of You!*, 1997

Gary Zukav, *The Seat of the Soul*, 1989

619

LUCINDA VARDEY, Editor

God in All Worlds: An Anthology of Contemporary Spiritual Writing

(New York: Pantheon Books, 1995)

Category: Essays
Subject(s): Poetry; Meditation; Spirituality
Age range(s): Adult

Summary: *God in All Worlds* offers an anthology of writings from many traditions designed to highlight a wide range of contemporary spiritual thought and philosophy. Twentieth-century theology is side-by-side with personal and spiritual contributions from poets, novelists, feminists, social activists, and scientists. Each of the twenty-two chapters is introduced

by Varney, whose notes place the chapter's writings within the context of a journey toward enlightenment.

Other books by the same author:

The Flowering of the Soul: A Book of Prayers by Women, 1999

Belonging: A Questioning Catholic Comes to Terms with the Church, 1989

Other books you might like:

C. Michael Curtis, *God: Stories*, 1998

Abraham Joshua Heschel, *I Asked for Wonder: A Spiritual Anthology*, 1982

Philip Zaleski, *The Best Spiritual Writing, 1998*, 1998

620

LLEWELLYN VAUGHAN-LEE

The Bond with the Beloved: The Mystical Relationship of the Lover and the Beloved

(Inverness, California: Golden Sufi Center, 1999)

Category: New Age (Nonfiction); Doctrine
Subject(s): Sufism; Mysticism; Dreams and Nightmares
Age range(s): Adult

Summary: In *The Bond with the Beloved*, Llewellyn Vaughan-Lee portrays the inner journey of returning to God as a return to "the beloved." The author describes the stages of the mystical journey in terms of Sufism and Jungian psychology, noting that practicing meditation and dreamwork are two ways of integrating one's spiritual journey into everyday life. Vaughan-Lee suggests that a mystical union with God as the beloved is at the core of personal and global transformation and enlightenment.

Other books by the same author:

Catching the Thread: Sufism, Dreamwork, and Jungian Psychology, 1998

The Paradoxes of Love, 1996

Travelling the Path of Love: Sayings of Sufi Masters, 1995

In the Company of Friends: Dreamwork Within a Sufi Group, 1994

Other books you might like:

Nasrollah S. Fatemi, *Love, Beauty and Harmony in Sufism*, 1978

Muzaffer Ozak, *Love Is the Wine: Talks of a Sufi Master in America*, 1987

William C. Chittick, *The Sufi Path of Love: The Spiritual Teachings of Rumi*, 1983

621

DOREEN VIRTUE

Divine Guidance: How to Have a Dialogue with God and Your Guardian Angels

(New York: St. Martin's Press, 1998)

Category: New Age (Nonfiction); Self-Help
Subject(s): Angels; Spirituality
Age range(s): Adult

Summary: Doreen Virtue shares clairvoyant techniques for communicating with God and the angels in *Divine Guidance*, a guide to angel spirituality. She describes the characteristics of true angelic guidance as positive and supportive, suggesting that feelings of fear or negativity as a result of angel communication are indicative of false guidance. She also outlines a method for making direct spiritual connections with God and the angels through meditative breathing, the use of specific questions, and the conscious pursuit of a spirit of trust.

Other books by the same author:

Angel Therapy: Healing Messages for Every Area of Your Life, 1997

The Lightworker's Way: Awakening Your Spiritual Power to Know and Heal, 1997

Other books you might like:

Rosalyn Bruyere, *Wheels of Light: Chakras, Auras, and the Healing Energy of the Body*, 1994

Arielle Ford, *Hot Chocolate for the Mystical Soul: 101 True Stories of Angels, Miracles, and Healings*, 1998

Julia Ingram, *The Messengers: A True Story of Angelic Presence and the Return to the Age of Miracles*, 1996
G.W. Hardin, co-author

Neale Donald Walsch, *Conversations with God: An Uncommon Dialogue*, 1996

622

JORDAN LEE WAGNER

The Synagogue Survival Kit

(Northvale, New Jersey: Jason Aronson, 1997)

Category: Self-Help
Subject(s): Judaism; Religious Life; Customs
Age range(s): Young Adult-Adult

Summary: Jordan Lee Wagner provides a simple, direct guide to Jewish worship that can benefit both newcomers and experienced attendees of Jewish synagogue worship services. With its roots in a letter to a non-Jewish friend explaining the rituals and components of synagogue worship, *The Synagogue Survival Kit* has evolved into a comprehensive yet accessible handbook for anyone who wishes to attend Jewish worship services and know how to fit in. From what to wear, when to stand, and how to cover one's head during prayer, to a vocabulary guide for Hebrew and Yiddish terms, Wagner's book offers practical information that will help readers focus more on the worship service than on their own unfamiliarity in a new situation. Wagner is careful to note the differences in custom and ritual among Orthodox, Conservative, and Reform traditions in modern Judaism.

Other books you might like:

Shimon Apisdorf, *Rosh Hashanah Yom Kippur Survival Kit*, 1997

Hayim Halevy Donin, *To Pray as a Jew: A Guide to the Prayer Book and the Synagogue Service*, 1980

Reuven Hammer, *Entering Jewish Prayer: A Guide to Personal Devotion and the Worship Service*, 1994

Adin Steinsaltz, *Teshuvah: A Guide for the Newly Observant Jew*, 1987

623

TERRY WAITE

Taken on Trust

(New York: Harcourt, Brace, 1993)

Category: Autobiography
Subject(s): Hostages; Prisoners and Prisons; Faith
Age range(s): Adult
Time period(s): 1980s; 1990s (1987-1991)
Locale(s): England; Lebanon

Summary: Terry Waite is a British clergyman who was taken hostage in Lebanon when he went to the country to try to free hostages. Among those being held in captivity were American Terry Anderson, a journalist and the author of *Den of Lions*, which recounts his many days as a hostage. *Taken on Trust* is Terry Waite's autobiographical account of his ordeal as a hostage, which lasted nearly four years. Begun as a mental exercise during his captivity, the book is an autobiographical survey of his life, with particular emphasis on the years of his captivity, from 1987 to 1991.

Other books by the same author:

Footfalls in Memory: Reflections From Solitude, 1997

Other books you might like:

Terry A. Anderson, *Den of Lions: Memoirs of Seven Years*, 1993

Brian Keenan, *An Evil Cradling*, 1992
Keenan was another of the hostages held in Lebanon.

Lawrence Martin Jenco, *Bound to Forgive: The Pilgrimate to Reconciliation of a Beirut Hostage*, 1995

Tom Sutherland, *At Your Own Risk: An American Chronicle of Crisis and Captivity in the Middle East*, 1996

Ben Weir, *Hostage Bound, Hostage Free*, 1987

624

DAN WAKEFIELD

Expect a Miracle: The Miraculous Things That Happen to Ordinary People

(San Francisco: HarperSanFrancisco, 1995)

Category: New Age (Nonfiction); Self-Help
Subject(s): Miracles; Spirituality
Age range(s): Adult
Time period(s): 20th century

Summary: Based firmly on twentieth-century experiences with miraculous life changes, Dan Wakefield's *Expect a Miracle* is an inspirational collection of modern-day miracles and uplifting stories, many from famous names including singer Judy Collins, Rabbi Harold Kushner, author Michael Crichton, and actress Kathy Baker. In addition, there are accounts from relative unknowns, including a factory worker in Ireland, a practicing Western Buddhist from California, and others from all walks of life and all over the world. No definition of miracles is offered, but everyday stories of unexpected good fortune are mixed with stories of the uncommon and improbable circumstances that may be recognized across faith traditions as miraculous in nature.

Other books by the same author:

Returning: A Spiritual Journey, 1997

The Story of Your Life: Writing a Spiritual Autobiography, 1990

Other books you might like:

Jodie Berndt, *Celebration of Miracles*, 1995

Arielle Ford, *Hot Chocolate for the Mystical Soul: 101 True Stories of Angels, Miracles, and Healings*, 1998

Ann Spangler, *A Miracle a Day: Stories of Heavenly Encounters*, 1996

625

JIM WALLIS

The Call to Conversion: Recovering the Gospel for These Times

(San Francisco: HarperSanFrancisco, 1992)

Category: Theology
Subject(s): Politics; Christian Life; Civil Rights
Age range(s): Adult
Locale(s): United States

Summary: Jim Wallis, social activist, Christian evangelical, and founder of the social action ministry, Sojourners, has updated his 1981 classic for the 1990s. *The Call to Conversion* is a fervent plea to those who call themselves Christians to commit their lives and resources to God's community and not to worldly standards of material and religious ''success.'' The editor of *Sojourners* magazine seeks a Christianity rooted in the compassion and service of Christ, rather than in what he characterizes as the self-righteous politics of the American right. Wallis espouses an evangelical, biblical faith that supports the family-friendly values of truth, honesty, and selflessness, and he calls individuals and churches to rethink their commitment to Christ in terms of these values.

Other books by the same author:

Who Speaks for God? An Alternative to the Religious Right— A New Politics of Compassion, Community, and Civility, 1996

The Soul of Politics: A Practical and Prophetic Vision for Change, 1994

Revive Us Again: A Sojourner's Story, 1983

Agenda for Biblical People, 1976

Other books you might like:

N. Gordon Cosby, *By Grace Transformed: Christianity for a New Millennium*, 1998

Millard J. Erickson, *The Evangelical Left: Encountering Postconservative Evangelical Theology*, 1997

Millard J. Erickson, *Postmodernizing the Faith: Evangelical Responses to the Challenge of Postmodernism*, 1998

Elizabeth O'Connor, *Cry Pain, Cry Hope: Thresholds to Purpose*, 1993

626

NEALE DONALD WALSCH

Conversations with God: An Uncommon Dialogue

(New York: Putnam, 1996)

Category: New Age (Nonfiction)
Subject(s): Spirituality; Heaven; God
Age range(s): Adult

Summary: With everything in his life falling apart, Walsch sits down and writes God an angry letter. Although he doesn't expect a reply, God does indeed talk back to Walsch. From that point, he and God begin having conversations about issues that affect Walsch's life. As outlined in this volume by the author, God and Walsch talk about everything from spiritual wealth to material blessings. This is the author's recording of those initial conversations.

Other books by the same author:

Friendship with God: An Uncommon Dialogue, 1999

Other books you might like:

Thom Hartmann, *The Prophet's Way: Touching the Power of Life*, 1997

Barbara Marx Hubbard, *The Revelation: A Message of Hope for the New Millennium*, 1995

Michael Lerner, *Jewish Renewal: A Path to Healing and Transformation*, 1994

Benjamin Shield, *For the Love of God: Handbook for the Spirit*, 1997

Marianne Williamson, *A Return to Love: Reflections on the Principles of a Course in Miracles*, 1992

627

MICHAEL WALSH, Editor

Butler's Lives of the Saints

(San Francisco: HarperSanFrancisco, 1991)

Category: Biography
Subject(s): Christianity; Catholicism; Saints
Age range(s): Young Adult-Adult

Summary: Alban Butler (1711-1773) compiled his original collection of biographies of the saints during the 1750s. Published in various formats in the centuries since then, the work has become a classic of religious literature. In this edition, which features the lives of 235 saints of the Roman Catholic tradition arranged according to their respective feast days, editor Michael Walsh is careful to preserve the original style of Butler's prose. The book also features illuminated illustrations from the 18th century.

Other books you might like:

Wendy Beckett, *Sister Wendy's Book of Saints*, 1998

John Foxe, *Foxe's Book of Martyrs and How They Found Christ: In Their Own Words*, 1998

Kenneth L. Woodward, *Making Saints: How the Catholic Church Determines Who Becomes a Saint, Who Doesn't, and Why*, 1990

628

MICHAEL WARNER, Editor

American Sermons: The Pilgrims to Martin Luther King, Jr.

(New York: The Library of America, 1999)

Category: Sermons
Subject(s): History; Literature; Christianity
Age range(s): Adult
Locale(s): United States

Summary: As a unique form of American literature, the sermon's roots extend to the very beginnings of America's history. Sermons in Puritan settlements were the public vehicle for exchanging and expounding ideas. The rhetorical speeches that gave rise to Revolutionary fervor had their origins in sermons. Some of the most moving and memorable moments in the civil rights movement, and prior to that, during the call for abolition of slavery, came within the context of sermons. The 58 sermons collected in *American Sermons: The Pilgrims to Martin Luther King, Jr.* reflect a history of more than 300 years of sermons in the United States. In their written form, they serve as a record of politics, philosophy, theology, and culture. In their spoken form, they represented spiritual and political discourse, public ritual, and, in many cases, popular entertainment and showmanship.

Other books by the same author:
Letters of the Republic: Publication and the Public Sphere in Eighteenth-Century America, 1990

Other books you might like:
Janice M. Bracken, *Women of the Word: Contemporary Sermons by Women Clergy*, 1985
Roslyn A. Karaban, *Extraordinary Preaching: Twenty Homilies*, 1996
Clarence E. MacArtney, *Great Sermons of the World: Sermons From 25 of the World's Greatest Preachers*, 1997
Darryl M. Trimiew, *Out of Mighty Waters: Sermons by African-American Disciples*, 1994
Kenneth L. Waters Sr., *Afrocentric Sermons: The Beauty of Blackness in the Bible*, 1993

629

PETER WASHINGTON

Madame Blavatsky's Baboon: A History of the Mystics, Mediums, and Misfits who Brought Spiritualism to America

(New York: Schocken Books, 1995)

Category: New Age (Nonfiction); History
Subject(s): Occult; Spiritualism; Mysticism
Age range(s): Adult
Time period(s): 19th century; 20th century
Locale(s): Europe; United States

Summary: Peter Washington explores the roots of New Age thought in Europe and America and chronicles its beginnings with the arrival of Russian theosophist Madame Blavatsky early in the 1900s. Madame Blavatsky founded the Theosophical Society to promote her belief that human beings evolved from spirit beings, rather than from apes. This was during the early age of Darwinism, a time when there were many new challenges to traditional Christian religion on both sides of the Atlantic. In this book, Washington focuses on the history and growth of this first "New Age" religion, Theosophy.

Other books by the same author:
Bach, 1997
Prayers, 1995
Fraud: Literary Theory and the End of English, 1989

Other books you might like:
Helena P. Blavatsky, *Key to Theosophy*, 1969
Helena P. Blavatsky, *The Secret Doctrine: The Synthesis of Science, Religion, and Philosophy*, 1938
Wouter J. Hanegraaff, *New Age Religion and Western Culture*, 1996
Roger Lipsey, *An Art of Our Own: The Spiritual in Twentieth-Century Art*, 1998

630

ALAN WATTS

Myth and Ritual in Christianity

(New York: Vanguard Press, 1953)

Category: Theology
Subject(s): Christianity; Art; Mythology
Age range(s): Adult

Summary: Alan Watts (1915-1973) was a Western-trained theologian and Episcopal priest who is best remembered as an interpreter of Eastern philosophy in general and Zen Buddhism in particular. From 1944, when he was ordained, until 1950, he served as an Episcopal chaplain at Northwestern University. As early as his teen years, he questioned Christian theology, and this questioning intensified throughout his affiliation with the church as a member of the clergy. By the mid-1950s, he had already been writing about Zen Buddhism for two decades, and he joined the faculty of the American Academy of Asian Studies in San Francisco in 1951. *Myth and Ritual in Christianity*, first published in 1953, has been reprinted frequently and has become a classic in theological studies for its dispassionate examination of the traditional narratives of Christianity in terms of mythology and symbolism.

Other books by the same author:
The Way of Zen, 1957
The Wisdom of Insecurity: A Message for the Age of Anxiety, 1951
Behold the Spirit: A Study in the Necessity of Mystical Religion, 1947
Outline of Zen Buddhism, 1933

Other books you might like:
Yves Bonnefoy, *Mythologies*, 1991
Joseph Campbell, *The Power of Myth*, 1988
   Bill Moyers, co-author
Neils C. Neilsen, *Fundamentalism, Mythos, and World Religions*, 1993

Robert A. Segal, *The Myth and Ritual Theory: An Anthology*, 1998

631

ALAN WATTS

The Way of Zen

(New York: Pantheon, 1957)

Category: History
Subject(s): Zen Buddhism; Mythology; Customs
Age range(s): Adult

Summary: Watts remains one of the great popularizers of Zen Buddhism in the West. His lectures and interviews introduce the ways of Zen to a larger audience and are responsible for its growth in the late 1950s and early 1960s. In this book, Watts provides a clear and thorough overview of Zen. He discusses the ideas of enlightenment and mindfulness in an engaging way. Although the contemporary spirituality landscape is littered with manuals on Zen practice, Watts' book remains an indispensable guide.

Other books by the same author:
Myth and Ritual in Christianity, 1953

Other books you might like:
Ram Dass, *Compassion in Action: Setting Out on the Path of Service*, 1992
Thich Nhat Hanh, *Peace Is Every Step: The Path of Mindfulness in Everyday Life*, 1991
Timothy Leary, *Psychedelic Prayers and Other Meditations*, 1997
Dan Millman, *The Life You Were Born to Live: A Guide to Finding Your Life Purpose*, 1993
Robert M. Pirsig, *Zen and the Art of Motorcycle Maintenance: An Inquiry into Values*, 1974

632

MARILYNN CARLSON WEBBER
WILLIAM D. WEBBER, Co-Author

A Rustle of Angels: Stories about Angels in Real-Life and Scripture

(Grand Rapids, Michigan: Zondervan, 1994)

Category: Theology
Subject(s): Angels; Christianity; Scripture
Age range(s): Young Adult-Adult

Summary: In response to the current popularity of angels and angel lore, *A Rustle of Angels* addresses the topic from a biblical and theological approach and a Christian perspective. The authors combine personal anecdotes and guided readings from the Bible and Christian theology in their assessment of the role of angels, past and present, in human life. Based on their research, the Webbers offer evidence that God is at work in the world through angels.

Other books by the same author:
How to Become a Sweet Old Lady Instead of a Grumpy Old Grouch, 1996

Other books you might like:
Billy Graham, *Angels: God's Secret Agents*, 1975
Nathalie Ladner-Bischoff, *An Angel's Touch: True Stories about Angels, Miracles, and Answers to Prayers*, 1998
Phil Phillips, *Angels, Angels, Angels: Embraced by the Light or Embraced by the Darkness?*, 1995
Ann Spangler, *An Angel a Day: Stories of Angelic Encounters*, 1994
Brad Steiger, *Angels over Their Shoulders: Children's Encounters with Heavenly Beings*, 1995

633

SIMONE WEIL

Waiting for God

(New York: Harper and Row, 1951)

Category: Devotionals; Autobiography
Subject(s): Christianity; Catholicism; Social Issues
Age range(s): Adult

Summary: Weil is a Jewish convert to Catholicism whose mysticism influenced later writers like Thomas Merton and Dorothy Day. She believes that God's presence comes to people most readily in God's absence, and as people experience absence they do experience His presence. Influenced by Talmudic masters as well as by mystics like Meister Eckhart, Weil provides her spiritual autobiography in this accessible little book. Her mysticism also penetrates this world as she articulates a vision of social justice. Translation by Emma Gruafurd.

Other books by the same author:
Gravity and Grace, 1952

Other books you might like:
Anonymous, *The Cloud of Unknowing*, c. 1300
Dorothy Day, *The Long Loneliness: The Autobiography of Dorothy Day*, 1952
Waltraud Herbstrith, *The Way of the Cross: Edith Stein*, 1974 Translation by Lee Marill
Friedrich Freiherr von Hugel, *Letters to a Niece*, 1950
Eric O. Springsted, *Simone Weil*, 1998
Springsted's volume is a part of Orbis Book's Modern Spiritual Masters series.

634

R.J. ZWI WERBLOWSKY, Editor
GEOFFREY WIGODER, Co-Editor

The Oxford Dictionary of the Jewish Religion

(New York: Oxford University Press, 1997)

Category: Religious Encyclopedias/Dictionaries
Subject(s): Judaism; Religious Life; Customs

Summary: This reference volume is first and foremost a guide to topics and people of religious, rather than cultural or historical, significance in the Jewish world. Entries are written from the religious perspective, even in cases where the topic itself has historical relevancy apart from the religious aspects-as in the Holocaust or the independence of Israel. The alphabetically arranged topic articles range from a paragraph to a full page in length. Many entries were newly written for this collection; others are incorporated from the editors' 1965 publication, *The Encyclopedia of the Jewish Religion*.

Other books by the same author:
Sacred Space: Shrine, City, Land, 1998 (Benjamin Z. Kedar, co-editor)
Beyond Tradition and Modernity: Changing Religions in a Changing World, 1976
The Encyclopedia of the Jewish Religion, 1965 (Geoffrey Wigoder, co-editor)

Other books you might like:
Ronald H. Isaacs, *The Jewish Bible Almanac*, 1997
Ronald H. Isaacs, *The Jewish Information Source Book: A Dictionary and Almanac*, 1993
Jacob Neusner, *Dictionary of Judaism in the Biblical Period*, 1999
Kerry M. Olitzky, *A Glossary of Jewish Life*, 1992
Dagobert D. Runes, *Dictionary of Judaism*, 1991

635

GAYLE COLQUITT WHITE

Believers and Beliefs: A Practical Guide to Religious Etiquette for Business and Social Occasions

(New York: Berkeley Books, 1997)

Category: History
Subject(s): World Religions; Customs; Religious Traditions
Age range(s): Young Adult-Adult

Summary: If you are visiting a Japanese Buddhist temple, how should you greet the monks? Should you say anything to them at all? If you are visiting Amish country, which orders will allow themselves to be photographed? The answers to these questions as well as a host of others can be found in White's helpful guide to religious etiquette. Given the great religious diversity in contemporary America, White's book is useful for those hoping to discover what they should and shouldn't do or say to their new neighbors who practice a different and unfamiliar religion.

Other books you might like:
Elizabeth Breuilly, *Religions of the World: The Illustrated Guide to Origins, Beliefs, Traditions, & Festivals*, 1997
Norine Dresser, *Multicultural Manners: New Rules of Etiquette for a Changing Society*, 1996
Arthur J. Magida, *How to Be a Perfect Stranger: A Guide to Etiquette in Other People's Religious Ceremonies*, 1996
Ann Marie Sabath, *Business Etiquette: 101 Ways to Conduct Business with Charm and Savvy*, 1998
Huston Smith, *Illustrated World's Religions: A Guide to Our Wisdom Traditions*, 1994

636

WARREN W. WIERSBE

Living with the Giants: The Lives of Great Men of the Faith

(Grand Rapids, Michigan: Baker Book House, 1993)

Category: Biography; History
Subject(s): Christianity; Protestantism
Age range(s): Adult

Summary: *Living with the Giants* is a collection of biographical essays about more than thirty preachers and theologians influential in the development of conservative Protestant Christianity from the mid-seventeenth century through the 1960s. Included are profiles of such men as Charles H. Spurgeon and Dwight L. Moody, whose legacy in print keeps their names familiar generations after their death, alongside profiles of men like W.E. Sangster, pastor of a Methodist church in the shadow of London's Westminster Abbey where he ran a nightly bomb shelter for more than four years during World War II. Wiersbe's selection was based on the standing of these men as inspirational Christian leaders-spiritual giants—during their lifetimes, and not on their standing in church history today. The essays in *Living with the Giants* were previously published in *Listening to the Giants* and *Walking with the Giants*.

Other books by the same author:
Be Myself, 1994 (autobiography)
Preaching and Teaching with Imagination, 1994
So That's What a Christian Is!, 1988
A Basic Library for Bible Students, 1981

Other books you might like:
Os Guinness, *Character Counts: Leadership Qualities in Washington, Wilberforce, Lincoln, Solzhenitsyn*, 1999
Barbara Anne Keely, *Faith of Our Foremothers: Women Changing Religious Education*, 1997
David Lindstedt, *Faith's Great Heroes*, 1999
William J. Peterson, *25 Surprising Marriages: Faith-Building Stories From the Lives of Famous Christians*, 1997
Judith Weisenfeld, *This Far by Faith: Readings in African-American Women's Religious Biography*, 1996

637

ELIE WIESEL

Messengers of God: Biblical Portraits and Legends

(New York: Random House, 1976)

Category: Theology
Subject(s): Judaism; Bible; Legends
Age range(s): Adult

Summary: Wiesel brings new life to several biblical and Talmudic figures by retelling their stories. The intense religious vision of the prophet Jeremiah and the loneliness that his vision brings him haunt Wiesel's portrait of the prophet. Wiesel animates the great Talmudic storyteller and sage Baal Shem Tov as he imagines him sitting in the forest telling stories. Wiesel's own lyrical storytelling recovers these legends for every generation that encounters this remarkable book.

Other books by the same author:
All Rivers Run to the Sea: Memoirs, 1995
Night, 1960

Other books you might like:
Thomas Cahill, *The Gifts of the Jews: How a Tribe of Desert Nomads Changed the Way Everyone Thinks and Feels*, 1998
Primo Levi, *The Drowned and the Saved*, 1988
Chaim Potok, *Wanderings: Chaim Potok's History of the Jews*, 1978
Gershom Scholem, *On the Kabbalah and Its Symbolism*, 1965
Herbert Weiner, *9 1/2 Mystics: The Kabbala Today*, 1969

638

ELIE WIESEL

Night

(New York: Hill & Wang, 1960)

Category: Autobiography
Subject(s): Holocaust; History; Judaism
Age range(s): Young Adult-Adult
Time period(s): 1940s (1944-1945)
Locale(s): Auschwitz, Germany

Summary: *Night* is Elie Wiesel's searing autobiographical account of a year inside the barbed wire boundaries of Auschwitz, an infamous concentration camp in Germany. Thousands of Jews were forced from their homes, communities, and synagogues into the hellish world of Nazi death camps throughout World War II. Then a teenager, Elie Wiesel was imprisoned in Auschwitz from April 1944 until the liberation of the camps in April 1945. Like many others, he lost his family to the death camps, but he himself survived. *Night* is the first of several works by the author on this dark period of modern history, but it remains his most powerful literary account of the Holocaust. This edition is translated from the French by Stella Rodway.

Other books by the same author:
All Rivers Run to the Sea: Memoirs, 1995
The Accident, 1962
Dawn, 1961

Other books you might like:
Anne Frank, *The Diary of a Young Girl*, 1952
Solomon Perel, *Europa, Europa*, 1997
    Margot Bettauer Dembo, translator
Jack Pomerantz, *Run East: Flight From the Holocaust*, 1997
Levi Primo, *Survival in Auschwitz: The Nazi Assault on Humanity*, 1986
Dawid Sierakowiak, *The Diary of Dawid Sierakowiak*, 1996
Simon Wiesenthal, *The Sunflower*, 1998

639

ELIE WIESEL

Sages and Dreamers: Biblical, Talmudic, and Hasidic Portraits and Legends

(New York: Summit Books, 1991)

Category: Biography
Subject(s): Judaism; History; Literature
Age range(s): Adult

Summary: *Sages and Dreamers* is a collection of essays and lectures by the author about the writers whose works are the stories and myths of Jewish folklore. Elie Wiesel writes anedoctally in this setting, so the portraits of the prophets and scribes take on an intimate tone, and his written commentary on the works themselves seems as personal and conversational as when the lectures were delivered in person.

Other books by the same author:
Four Hasidic Masters and Their Struggle Against Melancholy, 1978
Messengers of God: Biblical Portraits and Legends, 1976
Souls on Fire: Portraits and Legends of Hasidic Masters, 1972

Other books you might like:
Shulamis Frieman, *Who's Who in the Talmud*, 1995
Yokheved Segel, *Our Sages Showed the Way*, 1988
Adin Steinsaltz, *Talmudic Images*, 1997

640

LEON WIESELTIER

Kaddish

(New York: Knopf, 1998)

Category: Journals/Letters
Subject(s): Death; Grief; Judaism
Age range(s): Adult

Summary: *Kaddish* is Leon Wieseltier's account of the period of time following his father's death during which he participated in the recitation of the Jewish ritual prayer of mourning, the kaddish, three times each day, despite the fact that up to the time when his father died he had not been a particulary observant Jew. During the months of mourning, he also kept a journal, and he rediscovered the writings and traditions of his Jewish heritage. While *Kaddish* is especially resonant with Jewish readers, the themes of grief, mourning, healing, and remembering loved ones make it relevant to those of other faiths as well.

Other books by the same author:
Against Identity, 1996
Nuclear War, Nuclear Peace, 1983

Other books you might like:
Anita Diamant, *Saying Kaddish: How to Comfort the Dying, Bury the Dead, and Mourn as a Jew*, 1998
Ronald H. Isaacs, *Every Person's Guide to Death and Dying in the Jewish Tradition*, 1999
Michael Katz, *Swimming in the Sea of the Talmud: Lessons for Everyday Living*, 1998

Alfred J. Kolatch, *The Jewish Mourner's Book of Why*, 1995 revised edition

Kerry M. Olitzky, *Grief in Our Seasons: A Mourner's Kaddish Companion*, 1998

641

SIMON WIESENTHAL

The Sunflower

(New York: Schocken Books, 1976)

Category: Essays; Autobiography
Subject(s): Holocaust; Forgiveness
Age range(s): Young Adult-Adult

Summary: Simon Wiesenthal's memories of the hellish life of the Nazi concentration camps are recounted here, including his account of the indelibly memorable day when he was asked for forgiveness by a dying German SS trooper. Wiesenthal describes that event and asks, "What would you do?" of readers and of a global panel of 46 political, intellectual, and spiritual leaders of the latter half of the 20th century, including the Dalai Lama, Matthew Fox and Robert McAfee Brown (Protestant clergy), Archbishop Desmond Tutu of South Africa, Rabbi Harold S. Kushner, and others. Their thought-provoking answers reflect a range of personal and spiritual backgrounds and perspectives on vengeance, forgiveness, and the limits on each. The work was reissued in 1998 as *The Sunflower: On the Possibilities and Limits of Forgiveness*. The recent edition includes ten responses from panelists queried for the original edition.

Other books by the same author:
Krystyna: The Tragedy of Polish Resistance, 1991
Justice, Not Vengeance, 1989 (Ewald Osers, translator)
Every Day Remembrance Day: A Chronicle of Jewish Martyrdom, 1987
Max and Helen, 1981 (Catherine Hutter, translator)
The Murderers Among Us, 1967

Other books you might like:
Martha Minow, *Between Vengeance and Forgiveness: Facing History After Genocide and Mass Violence*, 1998
Jeffrie G. Murphy, *Forgiveness and Mercy*, 1988
Solomon Perel, *Europa, Europa*, 1997
    Margot Bettauer Dembo, translator
Donald W. Shriver, *An Ethic for Enemies: Forgiveness in Politics*, 1995
Corrie ten Boom, *The Hiding Place*, 1971

642

KEN WILBER

The Eye of Spirit: An Integral Vision for a World Gone Slightly Mad

(Boston: Shambhala, 1997)

Category: New Age (Nonfiction)
Subject(s): Religion; Science; Psychology
Age range(s): Adult

Summary: Wilber is a polymath whose work embraces science, spirituality, art, and psychology. In this book, Wilber names the problems of the world in which we live. Our tendency to separate the soul from the body and not to understand the integration of the spiritual and material has resulted in chaos. He claims that we need to recover our spiritual sight and to reintegrate the spiritual and the material to live holistically. Wilber is a popular writer who captures well the esoteric tradition of Rudolf Steiner and others and makes their vision accessible to a wide audience.

Other books by the same author:
The Marriage of Sense and Soul: Integrating Science and Religion, 1998

Other books you might like:
Stanislav Grof, *Ancient Wisdom and Modern Science*, 1984
Donald Rothberg, *Ken Wilber in Dialogue: Conversations with Leading Transpersonal Thinkers*, 1998
Frithjof Schuon, *To Have a Center*, 1990
Frances Vaughan, *Paths Beyond Ego: The Transpersonal Vision*, 1993
Michael Washburn, *The Ego and the Dynamic Ground: A Transpersonal Theory of Human Development*, 1988

643

WILLIAM WILBERFORCE

Real Christianity: Contrasted with the Prevailing Religious System

(Portland, Oregon: Multnomah, 1982)

Category: Doctrine
Subject(s): Christianity; Theology; Religious Life

Summary: Published in its first edition in England in 1796, William Wilberforce's *Real Christianity* is a classic in evangelical Christian literature. Wilberforce was a prominent member of Parliament and a strong voice in the anti-slavery movement in England. He was also a staunch campaigner for what he termed "real Christianity," which acknowledges Original Sin and demands honest and public repentence and commitment to the ways of Christ. This volume outlines the differences between the real faith and the false teachings he observed in his day. His evangelical message came to American audiences in 1829, and *Real Christianity* has been updated for contemporary readers in late 20th-century editions such as this one.

Awards the book has won:
Gold Medallion Book Award, Classics, 1983

Other books by the same author:
Private Papers of William Wilberforce, 1897
The Correspondence of William Wilberforce, 1840

Other books you might like:
Jimmy Carter, *Living Faith*, 1996
Charles Colson, *How Now Shall We Live?*, 1999
Garth Lean, *God's Politician: William Wilberforce's Struggle*, 1980
Jack Hayward, *Out of Slavery: Abolition and After*, 1985

644

DAVID WILKERSON
JOHN SHERRILL, Co-Author
ELIZABETH SHERRILL, Co-Author

The Cross and the Switchblade

(New York: Berkley, 1962)

Category: Autobiography
Subject(s): Gangs; Drugs; Christianity
Age range(s): Young Adult-Adult
Time period(s): 1960s
Locale(s): New York, New York

Summary: In 1958, David Wilkerson felt an undeniable call from God to go to New York to minister to the street kids in gangs. With nothing but a heart for the work and a lot of prayer, he and his prayer partners navigated their way through the uncertainties of starting and maintaining a street ministry. The work was hard and dangerous, but Wilkerson's passion for reaching every reachable heart and saving kids from lives of crime, drug abuse, and poverty was stronger than any fear he had. *The Cross and the Switchblade*, which was made into a movie in 1970, tells the story of this street ministry and the dramatic and unlikely conversion of Mau Mau gang leader Nicky Cruz, who later devoted his life to the same type of ministry to gang members.

Other books by the same author:
America's Last Call, 1998
Hungry for More of Jesus, 1992
Beyond the Cross and the Switchblade, 1974
The Untapped Generation, 1971
Hey, Preach—You're Comin' Through!, 1968

Other books you might like:
Brother Andrew, *God's Smuggler*, 1967
    John Sherrill, Elizabeth Sherrill, co-authors
Charles Colson, *Born Again*, 1976
Nicky Cruz, *Run, Baby, Run*, 1968
Don Wilkerson, *The Cross Is Still Mightier than the Switchblade*, 1996

645

PAUL WILKES

And They Shall Be My People: An American Rabbi and His Congregation

(New York: Atlantic Monthly Press, 1994)

Category: Biography
Subject(s): Judaism; Religious Life; Conduct of Life
Age range(s): Adult
Time period(s): 20th century
Locale(s): Worcester, Massachusetts

Summary: What is the place of religion-in this case, the Jewish religion-in a contemporary lifestyle? This is the question asked by Rabbi Jay Rosenbaum. Author Paul Wilkes follows Rosenbaum's work for a year in a suburban Conservative Jewish synagogue in Worcester, Massachusetts. He records Rosenbaum's comments in various settings, from worship services to synagogue board meetings to day care center story

times, and interviews congregants about their rabbi and his work among them. The portrait that emerges is of a man deeply committed to his vocation and frustrated by the apparent lack of interest in Jewish religious life on the part of his congregants. It is also a snapshot of upper middle class American Judaism at the end of the 20th century.

Other books by the same author:
Beyond the Walls: Monastic Wisdom for Everyday Life, 1999
The Seven Secrets of Successful Catholics, 1998
The Good Enough Catholic: A Guide for the Perplexed, 1996
In Mysterious Ways: The Death and Life of a Parish Priest, 1990
These Priests Stay, 1973

Other books you might like:
Tom Beaudoin, *Virtual Faith: The Irreverent Spiritual Quest of Generation X*, 1998
Dan Cohn-Sherbok, *The American Jew: Voices From an American Jewish Community*, 1994
    Lavinia Cohn-Sherbok, co-author
Gary Dorsey, *Congregation: The Journey Back to Church*, 1995
Neil Gillman, *Conservative Judaism: The New Century*, 1993
Penelope Ryan, *Practicing Catholic: The Search for a Livable Catholicism*, 1998

646

PAUL WILKES

The Good Enough Catholic: A Guide for the Perplexed

(New York: Ballantine Books, 1996)

Category: Self-Help
Subject(s): Catholicism; Religious Life; Conduct of Life
Age range(s): Adult

Summary: Award-winning writer and practicing Catholic Paul Wilkes considers the question of how to be a "good" Catholic while remaining open to change and new ideas. Noting that the Catholic church suffers from a "crisis of authority" in the United States, Wilkes describes Catholics who wish to be loyal to their church yet who disagree with official church positions on such issues as contraception, ordination of women, and celibacy of priests. Addressing the resulting tension between belief and action, Wilkes suggests ways for Catholics of good faith to embrace their church, make thoughtful choices, and recognize that being "good enough" is to be really quite good.

Other books by the same author:
Beyond the Walls: Monastic Wisdom for Everyday Life, 1999
The Seven Secrets of Successful Catholics, 1998
In Mysterious Ways: The Death and Life of a Parish Priest, 1990
Merton: By Those Who Knew Him Best, 1984
These Priests Stay, 1973

Other books you might like:
Thomas J. Ferraro, *Catholic Lives, Contemporary America*, 1997
Andrew M. Greeley, *The Catholic Myth: The Behavior and Beliefs of American Catholics*, 1990

Kevin Orlin Johnson, *Why Do Catholics Do That?: A Guide to the Teachings and Practices of the Catholic Church*, 1994

Penelope Ryan, *Practicing Catholic: The Search for a Livable Catholicism*, 1998

647

DALLAS WILLARD

The Divine Conspiracy: Rediscovering Our Hidden Life in God

(San Francisco: HarperSanFrancisco, 1998)

Category: Self-Help
Subject(s): Christianity; Spirituality; Christian Life
Age range(s): Adult

Summary: Dallas Willard, theologian and philosophy professor, criticizes what he terms "consumer Christianity" and "bumper sticker" faith that doesn't acknowledge the true meaning of Christian discipleship. In the steps of classic writers including Brother Lawrence, Willard advocates new ways of experiencing God in the day-to-day activities of life, not reserving Christianity for Sundays and Bible study sessions, but knowing God as a constant companion and guide for daily living. He challenges readers to confront their own comfort zones and move from a pious, polite faith to an authentic, dynamic, life-changing, relationship-based faith in Jesus.

Other books by the same author:
The Spirit of the Disciplines: Understanding How God Changes Lives, 1988
In Search of Guidance: Developing a Conversational Relationship with God, 1983

Other books you might like:
Brother Lawrence, *The Practice of the Presence of God*, 1945
Richard J. Foster, *Celebration of Discipline: The Path to Spiritual Growth*, 1978
Richard J. Foster, *Streams of Living Water: Celebrating the Great Traditions of Christian Faith*, 1998
Os Guinness, *The Call: Finding and Fulfilling the Central Purpose of Your Life*, 1998
J.I. Packer, *Knowing God*, 1973

648

JEAN KINNEY WILLIAMS

The Christian Scientists

(New York: Franklin Watts, 1997)

Category: Biography
Subject(s): Christian Science; History
Age range(s): Young Adult-Adult

Summary: Jean Kinney Williams offers an overview of the life of Mary Baker Eddy, founder of the Church of Christ, Scientist. She traces the events of Mary Baker Eddy's life that led to her interest in biblical and faith-based healing. She also provides an outline of the basic tenets of the practice of Christian Science.

Other books by the same author:
The Quakers, 1998
The Shakers, 1997
The Amish, 1996
The Mormons, 1996

Other books you might like:
Georgine Milmine, *The Life of Mary Baker G. Eddy and the History of Christian Science*, 1909
Doris Grekel, *The Founding of Christian Science (1888-1900): Being the Gospel According to Doris Grekel*, 1987
Bliss Knapp, *The Destiny of the Mother Church*, 1947
Stuart E. Knee, *Christian Science in the Age of Mary Baker Eddy*, 1994

649

MARIANNE WILLIAMSON

A Return to Love: Reflections on the Principles of a Course in Miracles

(New York: HarperCollins, 1992)

Category: New Age (Nonfiction); Self-Help
Subject(s): Spirituality; Miracles
Age range(s): Adult

Summary: In a series of essays, 20th century spiritual philosopher Marianne Williamson offers her personal reflections on the teachings of *A Course in Miracles*, a popular treatise in New Age spirituality. Williamson encourages readers to apply unconditional love to life's problems and to expect unexpected solutions to emerge as a result. She offers guidance in creating a loving, peaceful environment in which to raise families, have careers, and create meaningful relationships with others.

Other books by the same author:
Illuminata: Thoughts, Prayers, Rites of Passage, 1994
A Woman's Worth, 1993

Other books you might like:
Arlene Boday, *The Third Time Is Now*, 1996
James Redfield, *The Celestine Prophecy: An Adventure*, 1993
Neale Donald Walsch, *Conversations with God: An Uncommon Dialogue*, 1996

650

A.N. WILSON

Jesus

(New York: Norton, 1992)

Category: Biography
Subject(s): History; Archaeology; Bible
Age range(s): Adult

Summary: Taking a historical and archaeological perspective, A. N. Wilson writes a biography of Jesus based on contemporary biblical scholarship, rather than on what is popularly considered to be the authoritative documentation of the life of Christ-the translated, English language New Testament. He provides a reading of relevant portions of the Dead Sea Scrolls, and offers his own interpretations of language from the Old and New Testaments. Because Wilson ''demytho-logizes'' the traditional stories of Christianity throughout this volume, some readers may be disappointed or offended at his conclusions. At the same time, Wilson does nothing to downplay the impact that Jesus has had since his life and death on Earth.

Other books by the same author:

God's Funeral, 1999

Paul: The Mind of the Apostle, 1997

How Can We Know?, 1985

Other books you might like:

Charlotte Allen, *The Human Christ: The Search for the Historical Jesus*, 1998

Geza Bermes, *Jesus the Jew: A Historian's Reading of the Gospels*, 1973

Marcus J. Borg, *Meeting Jesus Again for the First Time: The Historical Jesus and the Heart of Contemporary Faith*, 1994

John Dominic Crossan, *The Historical Jesus: The Life of a Mediterranean Jewish Peasant*, 1991

E.P. Sanders, *The Historical Figure of Jesus*, 1993

Ben Witherington III, *The Jesus Quest: The Third Search for the Jew of Nazareth*, 1995

651

COLIN WILSON

The Atlas of Holy Places & Sacred Sites

(New York: D.K. Publishing, 1996)

Category: Religious Encyclopedias/Dictionaries

Subject(s): Travel; Pilgrims and Pilgrimages; History

Age range(s): Young Adult-Adult

Summary: *The Atlas of Holy Places & Sacred Sites* is a lavishly-illustrated guide to the 100 holiest spots in the world for religious adherents of different faith systems. A large portion of the book is devoted to overviews of each of these sites, with historical background and color photographs for each. In addition, twenty full-color maps show the locations of more than 1,000 holy places, each of which is keyed to a list that provides brief notes about the significance of the site, its age, and the country in which it can be found.

Other books by the same author:

Mysteries of the Universe, 1997

Beyond the Occult: A Twenty-Year Investigation into the Paranormal, 1989

Other books you might like:

Bernyce Barlow, *Sacred Sites of the West*, 1996

John Bowker, *World Religions*, 1997

Paul Lamborne Higgins, *Pilgrimages to Rome and Beyond*, 1987

Jennifer Westwood, *Sacred Journeys: An Illustrated Guide to Pilgrimages around the World*, 1997

652

EDMUND WILSON

The Dead Sea Scrolls: 1947-1969

(New York: Oxford University Press, 1969)

Category: Scripture

Subject(s): Archaeology; History; Bible

Age range(s): Adult

Summary: *The Dead Sea Scrolls: 1947-1969*, a revision of Edmund Wilson's 1955 publication *The Scrolls from the Dead Sea*, is notable more as one of the earliest publications on the Dead Sea Scrolls than as an authoritative one. Because control of the Dead Sea Scrolls opened to scholars worldwide in the 1980s and 1990s, much more is known about the archaeological fragments, their origin, and their possible significance in Christian and pre-Christian teachings and history. However, Edmund Wilson's narrative delves into the context of the 1947 discovery of the scrolls, bringing to life for readers the excitement that accompanied the unprecedented find and providing a portrait of people whose stories would otherwise go untold.

Other books by the same author:

The Edmund Wilson Reader, 1997

A Piece of My Mind: Reflections at Sixty, 1956

Red, Black, Blond, Olive: Studies in Four Civilizations, 1956

Other books you might like:

Ilene Cooper, *The Dead Sea Scrolls*, 1997

Harold Scanlin, *The Dead Sea Scrolls and Modern Translations of the Old Testament*, 1993

Lawrence H. Schiffman, *Reclaiming the Dead Sea Scrolls: The History of Judaism, the Background of Christianity, and the Lost Library of Qumran*, 1994

James C. Vanderkam, *The Dead Sea Scrolls Today*, 1994

653

ALBERT CURRY WINN

A Christian Primer: The Prayer, the Creed, the Commandments

(Louisville: Westminster/John Knox Press, 1990)

Category: Doctrine

Subject(s): Prayer; Scripture; Presbyterians

Age range(s): Adult

Summary: Using three well-known Christian documents as touchstones, Albert Curry Winn, retired Presbyterian pastor and former president of Louisville Presbyterian Theological Seminary, discusses the basics of Christianity. He starts with the Lord's Prayer, the Apostles' Creed, and the Ten Commandments-which he recasts as ''the ten promises''-and explains that these are the foundation many Christians have unconsciously internalized as a result of reading and interacting with them. Using stories and a conversational tone, Winn offers insight and inspiration for the spiritual journey from mainstream Protestantism.

Other books by the same author:

Christ the Peacemaker, 1982

Epiphany, 1980

Other books you might like:

Milton J. Coalter, *The Confessional Mosaic: Presbyterians and Twentieth-Century Theology*, 1991

Samuel Hudson, *Anthology of Presbyterian and Reformed Literature*, 1992

John H. Leith, *The Church: A Believing Fellowship*, 1982

Louis B. Weeks, *The Presbyterian Source: Bible Words That Shape a Faith*, 1990

654

SHERWOOD ELIOT WIRT

Billy: A Personal Look at Billy Graham, the World's Best-Loved Evangelist

(Wheaton, Illinois: Crossway, 1997)

Category: Biography
Subject(s): Christian Life; Ministry; Friendship
Age range(s): Young Adult-Adult
Time period(s): 20th century
Locale(s): United States

Summary: Sherwood Eliot Wirt has been a friend of Billy Graham for more than 40 years and was part of the Billy Graham organization for nearly two decades. In a book that is more memoir than biography, Wirt offers an insider's glimpse at the life of Billy Graham, revealing a private man as unpretentious and humble as the public figure has always appeared to be. This volume covers Billy Graham's career from the start of his ministry through the late 90s, when his schedule has been slowed due to age and the effects of Parkinson's disease. Black-and-white photos highlight events throughout the volume.

Other books by the same author:

The Inner Life of the Believer, 1989
The Making of a Writer, 1987
A Thirst for God, 1980

Other books you might like:

Betty Frist, *My Neighbors, the Billy Grahams*, 1983

Billy Graham, *Just as I Am: The Autobiography of Billy Graham*, 1997

Janet Lowe, *Billy Graham Speaks: Insight From the World's Greatest Preacher*, 1999

William Martin, *A Prophet with Honor: The Billy Graham Story*, 1991

Gerald S. Strober, *Graham: A Day in Billy's Life*, 1976

655

MICHAEL WISE
MARTIN ABEGG JR., Co-Author
EDWARD COOK, Co-Author

The Dead Sea Scrolls: A New Translation

(San Francisco: HarperSanFrancisco, 1996)

Category: Scripture
Subject(s): Archaeology; History

Summary: This is the first complete translation and interpretation of nearly every fragment of the Dead Sea Scrolls, which were found in a cave in 1947. The authors provide background information about the scrolls-where and how they were found, why they were inaccessible to researchers and translators for more than forty years, and more-and offer guidance on how to read the scrolls. The texts are provided in Aramaic and Hebrew with English translations and commentary for each, placing the scrolls and fragments within the context of other writings of the Biblical era.

Other books by the same author:

The First Messiah: Investigating the Savior Before Jesus, 1999

Methods of Investigation of the Dead Sea Scrolls and the Khirbet Qumran Site, 1994

Other books you might like:

James H. Charlesworth, *Jesus and the Dead Sea Scrolls*, 1992

John Joseph Collins, *The Scepter and the Star: The Messiahs of the Dead Sea Scrolls and Other Ancient Literature*, 1995

Robert H. Eisenman, *The Dead Sea Scrolls and the First Christians*, 1997

Hershel Shanks, *The Mystery and Meaning of the Dead Sea Scrolls*, 1998

Geza Vermes, *The Complete Dead Sea Scrolls in English*, 1997

656

MICHAEL WOLFE, Editor

One Thousand Roads to Mecca: Ten Centuries of Travelers Writing about the Muslim Pilgrimage

(New York: Grove Press, 1997)

Category: Essays
Subject(s): Pilgrims and Pilgrimages; Islam; History

Summary: The pilgrimage to Mecca, the *hajj*, is something that Islamic believers must try to do at least once in life. As one of the Five Pillars of Islam, the *hajj* is the primary topic of Islamic travel writing, as it has been for centuries. *One Thousand Roads to Mecca* is a collection of personal accounts of such pilgrimages that spans ten centuries. More than twenty records of journeys are here, pilgrimage accounts by believers from Morocco, Persia, India, the United States, and more. The essays provide excellent travel narratives and shed light on a world religion that is still quite misunderstood throughout the West.

Other books by the same author:

The Hadj: An American's Pilgrimage to Mecca, 1993
Invisible Weapons, 1986
In Morocco, 1980

Other books you might like:

Sir Richard Francis Burton, *Personal Narrative of a Pilgrimage to El-Medinah and Meccah*, 1855

Simon Coleman, *Pilgrimage: Past and Present in the World Religions*, 1995

John Elsner, co-author

Rick Jarow, *In Search of the Sacred: A Pilgrimage to Holy Places*, 1986

Amin Maalouf, *The Crusades through Arab Eyes*, 1989

Kazuyoshi Nomachi, *Mecca the Blessed, Medina the Radiant: The Holiest Cities of Islam*, 1997

Robert H. Stoddard, *Sacred Places, Sacred Spaces: The Geography of Pilgrimages*, 1997

657

JOHN WOODBRIDGE, Editor

Ambassadors for Christ

(Chicago: Moody Press, 1994)

Category: Biography
Subject(s): Evangelism; Christianity
Age range(s): Young Adult-Adult

Summary: *Ambassadors for Christ* is a collection of stories about Christians who have spread the gospel throughout the world. Not necessarily famous for their work or their lives, the people profiled have overcome difficulties to share the love of God with others.

Other books by the same author:
More than Conquerors, 1992
Great Leaders of the Christian Church, 1988
The Gospel in America, 1979
The Evangelicals: What They Believe, Who They Are, Where They Are Changing, 1975 (David F. Wells, co-editor)

Other books you might like:
Nathan Aaseng, *Explorers for God*, 1998
Timothy Crater, *In God We Trust: Stories of Faith in American History*, 1997
J. Gilchrist Lawson, *Deeper Experiences of Famous Christians*, 1998
Donald M. Lewis, *The Blackwell Dictionary of Evangelical Biography*, 1995
David Lindstedt, *Faith's Great Heroes*, 1999

658

JOHN WOODBRIDGE, Editor

Great Leaders of the Christian Church

(Chicago: Moody Press, 1988)

Category: Biography
Subject(s): Christianity; History
Age range(s): Young Adult-Adult

Summary: In *Great Leaders of the Christian Church*, John Woodbridge offers profiles of people who have made a difference in the growth and vitality of Christianity in the world. This is one of a collection of inspirational Christian biographies written by Woodbridge.

Awards the book has won:
Gold Medallion Book Award, Reference/Text, 1989

Other books by the same author:
Ambassadors for Christ, 1994
More than Conquerors, 1992
The Gospel in America, 1979

The Evangelicals: What They Believe, Who They Are, Where They Are Changing, 1975 (David F. Wells, co-editor)

Other books you might like:
Nathan Aaseng, *Explorers for God*, 1998
Timothy Crater, *In God We Trust: Stories of Faith in American History*, 1997
J. Gilchrist Lawson, *Deeper Experiences of Famous Christians*, 1998
Donald M. Lewis, *The Blackwell Dictionary of Evangelical Biography*, 1995
David Lindstedt, *Faith's Great Heroes*, 1999

659

JOHN WOODBRIDGE, Editor

More than Conquerors

(Chicago: Moody Press, 1992)

Category: Biography
Subject(s): Christianity; Christian Life
Age range(s): Young Adult-Adult

Summary: *More than Conquerors* offers more than sixty stories about men and women who turned to God for the strength to overcome the difficulties and temptations that affect all Christians. Featuring the famous and the unknown, the young and the old, these inspirational profiles show how God works in the lives of all kinds of people and how God's love helps people handle adversity.

Other books by the same author:
Ambassadors for Christ, 1994
Great Leaders of the Christian Church, 1988
The Gospel in America, 1979
The Evangelicals: What They Believe, Who They Are, Where They Are Changing, 1975 (David F. Wells, co-editor)

Other books you might like:
Nathan Aaseng, *Explorers for God*, 1998
Timothy Crater, *In God We Trust: Stories of Faith in American History*, 1997
J. Gilchrist Lawson, *Deeper Experiences of Famous Christians*, 1998
Donald M. Lewis, *The Blackwell Dictionary of Evangelical Biography*, 1995
David Lindstedt, *Faith's Great Heroes*, 1999

660

KENNETH L. WOODWARD

Making Saints: How the Catholic Church Determines Who Becomes a Saint, Who Doesn't, and Why

(New York: Simon and Schuster, 1990)

Category: Doctrine
Subject(s): Catholicism; Saints
Age range(s): Young Adult-Adult

Summary: Kenneth L. Woodward traces nearly 2000 years of canonization history in the church to explain how the Catholic church names saints. He describes the process of investigating the lives and purported miracles of people nominated for sainthood, and discusses how political pressures inside the church and in the larger world can play a significant role in the selection and approval process.

Other books by the same author:
Grandparents, Grandchildren: The Vital Connection, 1981 (Arthur Kornhaber, co-author)

Other books you might like:
Wendy Beckett, *Sister Wendy's Book of Saints*, 1998
Stephen Bunson, *Our Sunday Visitor's Encyclopedia of Saints*, 1998
Sean Kelly, *Saints Preserve Us!: Everything You Need to Know about Every Saint You'll Ever Need*, 1993

661

HERMAN WOUK

This Is My God: The Jewish Way of Life

(Boston: Little, Brown, and Co., 1988)

Category: Doctrine
Subject(s): Judaism; Conduct of Life
Age range(s): Adult

Summary: Originally published in 1959 as *This is My God*, this volume by novelist Herman Wouk has become a classic introduction to Judaism, remarkable in its simplicity and directness. It is a personal account of the Jewish faith and its significance in daily life. In this edition, Wouk has added a chapter about the modern state of Israel forty years after independence.

Other books by the same author:
The Glory, 1994
The Hope, 1994
War and Remembrance, 1978
The Winds of War, 1971

Other books you might like:
Hayim Halevy Donin, *To Be a Jew: A Guide to Jewish Observance in Contemporary Life*, 1972
Hayim Halevy Donin, *To Pray as a Jew: A Guide to the Prayer Book and the Synagogue Service*, 1980
Blu Greenberg, *How to Run a Traditional Jewish Household*, 1983
Louis Jacobs, *The Book of Jewish Belief*, 1984

662

DON WYRTZEN

A Musician Looks at the Psalms

(Grand Rapids, Michigan: Daybreak Books, 1988)

Category: Devotionals
Subject(s): Music and Musicians; Bible
Age range(s): Young Adult-Adult

Summary: The Psalms of the Bible, many of which have been set to music, may have been sung before they were ever recorded in written form. They represent an important link between God and the arts and literature. Contemporary composer Don Wyrtzen reflects on the significance of the Psalms

as a living record of psalm writers' struggles in life, which parallel the struggles believers face in modern times. *A Musician Looks at the Psalms* is a devotional guide that offers a new perspective on some of the most familiar passages of scripture in the Bible.

Awards the book has won:
Gold Medallion Book Award, Devotional, 1989

Other books you might like:
Ronald B. Allen, *Lord of Song: The Messiah Revealed in the Psalms*, 1985
W.H. Bellinger Jr., *The Testimony of Poets and Sages: The Psalms and Wisdom Literature*, 1998
Leslie F. Brandt, *Psalms Now*, 1996
Thomas Merton, *Bread in the Wilderness*, 1953

663

PHILIP YANCEY

Disappointment with God: Three Questions No One Asks Aloud

(Grand Rapids, Michigan: Zondervan, 1988)

Category: Theology
Subject(s): Christianity; Prayer; Nature of God
Age range(s): Young Adult-Adult

Summary: If God wants the love of humankind, why do bad things happen? Why does God seem so distant? What can believers expect of God? These and other questions about the nature of God are addressed by Philip Yancey from a Christian point of view.

Awards the book has won:
Gold Medallion Book Award, Inspirational, 1989

Other books by the same author:
What's So Amazing about Grace?, 1997
Finding God in Unexpected Places, 1995
Where Is God When It Hurts, 1977

Other books you might like:
George Carey, *Why I Believe in a Personal God: The Credibility of Faith in a Doubting Culture*, 1991
Roy A. Clouser, *Knowing with the Heart: Religious Experience and Belief in God*, 1999
Joni Eareckson Tada, *When God Weeps: Why Our Sufferings Matter to the Almighty*, 1997
Mark Wynn, *God and Goodness: A Natural Theological Perspective*, 1999

664

PHILIP YANCEY

Finding God in Unexpected Places

(Nashville: Moorings, 1995)

Category: Self-Help
Subject(s): Christianity; Prayer; Christian Life
Age range(s): Adult

Summary: Where is God? God is where I am. This is the message of this collection of inspirational essays and stories. Yancey shares personal observations on the ease with which

Christians forget that God is in every circumstance and situation, and he offers suggestions to become more aware of God's presence in every moment and event of life.

Awards the book has won:
Gold Medallion Book Award, Inspirational, 1996

Other books by the same author:
What's So Amazing about Grace?, 1997
I Was Just Wondering, 1989
Where Is God When It Hurts, 1977

Other books you might like:
Emilie Barnes, *Fill My Cup, Lord: A Teatime Devotional*, 1996
   Anne Christian Buchanan, co-author
John T. Catoir, *Enjoy the Lord: A Path to Contemplation*, 1989
Sharon Elwell, *Driving Lessons: Christian Meditations about Life From the Not So Fast Lane*, 1995
Kathy Collard Miller, *God's Unexpected Blessings*, 1998

665

PHILIP YANCEY

The Jesus I Never Knew

(Grand Rapids, Michigan: Zondervan, 1995)

Category: Biography
Subject(s): Bible; Christianity
Age range(s): Young Adult

Summary: Addressing three basic questions-who was Jesus, why did he come, and what did he leave behind-Yancey shares his personal search to understand the nature of Jesus. He examines the culture into which Jesus was born, re-reads accounts of his teachings, miracles, mission, and interaction with other people, and traces the legacy that has remained following his life on earth.

Awards the book has won:
Charles ''Kip'' Jordan Christian Book of the Year, 1996

Other books by the same author:
Church, Why Bother?: My Personal Pilgrimage, 1998
I Was Just Wondering, 1989

Other books you might like:
Max E. Anders, *Jesus: Knowing Our Savior*, 1995
Ricky A. Mayotte, *The Complete Jesus*, 1997
Pheme Perkins, *Jesus as Teacher*, 1990
Charlton Smith, *Jesus Didn't Go To Church*, 1994

666

PHILIP YANCEY

What's So Amazing about Grace?

(Grand Rapids, Michigan: Zondervan, 1997)

Category: Doctrine
Subject(s): Christianity; Bible; Christian Life
Age range(s): Adult

Summary: What is ''grace'' to a Christian? Philip Yancey uses stories to demonstrate and clarify the concept of God's grace, much as Jesus did in the telling of parables. Yancey avoids the use of platitudes and familiar evangelical phrases in his discussion of what it means to be either the recipient or the giver of grace, and he calls on everyone, believer or not, to choose to be an agent of grace rather than one of vengeance, anger, or indifference.

Awards the book has won:
Gold Medallion Book Award, Inspirational, 1998
Charles ''Kip'' Jordan Christian Book of the Year, 1998

Other books by the same author:
Church, Why Bother?: My Personal Pilgrimage, 1998
I Was Just Wondering, 1989

Other books you might like:
Carlton Allen, *Stories of Falling Toward Grace*, 1995
Jerry Bridges, *The Discipline of Grace: God's Role and Our Role in the Pursuit of Holiness*, 1994
Max Lucado, *In the Grip of Grace*, 1996
Charles R. Swindoll, *The Grace Awakening*, 1990

667

PHILIP YANCEY

Where Is God When It Hurts

(Grand Rapids, Michigan: Zondervan, 1977)

Category: Self-Help
Subject(s): Christianity; Nature of God; Prayer
Age range(s): Young Adult-Adult

Summary: This longtime bestseller grew out of the author's experience as a writer for *Campus Life* magazine. He wrote many articles about people's tragedies and he began wondering why God allows the kind of pain that exists in the world. Yancey writes of experiences-his own and others'-that have helped him work through the answers to his questions, and he directs readers to biblical teachings on the purpose of pain in the world. Since its publication in 1977, *Where Is God When It Hurts* has been expanded and revised with study guides added for personal and group use.

Awards the book has won:
Charles ''Kip'' Jordan Christian Book of the Year, 1978
Gold Medallion Book Award, Inspirational, 1978

Other books by the same author:
Church, Why Bother?: My Personal Pilgrimage, 1998
I Was Just Wondering, 1989

Other books you might like:
Kay Arthur, *As Silver Refined: Learning to Embrace Life's Disappointments*, 1998
James C. Dobson, *In the Arms of God*, 1997
Charles R. Swindoll, *For Those Who Hurt*, 1994
Terry Wardle, *Draw Close to the Fire: Finding God in the Darkness*, 1998

668

FRANCIS A. YATES

The Rosicrucian Enlightenment

(Boston: Routledge, 1972)

Category: New Age (Nonfiction); History

Subject(s): Secrets; History; Alchemy
Age range(s): Adult

Summary: British Renaissance historian Yates offers this now-definitive history of the Rosicrucian Enlightenment. Yates tells the tale of Frederick and Elizabeth, the Winter King and Queen of Bohemia, who came to the throne in 1619 at the time of a heightened spiritual optimism. Yates narrates the discovery of the Rosicrucian manifestos, which had been circulated just a few years before the king and queen came to power and which promised a new era of spiritual wisdom. These documents encourage the practice of alchemy and the search for hermetic knowledge. Yates' book contains the enthralling stories of figures like the alchemist Paracelsus and the great hermetic philosopher Giodarno Bruno.

Other books by the same author:
The Art of Memory, 1966

Other books you might like:
Giordano Bruno, *Expulsion of the Triumphant Beast*, 1964
    Bruno was an Italian Renaissance philosopher and poet who lived from c. 1548 to 1600.
Brian P. Copenhaver, *Hermetica: The Greek Corpus Hermeticum and the Latin Asclepius in a New English Translation*, 1992
Jacques Lacarriere, *The Gnostics*, 1977
Bentley Layton, *The Gnostic Scriptures: A New Translation with Annotations and Introductions*, 1987
John Matthews, *The Rosicrucian Enlightenment Revisited*, 1999

669

CAROL ZALESKI

Otherworld Journeys: Accounts of Near-Death Experience in Medieval and Modern Times

(New York: Oxford University Press, 1987)

Category: History
Subject(s): Death; Near-Death Experience; Unexplained Phenomena
Age range(s): Adult

Summary: With a well-researched and scholarly approach to the subject, Carol Zaleski traces the occurrence of near-death experiences from medieval times to the present. She discusses the literary tradition of near-death experience personal narratives, the scientific methodologies being used to investigate near-death experiences, and the general impact of visions and similar paranormal phenomena on those who experience them-as well as on those who hear about them. No conclusion is drawn as to the veracity of near-death visions and their ability to accurately foretell anything about an afterlife.

Other books by the same author:
The Life of the World to Come: Near-Death Experience and Christian Hope: The Albert Cardinal Meyer Lectures, 1996

Other books you might like:
Lee Worth Bailey, *The Near-Death Experience: A Reader*, 1996

P.M.H. Atwater, *Beyond the Light: What Isn't Being Said about Near-Death Experience*, 1994
P.B.C. Fenwick, *The Truth in the Light: An Investigation of over 300 Near-Death Experiences*, 1997
Kenneth Ring, *Lessons From the Light: What We Can Learn From the Near-Death Experience*, 1998
    Evelyn Elsaesser Valarino, co-author
Michael B. Sabom, *Light and Death: One Doctor's Fascinating Account of Near-Death Experiences*, 1998

670

PHILIP ZALESKI, Editor

The Best Spiritual Writing, 1998

(San Francisco: HarperSanFrancisco, 1998)

Category: Essays
Subject(s): Religion; Self-Perception; Poetry
Age range(s): Adult

Summary: In this volume, editor Philip Zaleski has collected contemporary perspectives on spirituality representing many faith traditions. Writers (including Andre Dubus, Natalie Goldberg, Anne Lamott, Madeleine L'Engle, Reynolds Price, and Cynthia Ozick) offer their thoughts in articles, essays, and poems on such subjects as prayer and meditation, worship traditions, sin, and spiritual heritage.

Other books by the same author:
Gifts of the Spirit: Living the Wisdom of the Great Religious Traditions, 1997

Other books you might like:
J.P. Maney, *A Celestial Omnibus: Short Fiction on Faith*, 1997
Robert Lawrence Smith, *A Quaker Book of Wisdom: Life Lessons in Simplicity, Service, and Common Sense*, 1998
Lucinda Vardey, *God in All Worlds: An Anthology of Contemporary Spiritual Writing*, 1995

671

STEVEN J. ZEITLIN, Editor

Because God Loves Stories: An Anthology of Jewish Storytelling

(New York: Simon & Schuster, 1997)

Category: Morality Tales
Subject(s): Judaism; Folklore
Age range(s): Young Adult-Adult

Summary: In this volume, Zeitlin has collected the work of thirty-six contemporary storytellers, each of whom offers a unique reflection of Jewish culture in America. At once a look at the past and a prism of the present, these stories demonstrate that the tradition of storytelling long associated with East European Jewish culture continues to evolve in twentieth-century America. The collection includes family stories, memories, anecdotes, and folktales.

Other books by the same author:
While Standing on One Foot, 1993 (Nina Jaffe, co-author)

Other books you might like:

Nathan Ausubel, *A Treasury of Jewish Folklore*, 1948

Ellen Frankel, *The Jewish Spirit: A Celebration in Stories and Art*, 1997

Irving Howe, *A Treasury of Yiddish Stories*, 1989

672

ROLF ZETTERSTEN

Dr. Dobson: Turning Hearts Toward Home: The Life and Principles of America's Family Advocate

(Dallas: Word, 1989)

Category: Biography

Subject(s): Christian Life; Family Life; Evangelism

Age range(s): Adult

Summary: Rolf Zettersten writes of the life and work of Dr. James C. Dobson, a Christian psychologist, author, and radio personality whose life's work has been centered around strengthening families through Christian principles and prayer. The "Focus on the Family" ministry of parenting support groups and radio programming, books, and magazines for people of all ages was begun by Dr. Dobson during his days as a practicing psychologist.

Awards the book has won:

Gold Medallion Book Award, Biography/Autobiography, 1990

Other books by the same author:

Sex, Lies, &—the Truth: A Message From Focus on the Family, 1994

Train Up a Child: Giving the Values That Last a Lifetime, 1991

Other books you might like:

James C. Dobson, *Coming Home: Timeless Wisdom for Families*, 1999

James C. Dobson, *Home with a Heart*, 1996

James C. Dobson, *Solid Answers: American's Foremost Family Counselor Responds to Tough Questions Facing Today's Families*, 1997

673

GARY ZUKAV

The Seat of the Soul

(New York: Simon & Schuster, 1989)

Category: New Age (Nonfiction)

Subject(s): Essays; Extrasensory Perception; Spirituality

Age range(s): Adult

Summary: Synthesizing "new physics" and spirituality, Gary Zukav explores his theory that human beings are evolving from a species whose power comes from mastering the five "external" senses—vision, hearing, taste, touch, smell—into a one whose power comes from non-physical realities of perception, soul values, and extrasensory, intuitive abilities. Zukav introduced his ideas about the significance of invisible realities in his bestselling *The Dancing Wu Li Masters: An Overview of the New Physics*. In this sequel, he blends science and philosophy to illustrate the emerging significance of spirituality in all of daily life.

Other books by the same author:

Thoughts From the Seat of the Soul: Meditations for Souls in Process, 1994

The Dancing Wu Li Masters: An Overview of the New Physics, 1979

Other books you might like:

Fritjof Capra, *The Tao of Physics: An Exploration of the Parallels between Modern Physics and Eastern Mysticism*, 1991

third edition

Michael Talbot, *The Holographic Universe*, 1991

Ken Wilber, *Quantum Questions: Mystical Writings of the World's Great Physicists*, 1984

Fiction Titles

674

EDWIN ABBOTT

Flatland

(London: Seeley & Co., 1884)

Category: Fantasy; Science Fiction
Subject(s): Mathematics; Philosophy; Science
Age range(s): Young Adult-Adult
Time period(s): 1880s
Locale(s): Fictional Country (Flatland)

Summary: *Flatland* is a highly imaginative and metaphorical adventure that deals with mathematics, relativity, and the dynamics of space and time. The residents of the world of Flatland are two-dimensional geometric shapes. As far as they are concerned, the world is literally flat. One curious inhabitant, however, discovers that a third dimension exists, and once that boundary is broken, he imagines a fourth dimension. While this novel is appreciated by physicists and mathematicians for its deft and accurate treatment of higher level concepts in their disciplines, it is also a pointed satire of the Victorian culture in which the author lived. At yet another level, the novel supports a rational approach to religious faith, one that separates belief in superstition, as represented by the two-dimensional thinkers, from belief in the supernatural—that which cannot be seen or experienced in familiar ways—as represented by the breakthrough thinkers. Edwin A. Abbott (1839-1926) was a British professor and member of the ordained clergy.

Other books you might like:
Robert Gilmore, *Alice in Quantumland: An Allegory of Quantum Physics*, 1995
P. Stephen Peterson, *The Quantum Particle Internet*, 1997
Rudy Rucker, *All the Visions*, 1990
    science fiction poems
Rudy Rucker, *Mathenauts: Tales of Mathematical Wonder*, 1987
Rudy Rucker, *White Light*, 1997

675

PEARL ABRAHAM

The Romance Reader

(New York: Riverhead Books, 1995)

Category: Gentle Reads
Subject(s): Jews; Marriage; Family Relations
Age range(s): Young Adult-Adult
Major character(s): Rachel Benjamin, Teenager
Time period(s): 1990s
Locale(s): Ashley, New York

Summary: Rachel, a 12-year-old Hassidic Jew, is the eldest child and daughter of a rabbi. Unlike her younger siblings, who are content to follow the conservative ways of the Hassidic tradition, Rachel is driven by curiosity about the world of her non-Jewish classmates and friends. As a role model, however, Rachel is expected to embrace and follow the rules of her home and her faith. The conflict leads her to stretch the boundaries in surreptitious ways: wearing sheer hose to school instead of opaque tights; swimming in public in defiance of modesty restrictions; and smuggling forbidden romance novels into her room. She is also fully aware that according to Hassidic custom, her father will arrange a marriage for her, to take place when she is 18 years old. How will Rachel resolve the tension between her ties to family and tradition and her desire for independence?

Other books by the same author:
Giving Up America, 1998

Other books you might like:
Chaim Potok, *My Name Is Asher Lev*, 1972
S.J. Rozan, *China Trade*, 1994
Suzanne Fisher Staples, *Shabanu: Daughter of the Wind*, 1989

STEPHEN P. ADAMS

October Holiday: A Novel

(Chicago: Moody Press, 1993)

Category: Thrillers
Subject(s): Halloween; Spiritualism
Age range(s): Young Adult-Adult
Major character(s): Neal McBride, Judge
Time period(s): 2020s
Locale(s): Ohio

Summary: More than twenty years after the end of the 20th century, Halloween has become the primary national holiday of the United States. On October 31, while most people indulge in their annual revelry, the police take a hands-off approach. During the chaotic celebrations of darkness, people and property are left virtually without protection from those who wish to take advantage of the lack of external control on their basest instincts. The creation of an artificial intelligence with the capacity to act with evil intent is imminent, as well, and Christianity has virtually disappeared as a positive force on society. In this world, Judge Neal McBride finds himself presiding over a court case that will have a major impact on the world.if the judge eludes threats against his life and family long enough to see the trial through.

Other books by the same author:
The Temple Scroll, 1996
The Hofburg Treasures, 1995

Other books you might like:
Tim LaHaye, *Left Behind: A Novel of the Earth's Last Days*, 1995
   Jerry B. Jenkins, co-author
Paul Meier, *Beyond the Millennium*, 1998
Paul Meier, *The Fourth Millennium: The Sequel*, 1996
Bill Myers, *Threshold*, 1997

DAVID AIKMAN

When the Almond Tree Blossoms

(Dallas: Word, 1993)

Category: Thrillers
Subject(s): Political Thriller; Civil War; Politics
Age range(s): Adult
Major character(s): Douglas Richfield, Spy; Alexei Ilyich Ponomarev, Leader (of People's Movement)
Time period(s): 1990s (1998)
Locale(s): United States

Summary: In this post-Cold War political thriller, the United States is under the control of a collectivist political regime known as the People's Movement. The Constitution has been abolished and the power-brokers of the United States now contend with a Fascist Russia and a market economy-based China. In the United States, civil war is being waged between the People's Movement and the Constitutionalists. Russian Alexei Ilyich Ponomarev has been recruited by the People's Movement to crush the resistance, and he has sent loyal supporter Douglas Richfield on a mission to infiltrate the Constitutionalist organization and uncover information about Project Almond, the code name for a nuclear arsenal maintained by the Constitutionalists. Love and conservative Christian values overcome Richfield, however, and his role as a spy becomes that of a double agent.

Other books by the same author:
Great Souls: Six Who Changed the Century, 1996

Other books you might like:
Randy Alcorn, *Deadline: A Novel*, 1994
Randy Alcorn, *Dominion*, 1996
Tim LaHaye, *Left Behind: A Novel of the Earth's Last Days*, 1995
   Jerry B. Jenkins, co-author

RANDY ALCORN

Deadline: A Novel

(Sisters, Oregon: Multnomah, 1994)

Category: Thrillers
Subject(s): Christian Life; Conspiracies
Age range(s): Adult
Major character(s): Jake Woods, Journalist
Time period(s): 1990s

Summary: Jake Woods is a journalist without much interest in God, until he is nearly killed in a suspicious automobile accident that robs him of two of the most important people in his life. His priorities come under new scrutiny as he struggles to solve a murder mystery. His journey through grief and a search for legal truth lead him to discover another kind of truth, plus answers to questions he didn't know he had.

Other books by the same author:
Edge of Eternity, 1998
Dominion, 1996

Other books you might like:
Paul Meier, *The Third Millennium: A Novel*, 1993
Bill Myers, *Threshold*, 1997
Frank E. Peretti, *The Oath*, 1995
Michael Phillips, *A Rift in Time*, 1997

RANDY ALCORN

Dominion

(Sisters, Oregon: Multnomah, 1996)

Category: Thrillers
Subject(s): Christian Life; Conspiracies; African Americans
Age range(s): Adult
Major character(s): Clarence Abernathy, Journalist; Jake Woods, Journalist; Ollie Chandler, Detective—Police
Time period(s): 1990s
Locale(s): Oregon

Summary: Jake Woods, first introduced in *Deadline*, is back again in *Dominion*. His colleague, Clarence Abernathy, is a black man from a middle-class suburban background who has been drawn into the seamy world of inner-city racial turmoil and gang violence. At Jake's suggestion, Clarence networks with Ollie Chandler, a homicide detective, in an effort to address Clarence's personal tragedies. The more they learn, though, the more the evils of prejudice and distance from God threaten to overtake Clarence's life. Alcorn's storytelling keeps readers in suspense and underscores the difficulty of achieving true racial reconciliation apart from God.

Other books by the same author:
Edge of Eternity, 1998
Deadline: A Novel, 1994

Other books you might like:
Paul Meier, *The Third Millennium: A Novel*, 1993
Bill Myers, *Threshold*, 1997
Frank E. Peretti, *The Oath*, 1995
Michael Phillips, *A Rift in Time*, 1997

680

ISABELLA MACDONALD ALDEN

Julia Ried

(Boston, 1900)

Category: Romance
Subject(s): Christian Life; Conduct of Life
Age range(s): Young Adult-Adult
Major character(s): Julia Ried, 16-Year-Old, Office Worker; Dr. Douglas, Doctor; Mrs. Tyndall, Landlord

Summary: Isabella Macdonald Alden (1841-1930) was a novelist and pastor's wife who was also "Auntie Belle" to Grace Livingston Hill (1865-1947), another prolific writer of Christian fiction. *Julia Ried* was originally published in 1900. It is the story of a young girl stepping out from the world of her childhood into life as a bookkeeper, boarder, and-ultimately-a woman in love, testing the Christian beliefs taught to her by a devoted mother and strengthened by loving friends and family members. The Tyndale House edition includes a preface originally written for another Isabella Alden book by Grace Livingston Hill, in honor of her aunt and mentor.

Other books by the same author:
Ester Ried Yet Speaking, 1998
The Sunset Gate, 1994
Ester Ried's Awakening, 1992 (originally published in 1870 as *Ester Ried*)

Other books you might like:
Grace Livingston Hill, *Crimson Roses*, 1928
Evangeline Booth, *The War Romance of the Salvation Army*, 1919
    Grace Livingston Hill, co-author
Grace Livingston Hill, *Where Two Ways Met*, 1947

681

JORGE AMADO

The War of the Saints

(New York: Bantam Books, 1993)

Category: Fantasy; Mainstream Fiction
Subject(s): Religion; Saints; Love

Age range(s): Adult
Major character(s): Barbara, Saint (used to be a statue); Manela, Niece (of Adalgisa); Adalgisa, Aunt (of Manela), Guardian (of Manela)
Time period(s): 1970s
Locale(s): Bahia, Brazil

Summary: The statue of St. Barbara of the Thunder is intended for a place of honor in the Museum of Sacred Art. Instead, after being transported from the church of Santo Amaro da Purificacao, the statue comes to life and jumps ship, wandering the streets of Bahia. Saint Barbara, a combination of the Christian saint and the Afro-Brazilian spirit Oya, leaves magic in her wake as she travels. Meanwhile, Manela is suffering dreadfully at the hands of her devout and repressive aunt over her love for a taxi driver, and only the saint can set the young lovers free. Amado's magic realism and a fascinating depiction of Bahian religious syncretism work together to create this kaleidoscopic view of Brazilian life, translated by Gregory Rabassa.

Other books by the same author:
The Golden Harvest, 1992 (Clifford E. Landers, translator)
The Swallow and the Tom Cat: A Love Story, 1982 (Barbara Shelby Merello, translator)
Tent of Miracles, 1971 (Barbara Shelby, translator)
Dona Flor and Her Two Husbands: A Moral and Amorous Tale, 1969 (Harriet de Onis, translator)
Gabriela, Clove and Cinnamon, 1962 (James L. Taylor, William L. Grossman, translators)

Other books you might like:
Euclides Da Cunha, *Rebellion in the Backlands*, 1985
Gabriel Garcia Marquez, *The Autumn of the Patriarch*, 1976
Gabriel Garcia Marquez, *Strange Pilgrims: Twelve Stories*, 1993

682

U.R. ANANTHA MURTHY

Samskara: A Rite for a Dead Man

(Delhi: Oxford University Press, 1976)

Category: Gentle Reads
Subject(s): Hinduism; Spirituality; Mythology
Age range(s): Adult
Major character(s): Praneschacharya, Religious (holy man)
Time period(s): 1960s
Locale(s): Karnataka, India

Summary: *Samskara* is a Kannada novel originally published in 1965, translated later into English by A.K. Ramanujan. The author depicts hierarchical life and the very slow pace of change in an orthodox Brahmin community in southern India. The central figure in the novel is the well-liked and very holy Praneschacharya. When an unpopular member of the community dies, the aftermath of his death brings out the worst in his former colleagues. As life starts disintegrating all around him, Praneschacharya remains focused on his personal journey of spirituality. Murthy uses the vehicle of this poetic fiction to illuminate hypocrisy and inconsistencies in Brahmin thinking and social stratification.

Other books by the same author:
Bhava, 1998 (Judith Kroll, co-translator)
Indian Culture: An End of the Century View, 1998
Bharathipura, 1996 (P. Sreenivasa Rao, translator)
Modernism in Indian Writing, 1992 (Ramachandra Sharma, D.R. Nagaraj, co-editors)

Other books you might like:
Vikram Chandra, *Red Earth and Pouring Rain*, 1997
Kiran Desai, *Hullabaloo in the Guava Orchard*, 1998
Kirin Narayan, *Mondays on the Dark Night of the Moon: Himalayan Foothill Folktales*, 1997

683

FRANCENA H. ARNOLD

Not My Will

(Chicago: Moody Press, 1946)

Category: Gentle Reads
Subject(s): Christian Life; Conduct of Life; Love
Age range(s): Young Adult-Adult
Major character(s): Eleanor Stewart, Scientist; Chad Stewart, Spouse (of Eleanor); Dr. Philip King, Religious, Professor
Time period(s): 1940s
Locale(s): United States

Summary: Eleanor Stewart has always been stubborn and determined to have her own way. Orphaned as a child and raised by an equally willful aunt, she has always been proud of her independent ways. But the Christian faith that she has isolated herself from gradually breaks through as she discovers that life's blows are easier to bear when she is following the will of God. When her happy marriage to Chad ends sadly, and she suffers other losses in her life, she alternates between relying on God and fighting against her faith. Ultimately, the Rev. Dr. Philip King helps her find the path she has been preparing for all along.

Other books by the same author:
The Deepening Stream, 1963
A Brother Beloved, 1957
Then Am I Strong, 1951
Light in My Window, 1950

Other books you might like:
Isabella Macdonald Alden, *Julia Ried*, 1900
Grace Livingston Hill, *The Beloved Stranger*, 1933
Christmas Carol Kauffman, *Light From Heaven*, 1948

684

RANDALL ARTHUR

Wisdom Hunter

(Sisters, Oregon: Questar, 1991)

Category: Gentle Reads
Subject(s): Family Problems; Conduct of Life; Religion
Age range(s): Young Adult-Adult
Major character(s): Pastor Jason Faircloth, Religious (minister), Father

Summary: In *Wisdom Hunter*, Randall Arthur explores the devastating effects of hypocrisy and Christian legalism, and the ways in which well-meaning Christians can hurt themselves and the ones they love when they forget to temper the letter of the law with the spirit of the Lord. Pastor Jason Faircloth is a man of discipline and principle whose zealous adherence to man-made standards drives his daughter out of his life. This is the story of the physical and spiritual journey Faircloth undertakes to salvage the shreds of a family torn apart by unrealistic expectations and the demand for blind obedience that is rooted in fear, rather than in love.

Other books by the same author:
Betrayal, 1999
Jordan's Crossing, 1993

Other books you might like:
Charles Laird Calia, *The Unspeakable*, 1998
Suzanne Newton, *I Will Call It Georgie's Blues*, 1983
Lee Smith, *Saving Grace*, 1995
Harold Bell Wright, *The Calling of Dan Matthews*, 1909

685

SHOLEM ASCH

The Nazarene

(New York: G.P. Putnam's Sons, 1939)

Category: Historical Fiction
Subject(s): Christianity; History; Judaism
Age range(s): Adult
Major character(s): Pan Viadomsky, Scholar; Joseph of Arimathea, Historical Figure, Biblical Figure; Yeshua, Biblical Figure (Jesus), Historical Figure
Time period(s): 1st century
Locale(s): Jerusalem, Israel

Summary: Pan Viadomsky is a scholar and a zealous anti-Semite. In his employ is a young Jewish man hired to assist Viadomsky with a translation of Hebrew texts. Soon after *The Nazarene* gets underway, Viadomsky suddenly and feverishly launches into an account of the life of Jesus as one who was there when he died—indeed, as one who believes his actions led directly to the crucifixion. The rest of the novel focuses on the story of Jesus, or Yeshua, as seen through several viewpoints, all narrated by Viadomsky, who is overcome by his visions and memories. In a sophisticated and elegant way, Sholem Asch portrays Christianity and Judaism as the relatives they are, rather than as the enemies that centuries of organized religious doctrine has made them out to be.

Other books by the same author:
Mary, 1949
Tales of My People, 1948
Children of Abraham, 1942
In the Beginning, 1935

Other books you might like:
Lloyd C. Douglas, *The Robe*, 1942
Michael L. Monhollon, *Divine Invasion*, 1998
Reynolds Price, *The Three Gospels*, 1996
Lew Wallace, *Ben-Hur: A Tale of the Christ*, 1880

686

RICHARD BACH

Illusions: The Adventures of a Reluctant Messiah

(New York: Delacorte, 1977)

Category: Gentle Reads
Subject(s): Self-Perception; Airplanes
Age range(s): Young Adult-Adult
Major character(s): Richard Bach, Writer, Pilot; Donald Shimoda, Pilot
Time period(s): 20th century
Locale(s): United States

Summary: In *Jonathan Livingston Seagull*, Richard Bach introduced a seagull whose purpose and mission in life was to break through the barriers of thought, habit, and matter that put limits on the flight of all seagulls, and to teach others the joy of doing the same. In *Illusions*, Bach again uses flight as a metaphor for living within and beyond limits. A disillusioned writer named Richard meets a drop-out messiah, Donald Shimoda. The two share a love for barnstorming and a lack of roots. One teaches the other to soar above the physical and spiritual clouds that obscure vision and dampen dreams.

Other books by the same author:
Above the Clouds: A Reunion of Father and Son, 1993
There's No Such Place as Far Away, 1990
Jonathan Livingston Seagull, 1970

Other books you might like:
Robert Barnes, *The Blue Dolphin*, 1994
Antoine de Saint-Exupery, *The Little Prince*, 1943
Erik Quisling, *The Angry Clam*, 1998

687

RICHARD BACH
RUSSELL MUNSON, Illustrator

Jonathan Livingston Seagull

(New York: Macmillan, 1970)

Category: Gentle Reads
Subject(s): Self-Confidence; Self-Perception; Animals/Birds
Age range(s): Young Adult-Adult
Major character(s): Jonathan Livingston Seagull, Bird (seagull), Adventurer

Summary: Jonathan Livingston Seagull is not content to do what other seagulls do: circle their territory slowly, at low altitudes, fighting over every morsel of food that appears. He is a bird who wants to fly faster, higher, and farther than any gull has ever flown before. Cast out of the flock for his unorthodox ways, Jonathan Livingston discovers new dimensions to flight and new purpose in life, and despite his desire to simply enjoy his new-found freedom, he is given the mission of returning to his flock, against the Law of the Outcast, to share his revelation with any from the flock who will hear and follow. This is a non-sectarian, allegorical story of a prophet, or savior, who breaks the bonds of what is known, brings hope to others, and testifies to the existence of life beyond what can be seen.

Awards the book has won:
Nene Award, 1974

Other books by the same author:
Above the Clouds: A Reunion of Father and Son, 1993
There's No Such Place as Far Away, 1990
Illusions: The Adventures of a Reluctant Messiah, 1977

Other books you might like:
Robert Barnes, *The Blue Dolphin*, 1994
Antoine de Saint-Exupery, *The Little Prince*, 1943
Erik Quisling, *The Angry Clam*, 1998

688

JUNE MASTERS BACHER

The Journey West: Love Is a Gentle Stranger

(NewYork: Inspirational Press, 1996)

Category: Romance; Westerns
Series: Love Is a Gentle Stranger
Subject(s): Frontier and Pioneer Life; Christian Life
Age range(s): Young Adult-Adult
Major character(s): Chris Beth Kelly, Settler, Teacher
Time period(s): 19th century
Locale(s): Oregon

Summary: June Masters Bacher shares the triumphs and tragedies of a pioneer family braving the wilds of the Oregon frontier in the 19th century. Among the challenges that beset Chris Beth Kelly and her fellow settlers are dangerous floods and Indian attacks. These three novels tell a continuing story of bravery, adventure, loyalty, and love as the young schoolteacher seeks a new life in a strange, wonderful, and awe-inspiring land. The titles published in this volume include *Love Is a Gentle Stranger* (1983), *Love's Silent Song* (1983), and *Diary of a Loving Heart* (1984).

Other books by the same author:
Homeward Bound: Love Is a Gentle Stranger, 1998
No Time for Tears, 1992
Love's Soft Whisper, 1986
Seasons of Love, 1986

Other books you might like:
Lori Copeland, *Faith*, 1998
Catherine Marshall, *Christy*, 1967
Janette Oke, *Heart of the Wilderness*, 1993
Janette Oke, *When Calls the Heart*, 1983
Jane Peart, *Where Tomorrow Waits*, 1995
Lori Wick, *Whatever Tomorrow Brings*, 1992

689

MARGARET AYER BARNES

Years of Grace

(Boston: Houghton Mifflin, 1930)

Category: Gentle Reads
Subject(s): Family Life; Marriage
Age range(s): Young Adult-Adult

Major character(s): Jane Ward Carver, Daughter, Spouse (of Stephen), Mother; Andre, Artist; Stephen Carver, Spouse (of Jane)
Time period(s): 19th century; 20th century (1890s-1930s)
Locale(s): Chicago, Illinois

Summary: Margaret Ayer Barnes' novel *Years of Grace* chronicles the adult life of Jane Ward Carver, who lives by the manners and mores of her upper middle class upbringing despite the loosening of social structures at the turn of the century and during the early decades of the 20th century. As a teenager in Chicago, Jane is in love with Andre, a French artist on his way back home to continue his studies. Neither family approves of the match, and when she dutifully breaks off contact with him, her father sends her to the exclusive women's college Bryn Mawr, as a reward. Within the next decade, Jane makes her social debut, marries Stephen Carver—a suitable match for her social standing, and settles into life as a respectable wife, mother and woman of leisure. As time passes, she observes that the standards and expectations set for women are changing, yet she chooses to live by the code of behavior generally adhered to by her mother's generation. This governs the direction of her friendship with Jimmy, a man who might otherwise have become her lover, and it creates conflict for Jane as she watches her children choose paths that lead to divorce and independent careers that take them away from the heart of the family in Chicago. An opportunity to reconnect with Andre during their later years causes Jane to examine their respective philosophies on life and love, and leads her to make a decision that is, not surprisingly, strongly influenced by the traditional values by which she has lived her life.

Awards the book has won:
Pulitzer Prize, Fiction, 1931

Other books by the same author:
Wisdom's Gate, 1938
Edna His Wife, 1935
Within This Present, 1933
Prevailing Winds, 1928

Other books you might like:
Francena H. Arnold, *Not My Will*, 1946
Grace Livingston Hill, *According to the Pattern*, 1903
Grace Livingston Hill, *Happiness Hill*, 1932
L.T. Meade, *Priscilla's Promise*, 1998

690

BYRD BAYLOR
PETER PARNALL, Illustrator

Hawk, I'm Your Brother
(New York: Scribner, 1976)

Category: Gentle Reads
Subject(s): Animals/Birds; Indians of North America
Age range(s): Children
Major character(s): Rudy, Child
Time period(s): 20th century
Locale(s): United States

Summary: Rudy has always wanted to fly. He thinks that perhaps if he were a brother to a hawk, he might learn. He takes a young hawk from a cliff and keeps it on a string, hoping to learn to fly alongside the hawk. Instead, the bird grows tame and Rudy learns an unexpected lesson.

Other books by the same author:
The Best Town in the World, 1983 (Ronald Himler, illustrator)
The Other Way to Listen, 1978 (Peter Parnall, co-author)
The Way to Start a Day, 1978 (Peter Parnall, illustrator)
Coyote Cry, 1972 (Symeon Shimin, illustrator)

Other books you might like:
Anne Eliot Compton, *The Ice Trail*, 1980
Sheryl McFarlane, *Eagle Dreams*, 1994
Joyce Rockwood, *Groundhog's Horse*, 1978
Beatrice Siegel, *The Basket Maker and the Spinner*, 1987

691

CARRIE BENDER

A Fruitful Vine
(Scottdale, Pennsylvania: Herald Press, 1993)

Category: Gentle Reads
Series: Miriam's Journal
Subject(s): Family Life; Love; Amish
Age range(s): Young Adult-Adult
Major character(s): Miriam, Religious (Amish); Nate, Religious (Amish)

Summary: Miriam is entering a new stage of life in her Amish community. Now forty, she has spent her adult life caring for her parents, and both have passed away. But as a single woman, she is outside the mainstream of Amish community life for women her age. When she spends time over the course of one summer with Nate, she finds herself falling in love and hoping for the marriage and family life she has always wanted. When conflicts threaten her dreams, she chooses to trust God and accept whatever the future brings.

Other books by the same author:
Miriam's Cookbook, 1998
A Golden Sunbeam, 1996
A Treasured Friendship, 1996
A Joyous Heart, 1994

Other books you might like:
Beverly Lewis, *The Confession*, 1997
Beverly Lewis, *The Reckoning*, 1998
Beverly Lewis, *The Shunning*, 1997
Louise Stoltzfus, *Amish Women: Lives and Stories*, 1994

692

GEORGES BERNANOS

The Diary of a Country Priest
(New York: Macmillan, 1937)

Category: Biographical Fiction
Subject(s): Ministry; Greed; Catholicism
Age range(s): Adult
Major character(s): Unnamed Character, Narrator, Religious (priest)
Time period(s): Indeterminate Past
Locale(s): France

Summary: A young French priest with idealistic and unorthodox plans for his parish ministry meets with opposition from both his parishioners and his superiors. A man of faith and compassion who believes the poor should have opportunities to better themselves, the anonymous priest writes of his growing frustration with those in positions of power who prefer to maintain control over the poor. As the story unfolds, it becomes obvious that the young priest is ill. He is not a very effective leader even when he is in good health, and as his physical condition worsens, so too do his relationships with peers, superiors, and parishioners. Ultimately, a cancer destroys his life and ministry, just as their lack of faith proves fatal to his congregation.

Other books by the same author:
Georges Bernanos and the Saints, 1996
The Crime, 1936
The Star of Satan, 1927

Other books you might like:
Cardinal Joseph Bernardin, *The Gift of Peace: Personal Reflections*, 1997
Jon Hassler, *North of Hope: A Novel*, 1990
Henri J.M. Nouwen, *The Wounded Healer: Ministry in Contemporary Society*, 1972
J.F. Powers, *Wheat That Springeth Green*, 1988

`693`

MARCELLE BERNSTEIN

Body and Soul

(New York: St. Martin's Press, 1991)

Category: Gentle Reads
Subject(s): Catholicism; Religious Life; Self-Perception
Age range(s): Adult
Major character(s): Sister Gabriel, Religious (nun; also known as Anna); Lynn, Single Mother (sister-in-law of Anna)
Time period(s): 20th century
Locale(s): Wales

Summary: Sister Gabriel, whose pre-convent name was Anna, is a member of a conservative, contemplative order of nuns in Wales. When her brother dies suddenly, she is summoned to help her sister-in-law, Lynn, and she finds more than she bargained for in "the world." While living with Lynn, a single mother about to give birth to her third child, Anna feels guilty as she enjoys the luxuries of hot coffee and bubble baths. She must set her quick intellect to the task of managing the family business left in disarray by her brother's suicide, and unexpectedly discovers the pleasures of romantic love. In the process of entering life outside the convent as a woman and a businessperson, she gradually finds the fulfillment that was missing in her cloistered life. Because she still loves the Church, she must figure out how to blend her love for Christ with a newfound zest for life outside the boundaries of the convent.

Other books by the same author:
Russian Bride, 1986
Sadie, 1983
Nuns, 1976

Other books you might like:
Veronica Black, *A Vow of Sanctity*, 1993
Walter Keady, *Mary McGreevy*, 1998
Mary Pat Kelly, *Special Intentions*, 1997
Muriel Spark, *The Abbess of Crewe*, 1974

`694`

DORIS BETTS

Souls Raised From the Dead: A Novel

(New York: Knopf, 1994)

Category: Biographical Fiction
Subject(s): Death; Family Life; Illness
Age range(s): Adult
Major character(s): Mary Grace Thompson, Teenager; Frank Thompson, Police Officer, Father (of Mary Grace)
Time period(s): 1990s
Locale(s): North Carolina

Summary: Mary Grace Thompson was only 12 when her mother left the family. She and her highway patrolman father have managed on their own ever since. As a teenager, however, Mary Grace is faced with a rare and life-threatening kidney disease. Because of injuries sustained in a shooting years earlier, her father cannot donate an organ to his much-loved daughter. Can Mary Grace count on her mother to be there for her in this life-and-death struggle? The author presents emotionally realistic characters who search for spiritual meaning in the face of tragedy, despite the recognition that their seeking may not yield the answers they most desire.

Awards the book has won:
Reference and User Service Association (RUSA) Award, Fiction, 1995

Other books by the same author:
The Sharp Teeth of Love, 1997
Heading West: A Novel, 1981
Tall Houses in Winter, 1957

Other books you might like:
Dee Henderson, *Danger in the Shadows*, 1999
Laurel Schunk, *Black and Secret Midnight*, 1998
Ed Stewart, *Terminal Mercy: A Novel*, 1999

`695`

TERRI BLACKSTOCK

Justifiable Means

(Grand Rapids, Michigan: Zondervan, 1996)

Category: Thrillers
Subject(s): Rape; Ethics; Serial Killer
Age range(s): Adult
Major character(s): Melissa Nelson, Abuse Victim, Sister (of murder victim); Larry Millsaps, Detective
Time period(s): Multiple Time Periods

Summary: Melissa Nelson is the key witness in a case against a psychopathic rapist. Detective Larry Millsaps believes that Melissa's testimony can put an end to the rapist's violent career of assaults on women. Before long, however, he discovers that the victim herself knows more about the evidence than she possibly could unless she had been involved in planting it. By the time he learns why she might be willing to cross the line of law and ethics to convict this man, he is in love with Melissa. Torn between his personal feelings and the demands of the law, he must rely on his faith and Christian ethics to help him do the right thing.

Other books by the same author:
Presumption of Guilt, 1997
Ulterior Motives, 1996
Evidence of Mercy, 1995

Other books you might like:
B.J. Hoff, *The Captive Voice*, 1995
Gilbert Morris, *Guilt by Association*, 1991
Hilda Stahl, *The Boning Knife*, 1992

STEPHEN BLY

The Final Chapter of Chance McCall
(Wheaton, Illinois: Crossway Books, 1996)

Category: Westerns
Series: Austin-Stoner Files
Subject(s): Treasure; Mystery
Age range(s): Young Adult-Adult
Major character(s): Lynda Dawn Austin, Editor; Brady Stoner, Guide
Locale(s): Jackson, Wyoming; Great Falls, Montana

Summary: In an adventure that takes editor Lynda Dawn Austin across the American West, *The Final Chapter of Chance McCall* tells the story of a yet-to-be-published novel and the wild search to find its missing chapter, which contains detailed treasure maps of Montana rumored to hold deposits of gold. Austin and her partner, Brady Stoner, encounter and overcome challenges and obstacles in their travels from Jackson, Wyoming, to Great Falls, Montana. Bly's storytelling evokes the westerns of Zane Grey, with a Christian message.

Other books by the same author:
Copper Hill, 1997
The Kill Fee of Cindy LaCoste, 1997 (Austin-Stoner Files, #3)
The Lost Manuscript of Martin Taylor Harrison, 1995 (Austin-Stoner Files, #1)
Final Justice at Adobe Wells, 1993
Last Hanging at Paradise Meadow, 1992

Other books you might like:
Al Lacy, *Circle of Fire*, 1996
Al Lacy, *Legacy*, 1994
Gilbert Morris, *Reno*, 1992
Jim Walker, *The Dreamgivers*, 1994

697

STEPHEN BLY

Hard Winter at Broken Arrow Crossing
(Wheaton, Illinois: Crossway Books, 1991)

Category: Westerns
Series: Stuart Brannon

Subject(s): Good and Evil; Christian Life
Age range(s): Young Adult-Adult
Major character(s): Stuart Brannon, Cowboy

Summary: Stuart Brannon has lost his family in tragic circumstances and now he's confronted with more challenges. He has moved to Broken Arrow Crossing to get away from everything for a while. But wherever he goes, he finds someone who needs him, even when he thinks he'd rather not get involved. In the spirit of old-fashioned westerns, this story packs adventure, courage, and strong moral values.

Other books by the same author:
Final Justice at Adobe Wells, 1993 (Stuart Brannon, #5)
Son of an Arizona Legend, 1993 (Stuart Brannon, #6)
Standoff at Sunrise Creek, 1993 (Stuart Brannon, #4)
False Claims at the Little Stephen Mine, 1992 (Stuart Brannon, #2)
Last Hanging at Paradise Meadow, 1992 (Stuart Brannon, #3)

Other books you might like:
Al Lacy, *Circle of Fire*, 1996
Al Lacy, *Legacy*, 1994
Gilbert Morris, *Reno*, 1992
Jim Walker, *The Dreamgivers*, 1994

698

MARY CHRISTOPHER BORNTRAGER

Ellie
(Scottsdale, Pennsylvania: Herald Press, 1988)

Category: Biographical Fiction
Series: Ellie's People
Subject(s): Amish; Childhood; Culture
Age range(s): Children-Young Adult

Summary: Ellie is a young girl born into the Amish way of life. This book, written by the author to preserve her family heritage, became the first in a series of stories told from the point of view of young Amish boys and girls. It provides a glimpse into the everyday life of the Amish, from an adventure with a runaway buggy to preparing and sleeping on straw-filled mattresses.

Other books by the same author:
Polly, 1994
Andy, 1993
Reuben, 1992
Daniel, 1991
Rachel, 1990

Other books you might like:
Richard Ammon, *An Amish Christmas*, 1996
Raymond Bial, *Amish Home*, 1993
Alma T. Hershberger, *Amish Life through a Child's Eyes*, 1987
Carol M. Highsmith, *The Amish: A Photographic Tour*, 1999
John A. Hostetler, *Amish Life*, 1952
Lucian Niemeyer, *Old Order Amish: Their Enduring Way of Life*, 1993

699
JOAN BRADY

God on a Harley: A Spiritual Fable
(New York: Pocket Books, 1995)

Category: New Age (Fiction)
Subject(s): Spirituality; Peace
Age range(s): Adult
Major character(s): Christine Moore, Religious (spiritual seeker)
Time period(s): 1990s

Summary: The Harley-Davidson is a head-turner. So is the guy riding it. A long-haired stranger in a T-shirt and leather jacket calls out to Christine Moore, who, at 37 with a boring job and no special relationship in her life, is feeling more than a little washed up. Without knowing why, she is drawn to the man, trusting that this biker who speaks softly and knows everything about her is not what he appears to be at first glance. As a result, Christine is launched on a spiritual journey that leads her to inner peace and a renewed outlook on life. Although the stranger moves on, Christine's life is forever changed.

Other books by the same author:
I Don't Need a Baby to Be Who I Am: Thoughts and Affirmations on a Fulfilling Life, 1998
Heaven in High Gear, 1997

Other books you might like:
Richard Bach, *Illusions: The Adventures of a Reluctant Messiah*, 1977
Richard Bach, *Jonathan Livingston Seagull*, 1970
James Redfield, *The Celestine Prophecy: An Adventure*, 1993
Iyanla Vanzant, *One Day My Soul Just Opened Up: 40 Days and 40 Nights Toward Spiritual Strength and Personal Growth*, 1998

700
SIGMUND BROUWER

Blood Ties
(Dallas: Word, 1996)

Category: Thrillers
Subject(s): Serial Killer; Family Relations; Faith
Age range(s): Adult
Time period(s): 1990s

Summary: The Federal Bureau of Investigation is once again on the trail of a serial killer whose crimes date back more than two decades. A former "profiler" for the FBI is wrenched out of retirement to match wits with this criminal mind when his own family members are kidnapped. In the face of grisly crimes and the darkest of human experiences, the author explores what it means to believe in God amid the evils of the world.

Other books by the same author:
Double Helix, 1997
Magnus, 1995

Other books you might like:
Frank E. Peretti, *The Oath*, 1995

701
SIGMUND BROUWER

Double Helix
(Dallas: Word, 1997)

Category: Thrillers
Subject(s): Abortion; Genetic Engineering; Ethics
Age range(s): Adult
Major character(s): Paige Stevens, Widow(er); Peter Van Klees, Professor; Slater Ellis, Detective—Amateur
Time period(s): 1990s
Locale(s): New Mexico

Summary: Deep in the rural mountain terrain of New Mexico, professor and genetic engineer Peter Van Klees is secretly using fetal tissue to perform genetic experiments and forcing women to participate in the bearing of experimental babies. His clandestine work is supported by unsuspecting donors who contribute large amounts of money to a phony world relief organization. Paige Stevens is the widow of a man who committed suicide, possibly due to his association with The Institute. Slater Ellis is a man who discovers a naked, wild boy with a tattooed forehead along a deserted mountain road. As Stevens and Ellis individually seek to unravel the mystery behind their own experiences, they discover The Institute and encounter its evil and danger.

Other books by the same author:
Blood Ties, 1996
Magnus, 1995

Other books you might like:
Michael D. O'Brien, *Plague Journal: A Novel*, 1999
Greg Rucka, *Keeper*, 1996

702
SIGMUND BROUWER

Magnus
(Wheaton, Illinois: Victor Books, 1995)

Category: Historical Fiction
Subject(s): Middle Ages; Druids and Druidism; Good and Evil
Age range(s): Adult
Time period(s): 14th century

Summary: Set in the 14th century, this is historic adventure and mystery fiction with Christian overtones. A young knight is caught between the forces of good and evil, but finds it hard to tell one from the other. As the Druids and the Merlins battle for supremacy, an ancient secret is the prize, and the young knight is the only one with the knowledge that all the others seek. The novel brings to life the world of the Middle Ages, Marco Polo, and the Crusades.

Other books by the same author:
Wings of the Dawn, 1999

Other books you might like:
Gillian Bradshaw, *Islands of Ghosts*, 1998

Linda Chaikin, *Swords & Scimitars*, 1993

703
SIGMUND BROUWER

Rebel Glory
(Dallas: Word, 1995)

Category: Mystery
Series: Lightning on Ice
Subject(s): Sports/Hockey; Ethics; Christian Life
Age range(s): Children-Young Adult
Major character(s): B.T. McPhee, 17-Year-Old, Sports Figure (hockey player)

Summary: While hoping for a playoff championship, B.T. McPhee's hockey team is suddenly struck with a string of mishaps and injuries. What's going on and why? The 17-year-old star of the team sets out to solve the mystery in this first volume of the ''Lightning on Ice'' series of books for young hockey lovers.

Other books by the same author:
Thunderbird Spirit, 1996
Winter Hawk Star, 1996
All-Star Pride, 1995

Other books you might like:
Stephen Bly, *Hazards of the Half-Court Press*, 1998
Bruce Brooks, *The Wolfbay Wings Series*, 1997-
Roy MacGregor, *The Screech Owls Series*, 1995-

704
SIGMUND BROUWER

Snowboarding—To the Extreme—Rippin'
(Dallas: Word, 1996)

Category: Mystery
Subject(s): Sports/Skiing
Age range(s): Children-Young Adult
Major character(s): Keegan Bishop, Skier

Summary: A talented young skier with all the right moves, Keegan Bishop is ready to join the hip world of snowboarding-rippin'. But what's going on with that crowd? Mysterious things are happening, and Keegan's about to experience the weirdness firsthand.

Other books by the same author:
Sky Diving—To the Extreme—'Chute Roll, 1997
Mountain Biking—To the Extreme—Cliff Dive, 1996
Scuba Diving—To the Extreme—Off the Wall, 1996

Other books you might like:
Stephen Bly, *Hazards of the Half-Court Press*, 1998
Bruce Brooks, *The Wolfbay Wings Series*, 1997-
Roy MacGregor, *The Screech Owls Series*, 1995-

705
SIGMUND BROUWER

The Weeping Chamber
(Nashville: Word, 1998)

Category: Historical Fiction
Subject(s): Christianity; Bible
Age range(s): Young Adult-Adult

Summary: A man whose personal world is crumbling around him travels to Jerusalem for Passover. It's the last week of Jesus's life. As the man is drawn to the healing words of the great teacher, he discovers that not everyone is friendly toward the rabbi. He witnesses and is deeply saddened by the political, personal, and public betrayal of Jesus that results in his crucifixion. Desperate for solace, he hears and believes rumors that Jesus has come back to life, and this changes the direction of his life.

Other books by the same author:
The Carpenter's Cloth, 1997

Other books you might like:
Orson Scott Card, *Stone Tables: A Novel*, 1997
Marianne Fredriksson, *According to Mary Magdalene*, 1999
Maria Isabel Hodges, *The Promise*, 1999
Norman Mailer, *The Gospel According to the Son*, 1997

706
PEARL S. BUCK

The Good Earth
(New York: John Day, 1931)

Category: Biographical Fiction
Subject(s): Farm Life; Poverty; Family Relations
Age range(s): Young Adult-Adult
Major character(s): Wang Lung, Farmer (Chinese peasant); O-lan, Spouse (of Wang Lung)
Time period(s): 19th century
Locale(s): China (rural)

Summary: Wang Lung, farmer and peasant, tills the soil with his wife, O-lan, until famine forces them to abandon their rural way of life. Their escape from farming, however, brings new suffering, as both husband and wife must beg to survive. During a peasant uprising, their fortunes shift, and they are able to return to living off the land. Gradually Wang Lung's hard work turns to wealth, but the family's new economic comfort brings complacency for the sons and pleasure-seeking for the father. As the younger men in the family turn away from the old values, they no longer cherish the land that has made their success possible. By the time Wang Lung realizes how his behavior has hurt his family, it is too late to make amends.

Awards the book has won:
William Dean Howells Medal, 1935
Pulitzer Prize, Fiction, 1932

Other books by the same author:
The Big Wave, 1948
Dragon Seen, 1942

Today and Forever: Stories of China, 1941
Other books you might like:
Edith Schaeffer, *Mei Fuh: Memories From China*, 1998
Amy Tan, *The Kitchen God's Wife*, 1992
Gail Tsukiyama, *Women of the Silk*, 1991

707

FREDERICK BUECHNER

The Book of Bebb
(New York: Atheneum, 1979)

Category: Gentle Reads
Subject(s): Religion; Dishonesty; Humor
Age range(s): Adult
Major character(s): Leo Bebb, Con Artist; Antonio Parr, Detective—Amateur

Summary: Leo Bebb's many adventures are collected in this omnibus volume of four novels by Frederick Buechner. Included are *Lion Country* (1971), *Open Heart* (1972), *Love Feast* (1974), and *Treasure Hunt* (1977). Leo Bebb is the founder of the Church of Holy Love, Inc. The primary "mission" of this church is for Bebb to make a living through mail-order requests for diplomas and ordinations in his religious organization. As Antonio Parr discovers, though, Bebb's good qualities at least partially offset his con artist personality, and even those who don't buy his gospel-literally or figuratively-are drawn to him. Things are not always as black-and-white as they seem.

Other books by the same author:
The Eyes of the Heart: A Memoir of the Lost and Found, 1999
The Storm: A Novel, 1998
The Longing for Home: Recollections and Reflections, 1996
Listening to Your Life: Daily Meditations with Frederick Buechner, 1992 (George Connor, compiler)

Other books you might like:
Sinclair Lewis, *Elmer Gantry*, 1927
T.R. Pearson, *Gospel Hour*, 1991
Frank G. Slaughter, *Gospel Fever: A Novel about America's Most Beloved TV Evangelist*, 1980

708

FREDERICK BUECHNER

Godric
(New York: Atheneum, 1980)

Category: Historical Fiction
Subject(s): Middle Ages; Religious Life
Major character(s): Godric, Historical Figure, Religious, Recluse (hermit); Ranulf Flambard, Historical Figure, Religious (bishop)
Time period(s): 12th century
Locale(s): Finchale, England

Summary: Godric narrates the story of his life, during which he engages in many occupations. A peddler and a trader, he travels far and wide in 12th-century Europe and beyond. He also makes two religious pilgrimages, one each to Rome and to Jerusalem. His search to find sanctity and holiness in the everyday activities of his life eventually leads Godric into a life of solitude, contemplation, and reflection. At life's end, he is a hermit leaving behind the writings that tell the story of his physical and spiritual journey on Earth. The author, a Presbyterian minister, is known for writing works of fiction and nonfiction that explore spiritual matters with creativity and gentle wit.

Other books by the same author:
The Storm: A Novel, 1998
The Longing for Home: Recollections and Reflections, 1996
Now and Then, 1983
The Book of Bebb, 1979

Other books you might like:
Thomas Mann, *The Holy Sinner*, 1951

709

FREDERICK BUECHNER

Lion Country
(New York: Atheneum, 1971)

Category: Gentle Reads
Subject(s): Religion; Dishonesty; Humor
Age range(s): Adult
Major character(s): Leo Bebb, Con Artist, Spouse (of Lucille); Antonio Parr, Detective—Amateur; Lucille Bebb, Spouse (of Leo)
Locale(s): Armadillo, Florida

Summary: Leo Bebb is a con artist who runs a mail-order Bible college from his garage in Armadillo, Florida. He confers a degree and ordination as a member of the clergy of the Church of Holy Love, Inc., upon any male adult who writes and is willing to pay the fee. Antonio Parr is a rather sorry soul who sends away for his ordination papers-but not to become a minister in Bebb's hypothetical religious institution. Antonio intends to expose Bebb as a fraud. Once ordained, Antonio sets out to gather the evidence that he needs to prove that Bebb is a charlatan, but the closer he gets to the core of Bebb's universe, the more he is drawn in, despite of the weirdness of it all. Bebb may not be a legitimate man of the cloth, but his "religion" is lively, contagious, mysterious and, most of all, real.

Other books by the same author:
The Eyes of the Heart: A Memoir of the Lost and Found, 1999
The Storm: A Novel, 1998
Treasure Hunt, 1977
Love Feast, 1974
Open Heart, 1972

Other books you might like:
Clyde Edgerton, *Killer Diller: A Novel*, 1991
Jon Hassler, *North of Hope: A Novel*, 1990
Jon Hassler, *Simon's Night*, 1979
T.R. Pearson, *Gospel Hour*, 1991

710

FREDERICK BUECHNER

On the Road with the Archangel: A Novel

(San Francisco: HarperSanFrancisco, 1997)

Category: Gentle Reads
Subject(s): Angels; Prayer; Humor
Age range(s): Adult
Major character(s): Raphael, Angel (one of the seven archangels)
Time period(s): 2nd century B.C.

Summary: This gentle fable takes the apocryphal book of Tobit as its departure point, and weaves a poignant tale of providence and faith. Raphael is one of the seven archangels. It is his job to gather prayers from the creatures on earth and transport them to God, returning with answers if they are warranted. Among the petitions are things such as prayers of thanksgiving from a fish grateful for its surroundings. But Raphael's real work is among humans, and working out "the will of God" in answer to prayers means intervening in the lives of people whose prayerful pleas requested results other than those delivered. In a light-hearted parable, Buechner addresses big questions about the existence and nature of God.

Other books by the same author:
The Eyes of the Heart: A Memoir of the Lost and Found, 1999
The Storm: A Novel, 1998
The Longing for Home: Recollections and Reflections, 1996
Listening to Your Life: Daily Meditations with Frederick Buechner, 1992 (George Connor, compiler)

Other books you might like:
Jan Cooper, *Argument with an Angel*, 1996
Roger Elwood, *Angelwalk: A Modern Fable*, 1988
Stephen Mitchell, *Meetings with the Archangel*, 1998
David Swenson, *The Interfacers*, 1998

711

T. DAVIS BUNN

Gibraltar Passage

(Minneapolis: Bethany House, 1994)

Category: Thrillers
Series: Rendezvous with Destiny
Subject(s): Brothers; Nazis; World War II
Age range(s): Young Adult-Adult
Major character(s): Pierre Servais, Brother (of Patrique); Patrique Servais, Brother (of Pierre), Leader (in French Resistance); Jake Burnes, Friend (of Pierre)
Time period(s): 1940s (World War II)
Locale(s): Morocco; Europe

Summary: Pierre Servais lost his twin brother, Patrique, in an ambush attack against him as a leader of the French Resistance. But later, Pierre learns from a young refugee that Patrique is alive and hiding in Morocco. Fighting against the Nazi terror in Europe and North Africa, Pierre and Jake Burnes are on an urgent mission to find Patrique before his assassins do. Faith in God's protection and commitment to

principles of freedom and honor sustain Pierre in his desperate search.

Other books by the same author:
Berlin Encounter, 1995 (Rendezvous with Destiny, #5)
Istanbul Express, 1995 (Rendezvous with Destiny, #4)
Sahara Crosswind, 1994 (Rendezvous with Destiny, #3)
Rhineland Inheritance, 1993 (Rendezvous with Destiny, #1)

Other books you might like:
Jack Cavanaugh, *The Allies*, 1997
Jack Cavanaugh, *The Victors*, 1998
Michael Phillips, *Escape to Freedom*, 1994
Bodie Thoene, *The Gates of Zion*, 1986

712

T. DAVIS BUNN

One Shenandoah Winter: A Novel

(Nashville: Thomas Nelson, 1998)

Category: Gentle Reads
Subject(s): Friendship; Rural Life; Christmas
Age range(s): Young Adult-Adult
Major character(s): Connie Wilkes, Political Figure (assistant mayor), Government Official; Dr. Nathan Reynolds, Doctor; Poppa Joe, Uncle (Connie's)
Time period(s): 1960s (1961)
Locale(s): Hillsboro, Virginia

Summary: The rural town of Hillsboro is finally getting its own doctor. It is late in 1961 when gruff Nathan Reynolds assumes the job of physician to the community, and first locks horns with assistant mayor Connie Wilkes. Her life is complicated enough without the problems Dr. Reynolds leaves in his wake, especially with her worries about Poppa Joe, her aging uncle who refuses to leave his isolated mountain home. Town hall concerns and personal issues combine to make this a dark season for Connie. When Dr. Reynolds decides things just aren't working out in Hillsboro, Connie isn't sure whether to be grateful or regretful, and it isn't until everything takes a turn for the worse that the answer becomes clear, and the darkness lifts for both Connie and the ill-natured doctor. T. Davis Bunn spins a gentle tale of friends, family, and down-home Christian faith in *One Shenandoah Winter*.

Other books by the same author:
Another Homecoming, 1997
The Quilt, 1993

Other books you might like:
Jan Karon, *The Mitford Series*, 1994-
Janette Oke, *Nana's Gift*, 1996
Janette Oke, *The Red Geranium*, 1995
Francine Rivers, *The Last Sin Eater*, 1998

713

T. DAVIS BUNN

The Quilt

(Minneapolis: Bethany House, 1993)

Category: Gentle Reads
Subject(s): Quilts; Prayer; Family Life

Age range(s): Young Adult-Adult
Major character(s): Mary, Grandmother; Jody, Relative (daughter-in-law); Lou Ann, Relative (daughter-in-law)

Summary: In an unnamed small town, a woman named Mary is everybody's grandmother at heart. Beautiful Mary, as many think of her, is old and slowed by the ravages of arthritis, but she knows God has called her to do one last task, and that is to make a quilt. Mary's gnarled hands can't sew a stitch anymore, but the women of the town, even the ones who have never gone in for such things, spend many hours helping Mary make the quilt. Every stitch is sewn with a prayer of thanks, just as Mary has decreed. Everyone who sees the quilt agrees that it is beautiful, but they know that its beauty comes from something more precious than lovely fabric.

Other books by the same author:
One Shenandoah Winter: A Novel, 1998
The Messenger, 1995
The Gift, 1994

Other books you might like:
Janette Oke, *Nana's Gift*, 1996
Janette Oke, *The Red Geranium*, 1995
Catherine Palmer, *A Victorian Christmas Quilt*, 1998
   Debra White Smith, Ginny Aiken, Peggy Stokes, co-authors
Jane Peart, *The Pattern*, 1996
   American Quilt, #1

714
JOHN BUNYAN
The Pilgrim's Progress
(London: Nathaniel Ponder, 1678)

Category: Morality Tales
Subject(s): Christianity; Pilgrims and Pilgrimages; Christian Life
Age range(s): Young Adult-Adult
Major character(s): Christian, Traveler; Mr. Worldly Wiseman, Villain; Evangelist, Guide
Time period(s): 17th century
Locale(s): Bedford, England

Summary: *The Pilgrim's Progress* was written by John Bunyan, a Puritan minister imprisoned for conducting worship services outside the structure of the Church of England. It is a prose allegory of the journey of a soul to salvation, in which a soul named Christian sets out to find his way to Heaven. He is met along the way by Evangelist, who serves as his guide for a good part of his journey. He also encounters Mr. Worldly Wiseman whose counsel is deceitful, as Christian soon discovers. *The Pilgrim's Progress* is considered one of the premiere allegories in English literature.

Other books by the same author:
The Holy War Made by Shaddai upon Diabolus for the Regaining of the Metropolis of the World; Or, the Losing and Taking Again of the Town of Mansoul, 1682
The Life and Death of Mr. Badman Presented to the World in a Familiar Dialogue between Mr. Wiseman, and Mr. Attentive, 1680
Grace Abounding to the Chief of Sinners, 1666

Other books you might like:
Hannah Hurnard, *Hind's Feet on High Places*, 1977
Hannah Hurnard, *Mountains of Spices*, 1976
James Pappas Jr., *The New Amplified Pilgrim's Progress*, 1999
Mark Twain, *The Innocents Abroad, or, the New Pilgrims' Progress; Being Some Account of the Steamship Quaker City's Pleasure Excursion to Europe and the Holy Land*, 1869

715
LARRY BURKETT
The Illuminati
(Nashville: T. Nelson, 1991)

Category: Thrillers
Subject(s): End-Times; Conspiracies; Christianity
Age range(s): Adult
Major character(s): Mark Hunt, Political Figure (U.S. President); Jeff Wells, Computer Expert
Time period(s): 2000s (2001)
Locale(s): United States

Summary: Larry Burkett's first fiction bestseller is an apocalyptic tale based on the prophecies of the book of Revelation, which is at the end of the Christian Bible. During 2001, a secret group known as the Illuminati is poised to take over the world with the power of technology and the office of the U.S. Presidency. The group's plan begins to unfold when newly elected President Mark Hunt first shuts down Congress with a line-item veto of the entire budget and then clears the way for implementation of Data-Net—a global, computer-based economy and social engineering system. Data-Net technology allows the Illuminati to control the wealth—indeed, the basic survival—of every American through the mandatory use of implanted microchips and a Data-Net card. The same technology makes it possible to follow and punish individual Christians who oppose the power of the Illuminati, and to coerce everyone else to fall into line with the Illuminati's vision for world domination. When computer hacker extraordinaire Jeff Wells is recruited by the Christian underground to disable the Data-Net system, the balance of power begins to shift, but not before thousands of Christians are detained in concentration camps, and natural disasters decimate the population of California.

Other books by the same author:
Solar Flare, 1997
The Thor Conspiracy: The Seventy-Hour Countdown to Disaster, 1995

Other books you might like:
Tim LaHaye, *Left Behind: A Novel of the Earth's Last Days*, 1995
   Jerry B. Jenkins, co-author
Bill Myers, *Blood of Heaven*, 1996
Michael Phillips, *A Rift in Time*, 1997
William J. Sutton, *Illuminati 666*, 1995

716

FRANCES HODGSON BURNETT

The Secret Garden

(New York: F.A. Stokes, 1911)

Category: Gentle Reads
Subject(s): Friendship; Gardens and Gardening; Physically Handicapped
Age range(s): Children-Young Adult
Major character(s): Mary Lennox, Orphan, 10-Year-Old; Dickon, Neighbor, Friend, 12-Year-Old; Colin Craven, Son (of Archibald Craven), Handicapped, 10-Year-Old
Time period(s): 1900s
Locale(s): Yorkshire, England

Summary: Orphaned after her parents die of cholera, Mary Lennox is sent to live with Archibald Craven, an uncle who owns Misslethwaite Manor. The old manor holds many secrets and locked doors, and Mary is quite unhappy with her circumstances. Among the mysteries of the house is a child, Colin, who has been hidden away from the rest of the world. With friend and neighbor Dickon, Mary befriends Colin, and the three of them discover a locked garden that has been untouched for many years. As they join together to tend the garden, all three children are themselves nurtured and healed of the various hurts that have burdened their young lives. Burnett offers a vivid and convincing portrait of the spiritual and emotional development of young people who find that they have something of value to contribute to their world.

Other books by the same author:
The Lost Prince, 1915
A Little Princess, 1905
Sara Crewe; or, What Happened at Miss Minchin's, 1889
Little Lord Fauntleroy, 1886

Other books you might like:
Madeleine L'Engle, *A Wrinkle in Time*, 1962
C.S. Lewis, *The Lion, the Witch, and the Wardrobe*, 1950
Margaret Mahy, *The Other Side of Silence*, 1995
Philippa Pearce, *Tom's Midnight Garden*, 1958

717

NICK BUTTERWORTH
MICK INKPEN, Co-Author

Stories Jesus Told

(Sister, Oregon: Gold'n'Honey, 1994)

Category: Morality Tales
Subject(s): Children; Christianity; Christian Life
Age range(s): Children
Time period(s): 1st century (20s-30s)
Locale(s): Israel

Summary: For the very youngest members of a Christian family, Nick Butterworth's *Stories Jesus Told* is an age-appropriate introduction to the parables of Jesus. A perennial favorite with toddlers, Butterworth's picture books are popular with adults, too, for their gentle humor and child-like characters. This collection of eight parables helps teach basic principles of Christian living.

Awards the book has won:
Gold Medallion Book Award, Pre-School Children, 1995

Other books by the same author:
The House on the Rock, 1986
The Lost Sheep, 1986
The Precious Pearl, 1986
The Two Sons, 1986

Other books you might like:
Carolyn Nabors Baker, *The Beginners' Bible for Toddlers*, 1995
Ken Taylor, *Big Thoughts for Little People*, 1982
Ken Taylor, *Wise Words for Little People*, 1987
Mack Thomas, *Once upon a Parable: Bringing Heaven Down to Earth*, 1995

718

TAYLOR CALDWELL

Ceremony of the Innocent

(Garden City, New York: Doubleday, 1976)

Category: Romance
Subject(s): History; Politics; World War I
Age range(s): Adult
Major character(s): Jeremy Porter, Political Figure, Spouse (of Ellen); Ellen Watson Porter, Spouse (of Jeremy)
Time period(s): 19th century; 20th century (1890s-1930s)
Locale(s): Pennsylvania; New York, New York (USA); Washington, District of Columbia

Summary: Taylor Caldwell's *Ceremony of the Innocent* is a tale of political corruption and betrayal. Ellen Watson marries Jeremy Porter and enters his world of politics, wealth, and power. The story illustrates America's loss of innocence during the turbulent opening decades of the 20th century. Caldwell's love stories often explore the worlds of politics or business from a moral standpoint.

Other books by the same author:
Great Lion of God, 1970
Testimony of Two Men, 1968
No One Hears but Him, 1966
The Devil's Advocate, 1952

Other books you might like:
Elaine Barbieri, *Wishes on the Wind*, 1991
Meagan McKinney, *Lions and Lace*, 1992

719

TAYLOR CALDWELL

Dear and Glorious Physician

(Garden City, New York: Doubleday, 1959)

Category: Historical Fiction
Subject(s): Bible; Christianity; Roman Empire
Age range(s): Young Adult-Adult
Major character(s): Luke, Historical Figure, Biblical Figure, Doctor; Mary, Historical Figure, Biblical Figure; Pontius Pilate, Historical Figure, Government Official (procurator of Jerusalem), Biblical Figure; Tiberius, Historical Figure, Ruler (Roman emperor)

Time period(s): 1st century
Locale(s): Jerusalem, Israel; Athens, Greece; Rome, Roman Empire

Summary: Taylor Caldwell portrays the life of St. Luke as she imagines it might have been, from his childhood and youth as an apprentice, to his career as a physician and his life-changing experience as a disciple of Jesus and writer of what is now known as the New Testament book of Luke. The author weaves together history, biblical record, and creative narrative in what has become one of the classics of spiritual fiction.

Other books by the same author:
Great Lion of God, 1970

Other books you might like:
Sigmund Brouwer, *The Weeping Chamber*, 1998
Gene Edwards, *The Prisoner in the Third Cell*, 1991
Marjorie Holmes, *Three From Galilee: The Young Man From Nazareth*, 1985
Marjorie Holmes, *Two From Galilee: A Love Story*, 1972

720

TAYLOR CALDWELL

Great Lion of God

(Garden City, New York: Doubleday, 1970)

Category: Historical Fiction
Subject(s): Bible; Faith; Christianity
Age range(s): Young Adult-Adult
Major character(s): Saul of Tarsus, Historical Figure, Biblical Figure; Jesus, Historical Figure, Biblical Figure; Pontius Pilate, Historical Figure, Government Official (procurator of Jerusalem), Biblical Figure; Joseph of Arimathea, Historical Figure, Biblical Figure; Peter, Historical Figure, Biblical Figure (apostle)
Time period(s): 1st century (15-65)
Locale(s): Jerusalem, Israel; Tarsus, Roman Empire

Summary: Drawing on biblical, historical and creative sources, Taylor Caldwell creates a fictional account of the life of St. Paul, who started out in life as Saul of Tarsus, the intellectual son of a wealthy Roman-Jewish family. The story chronicles events in the life of the man whose conversion from Christian persecutor to believer eventually resulted in many of the writings that are gathered in the New Testament of the *Bible*. From his early years as the teenager Saul to his death as a martyr, now renamed Paul, the central figure in this novel emerges as a complex blend of religious faith and human frailties.

Other books by the same author:
Dear and Glorious Physician, 1959

Other books you might like:
Gene Edwards, *The Silas Diary*, 1998
Gene Edwards, *The Titus Diary*, 1999
Marjorie Holmes, *Three From Galilee: The Young Man From Nazareth*, 1985
Marjorie Holmes, *Two From Galilee: A Love Story*, 1972

721

TAYLOR CALDWELL
JESS STEARN, Co-Author

I, Judas

(New York: Atheneum, 1977)

Category: Historical Fiction
Subject(s): Bible; Christianity; Jesus
Age range(s): Young Adult-Adult
Major character(s): Jesus, Historical Figure, Biblical Figure; Judas Iscariot, Historical Figure, Biblical Figure, Traitor; John the Baptist, Historical Figure, Biblical Figure; Mary, Historical Figure, Biblical Figure; Mary Magdalene, Historical Figure, Biblical Figure; Pontius Pilate, Historical Figure, Government Official (procurator of Jerusalem), Biblical Figure
Locale(s): Jerusalem, Israel; Roman Empire

Summary: Judas Iscariot tells his own story and emerges not as the wicked villain of Christian scripture. The son of a rich and powerful Pharisee Jewish family, Judas becomes a zealot opposing Roman rule. He becomes a disciple of Jesus, and his ultimate betrayal of Jesus is far more complex than the desire for a few pieces of silver.

Other books by the same author:
Great Lion of God, 1970
Testimony of Two Men, 1968
No One Hears but Him, 1966
The Devil's Advocate, 1952

Other books you might like:
Sholem Asch, *The Nazarene*, 1939
    Maurice Samuel, translator
Jim Bishop, *The Day Christ Died*, 1957
Nikos Kazantzakis, *The Last Temptation of Christ*, 1960
Lew Wallace, *Ben-Hur: A Tale of the Christ*, 1880

722

TAYLOR CALDWELL

Testimony of Two Men

(Garden City, New York: Doubleday, 1968)

Category: Gentle Reads
Subject(s): Crime and Criminals; Doctors; Medicine
Age range(s): Young Adult-Adult
Major character(s): Robert Morgan, Doctor; Jonathan Ferrier, Doctor
Time period(s): 19th century; 20th century (turn of the century)
Locale(s): Hambledon, Pennsylvania

Summary: Sheltered and naive, Robert Morgan is an idealistic young physician who has recently graduated from medical school. Morgan's formal medical education may be just completed, but his life education is just about to begin. In his first job as a physician, he begins work with a small-town doctor, Jonathan Ferrier—who has recently been acquitted in the mysterious death of his wife. The folks in town may one day forget the lies spoken of their brilliant physician, but they'll never get over the truths he revealed about themselves. Taylor

Caldwell spins a dramatic tale of despair and redemption set in the context of the medical advances at the turn of the century.

Other books by the same author:
Ceremony of the Innocent, 1976
Great Lion of God, 1970
No One Hears but Him, 1966
The Devil's Advocate, 1952

Other books you might like:
T. Coraghessan Boyle, *The Road to Wellville*, 1993
Bill Crider, *Medicine Show*, 1990
Larry Watson, *Montana 1948: A Novel*, 1993

723

ORSON SCOTT CARD

Stone Tables: A Novel

(Salt Lake City: Deseret Book Company, 1997)

Category: Historical Fiction
Subject(s): Bible; History
Age range(s): Young Adult-Adult
Major character(s): Moses, Biblical Figure, Historical Figure, Brother (of Aaron and Miriam); Aaron, Biblical Figure, Brother (of Moses); Miriam, Biblical Figure, Sister (of Moses)
Locale(s): Israel; Egypt

Summary: *Stone Tables* is a novel based on a musical play written by Orson Scott Card and Robert Stoddard. The story focuses on the life of Moses and his siblings, Aaron and Miriam, and on other members of Moses's family. In imagining what Moses's personal life might have been like, Card weaves into the narrative a glimpse of God and the ways in which God used Moses to foreshadow the coming of Jesus into human history. The purpose of humankind is explored through an examination of Moses and his purpose.

Other books by the same author:
Treasure Box: A Novel, 1996
Turning Hearts: Short Stories on Family Life, 1994 (David C. Dollahite, co-editor)
A Woman of Destiny, 1983
Saintspeak: The Mormon Dictionary, 1981

Other books you might like:
Stanley Burnshaw, *The Refusers: An Epic of the Jews: A Trilogy of Novels Based on Three Heroic Lives*, 1981
Carla Gredley, *Seal of the Mysteries*, 1993
Zora Neale Hurston, *Moses, Man of the Mountain*, 1939
Ursula Synge, *The People and the Promise*, 1974
Ellen Gunderson Traylor, *Moses: The Deliverer*, 1990

724

JAMES P. CARSE

The Gospel of the Beloved Disciple

(San Francisco: HarperSanFranciso, 1997)

Category: Historical Fiction; Biographical Fiction
Subject(s): Bible; Christianity
Age range(s): Adult

Major character(s): Jesus, Historical Figure, Biblical Figure
Time period(s): 1st century
Locale(s): Israel

Summary: Religion professor James P. Carse interprets the life and times of Jesus through the eyes and voice of a Samaritan woman befriended by Jesus at the outset of his wandering career. As the novel opens, the author explains the ancient tradition of gospel writing, in which eye-witnesses recorded stories on scrolls from their own memories and unique points of view. He notes that although there are only four gospels that have been accepted as part of the canonical writings called the New Testament, there are other writings that record the same events from other perspectives, and he offers this novel, written in poetic language and 95 short, parable-like sections, as an example that might have been recorded by a woman who was part of the inner circle of Jesus' group.

Other books by the same author:
Breakfast at the Victory: The Mysticism of Ordinary Experience, 1994
The Silence of God: Meditations on Prayer, 1985

Other books you might like:
Mary Ellen Ashcroft, *The Magdalene Gospel*, 1995
Marianne Fredriksson, *According to Mary Magdalene*, 1999
Norma Rosen, *Biblical Women Unbound: Counter-Tales*, 1996

725

BETTY SMARTT CARTER

I Read It in the Wordless Book: A Novel

(Grand Rapids, Michigan: Baker, 1996)

Category: Gentle Reads
Subject(s): Family Relations; Christian Life; Growing Up
Age range(s): Young Adult-Adult
Major character(s): Carrie Grietkirk, 12-Year-Old; Ginger Jordan, Actress
Time period(s): 1970s
Locale(s): Dutch Falls, Virginia

Summary: Carrie Grietkirk is a mature 12-year-old living with her grandmother in Dutch Falls, Virginia. Carrie's father is a chaplain still serving the U.S. armed forces in southeast Asia following the withdrawal of troops from Vietnam. Members of the local Dutch Reformed church, Carrie and her grandmother regularly attend services and other church functions together and separately. Carrie's peaceful, conservative community and family life are disrupted with the arrival of outgoing and worldly former actress Ginger Jordan, who takes the place of a long-time Sunday school teacher working with the young teen group of students. Although Carrie loves her family's ways and is happy in her church life, she is enticed by the freedom represented by her new adult friend. *I Read It in the Wordless Book* is the story of Carrie's journey toward adulthood and the classic push-and-pull relationship she has with the people and values of her childhood.

Other books by the same author:
The Tower, the Mask and the Grave: A Mystery Novel, 1997

Other books you might like:
Clyde Edgerton, *Raney: A Novel*, 1985

Gail Godwin, *Father Melancholy's Daughter*, 1991
Sheri Reynolds, *The Rapture of Canaan*, 1995
Lee Smith, *The Devil's Dream*, 1992
Lee Smith, *Saving Grace*, 1995

726

LINDA CHAIKIN

Captive Heart

(Eugene, Oregon: Harvest House, 1998)

Category: Romance
Series: Trade Winds
Subject(s): Love; Romance; Pirates
Age range(s): Young Adult-Adult
Major character(s): Devora Ashby, Daughter (of a countess); Nicklas Valentin, Nobleman (Spanish Don); Captain Bruce Hawkins, Pirate
Time period(s): Indeterminate Past

Summary: In this romantic tale of English pirates, Spanish conquerors, and young love, a countess has arranged a marriage for her unwilling daughter, Devora Ashby. Devora believes she has already found her true love in Barbados, where she lives with her uncle, and she is not pleased to be traveling to Spain with her mother. En route to meet the Spanish Don her mother has chosen for her, Devora encounters, and begins to fall in love with, Captain Bruce Hawkins, a mysterious pirate whose true identity will surprise and shock Devora.

Other books by the same author:
Island Bride, 1999
Silver Dreams, 1998

Other books you might like:
Jim Kraus, *Pirates of the Heart*, 1996
    Terri Kraus, co-author
Jane Peart, *Ransomed Bride*, 1989
Lisa Samson, *Indigo Waters*, 1999

727

LINDA CHAIKIN

Silk

(Eugene, Oregon: Bethany House, 1993)

Category: Historical Fiction
Series: Heart of India
Subject(s): Indian Empire; Family Relations
Age range(s): Young Adult-Adult
Major character(s): Coral Kendall, Heiress (of silk plantation)
Time period(s): 18th century
Locale(s): India

Summary: This story is set in the late 18th century on India's northern frontier. Coral Kendall, whose British family owns a significant silk plantation in India, adopts an orphan—an "untouchable"—against the wishes of her wealthy and powerful family. Not long afterward, the boy is abducted by Indian soldiers. During the struggle to reunite with her son, Coral demonstrates courage and the strength of love against all odds.

Other books by the same author:
Silk, 1993

Other books you might like:
Irene Brand, *Child of Her Heart*, 1998
Chitra Banerjee Divakaruni, *Sister of My Heart*, 1999

728

LINDA CHAIKIN

Swords & Scimitars

(Nashville: Thomas Nelson, 1993)

Category: Historical Fiction
Series: Royal Pavilions
Subject(s): Middle Ages; Good and Evil; Romance
Age range(s): Young Adult-Adult
Major character(s): Tancred Redwan, Knight; Helena, Heiress

Summary: Tancred Redwan is a knight in hiding, falsely accused of a murder. During the days preceding the first wave of Crusades through the Holy Land, Redwan rescues Helena, a Byzantine princess, from peril, and finds that she is a worthy survivor on her own terms. Choices must be made amidst the chaos of the Peasant Crusade, and Redwan struggles to do what he believes is right.

Other books by the same author:
Behind the Veil, 1998
Golden Palaces, 1996

Other books you might like:
Gillian Bradshaw, *Islands of Ghosts*, 1998
Sigmund Brouwer, *Magnus*, 1995
Deanna Julie Dodson, *To Grace Surrendered*, 1998

729

LINDA CHAIKIN

Under Eastern Stars

(Minneapolis, Minnesota: Bethany House, 1993)

Category: Historical Fiction; Romance
Series: Heart of India
Subject(s): Indian Empire; Family Relations; Social Classes
Age range(s): Young Adult-Adult
Major character(s): Coral Kendall, Heiress (of silk plantation); Dr. Ethan Boswell, Doctor; Major Jace Buckley, Military Personnel
Time period(s): 18th century
Locale(s): India

Summary: This is the second book in Chaikin's "Heart of India" trilogy. Coral Kendall's young son was kidnapped shortly after she adopted him, and in this volume, she is still searching for him. As a wealthy young woman with an uncharacteristic concern for the "Untouchables" of her society, Miss Kendall is also working to establish a school for the poor young orphans who are social outcasts in the hierachical caste system of 18th-century India. Adding to the drama of Coral's life, Dr. Ethan Boswell and Major Jace Buckley are both in love with her, and each is willing to fight to win her affection. The heroine portrays the power of love and faith in overcoming obstacles.

Fiction

Other books by the same author:
Kingscote, 1994
Silk, 1993

Other books you might like:
Irene Brand, *Child of Her Heart*, 1998
Chitra Banerjee Divakaruni, *Sister of My Heart*, 1999
M.M. Kaye, *The Far Pavilions*, 1978

730

DEEPAK CHOPRA

The Return of Merlin

(New York: Harmony Books, 1995)

Category: New Age (Fiction)
Subject(s): Arthurian Legend; Self-Acceptance; Self-Perception
Age range(s): Adult
Major character(s): Arthur McCallum, Police Officer; Melchior, Apprentice (of Merlin)
Time period(s): 20th century
Locale(s): England

Summary: Deepak Chopra uses the King Arthur legend as a vehicle for communicating his ideas about the quest for self-fulfillment and spiritual peace. Arthurian characters are portrayed through 20th-century counterparts. Chief among these modern-day Arthurian figures is police officer Arthur McCallum, who discovers an old man nicknamed "Merlin" dead on the streets. In this novel, Chopra explores the themes of healing and self-awareness that are characteristic of his nonfiction bestsellers.

Other books by the same author:
The Way of the Wizard: Twenty Spiritual Lessons in Creating the Life You Want, 1995
Journey into Healing: Awakening the Wisdom Within You, 1994
The Seven Spiritual Laws of Success: A Practical Guide to the Fulfillment of Your Dreams, 1994
Return of the Rishi: A Doctor's Search for the Ultimate Healer, 1988

Other books you might like:
Peter Goodrich, *The Romance of Merlin*, 1990
Katherine Paterson, *Parzival: The Quest of the Grail Knight*, 1998

731

ANDREI CODRESCU

Messiah

(New York: Simon & Schuster, 1999)

Category: New Age (Fiction)
Subject(s): Family Relations; Revenge; Millennium
Age range(s): Adult
Major character(s): Felicity LeJeune, Detective—Private; Jeremy "Elvis" Mullin, Religious (evangelist); Andrea Isbik, Orphan, Friend, of Felicity
Time period(s): 1990s (1999)
Locale(s): New Orleans, Louisiana

Summary: Felicity LeJeune is a boyish young private investigator living in New Orleans in 1999, on the eve of the new millennium. Her grandmother has just died, after donating a 2 million dollar winning lottery ticket to the dubious ministry of evangelist Jeremy "Elvis" Mullins. Felicity vows to destroy the organization of the man she believes took advantage of her grandmother's fragile mental state. Joining forces with Sarajevan orphan Andrea Isbik, Felicity gains a following of spiky-haired, pierced, and tattooed young people seeking a millennial messiah. Together, they take on Mullins in this spoof-like commentary on millennial fears and anxieties.

Other books by the same author:
Hail Babylon: In Search of the American City at the End of the Millennium, 1998

Other books you might like:
Stanley C. Baldwin, *1999: A Novel*, 1994
Larry Burkett, *The Illuminati*, 1991
Michael Phillips, *A Rift in Time*, 1997

732

PAULO COELHO

The Fifth Mountain

(New York: HarperFlamingo, 1998)

Category: Historical Fiction
Subject(s): Bible; Miracles
Age range(s): Young Adult-Adult
Major character(s): Elijah, Biblical Figure (Old Testament prophet), Historical Figure
Time period(s): 9th century B.C.

Summary: Set in the 9th century B.C., this is an imaginative yet believable tale about the Biblical prophet Elijah, whose call from God tears him away from an unexpected love and threatens his life. Phoenecian queen Jezebel wants Elijah and all Hebrew prophets dead. Elijah flees from Gilead to Zarephath, where he is instructed by an angel to live with a widow and her young son. The boy dies shortly after Elijah's arrival. Accused by the village elders of causing the boy's death, Elijah is sent to Baal's Fifth Mountain, where an angel appears to him with instructions to go back and raise the child from the dead. Events afterward continue to test his faith and faithfulness. Ultimately his enemies are overcome and left behind as he is transported to heaven in his chariot of fire.

Other books by the same author:
By the River Piedra I Sat Down and Wept, 1996
The Pilgrimage: A Contemporary Quest for Ancient Wisdom, 1995
Alchemist, 1993

Other books you might like:
Shulamith Hareven, *The Prophet*, 1990
Shulamith Hareven, *Thirst: The Desert Triology*, 1996

733

MARC CONNELLY
ROBERT EDMUND JONES, Illustrator

The Green Pastures: A Fable Suggested by Roark Bradford's Southern Sketches, "Ol' Man Adam an' His Chillun"

(New York: Farrar & Rinehart, 1929)

Category: Plays
Subject(s): Christianity; African Americans; God
Age range(s): Adult
Major character(s): Mr. Deshee, Religious (preacher); Myrtle, Religious (member of Deshee's church); De Lawd, Deity (God)
Locale(s): South

Summary: *The Green Pastures*, which won the Pulitzer Prize for Drama in 1930, is the only one of Marc Connelly's plays to be much remembered several decades after they were written. The play was unusual for its time as it was written for general audiences about "the simple faith" of black Christians in the Deep South, and acted by an all-black cast. The play's interpretations of episodes from Christian scripture revolve around the themes of sin and suffering-sin is universal and the cause of punishment and renunciation by God, and suffering is also universal, but beneficial as a vehicle for learning. Written in 1920s vernacular and dialect attributed to black Americans by the playwright, *The Green Pastures* is a play whose aesthetics and cultural sensibilities do not translate well to the latter 20th century. It is considered by critics to be an important play in the development of American drama, but not a classic.

Awards the book has won:
Pulitzer Prize, Drama, 1930

Other books by the same author:
Voices Off-Stage: A Book of Memories, 1968
The Wisdom Tooth: A Fantastic Comedy, 1927

Other books you might like:
Roark Bradford, *Ol' Man Adam an' His Chillun: Being the Tales They Tell about the Time When the Lord Walked the Earth Like a Natural Man*, 1928
   A.B. Walker, illustrator
Paul Green, *In Abraham's Bosom*, 1929
Hatcher Hughes, *Hell-Bent for Heaven: A Play in Three Acts*, 1924
Clarence L. Jordan, *The Substance of Faith and Other Cotton Patch Sermons*, 1972
   Dallas Lee, editor

734

SUSAN COOPER

The Dark Is Rising Sequence

(1965-1977)

Category: Fantasy; Mainstream Fiction
Series: Dark Is Rising Sequence
Subject(s): Good and Evil; Legends; Quest

Age range(s): Young Adult
Major character(s): Merriman, Uncle (of Barney, Jane, and Simon), Hero (first Old One of the Light)
Locale(s): United Kingdom; Europe

Summary: The Dark Is Rising Sequence is a masterpiece of young adult fantasy consisting of five novels written between 1965 and 1977. Drawing on Arthurian legends, Cooper draws a strong picture of a pitched battle between good, the Light, and evil, the Dark, the success of which depends on five children and their mentor. The Drew children are Barney, Jane, and Simon, and their Uncle Merriman is, in fact, the first Old One of the Light, an immortal who is pledged to battle the Dark. Will Stanton, 11 years old at the time, discovers he also has a bond to Merriman: Will is the last of the Old Ones of the Light, and must share in Merriman's quest. Also involved is Bran Davies, a Welsh boy. Together these six people begin a long and perilous journey to save the world from the forces of the Dark. The five novels of the series are: *Over Sea, Under Stone* (1965), in which the Drew children search for a grail to help them combat the Dark; *The Dark Is Rising* (1973), in which Will discovers his destiny as an Old One; *Greenwitch* (1974), in which the Drew children must recover the grail from the forces of the Dark; *The Grey King* (1975), a Newbery Medal winner in which Bran and Will team up on a quest for the Light; and *Silver on the Tree*, in which the final, desperate battle between the Light and the Dark takes place.

Other books by the same author:
King of Shadows, 1999
The Boggart, 1995
Seaward, 1983
Dawn of Fear, 1970

Other books you might like:
Lloyd Alexander, *The Castle of Llyr*, 1966
Lloyd Alexander, *Taran Wanderer*, 1967
Thomas A. Barrow, *The Ancient One*, 1992
Debra Doyle, *City by the Sea*, 1991
Madeleine L'Engle, *A Wrinkle in Time Quartet*, 1962-1986
C.S. Lewis, *Chronicles of Narnia*, 1950-1956

735

LORI COPELAND

Faith

(Wheaton, Illinois: Tyndale House, 1998)

Category: Romance; Historical Fiction
Series: Brides of the West 1872
Subject(s): Marriage; Love
Age range(s): Young Adult-Adult
Major character(s): Faith Kallahan, 19-Year-Old, Mail Order Bride; Nicholas Shepherd, Rancher, Son (of Liza); Liza Shepherd, Mother (of Nicholas)
Time period(s): 19th century
Locale(s): Deliverance, Texas

Summary: At age 19, Faith Kallahan travels from Michigan to Deliverance, Texas, to be the mail order bride of rancher Nicholas Shepherd. Her father has died, leaving behind Faith and her two younger sisters, all of whom are of marrying age. With few prospects in their small town, they reply to an ad for mail order brides, and Faith's adventure begins. Though she is sure this is God's will for her, and she is determined to make a good wife, she runs up against two major obstacles: a slightly reluctant husband-to-be, and his hostile mother, Liza Shepherd. Adding to the complications: she and Nicholas are equally headstrong, independent people used to doing things their own ways. What kind of future is in store for Faith and Nicholas if their wedding plans ever do take place?

Other books by the same author:
Hope, 1999 (Brides of the West 1872)
June, 1999 (Brides of the West 1872)
All or Nothing: Rainbow's End, 1995
Promise Me Forever, 1994

Other books you might like:
Al Lacy, *Secrets of the Heart*, 1998
Al Lacy, *A Time to Love*, 1998
Janette Oke, *Love Comes Softly*, 1979
Catherine Palmer, *Prairie Rose*, 1997
Catherine Palmer, *Prairie Storm*, 1999

736

THOMAS BERTRAM COSTAIN

The Silver Chalice: A Novel

(Garden City, New York: Doubleday, 1952)

Category: Historical Fiction
Subject(s): Bible; Christianity; Romance
Age range(s): Young Adult-Adult
Major character(s): Basil of Antioch, Artisan (silversmith), Slave; Deborah, Gentlewoman; Simon Magus, Historical Figure, Magician; Paul, Biblical Figure (apostle), Historical Figure; Luke, Biblical Figure (evangelist), Historical Figure; Nero, Historical Figure, Ruler (Roman emperor); Peter, Historical Figure (apostle), Biblical Figure
Time period(s): 1st century
Locale(s): Antioch, Syria; Jerusalem, Israel; Rome, Roman Empire

Summary: Basil is an enslaved silversmith who was cheated out of his inheritance. He is purchased and freed by Luke, who hires him to make a likeness of the dying Joseph of Arimathea. Basil is then commissioned to design a silver chalice to house the cup used by Jesus during the Last Supper. While carrying out his commission, Basil works to regain his inheritance, is torn between two beautiful women, and experiences the promise of Christianity versus the charlatanism of the false messiah, magician Simon Magus. With a blend of fiction, history, and scriptural sources, Costain's work has become a classic of inspirational literature.

Other books by the same author:
The Last Love, 1963
The Darkness and the Dawn, 1959
Son of a Hundred Kings: A Novel of the Nineties, 1950

Other books you might like:
Gene Edwards, *The Silas Diary*, 1998
Gene Edwards, *The Titus Diary*, 1999
Lew Wallace, *Ben-Hur: A Tale of the Christ*, 1880

737

NEVA COYLE

Sharon's Hope

(Nashville: Thomas Nelson, 1996)

Category: Romance
Subject(s): Love; Parenthood; Trust
Age range(s): Young Adult-Adult
Major character(s): Sharon Potter, Abuse Victim, Single Mother; Kenneth, Boyfriend (of Sharon Potter), Veteran

Summary: A survivor of an abusive marriage, Sharon Potter is now struggling to raise two children as a single mother, fearful that she will never find the right kind of love. Instead, Sharon is surprised by a new relationship with Kenneth, a Vietnam War veteran whose own problems are overcome by their shared love. This is a story of human resiliency, hope in the face of obstacles, and a faith in God that transforms fear and anger into trust and love.

Other books by the same author:
Door of Hope, 1995

Other books you might like:
Carrie Brown, *Lamb in Love*, 1999
Carrie Brown, *Rose's Garden*, 1998
Patricia Haley-Brown, *Nobody's Perfect*, 1998

738

JIM CRACE

Quarantine

(New York: Farrar Straus and Giroux, 1997)

Category: Historical Fiction; Biographical Fiction
Subject(s): Scripture; Bible
Age range(s): Adult
Major character(s): Jesus, Historical Figure, Biblical Figure

Summary: Jim Crace's controversial novel *Quarantine* reimagines the 40-day wilderness experience of Jesus as rooted in natural and rational rather than supernatural and miraculous terms. Archangels and demons do not tempt the Jesus of Crace's reinterpretation: a motley crew of human beings do, one of whom is the embodiment of Satan. The wilderness sojourn is not the beginning of an itinerant ministry; it is the end of an earthly life when Jesus perishes of starvation, suffering from visions and hallucinations, after thirty days of fasting. Yet the possibility of resurrection is not firmly eliminated. Crace paints an unfamiliar picture of Jesus that highlights the harsh physical and cultural landscape of the time during which he lived, which in turn may shed new light on readings of the more traditional portrayals of the life and work of Jesus.

Awards the book has won:
Whitbread Prize, Novel, 1997

Other books by the same author:
Signals of Distress, 1995
Arcadia, 1991
The Gift of Stones, 1988
Continent, 1986

Other books you might like:
Robert Graves, *King Jesus*, 1946
Nikos Kazantzakis, *The Last Temptation of Christ*, 1960
Norman Mailer, *The Gospel According to the Son*, 1997
Robert Stone, *Damascus Gate*, 1998

739

MARGARET CRAVEN

I Heard the Owl Call My Name

(Toronto, Ontario, Canada: Clarke, Irwin, 1967)

Category: Gentle Reads
Subject(s): Death; Indians of North America; Missionaries
Age range(s): Young Adult-Adult
Major character(s): Mark Brian, Religious (Anglican vicar); Jim, Assistant (Kwakiutl guide for the vicar); Marta Stephens, Aged Person (Kwakiutl elder)
Time period(s): 1960s
Locale(s): Kingcome, British Columbia, Canada

Summary: Mark Brian, a young Anglican priest, is sent by his bishop to Kingcome, a remote village in British Columbia, to live with the Kwakiutl Indians as their vicar. Brian is unaware that he is mortally ill and has less than three years to live, though his bishop is cognizant of this. When he arrives in his new home, he is struck by the gentle nature of the Kwakiutl people and by the unprovoked insensitivity exhibited toward them by most of the non-Indians they encounter in trade and interactions with government authorities. Gradually, the Kwakiutl come to accept Brian among them, in large part because he is respectful of their customs and genuine in his mourning with them at times of death. During the course of the novel, death, dying, and grieving the passing of loved ones are central themes. Brian gradually becomes aware of his own impending mortality when he "hears the owl call his name," and he mourns the likelihood that he will be removed from the village and sent to a hospital in a white culture that now seems alien to him. However, his Kwakiutl family intervenes and persuades the bishop to allow the young priest to remain surrounded by people who love him until it is his time to die.

Other books by the same author:
The Home Front: Collected Stories, 1981
Again Calls the Owl, 1980
Walk Gently This Good Earth, 1977

Other books you might like:
Rayna M. Gangi, *Mary Jemison: White Woman of the Seneca*, 1996
Janet Campbell Hale, *Owl's Song*, 1974
Frank Herbert, *Soul Catcher*, 1972
James Sewid, *Guests Never Leave Hungry: The Autobiography of James Sewid, A Kwakiutl Indian*, 1969

740

HARRY CREWS

Gospel Singer

(New York: Morrow, 1968)

Category: Morality Tales

Subject(s): Racial Conflict; Popular Culture; Murder
Age range(s): Adult
Major character(s): Gospel Singer, Singer; Willalee Bookatee Hull, Murderer (accused)
Time period(s): 1960s
Locale(s): Enigma, Georgia

Summary: Harry Crews' first novel, *Gospel Singer*, tells the story of a small-town boy who has made it big in the world of pop gospel singing and Bible Belt preaching. He is Enigma's one claim to fame, a golden boy, and he is coming home. The people of the rural Georgia town are eagerly awaiting the arrival of their hero. The Gospel Singer (who is never named but always referred to as Gospel Singer) knows there is a dark side to his life, however, and that is what is driving him home, back to MaryBell Carter, the town's "golden girl," and the Gospel Singer's only true confidante. Only thing is, MaryBell has just been raped and murdered, and one of the town's black men, Willalee Bookatee Hull, is sitting in jail, accused but not guilty of her murder. Willalee's friendship with the Gospel Singer goes way back, and Willalee is sure that once his old friend is back in town, he'll stick by him and help him clear his name. The emotionally bankrupt Gospel Singer does find himself by his friend's side, but not in a way that either one of them has anticipated. As community fervor against Willalee reaches fever pitch, the Gospel Singer unexpectedly reveals his darker side, and that of the deceased MaryBell Carter. Then the wrath of the town turns itself on the one-time hero.

Other books by the same author:
Blood and Grits, 1979
Karate Is a Thing of the Spirit: A Novel, 1971
This Thing Don't Lead to Heaven, 1970

Other books you might like:
T.R. Pearson, *Gospel Hour*, 1991
Frank G. Slaughter, *Gospel Fever: A Novel about America's Most Beloved TV Evangelist*, 1980

741

DONNA FLETCHER CROW

The Banks of the Boyne: A Quest for a Christian Ireland

(Chicago: Moody Press, 1998)

Category: Historical Fiction
Subject(s): Religious Conflict; Family Life; Christianity
Age range(s): Young Adult-Adult
Major character(s): Mary, Young Woman Gareth, Young Man
Time period(s): 20th century
Locale(s): Northern Ireland

Summary: Married life is not starting out easily for Mary and Gareth. Having just started out their lives together with a wedding in Scotland, they find themselves heading to northern Ireland, where Gareth has pledged to help bring peace to a people divided by political and religious strife. The author weaves historical background into their contemporary story. As Mary and Gareth travel around their adopted country, they learn about the politics and religious dogma that have fueled more than three centuries of hatred between Catholic and Protestant constituencies in the small island country. Readers come to understand how difficult it is to overcome generations of mistrust and mistreatment, and why people of principle and religious conviction still try to do so.

Other books by the same author:
Encounter the Light, 1999
Where Love Begins, 1995
The Castle of Dreams, 1992
A Gentle Calling, 1987

Other books you might like:
Beatrice Coogan, *The Big Wind: A Novel of Ireland*, 1995
Elaine Crowley, *A Dublin Girl: Growing Up in the 1930s*, 1998
Alice Taylor To Sch, *To School Through the Fields: An Irish Country Childhood*, 1988

742

MARELE DAY

Lambs of God

(New York: Riverhead Books, 1998)

Category: Thrillers
Subject(s): Catholicism; Religious Life
Age range(s): Adult
Major character(s): Sister Carla, Religious (nun); Sister Iphigenia, Religious (nun); Sister Margarita, Religious (nun); Father Ignatius, Religious (priest)
Locale(s): Australia

Summary: A flock of sheep and an abandoned monastery are the trappings of daily life for three forgotten nuns—Carla, Margarita, and Iphigenia—on a remote island in Australia. The three women are all that's left of an order of nuns whose simple life was one of prayer, sheep-tending, wool-spinning, and knitting. One day Father Ignatius arrives on the island with a cellular phone and big plans to convert what he believes is an empty piece of church property into a money-making resort, thus boosting his opportunities to move up in the church hierarchy. No matter that he is a Catholic cleric; the nuns know that his presence on the island doesn't bode well for the continuation of their simple existence. The unsuspecting and enterprising priest is captured by the three women, the youngest of whom has never seen a man, and his fate from that point on provides both suspenseful and funny moments in this tale of a clash of cultures and genders.

Other books by the same author:
The Disappearances of Madalena Grimaldi: A Claudia Valentine Mystery, 1994
The Case of the Chinese Boxes, 1990

Other books you might like:
Marcy Heidish, *Miracles: A Novel about Mother Seton, the First American Saint*, 1984
Alison Joseph, *The Hour of Our Death: A Sister Agnes Mystery*, 1997
Mary Pat Kelly, *Special Intentions*, 1997

743

SANDRA DENGLER

Code of Honor

(Minneapolis: Bethany House, 1988)

Category: Romance; Historical Fiction
Subject(s): Adventure and Adventurers
Age range(s): Young Adult-Adult
Major character(s): Samantha Connolly, Immigrant, Sister (of Meg and Linnet); Margaret Connolly, Immigrant, Sister (of Samantha and Linnet); Linnet Connolly, Immigrant, Sister (of Samantha and Meg); Luke Vinson, Religious (minister); Cole Sloan, Plantation Owner
Time period(s): 1900s (1905)
Locale(s): County Cork, Ireland; Australia

Summary: Trouble is brewing in County Cork, Ireland as the revolutionary group Sinn Fein is being formed to procure independence from England. With few prospects for marriage or happiness in their native land, the Connolly girls-Samantha, Margaret, and their little sister Linnet-leave Ireland to work as indentured servants in Australia. Margaret finds love with Luke Vinson, a minister with a mission to end the practice of indenture in Queensland. Linnet learns a little independence and self-reliance. And Samantha, the sensible eldest sister, finds herself drawn to Cole Sloan, the plantation owner who plays fast and loose with the law and has no regard for the God Samantha is struggling to understand. Life is harsh in Samantha's new land; will she find the strength to do the job she is expected to do and be true to herself and her values at the same time?

Other books by the same author:
East of Outback, 1990
The Power of Pinjarra, 1989
Taste of Victory, 1989

Other books you might like:
Madeline Brent, *Golden Urchin*, 1986
Lori Copeland, *Faith*, 1998
Patricia Hickman, *Angel of the Outback*, 1995
Patricia Hickman, *Voyage of the Exiles*, 1995
David Malouf, *The Conversations at Curlow Creek*, 1997

744

KIRAN DESAI

Hullabaloo in the Guava Orchard

(New York: Atlantic Monthly Press, 1998)

Category: New Age (Fiction)
Subject(s): Coming of Age; Religion; Hinduism
Age range(s): Adult
Major character(s): Sampath Chawla, Young Man; Kulfi, Mother; Mr. Chawla, Father
Time period(s): 1990s
Locale(s): India

Summary: When a young Hindu man with little ambition in life runs away from home and takes up residency in a guava tree, the town mistakes him for a holy man. Each member of his eccentric family is affected by this, especially his father, who decides to exploit the situation for monetary gain. The people of the town are mystified by the presence of this unusual holy man and undecided about his rightful place in the beliefs of the village. Suspicious tourists and a band of alcoholic monkeys season Kiran Desai's first novel with humor and excitement.

Awards the book has won:
Betty Trask Prize, 1988

Other books you might like:
Rohinton Mistry, *Such a Long Journey*, 1991
Daniel Manus Pinkwater, *The Last Guru*, 1978
Salman Rushdie, *The Satanic Verses*, 1988

745

JUDE DEVERAUX

An Angel for Emily
(New York: Pocket Books, 1998)

Category: Romance
Subject(s): Angels; Libraries; Love
Age range(s): Adult
Major character(s): Emily Todd, Librarian; Michael Chamberlain, Angel

Summary: Emily Todd is a small-town librarian whose life is in a bit of a rut. One disappointing evening after she receives an award at a ceremony that her boyfriend was too busy to attend with her, she is driving home alone when she realizes she has hit a man with her car. Horrified, she gets out to help him, only to discover that the injuries he has came from another cause, and that for a guy who was just hit by a car he's in remarkably good shape. Who is this Michael Chamberlain? He calls himself an angel and says he has been sent to save Emily. For her part, Emily is not sure she needs a guardian angel, particularly not one as handsome and charming as Michael appears to be, but that doesn't deter the angel of love and happiness. Jude Deveraux is well-known as a romance novelist. *An Angel for Emily* features an ethically strong heroine who ultimately makes good choices and a handsomely strong hero who places the best interests of others ahead of his own.

Other books by the same author:
Blessing, 1998
Eternity, 1992
A Knight in Shining Armor, 1989

Other books you might like:
Elizabeth Chandler, *Kissed by an Angel*, 1998
Andrew M. Greeley, *Angel Light: An Old-Fashioned Love Story*, 1995
Lurlene McDaniel, *Angels Watching over Me*, 1996

746

FYODOR DOSTOEVSKY

The Brothers Karamazov
(New York: Macmillan, 1912)

Category: Morality Tales
Subject(s): Brothers; Fathers and Sons; Family Problems

Age range(s): Adult
Major character(s): Fyodor Karamazov, Father, Landowner; Dmitri Karamazov, Relative (stepbrother of Ivan, Alyosha), Military Personnel; Ivan Karamazov, Brother (of Alyosha), Relative (stepbrother of Dmitri), Professor; Alyosha Karamazov, Brother (of Ivan), Relative (stepbrother of Dmitri), Religious (student); Smerdyakov, Bastard Son (of Fyodor Karamazov)
Time period(s): 19th century (mid-century)
Locale(s): Skotoprigonyvski, Russia

Summary: In this novel, which was first published in Russia in 1880, Dostoyevsky explores themes of generational conflict, sibling rivalry, the search for truth, and the futility of living in separation from God. Each of the four sons of Fyodor Karamazov has reason to hate his father. The elder Karamazov mistreated his two wives, neglected the three sons of those marriages, and fathered an illegitimate son who became his servant. The oldest son, Dmitri, is his rival for the affection of a mutual lover. Ivan, the next eldest, has distanced himself from his father as an intellectual and a writer of parables. Ivan's natural brother, Alyosha, is a young seminarian studying for the priesthood, loved by many and good-natured to all, in contrast to the rest of his family. The illegitimate son, Smerdyakov, raised by his father's servants, is a generally shallow and unpleasant character. Despite their differences and their separate lives, all four sons figure into the death of their father. And although one is eventually punished through the legal system based on visible evidence, all four suffer various fates as a consequence of their real or perceived roles in the murder.

Other books by the same author:
Crime and Punishment, 1866
The Idiot, 1868
Notes From the Underground, 1864

Other books you might like:
Leo Tolstoy, *Anna Karenina*, 1889
Leo Tolstoy, *Ivan Ilyitch, and Other Stories*, 1887
Leo Tolstoy, *The Kingdom of God Is Within You: Christianity Not as a Mystic Religion but as a New Theory of Life*, 1894

747

LLOYD C. DOUGLAS

The Big Fisherman
(Boston: Houghton Mifflin, 1948)

Category: Historical Fiction
Subject(s): Christianity; Bible
Age range(s): Adult
Major character(s): Fara, Royalty (Arabian princess); Voldi, Nobleman (Arabian); Nicator Mencius, Government Official (Roman proconsul); Peter, Historical Figure, Biblical Figure; Jesus, Historical Figure, Biblical Figure; Herod Antipas, Historical Figure, Ruler (Tetrarch of Judea), Biblical Figure; John the Baptist, Historical Figure, Biblical Figure
Locale(s): Arabia; Roman Empire; Jerusalem, Israel

Summary: The story of early Christianity and Jesus' later life, teachings, miracles, death, resurrection, and the gathering of the disciples is told from different points of view. These viewpoints come from Peter; Fara, the half-Arabian, half-Jewish daughter of Antipas; Voldi, Fara's betrothed; and Mencius, a sympathetic Roman proconsul. John the Baptist's last days and death are also described.

Other books by the same author:
The Robe, 1942
Disputed Passage, 1939
White Banners, 1936
Forgive Us Our Trespasses, 1932
Magnificent Obsession, 1929

Other books you might like:
Sholem Asch, *The Apostle*, 1943
Sholem Asch, *The Nazarene*, 1939
Taylor Caldwell, *I, Judas*, 1977
Thomas Bertram Costain, *The Silver Chalice: A Novel*, 1952
Robert Graves, *King Jesus*, 1946

748

LLOYD C. DOUGLAS

The Robe
(Boston: Houghton Mifflin, 1942)

Category: Historical Fiction
Subject(s): Christianity; Roman Empire; Jesus
Age range(s): Young Adult-Adult
Major character(s): Marcellus Gallio, Military Personnel (Roman tribune); Demetrius, Slave; Diana Gallus, Young Woman; Tiberius, Historical Figure, Ruler (Roman emperor); Caligula, Historical Figure, Ruler (Roman emperor); Pontius Pilate, Historical Figure, Government Official (procurator of Jerusalem), Biblical Figure; Peter, Historical Figure, Biblical Figure; Salome, Historical Figure, Biblical Figure
Time period(s): 1st century
Locale(s): Rome, Roman Empire; Jerusalem, Israel; Athens, Greece

Summary: In this inspirational classic, Douglas blends fiction, history, and biblical sources to create the story of Marcellus Gallio, an upperclass Roman tribune assigned to crucify Jesus. When Marcellus wins Jesus' robe in a dice game and dons the garment in a fit of drunkenness, he becomes emotionally distraught over the crucifixion. The robe's healing powers later restore Marcellus' equanimity, and with his loyal, resourceful slave, Demetrius, he embarks upon a quest to learn all he can about Jesus and his teachings, eventually becoming a Christian in defiance of Roman law.

Other books by the same author:
Time to Remember, 1951
The Big Fisherman, 1948
Magnificent Obsession, 1929

Other books you might like:
Marjorie Holmes, *The Messiah*, 1987
Charles R. Swindoll, *Suddenly One Morning: The Shopkeeper's Story*, 1998
Lew Wallace, *Ben-Hur: A Tale of the Christ*, 1880

749

DAVID JAMES DUNCAN

The River Why
(San Francisco: Sierra Club Books, 1983)

Category: Gentle Reads
Subject(s): Nature; Rivers; Fishing
Age range(s): Adult
Major character(s): Gus Orviston, Fisherman
Locale(s): Oregon

Summary: Set in the outdoors of Oregon, *The River Why* is a comic, yet poignant, novel on the relationship between human beings and the natural world. The story is told through the eyes and adventures of Gus Orviston, whose passion in life is fly-fishing. Through Orviston's interactions with people and nature, Duncan explores themes of conservation and respect for the land in the first novel ever pubished by the Sierra Club.

Other books by the same author:
River Teeth: Stories and Writings, 1995
The Brothers K, 1992

Other books you might like:
Amy Blackmarr, *Going to Ground: Simple Life on a Georgia Pond*, 1997
Annie Dillard, *Pilgrim at Tinker Creek*, 1974
Stephanie Kaza, *The Attentive Heart: Conversations with Trees*, 1993
Kathleen Norris, *Dakota: A Spiritual Geography*, 1993

750

UMBERTO ECO

The Name of the Rose
(San Diego: Harcourt, 1983)

Category: Mystery
Subject(s): Catholicism; Mystery; Murder
Age range(s): Adult
Major character(s): Brother William of Baskerville, Religious (monk); Jorge of Burgos, Religious (monk); Adso, Assistant (scribe to Brother William)
Time period(s): 14th century (1327)
Locale(s): Italy (a Benedictine monastery)

Summary: In 1327, a conflict is brewing among Franciscan Catholic monks in northern Italy. The Spiritualists, allied with Emperor Louis IV, stand for vows of poverty among monks and evangelical poverty for the church. Allies of corrupt Pope John XXII, however, fear that vows of poverty will weaken the economic and political power of the church. To mediate the disputes and ward off impending violence, Brother William of Baskerville and his scribe, Adso, arrive at a neutral Benedictine monastery where the two factions have agreed to meet together. Before the gathering can begin, however, a monk is found dead. Thus begins Brother William's role as a detective. With Adso as his assistant, he will eventually have to figure out why seven monks are murdered in seven days' time. Although the novel, first published in Italian in 1980, is an intricate murder mystery, it is also considered to be a parable of modern religion and politics in Italy, couched in the language of the church-state conflict of the 14th century.

Awards the book has won:
Association of Logos Bookstores Best Fiction Book Award, 1983

Other books by the same author:
The Cult of Vespa, 1997
The Island of the Day Before, 1995
Foucault's Pendulum, 1989
Postscript to "The Name of the Rose", 1984

Other books you might like:
Ralph McInerny, *The Red Hat: A Novel*, 1998
Brian Moore, *The Color of Blood*, 1987
Michael D. O'Brien, *Father Elijah: An Apocalypse*, 1996
Richard Zimler, *The Last Kabbalist of Lisbon*, 1998

751

CLYDE EDGERTON

Killer Diller: A Novel
(Boston: G.K. Hall, 1991)

Category: Comedy
Subject(s): College Life; Baptists; Mentally Handicapped
Age range(s): Young Adult-Adult
Major character(s): Vernon Jackson, Musician (guitarist), 16-Year-Old, Handicapped; Wesley Benfield, Worker (bricklayer), Musician (guitarist)
Time period(s): 1990s
Locale(s): Listre, North Carolina

Summary: First introduced in Edgerton's *Walking Across Egypt,* Wesley Benfield is a former car thief who had changed his old ways, but couldn't resist the temptation of keys left in a white Lincoln Continental. He's now part of the "Back on Track Again" project sponsored by a Baptist college whose president and provost love to receive credit for helping underdogs. Wesley's assigned task is to teach bricklaying to teenaged Vernon, a mentally handicapped but musically talented young man. The irrepressible Wesley settles in and organizes a band that plays fast and loose with gospel music. He also dates a girl from campus and, with an infectious sense of humor, tweaks his nose at certain holier-than-thou Christian members of Ballard University. The novel offers a warm-hearted and comic poke at judgmental behavior and attitudes occasionally associated with some Christian denominations.

Other books by the same author:
The Floatplane Notebooks, 1988
Walking Across Egypt: A Novel, 1987
Raney: A Novel, 1985

Other books you might like:
Robert A. Heinlein, *Job: A Comedy of Justice*, 1984
Chaim Potok, *My Name Is Asher Lev*, 1972
Terry Pringle, *The Preacher's Boy: A Novel*, 1988

752

CLYDE EDGERTON

Raney: A Novel
(Chapel Hill, North Carolina: Algonquin, 1985)

Category: Comedy
Subject(s): Baptists; Marriage; Women
Age range(s): Young Adult-Adult
Major character(s): Raney Bell, Young Woman; Charles Shepherd, Librarian
Time period(s): 1970s (1975)
Locale(s): Listre, North Carolina

Summary: Edgerton's hilarious first novel chronicles Raney Bell's first year of marriage to Charles Shepherd. Their marriage is a study in contrasts. Charles is an Episcopalian from Atlanta, the New South; he is an only child. Raney is a dyed-in-the wool Southern Baptist from the small town South where family values are grounded in a literal view of *The Bible*. In a number of comic scenes, Raney's faith is sorely tested by Charles' views on sex, race, family, and religion.

Other books by the same author:
Redeye, 1995
Killer Diller: A Novel, 1991
Walking Across Egypt: A Novel, 1987

Other books you might like:
Pearl Abraham, *The Romance Reader*, 1995
  Though Abraham's novel is about a young Orthodox Jewish girl's coming-of-age, its themes and its humor are similar to *Raney.*
Connie May Fowler, *Before Women Had Wings*, 1995
Sheri Reynolds, *The Rapture of Canaan*, 1995
Lee Smith, *Saving Grace*, 1995
Rebecca Wells, *Little Altars Everywhere*, 1992

753

CLYDE EDGERTON

Walking Across Egypt: A Novel
(Chapel Hill, North Carolina: Algonquin Books, 1987)

Category: Gentle Reads
Subject(s): Baptists; Christian Life; Family Life
Age range(s): Young Adult-Adult
Major character(s): Mattie Rigsbee, Widow(er), Aged Person (78 years old); Wesley Benfield, Teenager, Orphan
Time period(s): 1990s
Locale(s): North Carolina

Summary: Mattie Rigsbee is a 78-year-old widow determined to live independently and rather impatiently waiting for her children to marry and provide her with grandchildren. Although she is active in her Baptist church and small-town community life, she is lonely and in need of someone to take care of. A stray dog fills the bill for awhile. Then along comes Wesley Benfield, juvenile delinquent and orphan, who needs Mattie as much as she needs him. Despite the disapproval of her neighbors, friends, family, and the local sherriff's office, Mattie sets her mind on being the grandmother Wesley has never had.

Other books by the same author:
Where Trouble Sleeps, 1997
Killer Diller: A Novel, 1991
Raney: A Novel, 1985

Other books you might like:
Robert A. Heinlein, *Job: A Comedy of Justice*, 1984
Jan Karon, *At Home in Mitford*, 1994
Terry Pringle, *The Preacher's Boy: A Novel*, 1988

754

GENE EDWARDS

The Birth

(Wheaton, Illinois: Tyndale House, 1991)

Category: Historical Fiction
Series: Chronicles of the Door
Subject(s): Scripture; Christianity
Age range(s): Young Adult-Adult
Major character(s): Mary, Biblical Figure, Historical Figure; Joseph, Historical Figure, Biblical Figure
Locale(s): Heaven

Summary: In his Chronicle of the Door series, Gene Edwards retells familiar stories from the Old and New Testaments of the Bible with a twist. Each episode is told from two perspectives: that of the angels in Heaven and that of the witnesses and participants on Earth. In *The Birth*, the author focuses on the story of the incarnation of Jesus and his birth.

Other books by the same author:
The Return, 1996
The Triumph, 1995
The Escape, 1993
The Beginning, 1992

Other books you might like:
Maria Isabel Hodges, *The Promise*, 1999
Marjorie Holmes, *The Messiah*, 1987
Marjorie Holmes, *Three From Galilee: The Young Man From Nazareth*, 1985
Marjorie Holmes, *Two From Galilee: A Love Story*, 1972
Charles R. Swindoll, *Suddenly One Morning: The Shopkeeper's Story*, 1998

755

ROGER ELWOOD

Angelwalk: A Modern Fable

(Westchester, Illinois: Crossway Books, 1988)

Category: Fantasy
Series: Angelwalk Trilogy
Subject(s): Angels; Good and Evil; Religion
Age range(s): Adult
Major character(s): Darien, Angel
Time period(s): 1980s
Locale(s): Earth; Heaven

Summary: Angel Darien doesn't believe that Lucifer should have been thrown out of Heaven. He is granted a chance to go to Earth himself to see what kinds of sadness and pain Lucifer caused. What he sees is both repulsive and horribly fascina-

ting. When his time on Earth comes to an end, he must decide between good and evil-and as he does, the powers of Heaven and Hell prepare for the confrontation of the end times.

Other books by the same author:
Where Angels Dare, 1999
Angels in Atlantic City: The New Angelwalk Novel, 1998
Darien: Guardian Angel of Jesus, 1994
Stedfast: Guardian Angel, 1992 (Angelwalk, #3)
Fallen Angel: A Novel, 1990 (Angelwalk, #2)

Other books you might like:
Randy Alcorn, *Deadline: A Novel*, 1994
Randy Alcorn, *Dominion*, 1996
Andrew M. Greeley, *Angel Fire*, 1988
C.S. Lewis, *Perelandra: A Novel*, 1944
Frank E. Peretti, *Piercing the Darkness*, 1989
Frank E. Peretti, *This Present Darkness*, 1986

756

ROGER ELWOOD

Fallen Angel: A Novel

(Dallas: Word, 1990)

Category: Fantasy
Series: Angelwalk Trilogy
Subject(s): Angels; Good and Evil; Religion
Age range(s): Adult
Major character(s): Observer, Angel
Time period(s): 1980s

Summary: In *Fallen Angel*, a dark angel named Observer is sent by Satan on a journey through time and space to document world events from Lucifer's point of view. From the Old Testament flood to the assassination of President Kennedy, from Auschwitz to the Middle East tensions of the late 20th century, Observer's chronicle of events is supposed to be a complete account of Satan's success at destroying God's creation. But as his work progresses, Observer begins to wonder if he has made a mistake in following Satan. More importantly, he wonders if he will ever have a chance to change his mind.

Other books by the same author:
Where Angels Dare, 1999
Angels in Atlantic City: The New Angelwalk Novel, 1998
Darien: Guardian Angel of Jesus, 1994
Stedfast: Guardian Angel, 1992 (Angelwalk, #3)
Angelwalk: A Modern Fable, 1988 (Angelwalk, #1)

Other books you might like:
Randy Alcorn, *Deadline: A Novel*, 1994
Randy Alcorn, *Dominion*, 1996
Andrew M. Greeley, *Angel Fire*, 1988
C.S. Lewis, *Perelandra: A Novel*, 1944
Frank E. Peretti, *Piercing the Darkness*, 1989
Frank E. Peretti, *This Present Darkness*, 1986

757

ROGER ELWOOD

Stedfast: Guardian Angel

(Dallas: Word, 1992)

Category: Fantasy
Series: Angelwalk Trilogy
Subject(s): Angels; Good and Evil; Religion
Age range(s): Adult
Major character(s): Stedfast, Angel
Time period(s): 1990s

Summary: In the third volume of the Angelwalk Trilogy, Roger Elwood tells a story of good and evil, of the seen and the unseen world of humans and angels, through the eyes of Stedfast, the rock-steady guardian angel. Once the guardian of Adam in the Garden of Eden, Stedfast is a guardian to souls passing from earthly life into heaven's peace. As people die, Stedfast-and other angels-take on the pain and sadness of their human souls so that they may enter the life of heaven free of tears. Stedfast is determined that Lucifer, who defeated him in the very first battle between good and evil in Eden, will take no more souls from their heavenly reward while Stedfast is on guardian duty.

Other books by the same author:
Where Angels Dare, 1999
Angels in Atlantic City: The New Angelwalk Novel, 1998
Darien: Guardian Angel of Jesus, 1994
Fallen Angel: A Novel, 1990 (Angelwalk, #2)
Angelwalk: A Modern Fable, 1988 (Angelwalk, #1)

Other books you might like:
Randy Alcorn, *Deadline: A Novel*, 1994
Randy Alcorn, *Dominion*, 1996
Andrew M. Greeley, *Angel Fire*, 1988
C.S. Lewis, *Perelandra: A Novel*, 1944
Frank E. Peretti, *Piercing the Darkness*, 1989
Frank E. Peretti, *This Present Darkness*, 1986

758

RICHARD PAUL EVANS

The Christmas Box

(New York: Simon & Schuster, 1993)

Category: Gentle Reads
Series: Christmas Box
Subject(s): Christmas; Gifts; Love
Age range(s): Young Adult-Adult
Major character(s): Mary Parkin, Widow(er), Aged Person; Richard, Narrator, Spouse (of Keri); Keri, Spouse (of Richard)
Time period(s): Indeterminate Past

Summary: A sentimental tale of Christmas-inspired revelations, *The Christmas Box* is narrated by Richard who, with his wife, has moved into the home of elderly widow Mary Parkin so that she might continue to live in her home with their assistance. In her lovely Victorian mansion, Mrs. Parkin sees trouble ahead for Richard, who puts in long hours at work to get ahead, at the expense of his young family. He disregards her hints, however, until it is nearly too late. The contents of a special Christmas Box reveal the depth of her concern, and help him discover what is really important in life while there is still time to do something about it.

Other books by the same author:
The Dance, 1999
The Locket, 1998
The Letter, 1997
Timepiece, 1996

Other books you might like:
Max Lucado, *The Christmas Cross: A Story about Finding Your Way Home for the Holidays*, 1998
Joe Wheeler, *Christmas in My Heart: A Third Treasury: Further Tales of Holiday Joy*, 1998

759

RICHARD PAUL EVANS

The Letter

(New York: Simon & Schuster, 1997)

Category: Gentle Reads
Series: Christmas Box
Subject(s): Relationships; Love; Family Life
Age range(s): Adult
Major character(s): David Parkin, Spouse (of Mary Anne); Mary Anne Parkin, Spouse (of David); Lawrence Flake, Friend (of David)
Time period(s): 1930s (1933)
Locale(s): Salt Lake; Chicago, Illinois

Summary: In the final volume of the Christmas Box collection, Richard Paul Evans picks up the Parkin family story twenty years after the death of David and Mary Anne Parkin's little daughter. David has closed himself off from his feelings and his loved ones during the decades since his unbearable loss, and as a result, Mary Anne finally leaves him, hoping to find the love and support she so desperately needs. In his despair, David deals with old feelings of abandonment and, having found a mysterious letter on his daughter's grave, decides to go to Chicago to search for the mother he hardly knew as a child. During his search, he confronts many issues in his life, until he is summoned back home when long-time friend Lawrence Flake has a stroke. The sentimental resolution will not disappoint fans of *The Christmas Box* and *Timepiece*, the first two books in the series.

Other books by the same author:
The Dance, 1999
The Locket, 1998
Timepiece, 1996
The Christmas Box, 1993

Other books you might like:
Max Lucado, *The Christmas Cross: A Story about Finding Your Way Home for the Holidays*, 1998
Julie Salamon, *The Christmas Tree*, 1996
Joe Wheeler, *Christmas in My Heart: A Third Treasury: Further Tales of Holiday Joy*, 1998

760

MICHAEL J. FARRELL

Papabile: The Man Who Would Be Pope: A Novel

(New York: Crossroad Publishing, 1998)

Category: Thrillers
Subject(s): Catholicism; Identity; Religious Life
Age range(s): Adult
Major character(s): Hugo Orvath, Religious (priest)
Time period(s): 20th century (1940s-1980s)
Locale(s): Europe (eastern European village); Rome, Italy

Summary: In a small village in an unspecified East European country, shortly after the end of World War II, a young boy dreams of doing something important within the Communist Party. Hugo Orvath is assigned by party leaders to attend seminary and become a Catholic priest, so he'll be able to work from within the church to promote the Communist agenda. He does so. A gifted writer and speaker, he is noticed favorably by the Vatican and is eventually appointed a Cardinal, putting him in line for the papacy. Unfortunately, though by this time his youthful zeal for Communism has subsided, it has not been replaced with a belief in God. Now he is caught in a fearsome web of conscience and consequences. He realizes that his deceptive actions have hurt the ones he loves most, and he himself is torn between duty and personal happiness. It is only after he has been elected pope that Orvath confronts his guilt, with unpredictable consequences.

Other books you might like:
Ignazio Silone, *Bread and Wine*, 1937
Morris L. West, *Eminence*, 1998
Morris L. West, *The Shoes of the Fisherman*, 1963

761

SUSAN FELDHAKE

In Love's Own Time

(Grand Rapids, Michigan: Zondervan, 1984)

Category: Romance
Series: Enduring Faith
Subject(s): Love; Frontier and Pioneer Life
Age range(s): Young Adult-Adult
Major character(s): Alton Wheeler, Drifter, Gambler; Sue Ellen Stone, Young Woman
Time period(s): 19th century
Locale(s): Illinois

Summary: In the wilderness of nineteenth-century Illinois, Alton Wheeler is a man to match the territory—a tough drifter and gambler who can be tamed by no laws. Sue Ellen Stone is a woman of faith whose loving ways make an impression on Wheeler. No matter how hard he tries, he cannot forget about her. Is he willing to do what it takes to spend his life with her?

Other books by the same author:
The Darkness and the Dawn, 1996
From This Day Forward, 1994
For Ever and Ever, 1993
Seasons of the Heart, 1986

Other books you might like:
Janette Oke, *A Bride for Donnigan*, 1993
Jane Peart, *Promise of the Valley*, 1995
Jane Peart, *Runaway Heart*, 1994
Lori Wick, *Where the Wild Rose Blooms*, 1996

762

JOHN FISCHER

Saint Ben

(Minneapolis: Bethany House, 1993)

Category: Gentle Reads
Subject(s): Friendship; Christianity; Adolescence
Age range(s): Young Adult
Major character(s): Jonathan, Narrator, Son (of a pastor); Ben, Friend (of Jonathan)
Time period(s): 1950s
Locale(s): Pasadena, California

Summary: This is a story of friendship between two boys and their unique journeys toward God. Jonathan is the son of a pastor, living in Pasadena, California, during the 1950s. Ben is his best friend, considered by many to be a trouble-maker. Jonathan tells a story of boyhood pranks, fun, secrets, and misfortune. Readers discover that there is more than one way to find God, and that spiritual growth and character development cannot always be measured by observers.

Other books by the same author:
The Saints' and Angels' Song, 1994 (sequel to *Saint Ben*)
Making Real What I Already Believe, 1991
Dark Horse: The Story of a Winner, 1983

Other books you might like:
Clair Bee, *Pitcher's Duel*, 1950
Paul Buchanan, *Anything You Can Do I Can Do Better*, 1998
Paul Hutchens, *The Chicago Adventure*, 1996
  Sugar Creek Gang, #5

763

ELLEN FRANKEL, Editor

The Classic Tales: 4,000 Years of Jewish Lore

(Northvale, New Jersey: J. Aronson, 1989)

Category: Morality Tales
Subject(s): Judaism; Folklore
Age range(s): Young Adult-Adult

Summary: To create this collection of 300 classic Jewish stories, Ellen Frankel has drawn folk tales and scripture-based stories from Talmudic, Hasidic, and Midrashic sources. Many of the tales date back 4,000 years. Together, the stories present a literary and spiritual anthology of age-old Jewish wisdom and culture.

Other books by the same author:
The Jewish Spirit: A Celebration in Stories and Art, 1997
The Encyclopedia of Jewish Symbols, 1992
Choosing to Be Chosen, 1985

Other books you might like:
Adele Geras, *A Treasury of Jewish Stories*, 1996
Fred Kogos, *1001 Yiddish Proverbs*, 1990
Julius Lester, *When the Beginning Began*, 1999
Stanley Mack, *The Story of the Jews: A 4,000 Year Adventure*, 1999

764

MARIANNE FREDRIKSSON

According to Mary Magdalene

(Charlottesville, Virginia: Hampton Roads Publishing, 1999)

Category: Historical Fiction
Subject(s): Scripture; Bible
Age range(s): Adult
Major character(s): Mary Magdalene, Historical Figure, Biblical Figure; Jesus, Historical Figure, Biblical Figure

Summary: Swedish novelist Marianne Fredriksson depicts the story of early Christianity from the perspective of Mary Magdalene, offering a feminist-revisionist perspective on the life and work of Jesus Christ. Mary's narrative suggests that if patriarchal societies hadn't controlled the written and oral accounts of the life of Christ, records would demonstrate that Jesus honored gender equality, and the Christian religion would be founded on principles of reconciliation, responsibility, and forgiveness, rather than on law and patriarchal power.

Other books by the same author:
Simon's Family, 1999
Hanna's Daughters, 1998

Other books you might like:
Mary Ellen Ashcroft, *The Magdalene Gospel*, 1995
David W. Frasure, *Mary: A Novel*, 1996
Graham Joyce, *Requiem*, 1998
Brenton G. Yorgason, *The Carpenter's Son: Letters From Magdala*, 1995

765

ELIZABETH GIBSON

The Water Is Wide: A Novel of Northern Ireland

(Grand Rapids, Michigan: Zondervan, 1984)

Category: Gentle Reads
Subject(s): Religious Conflict; Interpersonal Relations; College Life
Age range(s): Young Adult-Adult
Major character(s): Kate, Student—College; Deirdre, Student—College; Sheila, Student—College; Roger, Student—College; Liam, Student—College; Jack, Student—College
Time period(s): 1960s; 1970s
Locale(s): Ulster, Northern Ireland

Summary: *The Water is Wide* is set in Northern Ireland during the troubled years of the late 1960s and early 1970s. Six students at the New University of Ulster-Deirdre, Jack, Kate, Liam, Roger, and Sheila-try to overcome their differences and find common ground amidst the religious and political turmoil of the age. Sorting out their labels—Christian, Catholic, Protestant, Irish, male, female—the classmates seek their identities and struggle with whether or not individual reconciliation can transcend political differences and forces beyond their control.

Awards the book has won:
Gold Medallion Book Award, Fiction, 1985

Other books by the same author:
The Daisy Ring, 1995
Fragile Dreams and Old Photographs, 1991
Men of Kent, 1988

Other books you might like:
Jennifer C. Cornell, *Departures*, 1995
Donna Fletcher Crow, *The Banks of the Boyne: A Quest for a Christian Ireland*, 1998
Bernard MacLaverty, *Grace Notes*, 1997

766

JOSEPH F. GIRZONE

Joshua

(New York: Collier Books, 1987)

Category: Gentle Reads
Series: Joshua
Subject(s): Christianity; Small Town Life; Religious Conflict
Age range(s): Young Adult-Adult
Major character(s): Joshua, Artisan (woodcarver)
Time period(s): 20th century
Locale(s): New York

Summary: Joshua is an unassuming woodcarver who lives simply in a little cabin outside a small town in New York. He sells his carvings to make a living and tries to make peace with his new neighbors, who are a little puzzled by this stranger in their midst. Joshua visits churches of all denominations, sharing his message of God as the source of serenity, strength, liberation, and all knowledge, and he pointedly rebukes church leaders whose ministries exclude others through prejudice and exclusivity. Ultimately, Joshua is called to explain himself at the Vatican, where his true identity is made clear. Joseph F. Girzone's parable about a modern-day return of Jesus was first published privately in 1982. Its popularity led to commercial publication five years later and a number of additional stories about Joshua.

Other books by the same author:
Joshua, the Homecoming, 1999 (Joshua)
Joshua and the City, 1995 (Joshua)
Joshua in the Holy Land, 1992 (Joshua)
The Shepherd, 1990 (Joshua)
Joshua and the Children, 1989 (Joshua)

Other books you might like:
Frederick Buechner, *The Book of Bebb*, 1979
John Bunyan, *The Pilgrim's Progress*, 1678-1684
James Byron Huggins, *A Wolf Story*, 1993
Laurie Beth Jones, *Jesus in Blue Jeans: A Practical Guide to Everyday Spirituality*, 1997
Max Lucado, *When God Whispers Your Name*, 1994

767

JOSEPH F. GIRZONE

Joshua and the Children

(New York: Macmillan, 1989)

Category: Gentle Reads
Series: Joshua
Subject(s): Christianity; Small Town Life; Religious Conflict
Age range(s): Young Adult-Adult
Major character(s): Joshua, Artisan (woodcarver)
Locale(s): Northern Ireland

Summary: In this sequel to *Joshua*, Joshua appears in another village where hatred and mistrust result in a violent atmosphere and only the children are open enough to receive Joshua's message of trust and love. The long-standing division between the adults gradually melts as the children lead them into a future of peace based on the message of the stranger, Joshua.

Other books by the same author:
Joshua, the Homecoming, 1999 (Joshua)
Joshua and the City, 1995 (Joshua)
Joshua in the Holy Land, 1992 (Joshua)
The Shepherd, 1990 (Joshua)
Joshua, 1987 (Joshua)

Other books you might like:
Frederick Buechner, *The Book of Bebb*, 1979
John Bunyan, *The Pilgrim's Progress*, 1678-1684
James Byron Huggins, *A Wolf Story*, 1993
Laurie Beth Jones, *Jesus in Blue Jeans: A Practical Guide to Everyday Spirituality*, 1997
Max Lucado, *When God Whispers Your Name*, 1994

768

JOSEPH F. GIRZONE

Joshua and the City

(New York: Doubleday, 1995)

Category: Gentle Reads
Series: Joshua
Subject(s): Christianity; Poverty; City Life
Age range(s): Young Adult-Adult
Major character(s): Joshua, Artisan (woodcarver)
Time period(s): 20th century
Locale(s): United States

Summary: In the fourth book chronicling the intervention of Joshua in modern lives, the protagonist is found in a contemporary metropolitan area, living and working among people who need his healing touch, from prostitutes and troubled street teens to wealthy folks whose purpose in life isn't clear. Joshua's gentle spirit and good works are directed toward the problems of today's inner-city societies, which include drug addiction, poverty, and street crime.

Other books by the same author:
Joshua, the Homecoming, 1999 (Joshua)
Joshua in the Holy Land, 1992 (Joshua)
The Shepherd, 1990 (Joshua)
Joshua and the Children, 1989 (Joshua)

Joshua, 1987 (Joshua)

Other books you might like:
Frederick Buechner, *The Book of Bebb*, 1979
John Bunyan, *The Pilgrim's Progress*, 1678-1684
James Byron Huggins, *A Wolf Story*, 1993
Laurie Beth Jones, *Jesus in Blue Jeans: A Practical Guide to Everyday Spirituality*, 1997
Max Lucado, *When God Whispers Your Name*, 1994

769

JOSEPH F. GIRZONE

Joshua in the Holy Land

(New York: Macmillan, 1992)

Category: Gentle Reads
Series: Joshua
Subject(s): Christianity; Religious Conflict
Age range(s): Young Adult-Adult
Major character(s): Joshua, Artisan (woodcarver)
Time period(s): 20th century
Locale(s): Jerusalem, Israel

Summary: *Joshua in the Holy Land* finds the modern-day savior back in the land of his earthly birth, where the same hatreds that divided one tribe from another still fuel violence between factions in towns such as Nazareth, Bethany, and Capernaum. Joshua's good works for others include returning a lost lamb to a sheik and healing the sheik's daughter of a venomous snakebite. These gestures earn Joshua the trust of a prominent Arab leader and result in his sharing his message of reconciliation with Christians, Jews, and Moslems.

Other books by the same author:
Joshua, the Homecoming, 1999 (Joshua)
Joshua and the City, 1995 (Joshua)
The Shepherd, 1990 (Joshua)
Joshua and the Children, 1989 (Joshua)
Joshua, 1987 (Joshua)

Other books you might like:
Frederick Buechner, *The Book of Bebb*, 1979
John Bunyan, *The Pilgrim's Progress*, 1678-1684
James Byron Huggins, *A Wolf Story*, 1993
Laurie Beth Jones, *Jesus in Blue Jeans: A Practical Guide to Everyday Spirituality*, 1997
Max Lucado, *When God Whispers Your Name*, 1994

770

GAIL GODWIN

Evensong

(New York: Ballantine Books, 1999)

Category: Gentle Reads
Subject(s): Religion; Marriage; Clergy
Age range(s): Adult
Major character(s): Margaret Gower Bonner, Religious (Episcopal rector), Spouse (of Adrian); Adrian Bonner, Religious (chaplain at a boys' school), Spouse (of Margaret); Chase Zorn, 16-Year-Old, Student
Time period(s): 1990s

Locale(s): High Balsam, North Carolina

Summary: *Evensong* is the story of a woman who followed in her father's footsteps and became an Episcopal parish priest. Margaret Bonner is the rector of All Saints Episcopal Church in High Balsam, North Carolina. She finds herself caught between family concerns and parish needs. Her husband is the chaplain and headmaster of a local high school, which is where troubled student Chase Zorn has found the one person in his life who makes it his mission to turn the young man around-Adrian Bonner. Church and community circumstances, plus ongoing marital tensions complicate matters for Margaret and Adrian.

Other books by the same author:
The Good Husband, 1994
Father Melancholy's Daughter, 1991
A Southern Family, 1987
Dream Children: Stories, 1976

Other books you might like:
Jan Karon, *The Mitford Series*, 1994-
Jan Karon, *A New Song*, 1999
Lee Smith, *News of the Spirit*, 1997
Lee Smith, *Saving Grace*, 1995

771

GAIL GODWIN

Father Melancholy's Daughter

(New York: Morrow, 1991)

Category: Gentle Reads
Subject(s): Family Relations; Religion; Fathers and Daughters
Age range(s): Adult
Major character(s): Margaret Gower, Daughter (of Walter); Walter Gower, Religious (Episcopal priest), Father (of Margaret)
Locale(s): North Carolina

Summary: Author Gail Godwin explores themes of loss, abandonment, and father-daughter relationships in *Father Melancholy's Daughter*. Margaret Gower is a young woman who was raised by her father, the rector of St. Cuthbert's Episcopal parish in Romulus, North Carolina, after her mother abandoned the family then was killed in an accident not long afterward. Margaret has always struggled to figure out where she fits into the world. Her father, a deeply religious man, is prone to depression, and he, too, seems to be on a perpetual quest to discover his place in the world. The question that seems to form a common theme through their lives is, "How can one learn to live a decent, passionate, and honorable life?"

Other books by the same author:
Evensong, 1999
The Good Husband, 1994
A Southern Family, 1987
Dream Children: Stories, 1976

Other books you might like:
Jan Karon, *The Mitford Series*, 1994-
Jan Karon, *A New Song*, 1999
Lee Smith, *News of the Spirit*, 1997
Lee Smith, *Saving Grace*, 1995

772

REBECCA GOLDSTEIN

Mazel

(New York: Viking, 1995)

Category: Gentle Reads
Subject(s): Judaism; Family Saga; Family Relations
Age range(s): Young Adult-Adult
Major character(s): Sasha Saunders, Actress, Mother (Chloe's), Grandmother (Phoebe's); Chloe Saunders, Daughter (Sasha's), Professor, Mother (Phoebe's); Phoebe Saunders, Daughter (Chloe's), Scientist
Locale(s): New York, New York; Warsaw, Poland; Lipton, New Jersey

Summary: *Mazel* tells the story of three generations of accomplished Jewish women, the youngest of whom chooses the traditional lifestyle rejected by her grandmother and never considered by her mother. Sasha, the eldest of the clan, struck out on her own to become a stage actress in Poland. Once she settled in New York City, she stayed and enjoyed a life that kept the tradition suburban Jewish life at arm's length. Her daughter Chloe was raised as a free spirit who pursued motherhood in an unconventional way and raised her own daughter Phoebe to be a strong, independent soul. It is Phoebe's decision to marry into a most conventional Jewish American family that brings out the stories behind the lives and choices of the two generations that preceded her. In flashbacks and memories, the scene shifts from the city to the suburbs to the Old Country and back again in a gentle tale of women, spirituality, social and personal choices, and changing times.

Other books by the same author:
Strange Attractors, 1994
The Dark Sister, 1993

Other books you might like:
Pearl Abraham, *Giving Up America*, 1998
Pearl Abraham, *The Romance Reader*, 1995
Allegra Goodman, *The Family Markowitz*, 1996
Naomi Ragen, *The Ghost of Hannah Mendes*, 1998
Anne Richardson Roiphe, *Lovingkindness*, 1987

773

ALLEGRA GOODMAN

Kaaterskill Falls: A Novel

(New York: Dial Press, 1998)

Category: Gentle Reads
Subject(s): Judaism; Religious Life; Small Town Life
Age range(s): Young Adult-Adult
Major character(s): Elizabeth Shulman, Spouse, Mother; Rav Kirshner, Religious (rabbi), Aged Person
Time period(s): 1970s (1976-1978)
Locale(s): Kaaterskill Falls, New York

Summary: The "summer people" in Kaaterskill Falls are a community of Orthodox Jewish families who spend their summers away from the heat and oppression of the city. Allegra Goodman creates a richly textured fabric of individuals whose relationships to each other and their Orthodox religious tradition take on multiple layers. Reflective narrative reveals that some are devoted, some are detached, and some are merely on the cusp of questioning the structure of their lives under the strict guidance of elderly Rabbi Rav Kirshner. The most predominant point of view is that of Elizabeth Shulman, a 34-year-old mother of five whose contemplation of her circumstances causes her to begin gently nudging at the boundaries. Over the course of two summers, change inevitably winds its way slowly through the Orthodox community, where time only seems to stand still, yet the safety and comfortable security of life in a loving community with a long heritage remain.

Other books by the same author:
The Family Markowitz, 1996
Total Immersion: Stories, 1989

Other books you might like:
Pearl Abraham, *Giving Up America*, 1998
Pearl Abraham, *The Romance Reader*, 1995
Rebecca Goldstein, *Mazel*, 1995
Naomi Ragen, *The Ghost of Hannah Mendes*, 1998
Anne Richardson Roiphe, *Lovingkindness*, 1987

774

ROBERT GRAVES

King Jesus
(New York: Minerva, 1946)

Category: Historical Fiction
Subject(s): Christianity; Bible
Age range(s): Adult

Summary: Robert Graves' 1946 novel *King Jesus* reflects a high degree of biblical knowledge, research, and sensitivity toward (if not agreement with) the basic tenets of Christian belief. Graves successfully integrates what is generally known about his subject, Jesus, with aspects rooted solely in the author's imagination. Despite Graves' unconventional and occasionally controversial departures from the familiar story of Jesus in this novel, his tone and the story action always remain respectful toward the man upon whom one of the major Western religions is based.

Other books by the same author:
The Golden Fleece, 1944
I, Claudius: From the Autobiography of Tiberius Claudius, Born B.C. 10, Murdered and Deified A.D. 54, 1934

Other books you might like:
Sholem Asch, *The Nazarene*, 1939
Jim Crace, *Quarantine*, 1997
Nikos Kazantzakis, *The Last Temptation of Christ*, 1960

775

ANDREW M. GREELEY

Angel Light: An Old-Fashioned Love Story
(New York: Forge, 1995)

Category: Romance
Subject(s): Fantasy; Angels
Age range(s): Adult

Major character(s): Toby Tobin, Computer Expert, Cousin (distant, of Sara); Sara Anne Elizabeth Tobin, Cousin (distant, of Toby); Raphaella, Angel, Travel Agent
Locale(s): United States; Ireland

Summary: Toby Tobin is a man with a mission not his own. The nearly 25-year-old computer hacker has just one month to travel to Ireland, court and marry a distant cousin, and handle a few other mildly disconcerting details in order to inherit ten million dollars, as promised in his great-uncle's will. The problem is, Toby doesn't care much about inheriting the money and he certainly isn't interested in doing what the will directs him to. Urged on by the family, however, he goes about making travel plans with the help of Raphaella, a most unusual travel agent who also happens to be an angel. With the help of this self-appointed guardian angel, Toby manages to connect with his beautiful cousin Sara, but not without mishaps and side adventures along the way.

Other books by the same author:
Irish Lace, 1996
Irish Gold, 1994
Angel Fire, 1988
Thy Brother's Wife, 1982

Other books you might like:
Walter Keady, *Mary McGreevy*, 1998
Bodie Thoene, *Of Men & of Angels: A Novel*, 1998
Bodie Thoene, *Only the River Runs Free*, 1997

776

GRAHAM GREENE

The Power and the Glory
(London: W. Heinemann, 1940)

Category: Historical Fiction; Mainstream Fiction
Subject(s): Catholicism; Martyrs; Revolution
Age range(s): Adult
Major character(s): Whiskey Priest, Religious; Lieutenant of Police, Police Officer
Time period(s): 1910s
Locale(s): Mexico

Summary: Graham Greene's *The Power and the Glory* was first published in the United States as *The Labyrinthine Ways*. Set during the Mexican Revolution of the early 20th century, it is the story of the last Roman Catholic priest in Mexico, who is being hunted by a Communist police lieutenant. Although the story is set in political circumstances that result in the death of the priest, Greene focuses on the inner struggle of the man his people call ''the whisky priest'' due to his advanced alcoholism. The man who feels compelled to perform his clerical duties has broken most of his vows and considers himself unworthy of whatever grace has come his way in life. This personal conflict continues to the very end, when he ultimately finds redemption in martyrdom.

Other books by the same author:
The End of the Affair, 1951
The Heart of the Matter, 1948
Brighton Rock, 1938

Other books you might like:

Mariano Azuela, *The Underdogs: A Novel of the Mexican Revolution*, 1962
  E. Munguia, translator; J.C. Orozco, illustrator
Harriet Doerr, *Stones for Ibarra*, 1984
William X. Kienzle, *No Greater Love*, 1999
Malcolm Lowry, *Under the Volcano*, 1947
Michael F. McCauley, *In the Name of the Father: Stories about Priests*, 1983
Edwin O'Connor, *The Edge of Sadness*, 1961

777

ELGIN GROSECLOSE

The Kiowa

(Elgin, Illinois: D.C. Cook, 1978)

Category: Historical Fiction
Subject(s): Indians of North America; Religion; Culture
Age range(s): Young Adult-Adult
Major character(s): Ileeta, Hostage (from Mexico); Sanjak, Indian (Kiowa leader)
Time period(s): 19th century (1850s-1870s)
Locale(s): Southwest

Summary: Sanjak is a leader in the Kiowa tribe of native North Americans preceding the Civil War in the United States. Similar in nature to the Comanche, the Kiowa are an aggressive people, given to expanding their influence rather forcefully. During raids across the border in Mexico, Sanjak and his warriors bring back horses, blankets and supplies, and, quite often, women. Ileeta is one such Mexican woman. Sanjak is fascinated by the "medicine" she wears around her neck—a gold crucifix—and as time goes by, he is drawn into her world of faith and Christian belief, which becomes a comfort to him during an unexpected tragedy. Meanwhile, confrontations between the Kiowa and the encroaching European Americans who forged the West are increasing, and Kiowa finds himself caught in a clash of cultures that is characterized by lack of communication and understanding. Reflecting the realities of history in the region, the Kiowas' ways are no match for the bullets and frontier law of the white man. *The Kiowa* is a poignant tale of love, faith, injustice, and redemption.

Awards the book has won:
Gold Medallion Book Award, Fiction, 1979

Other books by the same author:
Olympia: A Novel, 1980
The Scimitar of Saladin, 1956
Carmelite, a Novel, 1955
Ararat, 1939
The Persian Journey of the Reverend Ashley Wishard and His Servant Fathi, 1937

Other books you might like:
Maurice Boyd, *Kiowa Voices: Ceremonial Dance, Ritual and Song*, 1981
Maurice Boyd, *Kiowa Voices: Myths, Legends and Folktales*, 1983
Isabel Crawford, *Kiowa: A Woman Missionary in Indian Territory*, 1998

new edition of *Kiowa: The History of a Blanket Indian Mission*, 1915
Cynthia Haseloff, *The Kiowa Verdict: A Western Story*, 1997

778

RON HANSEN

Mariette in Ecstasy

(New York: E. Burlingame Books, 1991)

Category: Mystery
Subject(s): Catholicism; Mysticism
Age range(s): Adult
Major character(s): Mariette Baptiste, 17-Year-Old, Religious (postulant)
Time period(s): 1900s (1906)
Locale(s): New York

Summary: It is late summer 1906 in rural, upstate New York, and 17-year-old Mariette Baptiste has just entered the local convent, purely by her choice, out of her unusually passionate love for Jesus. The Sisters of the Crucifixion spend their days inside the convent of Our Lady of Afflictions in farm work, religious study, and structured prayer. It is a highly ordered life disrupted by Mariette's intense devotion and quietly emotional Christian experience that begins to manifest itself in trances from which she awakens with unexplained bleeding from her hands, feet, and side-stigmata, to reflect the wounds inflicted on Christ during the crucifixion. *Mariette in Ecstasy* is the richly-textured story of the nuns' response to this mystical phenomenon, its effects on the cloistered community, and the results of an official church investigation into Mariette's uncommon religious experience.

Other books by the same author:
Hitler's Niece: A Novel, 1999
Atticus: A Novel, 1996
Mexican Mystery, 1993
Nebraska Stories, 1989
Desperadoes: A Novel, 1979

Other books you might like:
Katherine Hulme, *Nun's Story*, 1956
Mary Pat Kelly, *Special Intentions*, 1997
Candace M. Robb, *The Nun's Tale*, 1996

779

WARREN HANSON, Author/Illustrator

The Next Place

(Minneapolis: Waldman House, 1999)

Category: Gentle Reads
Subject(s): Afterlife; Children; Death
Age range(s): Children-Adult

Summary: *The Next Place* offers an inspirational non-sectarian look at what life after death might be like. Despite its status as a picture book, *The Next Place* is challenging on both an intellectual and a spiritual level. Author and illustrator Warren Hanson prompts readers to contemplate the relationships between life on earth and life after death, and encourages readers to think beyond their stereotypes of heaven as either a place or a concept. The book is already becoming a favorite with readers of all ages who are grieving the death of loved ones.

Awards the book has won:
Midwest Independent Publishers Association Book Award, Spiritual, 1999

Other books by the same author:
Older Love, 1999
A is for Adult: An Alphabet Book for Grown-Ups, 1993

Other books you might like:
Leo Buscaglia, *The Fall of Freddie the Leaf*, 1982
Pat Palmer, *I Wish I Could Hold Your Hand—: A Child's Guide to Grief and Loss*, 1994
Susan Varley, *Badger's Parting Gifts*, 1984

780

JON HASSLER

North of Hope: A Novel
(New York: Ballantine Books, 1990)

Category: Biographical Fiction
Subject(s): Catholicism; Ministry; Indians of North America
Age range(s): Adult
Major character(s): Father Frank Healy, Religious; Libby Girard, Friend (of Father Healy)
Locale(s): Minnesota (Basswood Reservation)

Summary: After 20 years of parish ministry, Father Frank Healy is struggling with doubts about his vocation, in spite of his love for the church. Seeking solace in his family roots, Father Healy requests an assignment in the parish where he grew up, where he will also minister to the Ojibway on the Basswood Reservation. Faith, hope, and love, all central themes of Father Healy's faith, are also central themes in this story. However, societal problems—including alcoholism, drug abuse, murder, and widespread despair—test the priest's solid values and commitment to his ministry, as does the unexpected return to his life of the woman he has loved since he was a boy.

Other books by the same author:
Grand Opening, 1987
Simon's Night, 1979

Other books you might like:
Jim Kraus, *Journey to the Crimson Sea*, 1997
    Terri Kraus, co-author
J.F. Powers, *Morte d'Urban*, 1962
J.F. Powers, *Wheat That Springeth Green*, 1988

781

JON HASSLER

Simon's Night
(New York: Atheneum, 1979)

Category: Gentle Reads
Subject(s): Aging; Retirement; Independence
Age range(s): Adult

Major character(s): Simon Peter Shea, Professor (retired), Aged Person
Locale(s): Minnesota

Summary: *Simon's Night* tells the story of a retired professor who fears he is unable to live alone any longer after he accidentally causes a fire in his home. Simon Peter Shea decides to commit himself to the Norman Home, where the elderly receive full-time supervision and care. Within a few days, however, he comes to the realization that he has made a big mistake. If he stays on at the Norman Home, he will quickly wither and die, both mentally and physically. The novel explores Simon's attempts, with the support and encouragement of a young doctor, to regain his independence and find the balance he needs to continue living productively and happily. *Simon's Night* offers an uplifting tale of courage, spirit, creativity, and wisdom during a major life transition.

Other books by the same author:
The Dean's List, 1997
North of Hope: A Novel, 1990
Grand Opening, 1987
A Green Journey, 1985
The Love Hunter, 1981

Other books you might like:
Robert Cormier, *Take Me Where the Good Times Are*, 1991
Barbara M. Dickinson, *A Rebellious House*, 1997
Virginia Myers, *Vessels of Honor*, 1995
Daniel R. Seagren, *I'll Retire Tomorrow*, 1997

782

JON HENDERSON

Tigers & Dragons
(Wheaton, Illinois: Tyndale House, 1993)

Category: Thrillers
Subject(s): Christianity; Buddhism; Religious Conflict
Age range(s): Young Adult-Adult

Summary: In 1992, Jon Henderson made an extended visit to Tibet. The story he tells in *Tigers & Dragons* is based on his experiences in that country, speaking with natives living under the hand of Chinese Communism and persecution. The novel's title and story line are based directly on a real underground insurrectionist group called the Tigers and Dragons whose dangerous mission is to fight to restore freedom and independence once again to "The Sky People."

Other books by the same author:
Nightwatch, 1995
Tourmaline, 1992

Other books you might like:
Eleanor Cooney, *Shangri-la: The Return to the World of Lost Horizon*, 1996
Alexandra David-Neel, *Magic and Mystery in Tibet*, 1932
Charlotte Painter, *Conjuring Tibet*, 1996

783

JON HENDERSON

Tourmaline

(Wheaton, Illinois: Tyndale House, 1992)

Category: Thrillers
Subject(s): Romance
Age range(s): Young Adult-Adult
Major character(s): Jake MacIntyre, Journalist
Time period(s): 20th century (late)
Locale(s): Cairo, Egypt

Summary: Jake MacIntyre is a photojournalist covering an important political story in Cairo, Egypt. While shooting rolls of film related to the signing of a Mideast peace treaty, he inadvertently finds himself on the trail of an assassination plot. After he gets photographs of the crime, Jake is desperate to protect himself and the evidence. One thing leads to another, and suddenly other innocent people are involved, in this page-turning suspense with a Christian perspective.

Other books by the same author:
Nightwatch, 1995
Tigers & Dragons, 1993

Other books you might like:
Calvin Miller, *Symphony in Sand*, 1990
Ray Rosenbaum, *Condors*, 1995
Bodie Thoene, *The Gates of Zion*, 1986

784

HERMANN HESSE

Siddhartha

(New York: New Directions, 1951)

Category: Morality Tales; Mainstream Fiction
Subject(s): Mysticism; Hinduism; Buddhism
Age range(s): Young Adult-Adult
Major character(s): Siddhartha, Young Man; Govinda, Friend (of Siddhartha)
Locale(s): India

Summary: *Siddhartha* is an allegorical tale of a young mystic in search of Nirvana. His quest takes him through various stages of earthly life as a wanderer, a lover, a father, a merchant, and a loner. He realizes again and again throughout the journey that it is only by experiencing life's pain that one can hope to achieve the ultimate state of Nirvana. His friend Govinda sets out on the journey with him, takes his own paths, and ultimately joins Siddhartha near the end of their earthly roads, having found what he was seeking as well. Although Siddhartha was originally published in Germany in 1922, this first English version, translated by Hilda Rosner, was published in 1951.

Other books by the same author:
Narcissus and Goldmund, 1968
The Journey to the East, 1957
Steppenwolf, 1927

Other books you might like:
Padmasri Adiccabuandhu, *Siddhartha and the Swan*, 1999

David J. Kalupahana, *Way of Siddhartha: A Life of the Buddha*, 1982
U.R. Anantha Murthy, *Samskara: A Rite for a Dead Man*, 1976
A.K. Ramanujan, translator

785

LIZ CURTIS HIGGS
NANCY MUNGER, Illustrator

The Parable of the Lily

(Nashville: Thomas Nelson, 1997)

Category: Morality Tales
Subject(s): Children; Nature; Christianity
Age range(s): Children
Major character(s): Maggie, Child, Daughter (of the Farmer); Farmer, Father (Maggie's)

Summary: Maggie is a little girl who doesn't know what to make of the gift she has received: a box of dirt and some instructions for doing something with it in the springtime. When the early days of spring arrive, she tosses the box out the door. Much to her surprise, something interesting happens to that pile of dirt. When Easter arrives, there is a beautiful lily in the yard growing from the gift she had discarded. Along with the story of Maggie, her father, and the lily, the illustrations and text tell a parallel story about Jesus, his death, and his resurrection-new life, like the lily-on the day now commemorated as Easter.

Awards the book has won:
Gold Medallion Book Award, Pre-School Children, 1998

Other books by the same author:
''While Shepherds Washed Their Flocks'' and Other Funny Things Kids Say and Do, 1998 (Dennis Hill, illustrator)
Bad Girls of the Bible and What We Can Learn From Them, 1997
The Pumpkin Patch Parable, 1995 (Nancy Munger, illustrator)
The Pine Tree Parable, 1997 (Nancy Munger, illustrator)
The Sunflower Parable, 1997 (Nancy Munger, illustrator)

Other books you might like:
Brian Cochran, *The Easter Promise*, 1998
Angela Elwell Hunt, *The Tale of Three Trees: A Traditional Folktale*, 1989
Lori Walburg, *The Legend of the Easter Egg*, 1999

786

OSCAR HIJUELOS

Mr. Ives' Christmas

(New York: HarperCollins, 1995)

Category: Gentle Reads; Mainstream Fiction
Subject(s): Christmas; Family Life; Spirituality
Age range(s): Adult
Major character(s): Edward Ives, Artist, Spouse (of Annie); Annie Ives, Teacher, Spouse (of Edward)
Time period(s): 20th century
Locale(s): New York, New York

Summary: The story of Edward Ives—orphan, artist, husband, and father—unfolds on several levels in this gentle tale that has been compared to Charles Dickens' *A Christmas Carol*. After a difficult early life, Ives makes his way comfortably in the world, settling into work he enjoys, marrying, and raising a much-loved son. In 1967, however, his son is murdered on the street a few days before Christmas. No matter how much time passes, Ives can never quite find the way to deal with his grief, which causes him much trouble in his marriage and his life in general. The novel ends at Christmastime in the 1990s, and somehow, magically or mystically, the grief that has overshadowed Edward Ives' life loosens its hold on him.

Other books by the same author:
The Empress of the Splendid Season, 1999
The Fourteen Sisters of Emilio Montez O'Brien: A Novel, 1993
The Mambo Kings Play Songs of Love, 1989
Our House in the Last World: A Novel, 1983

Other books you might like:
Charles Dickens, *A Christmas Carol, in Prose: Being a Ghost Story of Christmas*, 1843
John Fante, *1933 Was a Bad Year*, 1985
Paul L. Gaus, *Blood of the Prodigal*, 1999
Chaim Potok, *The Chosen*, 1976
Dale C. Willard, *My Son, My Brother, My Friend: A Novel in Letters*, 1995

787

GRACE LIVINGSTON HILL

The Beloved Stranger

(Philadelphia, J.B. Lippincott, 1933)

Category: Romance
Subject(s): Marriage
Age range(s): Young Adult-Adult
Major character(s): Sherrill, Bride; Carter McArthur, Bridegroom; Graham Copeland, Young Man
Time period(s): 1930s

Summary: On Sherrill's wedding day, things are going as planned until she sees Carter McArthur, the man she is about to marry, kissing another girl. Suddenly she changes her mind and sends the other woman to the altar in her place. Outside the church, in the midst of her turmoil over the way things are turning out, she falls into the arms of Graham Copeland, a stranger who seems to have appeared out of nowhere. He stays by her side throughout the ceremony and the reception and before long he has won her heart. Grace Livingston Hill's novels typically feature high moral standards and characters whose actions are based on their personal faith in Christ.

Other books by the same author:
Girl to Come Home To, 1945
Christmas Bride, 1934
Happiness Hill, 1932
The Angel of His Presence, 1902

Other books you might like:
Irene Brand, *To Love and Honor*, 1999
Melody Carlson, *Awakening Heart*, 1998
Sherrie Lord, *Airwaves*, 1998

Penelope Stokes, *Home Fires Burning*, 1996

788

GRACE LIVINGSTON HILL

Crimson Roses

(Philadelphia: J.B. Lippincott, 1928)

Category: Romance
Subject(s): Music and Musicians; Love
Age range(s): Young Adult-Adult
Major character(s): Marion Warren, Young Woman, Clerk (store); Jeff Lyman, Young Man, Wealthy

Summary: Marion Warren is all alone in the world now. Her parents have died, her brother has abandoned her, she has lost the home she lived in for so many years, and she must figure out how to make ends meet on her own. But years of nursing her aging parents have taught her patience, endurance, and courage. Although her salary as a store clerk can barely support it, she buys a season ticket to the symphony orchestra. And every week, without a hint as to how they get there, she finds one beautiful, red rose on her assigned seat when she arrives. Who could be sending these? Surely it's not wealthy, handsome Jeff Lyman, is it? Prolific novelist Grace Livingston Hill wrote light, romantic fiction, often featuring godly young women like Marion who endured hardships quietly and were rewarded with worthy romances.

Other books by the same author:
Girl to Come Home To, 1945
Christmas Bride, 1934
The Beloved Stranger, 1933
Happiness Hill, 1932
The Angel of His Presence, 1902

Other books you might like:
Irene Brand, *To Love and Honor*, 1999
Marion Duckworth, *Remembering the Roses*, 1998
Robin Jones Gunn, *Secrets*, 1999
Sally John, *In the Shadow of Love*, 1998

789

GRACE LIVINGSTON HILL

Silver Wings

(Philadelphia: Lippincott, 1931)

Category: Romance
Subject(s): Grief; Love; Christianity
Age range(s): Young Adult-Adult
Major character(s): Amory Lorrimer, Secretary; Mrs. Whitney, Socialite

Summary: Amory Lorrimer watches Ted's plane take off over the snowy Alaska landscape, not knowing whether she will ever see him again. She returns home to her job as Mrs. Whitney's social secetary, but she doesn't enjoy being in the snobby, sophisticated crowd that surrounds her. She dislikes the way the young women toy with the affections of Mrs. Whitney's nephew, a handsome young minister. Fortunately, he holds his own and is a comfort to Amory when news arrives that Ted's plane is lost in the Arctic snows. In spite of her faith and daily prayers, Amory wonders, will she ever be happy again?

Other books by the same author:
Girl to Come Home To, 1945
Christmas Bride, 1934
The Beloved Stranger, 1933
Happiness Hill, 1932
The Angel of His Presence, 1902

Other books you might like:
Terri Blackstock, *Broken Wings*, 1998
Lynn Bullock, *Dalton's Dilemma*, 1998
Robin Jones Gunn, *Closer than Ever*, 1999
Yvonne Lehman, *A Fighting Chance*, 1997

790

GRACE LIVINGSTON HILL

Where Two Ways Met

(Philadelphia: J.B. Lippincott, 1947)

Category: Romance
Subject(s): Real Estate; Love; Conduct of Life
Age range(s): Young Adult-Adult
Major character(s): Paige Madison, Real Estate Agent; Reva Chalmers, Daughter (of Paige's boss); June Culbertson, Daughter (of Paige's minister)

Summary: In *Where Two Ways Met*, a young man takes center stage. Paige Madison is home from the war and ready to start a promising career in real estate, but he runs into ethical conflicts with his boss, an unscrupulous man who is used to getting his way. He expects Paige to do what he is told to do, regardless of conflicts with his religious beliefs. The boss's daughter, Reva Chalmers, has her eye on the handsome new addition to the family business, and she's used to getting what she wants, too. Paige has met the minister's daughter, June Culbertson, who becomes his friend and ally in rectifying some of the wrongs brought about by his boss's underhanded business tactics. With two beautiful women in love with him and his job on the line, Paige has some big decisions to make.

Other books by the same author:
Girl to Come Home To, 1945
Christmas Bride, 1934
The Beloved Stranger, 1933
Happiness Hill, 1932
The Angel of His Presence, 1902

Other books you might like:
Judy Baer, *Reunited*, 1998
Robin Jones Gunn, *Secrets*, 1999
Janette Oke, *Another Homecoming*, 1997

791

B.J. HOFF

The Captive Voice

(Wheaton, Illinois: Tyndale House, 1995)

Category: Mystery
Series: Daybreak Mysteries
Subject(s): Marriage; Vacations; Christian Life

Age range(s): Young Adult-Adult
Major character(s): Daniel Kaine, Spouse (of Jennifer); Jennifer Kaine, Spouse (of Daniel); Vali Tremayne, Singer (Christian)
Time period(s): 1990s
Locale(s): Lake Erie; USA

Summary: While on their honeymoon, Daniel and Jennifer Kaine meet Christian music star Vali Tremayne. The singer has been out of the public eye since the death of her fiance in an accidental plane crash. Or was it an accident? It soon becomes clear that someone is stalking the frightened young woman, and the Kaines are targets, too, because they're trying to help. The vacation turns into a fight for their lives, until the truth of God begins to shed light on shady circumstances, and their trust in God pays off. This title was originally published in 1987 as *The Domino Image*.

Other books by the same author:
Ashes and Lace, 1999
Dark River Legacy, 1997 (Daybreak Mysteries)
The Tangled Web, 1997 (Daybreak Mysteries, #3)
Vow of Silence, 1997 (Daybreak Mysteries, #4)
Storm at Daybreak, 1995 (Daybreak Mysteries, #1)

Other books you might like:
Terri Blackstock, *Blind Trust*, 1997
Terri Blackstock, *Justifiable Means*, 1996
T. Davis Bunn, *Promises to Keep*, 1991
Athol Dickson, *Every Hidden Thing*, 1998
    A Garr Reed Mystery, #2
Hilda Stahl, *The Boning Knife*, 1992
    Carolyn Burgess Mysteries, #1

792

B.J. HOFF

Dawn of the Golden Promise

(Minneapolis: Bethany House, 1994)

Category: Historical Fiction
Series: Emerald Ballad
Subject(s): Romance; Family Saga; Emigration and Immigration
Age range(s): Young Adult-Adult
Major character(s): Morgan Fitzgerald, Invalid; Michael Burke, Police Officer
Time period(s): 1850s
Locale(s): New York, New York; Ireland

Summary: B.J. Hoff's Emerald Ballad series continues with this fifth installment of the saga of Irish immigrants in the United States and family members left behind in famine-plagued Ireland. Morgan Fitzgerald, now confined to a wheelchair due to a gunshot wound to the spine, is caught between his faith and a decision that could cost him everything he cares about. Michael Burke, a police officer in New York City, is obsessed with bringing a criminal to justice, and it is coming between him and God. In the Irish immigrant settlement in New York City, people arrive daily, seeking hope in a new land that is undergoing strains of its own in the decade preceding the War Between the States.

Other books by the same author:
Ashes and Lace, 1999 (Song of Erin, #2)
Sons of an Ancient Glory, 1993 (Emerald Ballad, #4)
Land of a Thousand Dreams, 1992 (Emerald Ballad, #3)
Heart of the Lonely Exile, 1991 (Emerald Ballad, #2)
Song of the Silent Harp, 1991 (Emerald Ballad, #1)

Other books you might like:
Bodie Thoene, *Of Men & of Angels: A Novel*, 1998
Bodie Thoene, *Only the River Runs Free*, 1997
Bodie Thoene, *To Gather the Wind*, 1998
Bodie Thoene, *Winds of Promise*, 1997

793

B.J. HOFF

Sons of an Ancient Glory

(Minneapolis: Bethany House, 1993)

Category: Historical Fiction
Series: Emerald Ballad
Subject(s): Family Saga; Romance; Emigration and Immigration
Age range(s): Young Adult-Adult
Major character(s): Quinn O'Shea, Young Woman; Billy Hogan, Abuse Victim; Michael Burke, Police Officer; Evan Whittaker, Musician
Locale(s): New York, New York; Ireland

Summary: In the fourth installment of B.J.Hoff's Emerald Ballad series, Irish immigrant Michael Burke is a New York City police officer, doing his part to get rid of the city's organized crime bosses. His wife is fighting poverty and discrimination in the over-populated immigrant slums. Quinn O'Shea has come to the United States to escape her dark past, but she will need more than a new home to bring true light into her life. Young Billy Hogan is alone in the world, and what he needs most is a father's love. And Evan Whitakker is finding his way musically through his new culture. Suspense, disappointment, hope, fear, courage, and faith all play a role in this saga of Irish pilgrims seeking new life in a new world.

Other books by the same author:
Ashes and Lace, 1999 (Song of Erin, #2)
Dawn of the Golden Promise, 1994 (Emerald Ballad, #5)
Land of a Thousand Dreams, 1992 (Emerald Ballad, #3)
Heart of the Lonely Exile, 1991 (Emerald Ballad, #2)
Song of the Silent Harp, 1991 (Emerald Ballad, #1)

Other books you might like:
Bodie Thoene, *Of Men & of Angels: A Novel*, 1998
Bodie Thoene, *Only the River Runs Free*, 1997
Bodie Thoene, *To Gather the Wind*, 1998
Bodie Thoene, *Winds of Promise*, 1997

794

MARJORIE HOLMES

The Messiah

(New York: Harper & Row, 1987)

Category: Historical Fiction
Subject(s): Christianity; Miracles; Jesus

Age range(s): Young Adult-Adult
Major character(s): Jesus, Historical Figure, Biblical Figure; John the Baptist, Historical Figure, Biblical Figure; Mary Magdalene, Historical Figure, Biblical Figure; Lazarus, Historical Figure, Biblical Figure; Peter, Historical Figure, Biblical Figure; John, Biblical Figure (apostle), Historical Figure
Time period(s): 1st century
Locale(s): Nazareth, Israel; Jerusalem, Israel; Roman Empire

Summary: This third volume of the author's fictional retelling of the life of Christ follows *Two from Galilee: A Love Story* and *Three from Galilee: The Young Man from Nazareth*. Holmes focuses here on the years of Jesus' ministry as rabbi, leader, and finally martyr. The author renders the famous scenes of Jesus' miracles, his sermons, trial, and crucifixion with the novelist's eye for period details and plausible motives.

Other books by the same author:
Three From Galilee: The Young Man From Nazareth, 1985
Two From Galilee: A Love Story, 1972

Other books you might like:
Lloyd C. Douglas, *The Robe*, 1942
Maria Isabel Hodges, *The Promise*, 1999
Charles R. Swindoll, *Suddenly One Morning: The Shopkeeper's Story*, 1998
Lew Wallace, *Ben-Hur: A Tale of the Christ*, 1880

795

MARJORIE HOLMES

Three From Galilee: The Young Man From Nazareth

(New York: Harper & Row, 1985)

Category: Historical Fiction
Subject(s): Bible; Christianity; Jesus
Age range(s): Young Adult-Adult
Major character(s): Jesus, Historical Figure, Biblical Figure; Joseph, Historical Figure, Biblical Figure; Mary, Historical Figure, Biblical Figure
Time period(s): 1st century (12-30)
Locale(s): Nazareth, Israel

Summary: In the sequel to her bestselling *Two From Galilee: A Love Story*, the author portrays what might have happened during the "lost years" of Jesus. The book follows Jesus from the age of 12 when the New Testament describes his debate with the elders in the temple, to the age of 30 when he begins his ministry.

Other books by the same author:
The Messiah, 1987
Two From Galilee: A Love Story, 1972

Other books you might like:
Madeleine L'Engle, *Sold into Egypt: Joseph's Journey into Human Being*, 1989
Madeleine L'Engle, *A Stone for a Pillow*, 1986
Lew Wallace, *Ben-Hur: A Tale of the Christ*, 1880

796

MARJORIE HOLMES

Two From Galilee: A Love Story

(Old Tappan, New Jersey: F.H. Revell, 1972)

Category: Historical Fiction
Subject(s): Bible; Christianity; Jesus
Major character(s): Joseph, Historical Figure, Biblical Figure; Mary, Historical Figure, Biblical Figure
Time period(s): 1st century B.C.
Locale(s): Galilee, Israel; Nazareth, Israel; Jerusalem, Israel

Summary: Remaining faithful to the Biblical account, Marjorie Holmes tells the story of the birth of Jesus Christ through the love story of Mary and Joseph. They appear as two human beings genuinely in love with one another, looking forward to their wedding and future together, and contending with the unexpected news of Mary's pregnancy. This bestselling novel is the first of three to focus on the life of Christ.

Other books by the same author:
The Messiah, 1987
Three From Galilee: The Young Man From Nazareth, 1985

Other books you might like:
Anthony Burgess, *Man of Nazareth*, 1979
Madeleine L'Engle, *Sold into Egypt: Joseph's Journey into Human Being*, 1989
Madeleine L'Engle, *A Stone for a Pillow*, 1986
Daniel A. Poling, *He Came From Galilee*, 1965

797

SUSAN HOWATCH

Absolute Truths: A Novel

(New York: Knopf, 1995)

Category: Gentle Reads
Subject(s): Clergy; Grief; Faith
Age range(s): Adult
Major character(s): Charles Ashworth, Religious (Anglican bishop)
Time period(s): 1960s (1965)
Locale(s): Starbridge, England

Summary: The sixth and last installment of Susan Howatch's series of novels focusing on the Church of England, *Absolute Truths* continues the author's psychological and theological examination of the human condition within the context of the church's long tradition of belief and practice. *Absolute Truths* is set in the English town of Starbridge in 1965. Bishop Charles Ashworth is trying to preserve the traditions, decorum, and moral standards of the church amidst the social turmoil of the 1960s that is setting traditional values on end and forever altering the longstanding relationship between the church and society. But Ashworth's public role as defender of the faith stands in stark contrast to the personal disintegration that begins to take place following a personal tragedy more devastating than anything he has previously had to face. Howatch chronicles his downward spiral and its ultimate consequences with sensitivity, exploring some of the absolute truths of life, death, love, and faith.

Other books by the same author:
Mystical Paths: A Novel, 1992
Scandalous Risks: A Novel, 1990
Ultimate Prizes, 1989
Glamorous Powers, 1988
Glittering Images, 1987

Other books you might like:
Gail Godwin, *Evensong*, 1999
Gail Godwin, *Father Melancholy's Daughter*, 1991
Jon Hassler, *North of Hope: A Novel*, 1990
Jan Karon, *The Mitford Series*, 1994-
Jan Karon, *A New Song*, 1999

798

JAMES BYRON HUGGINS

A Wolf Story

(Eugene, Oregon: Harvest House, 1993)

Category: Fantasy
Subject(s): Good and Evil; Peace; Courage
Age range(s): Young Adult-Adult
Major character(s): Aramus, Wolf (Silver Wolf); Baalkor, Wolf (enemy of the Lightmaker)

Summary: Near the beginning of time, the deep woods creatures had to choose whether to follow the Silver Wolf and the Lightmaker or to follow the dark forces of Corbis, led by Baalkor. The way of light would lead to strength and peace, but the price would be confrontation with the forces of darkness. The path of darkness, by contrast, would allow the creatures to follow their own desires, but the unseen consequences of such a choice would be fear and constant battling, one against another, to preserve one's own rights against the wishes of the others. Courage would be needed by those who chose the path of light. This is the story of the wolves, the creatures, the choices they made, and the consequences that came to pass.

Other books by the same author:
Hunter, 1999
Cain, 1997
Leviathan, 1995
The Reckoning: A Novel, 1994

Other books you might like:
Richard Adams, *Watership Down*, 1972
Sergio Bambaren, *The Dolphin: Story of a Dreamer*, 1997
C.S. Lewis, *Chronicles of Narnia*, 1950-1956
J.R.R. Tolkien, *The Hobbit; or, There and Back Again*, 1937

799

ANGELA ELWELL HUNT

Afton of Margate Castle

(Wheaton, Illinois: Tyndale House, 1993)

Category: Historical Fiction; Romance
Series: Theyn Chronicles
Subject(s): Adventure and Adventurers; Christianity; Dark Ages
Age range(s): Young Adult-Adult

Major character(s): Afton, Young Woman
Time period(s): Indeterminate Past (medieval times)
Locale(s): Ireland

Summary: Afton is a peasant child who is taken from her parents and raised as the daughter of an earl. As a young woman, however, she is cast out, sent back to her humble roots, and promised in marriage to a man she does not love. In response, Afton plans all manner of revenge, but discovers, much to her surprise, that a heart filled with love and faith cannot also hold vengeance. *Afton of Margate Castle*, the first installment of the Theyn Chronicles, was Angela Elwell Hunt's first novel. According to the author, it is a story that recognizes and celebrates the sparks of faith and courage that kept Christianity alive during the Dark Ages.

Other books by the same author:
The Emerald Isle, 1999
Flee the Darkness, 1998
Ingram of the Irish, 1994 (Theyn Chronicles, #3)
The Troubadour's Quest, 1993 (Theyn Chronicles, #2)

Other books you might like:
Sigmund Brouwer, *Barbarians From the Isle*, 1992
    Winds of Light, #2
Sigmund Brouwer, *Merlin's Destiny*, 1993
    Winds of Light, #6
B.J. Hoff, *Dawn of the Golden Promise*, 1994
    Emerald Ballad, #5
B.J. Hoff, *Land of a Thousand Dreams*, 1992
    Emerald Ballad
Bodie Thoene, *Of Men & of Angels: A Novel*, 1998
    Brock Thoene, co-author; Galway Chronicles

800

DAVE HUNT

The Mind Invaders: A Novel
(Eugene, Oregon: Harvest House, 1998)

Category: Thrillers
Subject(s): Psychology; End-Times; Christianity
Age range(s): Young Adult-Adult
Major character(s): Carla Bertelli, Journalist
Time period(s): 1990s

Summary: Carla Bertelli is an accomplished, well-known journalist with a conscience and an understanding of the hidden powers of darkness. When she discovers that the CIA and the Russian intelligence agency are battling each other for psychic control of the world, she heads straight for danger in a search for truth. Racing against time, Bertelli hopes that the latest breakthrough in mind research will not result in the unleashing of psychic powers the likes which of the world has never before seen. This end-times story was previously published as *The Archon Conspiracy* in 1989.

Other books by the same author:
Occult Invasion, 1998
A Cup of Trembling, 1995
How Close Are We?, 1993
Seduction of Christianity: Spiritual Discernment in the Last Days, 1985 (T.A. McMahon, co-author)

Other books you might like:
Tim LaHaye, *Left Behind: A Novel of the Earth's Last Days*, 1995
    Jerry B. Jenkins, co-author
Paul Meier, *The Third Millennium: A Novel*, 1993
Frank E. Peretti, *Piercing the Darkness*, 1989
Frank E. Peretti, *This Present Darkness*, 1986

801

HANNAH HURNARD

Mountains of Spices
(Wheaton, Illinois: Tyndale, 1976)

Category: Morality Tales
Subject(s): Allegories; Christian Life; Bible
Age range(s): Young Adult-Adult
Major character(s): Mrs. Dismal Foreboding, Widow(er) (becomes Mrs. Thanksgiving), Friend (of Mrs. Valiant); Mrs. Valiant, Friend (of Mrs. Dismal Foreboding); Chief Shepherd, Deity (God)
Time period(s): Indeterminate
Locale(s): Mythical Place (Valley of Humiliation); Mythical Place (Mountains of Spices)

Summary: *Mountains of Spices* is a sequel to Hannah Hurnard's popular *Hind's Feet on High Places*. Hurnard's allegory personifies negative attitudes such as fear, resentment, and arrogance, and sets them in an imaginary land also peopled by positive attitudes including mercy, joy, and peace-once negative attitudes that have been transformed through their relationship with the Chief Shepherd. Mrs. Dismal Foreboding has nothing positive to think, say, or do, but her friend, Mrs. Valiant, and others in the Valley of Humiliation will not give up on her. Ultimately the influence of the Shepherd and continued interaction with her neighbors helps Mrs. Dismal become Mrs. Thanksgiving. The nine mountains of spices, including saffron, cinnamon, and myrrh, each represent one of the nine ''fruit of the spirit''-love, joy, peace, patience, gentleness, goodness, faith, meekness, and self-control.

Other books by the same author:
Way of Healing, 1986
Steps to the Kingdom, 1985
Eagles' Wings to the Higher Places, 1981
Hind's Feet on High Places, 1977

Other books you might like:
Charles G. Coleman, *The Shining Sword*, 1956
Bill Hybels, *Fruit of the Spirit*, 1997
Dick King-Smith, *Godhanger*, 1997
    Andrew Davidson, illustrator
Michael L. McCoy, *The Bestman, the Bride, and the Wedding*, 1998

802

JOHN IRVING

A Prayer for Owen Meany: A Novel
(New York: Morrow, 1989)

Subject(s): Adolescence; Allegories; Religion
Age range(s): Young Adult-Adult
Major character(s): Owen Meany, Friend (of Johnny Wheelwright); Johnny Wheelwright, Friend (of Owen Meany)
Time period(s): 1950s
Locale(s): New Hampshire

Summary: Owen Meany is a child whose life circumstances, including a physical limitation that affects the sound of his voice and an inner conviction that he is an instrument of God, set him apart from the average. One fateful afternoon in 1953, a foul ball hit by Owen during a Little League game strikes and kills the mother of his best friend, Johnny Wheelwright. As tragic an event as this is, it eventually serves as a catalyst to reveal something significant from Johnny's past that dramatically affects his future. In this and other ways, Owen's life unpredictably affects Johnny's. Of one event in his life, however, Owen is certain: as an instrument of God, he will be martyred, and he knows when. Through the story of young Owen Meany, author John Irving explores the aspect of destiny in the inner and public life of Jesus who, as the ultimate instrument of God, lived his life with foreknowledge of the circumstances and timing of his death.

Other books by the same author:
A Widow for One Year, 1998
The Cider House Rules, 1985
The World According to Garp, 1978

Other books you might like:
Garrison Keillor, *Lake Wobegon Days*, 1985
Herman Melville, *Billy Budd, and Other Prose Pieces*, 1924
Anna Quindlen, *One True Thing*, 1989

803

JAN KARON

At Home in Mitford
(Elgin, Illinois: Lion, 1994)

Category: Biographical Fiction
Series: Mitford
Subject(s): Christian Life; Small Town Life; Episcopalians
Age range(s): Young Adult-Adult
Major character(s): Father Tim Kavanaugh, Religious (Episcopal rector); Dooley Barlowe, Abandoned Child; Cynthia Coppersmith, Writer (of children's books), Neighbor, Artist (illustrator, children's books); Barnabas, Dog
Time period(s): 1990s
Locale(s): Mitford, North Carolina

Summary: Father Tim, an Episcopalian rector, receives a letter from his bishop and the unwelcome attentions of a large, filthy dog on the same day. He takes to heart the bishop's concern about his stress level and takes in the dog as a pet. But daily life in Mitford continues to present challenges to Father Tim, including a homeless boy in need of a great deal of love and patience. The pastor's life is further complicated by a new scooter, the disappearance of his new pet, the discovery of a painting that might be valuable, mysterious goings-on in the church building, and—most significantly for the lifelong bachelor—a lovely new neighbor named Cynthia.

Other books by the same author:
A New Song, 1999
Out to Canaan, 1997
A Light in the Window, 1996
These High, Green Hills, 1996

Other books you might like:
Gail Godwin, *Evensong*, 1999
Gail Godwin, *Father Melancholy's Daughter*, 1991
Harold Bell Wright, *The Calling of Dan Matthews*, 1909
Harold Bell Wright, *The Shepherd of the Hills*, 1907

804

JAN KARON

A Light in the Window
(New York: Penguin, 1996)

Category: Biographical Fiction
Series: Mitford
Subject(s): Christian Life; Small Town Life; Clergy
Age range(s): Young Adult-Adult
Major character(s): Father Tim Kavanaugh, Religious (Episcopal rector); Cynthia Coppersmith, Writer (of children's books), Neighbor, Artist (illustrator, children's books); Dooley Barlowe, Child; Barnabas, Dog; Edith Mallory, Widow(er)
Time period(s): 1990s
Locale(s): Mitford, North Carolina

Summary: In this second of the Mitford books, Episcopalian Father Tim finds himself becoming more interested in his artistic neighbor, Cynthia. At the same time he is pursued relentlessly by the wealthy and altogether offensive widow Edith Mallory. As if life were not complicated enough, he is surprised by a "cousin" from Ireland he doesn't recall ever meeting. She turns out to be the house guest from Hell, and Father Tim is at a loss as to how to get her to leave or even to discover what she is up to at all hours behind the locked guest room door. Meanwhile, Father Tim struggles to understand and express his feelings for Cynthia while continuing to cope with the education, care, and civilization of Dooley Barlow, the abandoned boy he unofficially adopted in *At Home in Mitford*.

Other books by the same author:
A New Song, 1999
Out to Canaan, 1997
These High, Green Hills, 1996
At Home in Mitford, 1994

Other books you might like:
Gail Godwin, *Evensong*, 1999
Gail Godwin, *Father Melancholy's Daughter*, 1991
Harold Bell Wright, *The Calling of Dan Matthews*, 1909
Harold Bell Wright, *The Shepherd of the Hills*, 1907

805

JAN KARON

A New Song
(New York: Viking, 1999)

Category: Biographical Fiction
Series: Mitford
Subject(s): Christian Life; Small Town Life; Clergy
Age range(s): Young Adult-Adult
Major character(s): Father Tim Kavanaugh, Religious (Episcopal rector), Spouse (of Cynthia); Cynthia Kavanaugh, Writer (of children's books), Spouse (of Father Tim), Artist (illustrator, children's books)
Time period(s): 1990s
Locale(s): Mitford, North Carolina; Outer Banks, North Carolina

Summary: The locale for this fifth novel in the Mitford series shifts from North Carolina's Blue Ridge Mountains to its Outer Banks. But, just as Father Tim is only semi-retired, he also hasn't completely left the town of Mitford behind. As interim priest at St. John's in the Grove on Whitecap Island, he ministers to a new flock, including a lonely bachelor and a depressed mother. However, members of his old flock keep Father Tim and his wife, Cynthia, up-to-date on Mitford's latest events.

Other books by the same author:
Out to Canaan, 1997
A Light in the Window, 1996
These High, Green Hills, 1996
At Home in Mitford, 1994

Other books you might like:
Gail Godwin, *Evensong*, 1999
Gail Godwin, *Father Melancholy's Daughter*, 1991
Harold Bell Wright, *The Calling of Dan Matthews*, 1909
Harold Bell Wright, *The Shepherd of the Hills*, 1907

806

JAN KARON

Out to Canaan
(New York: Viking, 1997)

Category: Biographical Fiction
Series: Mitford
Subject(s): Christian Life; Small Town Life; Clergy
Age range(s): Young Adult-Adult
Major character(s): Father Tim Kavanaugh, Religious (Episcopal rector), Spouse (of Cynthia); Cynthia Kavanaugh, Writer (of children's books), Spouse (of Father Tim), Artist (illustrator, children's books); Dooley Barlowe, Student—Boarding School, Son ("adopted" by Father Tim)
Time period(s): 1990s
Locale(s): Mitford, North Carolina

Summary: In this fourth book in the Mitford series, Episcopalian Father Tim and his wife, Cynthia, contemplate retirement, Mitford's mayoral race heats up, the abused Lacey Turner finds a new home, Father Tim solves a mystery related to a shady real estate deal, and Dooley Barlowe, the aban-

doned boy "adopted" by Father Tim, is reunited with his mother and younger brother. As in previous volumes, the goings-on of church and community keep Father Tim active and involved, even as he considers his options for the future.

Other books by the same author:
A New Song, 1999
A Light in the Window, 1996
These High, Green Hills, 1996
At Home in Mitford, 1994

Other books you might like:
Gail Godwin, *Evensong*, 1999
Gail Godwin, *Father Melancholy's Daughter*, 1991
Harold Bell Wright, *The Calling of Dan Matthews*, 1909
Harold Bell Wright, *The Shepherd of the Hills*, 1907

807

JAN KARON

These High, Green Hills
(New York: Viking, 1996)

Category: Biographical Fiction
Series: Mitford
Subject(s): Christian Life; Small Town Life; Clergy
Age range(s): Young Adult-Adult
Major character(s): Father Tim Kavanaugh, Religious (Episcopal rector), Spouse (of Cynthia); Cynthia Kavanaugh, Writer (of children's books), Spouse (of Father Tim), Artist (illustrator, children's books); Dooley Barlowe, Child; Lacey Turner, Abuse Victim; Barnabas, Dog
Time period(s): 1990s
Locale(s): Mitford, North Carolina

Summary: The third book in the Mitford series finds Episcopalian Father Tim and his new bride and former neighbor Cynthia adjusting to married life. His status as a married man is only the latest in many changes for Father Tim. His "adopted" son Dooley is off at school; his maid, Puny, now brings her newborn twins to work; his eccentric and outspoken secretary must adjust to the church's first computer; a young abused girl finds her way to his door and into his life; and his old and dear friend, Miss Sadie, begins to feel her 90 years.

Other books by the same author:
A New Song, 1999
Out to Canaan, 1997
A Light in the Window, 1996
At Home in Mitford, 1994

Other books you might like:
Gail Godwin, *Evensong*, 1999
Gail Godwin, *Father Melancholy's Daughter*, 1991
Harold Bell Wright, *The Calling of Dan Matthews*, 1909
Harold Bell Wright, *The Shepherd of the Hills*, 1907

808

CHRISTMAS CAROL KAUFFMAN

Hidden Rainbow

(Harrisonburg, Virginia: Christian Light Publications, 1997)

Category: Gentle Reads
Subject(s): Mennonites; Protestantism; Missionaries
Age range(s): Young Adult-Adult
Major character(s): John Olesh, Young Man; Anna Olesh, Young Woman
Locale(s): Yugoslavia

Summary: Christmas Carol Kauffman's *Hidden Rainbow* tells the story of two young people, John and Anna Olesh, who were born in Yugoslavia to Catholic parents. Through the outreach efforts of a Mennonite missionary, they are converted to Protestantism. The novel reveals a certain bias against Catholicism, but it is reflective of doctrinal biases that continue to exist in some American Protestant denominations-although not necessarily the Mennonite tradition-at the end of the 20th century.

Other books by the same author:
For One Moment: A Biographical Story, 1992
Search to Belong, 1963
Not Regina, 1954
Light From Heaven, 1948
Lucy Winchester, 1945

Other books you might like:
Dave Elias, *Places of Grace*, 1997
Alan B. Morris, *Bright Sword of Justice*, 1998
Helen Wells Quintela, *Out of Ashes*, 1991
Marian Kleinsasser Towne, *Bread of Life: Diaries and Memories of a Dakota Family, 1936-1945*, 1994

809

CHRISTMAS CAROL KAUFFMAN

Light From Heaven

(Scottdale, Pennsylvania: Herald Press, 1948)

Category: Historical Fiction
Subject(s): Family Life; Prayer; Mennonites
Age range(s): Young Adult-Adult
Major character(s): Joseph Armstrong, Young Man
Time period(s): 19th century
Locale(s): United States

Summary: *Light From Heaven* focuses on the life of Joseph Armstrong, the eldest son in a Mennonite family with three children. All of the children are under constant scrutiny from their father, a strict disciplinarian who doesn't seem to love or care for his offspring, but Joseph bears the brunt of his father's temper. Despite the harsh relationship the children have with their father, they are taught by their mother's words and example to love, respect, and pray for their father. Primary themes of the novel include perseverance in difficult family relationships, the value of prayer and love in marriage and family life, and the unique bond of mother-child relationships throughout life.

Other books by the same author:
Hidden Rainbow, 1997
For One Moment: A Biographical Story, 1992
Search to Belong, 1963
Not Regina, 1954
Lucy Winchester, 1945

Other books you might like:
Dave Elias, *Places of Grace*, 1997
Helen Wells Quintela, *Out of Ashes*, 1991
Marian Kleinsasser Towne, *Bread of Life: Diaries and Memories of a Dakota Family, 1936-1945*, 1994

810

NIKOS KAZANTZAKIS

The Greek Passion

(New York: Simon & Schuster, 1953)

Category: Morality Tales
Subject(s): Christianity; Rural Life
Age range(s): Adult
Major character(s): Priest Grigoris, Religious (priest); Manolios, Shepherd, Young Man (selected to play Jesus); Panayotaros, Young Man (selected to play Judas)
Locale(s): Lycovrissi, Greece

Summary: Set during an occupation of Lycovrissi by Turkish forces, *The Greek Passion* focuses on what happens to the rural Greek villagers who have been selected to participate in one year's portrayal of the crucifixion of Christ. The old priest, Grigoris, is a domineering man who allows nothing and no one to stand between him and his will for the people and the community. He has tapped a young shepherd, Manolios, to play the role of Jesus. A young man by the name of Panayotaros has been selected to portray Judas, despite his desire not to do this. During the experience, young Manolios sees a vision of Jesus and his life is transformed. He begins to share the message he believes he has been given to tell the people. At the same time, Panayotaros is scorned and reviled by his townspeople, and he blames Manolios for his plight. Unfortunately for Manolios, the message he believes he has been called by God to share speaks against the religious establishment of the Greek village, threatening the control that Grigoris and other priests exert over their people. What happens to those who portray the sacrifice of Christ and the actions of his persecutors becomes a terrible parallel to the biblical story they are acting out.

Other books by the same author:
The Last Temptation of Christ, 1960
Zorba the Greek, 1952

Other books you might like:
Arnoul Greban, *The Mystery of the Passion: The Third Day*, 1996
Piers Paul Read, *On the Third Day*, 1990
Bernard Sahlins, *The Mysteries—The Passion*, 1993

811

NIKOS KAZANTZAKIS

The Last Temptation of Christ

(New York: Simon & Schuster, 1960)

Category: Historical Fiction
Subject(s): Christianity; Death; Jesus
Age range(s): Adult
Major character(s): Jesus, Historical Figure, Biblical Figure; Mary, Historical Figure, Biblical Figure; Joseph, Historical Figure, Biblical Figure; Mary Magdalene, Historical Figure, Biblical Figure; Herod Antipas, Historical Figure, Ruler (king of the Jews), Biblical Figure; Pontius Pilate, Historical Figure, Government Official (Roman procurator), Biblical Figure; John the Baptist, Historical Figure, Biblical Figure; Judas Iscariot, Historical Figure, Biblical Figure; Lazarus, Historical Figure, Biblical Figure
Time period(s): 1st century
Locale(s): Israel; Roman Empire

Summary: In this attempt to humanize the life of Jesus, the author offers an interpretation not of a confident Son of God with a prearranged mission, but of a hesitant man who, to serve God, conspires with Judas to arrange his own execution. The details in Kazantzakis' novel do not always parallel those in the *Bible*. Perhaps the most controversial suggestion is the treatment of Mary Magdalene as Jesus' greatest temptation, and the presentation of Lazarus as having been restored to life, but not to health. The novel was the basis of the much-debated 1988 film by the same name.

Other books by the same author:
Saint Francis: A Novel, 1962 (P.A. Bien, translator)

Other books you might like:
Jim Crace, *Quarantine*, 1997
Norman Mailer, *The Gospel According to the Son*, 1997
Jose Saramago, *The Gospel According to Jesus Christ*, 1993

812

NIKOS KAZANTZAKIS

Saint Francis: A Novel

(New York: Simon & Schuster, 1962)

Category: Historical Fiction
Subject(s): Middle Ages; Religious Life; Saints
Age range(s): Adult
Major character(s): Brother Leo, Religious (monk); Francis of Assisi, Historical Figure, Religious (monk)
Time period(s): 13th century
Locale(s): Assisi, Italy; Rome, Roman Empire; Egypt

Summary: In this fictional account of St. Francis of Assisi, the monk struggles to gain sanctity of spirit through intensifying asceticism. This is a sympathetic account, not a psychological study of Francis' self-punishment. It celebrates his triumph of spirit and essential holiness. The narrative is written from the perspective of Brother Leo, one of Francis' closest disciples, who chronicles their journeys. The volume was translated by P.A. Bien.

Other books by the same author:
The Last Temptation of Christ, 1960

Other books you might like:
Wendy Beckett, *Sister Wendy's Book of Saints*, 1998
G.K. Chesterton, *St. Francis of Assisi*, 1924
G.K. Chesterton, *St. Thomas Aquinas*, 1933

813

LEVI KEIDEL

Caught in the Crossfire: The Trials and Triumphs of African Believers through an Era of Tribulation

(Scottdale, Pennsylvania: Herald Press, 1979)

Category: Biographical Fiction
Subject(s): Christianity; Religious Conflict; Political Prisoners
Age range(s): Young Adult-Adult
Time period(s): 1960s (1964-1965)
Locale(s): Zaire (Congo)

Summary: American Levi Keidel spent three decades in the Congo, later called Zaire, as a missionary with the Mennonite Church. *Caught in the Crossfire* is a novel based on his experiences during the political unrest of the mid-1960s. It is the story of three African men and the consequences of the choices they make-to compromise, collaborate or resist-while trying to live as Christians under a new and unsympathetic regime following several years of instability and political turmoil culminating in an uprising in 1964.

Awards the book has won:
Gold Medallion Book Award, Fiction, 1980

Other books by the same author:
Conflict or Connection: Interpersonal Relationships in Cross-Cultural Settings, 1996
Black Samson, 1975
Stop Treating Me Like God, 1971
Footsteps to Freedom, 1969

Other books you might like:
Lillian Craig Harris, *The Sins of the Father*, 1989
Alan Paton, *Cry, the Beloved Country*, 1948
Homer A. Rodeheaver, *Singing Black: Twenty Thousand Miles with a Music Missionary*, 1975

814

CLINT KELLY

Deliver Us From Evil

(Minneapolis: Bethany House, 1998)

Category: Historical Fiction
Series: In the Shadow of the Mountain
Subject(s): Massacres; Prisoners and Prisons
Age range(s): Young Adult-Adult
Major character(s): Tatul ''The Fox'' Sarafian, Spy; Adrine Tevian, Captive; Lieutenant Leslie Davis, Diplomat (in U.S. consulate in Turkey)
Time period(s): 1910s (1914-1918)
Locale(s): Turkey

Summary: In this novel about the persecution and massacre of Armenians by the Turkish during the early decades of the 20th century, author Clint Kelly introduces two Armenians and an American diplomat who each fight the forces of evil and hate in their own way. Adrine Tevian is a young woman held prisoner in a military camp and in love with a man she knows only as "The Fox." Tatul Sarafian is "The Fox." He has joined a resistance group whose mission is to save the Armenians from slaughter. Lieutenant Leslie Davis is an American diplomat whose only recourse against the killing is to deceive Turkish governmental officials. Refugees struggle to survive by hiding wherever they can-in the mountains, in basements, and even right under the noses of Turkish soldiers. The story of courage and faith in God's power to redeem even the worst of circumstances continues in *The Power and the Glory*.

Other books by the same author:
The Power and the Glory, 1999
The Aryan, 1995
Me Parent, You Kid!: Taming the Family Zoo: Developing a Sense of Adventure, Purpose, and Humor in Your Child, 1993

Other books you might like:
Stina Katchadourian, *Efronia: An Armenian Love Story*, 1993
Arelo Sederbert, *Zora*, 1989
Marsha Skrypuch, *The Hunger*, 1999

815

AL LACY

Legacy

(Sisters, Oregon: Multhomah Books, 1994)

Category: Westerns
Series: Journeys of the Stranger
Subject(s): Romance; Frontier and Pioneer Life; Mystery
Age range(s): Young Adult
Major character(s): Breanna Baylor, Heroine; John Stranger, Hero
Time period(s): 1860s

Summary: Al Lacy's *Legacy*, the opening volume of his "Journeys of the Stranger" series, features action and romance in equal portions, set in the old West. A mysterious man appears just in time to confront one danger after another. Is he a drifter? Has he no roots? Where will he appear next? The episodic story of love, courage, faith, and the frontier is told through the eyes of both Breanna Baylor and John Stranger in small, vignette-like sequences.

Other books by the same author:
Snow Ghost, 1997 (Journeys of the Stranger, #7)
Circle of Fire, 1996 (Journeys of the Stranger, #5)
Quiet Thunder, 1996 (Journeys of the Stranger, #6)
Blizzard, 1995 (Journeys of the Stranger, #3)
Silent Abduction, 1994 (Journeys of the Stranger, #2)

Other books you might like:
Jack Cavanaugh, *The Adversaries*, 1996
Charles Frazier, *Cold Mountain*, 1997
Irene Hunt, *Across Five Aprils*, 1964
Gilbert Morris, *Bring the Boys Home*, 1997
Gilbert Morris, *The Last Confederate*, 1990

Miriam Freeman Rawl, *From the Ashes of Ruin*, 1999

816

TIM LAHAYE
JERRY B. JENKINS, Co-Author

Apollyon: The Destroyer Is Unleashed

(Wheaton, Illinois: Tyndale House, 1999)

Category: Thrillers
Series: Left Behind
Subject(s): Fundamentalism; Religious Conflict; End-Times
Age range(s): Adult
Major character(s): Rayford Steele, Pilot; Cameron "Buck" Williams, Journalist; Nicolae Carpathia, Leader
Time period(s): Indeterminate Future

Summary: This is the fifth volume in the Left Behind series of novels based on New Testament prophecies about the end of life on Earth. According to the authors, new titles in the series, which have been released yearly through this volume, will be published twice a year from this point on, for a projected series total of twelve volumes. In this installment, the world has been visited by a plague of demon locusts that attack anyone without the seal of God etched on their foreheads. Internet communication is becoming the primary means of maintaining unity within the underground resistance movement of believers. New global warfare threatens a third of the world's population. And the Tribulation Force members deal with personal crises, including pregnancies and lost family members.

Other books by the same author:
Soul Harvest: The World Takes Sides, 1998 (Jerry B. Jenkins, co-author)
Nicolae: The Rise of Antichrist, 1997 (Jerry B. Jenkins, co-author)
Tribulation Force: The Continuing Drama of Those Left Behind, 1996 (Jerry B. Jenkins, co-author)
Left Behind: A Novel of the Earth's Last Days, 1995 (Jerry B. Jenkins, co-author)

Other books you might like:
Paul Meier, *The Fourth Millennium: The Sequel*, 1996
Paul Meier, *The Third Millennium: A Novel*, 1993
Frank E. Peretti, *Piercing the Darkness*, 1989
Frank E. Peretti, *This Present Darkness*, 1986

817

TIM LAHAYE
JERRY B. JENKINS, Co-Author

Left Behind: A Novel of the Earth's Last Days

(Wheaton, Illinois: Tyndale House, 1995)

Category: Thrillers
Series: Left Behind
Subject(s): Fundamentalism; Religious Conflict; End-Times
Age range(s): Adult
Major character(s): Rayford Steele, Pilot; Cameron "Buck" Williams, Journalist; Nicolae Carpathia, Leader

Time period(s): Indeterminate Future

Summary: This is the first book in the Left Behind series of novels depicting a New Testament vision of the last years of life on Earth. The series is projected to consist of twelve volumes by its completion. In this opening novel, Christians around the world have been swept up into heaven in the Rapture of the Saints. Cars are without drivers, planes are missing passengers in mid-air. Pilot Rayford Steele had belittled his wife's belief that this would happen, and now here he is, left behind. Nicolae Carpathia is an Eastern European leader who intends to take advantage of the chaos to create one world government and religion, under his control. Steele, journalist Buck Williams, and others form an underground network to battle the forces of evil.

Other books by the same author:

Apollyon: The Destroyer Is Unleashed, 1999 (Jerry B. Jenkins, co-author)

Soul Harvest: The World Takes Sides, 1998 (Jerry B. Jenkins, co-author)

Nicolae: The Rise of Antichrist, 1997 (Jerry B. Jenkins, co-author)

Tribulation Force: The Continuing Drama of Those Left Behind, 1996 (Jerry B. Jenkins, co-author)

Other books you might like:

Paul Meier, *The Fourth Millennium: The Sequel*, 1996

Paul Meier, *The Third Millennium: A Novel*, 1993

Frank E. Peretti, *Piercing the Darkness*, 1989

Frank E. Peretti, *This Present Darkness*, 1986

818

TIM LAHAYE

JERRY B. JENKINS, Co-Author

Nicolae: The Rise of Antichrist

(Wheaton, Illinois: Tyndale House, 1997)

Category: Thrillers
Series: Left Behind
Subject(s): Fundamentalism; Religious Conflict; End-Times
Age range(s): Adult
Major character(s): Rayford Steele, Pilot; Cameron "Buck" Williams, Journalist; Nicolae Carpathia, Leader
Time period(s): Indeterminate Future

Summary: Two years after the Rapture of the Saints, Rayford Steele and Buck Williams are still working, together with others who were left behind, to counteract the evils of the Antichrist, Nicolae Carpathia. The world is at war. The biblical prophecies of trial and persecution are coming true. The Tribulation Force has infiltrated the regime of the would-be world ruler, and the actions they are about to take will set them on a course for direct confrontation with the man they are supposedly working for.

Other books by the same author:

Apollyon: The Destroyer Is Unleashed, 1999 (Jerry B. Jenkins, co-author)

Soul Harvest: The World Takes Sides, 1998 (Jerry B. Jenkins, co-author)

Tribulation Force: The Continuing Drama of Those Left Behind, 1996 (Jerry B. Jenkins, co-author)

Left Behind: A Novel of the Earth's Last Days, 1995 (Jerry B. Jenkins, co-author)

Other books you might like:

Paul Meier, *The Fourth Millennium: The Sequel*, 1996

Paul Meier, *The Third Millennium: A Novel*, 1993

Frank E. Peretti, *Piercing the Darkness*, 1989

Frank E. Peretti, *This Present Darkness*, 1986

819

TIM LAHAYE

JERRY B. JENKINS, Co-Author

Soul Harvest: The World Takes Sides

(Wheaton, Illinois: Tyndale House, 1998)

Category: Thrillers
Series: Left Behind
Subject(s): Fundamentalism; Religious Conflict; End-Times
Age range(s): Adult
Major character(s): Rayford Steele, Pilot; Cameron "Buck" Williams, Journalist; Nicolae Carpathia, Leader
Time period(s): Indeterminate Future
Locale(s): Iraq; United States

Summary: In the fourth installment of the Left Behind series of "end-times" novels, the world has suffered a massive earthquake. More than 100,000 Jews have converted to Christianity and they are evangelizing the world, which angers world leader Nicolae Carpathia. The newly converted and those who repented after the Rapture are being persecuted by the Antichrist and the Tribulation is barely halfway over.

Other books by the same author:

Apollyon: The Destroyer Is Unleashed, 1999 (Jerry B. Jenkins, co-author)

Nicolae: The Rise of Antichrist, 1997 (Jerry B. Jenkins, co-author)

Tribulation Force: The Continuing Drama of Those Left Behind, 1996 (Jerry B. Jenkins, co-author)

Left Behind: A Novel of the Earth's Last Days, 1995 (Jerry B. Jenkins, co-author)

Other books you might like:

Paul Meier, *The Fourth Millennium: The Sequel*, 1996

Paul Meier, *The Third Millennium: A Novel*, 1993

Frank E. Peretti, *Piercing the Darkness*, 1989

Frank E. Peretti, *This Present Darkness*, 1986

820

TIM LAHAYE

JERRY B. JENKINS, Co-Author

Tribulation Force: The Continuing Drama of Those Left Behind

(Wheaton, Illinois: Tyndale House, 1996)

Category: Thrillers
Series: Left Behind
Subject(s): Fundamentalism; Religious Conflict; End-Times
Age range(s): Adult
Major character(s): Rayford Steele, Pilot; Cameron "Buck" Williams, Journalist; Nicolae Carpathia, Leader

Time period(s): Indeterminate Future

Summary: In book two of the Left Behind series of end-times fiction by LaHaye and Jenkins, Rayford Steele and Buck Williams band together with others who were left behind after the Rapture to form the Tribulation Force. Their lot is to fight the forces of the Antichrist, Nicolae Carpathia. They do this in part by infiltrating his organization, which is a global government under the auspices of the United Nations.

Other books by the same author:
Apollyon: The Destroyer Is Unleashed, 1999 (Jerry B. Jenkins, co-author)
Soul Harvest: The World Takes Sides, 1998 (Jerry B. Jenkins, co-author)
Nicolae: The Rise of Antichrist, 1997 (Jerry B. Jenkins, co-author)
Left Behind: A Novel of the Earth's Last Days, 1995 (Jerry B. Jenkins, co-author)

Other books you might like:
Paul Meier, *The Fourth Millennium: The Sequel*, 1996
Paul Meier, *The Third Millennium: A Novel*, 1993
Frank E. Peretti, *Piercing the Darkness*, 1989
Frank E. Peretti, *This Present Darkness*, 1986

821

JOYCE LANDORF

I Came to Love You Late

(Old Tappan, New Jersey: F.H. Revell, 1977)

Category: Biographical Fiction
Subject(s): Bible; Relationships; Saints
Age range(s): Young Adult-Adult
Major character(s): Martha, Biblical Figure, Historical Figure; Jesus, Historical Figure, Biblical Figure; Mary, Historical Figure, Biblical Figure, Sister (of Martha)

Summary: Prolific Christian writer Joyce Landorf turns to fiction to explore the story of Martha, one of two sisters whose interaction with Jesus is recorded in the New Testament. In a gentle tale of spiritual journey, Landorf imagines how Martha may have responded to her growing awareness of Jesus' divine nature and being.

Awards the book has won:
Gold Medallion Book Award, Fiction, 1978

Other books by the same author:
Silent September, 1984
He Began with Eve, 1983
Change Points: When We Need Him Most, 1981
The High Cost of Growing, 1978

Other books you might like:
Gloria Howe Bremkamp, *Mara: The Woman at the Well*, 1991
Gloria Howe Bremkamp, *Martha and Mary of Bethany: A Novel*, 1991
Patricia McGerr, *Martha, Martha: A Biblical Novel*, 1960

822

BOB LARSON

Dead Air

(Nashville: T. Nelson, 1991)

Category: Thrillers
Subject(s): Kidnapping; Child Abuse; Radio
Age range(s): Adult
Major character(s): Jennifer, Kidnap Victim, 9-Year-Old; Wes Bryant, Radio Personality

Summary: Radio talk show personality Wes Bryant takes a mysterious call from a young girl who has been kidnapped. She doesn't know where she is or who has taken her. The host of "Talk of the Town" becomes obsessed with solving the mystery and rescuing Jennifer. What force is motivating Bryant to step into this darkness?

Other books by the same author:
In the Name of Satan, 1996
The Senator's Agenda, 1995

Other books you might like:
Margaret Humphreys, *Empty Cradles*, 1994
Candida Lawrence, *Change of Circumstance*, 1995
Janie Webster, *Fingernail Moon*, 1999

823

STEPHEN R. LAWHEAD

Byzantium

(New York: HarperPrism, 1996)

Category: Fantasy
Subject(s): Adventure and Adventurers; Religious Life; Dark Ages
Age range(s): Young Adult-Adult
Major character(s): Aidan Mac Cainnech, Religious (monk), Linguist; Harold Bull-Roar, Ruler (king of the Danes), Adventurer; Gunnar, Warrior, Traveler
Time period(s): 10th century
Locale(s): Byzantine Empire

Summary: Assigned to join a group of Irish monks transporting a valuable copy of what is now known as *The Book of Kells* to Byzantium, Aidan is captured in a Viking raid. His language skills prove valuable to his captors during an attack on the Byzantium enclave of Miklagard; Aidan's abilities saved King Harold Bull-Roar and his warriors from disaster. Eventually, Aidan becomes a spy for the emperor, endures imprisonment in the desert, and faces many other turns of fate in his quest to fulfill his destiny and protect his spiritual heritage.

Other books by the same author:
Grail, 1997
The Pendragon, 1994
Arthur, 1989

Other books you might like:
Jeffrey Gantz, *Early Irish Myths and Sagas*, 1981
J.R.R. Tolkien, *The Lord of the Rings Trilogy*, 1954-1956

824

STEPHEN R. LAWHEAD

In the Hall of the Dragon King

(Westchester, Illinois: Crossway, 1982)

Category: Fantasy
Series: Dragon King
Subject(s): Religion; Quest; Magic
Age range(s): Young Adult-Adult
Major character(s): Eskvar, Royalty (king); Nimrood, Wizard (evil); Quentin, Religious (acolyte)
Time period(s): Indeterminate
Locale(s): Mensandor, Mythical Place

Summary: King Eskvar has been captured by Nimrood, the evil necromancer, as part of a plot to take control of the kingdom. Quentin leaves his service to the god Ariel to rescue his captive king. The physical and spiritual quest tests Quentin's courage to the utmost and opens his eyes to the One True God.

Other books by the same author:
The Endless Knot, 1998
The War Lords of Nin, 1996
The Silver Hand, 1992
The Sword and the Flame, 1984

Other books you might like:
David Eddings, *The Diamond Throne*, 1989
 Elenium, 1
David Eddings, *Pawn of Prophecy*, 1982
 Belgariad, 1

825

STEPHEN R. LAWHEAD

The Iron Lance

(New York: HarperPrism/Zondervan, 1998)

Category: Historical Fiction
Series: Celtic Crusades
Subject(s): Crusades; Travel; Time Travel
Age range(s): Young Adult-Adult
Major character(s): Gordon Murray, Lawyer; Murdo Ranulfson, Young Man
Time period(s): 1890s (1899); 11th century (1095)
Locale(s): Scotland; Turkey

Summary: *The Iron Lance* opens as Scottish lawyer Gordon Murray is being initiated into a secret society in 1899. Deep inside a cavern, he falls upon an iron lance that mystically transports him to the time of the Crusades. Suddenly, it's the year 1095, and the nobles and royalty of Scotland are off to join the Crusades. Murdo Ranulfson has been charged with protecting the family home and property while the elder males are fighting for Jerusalem. But corrupt powers intervene, and it falls to Murdo to follow the Crusades in order to preserve his family's inheritance and legacy for future generations. The iron lance is the key to one man's past and another man's present in this story of pilgrimage, courage, and religious warfare.

Other books by the same author:
The Pendragon, 1994
The Endless Knot, 1998
The Sword and the Flame, 1984
In the Hall of the Dragon King, 1982

Other books you might like:
Linda Chaikin, *Behind the Veil*, 1998
Linda Chaikin, *Swords & Scimitars*, 1993
Susan Schwartz, *Cross and Crescent*, 1997

826

STEPHEN R. LAWHEAD

The Paradise War

(Batavia, Illinois: Lion, 1991)

Category: Fantasy
Series: Song of Albion
Subject(s): Celts; Magic; Good and Evil
Age range(s): Young Adult-Adult
Major character(s): Lewis Gilles, Scholar; Simon Rawnson, Scholar; "Nettles" Nettleson, Professor
Time period(s): 20th century
Locale(s): The Otherworld, Mythical Place; Scotland

Summary: According to the ancient Celts, a delicate balance exists between the earthly world and the "Otherworld." In this novel, Lewis Gilles discovers that something is throwing this balance awry. A graduate student of Celtic studies at Oxford, he finds himself drawn into an age-old struggle between good and evil that threatens the existence of both worlds when his roommate, Simon Rawnson, disappears into the Otherworld through a stone cairn in Scotland. Professor Nettleson assists the young scholars as Gilles seeks to rescue Rawnson from a mythological world turned real. The author draws upon Anglo-Celtic myth and legend to tell this story of spiritual quest and exploration.

Other books by the same author:
The Endless Knot, 1998
The Silver Hand, 1992

Other books you might like:
Walter L. Brenneman Jr., *Crossing the Circle at the Holy Wells of Ireland*, 1995
Nadine Crenshaw, *Balor of the Evil Eye*, 1995
John Matthews, *Tales of the Celtic Otherworld*, 1998
Ward Rutherford, *Celtic Mythology: The Nature and Influence of Celtic Myth From Druidism to Arthurian Legend*, 1987

827

STEPHEN R. LAWHEAD

Taliesin

(Westchester, Illinois: Crossway, 1987)

Category: Fantasy
Series: Pendragon Cycle
Subject(s): Arthurian Legend; Dark Ages; Fantasy
Age range(s): Young Adult-Adult

Major character(s): Charis, Royalty (Princess of Atlantis), Dancer (bull dancer); Taliesin, Minstrel (bard)
Time period(s): 5th century
Locale(s): Atlantis, Mythical Place; England; Wales

Summary: Charis and her father, King Avallach, are among the few survivors of the cataclysm that destroys Atlantis. They take refuge in Britain, a country struggling to survive intertribal warfare and barbarian legions as Rome begins to withdraw her legions. Here Charis meets Taliesin, a man of mysterious origins who has a dream for unifying his country. Out of their love will come a son, Arthur, whose life adventures will become part of a magnificent, enduring legend.

Awards the book has won:
Gold Medallion Book Award, Fiction, 1988

Other books by the same author:
Grail, 1997
The Pendragon, 1994
Arthur, 1989
Merlin, 1988

Other books you might like:
Gillian Bradshaw, *Imperial Purple*, 1988
Nancy McKenzie, *The Child Queen: The Tale of Guinevere and King Arthur*, 1994

828

BEVERLY LEWIS

The Shunning

(Minneapolis: Bethany House, 1997)

Category: Gentle Reads
Subject(s): Amish; Family Life; Religious Life
Age range(s): Young Adult-Adult
Major character(s): Katie Lapp, Young Woman; Bishop John, Bridegroom (engaged to Katie)
Time period(s): 20th century
Locale(s): Hickory Hollow, Pennsylvania (Lancaster County)

Summary: In a quiet Amish community in Lancaster County, Pennsylvania, young Katie Lapp prepares for her wedding to stately, respectable Bishop John. Alone in the attic of her parents' home, she finds a beautifully embroidered baby's gown made of satin, locked away in a trunk. Not knowing what secrets will be revealed or what consequences might result, Katie presses her parents to explain the presence of the satin dress. What she discovers will change their lives forever.

Other books by the same author:
The Postcard, 1999
The Reckoning, 1998
The Confession, 1997

Other books you might like:
Carrie Bender, *A Winding Path*, 1994
Ted Wojtasik, *No Strange Fire*, 1996
Joseph W. Yoder, *Rosanna of the Amish*, 1995
  Joy Dunn Keenan, illustrator; centennial edition

829

C.S. LEWIS

The Lion, the Witch, and the Wardrobe

(New York: Macmillan, 1950)

Category: Fantasy
Series: Chronicles of Narnia
Subject(s): Good and Evil; Brothers and Sisters; Adventure and Adventurers
Age range(s): Children-Young Adult
Major character(s): Peter, Child; Edmund, Child; Lucy, Child; Susan, Child; Aslan, Lion
Time period(s): 1930s
Locale(s): England; Narnia, Fictional Country

Summary: Four English children are staying in an old estate outside London, sent there to escape World War II air raids. During their visit, they explore hidden rooms and find an old wardrobe that seems to be an ideal place to play. Once inside, however, they are mysteriously transported to the mythical land of Narnia. Returning often through the secret passageway, they have strange adventures; become kings and queens; meet the royal lion, Aslan; and are engaged in the struggle to protect good from evil. A classic of children's literature, this is the first in a series of Christian allegorical stories known as the *Chronicles of Narnia.*

Other books by the same author:
The Horse and His Boy, 1954
The Silver Chair, 1953
The Voyage of the Dawn Treader, 1952
Prince Caspian: The Return to Narnia, 1951

Other books you might like:
Madeleine L'Engle, *A Swiftly Tilting Planet*, 1978
Madeleine L'Engle, *A Wind in the Door*, 1973
Madeleine L'Engle, *A Wrinkle in Time*, 1962
J.R.R. Tolkien, *The Hobbit; or, There and Back Again*, 1937

830

SINCLAIR LEWIS

Elmer Gantry

(New York: Harcourt, Brace and Company, 1927)

Category: Biographical Fiction
Subject(s): Religious Life; Baptists; Ministry
Age range(s): Adult
Major character(s): Elmer Gantry, Religious (fundamentalist preacher)
Time period(s): 1920s
Locale(s): United States

Summary: This satire of organized Christianity met with censure on its publication in 1927. The story of an unsavory Baptist minister who becomes a traveling evangelist and later the head of a Methodist congregation, *Elmer Gantry* points up shortcomings within American fundamentalism of the early 20th century. Not only the stereotypical itinerant preacher was satirized in this novel; hypocrites abound in Sinclair Lewis's portrayal of small town religious folk.

Other books by the same author:
World So Wide, 1951
The God-Seeker, 1949
Main Street, 1920

Other books you might like:
T.R. Pearson, *Gospel Hour,* 1991
Frank G. Slaughter, *Gospel Fever: A Novel about America's Most Beloved TV Evangelist,* 1980
Lee Smith, *Saving Grace,* 1995

831

MICHAEL L. LINDVALL

The Good News From North Haven
(New York: Doubleday, 1991)

Category: Gentle Reads
Subject(s): Rural Life; Christian Life; Presbyterians
Age range(s): Young Adult-Adult
Time period(s): 1990s
Locale(s): North Haven, Minnesota

Summary: Presbyterian minister Michael L. Lindvall turns personal experience into short stories about life in a small-town parish. Through the eyes of a pastor and his wife, Lindvall explores timeless truths and the ways in which they reveal themselves through the most routine events of life in a rural Protestant congregation in Minnesota. The eighteen stories in this collection reveal familiar lessons of life that are easily overlooked until someone like Lindvall articulates them.

Other books you might like:
Jan Karon, *At Home in Mitford,* 1994
Jan Karon, *A New Song,* 1999
Garrison Keillor, *Lake Wobegon Days,* 1985
Garrison Keillor, *We Are Still Married: Stories and Letters,* 1989

832

BARRY LOPEZ
TOM POHRT, Illustrator

Crow and Weasel
(San Francisco: North Point Press, 1990)

Category: Westerns; Fantasy
Subject(s): Indians of North America; Adventure and Adventurers; Legends
Age range(s): Young Adult
Major character(s): Crow, Indian, Young Man; Weasel, Indian, Young Man
Time period(s): Indeterminate
Locale(s): Great Plains, Mythical Place

Summary: Set in a mythical time when all creatures spoke the same language, *Crow and Weasel* is told like a Native American legend. The two main characters dress in garments with accoutrements that illustrator Tom Pohrt modeled after Plains Indians attire and artifacts. As Barry Lopez's story begins, Crow and Weasel embark on a spiritual journey to the North. They plan to go far-farther away than others in their village

have ever traveled. During their quest, they experience many new things. They see the wonders of the earth, brave the various dangers that cross their path, and meet interesting new people and animals. Their journey is one of discovery and growing respect, not only of themselves but of the land, its inhabitants, and "the Above Ones."

Awards the book has won:
Parents' Choice Award, 1990

Other books by the same author:
Lessons From the Wolverine, 1997 (Tom Pohrt, illustrator)
Coyote Love: Native American Folktales, 1989
Of Wolves and Men, 1978
Giving Birth to Thunder, Sleeping with His Daughter: Coyote Builds North America, 1977

Other books you might like:
John Bierhorst, *On the Road of Stars: Native American Night Poems and Sleep Charms,* 1995
Judy Pedersen, co-author
Gretchen Will Mayo, *Earthmaker's Tales,* 1990
Gerald McDermott, *Raven: A Trickster Tale From the Pacific Northwest,* 1993
Jerrie Oughton, *How the Stars Fell into the Sky,* 1992
Gerald Vizenor, *Dead Voices: Natural Agonies in the Real World,* 1992
Rosebud Yellow Robe, *Tonweya and the Eagles,* 1992
Jerry Pinkney, co-author

833

MAX LUCADO

The Christmas Cross: A Story about Finding Your Way Home for the Holidays
(Nashville: Word, 1998)

Category: Gentle Reads
Subject(s): Christmas; Love; Family Life
Age range(s): Children-Adult

Summary: Read along with the man whose mail leads him on a journey into his past. Find out why someone sent him a picture of a little church in Texas. Travel with him as he visits the small town where he was born, and share in his happiness when he finally finds what he has been missing all along. *The Christmas Cross* is a lushly illustrated and interactive (featuring envelopes to open with surprises inside) Christmas story suitable for readers of all ages.

Other books by the same author:
Christmas Stories for the Heart, 1999
The Heart of Christmas, 1998
Cosmic Christmas, 1997

Other books you might like:
Richard Paul Evans, *The Christmas Box,* 1993
Carol Lynn Pearson, *The Modern Magi: A Christmas Fable,* 1995
Joe Wheeler, *Christmas in My Heart: A Treasury of Holiday Classics,* 1996

834

MAX LUCADO
GREG DEARTH, Illustrator

Cosmic Christmas

(Nashville: Word, 1997)

Category: Gentle Reads
Subject(s): Christianity; Heaven; Christmas
Age range(s): Young Adult-Adult

Summary: In *Cosmic Christmas*, storyteller Max Lucado weaves a tale of the Christmas story told from the perspective of the angels in heaven. Lucado's retelling is not the stereotypical angel-story-of-Christmas-glory, however. He explores the aspect of heavenly wars and the role of Lucifer in the conflict that preceded the birth of the baby whose life and death would change the world.

Other books by the same author:
Christmas Stories for the Heart, 1999
The Gift for All People, 1999
Let the Journey Begin, 1998
No Wonder They Call Him the Savior, 1996
God Came Near: Chronicles of Christ, 1987

Other books you might like:
Andrew Clements, *Bright Christmas: An Angel Remembers*, 1996
    children's title; Kate Kiesler, illustrator
Gene Edwards, *The Birth*, 1991
Walter Wangerin Jr., *The Book of God: The Bible as a Novel*, 1996

835

GEORGE MACDONALD
LINDA HILL GRIFFITH, Illustrator

The Christmas Stories of George MacDonald

(Elgin, Illinois: David C. Cook, 1981)

Category: Gentle Reads
Subject(s): Christmas; Children
Age range(s): Children-Adult
Locale(s): Scotland

Summary: George MacDonald (1824-1905) was a Scottish preacher, poet, novelist, and storyteller best known for his children's books. During his lifetime he published more than fifty popular books, but by the mid-twentieth century, only a few of his children's books were still in print. A late twentieth-century resurgence of interest in his works, however, has led to the re-release of many of his novels, some of which have been edited for younger contemporary audiences. This is a compilation of Christmas stories including "My Uncle Peter," "A Scot's Christmas Story," "The Angel's Song," and "The Christmas Child."

Other books by the same author:
For the Childlike: George MacDonald's Fantasies for Children, 1992

Diary of an Old Soul: 366 Writings for Devotional Reflection, 1965
Complete Fairy Stories of George MacDonald, 1962
George MacDonald: An Anthology by C.S. Lewis, 1947
At the Back of the North Wind, 1924

Other books you might like:
Charles Dickens, *A Christmas Carol, in Prose: Being a Ghost Story of Christmas*, 1843
Susan Hill, *The Christmas Collection*, 1994
Katherine Paterson, *Angels and Other Strangers: Family Christmas Stories*, 1988
Neil Philip, *Christmas Fairy Tales*, 1996

836

GEORGE MACDONALD

The Curate's Awakening

(Minneapolis: Bethany House, 1985)

Category: Gentle Reads
Subject(s): Clergy; Christian Life
Age range(s): Young Adult-Adult
Major character(s): Thomas Wingfold, Religious (curate)
Time period(s): 1870s
Locale(s): Scotland

Summary: *The Curate's Awakening* is a revised edition of MacDonald's classic *Thomas Wingfold, Curate*, which was originally published in 1876. The protagonist, Thomas Wingfold, is a young minister who enters a church vocation simply as a profession, yet comes to search for the truth of Christianity through his work. The sequel to the original story is *Paul Faber*, which has been republished as *The Lady's Confession*.

Other books by the same author:
The Lady's Confession, 1986
Diary of an Old Soul: 366 Writings for Devotional Reflection, 1965
Complete Fairy Stories of George MacDonald, 1962
George MacDonald: An Anthology by C.S. Lewis, 1947
At the Back of the North Wind, 1924

Other books you might like:
Jeanine Hathaway, *Motherhouse: A Novel*, 1992
Ignazio Silone, *Bread and Wine*, 1937
    Gwenda David, Eric Mosbacher, translators
Harold Bell Wright, *The Shepherd of the Hills*, 1907

837

GEORGE MACDONALD

The Minister's Restoration

(Minneapolis: Bethany House, 1988)

Category: Gentle Reads
Subject(s): Clergy; Christian Life; Marriage
Age range(s): Young Adult-Adult
Time period(s): 1890s
Locale(s): Scotland

Summary: *The Minister's Restoration* is a revised edition of *Salted with Fire*, published in 1897. As a minister himself, the life and work of the clergy were favorite topics for the Scottish novelist. This is the story of an aspiring young minister whose dabbling with romance distracts him from his purpose. After a good dose of ''salting with fire,'' he and his young love decide to wed, and he returns fully to his calling.

Other books by the same author:

Diary of an Old Soul: 366 Writings for Devotional Reflection, 1965

Complete Fairy Stories of George MacDonald, 1962

George MacDonald: An Anthology by C.S. Lewis, 1947

At the Back of the North Wind, 1924

Other books you might like:

Harold Frederic, *The Damnation of Theron Ware*, 1915

Jan Karon, *The Mitford Series*, 1994-

Harold Bell Wright, *The Calling of Dan Matthews*, 1909

838

GEORGE MACDONALD
LINDA HILL GRIFFITH, Illustrator

The Princess and the Goblin

(Elgin, Illinois: Chariot, 1985)

Category: Gentle Reads
Subject(s): Fairy Tales; Children; Good and Evil
Age range(s): Children-Adult
Locale(s): Scotland

Summary: *The Princess and the Goblin* (1872) is one of George MacDonald's best-known and best-loved stories. It is a tale of good vs. evil, in which the Children of the Light must battle the darkness of the underground world. There are many editions of the story available featuring different illustrators; this one won the Gold Medallion Book Award for Classics in 1986. *The Princess and Curdie* is the sequel to the story.

Awards the book has won:

Gold Medallion Book Award, Classics, 1986

Other books by the same author:

The Princess and Curdie, 1980 (Peter Wane, illustrator)

Diary of an Old Soul: 366 Writings for Devotional Reflection, 1965

Complete Fairy Stories of George MacDonald, 1962

George MacDonald: An Anthology by C.S. Lewis, 1947

At the Back of the North Wind, 1924

Other books you might like:

Susan Cooper, *The Dark Is Rising Sequence*, 1965-1977

Madeleine L'Engle, *A Wrinkle in Time*, 1962

C.S. Lewis, *The Lion, the Witch, and the Wardrobe*, 1950

Antoine de Saint-Exupery, *The Little Prince*, 1943

Carl Sandburg, *Rootabaga Stories*, 1922

839

GEORGE MACDONALD

The Wanderings of Clare Skymer

(Wheaton, Illinois: Victor Books, 1987)

Category: Gentle Reads
Subject(s): Orphans; Christianity; Survival

Age range(s): Young Adult
Major character(s): Clare Skymer, Orphan
Time period(s): 1880s
Locale(s): England

Summary: *The Wanderings of Clare Skymer* is a revised edition of MacDonald's 1890 story *A Rough Shaking*. Clare is a young boy whose parents die in an earthquake, leaving him to survive alone. He wanders throughout the English countryside, surviving in part because of his sensitivity to animals. He encounters adventures along his way with thieves, hobos, and others who are outcasts or runaways from society. Always, his devotion to God keeps him strong.

Other books by the same author:

Diary of an Old Soul: 366 Writings for Devotional Reflection, 1965

Complete Fairy Stories of George MacDonald, 1962

George MacDonald: An Anthology by C.S. Lewis, 1947

At the Back of the North Wind, 1924

Other books you might like:

Frances Hodgson Burnett, *The Secret Garden*, 1911

Peter Dickinson, *Suth's Story*, 1998

Sherry Garland, *The Silent Storm*, 1993

840

ARCHIBALD MACLEISH

''J.B.'': A Play in Verse

(Boston: Houghton Mifflin, 1957)

Category: Plays
Subject(s): Scripture; Religion; Survival
Age range(s): Adult
Major character(s): J.B., Father, Spouse (of Sara); Sara, Spouse (of J.B.)
Time period(s): 20th century (mid-century)

Summary: Archibald MacLeish's Pulitzer Prize-winning drama in verse depicts the biblical story of Job. J.B., the Job-like protagonist of the play, endures tragedy after tragedy, loss after loss, including the deaths of his children and desertion by his wife. The drama is structured as a play within a play-the Job story is the inner play, framed within the structure of a modern traveling circus. *''J.B''.: A Play in Verse* examines the themes of religion, God, and suffering in the context of twentieth-century culture and values.

Awards the book has won:

Pulitzer Prize, Drama, 1959

Other books by the same author:

Archibald MacLeish: Reflections, 1986

The Trojan Horse, 1952 (verse play)

The Son of Man, 1947 (play)

The Happy Marriage and Other Poems, 1924

Other books you might like:

Gustavo Gutierrez, *On Job: God-Talk and the Suffering of the Innocent*, 1987

Stephen Mitchell, *The Book of Job*, 1992

Thomas Moore, *The Book of Job*, 1998

841

PAUL L. MAIER

A Skeleton in God's Closet: A Novel

(Nashville: T. Nelson, 1994)

Category: Thrillers
Subject(s): Archaeology; Christianity; History
Age range(s): Young Adult-Adult
Major character(s): Jon Weber, Archaeologist
Time period(s): 1990s
Locale(s): Israel

Summary: Jon Weber is an archaeologist who has made the discovery of the millennium. There seems to be little doubt that the bones he found in a tomb in Israel are those of Jesus. The implications of this find are enormous, as are the potential consequences for those involved in every step of the investigation and study of the remains. Dr. Paul L. Maier, author of *A Skeleton in God's Closet*, is an esteemed professor of ancient history whose storytelling ability makes it possible to seamlessly blend many levels of scientific and historic reality with an exciting and not always predictable storyline. Just when everything seems to have fallen into place, the plot takes another twist, and there is a surprise at the end.

Other books by the same author:
The Flames of Rome, 1981 (novel)
First Christians: Pentecost and the Spread of Christianity, 1976
Pontius Pilate, 1968 (novel)

Other books you might like:
Michael L. Monhollon, *Divine Invasion*, 1998
Bill Myers, *Blood of Heaven*, 1996
Piers Paul Read, *On the Third Day*, 1990

842

NORMAN MAILER

The Gospel According to the Son

(New York: Random House, 1997)

Category: Biographical Fiction; Mainstream Fiction
Subject(s): Scripture; Christianity
Age range(s): Adult
Major character(s): Jesus, Historical Figure, Biblical Figure; Judas, Biblical Figure, Historical Figure; Satan, Biblical Figure
Time period(s): 1st century (0-33)
Locale(s): Palestine; Israel

Summary: *The Gospel According to the Son* is Norman Mailer's literary effort to write the story of the life of Jesus from the perspective of Jesus-imagined, of course. While the narrative follows the outlines of the scriptural accounts of the external events of Jesus' life, Mailer applies his literary license to interpreting the inner life of Christ. He depicts Jesus as a man who performs miracles that drain him physically and emotionally; a man who sometimes loses his temper and questions whether or not he has said or done the right thing; a man whose decision to write his own gospel is rooted in

exasperation at how he has been portrayed in the existing gospels of the New Testament.

Other books by the same author:
Oswald's Tale: An American Mystery, 1995
Marilyn, a Biography, 1987
The Executioner's Song, 1979
American Dream, 1965

Other books you might like:
Jim Crace, *Quarantine*, 1997
Nikos Kazantzakis, *The Last Temptation of Christ*, 1960
Reynolds Price, *The Three Gospels*, 1996

843

DAVID MAINS
KAREN BURTON MAINS, Co-Author
JACK STOCKMAN, Illustrator

Tales of the Kingdom

(Elgin, Illinois: Chariot Books, 1983)

Category: Morality Tales
Subject(s): Allegories; Christian Life; Conduct of Life
Age range(s): Children-Adult

Summary: Reminiscent of stories by J.R.R. Tolkien or C.S. Lewis, David and Karen Burton Mains present allegorical tales about the quest for redemption in Christian life. The stories in *Tales of the Kingdom* and its companion volumes, *Tales of the Resistance* and *Tales of the Restoration*, depict the eternal struggle between good and evil and the ultimate reward of unconditional love.

Awards the book has won:
Gold Medallion Book Award, Children's Books, 1984

Other books by the same author:
When the Troops Are Tired!: 8 Miraculous Energizers to Tap Into, 1997
Tales of the Restoration, 1996 (Karen Mains, co-author; Diana Magnuson, illustrator)
Abba: How God Parents Us, 1989 (Karen Mains, co-author)
Parenting: How God Does It, 1986
Tales of the Resistance, 1986 (Karen Mains, co-author; Jack Stockman, illustrator)

Other books you might like:
John R. Aurelio, *Colors: Stories of the Kingdom*, 1993
C.S. Lewis, *Chronicles of Narnia*, 1950-1956
Ron Mills, *Kingdom Tales: Five Stories Jesus Told*, 1998
J.R.R. Tolkien, *The Hobbit; or, There and Back Again*, 1937

844

BERNARD MALAMUD

The Fixer

(New York: Farrar, Straus, and Giroux, 1966)

Category: Biographical Fiction
Subject(s): Jews; Anti-Semitism; Russian Empire
Age range(s): Young Adult-Adult

Major character(s): Yakov Shepsovitch Bok, Handyman, Prisoner; B.A. Bibikov, Detective—Police; Grubeshov, Lawyer (prosecuting attorney)
Time period(s): 1900s; 1910s
Locale(s): Kiev, Russia

Summary: This novel is loosely based on the life of a turn-of-the-century Russian Jew, who is accused of the ritual murder of a Gentile child. The work traces the experiences of Yakov Bok, a handyman or ''fixer,'' who is coerced into confessing to the crime and is used as an excuse by Tsarist officials to begin a pogrom. While incarcerated, Bok begins to reconsider the meaning of his Jewishness. The novel, which explores themes of spiritual and cultural identity, ends with Bok's fate in doubt as his trial begins.

Awards the book has won:
National Book Award, Fiction, 1967
Pulitzer Prize, Fiction, 1967

Other books by the same author:
God's Grace, 1982
The Assistant, 1957
The Natural, 1952

Other books you might like:
Rodger Kamenetz, *Stalking Elijah: Adventures with Today's Jewish Mystical Masters*, 1997
Binjamin Wilkomirski, *Fragments: Memories of a Wartime Childhood*, 1996

845

OG MANDINO

The Christ Commission

(New York: Lippincott & Crowell, 1980)

Category: Fantasy
Subject(s): Time Travel; Scripture
Age range(s): Adult
Major character(s): Matt Lawrence, Writer
Time period(s): 1st century (26)
Locale(s): Judea

Summary: In *The Christ Commission*, mystery writer Matt Lawrence brags that, given one week in ancient Jerusalem after the crucifixion of Christ, he could prove that Christ was never resurrected from the dead, thereby disproving the foundation of Christianity. Much to his surprise, he finds himself transported in time, as the result of a knock-out punch, and walking the streets where Jesus had been just a few years earlier. Remembering his mission, he begins his investigation, despite some not-unexpected dangers and obstacles. He knows that eyewitness testimony could lead him to solve the biggest mystery ever.but exactly which mystery it is, he's not so sure about now. And will he be able to travel back to his own century to share the explosive discoveries he expects to make?

Other books by the same author:
Spellbinder's Gift, 1995
The Choice, 1984
The Greatest Miracle in the World, 1975

Other books you might like:
James Allen, *As a Man Thinketh*, 1910
George S. Clason, *The Richest Man in Babylon*, 1955
Russell H. Conwell, *Acres of Diamonds: All Good Things Are Possible, Right Where You Are, and Now!*, 1993

846

OG MANDINO

The Greatest Salesman in the World

(New York: F. Fell, 1968)

Category: Morality Tales
Subject(s): Success; Business
Age range(s): Adult
Major character(s): Hafid, Young Man

Summary: Og Mandino's bestselling book *The Greatest Salesman in the World* combines ancient storytelling and the world of business in a motivational tale with Christian overtones. Hafid is a poor camel boy whose life is changed through his encounter with ten scrolls containing mystical wisdom. The fable of Hafid's life implies that the mysterious scrolls were divine teachings that he passed on to Paul, whose letters of guidance and wisdom written to Christian communities throughout the Mediterranean region now make up much of the modern-day New Testament.

Other books by the same author:
Spellbinder's Gift, 1995
The Choice, 1984
The Greatest Miracle in the World, 1975

Other books you might like:
James Allen, *As a Man Thinketh*, 1910
George S. Clason, *The Richest Man in Babylon*, 1955
Russell H. Conwell, *Acres of Diamonds: All Good Things Are Possible, Right Where You Are, and Now!*, 1993

847

OG MANDINO

The Twelfth Angel

(New York: Fawcett Columbine, 1993)

Category: Gentle Reads
Subject(s): Family Life; Grief; Courage
Age range(s): Young Adult-Adult
Major character(s): John Harding, Businessman; Timothy Noble, Child
Time period(s): 1990s
Locale(s): Boland, New Hampshire

Summary: John Harding is a successful businessman at the helm of a profitable software company, Millennium Unlimited. He and his wife and young son have returned to John's hometown in New Hampshire to put down roots as a family. Then tragedy strikes, and John's world is turned upside down. With support and encouragement from his friends and associates, John begins reaching out to the world in new ways. As the manager of a Little League team, John is drawn toward charismatic little Timothy Noble. John teaches Tim to hit a ball; Tim teaches John to embrace life. When the next tragedy looms, John is more spiritually prepared to help himself and others. *The Twelfth Angel* is a non-sectarian inspirational fable of love and courage.

Other books by the same author:
Spellbinder's Gift, 1995
The Choice, 1984
The Greatest Miracle in the World, 1975

Other books you might like:
James Allen, *As a Man Thinketh*, 1910
George S. Clason, *The Richest Man in Babylon*, 1955
Russell H. Conwell, *Acres of Diamonds: All Good Things Are Possible, Right Where You Are, and Now!*, 1993

848

CATHERINE MARSHALL
JOE BODDY, Illustrator

Catherine Marshall's Storybook for Children

(Old Tappan, New Jersey: Chosen Books, 1987)

Category: Morality Tales
Subject(s): Children; Storytelling; Christian Life
Age range(s): Children

Summary: Catherine Marshall uses elegant prose and heartfelt spirituality to share Christian values with young readers in this collection of short stories. *Catherine Marshall's Storybook for Children* offers stories and poems that focus on faith, honesty, kindness, and other Christian attributes and values.

Awards the book has won:
Gold Medallion Book Award, Elementary Children, 1988

Other books by the same author:
Julie, 1984
Catherine Marshall's Story Bible, 1982
Christy, 1967

Other books you might like:
William J. Bennett, *The Children's Book of Virtues*, 1995
    Michael Hague, illustrator
Lawrence Castagnola, *Parables for Little People*, 1982
    Nancy LaBerge Muren, illustrator
Richard Gardiner, *Dr. Gardiner's Fables for Our Times*, 1981
Colin Greer, *A Call to Character: A Family Treasury: Of Stories, Poems, Plays, Proverbs, and Fables to Guide the Development of Values for You and Your Children*, 1995
    Herbert Kohl, co-editor

849

CATHERINE MARSHALL

Christy

(New York: McGraw-Hill, 1967)

Category: Biographical Fiction
Subject(s): Christian Life; Appalachia
Age range(s): Young Adult-Adult
Major character(s): Christy Huddleston, 19-Year-Old, Teacher
Time period(s): 1910s

Locale(s): Cutter Gap, Kentucky

Summary: In 1912, young Christy Huddleston leaves the stability of her comfortable family home to become a teacher in a tiny town in the Smoky Mountains. Cutter Gap, Kentucky, holds many challenges for the 19-year-old who nonetheless believes she is called to do this work. Adjusting to unfamiliar mountain life and rural customs, learning the ropes as a teacher, and dealing with the romantic attentions of two men are all part of Christy's new life. Based on the life of the author's mother, this novel has become a staple of inspirational Christian fiction.

Other books by the same author:
Christy's Choice, 1996
The Proposal, 1996
Julie, 1984

Other books you might like:
Louisa May Alcott, *Little Women; or Meg, Jo, Beth, and Amy*, 1868
June Masters Bacher, *The Journey West: Love Is a Gentle Stranger*, 1996
L.M. Montgomery, *Anne of Avonlea*, 1909
L.M. Montgomery, *Anne of Green Gables*, 1908
Laura Ingalls Wilder, *Little House on the Prairie*, 1935
Brenda Wilbee, *Sweetbriar Summer*, 1997

850

CATHERINE MARSHALL

Julie

(New York: McGraw-Hill, 1984)

Category: Biographical Fiction
Subject(s): Christian Life; Family Relations; Identity
Age range(s): Young Adult-Adult
Major character(s): Julie Paige Wallace, 18-Year-Old, Daughter (of newspaper editor), Journalist
Time period(s): 1930s
Locale(s): Alderton, Pennsylvania

Summary: In a novel set during the Great Depression years in Alderton, Pennsylvania, Catherine Marshall tells the story of Julie Paige Wallace. Julie's father, once a minister, is now the editor of the small local newspaper. His daughter is a talented young reporter making her way into the business while wrestling with the normal concerns of an 18-year-old who is seeking her place in the world. The novel follows Julie's spiritual and personal journey through family, romantic, and small-town community circumstances, bringing to life both a spunky heroine and a historically accurate snapshot of life in small-town America during the 1930s. As in the novel *Christy*, the author draws upon experiences from her own life to portray Julie and her world.

Other books by the same author:
Christy's Choice, 1996
The Proposal, 1996
Christy, 1967

Other books you might like:
Patricia Hagan, *The Daring*, 1991
Susan Kirby, *Prairie Rose*, 1997
Susan Kirby, *When Lilacs Bloom*, 1997

851

FRANCOIS MAURIAC

Vipers' Tangle

(London: V. Gollancz, Ltd., 1933)

Category: Morality Tales
Subject(s): Catholicism; Redemption
Age range(s): Adult
Major character(s): Louis, Wealthy, Spouse (of Isa); Isa, Spouse (of Louis)

Summary: Francois Mauriac was a Roman Catholic whose novels reflect conflicts between good and evil within the Catholic universe. In *Vipers' Tangle*, an elderly narrator recounts the circumstances of his life-those over which he had no control as well as those which he willed upon himself and others-in an effort to discover the source of his deep and lifelong unhappiness. An excessively wealthy man, Louis has committed any number of wrong-doings against others in the course of managing his business and personal affairs. He has caused and endured emotional estrangement from his wife, Isa, his children, and virtually everyone else in this life, except for his overbearing mother. Although he is a wretched and unlovable character, it is exactly love that is missing in his life, and it is only love that ultimately redeems the evil of his life.

Other books by the same author:
The Holy Terror, 1967
The Weakling, and the Enemy, 1952
The Desert of Love, 1949 (Gerard Hopkins, translator)
The Unknown Sea, 1948 (Gerard Hopkins, translator)
Woman of the Pharisees, 1946 (Gerard Hopkins, translator)

Other books you might like:
Charles Dickens, *A Christmas Carol, in Prose: Being a Ghost Story of Christmas*, 1843
George Eliot, *Silas Marner*, 1861
J.E. Flower, *A Critical Commentary on Mauriac's "Le Noeud de Vipres"*, 1969
Selma Lagerlof, *The Story of Gosta Berling*, 1894

852

JOSH MCDOWELL
DOTTIE MCDOWELL, Co-Author
ANN NIELSEN, Illustrator

Katie's Adventure at Blueberry Pond

(Elgin, Illinois: Chariot Books, 1988)

Category: Morality Tales
Subject(s): Christian Life; Children
Age range(s): Children
Major character(s): Katie, Child

Summary: Katie thinks that the family rule about having an adult go with her to Blueberry Pond is just to keep her from having fun. Naturally, she breaks the rule and heads to the pond on her own, encountering just the sort of circumstances the rule was made to avoid. In the end, she learns that both family rules and God's laws are made out of love, to protect her and keep her safe.

Awards the book has won:
Gold Medallion Book Award, Pre-School Children, 1989

Other books by the same author:
The Topsy-Turvy Kingdom, 1996 (Dottie McDowell, David Nathan Weiss, co-authors; Lydia Taranovic, illustrator)
New Friends, Good Friends?, 1992 (Dottie McDowell, co-author; Kathy Kulin-Sandel, illustrator)
Pizza for Everyone, 1988 (Dottie McDowell, co-author; Meredith Johnson, illustrator)

Other books you might like:
Paul Hutchens, *The Battle of the Bees*, 1999
Catherine Marshall, *Catherine Marshall's Storybook for Children*, 1987
Jane Belk Moncure, *Terry's Turnaround*, 1982
John Trent, *The Treasure Tree*, 1992

853

RALPH MCINERNY

The Red Hat: A Novel

(San Francisco: Ignatius Press, 1998)

Category: Thrillers
Subject(s): Catholicism; Murder; Politics
Age range(s): Adult
Major character(s): Archbishop Thomas Lannan, Religious (Archbishop)
Time period(s): 1990s
Locale(s): Washington, District of Columbia; Rome, Italy (Vatican)

Summary: *The Red Hat* is a novel of suspense, intrigue, and murder, revolving around one man's quest for the red hat of the title-an appointment to Cardinal in the Roman Catholic Church. Thomas Lannan has had that dream for a lifetime. As Archbishop of Washington, D.C., and in other influential positions within the hierarchy of the Catholic Church, he is poised to win the prize-indeed, he is called to the Vatican to receive his red hat-when circumstances begin to intervene. The plot involves the death of two popes, the kidnapping of Archbishop Lannan, the murder of a woman, and more. Just as it appears that Lannan will finally achieve his dream, rumors of an illegitimate child surface. McInerny, who is also the creator of the Father Dowling mystery series, uses his knowledge of the politics and history of the Roman Catholic church to great effect in his storytelling.

Other books by the same author:
Lack of the Irish: A Mystery Set at the University of Notre Dame, 1998
On This Rockne: A Notre Dame Mystery, 1998
What Went Wrong with Vatican II: The Catholic Crisis Explained, 1998
The Search Committee, 1991

Other books you might like:
Michael D. O'Brien, *Eclipse of the Sun: A Novel*, 1998
Edward R.F. Sheehan, *Cardinal Galsworthy: A Novel*, 1997
Philip Trower, *A Danger to the State: A Historical Novel*, 1998

854

L.T. MEADE

Priscilla's Promise

(Eugene, Oregon: Harvest House, 1998)

Category: Gentle Reads
Subject(s): College Life; Friendship; Christian Life
Age range(s): Young Adult-Adult
Major character(s): Priscilla Peel, 19-Year-Old, Student—College, Friend (of Maggie and Geoffrey); Maggie Oliphant, Friend (of Priscilla); Geoffrey Hammond, Friend (of Maggie and Priscilla)
Time period(s): 1890s
Locale(s): Kingsdene, England

Summary: *Priscilla's Promise* is a Victorian novel, first published in 1891 as *A Sweet Girl-Graduate*, about life in an exclusive women's college at the end of the 19th century. Priscilla Peel's social and economic background has not prepared her for the cliques of fashionable young women she encounters at St. Benet's College for Women. Naive, studious, and earnest, she is bewildered by the gossip and petty meanness of some of her new house-mates and fellow students. Her plan is to study the classics and earn a degree that will allow her to earn a comfortable living for herself, her aunt, and her three sisters. Her fondest wish is for the people she cares about to be happy, and that includes her family and her dear new friends Maggie Oliphant and Geoffrey Hammond. This book is an example of a turn-of-the-century girls' novel, reflecting the manners and mores of Victorian gentlewomen. It is one of several novels of its age revived by Harvest House Publishers in the Victorian Bookshelf collection.

Other books by the same author:
The Time of Roses, 1900
Stories From the Diary of a Doctor, 1895

Other books you might like:
Isabella Macdonald Alden, *Julia Ried*, 1900
Francena H. Arnold, *Not My Will*, 1946
Grace Livingston Hill, *Crimson Roses*, 1928
Florence Irwin, *Dear Theodora*, 1998
   new edition of *Poor Dear Theodora*, 1900
Dwight Tilton, *A Gift for Abigail*, 1998
   new edition of *Miss Petticoats*, 1902

855

PAUL MEIER
ROBERT WISE, Co-Author

The Fourth Millennium: The Sequel

(Nashville: T. Nelson, 1996)

Category: Thrillers
Subject(s): Millennium; Apocalypse
Age range(s): Adult
Major character(s): Ben Feinberg, Professor; Jimmy Harrison, Relative (brother-in-law of Ben)
Time period(s): Indeterminate (997 N.E. (New Era))

Summary: *The Fourth Millennium* is the sequel to Paul Meier's bestselling *The Third Millennium*. It is now the year 997 N.E. (New Era), the 1000th year of the reign of Yeshua, also known as Jesus. There has been world peace for more than 900 years and technological advances have led to a good life for virtually everyone. Life expectancy has increased dramatically. The central character in this installment of Meier's apocalyptic series is 1034-year-old Ben Feinberg, a political science professor. He has noticed a certain cynicism among the younger members of society—people who were not around to witness and live through the apocalyptic horrors he remembers so clearly from 1000 years ago. There are other worrisome signs that all is not right. AIDS, thought to have been eradicated, is showing up again. And with his brother-in-law, Jimmy Harrison, Ben discovers there is an undercover conspiracy making plans to stage a global revolution. After the millennium of peace, the final confrontation between Satan and Yeshua is looming, and Ben wonders if he will survive the mayhem that is sure to accompany this history-changing event.

Other books by the same author:
The Secret Code: A Novel, 1999 (Robert Wise, co-author)
Beyond the Millennium, 1998 (Robert Wise, co-author)
The Third Millennium: A Novel, 1993

Other books you might like:
Randy Alcorn, *Deadline: A Novel*, 1994
Tim LaHaye, *Left Behind: A Novel of the Earth's Last Days*, 1995
   Jerry B. Jenkins, co-author
Christopher A. Lane, *Appearance of Evil*, 1997
Bill Myers, *Blood of Heaven*, 1996
Michael Phillips, *A Rift in Time*, 1997

856

PAUL MEIER

The Third Millennium: A Novel

(Nashville: Thomas Nelson, 1993)

Category: Thrillers
Subject(s): Millennium; Apocalypse
Age range(s): Adult
Major character(s): Michael, Angel (guardian), Narrator; Dr. Larry Feinberg, Doctor (psychiatrist)
Time period(s): 1990s; 2000s
Locale(s): Newport Beach, California

Summary: At the dawning of the third millennium, the apocalyptic prophecies of the New Testament begin to be fulfilled as the final years of human history play out and the Antichrist appears, foreshadowing the return of Jesus. Paul Meier's novel *The Third Millennium* is narrated by Michael, a guardian angel assigned to protect psychiatrist Dr. Larry Feinberg and his family in California. He tells the story of end-times trials and tribulations creating chaos in the world and turmoil in the family. What will come to pass as the age of man winds down and the reign of Yeshua is ushered in?

Other books by the same author:
The Secret Code: A Novel, 1999 (Robert Wise, co-author)
Beyond the Millennium, 1998 (Robert Wise, co-author)

The Fourth Millennium: The Sequel, 1996 (Robert Wise, co-author)

Other books you might like:
Randy Alcorn, *Deadline: A Novel*, 1994
Tim LaHaye, *Left Behind: A Novel of the Earth's Last Days*, 1995
   Jerry B. Jenkins, co-author
Christopher A. Lane, *Appearance of Evil*, 1997
Bill Myers, *Blood of Heaven*, 1996
Michael Phillips, *A Rift in Time*, 1997

857
CALVIN MILLER

Walking with the Angels, the Valiant Papers & the Philippian Fragment
(Grand Rapids, Michigan: Baker Books, 1994)

Category: Fantasy
Subject(s): Angels
Age range(s): Adult

Summary: In three tales, one of which is published for the first time in this edition, Calvin Miller explores the unseen influence of angels on the visible world. What are guardian angels? Do they have limitations on their involvement in human life? Can they manipulate human activity, and if so, how? Miller weaves these questions and their answers into engrossing fiction in *Walking with the Angels, The Valiant Papers, & The Philippian Fragment.*

Other books by the same author:
Disarming the Darkness: A Guide to Spiritual Warfare, 1998
The Book of 7 Truths: A Tale of Hope and Restoration, 1997
The Singer Trilogy: The Mythic Retelling of the Story of the New Testament, 1990 (Joe DeVelasco, illustrator)
The Taste of Joy, 1983

Other books you might like:
Roger Elwood, *Angelwalk: A Modern Fable*, 1988
Roger Elwood, *Fallen Angel: A Novel*, 1990
Roger Elwood, *Stedfast: Guardian Angel*, 1992
Andrew M. Greeley, *Angel Fire*, 1988

858
CAROLINE MILLER

Lamb in His Bosom
(New York: Harper & Brothers, 1933)

Category: Gentle Reads; Historical Fiction
Subject(s): Family Life; Rural Life
Age range(s): Adult
Major character(s): Cean Carver, Spouse (of Lonzo), Mother; Lonzo Smith, Spouse (of Cean); Margot Kimbrough, Relative (sister-in-law of Cean)
Time period(s): 19th century (early to mid-century)
Locale(s): Georgia

Summary: *Lamb in His Bosom*, winner of the Pulitzer Prize for Fiction in 1934, is a story of rural pioneer life and the inner and outer lives of one family, the Carvers. While there is little plot, there are many episodes and vignettes that portray the daily lives of Cean Carver, her husband and children, and her other relatives by blood and by marriage. Women's self-identity is one theme that runs throughout Caroline Miller's novel: Cean Carver, newly married at the outset of the story, defines her identity as a woman, rather than as a girl, by her relationship to her husband and to the fact that she ''belonged'' to him, which in turn allows her to ''belong'' to herself. In contrast, Margot Kimbrough, Cean's sister-in-law, possesses a sense of self that is not shaped by her relationships, but is understood in relationship to them. The novel explores the small triumphs and daily hardships of families trying to live their lives as best they can.

Awards the book has won:
Pulitzer Prize, Fiction, 1934

Other books by the same author:
Lebanon, 1944

Other books you might like:
Gladys Hasty Carroll, *As the Earth Turns*, 1933
Harold Lenoir Davis, *Honey in the Horn*, 1935
Charles Frazier, *Cold Mountain*, 1997

859
STEPHEN MITCHELL

Meetings with the Archangel
(New York: HarperFlamingo, 1998)

Category: Fantasy
Subject(s): Allegories; Heaven; Angels
Age range(s): Adult
Major character(s): Gabriel, Angel (archangel); Stephen, Writer, Narrator; David Copland, Religious (Zen master)
Time period(s): 20th century (mid-to-late)

Summary: An author by the name of Stephen has written a book debunking the angel-centered spirituality of the late 20th century. His life is disrupted, to say the least, when the archangel Gabriel appears to him to confirm the existence of angels as the mirror of people's subconscious minds and thoughts. When Gabriel isn't revealing such previously unknown facts about angels as what their sex lives are like, he is engaging Stephen, the narrator of the story, in a spiritual journey that illuminates the relationship between his current work and his ongoing quest for spiriutal enlightenment. Gabriel leads Stephen on a spiritual trip down memory lane that reveals his youthful dabblings in mysticism and ultimate discovery of Zen spirituality through New York City-born Zen master David Copland. Through often funny fiction, the author of *Meetings with the Archangel* asks some of the big questions of religion: What is truth? Love? And what do the answers to these questions tell us about how we should live?

Other books by the same author:
An Enlightened Heart: An Anthology of Sacred Poetry, 1993
The Book of Job, 1992
The Gospel According to Jesus: A New Translation and Guide to His Essential Teachings for Believers and Unbelievers, 1991
Parables and Portraits, 1990

Other books you might like:
Nelson Foster, *The Roaring Stream: A New Zen Reader*, 1996
Seikan Hasegawa, *Mind to Mind: A Novel*, 1999
John Tarrant, *The Light Inside the Dark: Zen, Soul and the Spiritual Life*, 1998

860

N. SCOTT MOMADAY

House Made of Dawn

(New York: Harper and Row, 1968)

Category: Historical Fiction
Subject(s): Indians of North America; Race Relations; Identity
Age range(s): Adult
Major character(s): Francisco, Indian, Grandfather (of Abel); Abel, Indian, Convict, Relative (of Francisco)
Time period(s): 20th century (1945-1969)
Locale(s): Walatowa, New Mexico (a small Pueblo village); Los Angeles, California

Summary: This novel centers on a Native American named Abel, the illegitimate son of a Tanoan mother and a father of unknown origin. Born in the pueblo (village) of Walatowa, Abel is raised by his grandfather, Francisco. He leaves the village in young adulthood. Abel is portrayed as a Native American who feels lost and displaced in white America, reflecting the difficulty of navigating through two cultures. Shortly after returning from World War II, Abel is convicted of murder, and after serving seven years in jail, he relocates to Los Angeles. He eventually returns to Walatowa to perform the traditional Tanoan burial ritual for his grandfather. While singing a Navajo prayer called ''House Made of Dawn,'' Abel experiences a moment of peace and achieves a measure of the self-definition he is seeking. Throughout the novel, Momaday explores themes of spiritual and cultural identity and reverence for the earth.

Awards the book has won:
Pulitzer Prize, Fiction, 1969

Other books by the same author:
The Ancient Child, 1989
The Names: A Memoir, 1976

Other books you might like:
Michael Dorris, *A Yellow Raft in Blue Water*, 1987
Louise Erdich, *The Beet Queen*, 1986
Barbara Kingsolver, *Pigs in Heaven*, 1993
John Joseph Mathews, *Sundown*, 1934
Leslie Marmon Silko, *Ceremony*, 1977

861

GEORGE MOORE

The Brook Kerith: A Syrian Story

(New York: Macmillan, 1916)

Category: Biographical Fiction
Subject(s): History; Christianity; Bible
Time period(s): 1st century

Summary: George Moore (1852-1933) was an Irish poet and novelist whose best-remembered work is *Esther Waters*, the story of the difficult life of a religious girl. *The Brook Kerith* is an elaborate and unusual retelling of the life and crucifixion of Christ through the eyes of a would-be follower. While preparing to write the novel, Moore spent a great deal of time traveling through the Holy Land.

Other books by the same author:
Hail and Farewell, 1911-1914
The Apostle: A Drama in a Prelude and Three Acts, 1911
Esther Waters, 1894
Confessions of a Young Man, 1888

Other books you might like:
Sholem Asch, *The Nazarene*, 1939
Lloyd C. Douglas, *The Robe*, 1942
Anatole France, *Balthazar*, 1909
Robert Graves, *King Jesus*, 1946
Lew Wallace, *Ben-Hur: A Tale of the Christ*, 1880

862

JOHN L. MOORE

Bitter Roots

(Nashville: Thomas Nelson, 1993)

Category: Westerns
Subject(s): Family Saga; American West; Family Problems
Age range(s): Young Adult-Adult
Locale(s): Montana

Summary: John L. Moore, award-winning journalist and photographer, is a third-generation cattle rancher in Montana. His love for the land, long-time ranching experience, and Christian beliefs form the core of his realistic tales of life in the rugged West. In *Bitter Roots*, he explores the lives of the McColley family in Montana as they deal with the consequences of intergenerational conflict, the roots of which are buried in the past but which continue to bear bitter fruit in the family circle. Moore's characters ultimately experience the healing presence of God, but the journey to peace takes them along a dramatic and difficult road.

Other books by the same author:
The Land of Empty Houses: A Novel, 1998
The Limits of Mercy: A Novel, 1996
Leaving the Land, 1995
The Breaking of Ezra Riley, 1990
Letters to Jess, 1990

Other books you might like:
Jack Curtis, *Christmas in Calico*, 1998
Jane Orcutt, *The Hidden Heart*, 1998
Brock Thoene, *A Land Without Law: Saga of the Sierras*, 1999
Brock Thoene, *A New Frontier: Saga of the Sierras*, 1998

863

GILBERT MORRIS
BOBBY FUNDERBURK, Co-Author

A Call to Honor

(Dallas: Word, 1993)

Category: Historical Fiction

Series: Price of Liberty
Subject(s): World War II; Romance; Faith
Age range(s): Young Adult-Adult
Major character(s): Ben Logan, Young Man, Military Personnel
Time period(s): 1940s

Summary: Ben Logan is a troubled young man who just can't seem to keep his life on track. By the time he joins the navy to avoid going to jail, the only people who think he'll amount to anything in life are his mother and his friend Hanna. With their encouragement, he goes off to the service. There, he discovers that there is more to life than what he has known; maybe God has something in mind for him to do. But his faith in God is put to a severe test when the bombing of Pearl Harbor begins and Ben must truly trust God with his future.

Other books by the same author:
A Time to Heal, 1994 (Bobby Funderburk, co-author; Price of Liberty, #6)
All the Shining Young Men, 1993 (Bobby Funderburk, co-author; Price of Liberty, #3)
The Color of the Star, 1993 (Bobby Funderburk, co-author; Price of Liberty, #2)
The End of Glory, 1993 (Bobby Funderburk, co-author; Price of Liberty, #4)
A Silence in Heaven, 1993 (Bobby Funderburk, co-author; Price of Liberty, #5)

Other books you might like:
Jack Cavanaugh, *The Allies*, 1997
Clint Kelly, *The Power and the Glory*, 1999
Elsie J. Larson, *Dawn's Early Light*, 1996
   Tides of War, #1
Janette Oke, *Another Homecoming*, 1997

864

GILBERT MORRIS

The Captive Bride

(Minneapolis: Bethany House, 1987)

Category: Historical Fiction
Series: House of Winslow
Subject(s): American Colonies; Family Saga; Puritans
Age range(s): Young Adult-Adult
Major character(s): Gilbert Winslow, Settler; Rachel Winslow, Spouse (of Gilbert); Robert Howland, Settler
Time period(s): 17th century (1659-1691)
Locale(s): Plymouth, Massachusetts, American Colonies; Salem, Massachusetts, American Colonies

Summary: Rachel Winslow is a freethinking new bride who must somehow contend with the strict conformity of the Puritan hierarchy into which she has married. Life in the Puritan settlement of the Massachusetts Bay Colony is the focus of this second volume of the House of Winslow series of novels.

Other books by the same author:
The Gentle Rebel, 1988 (House of Winslow, #4)
Indentured Heart, 1988 (House of Winslow, #3)
The Saintly Buccaneer, 1988 (House of Winslow, #5)
The Honorable Imposter, 1986 (House of Winslow, #1)

Other books you might like:
Lucy Jane Bledsoe, *Colony of Fear*, 1989
Jack Cavanaugh, *The Colonists*, 1995
Jack Cavanaugh, *Puritans*, 1994
Lori Wick, *The Hawk and the Jewel*, 1993
Marly Youmans, *Catherwood*, 1996

865

GILBERT MORRIS

A Covenant of Love

(Wheaton, Illinois: Tyndale House, 1992)

Category: Historical Fiction
Series: Appomattox Saga
Subject(s): Civil War; Family Saga; War
Age range(s): Young Adult-Adult
Major character(s): Clay Rocklin, Young Man, Cousin (of Gideon); Gideon Rocklin, Young Man, Cousin (of Clay)
Time period(s): 1860s
Locale(s): United States

Summary: The author blends history and romance in this novel, which is the first volume in The Appomattox Saga series. Clay Rocklin and Gideon Rocklin are cousins whose lives are torn apart by love and war. In love with the same girl, they are also on opposite side of the conflict between the North and South during the Civil War. This is a story of personal and spiritual growth.

Other books by the same author:
Bring the Boys Home, 1997
Gate of His Enemies, 1992
The Last Confederate, 1990

Other books you might like:
Jack Cavanaugh, *The Adversaries*, 1996
Charles Frazier, *Cold Mountain*, 1997
Irene Hunt, *Across Five Aprils*, 1964
Miriam Freeman Rawl, *From the Ashes of Ruin*, 1999

866

GILBERT MORRIS

Guilt by Association

(Tarrytown, New York: F. H. Revell, 1991)

Category: Mystery
Series: Danielle Ross Mystery Series
Subject(s): Romance; Hostages; Faith
Age range(s): Adult
Major character(s): Danielle Ross, Detective
Time period(s): 1990s

Summary: This is the first in the Danielle Ross series of mystery novels written for adults. The series combines suspense, romance, intrigue, and solid Christian values. Set in contemporary times, each installment revolves around the work and life of detective Dani Ross. In the series opener, Dani and a friend are held hostage by a madman, testing her faith and skills.

Other books by the same author:
Race with Death, 1994

Quality of Mercy, 1993
Deadly Deception, 1992
Final Curtain, 1991

Other books you might like:
Terri Blackstock, *Justifiable Means*, 1996
Terri Blackstock, *Never Again Goodbye*, 1996
Terri Blackstock, *Ulterior Motives*, 1996
Hilda Stahl, *The Boning Knife*, 1992
Audrey Stallsmith, *Rosemary for Remembrance*, 1998

867

GILBERT MORRIS

The Honorable Imposter

(Minneapolis: Bethany House, 1986)

Category: Historical Fiction
Series: House of Winslow
Subject(s): American Colonies; Family Saga; Pilgrims and Pilgrimages
Age range(s): Young Adult-Adult
Major character(s): Gilbert Winslow, Religious (minister), Settler; William Bradford, Historical Figure, Leader (pilgrim); John Alden, Historical Figure, Leader (pilgrim); Miles Standish, Historical Figure, Leader (pilgrim)
Time period(s): 17th century
Locale(s): England; *Mayflower*, At Sea; Plymouth, Massachusetts, American Colonies

Summary: In the first of the author's House of Winslow series, Gilbert Winslow's family forces him to become a minister. As a member of the clergy in the Church of England, Winslow is asked to infiltrate the Pilgrims to identify and turn in their leaders, including William Bradford, John Alden, and Miles Standish. He crosses the Atlantic on the *Mayflower* and takes up life in the Plymouth colony. Before long, he has built friendships with the men he was supposed to betray, and he must now search his heart for guidance about his ongoing spy activity.

Other books by the same author:
The Gentle Rebel, 1988 (House of Winslow, #4)
Indentured Heart, 1988 (House of Winslow, #3)
The Saintly Buccaneer, 1988 (House of Winslow, #5)
The Captive Bride, 1987 (House of Winslow, #2)

Other books you might like:
Jack Cavanaugh, *The Colonists*, 1995
Jack Cavanaugh, *Puritans*, 1994
Francine Rivers, *A Voice in the Wind*, 1993
Lori Wick, *The Hawk and the Jewel*, 1993
Marly Youmans, *Catherwood*, 1996

868

GILBERT MORRIS

Reno

(Wheaton, Illinois: Tyndale House, 1992)

Category: Westerns
Series: Reno Western Saga

Subject(s): Ranch Life; Good and Evil; Frontier and Pioneer Life
Age range(s): Young Adult-Adult
Major character(s): Skull Carr, Rancher; Jim Reno, Drifter, Veteran (of Civil War)
Time period(s): 1860s; 1870s
Locale(s): "The Valley" (American West)

Summary: This is the first of a series of books about the adventures of Jim Reno, a drifter and sharpshooter who takes on injustice and shares spiritual values with those he encounters in his travels. In this volume, Reno, a veteran of the Civil War, finds himself the reluctant leader of a group of farmers and ranchers protesting the tactics of the Carrs, owners of Skull Ranch. The Carrs are a formidable force to reckon with on the western frontier, and Reno is caught in the middle of a fight between good and evil, armed with his values and his marksmanship skills.

Other books by the same author:
Lone Wolf, 1995 (Reno Western Saga, #6)
Valley Justice, 1995 (Reno Western Saga, #5)
Boomtown, 1992 (Reno Western Saga, #4)
Ride the Wild River, 1992 (Reno Western Saga, #3)
Rimrock, 1992 (Reno Western Saga, #2)

Other books you might like:
Stephen Bly, *Copper Hill*, 1997
Al Lacy, *Circle of Fire*, 1996
Al Lacy, *Legacy*, 1994
Alan Morris, *Between Earth and Sky*, 1998
Jim Walker, *The Nightriders*, 1994

869

LYNN MORRIS
GILBERT MORRIS, Co-Author

A City Not Forsaken

(Minneapolis: Bethany House, 1995)

Category: Historical Fiction
Series: Cheney Duvall
Subject(s): Medicine; Reconstruction; Love
Age range(s): Young Adult-Adult
Major character(s): Cheney Duvall, Doctor; Shiloh Irons, Nurse; Devlin Buchanan, Doctor; Ulysses S. Grant, Historical Figure, Military Personnel (general)
Time period(s): 1860s (1866)
Locale(s): New York, New York

Summary: This is the third in a series of novels about 19th-century doctor Cheney Duvall, whose goal is to help those in need through her medical skills. In this volume, she has returned to her home in New York City in 1866, determined to go into private practice with Devlin Buchanan, a physician who has asked her to marry him. When the city is threatened by an outbreak of cholera, he returns from London, and Cheney discovers that she must choose between treating the rich and powerful and caring for the needy during the epidemic. Professional conflicts and personal tragedy challenge Cheney's faith and resolve.

Other books by the same author:
Toward the Sunrising, 1996 (Cheney Duvall, #4)

Shadow of the Mountains, 1994 (Cheney Duvall, #2)
The Stars for a Light, 1994 (Cheney Duvall, #1)

Other books you might like:
Lori Copeland, *Faith*, 1998
Kristen Heitzmann, *Honor's Pledge*, 1998
Janette Oke, *They Called Her Mrs. Doc*, 1992

870

LYNN MORRIS
GILBERT MORRIS, Co-Author

The Stars for a Light

(Minneapolis: Bethany House, 1994)

Category: Historical Fiction
Series: Cheney Duvall, M.D.
Subject(s): Women; Medicine; Mountain Life
Age range(s): Young Adult-Adult
Major character(s): Cheney Duvall, Doctor; Shiloh Irons, Nurse (male); Asa Mercer, Businessman
Time period(s): 19th century (mid-century)
Locale(s): New York

Summary: Cheney Duvall has recently received her degree as a physician, but there aren't many jobs for women doctors in the United States during the post-Civil War years. Suddenly, just the right job becomes available. A ship carrying 200 women from New York City to the Washington Territory is in need of a doctor, and a woman is just what Asa Mercer needs to chaperone the women during a long and difficult journey. With time short before the ship leaves, Cheney hires a nurse, sight unseen, on the recommendation of a fellow doctor. When they finally meet, she is astonished to discover that nurse Shiloh Irons is a man. The two prove to be a volatile mix but valuable to each other during a voyage that includes disease, fire, and other dangers. Not surprisingly, the professional relationship takes on a personal tone, but Cheney Duvall is not about to get involved with someone who doesn't share her faith.

Other books by the same author:
In the Twilight, in the Evening, 1997 (Gilbert Morris, co-author; Cheney Duvall, M.D., #6)
Secret Place of Thunder, 1996 (Gilbert Morris, co-author; Cheney Duvall, M.D., #5)
Toward the Sunrising, 1996 (Gilbert Morris, co-author; Cheney Duvall, M.D., #4)
A City Not Forsaken, 1995 (Gilbert Morris, co-author; Cheney Duvall, M.D., #3)
Shadow of the Mountains, 1994 (Gilbert Morris, co-author; Cheney Duvall, M.D., #2)

Other books you might like:
Janette Oke, *They Called Her Mrs. Doc*, 1992
Janette Oke, *The Calling of Emily Evans*, 1990
Michael Phillips, *A Place in the Sun*, 1991
Michael Phillips, *Sea to Shining Sea*, 1992

871

BILL MYERS

Blood of Heaven

(Grand Rapids, Michigan: Zondervan, 1996)

Category: Thrillers
Subject(s): Christianity; Science
Age range(s): Adult
Major character(s): Philip O'Brien, Doctor; Michael Coleman, Prisoner, Convict
Time period(s): 1990s

Summary: In a suspenseful novel that revolves around the ethical use of genetics and the power of conscience on human behavior, Bill Myers speculates on the consequences of a collaboration between genetic researchers and biblical archaeologists. When DNA testing is performed on ancient blood stains believed to be the blood of Jesus, genetic scientists are forced to acknowledge that a lack of genetic markers indicates that the blood belongs to someone with no earthly father. Dr. Philip O'Brien wants to experiment with the DNA, but he needs a human volunteer to submit to experimentation. Michael Coleman is a man on death row, convicted of murder, and he's only too happy to exchange his death sentence for guinea pig status in O'Brien's lab. When DNA reproduced from the bloodstain is placed into Coleman's bloodstream, remarkable results take place. What happens next will depend on whether or not O'Brien is left free to pursue his unholy agenda, and whether Coleman, who now understands O'Brien's purpose for him, can summon the moral courage to stop him.

Other books by the same author:
Fire of Heaven, 1999
The Ancients, 1998 (Forbidden Doors, #10)
The Scream, 1998 (Forbidden Doors, #9)
Threshold, 1997
The Deceived, 1994 (Forbidden Doors, #2)

Other books you might like:
Jack Dann, *Clones*, 1998
   short stories
Christopher A. Lane, *Appearance of Evil*, 1997
Michael Phillips, *A Rift in Time*, 1997

872

BILL MYERS

My Life as a Smashed Burrito with Extra Hot Sauce

(Dallas: Word, 1993)

Category: Comedy
Series: Incredible Worlds of Wally McDoogle
Subject(s): Adolescence; Camps and Camping; Christianity
Age range(s): Young Adult
Major character(s): Wally McDoogle, 12-Year-Old, Camper; Gary the Gorilla, Bully, Camper; Dale, Counselor
Locale(s): Camp Wakkah Wakkah

Summary: From the moment they meet on the bus going to Camp Wakkah Wakkah, Wally McDoogle and Gary the Gorilla are a confrontation waiting to happen. Gary is the number one camp bully. Wally is the number one computer nerd in glasses. Somehow, he keeps making a fool out of Gary without even trying. Not a good idea when you're dealing with the biggest, baddest bully around. Bill Myers' first Wally McDoogle tale provides lots of fun and funny moments, along with the suspense of a river trip gone awry. Before they are in danger together, the boys at camp laugh at counselor Dale's talks about wisdom, but afterward, with their counselor and friend in the hospital, they recognize the truth in what he has said.

Other books by the same author:
My Life as a Mixed-Up Millennium Bug, 1999 (Incredible Worlds of Wally McDoogle, #17)
My Life as a Walrus Whoopee Cushion, 1999 (Incredible Worlds of Wally McDoogle, #16)
My Life as a Screaming Skydiver, 1998 (Incredible Worlds of Wally McDoogle, #14)
My Life as a Blundering Ballerina, 1997 (Incredible Worlds of Wally McDoogle, #13)
My Life as a Human Hockey Puck, 1994 (Incredible Worlds of Wally McDoogle, #7)

Other books you might like:
Paul Buchanan, *Anything You Can Do I Can Do Better*, 1998
Paul McCusker, *A Carnival of Secrets*, 1997
Paul McCusker, *Lights out at Camp What-a-Nut*, 1993
Nancy Speck, *The Lightning Escape*, 1997

873

BILL MYERS

Phantom of the Haunted Church

(Minneapolis: Bethany House, 1998)

Category: Mystery; Morality Tales
Series: Bloodhounds, Inc.
Subject(s): Haunted Houses; Treasure; Christianity
Age range(s): Children-Young Adult
Major character(s): Sean Hunter, Brother (of Melissa); Melissa Hunter, Sister (of Sean); Slobs, Dog
Time period(s): 1990s

Summary: *Phantom of the Haunted Church* is the third entry in Bill Myers' Bloodhounds, Inc. Christian fiction series for children and young adults. Sean and Melissa Hunter are siblings and amateur detectives. With their dog, Slobs, the two set out in search of a legendary cache of treasure hidden in an old church that will soon be torn down. The moral of the story is identified early and reinforced often. As the children become more and more obsessed with finding the treasure, nothing else matters. Ultimately they realize that the greed they have been warned about has dominated them, and they need to turn away from selfish pursuits and back to the values they know are right and good.

Other books by the same author:
The Case of the Missing Minds, 1999 (David Wimbish, co-author; Bloodhounds, Inc., #6)
Fangs for the Memories, 1999 (David Wimbish, co-author; Bloodhounds, Inc., #5)
Invasion of the UFOs, 1998 (Bloodhounds, Inc., #4)

The Ghost of KRZY, 1997 (Bloodhounds, Inc., #1)
The Mystery of the Invisible Knight, 1997 (Bloodhounds, Inc., #2)

Other books you might like:
Stephen Bly, *Revenge on Eagle Island*, 1998
Jerry B. Jenkins, *The Neighborhood's Scariest Woman*, 1996
Patricia H. Rushford, *Too Many Secrets*, 1993

874

BILL MYERS

The Portal

(Minneapolis: Bethany House, 1991)

Category: Morality Tales; Fantasy
Series: Journeys to Fayrah
Subject(s): Time Travel; Good and Evil
Age range(s): Children-Young Adult
Major character(s): Denise, Child; Nathan, Child
Time period(s): Indeterminate
Locale(s): Fictional Country (Fayrah)

Summary: In *The Portal*, the initial title in the Journeys to Fayrah series, selfishness has serious consequences for a young person trapped in a faraway land. For Nathan's birthday, Denise gives him an unusual gift: an odd-looking red stone. Neither one is aware of its powers, until they discover that it is a mystical gateway to the land of Fayrah. Before long, the two are swept away in a time travel adventure that involves a showdown between good and evil, and requires that they both choose to be on the side of good.

Other books by the same author:
The Tablet, 1992 (Journeys to Fayrah, #4)
The Whirlwind, 1992 (Journeys to Fayrah, #3)
The Experiment, 1991 (Journeys to Fayrah, #2)

Other books you might like:
Sigmund Brouwer, *Galilee Man*, 1998
    Cyberquest, #6
Thomas Locke, *Dream Voyager*, 1995
    Spectrum Chronicles
Paul McCusker, *Stranger in the Mist*, 1996
Gilbert Morris, *Escape with the Dream Maker*, 1997
    Seven Sleepers, #9

875

BILL MYERS

Threshold

(Grand Rapids, Michigan: Zondervan, 1997)

Category: Science Fiction
Subject(s): Extrasensory Perception; Demons; Occult
Age range(s): Adult
Major character(s): Gertie Morrison, Psychic; Sarah Weintraub, Scientist (neurobiologist), Researcher; Brandon Martus, Young Man, Psychic; Helmut Reichner, Administrator, Scientist (physicist)
Time period(s): 1990s
Locale(s): Bethel Lake, Indiana; Kathmandu, Nepal

Summary: Gertie Morrison prays and fasts to save the annointed one she sees in her dreams and thanks God for his approval. Brandon Martus discovers he can see into the future. Still suffering from her abortion three years earlier, Sarah Weintraub puts all her energy into her research into telekinesis, teaming up with Brandon and uncovering an unexpected secret. In this novel in which the characters study brain research and quantum physcis, the author explores parapsychology, demonology, and the supernatural, from the perspective of Christianity.

Other books by the same author:
Blood of Heaven, 1996

Other books you might like:
Christopher A. Lane, *Appearance of Evil*, 1997
Paul Meier, *Beyond the Millennium*, 1998
Frank E. Peretti, *This Present Darkness*, 1986
Michael Phillips, *A Rift in Time*, 1997

876

MICHAEL D. O'BRIEN

Eclipse of the Sun: A Novel

(San Francisco: Ignatius Press, 1998)

Category: Thrillers
Subject(s): Apocalypse; Catholicism; Freedom
Age range(s): Adult
Major character(s): Father Andrei, Religious (priest); Arrow Delaney, Brother; Anne Delaney, Mother; Stephen Delaney, Father
Time period(s): Indeterminate Future
Locale(s): British Columbia, Canada

Summary: Sometime in the not-distant future, the Delaney family from British Columbia runs afoul of an evolving, North American, totalitarian government. As publishers of a newspaper that is not controlled by the rising regime, the Delaneys are the targets of state enforcers because they have remained true to their Catholic beliefs and their constitutional heritage. As the Delaneys and their friends try to outlast those who would silence them, they are hunted relentlessly. Will there be courage enough to stand up to the evil? What price will there be to pay?

Other books by the same author:
Plague Journal: A Novel, 1999
Strangers and Sojourners: A Novel, 1997
Father Elijah: An Apocalypse, 1996

Other books you might like:
Ralph McInerny, *The Red Hat: A Novel*, 1998
Edward R.F. Sheehan, *Cardinal Galsworthy: A Novel*, 1997
Philip Trower, *A Danger to the State: A Historical Novel*, 1998

877

MICHAEL D. O'BRIEN

Father Elijah: An Apocalypse

(San Francisco: Ignatius Press, 1996)

Category: Thrillers

Subject(s): Apocalypse; Catholicism; End-Times
Age range(s): Adult
Major character(s): Father Elijah Schafer, Religious (Carmelite priest)
Time period(s): 1990s

Summary: At the end of the 20th century, Father Elijah Schafer is a Carmelite priest whose work for the Vatican is top secret and dangerous. He is a convert from Judaism and a Holocaust survivor whose quiet life of contemplation is interrupted by an assignment to become a spy in the house of the man believed to be the Antichrist. The mission is to call the Antichrist to repentance in order to postpone the tribulation of apocalyptic times. His complex new world brings him into contact with world powers, fellow priests from many nations, and ordinary citizens-saints and sinners among them all. He travels through Europe and the Middle East and encounters deception and conspiracy in places where he least expects to find it, and where it can do the most harm to the most innocent people. Will the mission succeed? Will his identity be discovered? Will honor and sacrifice prevail, or will Father Elijah find himself sacrificed for a lost cause?

Other books by the same author:
Plague Journal: A Novel, 1999
Eclipse of the Sun: A Novel, 1998
Strangers and Sojourners: A Novel, 1997

Other books you might like:
Ralph McInerny, *The Red Hat: A Novel*, 1998
Edward R.F. Sheehan, *Cardinal Galsworthy: A Novel*, 1997
Philip Trower, *A Danger to the State: A Historical Novel*, 1998

878

FLANNERY O'CONNOR

Wise Blood

(New York: Harcourt, Brace, 1952)

Category: Thrillers
Subject(s): Religious Life; Evangelism
Age range(s): Adult
Major character(s): Hazel Motes, Military Personnel (discharged serviceman), Religious (street preacher); Asa Hawks, Religious (street preacher); Lily Sabbath Hawks, Daughter (of Asa Hawks)
Time period(s): 1940s
Locale(s): Tennessee

Summary: Hazel Motes, a country boy from Tennessee, returns home after serving in World War II. Out of his league living in a big city, he discovers a brand-new world in street preaching, and decides to start his own "flock" under the name "Church Without Christ." Motes's cynical and immoral approach to life creates conflict with his mentor and competitor, Asa Hawks, and his own disciples turn on him as well. O'Connor's fierce, almost angry characterizations create a bizarre story of shifting alliances and religious absurdities.

Other books by the same author:
The Presence of Grace, and Other Book Reviews, 1983
Everything That Rises Must Converge, 1965
A Good Man Is Hard to Find, 1955

Other books you might like:

Caroline Gordon, *The Women on the Porch*, 1944
Caroline Gordon, *The Malefactors*, 1956
Herman Melville, *Billy Budd, and Other Prose Pieces*, 1924

879

JOAN OHANNESON

Scarlet Music: Hildegard of Bingen

(New York: Crossroads, 1997)

Category: Biographical Fiction
Subject(s): Saints; Music and Musicians
Age range(s): Young Adult-Adult
Time period(s): 11th century; 12th century (1098-1179)
Locale(s): Germany

Summary: A work of biographical fiction, *Scarlet Music* is based on the real life of Hildegard of Bingen (1098-1179), who lived with a community of nuns outside Bingen, Germany, from the age of eight. As an adult, she became the superior of the convent, and went on to start monastic orders elsewhere. A gifted and prolific writer and composer of music, including hymns and chants, Hildegard was also accomplished in medicine, natural science, and politics. She was proposed for sainthood after her death, but the Catholic Church has never canonized her. However, she is often referred to as Saint Hildegard. In this work, Ohanneson brings to life the legendary woman whose achievements set her apart from other women of her time.

Other books by the same author:

And They Felt No Shame: Christians Reclaim Their Sexuality, 1982
Woman: Survivor in the Church, 1980

Other books you might like:

Renate Craine, *Hildegard: Prophet of the Cosmic Christ*, 1997
Sabina Flanagan, *Hildegard of Bingen, 1098-1179: A Visionary Life*, 1989
Sabina Flanagan, *Secrets of God: Writings of Hildegard of Bingen*, 1996
Matthew Fox, *Illuminations of Hildegard of Bingen*, 1985

880

JANETTE OKE
T. DAVIS BUNN, Co-Author

Another Homecoming

(Minneapolis: Bethany House, 1997)

Category: Gentle Reads
Subject(s): Adoption; Family Relations; Christianity
Age range(s): Young Adult-Adult
Major character(s): Kyle Rothmore, Daughter (adopted by the Rothmores)
Time period(s): 20th century
Locale(s): United States

Summary: A little girl is born during World War II to a young woman whose husband is believed to be dead in action. Not wishing to deprive her little Katie of a two-parent home where she would be well-provided for, Martha gives the baby up for adoption to the Rothmores, a wealthy couple who re-name their daughter Kyle. Their only child grows up in luxury that her birth mother could never have provided, but there is little love in the home. Kyle's adoption remains a secret, as her parents wished, until a sudden tragedy tears the small family apart, and the secret is accidentally revealed. Kyle's subsequent search for her past yields unimagined surprises, which ultimately result in enough love and spiritual healing to mend all the hurting hearts in Kyle's life.

Other books by the same author:

The Meeting Place, 1999
A Searching Heart, 1998
Tomorrow's Dream, 1998
Return to Harmony: A Novel, 1996 (T. Davis Bunn., co-author)

Other books you might like:

Lori Wick, *Beyond the Picket Fence*, 1998
Lori Copeland, *Faith*, 1998
Lori Wick, *Pretense*, 1998
Lori Wick, *The Princess*, 1999

881

JANETTE OKE

The Calling of Emily Evans

(Minneapolis: Bethany House, 1990)

Category: Historical Fiction; Westerns
Series: Women of the West
Subject(s): Religious Life; Mennonites
Age range(s): Young Adult-Adult
Major character(s): Emily Evans, Religious (missionary)
Time period(s): 1900s; 1910s
Locale(s): Prairie Provinces, Canada

Summary: This novel, part of the Women of the West series, describes the experience of a missionary named Emily Evans. She sets out alone as a Ministry Sister to open a new church in a pioneer community on the Canadian Prairie.

Other books by the same author:

They Called Her Mrs. Doc, 1992
When Calls the Heart, 1983
Love's Abiding Joy, 1983
Love's Long Journey, 1982

Other books you might like:

Benedict Freedman, *Mrs. Mike: The Story of Katherine Mary Flannigan*, 1947
Catherine Palmer, *Prairie Fire*, 1998
Catherine Palmer, *Prairie Storm*, 1999

882

JANETTE OKE

A Gown of Spanish Lace

(Minneapolis: Bethany House, 1995)

Category: Historical Fiction; Westerns
Series: Women of the West
Subject(s): Romance; Family Saga

Age range(s): Young Adult-Adult
Major character(s): Ariana Benson, Teacher; Laramie Lawrence, Outlaw, Son (of outlaw leader)
Time period(s): 19th century
Locale(s): Montana

Summary: Ariana Benson is a very young schoolteacher in a small frontier town where she lives with the couple that raised her. The only link she has to her parents, who were massacred by Indians years before, is a wedding gown of Spanish lace, perfectly preserved except for a cuff missing from one sleeve. One night she is abducted from her schoolhouse by a band of outlaws. During her captivity, she prays for herself and her loved ones, and wonders whether she will ever have a chance to wear the heirloom dress. Impressed by her faith, the son of the outlaws' leader helps Ariana escape, and they ultimately fall in love. But a mystery involving the lace dress may stand in the way of their marriage.

Other books by the same author:
The Bluebird and the Sparrow, 1994
Heart of the Wilderness, 1993
A Bride for Donnigan, 1993
The Measure of a Heart, 1992

Other books you might like:
Jane Peart, *Dreams of a Longing Heart*, 1990
Jane Peart, *Homeward the Seeking Heart*, 1990
Lori Wick, *Where the Wild Rose Blooms*, 1996
Lori Wick, *Whispers of Moonlight*, 1996

883

JANETTE OKE

Love Comes Softly

(Minneapolis: Bethany Fellowship, 1979)

Category: Historical Fiction
Series: Love Comes Softly
Subject(s): Love; Frontier and Pioneer Life; Family Life
Age range(s): Young Adult-Adult
Major character(s): Marty Claridge Davis, Spouse (of Clark), Widow(er) (of Clem Claridge); Clark Davis, Father (of Missie), Widow(er), Spouse (of Marty); Missie Davis, Daughter (of Clark), Child
Time period(s): 19th century
Locale(s): West

Summary: Young Marty is pregnant and newly widowed on the American frontier. Her beloved Clem has died suddenly, before they could claim some property and build a prairie home together. Clark has recently lost his wife, too—the mother of toddler Missie. Together, Marty and Clark forge a marriage of convenience in order to survive. But Clark's God has other plans, and Marty discovers that God has a plan in mind for her, too. Despite their patience and faith, will either of them ever find love again?

Other books by the same author:
When Calls the Heart, 1983
Love's Long Journey, 1982
Love's Enduring Promise, 1980

Other books you might like:
June Masters Bacher, *No Time for Tears*, 1992

June Masters Bacher, *Songs in the Whirlwind*, 1992
Jane Peart, *Runaway Heart*, 1994
Jane Peart, *Valiant Bride*, 1989

884

JANETTE OKE

Love's Enduring Promise

(Minneapolis: Bethany Fellowship, 1980)

Category: Historical Fiction
Series: Love Comes Softly
Subject(s): Love; Frontier and Pioneer Life; Family Life
Age range(s): Young Adult-Adult
Major character(s): Marty Claridge Davis, Spouse (of Clark); Clark Davis, Father (of Missie), Spouse (of Marty); Missie Davis, Daughter (of Clark); Claridge Luke ''Clare'' Davis, Son (of Marty)
Time period(s): 19th century
Locale(s): West

Summary: In this sequel to *Love Comes Softly*, Marty and Clark are enjoying the happiness of being a real family at last. Missie and Clare welcome a new baby brother, and later two more sisters join the family. The settlers begin turning their homesteads into a proper town, with a school and a church. What does the future hold for the Davis family? Whatever it is, Marty and Clark trust that everything is in God's hands.

Other books by the same author:
When Calls the Heart, 1983
Love's Long Journey, 1982
Love's Enduring Promise, 1980

Other books you might like:
June Masters Bacher, *No Time for Tears*, 1992
June Masters Bacher, *Songs in the Whirlwind*, 1992
Jane Peart, *Dreams of a Longing Heart*, 1990
Lori Wick, *Where the Wild Rose Blooms*, 1996

885

JANETTE OKE

Love's Long Journey

(Minneapolis: Bethany House, 1982)

Category: Historical Fiction
Series: Love Comes Softly
Subject(s): Love; Frontier and Pioneer Life; Family Life
Age range(s): Young Adult-Adult
Major character(s): Missie LaHaye, Spouse (of Willie); Willie LaHaye, Spouse (of Missie); Nathan Isaiah, Son (of Missie and Willie)
Time period(s): 19th century
Locale(s): West

Summary: A new generation heads further West to find homes and build lives along the American frontier. In the sequel to *Love's Enduring Promise*, young Missie and her husband, Willie, leave their settled prairie town behind in order to claim their own land and start a family. Just as Missie's parents did, they face the hardships and joys of pioneer life with faith in God and love in their hearts.

Awards the book has won:
Gold Medallion Book Award, Fiction, 1983

Other books by the same author:
When Calls the Heart, 1983
Love's Long Journey, 1982
Love's Enduring Promise, 1980

Other books you might like:
June Masters Bacher, *No Time for Tears*, 1992
June Masters Bacher, *Songs in the Whirlwind*, 1992
Jane Peart, *Dreams of a Longing Heart*, 1990
Lori Wick, *Where the Wild Rose Blooms*, 1996

886

JANETTE OKE

The Matchmakers

(Minneapolis: Bethany House, 1997)

Category: Gentle Reads
Subject(s): Love; Family Life; Friendship
Age range(s): Young Adult-Adult
Major character(s): Cynthia, Widow(er); Judith, Friend
Time period(s): Indeterminate

Summary: A widow with two small sons, Cynthia is concerned about her father's future, as well as her own. Widowed himself, he has moved in with his daughter to help raise the boys following their father's death. While Cynthia appreciates his presence, she also wants to feel free to live her own life, and she doesn't quite know how to say so. Friend Judith suggests she introduce him to an older widow from church, but to do this, she must become acquainted with the woman's son, who seems rather distant and, to Cynthia's way of thinking, a little self-centered. As the two form an alliance, however, the outcome of their efforts is rather unexpected. Faith, love, friendship, and family ties neatly wrap up this gentle tale.

Other books by the same author:
Nana's Gift, 1996
The Red Geranium, 1995

Other books you might like:
Beverly Lewis, *The Reckoning*, 1998
Beverly Lewis, *The Sunroom*, 1998
LaVyrle Spencer, *Then Came Heaven*, 1997

887

JANETTE OKE

Nana's Gift

(Minneapolis: Bethany House, 1996)

Category: Gentle Reads
Subject(s): Love; Inheritance; Christian Life
Age range(s): Young Adult-Adult
Major character(s): Duncan, Spouse (of Lizzie), Grandfather; Lizzie, Spouse (of Duncan), Grandmother
Time period(s): 20th century
Locale(s): United States

Summary: Early in their marriage, Duncan promises Lizzie a string of pearls. He sets aside a small amount of money at the end of each year toward the gift, but it isn't until their 35th anniversary that he is finally able to fulfill his promise. Regretful that it has taken this long, since he had always hoped to see his daughters wear their mother's pearls as they themselves married, he is comforted by Lizzie's reminder that the granddaughters will have the chance to wear the pearls on their wedding days. Long after Duncan's death, the pearls become a very special legacy to a great-granddaughter he never knew. In this lavishly illustrated volume, which is a departure from Oke's usual format, the author offers a gentle tale of love and faithfulness that touches multiple generations.

Other books by the same author:
Another Homecoming, 1997 (T. Davis Bunn, co-author)
Return to Harmony: A Novel, 1996 (T. Davis Bunn, co-author)
Janette Oke's Reflections on the Christmas Story, 1994

Other books you might like:
Julie Salamon, *The Christmas Tree*, 1996
Wayne Skinner, *Journey to Christmas*, 1996

888

JANETTE OKE

Once upon a Summer

(Minneapolis: Bethany House, 1981)

Category: Gentle Reads
Series: Seasons of the Heart
Subject(s): Love; Family Relations; Christianity
Age range(s): Young Adult-Adult
Major character(s): Joshua, 12-Year-Old; Auntie Lou, 18-Year-Old
Time period(s): Indeterminate Past

Summary: Joshua is nearly a teenager, but he's not ready to face any more changes in his life. After his parents died, he moved in with his grandpa and young Auntie Lou who, despite her youth, had become a mother figure to him. She has her hands full taking care of a house full of men—her father, her grandfather, and young nephew Joshua. Now that she's eighteen, Auntie Lou finds the young men of the community are coming to call, and Joshua can't imagine what he'll do if she decides to get married and move away. Auntie Lou—Louisa Jennifer by birth—gently reassures him that family love continues, no matter how the family changes, and that God's love is the most certain of all.

Other books by the same author:
The Red Geranium, 1995
Spring's Gentle Promise, 1989
Winter Is Not Forever, 1988
The Winds of Autumn, 1987

Other books you might like:
Catherine Marshall, *Christy*, 1967
Arleta Richardson, *Prairie Homestead*, 1994

889

JANETTE OKE

The Red Geranium

(Minneapolis: Bethany House, 1995)

Category: Gentle Reads
Subject(s): Grandparents; Love; Family Relations
Age range(s): Young Adult-Adult
Major character(s): Gran Thomas, Grandmother; Tommy, Relative (grandson)
Time period(s): Indeterminate
Locale(s): United States

Summary: Gran Thomas is having a hard time adjusting to life after a stroke. No longer able to live in her lovely, cozy home with its lace curtains and bright potted flowers, she is in a nursing home where she can receive full-time care as she regains some strength. The house will never be home again, though, because she has agreed to sell it. Her great-grandson, Tommy, is unhappy, too. He misses their visits on the porch swing and he knows Gran Thomas is unhappy. One day just before his visit to Gran's new "home," Tommy runs a secret errand to Gran's old house and uses a hidden key that only he knows about to go retrieve something he hopes will brighten Gran's room and make it seem more like home. His gift of love does Gran more good than Tommy will ever know.

Other books by the same author:
Nana's Gift, 1996
Roses for Mama, 1991
Once upon a Summer, 1981

Other books you might like:
Larry Barkdull, *The Mourning Dove: A Story of Love*, 1996
Shea Darian, *Grandpa's Garden*, 1996
Richard Paul Evans, *The Locket*, 1998

890

JANETTE OKE
T. DAVIS BUNN, Co-Author

Return to Harmony: A Novel

(Minneapolis: Bethany House, 1996)

Category: Gentle Reads
Subject(s): Friendship; Family Life; Christian Life
Age range(s): Young Adult-Adult
Major character(s): Jodie Harland, Friend (of Bethan); Bethan Keane, Friend (of Jodie)
Time period(s): 1910s; 1920s (1915-1921)
Locale(s): Harmony, North Carolina

Summary: In the small North Carolina town of Harmony, Bethan Keane and Jodie Harland are unlikely but inseparable best friends. The differences between them strengthen their bond until their lives take decidedly separate directions. Jodie quietly leaves the town where her mother died and follows her dream to study biochemistry, despite the hardships of being the only woman in her college program. Bethan stays in the town she loves, always praying that her long-lost friend will some day return to the faith she turned her back on years

before. Can anything or anyone mend the torn fabric of this broken friendship?

Other books by the same author:
Tomorrow's Dream, 1998
Another Homecoming, 1997

Other books you might like:
John Irving, *A Prayer for Owen Meany: A Novel*, 1989
Jan Karon, *The Mitford Series*, 1994-
Kathryn Worth, *They Loved to Laugh*, 1996

891

JANETTE OKE

The Tender Years

(Minneapolis: Bethany House, 1997)

Category: Gentle Reads
Series: Prairie Legacy
Subject(s): Grandparents; Love; Family Relations
Age range(s): Young Adult-Adult
Major character(s): Virginia, Teenager, Relative (granddaughter of Marty & Clark); Jenny, Teenager; Marty Claridge Davis, Relative; Clark Davis, Relative
Time period(s): Indeterminate Past
Locale(s): United States

Summary: Marty and Clark Davis, whose story began in Janette Oke's first novel, *Love Comes Softly*, are great-grandparents now. Their spiritual heritage has been passed down through several generations, and they still pray for each and every grandchild, especially during the rough patches of life. Young Virginia has been in one of those times. In this first volume of the "Prairie Legacy" series of stories, the Davis's granddaughter is caught in the middle. She's the middle child of the family, she's between childhood and adulthood, and she can't seem to find the right ways to make her mark on the world. Then along comes a new friend, Jenny, whose lively personality and carefree manner contrast with Virginia's more cautious nature. Virginia finds life in Jenny's circle of friends much more exciting than the measured rhythms of home, but is it really better? And is there such a thing as too much fun and freedom?

Other books by the same author:
The Meeting Place, 1999
A Searching Heart, 1998
Tomorrow's Dream, 1998
Love's Unending Legacy, 1984

Other books you might like:
L.M. Montgomery, *Anne of Green Gables*, 1908
Laura Ingalls Wilder, *Little House on the Prairie*, 1935
Brenda Wilbee, *Sweetbriar Summer*, 1997

892

JANETTE OKE

They Called Her Mrs. Doc

(Minneapolis: Bethany House, 1992)

Category: Historical Fiction; Westerns
Series: Women of the West

Subject(s): Frontier and Pioneer Life; Women; Christian Life
Age range(s): Young Adult-Adult
Major character(s): Cassandra Dell Winston, Young Woman; Dr. Samuel Smith, Doctor
Time period(s): 19th century
Locale(s): Montreal, Quebec, Canada; Alberta, Canada

Summary: As Cassandra Dell Winston grew into young womanhood, her father, a doctor, frequently invited eligible young interns to dinner. Cassandra could have enjoyed a comfortable life in Montreal, Canada, but she has chosen instead to become the wife of a doctor in Alberta, where 19th-century life is not what she has been accustomed to. This novel, part of the Women of the West series, is the story of Cassandra's struggle to cope with the challenges of life on Canada's frontier.

Other books by the same author:
The Canadian West Saga, 1995
Heart of the Wilderness, 1993
Love's Long Journey, 1982

Other books you might like:
Benedict Freedman, *Mrs. Mike: The Story of Katherine Mary Flannigan*, 1947
Brenda Wilbee, *Sweetbriar Autumn*, 1998
Brenda Wilbee, *Sweetbriar Summer*, 1997
Lance Wubbels, *The Bridge over Flatwillow Creek*, 1998

893

JANETTE OKE

When Calls the Heart

(Minneapolis: Bethany House, 1983)

Category: Historical Fiction
Series: Canadian West
Subject(s): Romance
Age range(s): Young Adult-Adult
Major character(s): Beth Thatcher, Teacher; Wynn Delaney, Police Officer (Royal Canadian Mountie)
Time period(s): 1910s
Locale(s): Alberta, Canada

Summary: Elizabeth Thatcher is a young teacher assigned to a tiny school on the frontier in Alberta, Canada. A well-educated Easterner, she is not the least bit interested in finding a husband in this wild country, although there are plenty of men available and interested in marrying. Then she meets Wynn, a man she'd change her mind for. But can she change his mind about not mixing marriage and his career with the Royal Canadian Mounted Police? Her faith in God forces her to be honest with herself and with him, and she realizes that only God is in control of the circumstances of her life.

Other books by the same author:
When Breaks the Dawn, 1986
When Hope Springs New, 1986
When Comes the Spring, 1985

Other books you might like:
Benedict Freedman, *Mrs. Mike: The Story of Katherine Mary Flannigan*, 1947
Nancy Freedman, co-author

Christie Harris, *You Have to Draw the Line Somewhere*, 1964
Moira Johnston, illustrator
Alan Morris, *Bright Sword of Justice*, 1997

894

FULTON OURSLER

The Greatest Story Ever Told: A Tale of the Greatest Life Ever Lived

(Garden City, New York: Doubleday, 1949)

Category: Biographical Fiction
Subject(s): Christianity
Age range(s): Young Adult-Adult
Major character(s): Jesus, Historical Figure, Biblical Figure
Time period(s): 1st century (0-33)
Locale(s): Israel

Summary: This is a novelization of the life of Jesus, based on the Gospel accounts of Matthew, Mark, Luke, and John. The author faithfully retains the essence of each gospel writer's perspective while blending their stories together in what has become a classic of Christian literature. The novel served as the basis of a film by the same name. In both book and movie formats, Oursler's retelling of the life of Jesus remains popular among Christians of several generations.

Other books by the same author:
A Skeptic in the Holy Land, 1936

Other books you might like:
Sholem Asch, *The Nazarene*, 1939
Thomas Bertram Costain, *The Silver Chalice: A Novel*, 1952
Lloyd C. Douglas, *The Robe*, 1942
Walter Wangerin Jr., *The Book of God: The Bible as a Novel*, 1996

895

CATHERINE PALMER

Prairie Rose

(Wheaton, Illinois: Tyndale House, 1997)

Category: Westerns
Series: Town Called Hope
Subject(s): Ranch Life; Romance; Christian Life
Age range(s): Adult
Major character(s): Rosie Mills, Orphan; Seth Hunter, Settler; Chipper Hunter, Child
Time period(s): 1860s (1865)
Locale(s): Kansas City, Missouri; Hope

Summary: When Rosie Mills saves Seth Hunter's life, she finds a ticket out of the orphanage where she's lived since infancy. She goes west with widower Seth and his son, Chipper, to keep house for them. Since Rosie is now 19, this causes townsfolk to talk, even in the town of Hope. But Rosie and the Hunters rise above such problems, meeting the challenges of life in the West with faith and the courage and fortitude of true pioneers. Only when Rosie and Seth finally do begin to fall in love does an insurmountable problem arise. Rosie, haunted by a dark secret in her past, is convinced she can never marry, and can no longer live with Seth under their changed circumstances. This story of faith and determination is the first installment of A Town Called Hope, a Heartquest series of novels by Tyndale House.

Other books by the same author:
Prairie Storm, 1999
Prairie Fire, 1998
Victorian Christmas Tea, 1997

Other books you might like:
Lawana Blackwell, *Like a River Glorious*, 1995
Lori Copeland, *Faith*, 1998
Al Lacy, *A Time to Love*, 1998
Jane Peart, *The Heart's Lonely Secret*, 1994
Hilda Stahl, *Blossoming Love*, 1991

896

GARY E. PARKER

Death Stalks a Holiday: Sequel to Beyond a Reasonable Doubt

(Nashville: T. Nelson, 1996)

Category: Mystery
Subject(s): Murder; Christianity; Mystery
Age range(s): Adult
Major character(s): Burke Anderson, Religious (former pastor)
Time period(s): 1990s

Summary: It's the season of Advent, the weeks leading up to Christmas. Each Sunday, a woman has been murdered, and the police can't figure out why. Only one man sees a connection, and that is Burke Anderson, former pastor, who sees a similarity between murder detail reports and the description of injuries sustained by Jesus in the course of his crucifixion. Due to circumstances revealed in Parker's earlier novel, *Beyond a Reasonable Doubt*, Anderson must act on his own to solve the mystery before another victim is found. Can he do it in time?

Other books by the same author:
Beyond a Reasonable Doubt, 1994

Other books you might like:
Michael David Anthony, *The Becket Factor*, 1991
Michael David Anthony, *Dark Provenance*, 1995
Kate Charles, *The Snares of Death*, 1993

897

ALAN PATON

Cry, the Beloved Country

(New York: C. Scribner's Sons, 1948)

Category: Biographical Fiction
Subject(s): Africans; Fathers and Sons; Prejudice
Age range(s): Young Adult-Adult
Major character(s): Absalom Kumalo, Young Man
Time period(s): 1940s
Locale(s): South Africa

Summary: Absalom Kumalo is a young black African accused of murdering a white citizen. Written by one of South Africa's earliest proponents of racial equality, *Cry, the Beloved Country* follows the efforts of Kumalo's father, a South African minister, to defend and protect his son from the hostility and injustice of apartheid. The novel is unique for its blend of form and content: in addition to telling Absalom's story, Paton employs poetic language and lyrical passages to explore themes of fear, hate, prejudice, faith, and justice.

Other books by the same author:
Ah, But Your Land Is Beautiful, 1981
Too Late the Phalarope, 1953

Other books you might like:
James Michener, *The Covenant*, 1980
Ed Hazel Rochman, *Somehow Tenderness Survives: Stories of Southern Africa*, 1988
Norman Silver, *An Eye for Color*, 1993
Mildred D. Taylor, *Roll of Thunder, Hear My Cry*, 1976

898

T.R. PEARSON

Gospel Hour

(New York: William Morrow, 1991)

Category: Gentle Reads
Subject(s): Miracles; Humor; Rural Life
Age range(s): Adult
Major character(s): Donnie Huff, Lumberjack; Opal Criner, Relative (mother-in-law of Donnie)
Locale(s): Virginia

Summary: In the rural South, a miracle saves Donnie Huff's life—or so his mother-in-law believes—and that's all he needs to make a few bucks by spreading the word that Jesus saves. Though Donnie doesn't really seem to have a clue what he's talking about, he's out on the stump nonetheless, making his dubious case for the Lord. Not surprisingly, this doesn't mesh well with his lumberjack lifestyle or his penchant for kicking back with a beer or two or three.

Other books by the same author:
The Last of How It Was, 1987
Off for the Sweet Hereafter: A Novel, 1986
A Short History of a Small Place, 1985

Other books you might like:
Jan Karon, *The Mitford Series*, 1994-
Margaret Maron, *Killer Market*, 1997
Patty Sleem, *Back in Time*, 1997

899

T.R. PEARSON

Off for the Sweet Hereafter: A Novel

(New York: Linden Press/Simon & Schuster, 1986)

Category: Gentle Reads
Subject(s): Rural Life; Small Town Life
Age range(s): Adult
Major character(s): Raeford Benton Lynch, Worker (gravedigger); Jane Elizabeth Firesheets, Girlfriend (of Raeford)
Time period(s): 1990s
Locale(s): Neely, North Carolina

Summary: Neely, North Carolina is an imaginary town filled with quirky and realistically oddball characters. Folks and families go back a long way, but there's no mistaking this place for a bucolic rural retreat or a quiet little town nestled in the hills. T.R. Pearson's second novel centers around the chaotic relationship of Jane Elizabeth Firesheets and Raeford Benton Lynch, lovers who ricochet from one questionable enterprise to another, mowing down everyone and everything in their paths. Along the way, the adventure never stops, and the small-town faith that all will be well never dies.

Other books by the same author:
Gospel Hour, 1991
The Last of How It Was, 1987
A Short History of a Small Place, 1985

Other books you might like:
Jan Karon, *The Mitford Series*, 1994-
Margaret Maron, *Killer Market*, 1997
Patty Sleem, *Back in Time*, 1997

900

JANE PEART

The Heart's Lonely Secret
(Grand Rapids, Michigan: Fleming H. Revell, 1994)

Category: Romance; Historical Fiction
Subject(s): Orphans; Christian Life; Friendship
Age range(s): Young Adult-Adult
Major character(s): Ivy Austin, Orphan; Allison, Orphan
Time period(s): 1880s; 1890s (1887-1899)
Locale(s): Brookdale, Arkansas

Summary: Ivy Austin is on the Orphan Train with a group of children she has never seen before. Having been disappointed once by an adoption that didn't work out, she is especially worried that she will not find a good home. Pretty Allison is also on the train, and Ivy and Allison have become fast friends. Ivy privately schemes to switch outfits with Allison to boost her chances to land a good home, but when the supervisor later mistakes her for Allison and sends her to live with the mayor's family, Ivy feels that she has just cheated her new friend out of a happy future. The girls remain friends throughout their school years, sharing their special past as children of the Orphan Train. Each is happy in her new home, but Ivy's conscience bothers her until finally she reveals the lonely secret she has harbored in her heart for all these years.

Other books by the same author:
Love Takes Flight, 1994
Dreams of a Longing Heart, 1990
Homeward the Seeking Heart, 1990
Quest for Lasting Love, 1990

Other books you might like:
June Masters Bacher, *No Time for Tears*, 1992
Janette Oke, *Love Comes Softly*, 1979
Janette Oke, *Return to Harmony: A Novel*, 1996
Michael D. Patrick, *Orphan Trains to Missouri*, 1997
Evelyn Goodrich Trickel, co-author

901

JANE PEART

The Pledge
(Grand Rapids, Michigan: Zondervan, 1996)

Category: Romance; Historical Fiction
Series: American Quilt
Subject(s): Quilts; Civil War
Age range(s): Young Adult-Adult
Major character(s): JoBeth Davidson, Fiance(e) (of John Wesley Rutherford); John Wesley Rutherford, Military Personnel (Union soldier), Student (seminary), Fiance(e) (of JoBeth Davidson)
Time period(s): 1860s
Locale(s): North Carolina; Philadelphia, Pennsylvania

Summary: JoBeth Davidson and John Wesley Rutherford are in love. Wesley is a seminary student in Philadelphia, while JoBeth is living with relatives in a town in North Carolina. The Civil War moves closer, and the townspeople side with the Confederacy. Although he is from North Carolina, as well, Wesley has decided he cannot fight to protect slavery, so he sides with the Union and goes off to war, leaving JoBeth torn between the people she loves the most. Despite the heartache and family disapproval, the love between JoBeth and Wesley continues to grow, and they make plans to share their lives together. The American Quilt in this installment of Jane Peart's series is a commemorative quilt JoBeth makes following the assassination of Abraham Lincoln. It features a background of lilies framing three crosses, symbolizing God's sovereignty even in the turmoil and tragedy of war.

Other books by the same author:
The Pattern, 1996 (American Quilt, #1)
The Promise, 1996 (American Quilt, #3)
Runaway Heart, 1994
Valiant Bride, 1989

Other books you might like:
T. Davis Bunn, *The Quilt*, 1993
Gilbert Morris, *A Covenant of Love*, 1992
Esther Loewen Vogt, *The Enchanted Prairie*, 1992
Stephanie Grace Whitson, *Sarah's Patchwork*, 1998

902

JANE PEART

Sign of the Carousel
(Nashville: T. Nelson, 1985)

Category: Gentle Reads
Subject(s): Romance; Family Relations
Age range(s): Young Adult-Adult
Major character(s): Stacy, Art Dealer
Locale(s): California

Summary: Stacey receives some interesting news: a maiden aunt has left her some property and a mansion on the coast of Northern California. Leaving behind an art gallery job in San Francisco, she heads north to check on her surprise gift. When she decides to stay awhile, she finds everyone friendly and accepting of her-except for a wealthy rancher who has apparently had his eye on this property for some time. Is Stacy in over her head with this situation?

Other books by the same author:
Love Takes Flight, 1994
Autumn Encore, 1993
The House of Haunted Dreams, 1992
A Scent of Heather, 1985

Other books you might like:
Lisa Tawn Bergren, *Torchlight*, 1994
Audrey Stallsmith, *Rosemary for Remembrance*, 1998

903

JANE PEART

Valiant Bride

(Grand Rapids, Michigan: Zondervan, 1989)

Category: Romance; Historical Fiction
Series: Brides of Montclair
Subject(s): Marriage; Love
Age range(s): Young Adult-Adult
Major character(s): Noramary Marsh, Young Woman; Duncan Montrose, Young Man
Locale(s): Virginia, American Colonies

Summary: Noramary Marsh is a young lady with a problem, and not a solution is in sight. She is in love with a young man named Robert, but she is betrothed to one Duncan Montrose, who was promised to her cousin. In colonial Virginia, will Miss Marsh have to make a choice between doing her duty and following her heart? And where is God in the midst of all this?

Other books by the same author:
Folly's Bride, 1990 (Brides of Montclair, #4)
Gallant Bride, 1990 (Brides of Montclair, #6)
Yankee Bride, 1990 (Brides of Montclair, #5)
Fortune's Bride, 1986 (Brides of Montclair, #3)
Ransomed Bride, 1989 (Brides of Montclair, #2)

Other books you might like:
Lori Copeland, *Faith*, 1998
Al Lacy, *Secrets of the Heart*, 1998
Gilbert Morris, *Arrow of the Almighty*, 1997
    Liberty Bell, #4
Janette Oke, *Love Comes Softly*, 1979

904

M. SCOTT PECK

In Heaven as on Earth: A Vision of the Afterlife

(New York: Hyperion, 1996)

Category: New Age (Fiction)
Subject(s): Afterlife; Self-Awareness; Faith
Age range(s): Adult
Major character(s): Daniel Turpin, Doctor (psychiatrist), Writer, Aged Person
Time period(s): Indeterminate Future
Locale(s): Heaven; Hell

Summary: M. Scott Peck turns to allegorical fiction to explore questions of personal faith, spiritual growth, and the importance of having purpose in life-and afterlife. Daniel Turpin is a 73-year-old psychiatrist whose near-death experience takes him through a vortex and into the white light of the afterlife. He meets people he has known during his earthly life, and is nearly seduced by a beautiful spirit who, it turns out, is actually Satan. Themes of self-awareness, self-acceptance, and the need for spiritual purpose run throughout the story.

Other books by the same author:
The Road Less Traveled and Beyond: Spiritual Growth in an Age of Anxiety, 1997
The Friendly Snowflake: A Fable of Faith, Love, and Family, 1992
People of the Lie: The Hope for Healing Human Evil, 1983
The Road Less Traveled: A New Psychology of Love, Traditional Values, and Spiritual Growth, 1978

Other books you might like:
Mally Cox-Chapman, *The Case for Heaven: Near-Death Experiences as Evidence of the Afterlife*, 1995
Betty J. Eadie, *Embraced by the Light*, 1992
    Curtis Taylor, co-author
Maurice Rawlings, *Beyond Death's Door*, 1978
Barbara Harris Whitfield, *Final Passage: Sharing the Journey as This Life Ends*, 1998

905

JUDITH PELLA

Beloved Stranger

(Minneapolis: Bethany House, 1998)

Category: Gentle Reads
Subject(s): Marriage; Family Relations; Faith
Age range(s): Adult
Major character(s): Shelby Martin, Teacher; Frank Stefano, Businessman, Restaurateur
Time period(s): 1990s
Locale(s): Whittier, California; Redondo Beach, California; Puerto Vallarta, Mexico

Summary: Shelby Martin's life has just changed dramatically. Her beloved father died while trying to rescue an old man from danger, and now Shelby's mother, who left the family when her daughter was just a baby, wants to be part of her life again. During a hurriedly planned trip to Puerto Vallarta over Christmas, Shelby meets and falls in love with restaurateur Frank Stefano. But now, back home in California, she is discovering just how much she doesn't know about the man she has begun to build her life around. Shelby's faith, already rocked by the death of her father, is completely shaken. How much more can she be expected to bear, and who will share her burden of grief and confusion?

Other books by the same author:
Texas Angel, 1999
Blind Faith, 1996

Other books you might like:
Linda Chaikin, *Endangered*, 1997
Louise M. Gouge, *Once There Was a Way Back Home*, 1994
Lynn Morris, *The Balcony*, 1997

Tracie Peterson, *Framed*, 1998
Ann Tatlock, *A Room of My Own*, 1998

906

JUDITH PELLA

Frontier Lady

(Minneapolis: Bethany House, 1993)

Category: Historical Fiction; Westerns
Series: Lone Star Legacy
Subject(s): Civil War; Christianity
Age range(s): Young Adult-Adult
Major character(s): Deborah Graham, Young Woman
Time period(s): 1860s
Locale(s): Texas (Old West)

Summary: Deborah Graham has a rich life ahead of her, if she can only make it through the tough times. In this first book of Judith Pella's Lone Star Legacy trilogy, Deborah must put behind her the grief of the past in order to receive what God has in store for her. The challenges of life in the frontier West will be met with faith and strength and the independence of a young woman who trusts God's promises.

Other books by the same author:
Westward the Dream, 1999 (Tracie Peterson, co-author)
Warrior's Song, 1996
Stoner's Crossing, 1994

Other books you might like:
Janette Oke, *Love Comes Softly*, 1979
Catherine Palmer, *Prairie Fire*, 1998
Esther Loewen Vogt, *Song of the Prairie*, 1995
Lori Wick, *As Time Goes By*, 1992

907

JUDITH PELLA
TRACIE PETERSON, Co-Author

Westward the Dream

(Minneapolis: Bethany House, 1999)

Category: Historical Fiction
Series: Ribbons West
Subject(s): Frontier and Pioneer Life; Family Life; Civil War
Age range(s): Young Adult-Adult
Major character(s): Brenton Baldwin, Brother (of Jordana), Photographer, 18-Year-Old; Jordana Baldwin, Sister (of Brenton), 16-Year-Old
Time period(s): 1860s (1862)
Locale(s): California (Old West)

Summary: The Civil War is taking its toll on the eastern United States. When they must travel west while their parents are away, siblings Brenton and Jordana Baldwin accept the uncertainty of the unknown with the faith that God will be with them on their way to California. During their journey, the Baldwins help a young woman reunite with her family, and Brenton looks forward to honing his photographic talents and building a professional reputation in this new field of reporting. Surprises and challenges await the young people as they travel toward adventure and maturity.

Other books by the same author:
A Promise for Tomorrow, 1998
A Hope Beyond, 1997
Daughter of Grace, 1996 (Michael Phillips, co-author)

Other books you might like:
Constance Colson, *Chase the Dream*, 1996
Jane Peart, *A Distant Dawn*, 1995
Jim Walker, *The Rail Kings*, 1995

908

WALKER PERCY

The Last Gentleman

(New York: Farrar, Straus, and Giroux, 1966)

Category: Mystery
Subject(s): Self-Perception; Family Life; Relationships
Age range(s): Adult
Major character(s): Williston Bibb "Will" Barrett, Young Man, Recluse
Time period(s): 1960s
Locale(s): New York, New York

Summary: Williston Bibb Barrett, known as Will, is a Princeton dropout and loner living in New York City, something of a fish out of water away from his Southern roots. The more withdrawn he becomes, the more he lives his life through the high-powered telescope with which he views his world. Will doesn't dislike people, but he just can't seem to get along in groups. Besides people to relate to, there's something else significant missing in his life, although Will can't quite put a finger on just what that is. It seems to have something to do with the past, with his father, with memories he has spent a lifetime forgetting. An unexpected encounter with a family that knew his father leads him on a cross-country journey and a search for that undefined something—a sense of identity, perhaps?—without which he remains on the fringe of society.

Other books by the same author:
The Thanatos Syndrome, 1987
The Second Coming, 1980
Lancelot, 1977

Other books you might like:
Reynolds Price, *The Promise of Rest*, 1995
Reynolds Price, *The Source of Light*, 1981
Brian Regrut, *Stolen Identity: A Suspense Thriller*, 1993

909

WALKER PERCY

Love in the Ruins: The Adventures of a Bad Catholic at a Time Near the End of the World

(New York: Farrar, Straus, and Giroux, 1971)

Category: Thrillers
Subject(s): Civil Rights; Apocalypse; Fantasy
Age range(s): Adult
Major character(s): Dr. Tom More, Doctor, Bachelor, Inventor

Time period(s): Indeterminate Future
Locale(s): New Orleans, Louisiana

Summary: Dr. Tom More is a wealthy bachelor with a fantastic invention: the Ontological Lapsometer, a spiritual stethoscope with which he intends to change the world for the better. Not surprisingly, no one else has much faith in the doctor or his plans, and in the midst of civil unrest in his all-white club community in the Deep South, More is teetering on the fine line between madness and normalcy. His days and nights are spent maneuvering through an uncertain existence in which he seeks love and success (with little satisfaction on either front), all the while dodging the real bullets of radical civil rights snipers who are hiding in lowlands throughout the suburb. Written during the late 1960s, this novel creates a nightmarish world of apocalyptic civil unrest, race riots, and crises of faith that reflects its time.

Other books by the same author:
The Thanatos Syndrome, 1987
The Second Coming, 1980
The Last Gentleman, 1966

Other books you might like:
Connie Briscoe, *Big Girls Don't Cry*, 1996
Ann Fairbairn, *Five Smooth Stones: A Novel*, 1966
Patrick D. Smith, *The Beginning: A Novel*, 1967

910

FRANK E. PERETTI

The Oath

(Dallas: Word, 1995)

Category: Thrillers
Subject(s): Dragons; Allegories; Christianity
Age range(s): Adult
Major character(s): Steve Benson, Scientist; Tracy, Police Officer (deputy sheriff)
Time period(s): 1990s
Locale(s): Hyde River, Pacific Northwest

Summary: Steve Benson has arrived in mining town Hyde River following the mauling death of his brother. Although the death looks like the work of a grizzly bear, later evidence and more deaths suggest something far more sinister, and Benson sets out to discover what it is. Along the way, he hears tales of a sin-eating dragon that marks and kills those who have committed sins. Although he is skeptical, he entertains the possibility that such a creature exists, and then comes face to face with the monster as a result of having engaged in an affair with a married deputy sheriff. Following a dramatic confession-and-conversion, Benson takes on the dragon in a head-on battle of evil against righteousness.

Awards the book has won:
Gold Medallion Book Award, Fiction, 1996

Other books by the same author:
The Visitation, 1999
Piercing the Darkness, 1989
This Present Darkness, 1986

Other books you might like:
Randy Alcorn, *Deadline: A Novel*, 1994

Randy Alcorn, *Dominion*, 1996
Laurence Cosse, *A Corner of the Veil*, 1999
   Linda Asher, translator
Roger Elwood, *Where Angels Dare*, 1999
Gerald E. Goggins, *Half-Wits*, 1988

911

FRANK E. PERETTI

Piercing the Darkness

(Westchester, Illinois: Crossway, 1989)

Category: Thrillers
Subject(s): Angels; Demons; Fundamentalism
Age range(s): Adult
Major character(s): Sally Beth Roe, Young Woman
Locale(s): Bacon's Corner

Summary: Sally Beth Roe is a young woman whose troubled past hangs around her, no matter how she tries to shake it off. In the small town of Bacon's Corner, though, Sally's life affects everyone. As she tries to come to terms with her unhappy and chaotic past, she is supported by angels and attacked by demons. Demonic powers are taking over the community, as well, in Peretti's vision of late-twentieth-century spiritual warfare. At the heart of the community upheaval is the question over who controls the local school curriculum—the folks aligned with the angels? Or the others? Sally ultimately confronts the demons, undergoes a dramatic transformation, and becomes firmly aligned with the angels.

Awards the book has won:
Gold Medallion Book Award, Fiction, 1990

Other books by the same author:
The Visitation, 1999
The Prophet, 1992
This Present Darkness, 1986

Other books you might like:
Randy Alcorn, *Deadline: A Novel*, 1994
Randy Alcorn, *Dominion*, 1996
Roger Elwood, *Where Angels Dare*, 1999

912

FRANK E. PERETTI

This Present Darkness

(Westchester, Illinois: Crossway Books, 1986)

Category: Thrillers
Subject(s): Demons; Good and Evil; Clergy
Age range(s): Adult
Major character(s): Hank Busche, Religious (pastor)
Time period(s): 1990s
Locale(s): Ashton (a small college town)

Summary: In Peretti's first novel, a small college town is being threatened by the dark forces of demons who appear as a New Age minister, the leaders of a multinational corporation, a corrupt police officer, a Satanist professor, and the Universal Consciousness Society, a New Age group that plans to purchase the college and control humankind with godless philosophies and rhetoric. Pastor Hank Busche calls upon the power of heaven, and a legion of angels to do battle with the demons, resulting in the victory of good over evil. A conservative Christian theology is the basis for Peretti's bestselling novels, which generally deal with issues of spiritual warfare and the opposing forces of heaven and hell.

Other books by the same author:
The Oath, 1995
Piercing the Darkness, 1989

Other books you might like:
Orson Scott Card, *Ender's Game*, 1985
Tim LaHaye, *Left Behind: A Novel of the Earth's Last Days*, 1995
Tim LaHaye, *Nicolae: The Rise of Antichrist*, 1997

913

MICHAEL PHILLIPS

The Eleventh Hour
(Wheaton, Illinois: Tyndale House, 1993)

Category: Historical Fiction
Series: Secret of the Rose
Subject(s): Family Life; War; Romance
Age range(s): Young Adult-Adult
Major character(s): Sabina von Dortmann, Daughter (of the baron); Gustav, Neighbor (of Sabina and her father); Matthew, Military Personnel (American soldier)
Time period(s): 1930s; 1940s (1939-1945)
Locale(s): Prussia

Summary: As war threatens the nearby country of Poland, Baron von Dortmann and his daughter Sabina live peacefully in their Prussian home, he tending his roses and his family with loving care, she growing toward young womanhood under the watchful eye of her adoring father. The rose garden is a place of peace, prayer, and serenity for them until the day eight strangers find their way in, seeking shelter from the danger now so near. As the effects of war move closer to home, the Baron notices that young love is in the offing: the young American, Matthew, and their neighbor, Gustav, both seem interested in Sabina. The Baron knows that what is to come will change their lives forever.

Other books by the same author:
Dawn of Liberty, 1995 (Secret of the Rose, #4)
Escape to Freedom, 1994 (Secret of the Rose, #3)
A Rose Remembered, 1994 (Secret of the Rose, #2)

Other books you might like:
Neva Coyle, *Close to a Father's Heart: A Novel*, 1996
Doris Elaine Fell, *Before Winter Comes*, 1994
Carol Matas, *In My Enemy's House*, 1999
Maryann Minatra, *Before Night Falls*, 1996
Janette Oke, *Another Homecoming*, 1997
    T. Davis Bunn, co-author

914

MICHAEL PHILLIPS
JUDITH PELLA, Co-Author

The Heather Hills of Stonewycke
(Minneapolis: Bethany House, 1985)

Category: Historical Fiction
Series: Stonewycke Trilogy
Subject(s): Romance; Mystery; Adventure and Adventurers
Age range(s): Young Adult-Adult
Major character(s): Maggie Duncan, 17-Year-Old; Ian Duncan, Cousin (distant, of Maggie's father)
Time period(s): 19th century
Locale(s): Scotland

Summary: Inside the walls of the Duncan mansion at Stonewycke, all is not well. Daughter Maggie and her mother unobtrusively share an uneasy alliance against Maggie's father, a man prone to violent outbursts, whose secrets drive him further from his family all the time. A guest in the house, distant cousin Ian Duncan, is a city-bred young man who has been sent by his father to the country as a last resort to control his reckless behavior. During his visit, Ian and Maggie fall in love and Ian does some serious soul-searching about his past and his future. Meanwhile, her father has secretly made plans for an arranged marriage for Maggie as part of an unsavory business deal. When he discovers that she has no intention of marrying the man he has promised her to, his anger is the catalyst that tests the faith of Maggie and her mother. This is the first volume in two series of Stonewycke novels, the Stonewycke Trilogy and the Stonewycke Legacy.

Other books by the same author:
Stranger at Stonewycke, 1987 (Judith Pella, co-author; Stonewycke Legacy, #1)
The Lady of Stonewycke, 1986 (Judith Pella, co-author; Stonewycke Trilogy, #3)
Flight From Stonewycke, 1985 (Judith Pella, co-author; Stonewycke Trilogy, #2)

Other books you might like:
Robert McAfee Brown, *Dark the Night, Wild the Sea*, 1998
Sharon Gillenwater, *Song of the Highlands*, 1996
Grace Johnson, *Tempest at Stonehaven*, 1997

915

MICHAEL PHILLIPS

A Home for the Heart
(Minneapolis: Bethany House, 1994)

Category: Historical Fiction
Series: Journals of Corrie Belle Hollister
Subject(s): Romance; Family Life; Travel
Age range(s): Young Adult-Adult
Major character(s): Corrie Belle Hollister, Journalist; Christopher Braxton, Young Man
Time period(s): 1860s (1865)
Locale(s): Miracle Springs, California

Summary: Corrie Belle Hollister is on her way back to Miracle Springs, having traveled the country as an independent young woman and journalist during the Civil War. Recovering from a bullet wound, Corrie decides it's time to return to her roots as she figures out what's next in her life. But her old life isn't without ties to her recent adventures: her story unfolds in this novel through letters to and from Christopher, the young man she's ready to give her heart to. What will happen to their deepening friendship when they are separated by many miles of uninhabited territory? Will their love and faith be enough to keep them close? Although this is the last book in this series, Corrie's story continues in *The Braxtons of Miracle Springs*.

Other books by the same author:
A New Beginning, 1997
The Braxtons of Miracle Springs, 1996
Land of the Brave and the Free, 1993 (Journals of Corrie Belle Hollister, #7)
Into the Long Dark Night, 1992 (Journals of Corrie Belle Hollister, #6)

Other books you might like:
Lori Copeland, *Faith*, 1998
Lynn Morris, *Toward the Sunrising*, 1996
   Gilbert Morris, co-author
Jane Peart, *Promise of the Valley*, 1995
Bodie Thoene, *Winds of Promise*, 1997
   Brock Thoene, co-author; Wayward Winds, 1

916

MICHAEL PHILLIPS
JUDITH PELLA, Co-Author

A House Divided

(Minneapolis: Bethany House, 1992)

Category: Historical Fiction
Series: Russians
Subject(s): Family Saga; Russian Empire; Romance
Age range(s): Young Adult-Adult
Major character(s): Anna Yevnovna Berenin, Servant; Paul Berenin, Revolutionary; Sergei Fedorcencko, Royalty (prince); Katrina Fedorcencko, Royalty (princess)
Time period(s): 1870s; 1880s (1879-1880)
Locale(s): St. Petersburg, Russia

Summary: Anna Berenin is a servant girl who works for the aristocratic Fedorcencko family in St. Petersburg, Russia. Her homeland is at war with Turkey, and revolutionary fervor is building among the peasants, including Berenin's family. Prince Sergei returns from war and is reunited with Anna, but their love for each other is complicated by the tensions between their families. Anna turns to her faith in God in search of a solution.

Other books by the same author:
Travail and Triumph, 1992 (Judith Pella, co-author)
The Crown and the Crucible, 1991 (Judith Pella, co-author)

Other books you might like:
Orson Scott Card, *Enchantment*, 1999
Andrei Makine, *Dreams of My Russian Summers*, 1997

917

MICHAEL PHILLIPS

A Rift in Time

(Wheaton, Illinois: Tyndale House, 1997)

Category: Thrillers
Subject(s): Archaeology; Millennium; Christianity
Age range(s): Adult
Major character(s): Dr. Adam Livingstone, Archaeologist; Juliet Halsay, Young Woman
Time period(s): Indeterminate Future

Summary: Adam Livingstone is a British archaeologist who has made an astounding discovery—one that supports the biblical account of the great flood. Although he is not a very religious man, he begins to rethink his position when a terrorist group wants to stop him and his work because his findings might prove the Old Testament account of Noah's Ark more than a myth. Together, Livingstone and Juliet Halsay seek the truth—about those who are targeting him and about life in general—and they find more than they bargain for.

Other books by the same author:
Hidden in Time, 1999
The Garden at the Edge of Beyond, 1998
Grayfox, 1993

Other books you might like:
Christopher A. Lane, *Appearance of Evil*, 1997
Paul Meier, *The Third Millennium: A Novel*, 1993
Bill Myers, *Threshold*, 1997

918

MICHAEL PHILLIPS

Sea to Shining Sea

(Minneapolis: Bethany House, 1992)

Category: Historical Fiction
Series: Journals of Corrie Belle Hollister
Subject(s): American West; Civil War; Family Relations
Age range(s): Young Adult-Adult
Major character(s): Corrie Belle Hollister, Journalist; Cal Burton, Political Figure
Time period(s): 1860s (1860)
Locale(s): San Francisco, California; Sacramento, California

Summary: Away from the small town of Miracle Springs, young journalist Corrie Belle Hollister discovers a whole new world. While her life is exciting, serious events are underway as the United States moves closer to war between the North and South. Corrie finds herself working for Abraham Lincoln and the Republicans, risking conflict with the Hollister clan, and caught up in the politics that divides families and communities during the Civil War. Corrie's new perspective causes her to evaluate her faith and her loyalties.

Other books by the same author:
The Braxtons of Miracle Springs, 1996
A Place in the Sun, 1991
Daughter of Grace, 1990

Other books you might like:
Lynn Morris, *A City Not Forsaken*, 1995
Janette Oke, *Heart of the Wilderness*, 1993
Janette Oke, *The Measure of a Heart*, 1992
Judith Pella, *Lone Star Legacy*, 1993-1996

919

MICHAEL PHILLIPS
JUDITH PELLA, Co-Author

Travail and Triumph

(Minneapolis: Bethany House, 1992)

Category: Historical Fiction
Series: Russians
Subject(s): Family Saga; Russian Empire; Romance
Age range(s): Young Adult-Adult
Major character(s): Anna Yevnovna Berenin, Servant; Sergei Fedorcencko, Royalty (prince); Katrina Fedorcencko, Royalty (princess)
Time period(s): 1880s; 1890s
Locale(s): St. Petersburg, Russia

Summary: Peasant girl Anna and her prince, Sergei, have married, though they are now estranged from their families, and Sergei is sent to Siberia. Princess Katrina and Dmitri marry and live in the luxury to which they are accustomed, but without the maturity to overcome their own selfish ways, their marriage falls apart. What will happen to their young daughter Mariana when tragedy strikes? In pre-revolutionary Russia, is there faith enough to protect these young families from the unrest that lies ahead?

Other books by the same author:
A House Divided, 1992 (Judith Pella, co-author; Russians, #2)
The Crown and the Crucible, 1991 (Judith Pella, co-author; Russians #1)

Other books you might like:
Orson Scott Card, *Enchantment*, 1999
Andrei Makine, *Dreams of My Russian Summers*, 1997
Geoffrey Strachan, translator
Judith Pella, *The Dawning of Deliverance*, 1995
Russians, #5
Judith Pella, *Heirs of the Motherland*, 1993
Russians, #4
Judith Pella, *Passage into Light*, 1998
Russians, #7
Judith Pella, *White Nights, Red Morning*, 1996
Russians, #6

920

EUGENIA PRICE

The Beloved Invader

(Philadelphia: Lippincott, 1965)

Category: Historical Fiction
Series: St. Simons Trilogy
Subject(s): Family Saga; Clergy; Episcopalians
Age range(s): Young Adult-Adult

Major character(s): Anson Dodge, Historical Figure, Veteran (Union soldier), Religious (clergyman); Ellen Dodge, Historical Figure, Spouse; Anna Dodge, Historical Figure, Spouse
Time period(s): 19th century (1870s-1890s)
Locale(s): St. Simons Island, Georgia

Summary: This fictional biography of Anson Dodge is chronologically the end of the St. Simons Trilogy, although it was the first volume published in the series. Dodge is a Union veteran who comes to St. Simons in 1879, where he becomes an Episcopal minister. Despite the tensions of being a Northerner living in the war-ravaged South, he is driven to rebuild his war-torn church and community.

Other books by the same author:
Lighthouse, 1971
New Moon Rising, 1969

Other books you might like:
Jane Aiken Hodge, *Savannah Purchase*, 1971
Caroline Miller, *Lamb in His Bosom*, 1933
Anne Rivers Siddons, *Peachtree Road*, 1988

921

EUGENIA PRICE

Bright Captivity

(New York: Doubleday, 1991)

Category: Historical Fiction; Romance
Series: Georgia Trilogy
Subject(s): Antebellum South; Family Saga; War of 1812
Age range(s): Young Adult-Adult
Major character(s): Anne Couper, Gentlewoman; John Fraser, Military Personnel (British soldier); Sir Walter Scott, Historical Figure, Writer
Time period(s): 1810s (1815-1817)
Locale(s): St. Simons Island, Georgia; London, England; Scotland

Summary: This first volume of the author's Georgia Trilogy is set on St. Simons Island during and following the War of 1812. Anne Couper, the young daughter of a prominent St. Simons family, falls in love with a British officer on a mission to free the slaves. He returns after the war to marry Anne, and their life together takes them to England and Scotland while they struggle to decide whether to live in Europe or America. Themes of love, loyalty, and Christian faith are intertwined in this novel that blends history and romance in equal measure.

Other books by the same author:
Beauty From Ashes, 1995 (Georgia Trilogy, #3)
Where Shadows Go, 1993 (Georgia Trilogy, #2)

Other books you might like:
E. Randall Floyd, *Deep in the Heart*, 1998
Jane Aiken Hodge, *Savannah Purchase*, 1971
Caroline Miller, *Lamb in His Bosom*, 1933
Anne Rivers Siddons, *Peachtree Road*, 1988

922

EUGENIA PRICE

Lighthouse

(Philadelphia: Lippincott, 1971)

Category: Historical Fiction
Series: St. Simons Trilogy
Subject(s): Antebellum South; Family Saga; Faith
Age range(s): Young Adult-Adult
Major character(s): James Gould, Historical Figure, Land-owner, Spouse (of Jane); Jane Harris Gould, Historical Figure, Spouse (of James)
Time period(s): 1800s; 1810s
Locale(s): St. Simons Island, Georgia

Summary: This volume, though published last, is chronologically the first episode of the author's St. Simons Trilogy. The novel tells the story of the real James Gould and his family. Gould, from Massachusetts, settles on St. Simons Island in Georgia during the early years of the 19th century, drawn there by his dream of building a lighthouse. The author reveals the beginnings of the family saga first introduced in *The Beloved Invader*. Values including faith and integrity influence the family for generations.

Other books by the same author:
New Moon Rising, 1969
The Beloved Invader, 1965

Other books you might like:
Jane Aiken Hodge, *Savannah Purchase*, 1971
Caroline Miller, *Lamb in His Bosom*, 1933
Anne Rivers Siddons, *Peachtree Road*, 1988

923

EUGENIA PRICE

New Moon Rising

(Philadelphia: Lippincott, 1969)

Category: Historical Fiction
Series: St. Simons Trilogy
Subject(s): Antebellum South; Civil War; Slavery
Age range(s): Young Adult-Adult
Major character(s): Horace Gould, Historical Figure, Land-owner, Spouse (of Deborah); Deborah Gould, Historical Figure, Spouse (of Horace)
Time period(s): 19th century (1830s-1860s)
Locale(s): St. Simons Island, Georgia

Summary: The second novel of the author's St. Simons trilogy covers the period from the 1830s through the Civil War. Incorporating characteristic themes of trust and faithfulness, Eugenia Price tells the story of Horace Gould, who comes of age in the decade before the war starts. An outsider on the island, Gould struggles with the devastating impact of the Civil War on his life and the traditions of his home.

Other books by the same author:
Lighthouse, 1971
The Beloved Invader, 1965

Other books you might like:
Jane Aiken Hodge, *Savannah Purchase*, 1971
Caroline Miller, *Lamb in His Bosom*, 1933
Anne Rivers Siddons, *Peachtree Road*, 1988

924

EUGENIA PRICE

Savannah

(Garden City, New York: Doubleday, 1983)

Category: Historical Fiction
Series: Savannah Quartet
Subject(s): Antebellum South; Family Saga; War of 1812
Age range(s): Young Adult-Adult
Major character(s): Mark Browning, Gentleman, Spouse (of Caroline); Caroline Browning, Spouse (of Mark)
Time period(s): 1810s; 1820s (1812-1822)
Locale(s): Savannah, Georgia

Summary: The first volume of the Savannah Quartet describes life in Savannah, Georgia, during the War of 1812 and the years immediately afterward. The traditional southern city is seen through the experiences of Mark Browning, an orphan and outsider from Philadelphia, who makes his way in Georgia society while building a life with Caroline, his wife. The author interweaves history, romance, and traditional themes of faith and honor in a family saga that will conclude during the Civil War era in the fourth volume of the series, *Stranger in Savannah*.

Other books by the same author:
Stranger in Savannah, 1989
Before the Darkness Falls, 1987
To See Your Face Again: A Novel, 1985

Other books you might like:
Jane Aiken Hodge, *Savannah Purchase*, 1971
Caroline Miller, *Lamb in His Bosom*, 1933
Anne Rivers Siddons, *Peachtree Road*, 1988

925

REYNOLDS PRICE

The Tongues of Angels

(New York: Atheneum, 1990)

Category: Gentle Reads
Subject(s): Adolescence; Camps and Camping; Death
Age range(s): Adult
Major character(s): Bridge Boatner, Student—College, 21-Year-Old
Time period(s): 1950s (1954)
Locale(s): Camp Juniper (Smoky Mountains)

Summary: Set at a boys' camp in the Smoky Mountains, this novel tells the story of a young camp counselor and the events of one unforgettable summer. Bridge Boatner is at Camp Juniper to teach art to boys not quite in the throes of adolescence. It's the summer of 1954. Typically rowdy boys tumble from one outdoor activity to another, engaged in the usual horseplay and banter. Among the crowd, however, is one gifted boy whose camp experience, set within the context of a difficult life, will alter the course of his future. The story is told by a middle-aged Boatner whose recollections of that summer trace his development from boy to man.

Other books by the same author:
The Promise of Rest, 1995
Good Hearts, 1988
The Source of Light, 1981

Other books you might like:
Gail Godwin, *Evensong*, 1999
Gail Godwin, *Father Melancholy's Daughter*, 1991
Gail Godwin, *A Southern Family*, 1987

926
NAOMI RAGEN
Sotah
(New York: Crown, 1992)

Category: Gentle Reads
Subject(s): Judaism; Family Life
Age range(s): Adult
Major character(s): Dina Reich, Young Woman, Daughter (of Rabbi Reich), Spouse (of Judah); Judah, Carpenter, Spouse (of Dina)
Time period(s): 20th century
Locale(s): Jerusalem, Israel; New York, New York

Summary: Dina Reich is the daughter of Rabbi Reich, leader of an ultraorthodox sect in Jerusalem. When her family can't afford the dowry required for her to marry the man she loves, she is betrothed by the community matchmaker to a carpenter named Judah. He is a good man, but not much of an intellectual companion for the vibrant young woman who dreams of a wider world than that into which she was born. After bearing her first child, she becomes very friendly with a non-Jewish male neighbor. Although the relationship is not physical, she is accused by the elders of the community of being a sotah—an adultress—and she is forced to leave her home and family. Exiled in New York City, she takes a job as a maid and ultimately confesses all to the family she who employs her. Being kind and generous folk, they support her search for happiness and spiritual wholeness.

Other books by the same author:
The Ghost of Hannah Mendes, 1998
The Sacrifice of Tamar, 1994
Jephte's Daughter, 1989

Other books you might like:
Pearl Abraham, *Giving Up America*, 1998
Pearl Abraham, *The Romance Reader*, 1995
Rebecca Goldstein, *Mazel*, 1995
Allegra Goodman, *The Family Markowitz*, 1996
Allegra Goodman, *Kaaterskill Falls: A Novel*, 1998

927
JAMES REDFIELD
The Celestine Prophecy: An Adventure
(New York: Warner Books, 1993)

Category: New Age (Fiction)

Subject(s): Adventure and Adventurers; Quest; Spirituality
Age range(s): Adult
Major character(s): Wayne Dobson, Professor (of history), Historian; Wilson James, Researcher
Time period(s): 1990s
Locale(s): Andes Mountains, Peru

Summary: This is a spiritual mystery that begins when one friend meets another whose briefcase has been stolen. Before long, the narrator finds himself on a deadly race through the jungles of Peru in pursuit of a lost Peruvian manuscript containing nine secrets of spiritual awareness. His search for the ancient wisdom begins in the Andes Mountains, where he learns the first secret: the daily coincidences in our lives are not accidental, but are part of a universal synchronism. Throughout his journey, the seeker is pursued by agents for the government of Peru and by Catholic clergy. Neither group is willing to risk the possible loss of power and control that could result if these secrets are made available to the population at large. Nevertheless, the narrator encounters others along the way who reveal to him each of the remaining secrets.

Other books by the same author:
The Celestine Vision: Living the New Spiritual Awareness, 1997
The Tenth Insight: Holding the Vision, 1996

Other books you might like:
Arlene Boday, *The Third Time Is Now*, 1996
Neale Donald Walsch, *Conversations with God: An Uncommon Dialogue*, 1996

928
SHERI REYNOLDS
The Rapture of Canaan
(New York: G.P. Putnam's Sons, 1995)

Category: Gentle Reads
Subject(s): Pentecostal; Pregnancy
Age range(s): Adult
Major character(s): Ninah Huff, Teenager, 14-Year-Old; Herman Langston, Grandfather, Religious (preacher); Canaan, Baby, Son (of Ninah)
Time period(s): 1990s
Locale(s): South Carolina

Summary: Ninah Huff and her family are members of the Church of Fire and Brimstone and God's Almighty Baptizing Wind, an isolated, pentecostal, religious community in South Carolina. Grandpa Herman Langston is the fiery preacher whose dictates require Ninah to wear long dresses and never cut her hair. Ninah is obedient, but she privately questions the absolute mandates of her religion, especially when she and her young, male prayer partner discover a mutual attraction that is something other than spiritual. When Ninah becomes pregnant, she insists that she is innocent of sin and that her child is a miracle. In the end, Ninah learns about miracles of another kind in the world outside her closed community.

Other books by the same author:
A Gracious Plenty, 1997
Bitterroot Landing, 1994

Other books you might like:
Pearl Abraham, *The Romance Reader*, 1995
Kaye Gibbons, *Ellen Foster*, 1987
Jane Hamilton, *The Book of Ruth*, 1988
John Pielmeier, *Agnes of God*, 1982

929

PENNY RICHARDS

Unanswered Prayers

(New York: Harlequin, 1997)

Category: Romance
Subject(s): Pregnancy; Christianity; Love
Age range(s): Young Adult-Adult
Major character(s): Eva Carmichael, Young Woman; Howard Blake, Religious (minister)
Time period(s): 1990s

Summary: Can beautiful young Eva be happy as a minister's wife? Why would Howard Blake be willing to marry a woman bearing someone else's child? With God's love between them, Eva and Howard may be the answer to each other's prayers. This title is one of Harlequin's ''Love Inspired'' series of Christian romances.

Other books by the same author:
Where Dreams Have Been, 1995
Passionate Kisses, 1994
Eden, 1993

Other books you might like:
Irene Brand, *Child of Her Heart*, 1998
Irene Hannon, *A Groom of Her Own*, 1998
Ruth Scofield, *In God's Own Time*, 1998
Cheryl Wolverton, *A Father's Love*, 1998

930

FRANCINE RIVERS

The Atonement Child

(Wheaton, Illinois: Tyndale House, 1997)

Category: Gentle Reads
Subject(s): Christian Life; Rape; Abortion
Age range(s): Young Adult-Adult
Major character(s): Dynah Carey, Student, Daughter (of Hannah); Hannah Carey, Mother (of Dynah)
Time period(s): 1990s
Locale(s): United States

Summary: Dynah Carey is a young college student in love with one of the most sought-after young men on her Christian college campus, and the pair has begun making plans to marry. One night, on her way back to campus alone, Dynah is raped. When she finds herself pregnant, she struggles with whether or not to have an abortion. She doesn't want to. But Dynah isn't the only one feeling torn as a result of this experience. Her fiance can't understand why she won't just handle things quietly and discreetly. Dynah's choice opens wounds in three generations for women who had abortions and never told anyone. Dynah herself must face the realization that by doing what she believes her faith tells her she

must, she risks being expelled from her Christian school because pregnant students are not allowed. Francine Rivers deals sensitively with a highly charged topic, remaining faithful to her personal beliefs, yet acknowledging that there are no easy choices in this matter.

Other books by the same author:
The Last Sin Eater, 1998
The Scarlet Thread, 1996
An Echo in the Darkness, 1994

Other books you might like:
Judith Pella, *Beloved Stranger*, 1998
Bodie Thoene, *Only the River Runs Free*, 1997
    Brock Thoene, co-author
Jack Weyland, *Brittany*, 1997

931

FRANCINE RIVERS

The Last Sin Eater

(Wheaton, Illinois: Tyndale House, 1998)

Category: Historical Fiction
Subject(s): Christianity; Death; Sin
Age range(s): Adult
Major character(s): Cadi, 10-Year-Old, Relative (granddaughter)
Time period(s): 1850s
Locale(s): Smoky Mountains

Summary: Ten-year-old Cadi is broken-hearted. Her beloved grandmother has died, and she feels absolutely alone in the world and unloved. An earlier family tragedy is being blamed on her, and her mother can hardly bear to be in the same room with her. In her grief, Cadi looks at the forbidden graveside ''sin eater'' of 1850s mountain folklore at her grandmother's burial site. Burdened with her own guilt, she struggles to find a way for the sin eater to absolve her of all wrong-doing before death, rather than afterward. Her search for comfort leads her to Jesus and Christianity, which ultimately serves as a catalyst to family reconciliation. In her search for peace and comfort, Cadi finds forgiveness and faith.

Awards the book has won:
Gold Medallion Book Award, Fiction, 1999

Other books by the same author:
The Atonement Child, 1997
The Scarlet Thread, 1996

Other books you might like:
Catherine Marshall, *Christy*, 1967
Lee Smith, *The Devil's Dream*, 1992

932

FRANCINE RIVERS

The Scarlet Thread

(Wheaton, Illinois: Tyndale House, 1996)

Category: Gentle Reads
Subject(s): Marriage; Quilts; Love
Age range(s): Young Adult-Adult

Fiction

Major character(s): Sierra Madrid, Spouse (of Alex); Alex Madrid, Spouse (of Sierra); Mary Kathryn McMurray, Pioneer, Relative (ancestor of Sierra)
Time period(s): 1990s; 1890s
Locale(s): Los Angeles, California; Oregon Trail, California

Summary: Sierra Madrid is a happy wife and mother who loves her home and her community. When her husband, Alejandro, announces that the family will be moving to Los Angeles for his new job, she feels betrayed. Not only has he uprooted the family, he's also having an affair and spending money like crazy. While tending to home matters, Sierra discovers an old quilt made by a woman in her family tree, and a journal wrapped inside the quilt. As Sierra journeys through the obstacles of modern-day married life, she follows the journey of her ancestor, Mary Kathryn McMurray, who was herself uprooted and moved from her comfortable home to travel the Oregon Trail with her husband. Sierra draws strength from the spiritual insights of this writer whose life in a different century could have been Sierra's.

Other books by the same author:
The Last Sin Eater, 1998
The Atonement Child, 1997
A Voice in the Wind, 1993

Other books you might like:
James Scott Bell, *Circumstantial Evidence: A Novel*, 1997
Louise M. Gouge, *The Homecoming*, 1998
Sally John, *In the Shadow of Love*, 1998
Judith Pella, *Beloved Stranger*, 1998

933

FRANCINE RIVERS

A Voice in the Wind
(Wheaton, Illinois: Tyndale House, 1993)

Category: Historical Fiction
Series: Mark of the Lion
Subject(s): Slavery; Christianity; Roman Empire
Age range(s): Young Adult-Adult
Major character(s): Hadassah, Slave
Time period(s): 1st century (70 A.D.)
Locale(s): Roman Empire

Summary: Alone in a hostile place, Hadassah knows that to tell people about her faith could bring her harm. She knows that as a Benjamite, an early Christian, she risks persecution if she is discovered. But the young slave wants so much to share what she believes that she lives out her faith anyway, blessing the Roman family to whom she was sold after her city was destroyed. She also discovers that she is not as alone in her faith as she had originally thought, and that the rewards of sharing her faith far outweigh the risks.

Other books by the same author:
As Sure as the Dawn, 1995 (Mark of the Lion, #3)
An Echo in the Darkness, 1994 (Mark of the Lion, #2)

Other books you might like:
Thom Lemmons, *Daughter of Jerusalem*, 1999
Paul L. Maier, *The Flames of Rome*, 1981
Naomi Mitchison, *The Blood of the Martyrs*, 1939
Henryk Sienkiewicz, *Quo Vadis*, 1896

934

SALMAN RUSHDIE

The Satanic Verses
(New York: Viking, 1988)

Category: Fantasy
Subject(s): Good and Evil; Islam; Muhammad
Age range(s): Adult
Major character(s): Gibreel Farishta, Actor (film), Angel; Saladin Chamcha, Actor (star of a British TV show), Demon; Alleluia Cone, Leader (of pilgrimage to Mecca), Religious
Time period(s): 1890s (1899); 7th century
Locale(s): London, England; Bombay, India; Jahilia, Fictional Country

Summary: Gibreel, an Indian movie actor, and Saladin, the star of a British television show, both survive the terrorist bombing of a jumbo jet. After the crash, the two are mysteriously transformed into living incarnations of good and evil. Saladin grows the horns of a devil, and Gibreel develops an angel's halo. The book's titles refers to an Islamic story in which the prophet Muhammed removes two verses from the Koran, claiming that he should never have written them in the first place because they were inspired by Satan.

Awards the book has won:
Whitbread Prize, Novel, 1988

Other books by the same author:
The Moor's Last Sigh, 1995
Haroun and the Sea of Stories, 1990
Shame, 1983
Midnight's Children, 1981

Other books you might like:
Kiran Desai, *Hullabaloo in the Guava Orchard*, 1998
Godwin Parke, *The Snake Oil Wars*, 1989

935

MARY DORIA RUSSELL

Children of God: A Novel
(New York: Villard, 1998)

Category: Science Fiction
Subject(s): Religion; Space Travel; Catholicism
Age range(s): Adult
Major character(s): Father Emilio Sandoz, Religious (Jesuit priest)
Time period(s): 2060s (2060)
Locale(s): Rakhat, Planet—Imaginary (in Alpha Centauri system)

Summary: *Children of God* is the sequel to Mary Doria Russell's novel *The Sparrow*. It continues the brutal story of Father Emilio Sandoz, who had been living on Rakhat in the Alpha Centauri system. Following his rape and maiming in the conflict between two civilizations on the planet, he has returned to Earth to recover. No longer an active Jesuit, he has fallen in love with a young woman and wishes to pursue the happiness he has finally found. The Jesuits, however, want him to return to Rakhat, and despite his objections, he is compelled to do so. The situation is still dark, dangerous, and chaotic, but Sandoz ultimately prevails over the nightmares and horrors of the Rakhat conflict and returns to Earth once again. The story is filled with harsh and graphic scenes of cruelty, apathy, and war.

Other books by the same author:
The Sparrow, 1996

Other books you might like:
Glenn Kleier, *The Last Day*, 1997
Irene Martin, *Emerald Thorn*, 1991
Paul McCusker, *Catacombs*, 1997

936

MARY DORIA RUSSELL

The Sparrow
(New York: Villard, 1996)

Category: Science Fiction
Subject(s): Religion; Space Travel; Catholicism
Age range(s): Adult
Major character(s): Father Emilio Sandoz, Religious (Jesuit priest)
Time period(s): 2050s (2059)

Summary: In 2019, Jesuit priest Father Emilio Sandoz initiated a first contact mission with life forms that had just been discovered on Rakhat. Eight people went; only one came back. In the year 2059, the Vatican accuses Sandoz, the sole survivor, of having committed crimes that precipitated the death of his colleagues and caused the devastation of his physical and emotional health. The story alternates between the days of planning the trip, when the Jesuits had no idea what awaited them on Rakhat, and the time forty years later when Sandoz is reliving in his mind the years he spent there learning to love the civilizations that ultimately nearly killed him. The story, which deals with brutal aspects of war and societies without regard for human life, is continued in Russell's *Children of God*.

Awards the book has won:
Arthur C. Clarke Award, 1998
James Tiptree, Jr. Memorial Award, 1997

Other books by the same author:
Children of God: A Novel, 1998

Other books you might like:
Glenn Kleier, *The Last Day*, 1997
Irene Martin, *Emerald Thorn*, 1991
Paul McCusker, *Catacombs*, 1997

937

JULIE SALAMON

The Christmas Tree
(New York : Random House, 1996)

Category: Morality Tales
Subject(s): Christmas; Gifts; Love
Age range(s): Children-Adult
Major character(s): Anna, Orphan, Religious (Sister Anthony)

Locale(s): New York, New York; New Jersey

Summary: Sister Anthony is a nun at the convent in New Jersey where she grew up, not far from New York City. She is a much-loved teacher whose special appreciation of nature, and particularly of the tall evergreen she calls Tree, is shared by her students. Tree has been her companion since her early days at the convent as an orphan, when both were very young and small. Her story is told by an unnamed narrator, the chief gardener at Rockefeller Center, whose annual job it is to find a magnificent tree for the city's featured display. When Sister Anthony faces the possibility that her tree may die, she sacrificially chooses to make a very special gift.

Awards the book has won:
Audie Award, Inspirational/Spiritual, 1997

Other books by the same author:
The Net of Dreams, 1996 (novel for adults)
The Devil's Candy, 1991 (novel for adults)

Other books you might like:
Richard Paul Evans, *The Christmas Box*, 1993
Peter Maloney, *Redbird at Rockefeller Center*, 1997
Anna Quindlen, *The Tree That Came to Stay*, 1997
Richard M. Siddoway, *The Christmas Wish*, 1996
Charlotte Zolotow, *The Beautiful Christmas Tree*, 1999

938

SANDY EISENBERG SASSO
PHOEBE STONE, Illustrator

In God's Name
(Woodstock, Vermont: Jewish Lights, 1994)

Category: Gentle Reads
Subject(s): Religion; Mythology; Religious Conflict
Age range(s): Children

Summary: Eisenberg and Stone blend colorful text and poetic illustrations to tell a story of religious diversity that ends in harmony and understanding. Their modern fable explores an age-old question: What is God's name? Reflecting the reality of religious conflict, there are many who claim to know the answer. As the story unfolds, the reader discovers that each believer calls God by a name that reflects a single aspect of God's being, and that together, all the names reflect the whole, true nature of the same God. Although this is a picture book for children, its multicultural story of unity amidst diversity may be meaningful to adults, as well.

Other books by the same author:
God's Paintbrush, 1992

Other books you might like:
Kathleen Long Bostrom, *What Is God Like?*, 1998
Florence Mary Fitch, *A Book about God*, 1999
Nancy Sohn Swartz, *In Our Image: God's First Creatures*, 1998

939

DOROTHY L. SAYERS
FRITZ WEGNER, Illustrator

The Days of Christ's Coming

(London: Hamish Hamilton, 1953)

Category: Biographical Fiction
Subject(s): Christianity; Christmas
Age range(s): Children
Locale(s): Bethlehem, Judea

Summary: *The Days of Christ's Coming* is unusual among the works of Dorothy L. Sayers. Written specifically for children between the ages of five and ten, the volume is attractive to older readers, as well, because of the exceptionally detailed, medieval style illustrations. *The Days of Christ's Coming* tells the story of the birth of Jesus, from the time preceding the Nativity itself through the flight into Egypt of Mary, Joseph, and the baby.

Other books by the same author:
Letters of Dorothy L. Sayers, 1899-1986, 1996
Spiritual Writings, 1993
Creed or Chaos?: And Other Essays in Popular Theology, 1949
Even the Parrot: Exemplary Conversations for Enlightened Children, 1944

Other books you might like:
Georgie Adams, *The First Christmas*, 1997
Karen Ann Moore, *The Baby King*, 1999
Dennis Pepper, *The Oxford Book of Christmas Stories*, 1999

940

DOROTHY L. SAYERS

Gaudy Night

(London: V. Gollancz, Ltd., 1935)

Category: Mystery
Series: Lord Peter Wimsey
Subject(s): Reunions; College Life
Age range(s): Young Adult-Adult
Major character(s): Harriet Vane, Writer, Friend (of Lord Peter); Lord Peter Wimsey, Detective, Friend (of Harriet)
Time period(s): 1930s
Locale(s): London, England

Summary: Harriet Vane is attending a reunion of her graduating class from Shrewsbury College at Oxford, known as "the Gaudy." Harriet, a mystery writer, and her detective friend Lord Peter Wimsey are mystified by a series of elegantly-worded but threatening notes that appear under bizarre circumstances. As they begin to track down clues in this case that has cast a pall over the Gaudy Night celebrations, Harriet and Peter are drawn into a web of terror and suspense. In addition to being one of Dorothy L. Sayers' finely crafted mysteries featuring the highly-principled Lord Peter Wimsey, *Gaudy Night* also offers a portrayal of what can happen when otherwise intelligent and thoughtful people-in this case the women attending the reunion-become suspicious of each other, with or without good cause. Sayers was known for her

sharply-drawn mysteries with story lines that allowed for the exploration of ethics and values without heavy-handed moralism.

Other books by the same author:
Busman's Honeymoon: A Love Story with Detective Interruptions, 1937 (Lord Peter Wimsey)
The Nine Tailors: Changes Rung on an Old Theme in Two Short Touches and Two Full Peals, 1934 (Lord Peter Wimsey)
Have His Carcase, 1932 (Lord Peter Wimsey)
Strong Poison, 1930 (Lord Peter Wimsey)
Clouds of Witness, 1927 (Lord Peter Wimsey)

Other books you might like:
Agatha Christie, *The ABC Murders*, 1936
Agatha Christie, *Funerals Are Fatal*, 1953
Deborah Crombie, *All Shall Be Well*, 1994

941

ELAINE SCHULTE

With Wings as Eagles

(Elgin, Illinois: Life Journey Books, 1990)

Category: Romance
Series: California Pioneer
Subject(s): Frontier and Pioneer Life; Gold Discoveries; Christian Life
Age range(s): Young Adult-Adult
Major character(s): Betsy Talbot, Teacher
Time period(s): 1850s
Locale(s): Oak Hill, California

Summary: Elaine Schulte's California Pioneer series tells the story of the Talbot family and their desire to share their love for God in the American West. In the fourth book of the series, *With Wings as Eagles*, Betsy Talbot encounters some unhappy times after she leaves home to be a teacher in Oak Hill, California, a Gold Rush town. Her faith sustains her throughout her mishaps and adventures, however.

Other books by the same author:
Mercies So Tender, 1995 (California Pioneer)
Peace Like a River, 1993 (California Pioneer)
Eternal Passage, 1989 (California Pioneer)
Golden Dreams, 1989 (California Pioneer)
The Journey West, 1989 (California Pioneer)

Other books you might like:
Janette Oke, *A Gown of Spanish Lace*, 1995
Jane Peart, *Promise of the Valley*, 1995
Judith Pella, *Frontier Lady*, 1993
Hilda Stahl, *Blossoming Love*, 1991
Lori Wick, *Whatever Tomorrow Brings*, 1992

942

MARK SEBANC

Flight to Hollow Mountain

(Grand Rapids, Michigan: Eerdmans, 1996)

Category: Fantasy
Series: Talamadh

Subject(s): Adventure and Adventurers; Magic; Quest
Age range(s): Adult
Major character(s): Kalaquinn, Teenager, Adventurer; Gelly, Teenager, Adventurer; Wilum, Musician
Time period(s): Indeterminate
Locale(s): Lammermorn, Fictional Country

Summary: Centuries ago, King Ardiel used the Talamadh, an exquisitely crafted harp, to bind together the things of heaven and earth, thus establishing Middle Earth as a place of peace and harmony. But now the harp has been stolen, and chaos and social decay are unraveling the delicate balance of society. An evil force is ascending, and it is up to young Kalaquinn to recover the harp and restore the harmony of this once peaceful world. His quest requires the courage, faith, and wisdom of a hero, which he will become.

Other books you might like:
J.R.R. Tolkien, *The Book of Lost Tales*, 1984
J.R.R. Tolkien, *The Hobbit; or, There and Back Again*, 1937
J.R.R. Tolkien, *The Lord of the Rings Trilogy*, 1954-1956

943

DR. SEUSS

Oh, the Places You'll Go!

(New York: Random House, 1990)

Category: Gentle Reads; Mainstream Fiction
Subject(s): Growing Up; Self-Reliance; Success
Age range(s): Children-Adult
Time period(s): Indeterminate Future
Locale(s): Fictional Country

Summary: In his last book published before his death, Dr. Seuss reunites his trademarks: colorful, fuzzy creatures, a fantasy-like world of crooked landscapes and architecture, and an inimitable combination of rhyme and wisdom. The text and illustrations celebrate the wide world of opportunity that awaits each person, offering sage counsel about handling fears, loneliness, confusion, and disappointment along life's way. *Oh, The Places You'll Go!* has become a popular "transition" book for readers of all ages, from kindergarteners moving on to first grade, to college students, newlyweds, and retirees entering new stages of life.

Other books by the same author:
You're Only Old Once!, 1986
Oh, the Thinks You Can Think!, 1975
Great Day for Up!, 1974 (Quentin Blake, illustrator)
Did I Ever Tell You How Lucky You Are?, 1973
The Lorax, 1971

Other books you might like:
P.K. Hallinan, *Heartprints*, 1999
P.K. Hallinan, *That's What a Friend Is*, 1998
Gillian Heal, *The Halfpennys Find a Home*, 1995
Carol Lynn Pearson, *The Lesson: A Fable for Our Times*, 1998
J.K. Rowling, *Harry Potter and the Sorcerer's Stone*, 1998

944

GARRETT W. SHELDON
DEBORAH MORRIS, Co-Author

What Would Jesus Do?: A Contemporary Retelling of Charles M. Sheldon's Classic in His Steps

(Nashville: Broadman & Holman, 1993)

Category: Gentle Reads
Subject(s): Christian Life; Adolescence
Age range(s): Young Adult-Adult

Summary: This, the book that launched the W.W.J.D. bracelet, t-shirt, and key-chain industry, is an update of *In His Steps*, a book written in 1898 by author Garrett W. Sheldon's great-grandfather, Charles M. Sheldon. In both books the story is built around the idea that ordinary Christians can make a difference in the world by asking themselves, "What would Jesus do?" before making choices or taking action. In the original version, young people were tempted by such worldly diversions as the saloon and the opportunity to sing onstage in a popular, but not Christian, theater show. This 1990s version addresses the same human tendencies but introduces modern temptations, including drugs and a Hollywood acting debut in a less-than-inspirational film. Many editions of the new title are available; some include study guides and journals.

Other books by the same author:
What Would Jefferson Say?, 1998

Other books you might like:
Bruce Bikel, *What Would Jesus Do?: The Question Everyone Is Asking*, 1997
Mike Cope, *What Would Jesus Do Today?*, 1998
Beverly Courrege, *What Would Jesus Do?: Think About It*, 1998

945

JULIA SHUKEN

In the House of My Pilgrimage

(Wheaton, Illinois: Crossway Books, 1995)

Category: Romance
Subject(s): Pilgrims and Pilgrimages; Adventure and Adventurers; Refugees
Age range(s): Young Adult-Adult
Major character(s): Piotr Voloshin, Brother (of Nadya), Fiance(e) (of Fenya); Fenya Kostrikin, Fiance(e) (of Piotr); Nadya Voloshin, Sister (of Piotr), Refugee; Vaktang Rukhadze, Rescuer (of Nadya)
Time period(s): 1900s
Locale(s): Los Angeles, California; Transcaucasia, Russia

Summary: Piotr Voloshin and Fenya Kostrikin are Russian refugees living in the Molokan community in Los Angeles with assorted members of their families and neighbors from their village in the old country. The Molokans are a hardworking people of faith and goodwill toward their fellow workers of all ethnic and religious backgrounds. During the early years of the 1900s, there is much turmoil in their homeland, so there is a steady flow of refugees, including young Nadya Voloshin, a recent immigrant who came to Los Angeles to live with her brother. As Piotr and Fenya prepare for their wedding and celebrate holy days with others from their parish, Nadya secretly misses Vaktang Rukhadze, the young man who rescued her from dire circumstances in Russia and wanted to marry her. Wanting to make a new start, she had rejected his offer. Now that she is safe in America, her heart is drawn back to her old home. The narrative shifts between the daily life of the immigrants in Los Angeles and the suspense of Vaktang Rukhadze's search for Nadya across Transcaucasia—and the world.

Other books by the same author:
Day of the East Wind, 1993

Other books you might like:
B.J. Hoff, *Land of a Thousand Dreams*, 1992
Judith Pella, *The Dawning of Deliverance*, 1995
Judith Pella, *Heirs of the Motherland*, 1993
Michael Phillips, *The Crown and the Crucible*, 1991

946

ROBERT SIEGEL
KURT MITCHELL, Illustrator

Alpha Centauri

(Westchester, Illinois: Cornerstone Books, 1980)

Category: Fantasy
Subject(s): Time Travel; Ethics; Violence
Age range(s): Young Adult
Major character(s): Becky, Teenager
Time period(s): 20th century; Indeterminate Past (ancient Britain)
Locale(s): England

Summary: Robert Siegel's first novel for young adults, *Alpha Centauri* has won numerous awards. This inspirational tale of science fiction and time travel is the story of a young girl named Becky and her struggle to save innocent creatures in a previous time and place. During a visit to a farm in England, Becky is suddenly transported through time to ancient Britain, where she discovers cruel men trying to kill off an entire race of gentle, loving centaurs.

Awards the book has won:
Gold Medallion Book Award, Fiction, 1981
Campus Life Book of the Year, 1981

Other books by the same author:
The Ice at the End of the World, 1994
White Whale: A Novel, 1991
The Kingdom of Wundle, 1982 (Marilyn Churchill Theurer, illustrator)
Whalesong, 1981

Other books you might like:
Jan Adkins, *A Storm Without Rain*, 1983
Madeleine L'Engle, *A Swiftly Tilting Planet*, 1978
Betty Levin, *Mercy's Mill*, 1992
Paul McCusker, *Memory's Gate*, 1996
    Time Twists, #3
Margaret Meacham, *The Boy on the Beach*, 1992
    Marcy Dunn Ramsey, illustrator

Bill Myers, *The Portal*, 1991
    Journeys to Fayrah, #1

947

IGNAZIO SILONE

Bread and Wine

(New York: Harper & Brothers, 1937)

Subject(s): Politics; Religion; Identity, Concealed
Age range(s): Adult
Major character(s): Pietro Spina, Exile, Imposter (as Don Paolo), Religious (faux priest)
Time period(s): 1930s
Locale(s): Pietrasecca, Italy

Summary: In the years preceding World War II, Mussolini is in control of Italy and Pietro Spina is forced by his Communist philosophy to flee his homeland. After living abroad for some time, Spina finds his way back into Italy under the disguise of Don Paolo, priest. He settles in the mountain village of Pietrasecca, from which he intends to spread the message of Communism. Before long, however, his role as priest to the peasants begins to become less a disguise and more a reflection of his true leanings. His Communist ideals give way to a sort of Christian socialism, and he begins to see life, politics, and faith in a new light, which opens him up to new dangers. This first edition of *Bread and Wine*, translated by Gwenda David and Eric Mosbacher, was published in 1937 during the author's own exile from Italy.

Other books by the same author:
The Seed Beneath the Snow, 1965
The Fox and the Camelias, 1961

Other books you might like:
R.H.S. Crossman, *The God That Failed*, 1949
Grazia Deledda, *Reeds in the Wind*, 1999
    Martha King, translator
Carlo Levi, *Christ Stopped at Eboli: The Story of a Year*, 1947

948

FRANK G. SLAUGHTER

The Crown and the Cross: The Life of Christ

(Cleveland: World Pub. Co., 1959)

Category: Biographical Fiction
Subject(s): Christianity; Bible; Jesus
Age range(s): Young Adult-Adult
Major character(s): Jesus, Historical Figure, Biblical Figure; Mary, Mother (of Jesus); John the Baptist, Cousin (of Jesus)
Time period(s): 1st century
Locale(s): Israel; Judea

Summary: In *The Crown and the Cross*, prolific medical, historical, and biographical novelist Frank G. Slaughter offers a fictionalized biography of the life of Jesus Christ. Slaughter's approach is faithful to biblical accounts of Jesus' life and death.

Other books by the same author:
God's Warrior, 1967
David, Warrior and King: A Biblical Biography, 1962
The Road to Bithynia: A Novel of Luke, the Beloved Physician, 1951

Other books you might like:
Sholem Asch, *The Nazarene*, 1939
Taylor Caldwell, *I, Judas*, 1977
James P. Carse, *The Gospel of the Beloved Disciple*, 1997
Robert Graves, *King Jesus*, 1946
Marjorie Holmes, *The Messiah*, 1987

949

FRANK G. SLAUGHTER

David, Warrior and King: A Biblical Biography

(Cleveland: World, 1962)

Category: Biographical Fiction; Historical Fiction
Subject(s): Bible; Kings, Queens, Rulers, etc.
Age range(s): Young Adult-Adult
Major character(s): King David, Biblical Figure, Historical Figure, Royalty (King of Israel); Saul, Historical Figure, Ruler (King of Israel), Biblical Figure; Bathsheba, Historical Figure, Royalty (consort of David), Biblical Figure; Absalom, Historical Figure, Royalty (prince, son of David), Biblical Figure; Solomon, Historical Figure, Ruler (King of Israel), Biblical Figure; Samuel, Historical Figure, Religious, Biblical Figure (prophet)
Time period(s): 11th century B.C.
Locale(s): Jerusalem, Israel

Summary: Frank G. Slaughter's fictional biography chronicles the career of the biblical David, the shepherd boy who wrote psalms and grew up to unite the many tribes of Israel into a single nation. David achieves renown for slaying the Philistine giant, Goliath, and is alternately loved and persecuted by King Saul for many years. Upon Saul's death, David is crowned king, and he oversees a period of great glory and splendor in Israel. David's remarkable legacy of both triumphs and failures is chronicled in this novel that features his best moments as well as his deepest sins.

Other books by the same author:
No Greater Love, 1985
Gospel Fever: A Novel about America's Most Beloved TV Evangelist, 1980
The Crown and the Cross: The Life of Christ, 1959
The Galileans, a Novel of Mary Magdalene, 1953
The Road to Bithynia: A Novel of Luke, the Beloved Physician, 1951

Other books you might like:
F.W. Krummacher, *David, King of Israel*, 1983
Jerry M. Landay, *David: Power, Lust, and Betrayal in Biblical Times*, 1998
David Rosenberg, *The Book of David: A New Story of the Spiritual Warrior and Leader Who Shaped Our Inner Consciousness*, 1997
Charles R. Swindoll, *David: A Man of Passion and Destiny*, 1997

950

FRANK G. SLAUGHTER

Gospel Fever: A Novel about America's Most Beloved TV Evangelist

(Garden City, New York: Doubleday, 1980)

Category: Gentle Reads
Subject(s): Christianity; Evangelism; Healing
Age range(s): Adult
Major character(s): Brother Tim Douglas, Religious (television evangelist); Reverend Alex Porcher, Religious (faith healer); Lee Steadman, Assistant (to Brother Douglas)
Time period(s): 1970s
Locale(s): Weston, South Carolina

Summary: Brother Tim Douglas is a man of the cloth for the electronic media age; Lee Steadman is his young assistant. Both men genuinely care about the people they try to help through the Logos Club, a call-in prayer and religious talk show. Faith healer Alex Porcher is Brother Tim's on-air ''sidekick.'' More cynical than Brother Tim, Porcher is drawn to the power and prestige of the television ministry. Porcher is also leery of Tim's plan to take a more holistic approach to healing that focuses more on the behind-the-scenes treatment than on flashy instantaneous healing. Then one day, Lee Steadman discovers that someone is planting fake calls to the Logos Club to discredit Tim. Who would want to do such a thing, and why?

Other books by the same author:
Storm Haven, 1953
Spencer Brade, M.D.: A Novel, 1942

Other books you might like:
Marshall W. Fishwick, *God Pumpers: Religion in the Electronic Age*, 1987
John D. MacDonald, *One More Sunday*, 1984
Evelyn Minshull, *Familiar Terror: A Novel*, 1997
T.R. Pearson, *Gospel Hour*, 1991
Quentin J. Schultze, *Televangelism and American Culture: The Business of Popular Religion*, 1991
Ward Tanneberg, *September Strike*, 1994

951

FRANK G. SLAUGHTER

No Greater Love

(Garden City, New York: Doubleday, 1985)

Category: Thrillers
Subject(s): Hospitals; Doctors; Politics
Age range(s): Adult
Major character(s): Dr. Ted Bronson, Doctor (organ transplant specialist); Dr. Liz McGowan, Doctor (obstetrician)
Time period(s): 1980s

Summary: Dr. Ted Bronson is about to achieve a breakthrough in organ transplantation, when suddenly a friend is in big medical trouble following an assassination attempt-which was the result of his desire to clean up the neighborhood and close down Mafia drug trade in his community. Ted Bronson's colleague, Dr. Liz McGowan—also the woman he loves—is facing hospital and international pressure to take immediate action against her better medical judgment in the case of a Middle-Eastern princess whose life and the life of her unborn child hang in the balance. If he helps his friend, Ted will put himself in harm's way of the Mafia assassins. Liz's refusal to deliver a pre-term baby immediately could result in an international incident-and harm to the baby. In the midst of their life-and-death decisions, can they count on their faith to help them do the right thing?

Other books by the same author:
Transplant, 1987
Doctors' Wives, 1967
East Side General, 1952
Spencer Brade, M.D.: A Novel, 1942

Other books you might like:
Hannah Alexander, *Sacred Trust*, 1999
Alton Gansky, *By My Hands: A Novel*, 1996
Alton Gasky, *Through My Eyes: A Novel*, 1997
Harry Lee Kraus Jr., *Fated Genes*, 1996

952

LEE SMITH

The Devil's Dream

(New York: Putnam, 1992)

Category: Gentle Reads
Subject(s): Music and Musicians; Appalachia; Family Saga
Age range(s): Young Adult
Major character(s): Katie Cocker, Singer (country music star); Kate Malone, Musician (fiddle player), Spouse (of Moses Bailey); Moses Bailey, Spouse (of Kate Malone)
Time period(s): 19th century; 20th century (1830s-1960s)
Locale(s): Grassy Springs, Virginia; Nashville, Tennessee

Summary: In a rollicking family saga of Appalachian music and religion, several generations of musicians pass down traditions of fiddle-playing, gospel-singing, and music-making. The roots of this musical heritage are found in 1833 with great-grandmother Kate Malone, who defied her straight-laced husband, Moses Bailey, and continued to play her fiddle, despite his belief that such music was the Devil's laughter. Two generations later, there are the Grassy Branch Girls, and in the next generation, the Grassy Branch Quartet and Nashville country music star Katie Cocker. In addition to telling the story of a family, the author traces the development of country music from its roots in Baptist hymns and fiddling, through gospel sounds, sixties rockabilly and country western sounds. Religion and folk culture are inextricably woven together in this tale of joy and sorrow.

Other books by the same author:
News of the Spirit, 1997
Saving Grace, 1995
Appalachian Portraits, 1993
Family Linen, 1985

Other books you might like:
Donald Davidson, *The Big Ballad Jamboree*, 1996
Katherine Paterson, *Come Sing, Jimmy Jo*, 1985
Bland Simpson, *Heart of the Country: A Novel of Southern Music*, 1996

953

LAURAINE SNELLING

The Reapers' Song

(Minneapolis: Bethany House, 1998)

Category: Historical Fiction
Series: Red River of the North
Subject(s): Farm Life; Frontier and Pioneer Life
Age range(s): Young Adult-Adult
Major character(s): Zeb McAllister, Murderer
Time period(s): 19th century (mid-century)
Locale(s): Blessing (Dakota Territory)

Summary: The Bjorklund family, of Norwegian heritage, have settled in the town of Blessing in the Dakota Territory. Blessing is a community where pioneer families have established farms and are trying to build happy and productive lives. Naturally, the rigors of frontier living test their faith. One day, a trio of new faces arrives in Blessing. Zeb MacCallister is on the run from Missouri, where he accidentally killed a man. Now he is looking for a place to settle in with the two orphaned girls who traveled West with him, and the Bjorklund family's faith is about to be tested once again.

Other books by the same author:
A Land to Call Home, 1997
A New Day Rising, 1996
An Untamed Land, 1996

Other books you might like:
Carrie Bender, *A Joyous Heart*, 1994
Janette Oke, *Love Comes Softly*, 1979
Lance Wubbels, *Keeper of the Harvest*, 1995

954

HILDA STAHL

Blossoming Love

(Elkhart, Indiana: Bethel Publishing, 1991)

Category: Romance; Historical Fiction
Series: Prairie
Subject(s): Family Life; Frontier and Pioneer Life
Age range(s): Young Adult-Adult
Major character(s): Laurel Bennett, Teacher; Morgan Clements, Farmer
Time period(s): 1870s (1870)
Locale(s): Broken Arrow, Nebraska

Summary: Laurel Bennett is a schoolteacher in Broken Arrow, Nebraska. A single, pretty woman, she lives with a family in town and helps take care of their three little girls. But now she has suddenly lost her home and her job, and she has nowhere to turn. Morgan Clements is a recent widower with three young children and no one to take care of them. In the rough new land that is the new state of Nebraska, the children need a mother and Morgan needs someone to take care of the house and keep meals on the table. Are they meant for each other? But what about love? Has God abandoned them both in their respective losses?

Other books by the same author:
The Dream, 1993 (White Pine Chronicles, #3)

The Makeshift Husband, 1993 (Prairie, #3)
The Stranger's Wife, 1992
The Covenant, 1991 (White Pine Chronicles, #1)
Deadline, 1989 (Amber Ainslie, #1)

Other books you might like:
June Masters Bacher, *No Time for Tears*, 1992
Lori Copeland, *Faith*, 1998
Rhonda Graham, *Nowhere to Turn*, 1993
Janette Oke, *A Bride for Donnigan*, 1993
Janette Oke, *Love Comes Softly*, 1979

955

HILDA STAHL

The Boning Knife

(Tulsa: Victory House, 1992)

Category: Mystery
Series: Carolynn Burgess Mysteries
Subject(s): Murder; Family Life; Faith
Age range(s): Adult
Major character(s): Carolynn Burgess, Detective—Private
Time period(s): 1990s
Locale(s): Michigan

Summary: Carolynn Burgess is a wife, mother, and grand-mother with a secret. She's also an undercover detective. For years she has pretended to have a part-time secretarial job, when all the while she has been doing dangerous investigative business. Now she has decided it's time to quit, so as not to have to tell her family the secret that is heavy on her heart. The only thing is, there is a murder in the neighborhood, practically in the family, and one of the few people who knows her secret needs her help. As usual, one thing leads to another, and before long she's digging for clues in not one but two or three mysterious deaths. And as always, she prays that God, the source of all wisdom, will help her sort through the confusion before anyone else dies.

Other books by the same author:
The White Pine Chronicles, 1996 (omnibus edition contains *The Covenant, The Inheritance,* and *The Dream*)
Deadly Secrets, 1993 (Carolynn Burgess Mysteries, #2)
The Stranger's Wife, 1992
Blossoming Love, 1991 (Prairie, #1)

Other books you might like:
John F. Bayer, *Necessary Risk*, 1998
Terri Blackstock, *Blind Trust*, 1998
Terri Blackstock, *Justifiable Means*, 1996
Athol Dickson, *Every Hidden Thing*, 1998

956

HILDA STAHL

The Makeshift Husband

(Elkhart, Indiana: Bethel Publishing, 1993)

Category: Romance; Historical Fiction
Series: Prairie
Subject(s): Family Life; Marriage; Faith
Age range(s): Young Adult-Adult

Major character(s): Diane McGraw, Spouse (of Seth); Seth McGraw, Spouse (of Diane); Bobby Ryder, Gambler
Time period(s): 1890s (1891)
Locale(s): Broken Arrow, Nebraska

Summary: Diane McGraw has just given birth to a son. She hopes the baby will make her feel as if she's really happily married, but throughout their nine-month marriage, Seth has been distant and unhappy, and he won't even look at their beautiful dark-haired son. She often wonders if she should have tried to get Bobby Ryder to settle down and marry her. She has known them both all her life, and Bobby is darkly handsome, charming, and fun-loving-everything Seth isn't, it seems to her. Why did Seth change from the loving boy he had been before their wedding to the cold, barely civil man he has become? And why does he hate Bobby Ryder so? Can their marriage survive with all these unspoken secrets? Will God ever hear her prayers, or his?

Other books by the same author:
The Dream, 1993 (White Pine Chronicles, #3)
The Stranger's Wife, 1992
Blossoming Love, 1991 (Prairie, #1)
The Covenant, 1991 (White Pine Chronicles, #1)
Deadline, 1989 (Amber Ainslie, #1)

Other books you might like:
June Masters Bacher, *No Time for Tears*, 1992
Lori Copeland, *Faith*, 1998
Rhonda Graham, *Nowhere to Turn*, 1993
Janette Oke, *A Bride for Donnigan*, 1993
Janette Oke, *Love Comes Softly*, 1979

957

AUDREY STALLSMITH

Rosemary for Remembrance

(Colorado Springs: WaterBrook Press, 1998)

Category: Mystery
Series: Thyme Will Tell Mysteries
Subject(s): Death; Gardens and Gardening; Family Problems
Age range(s): Adult
Major character(s): Regan Culver, Daughter (of Alden); Alden Culver, Father (of Regan), Doctor
Locale(s): Pennsylvania

Summary: At the Thyme Will Tell herb farm, Regan Culver is suffering from a double shock. Her beloved father has just died, and it was a cup of tea she made that killed him. The primary heir to his estate, she is naturally the prime suspect. But she knows she didn't do it. How can she prove that to the police, and to the members of the family who stand to benefit if she is convicted of the crime? And who will stop the real killer from striking again? *Rosemary for Remembrance* is the first volume of Audrey Stallsmith's series of Thyme Will Tell mysteries set on the family herb farm in Pennsylvania. Stallsmith's novels don't ignore the darker side of life but do avoid graphic language.

Other books by the same author:
Marigolds for Mourning, 1999
Roses for Regret, 1999
The Body They May Kill, 1995

Other books you might like:
Terri Blackstock, *Blind Trust*, 1997
B.J. Hoff, *The Captive Voice*, 1995
Hilda Stahl, *The Boning Knife*, 1992
Hilda Stahl, *The Makeshift Husband*, 1993

958

ED STEWART

Millennium's Eve

(Wheaton, Illinois: Victor Books, 1993)

Category: Thrillers
Subject(s): Millennium; Christianity
Age range(s): Young Adult-Adult
Major character(s): Beth Scibelli, Journalist; Sergeant Reagan Cole, Police Officer (Los Angeles Police Department)
Time period(s): 1990s
Locale(s): Los Angeles, California

Summary: *Millennium's Eve* is the first of three related novels by Ed Stewart focusing on the conflict between good and evil as the 20th century draws to a close. Journalist Beth Scibelli and LAPD sergeant Reagan Cole find their paths crossing professionally during troubling times. What begins as a partnership built around the pursuit of a common goal develops into teamwork at another level. Their story is continued in *Millennium's Dawn* and *Doomsday Flight*. The author writes that it is his goal in these novels that readers will enjoy exciting action and suspense stories that support Christian values without being preachy.

Other books by the same author:
Terminal Mercy: A Novel, 1999
Doomsday Flight, 1995
Millennium's Dawn, 1994
A Window to Eternity: Twelve Short Stories of Fantasy and Fiction Based on the Sayings of Christ, 1985

Other books you might like:
Tim LaHaye, *Left Behind: A Novel of the Earth's Last Days*, 1995
   Jerry B. Jenkins, co-author
Paul Meier, *The Fourth Millennium: The Sequel*, 1996
   Robert Wise, co-author
Paul Meier, *The Third Millennium: A Novel*, 1993
Frank E. Peretti, *Piercing the Darkness*, 1989
Frank E. Peretti, *This Present Darkness*, 1986

959

PENELOPE STOKES

Home Fires Burning

(Wheaton, Illinois: Tyndale House, 1996)

Category: Romance
Series: Faith on the Home Front
Subject(s): Christian Life; World War II
Age range(s): Young Adult-Adult
Major character(s): Link Winsom, Military Personnel; Owen Slaughter, Military Personnel
Time period(s): 1940s (World War II)
Locale(s): Mississippi

Summary: Link Winsom and Owen Slaughter are soldiers fighting in France during World War II. Their loved ones are trying to cope with life on the homefront, trusting God to keep Link and Owen safe in battle. This is the first installment of the Faith on the HomeFront series of novels that reflects the patriotism, family love, and Christian faith of many Americans during the World War II years.

Other books by the same author:
Remembering You, 1997
Till We Meet Again, 1997
Grace under Pressure, 1990

Other books you might like:
June Masters Bacher, *Where Lies Our Hope*, 1992
Gilbert Morris, *All the Shining Young Men*, 1993
Gilbert Morris, *A Call to Honor*, 1993
Janette Oke, *Another Homecoming*, 1997
Judith Pella, *Shadows over Stonewycke*, 1988

960

BODIE THOENE

Danzig Passage

(Minneapolis: Bethany House, 1991)

Category: Historical Fiction
Series: Zion Covenant
Subject(s): Holocaust; Jews; War
Age range(s): Young Adult-Adult
Major character(s): Peter Wallich, Young Man; Lori Ibsen, Young Woman
Time period(s): 1930s (1938)
Locale(s): Germany; Austria

Summary: In this installment of the Zion Covenant series, the final days of prewar life in Germany are recounted as a number of Christians and Jews attempt to flee Nazi persecution. Peter Wallich and his family are trying to escape from Berlin, while the Ibsen family has been caught helping Jews escape. With two members of the family already arrested, danger is at the doorstep. They believe that Danzig, Poland, their destination, offers the prospect of a safe passage to freedom, but time is running out.

Other books by the same author:
Warsaw Requiem, 1991
Jerusalem Interlude, 1990
Munich Signature, 1990
Prague Counterpoint, 1989
Vienna Prelude, 1989

Other books you might like:
Malka Drucker, *Jacob's Rescue: A Holocaust Story*, 1993
Kathryn Winter, *Katarina*, 1998

961

BODIE THOENE

The Gates of Zion

(Minneapolis: Bethany House, 1986)

Category: Historical Fiction
Series: Zion Chronicles
Subject(s): Independence; Political Thriller; Religious Conflict
Age range(s): Young Adult-Adult
Major character(s): Ellie Warne, Journalist; David Meyer, Pilot (American); Moshe Sachar, Professor (Hebrew University)
Time period(s): 1940s (1947-1948)
Locale(s): Jerusalem, Israel (Zion)

Summary: Ellie Warne is an ambitious American photojournalist in Jerusalem on the eve of Israel's independence. As a staff photographer for an archeological society, she is doing her job when she captures on film a collection of ancient scrolls found in a nearby cave. Unbeknownst to her, the scrolls have great religious and political significance, and her life is now in danger. Two young men care deeply for her; David Meyer is a dear friend from her past, and Moshe Sacher is rooted in this new world of terror and intrigue. Both are part of her daily struggles now. But while Ellie is running for her life, she is also trying to find some direction for living. Caught up in the political strife created by clashing perspectives on God, she's not sure she can accept that God exists at all, especially in this place. As she is drawn into the conflicts tearing apart the Middle East in the aftermath of the Holocaust, Ellie comes to understand what compels others to forge ahead for Zion, and she begins to find her place in God's world.

Awards the book has won:
Gold Medallion Book Award, Fiction, 1987

Other books by the same author:
The Key to Zion, 1988 (Zion Chronicles, #5)
A Light in Zion, 1988 (Zion Chronicles, #4)
A Daughter of Zion, 1987 (Zion Chronicles, #2)
The Return to Zion, 1987 (Zion Chronicles, #3)

Other books you might like:
Shaw J. Dallal, *Scattered Like Seeds*, 1999
Mary Glazener, *The Cup of Wrath: A Novel Based on Dietrich Bonhoeffer's Resistance to Hitler*, 1996
Isabel R. Marvin, *Bridge to Freedom*, 1997

962

BODIE THOENE

In My Father's House

(Minneapolis: Bethany House, 1992)

Category: Historical Fiction
Series: Shiloh Legacy
Subject(s): Racial Conflict; Religious Conflict; World War I
Age range(s): Young Adult

Major character(s): Ellis Warne, Military Personnel (soldier); Birch Tucker, Military Personnel (soldier); Jefferson Canfield, Military Personnel (soldier)
Time period(s): 1910s
Locale(s): France; United States

Summary: This novel dramatizes America's role in the fighting of World War I and the racial and religious conflict on the homefront after the war. Three soldiers—Ellis Warne, Birch Tucker, and Jefferson Canfield—from different backgrounds are brought together for the fighting. As their lives and those of their families become intertwined, they find it difficult to claim the land of promise they risked their bodies and minds to protect. The action takes place on the battlefield of war as well as in the uncharted territory of early twentieth-century American culture. In spite of a certain sense of hopelessness and despair, it becomes clear that God has not abandoned them or their neighbors.

Awards the book has won:
Gold Medallion Book Award, Fiction, 1993

Other books by the same author:
Say to This Mountain, 1993
A Thousand Shall Fall, 1992

Other books you might like:
Alan Morris, *Heart of Valor*, 1996
Gilbert Morris, *Beyond the Quiet Hills*, 1997
Gilbert Morris, *A Time of War*, 1997
Penelope Stokes, *Till We Meet Again*, 1997

963

BODIE THOENE
BROCK THOENE, Co-Author

The Man From Shadow Ridge

(Minneapolis: Bethany House, 1990)

Category: Westerns
Series: Saga of the Sierras
Subject(s): Frontier and Pioneer Life; Civil War; Courage
Age range(s): Adult
Major character(s): Tom Dawson, Rancher, Brother; Nate Dawson, Rancher, Brother
Time period(s): 19th century; 20th century (1850-1950)
Locale(s): Shadow Ridge, California

Summary: The Dawson family, including brothers Tom and Nate, seem to have found a safe haven from the Civil War raging in the East. Their California ranch is remote from the battlefields and the questions of slavery and freedom. But a series of robberies, beginning with a bloody stage holdup, brings the war close to home. A band of Confederate sympathizers is stealing California gold to send back to the embattled South, and the Dawsons suddenly discover they're in the front lines of a small and undeclared war. Courage and faith are needed to deal with what they encounter next. This is the first of a series of novels that tell a multi-generational story.

Other books by the same author:
Cannons of the Comstock, 1992
Riders of the Silver Rim, 1990

Other books you might like:
Charles Frazier, *Cold Mountain*, 1997
Les Savage Jr., *Fire Dance at Spider Rock: A Western Story*, 1995

964

BODIE THOENE

Munich Signature

(Minneapolis: Bethany House, 1990)

Category: Historical Fiction
Series: Zion Covenant
Subject(s): Holocaust; Jews; Nazis
Age range(s): Young Adult-Adult
Major character(s): Elisa Murphy, Young Woman; Leah Feldstein, Young Woman
Time period(s): 1930s (1938)
Locale(s): Germany; Austria

Summary: In the third of the Zion Covenant series, Europe is on the brink of war as two friends struggle with the consequences of the German aggression against Jews. Leah Feldstein is trying to escape from Austria on foot through the Alps, while Elisa Murphy is involved in international intrigue that could hold the key to stopping Nazi leader Adolf Hitler's domination of Europe. Themes of faith and perseverance are interwoven with adventure and suspense.

Other books by the same author:
Danzig Passage, 1991
Warsaw Requiem, 1991
Jerusalem Interlude, 1990
Prague Counterpoint, 1989
Vienna Prelude, 1989

Other books you might like:
Malka Drucker, *Jacob's Rescue: A Holocaust Story*, 1993
Kathryn Winter, *Katarina*, 1998

965

BODIE THOENE
BROCK THOENE, Co-Author

Only the River Runs Free

(Nashville: Thomas Nelson, 1997)

Category: Historical Fiction
Series: Galway Chronicles
Subject(s): Independence; Christmas; Christianity
Age range(s): Young Adult-Adult
Major character(s): Kate Donovan Garrity, Widow(er); Mad Molly Fahey, Widow(er)
Time period(s): 1840s (1841)
Locale(s): Ballynockanor, Ireland

Summary: In the 1840s in poverty-stricken Irish village Ballynockanor, times are hard and hope for the future is nonexistent. The tenant farmers eke out a living under the iron fist of their English landlords. No trace of Irish culture or heritage is safe from the attacks of the English, and no season of the year brings relief from the troubles, least of all the season before Christmas. Yet one afternoon in December, 1841, a stranger named Joseph arrives in the village, and changes begin to take place. Is this the miracle predicted by the old woman, Mad Molly Fahey? And is this the beginning of a future of hope, once again, for the widow Kate Donovan Garrity? Or does the stranger's arrival signal the start of even greater hardships for the already weary folk of Ballynockanor? This is the first novel in the Galway Chronicles series by the Thoenes.

Awards the book has won:
Gold Medallion Book Award, Fiction, 1998

Other books by the same author:
Ashes of Remembrance, 1999 (Galway Chronicles)
To Gather the Wind, 1998
Of Men & of Angels: A Novel, 1998 (Galway Chronicles)
Winds of Promise, 1997

Other books you might like:
Donna Fletcher Crow, *The Banks of the Boyne: A Quest for a Christian Ireland*, 1998
Elizabeth Gibson, *The Water Is Wide: A Novel of Northern Ireland*, 1984
B.J. Hoff, *Land of a Thousand Dreams*, 1992
B.J. Hoff, *Song of the Silent Harp*, 1991
B.J. Hoff, *Sons of an Ancient Glory*, 1993

966

BODIE THOENE
BROCK THOENE, Co-Author

The Twilight of Courage: A Novel

(Nashville, Tennessee: T. Nelson, 1994)

Category: Historical Fiction
Subject(s): Ethics; Journalism; World War II
Age range(s): Adult
Major character(s): Josie Marlow, Journalist; David Mayer, Pilot (for British RAF); Captain Horst von Bockman, Military Personnel (German army officer)
Time period(s): 1930s; 1940s (1939-1940)
Locale(s): Germany; France

Summary: This is a historically detailed story of lives changed forever by the dawning of World War II in Europe with the invasion of Poland by Germany. Two American journalists must escape from the collapse of Warsaw; an orphaned Jewish baby is among scores of children sent to Jerusalem for safety; an American serving in the Royal Air Force finds himself unexpectedly in Normandy; and a German officer struggles to reconcile his personal beliefs and his professional responsibilities. At every turn, difficult decisions must be made, and there are no easy answers to questions of faith, fairness, and integrity.

Awards the book has won:
Gold Medallion Book Award, Fiction, 1995

Other books by the same author:
A Daughter of Zion, 1987
The Return to Zion, 1987

Other books you might like:
Jacob Boas, *We Are Witnesses: Five Diaries of Teenagers Who Died in the Holocaust*, 1995

Anne Frank, *The Diary of a Young Girl*, 1952
Maxine B. Rosenberg, *Hiding to Survive: Stories of Jewish Children Rescued From the Holocaust*, 1994
Ida Vos, *Anna Is Still Here*, 1993
Elie Wiesel, *All Rivers Run to the Sea: Memoirs*, 1995

967

BODIE THOENE

Vienna Prelude

(Minneapolis: Bethany House, 1989)

Category: Historical Fiction
Series: Zion Covenant
Subject(s): Holocaust; Jews; Nazis
Age range(s): Young Adult-Adult
Major character(s): Elisa Lindheim, Young Woman, Musician (violinist); Leah Feldstein, Young Woman, Musician (cellist); Shimon Feldstein, Spouse (of Leah)
Time period(s): 1930s (1938)
Locale(s): Germany; Austria

Summary: In the opening volume of the author's Zion Covenant series, Elisa Lindheim is a violinist who adopts an Aryan stage name that masks her Jewish heritage. Although her father has been detained by Nazis on a mission to rid Austria of Jews, Elisa is still able to help others, and she is driven to do so by her faith. A musician by profession, she has taken on the responsibility of helping Jews escape persecution in pre-World War II Europe, and she has no idea how far she'll have to go to achieve her goals.

Other books by the same author:
Danzig Passage, 1991
Warsaw Requiem, 1991
Jerusalem Interlude, 1990
Munich Signature, 1990
Prague Counterpoint, 1989

Other books you might like:
Malka Drucker, *Jacob's Rescue: A Holocaust Story*, 1993
Kathryn Winter, *Katarina*, 1998

968

BODIE THOENE

Warsaw Requiem

(Minneapolis: Bethany House, 1991)

Category: Historical Fiction
Series: Zion Covenant
Subject(s): Holocaust; Jews; World War II
Age range(s): Young Adult-Adult
Major character(s): Peter Wallich, Young Man; Lori Ibsen, Young Woman; Jacob Kalner, Young Man
Time period(s): 1930s
Locale(s): Warsaw, Poland; Danzig, Poland; London, England

Summary: In the finale of the author's Zion Covenant series, war breaks out, threatening a group of refugee children waiting in Danzig for a ship to England. Peter Wallich is also in danger now, because he is with the Jews in the Warsaw ghetto. This volume concludes a story of faith and uncertainty

that crosses political and religious boundaries in the pursuit of freedom for the oppressed and helpless.

Other books by the same author:
Danzig Passage, 1991
Jerusalem Interlude, 1990
Munich Signature, 1990
Prague Counterpoint, 1989
Vienna Prelude, 1989

Other books you might like:
Malka Drucker, *Jacob's Rescue: A Holocaust Story*, 1993
Kathryn Winter, *Katarina*, 1998

969

BROCK THOENE
BODIE THOENE, Co-Author

A New Frontier: Saga of the Sierras

(New York: Inspirational Press, 1998)

Category: Westerns; Historical Fiction
Series: Saga of the Sierras
Subject(s): Romance; Frontier and Pioneer Life; Family Life
Age range(s): Young Adult-Adult
Major character(s): Tom Dawson, Rancher, Brother (of Nate); Nate Dawson, Rancher, Brother (of Tom)
Time period(s): 19th century (mid-century)
Locale(s): California

Summary: *A New Frontier* is an omnibus edition of four popular westerns from Bodie and Brock Thoene. The storyline of each "Saga of the Sierras" novel stands on its own, but all deal with the adventures of ranchers and newcomers to California, starting with Tom and Nate Dawson, brothers and ranchers introduced in *The Man from Shadow Ridge*. Other novels included in this edition are *Riders of the Silver Rim*, *Gold Rush Prodigal*, and *Sequoia Scout*. The Thoenes' historical novels feature careful attention to detail, characterization, and action, all intertwined with an undercurrent of faith and values.

Other books by the same author:
Hope Valley War, 1997
The Legend of Storey County: A Novel, 1995
Shooting Star, 1993 (Bodie Thoene, co-author)
Cannons of the Comstock, 1992 (Bodie Thoene, co-author)
The Year of the Grizzly, 1992 (Bodie Thoene, co-author)

Other books you might like:
Stephen Bly, *Hard Winter at Broken Arrow Crossing*, 1991
Charles Frazier, *Cold Mountain*, 1997
Gilbert Morris, *Reno*, 1992
Gilbert Morris, *Valley Justice*, 1995
Les Savage Jr., *Fire Dance at Spider Rock: A Western Story*, 1995

970

JAKE THOENE
LUKE THOENE, Co-Author

Heart of Allegiance

(Nashville: Thomas Nelson, 1998)

Category: Historical Fiction
Series: Portraits of Destiny
Subject(s): Adventure and Adventurers; Napoleonic Wars; Sea Stories
Age range(s): Young Adult-Adult
Major character(s): Julia Sutton, Mother
Time period(s): 18th century; 19th century (1776-1805)
Locale(s): France; England

Summary: During a storm at sea and shipwreck in the English Channel on a winter's day in 1776, Julia Sutton loses her husband and one of her twin baby boys. When she and one son are rescued and taken back to England, she mourns the death of the other son and his father. Unbeknownst to her, however, the remaining twin is rescued and taken to France, where he is raised, unaware of the family he has been torn away from. Years later, their paths cross when they find themselves on opposite sides in the naval battle at Trafalgar, one of the most pivotal events of the Napoleonic Wars. Each young man is loyal to the country he has known since childhood. Can their shared roots ever overcome their divided patriotism? Will faith in the same God transcend loyalties to separate earthly kingdoms?

Other books by the same author:
Eyes of Justice, 1999 (Luke Thoene, co-author; Portraits of Destiny, #2)
The Jewelled Peacock of Persia, 1998 (Luke Thoene, co-author; Baker Street Mysteries, #3)
The Thundering Underground, 1998 (Luke Thoene, co-author; Baker Street Mysteries, #4)
The Giant Rat of Sumatra, 1995 (Luke Thoene, co-author; Baker Street Mysteries, #2)
Mystery Lights of Navajo Mesa, 1994 (Luke Thoene, co-author; Last Chance Detectives, #1)

Other books you might like:
Jack Cavanaugh, *The Colonists*, 1995
Jack Cavanaugh, *The Patriots*, 1995
David Howarth, *Trafalgar: The Nelson Touch*, 1969
Dudley Pope, *Decision at Trafalgar: The Story of the Greatest British Naval Battle of the Age of Nelson*, 1999
Alan Schom, *Trafalgar: Countdown to Battle, 1803-1805*, 1990

971

MACK THOMAS
NORMAND CHARTIER, Illustrator

A Mouse in Solomon's House: A Child's Book of Wisdom

(Sisters, Oregon: Questar, 1995)

Category: Morality Tales
Subject(s): Children; Ethics; Scripture

Age range(s): Children
Major character(s): Marble, Mouse

Summary: Marble is a little mouse who lives in the great halls of Solomon's fine home. Like the children for whom this picture book is written, Marble often gets into mischief because of his curiosity. Through his adventures, Marble learns to seek and apply God's wisdom in his little mouse life, and the author uses Marble's experiences to impart early lessons to young children about tapping the wisdom of God when making choices in their lives.

Awards the book has won:
Gold Medallion Book Award, Pre-School Children, 1996

Other books by the same author:
What Would Jesus Do?: An Adaptation for Children of Charles M. Sheldon's in His Steps, 1991 (Denis Mortenson, illustrator)
Quiet Times with God, 1996
Once upon a Parable: Bringing Heaven Down to Earth, 1995 (Hilber Nelson, illustrator)
The Bible Tells Me So: A Beginner's Guide to Loving and Understanding God's Word, 1992

Other books you might like:
Carolyn Nabors Baker, *The Beginners' Bible for Toddlers*, 1995
Ken Taylor, *Big Thoughts for Little People*, 1982
Ken Taylor, *Wise Words for Little People*, 1987

972

MACK THOMAS
DENIS MORTENSON, Illustrator

What Would Jesus Do?: An Adaptation for Children of Charles M. Sheldon's in His Steps

(Sisters, Oregon: Questar, 1991)

Category: Morality Tales
Subject(s): Christianity; Christian Life; Conduct of Life
Age range(s): Children
Major character(s): Claire, Child; Bill, Child; Parson Henry, Religious (minister)

Summary: In an adaptation for children of Charles M. Sheldon's classic *In His Steps*, Thomas tells the story of two children and a minister who help the needy and elderly in their community. At each point of decision, Bill, Claire, and Parson Henry learn the benefits of asking themselves first, ''What Would Jesus do?'' Values including truthfulness, generosity, and getting along with others are taught through word and picture. Discussion questions and related *Bible* readings for each chapter are included.

Awards the book has won:
Gold Medallion Book Award, Pre-School Children, 1992

Other books by the same author:
God's Best Promises for Kids, 1999
Once upon a Parable: Bringing Heaven Down to Earth, 1995 (Hilber Nelson, illustrator)
In His Hands: The Continuing Adventures of ''What Would Jesus Do?'', 1993

Other books you might like:
Carolyn Nabors Baker, *The Beginners' Bible for Toddlers*, 1995
Nick Harrison, *365 WWJD: Daily Answers to What Would Jesus Do?*, 1998
Ken Taylor, *Big Thoughts for Little People*, 1982
Ken Taylor, *Wise Words for Little People*, 1987

973

J.R.R. TOLKIEN

The Hobbit; or, There and Back Again

(London: Allen & Unwin, 1937)

Category: Fantasy
Subject(s): Adventure and Adventurers; Courage; Quest
Age range(s): Children-Adult
Major character(s): Bilbo Baggins, Mythical Creature (hobbit); Gandalf, Wizard; Smaug the Magnificent, Dragon
Time period(s): Indeterminate
Locale(s): Middle-Earth, Mythical Place

Summary: Bilbo Baggins, a respectable, home-loving hobbit, is quite happy to stay at home until he meets a wizard, Gandalf, and is enticed, cajoled, and encouraged into an adventure in which he becomes an "Expert Treasure Hunter." Together with Gandalf and a band of dwarves, Bilbo Baggins sets out to reclaim a fortune in gold that is now in the hands of Smaug the Magnificent, a terrifying dragon. Along the way they encounter threats in the guise of trolls, spiders, and wolves. Bilbo must draw upon his courage and strength of conviction to stand alone before the dragon and do what he has been chosen to do. In the end, Bilbo makes a discovery that will have far-reaching effects on the inhabitants of Middle-Earth.

Other books by the same author:
Unfinished Tales of Numenor and Middle-Earth, 1980
The Silmarillion, 1977
The Lord of the Rings Trilogy, 1954-1956

Other books you might like:
Lynn Abbey, *Unicorn and Dragon*, 1987
Lloyd Alexander, *The Remarkable Journey of Prince Jen*, 1991
Kenneth Grahame, *The Wind in the Willows*, 1908
R.A. Salvatore, *The Sword of Bedwyr*, 1995

974

J.R.R. TOLKIEN

The Lord of the Rings Trilogy

(Boston: Houghton Mifflin, 1954-1956)

Category: Fantasy
Subject(s): Elves; Magic; Quest
Age range(s): Children-Adult
Major character(s): Frodo Baggins, Mythical Creature (hobbit), Traveler; Sam Gamgee, Mythical Creature (hobbit), Servant; Gandalf, Wizard
Time period(s): Indeterminate Future (twilight of the third age)

Locale(s): Middle-Earth, Mythical Place

Summary: The Dark Lord Sauron has discovered that the Ring of Power is in the possession of a hobbit, Bilbo Baggins, in the far west of Middle-Earth. With the Ring, Sauron will have ultimate control over Middle-Earth. Before he can recover it, however, Bilbo's heir Frodo Baggins has begun a long, terrifying journey into the heart of the enemy's land to destroy the Ring, thereby stripping Sauron of his power. Frodo and his companions must contend with trolls, the Orcs, Sauron's henchmen, Gollum (the Ring's former owner), and the Ring itself, which feeds its wearer with the desire for power and domination. Frodo is fortified in his journey by courage, loyalty, and a sense of responsibility to future generations. *The Hobbit*, in which Bilbo first discovers the Ring, is the prequel to this trilogy. The individual titles of the series are: *The Fellowship of the Ring*, (1954), *The Two Towers* (1955), and *The Return of the King* (1956).

Other books by the same author:
Unfinished Tales of Numenor and Middle-Earth, 1980
The Silmarillion, 1977
The Hobbit; or, There and Back Again, 1937

Other books you might like:
Michael Scott Rohan, *The Forge in the Forest*, 1987
Tad Williams, *The Dragonbone Chair*, 1988

975

JOHN KENNEDY TOOLE

A Confederacy of Dunces

(Baton Rouge: Louisiana State University Press, 1980)

Category: Comedy; Mainstream Fiction
Subject(s): Sexual Behavior; Mental Illness
Age range(s): Adult
Major character(s): Ignatius J. Reilly, Unemployed, Eccentric
Time period(s): 20th century (mid-century)
Locale(s): New Orleans, Louisiana

Summary: As a novel, *A Confederacy of Dunces* practically defies description. It is one of only two novels ever written by John Kennedy Toole, who committed suicide in 1969 before seeing any of his literary efforts published. Toole's central character in this novel is Ignatius J. Reilly, a peripatetic, highly-opinionated, socially inept eccentric—or genius. Set in the seamiest streets of the French Quarter in New Orleans, the novel interweaves the stories of a flock of bizarre characters whose interactions with the frenetic Reilly and with each other provide much of the comedy. Reilly fancies himself a genius whose mission is to change the world. In each of his ill-fated endeavors, he places himself in the role of spokesperson against the oppression and organizer of the masses, with ironically comic consequences every time. Ultimately, he must leave town to escape from his alcoholic mother, who has had enough of his ranting and odd behavior and has decided to place him in a mental hospital. The outrage Ignatius J. Reilly vents against society at large seems to stem from his keenly idealistic religion-based morality and his expectations of others, which have been savaged by the insensitive, poverty-tinged economy in which he lives.

Other books by the same author:
The Neon Bible, 1989

Other books you might like:
Michael Malone, *Handling Sin*, 1993
Walker Percy, *The Last Gentleman*, 1966
Walker Percy, *The Moviegoer*, 1961
Jerry E. Strahan, *Managing Ignatius: The Lunacy of Lucky Dogs and Life in the Quarter*, 1998

976

ELLEN GUNDERSON TRAYLOR

John, Son of Thunder
(Wheaton, Illinois: Tyndale, 1979)

Category: Biographical Fiction
Subject(s): Christianity; Bible; History
Age range(s): Young Adult-Adult
Major character(s): John, Biblical Figure (apostle), Historical Figure
Time period(s): 1st century
Locale(s): Israel

Summary: Ellen Gunderson Traylor, writer of numerous biographical profiles of biblical figures, tells the story of the apostle John, one of the twelve disciples known to have traveled around with the itinerant Jesus. In this volume, Traylor depicts the life of a man whose path took him from desert paths to the courts of Jerusalem, and finally to exile on the island of Patmos. The story begins when John hears the words of John the Baptist and continues through the years he spent sharing the news of Jesus throughout the Holy Lands and beyond.

Other books by the same author:
The Priest, 1998
Jonah, 1987
Ruth, 1986
Song of Abraham, 1973

Other books you might like:
Taylor Caldwell, *Dear and Glorious Physician*, 1959
Taylor Caldwell, *Great Lion of God*, 1970
Taylor Caldwell, *I, Judas*, 1977
Francine Rivers, *The Mark of the Lion*, 1998

977

ELLEN GUNDERSON TRAYLOR

Mary Magdalene
(Wheaton, Illinois: Living Books, 1985)

Category: Biographical Fiction
Subject(s): History; Women; Jesus
Age range(s): Adult
Major character(s): Mary Magdalene, Historical Figure, Biblical Figure; Jesus, Historical Figure, Biblical Figure
Locale(s): Jerusalem, Israel; Roman Empire

Summary: Ellen Gunderson Traylor uses fiction to explore the shadowy world of an independent woman in 1st century Jewish society in *Mary Magdalene*, a novel of darkness, light, life, and hope. Mary Magdalene is a woman loved by every man but respected by none, except for Jesus. The author portrays her subject as the favored mistress of Magdala Inn whose profession brings her shame, though it pays her way in a society with few options for an unmarried woman. Haunted by her nightmare past and her unsavory present, Mary Magdalene is set free by the compassion of Jesus.

Other books by the same author:
Melchizedek, 1997
Samson, 1992
Ruth, 1986
John, Son of Thunder, 1979

Other books you might like:
Mary Ellen Ashcroft, *The Magdalene Gospel*, 1995
Esther de Boer, *Mary Magdalene: Beyond the Myth*, 1997
    John Bowden, translator
Mary R. Thompson, *Mary of Magdala: Apostle and Leader*, 1995
Anne Williman, *Mary of Magdala: A Novel*, 1990

978

ELLEN GUNDERSON TRAYLOR

Samson
(Wheaton, Illinois: Tyndale House, 1992)

Category: Biographical Fiction
Subject(s): Christianity; Bible
Age range(s): Young Adult-Adult
Major character(s): Samson, Biblical Figure, Historical Figure

Summary: Biblical novelist Ellen Gunderson Traylor portrays an Old Testament figure, Samson, in a balanced blend of historical, biblical, and fictional storytelling.

Other books by the same author:
The Priest, 1998
Jonah, 1987
Ruth, 1986
Song of Abraham, 1973

Other books you might like:
Taylor Caldwell, *Dear and Glorious Physician*, 1959
Taylor Caldwell, *Great Lion of God*, 1970
Zora Neale Hurston, *Moses, Man of the Mountain*, 1939
Francine Rivers, *The Mark of the Lion*, 1998

979

JOHN TRENT
CINDY TRENT, Co-Author
JUDY LOVE, Illustrator

The Treasure Tree
(Dallas: Word, 1992)

Category: Morality Tales
Subject(s): Treasure; Animals; Friendship
Age range(s): Children
Major character(s): Wise Old Owl, Owl

Summary: In this gentle tale about friendship and cooperation, four animal friends share the same birthday. Wise Old Owl presents them with a treasure map they can use to find the keys that will unlock the Treasure Tree. In order to be successful in their search, however, they must all use their own unique abilities and personalities, and they must appreciate the contributions and characteristics of all the others, as well. The values of friendship, acceptance, encouragement, and teamwork are emphasized.

Other books by the same author:
The Two Trails: A Treasure Tree Adventure, 1998

Other books you might like:
Janice Derby, *Are You My Friend*, 1993
Mona Gansberg Hodgson, *Smelly Tales*, 1998
Helena Clare Pittman, *The Angel Tree*, 1998

980

SUSAN TROTT

The Holy Man

(New York: Riverhead Books, 1995)

Category: Gentle Reads
Subject(s): Pilgrims and Pilgrimages; Buddhism; Religion
Age range(s): Young Adult-Adult
Major character(s): Joe, Religious (holy man); Anna, Traveler (pilgrim)

Summary: In this timeless, placeless tale, a holy man is visited by pilgrims, each of whom wants to ask for help with a problem. There are big problems and small ones, and in each tiny chapter of this small book, Joe—the holy man—offers a few words that lighten the load or enlighten the soul. One pilgrim is Anna, a woman whose connection with Joe is instantaneous. She recognizes him as the teacher she has been searching for and he sees in her the student he has waited for to carry on his work. But she must return to her husband and children, so with the discipline he has learned over the years, Joe urges her to move on, and she does. As the line of pilgrims winds down for the end of the season, a man and two boys appear, and then Anna. She has returned, whole now, and ready to move on in a new direction.

Other books by the same author:
The Holy Man's Journey, 1997
Divorcing Daddy, 1992

Other books you might like:
Gerald E. Goggins, *The Anonymous Disciple*, 1995
Judith Pella, *Beloved Stranger*, 1998
Gloria Whelan, *The Ambassador's Wife*, 1997

981

ANNE TYLER

Saint Maybe

(New York: Knopf, 1991)

Category: Gentle Reads
Subject(s): Family Life; Suicide
Age range(s): Adult
Major character(s): Danny Bedloe, Postal Worker; Lucy Bedloe, Waiter/Waitress; Ian Bedloe, Student—College, Carpenter
Time period(s): 1960s (1965)

Locale(s): Baltimore, Maryland

Summary: Danny, the eldest Bedloe son, marries Lucy, a divorcee with two children; seven months later they add a third child. Only Ian, Danny's younger brother, seems to notice that this new baby is not premature. When Lucy asks him to babysit for her, he wonders why she returns home with presents and new dresses but not shopping bags. He finally mentions his suspicions to his brother, who then commits suicide. After Lucy does the same, Ian's guilt is so strong that he seeks guidance from a fundamentalist sect known as the Church of the Second Chance, which is led by a charismatic preacher. The churchman directs Ian to become the caretaker of the children, so Danny gives up college to raise his nieces and nephew, hoping to atone for the havoc caused by his curiosity.

Other books by the same author:
A Patchwork Planet, 1998
Breathing Lessons, 1988
The Accidental Tourist, 1985

Other books you might like:
Margaret Atwood, *Cat's Eye*, 1988
Paul Horgan, *Whitewater*, 1970

982

JOHN UPDIKE

In the Beauty of the Lilies

(New York: Knopf, 1996)

Category: Biographical Fiction
Subject(s): Actors and Actresses; Family Saga; Presbyterians
Age range(s): Adult
Major character(s): Clarence Wilmot, Religious (Presbyterian clergyman), Father; Teddy Wilmot, Postal Worker, Son (of Clarence); Esther Wilmot, Actress, Daughter (of Teddy); Clark Lazlo, Cult Member, Son (of Esther)
Time period(s): 20th century (1910-1990)
Locale(s): Delaware; New Jersey; Colorado

Summary: This family saga traces four generations of the Wilmot family, beginning with Clarence Wilmot, a Presbyterian clergyman who becomes disenchanted with religion. After leaving the church, Clarence ends up as a mediocre salesman. His son Teddy, raised in the shadow of his father's dissatisfaction and failure, becomes a mail carrier. Teddy's beautiful daughter, Esther, climbs the Hollywood ladder to movie star fame and fortune. Esther's son Clark, neglected by his mother, is left to his own devices and joins a powerful religious cult. According to the author, the novel was inspired by the multi-generational lineage of Abraham, Isaac, and Joseph, as revealed in biblical writings, reflecting the truth that each generation is a member of all previous ancestral generations.

Other books by the same author:
Toward the End of Time, 1997
The Witches of Eastwick, 1984
A Month of Sundays, 1975

Other books you might like:
James Carroll, *An American Requiem: God, My Father, and the War That Came Between Us*, 1996

Gail Godwin, *Evensong*, 1999
Joanna Trollope, *The Rector's Wife*, 1994

983

JOHN UPDIKE

A Month of Sundays

(New York: Knopf, 1975)

Category: Comedy; Mainstream Fiction
Subject(s): Sexual Behavior; Clergy; Religious Life
Age range(s): Adult
Major character(s): Reverend Tom Marshfield, Religious (minister); Alicia, Musician (church organist)
Time period(s): 1970s
Locale(s): United States

Summary: The not-so-reverent Reverend Tom Marshfield is a handsome charmer who uses his charisma to attract women to himself rather than as believers to the church. In a succession of overlapping affairs with women of the parish, Marshfield manages to keep his bedroom behavior relatively private until a jilted lover—the just-fired church organist—goes to the church's administrative board with all the details. The minister is sent away for rest and rehabilitation, during which time he pens an account of his liaisons and dalliances. Updike's commentary on hypocrisy and human weakness in clerical circles contains language and situations that some readers may find offensive.

Other books by the same author:
In the Beauty of the Lilies, 1996

Other books you might like:
Susan Howatch, *The Wonder Worker*, 1997
Ivan Klima, *The Ultimate Intimacy*, 1998
Sinclair Lewis, *Elmer Gantry*, 1927
Morris L. West, *Eminence*, 1998
A.N. Wilson, *The Vicar of Sorrows*, 1994

984

JOHN UPDIKE

S.

(New York: Knopf, 1988)

Category: Comedy; Mainstream Fiction
Subject(s): Pilgrims and Pilgrimages; Religious Life; Self-Perception
Age range(s): Adult
Major character(s): Sarah P. Worth, Mother; Shri Arhat Mindadali, Religious (guru)
Time period(s): 1980s
Locale(s): Massachusetts; Arizona

Summary: Sarah Worth-the S. of the novel's title-is in her early forties and restless with her wealthy, suburban lifestyle. She leaves home, friends, and family behind and travels to Arizona to live as a ''sannyasin,'' a religious pilgrim, at the ashram of guru Shri Arhat Mindadali. The story of life at the ashram unfolds in the form of letters and cassette tapes sent by S. to the folks back home. Everyone from the daughter and the husband to the hairdresser and the psychiatrist gets news from

S. about her new-found Hindu lifestyle. As the novel progresses, it becomes clear that although Sarah purports to be seeking spiritual enlightenment away from the details of suburban American life, she really never lets go of the world she has run away from, nor does she ever fully embrace the world to which she has escaped.

Other books by the same author:
Toward the End of Time, 1997
In the Beauty of the Lilies, 1996
The Witches of Eastwick, 1984

Other books you might like:
Gail Godwin, *Father Melancholy's Daughter*, 1991
Alison Lurie, *Imaginary Friends*, 1967
Anne Tyler, *Ladder of Years*, 1995

985

ELIZABETH DEWBERRY VAUGHN

Many Things Have Happened Since He Died and Here Are the Highlights

(New York: Doubleday, 1990)

Category: Gentle Reads
Subject(s): Fundamentalism; Christianity; Religious Life
Age range(s): Adult
Time period(s): 1980s

Summary: A young woman raised in traditional Southern Christian fundamentalism tells the story of her life from the point of her father's suicide. The unnamed narrator reflects on the choices she has made and the turns her life has taken as a result in this poignant and funny novel. Among the ''highlights'' are an unhappy marriage to a deeply conservative man who abuses her in spite of-or perhaps as a consequence of-his Christian fundamentalist view of life, an unexpected and unwelcome pregnancy, and the death of her husband from a drug overdose. The juxtaposition of traditional faith, the narrator's dreams of fame and fortune as a writer, and the details of her sad and sorry life creates a picture of religion as both a foundational element and a destructive component in the life of the narrator, who is representative of many women in late twentieth-century America.

Other books by the same author:
Break the Heart of Me, 1994

Other books you might like:
Jan Karon, *The Mitford Series*, 1994-
Francine Rivers, *Redeeming Love*, 1997
Anne Tyler, *The Ladder of Years*, 1995
Lori Wick, *Pretense*, 1998

986

ELLEN VAUGHN

The Strand: A Novel

(Dallas: Word, 1997)

Category: Thrillers
Subject(s): Marriage; Death; Faith
Age range(s): Adult

Major character(s): Anne Lorelli, Spouse (Paul's); Paul Lorelli, Spouse (Anne's)
Time period(s): 1990s
Locale(s): Washington, District of Columbia
Summary: After ten years of marriage, Anne and Paul Lorelli are living the ideal suburban life just outside Washington, D.C., or so it seems to those who know them. But on the night of their anniversary, everything falls apart. In a mugging that escalates out of control, Paul is killed. Awash in her grief, Anne must contend with a detective who believes she set up the murder of her husband, only to discover that the truth is far more complicated and potentially devasating to Anne. Meanwhile, Anne finds solace in tutoring academically-challenged urban students, leaving behind the Junior League life that now seems empty and devoid of meaning. As Anne reconnects with herself and her personal faith, she develops the strength she'll need to deal with what she will soon discover about the reality of her marriage and her life with Paul.

Other books by the same author:
Gideon's Torch, 1995 (Charles Colson, co-author)
The God of Stones and Spiders: Letters to a Church in Exile, 1990 (Charles Colson, co-author)

Other books you might like:
Barbara Taylor Bradford, *Everything to Gain*, 1994
Gail Godwin, *Evensong*, 1999
Gail Godwin, *Father Melancholy's Daughter*, 1991
Anita Shreve, *The Pilot's Wife*, 1998
Anne Tyler, *The Ladder of Years*, 1995

987

ESTHER LOEWEN VOGT

The Enchanted Prairie

(Camp Hill, Pennsylvania: Horizon House, 1992)

Category: Romance
Subject(s): Christian Life; Civil War
Age range(s): Young Adult-Adult
Major character(s): Barbara Temple, 16-Year-Old, Orphan; Matthew Potter, Young Man
Time period(s): 1860s (1863)
Locale(s): Council Grove, Kansas

Summary: Barbara Temple is an orphan at sixteen. The Civil War is raging, and she has no option but to go live with relatives on the Kansas prairie until the war is over. Her dream is to return to Atlanta and marry handsome Matthew Potter, a Confederate Army officer to whom she has been betrothed for two years. But just as the war dashes her dreams and life on the prairie seems to hold out an endless future without hope or promise, something happens to change Barbara's outlook on life. With newfound faith, she discovers God's purpose for her and finds a new dream for her future.

Other books by the same author:
Song of the Prairie, 1995
The Wandering Trails, 1994
The Lonely Plains, 1993

Other books you might like:
Gilbert Morris, *Beyond the Quiet Hills*, 1997
Janette Oke, *The Bluebird and the Sparrow*, 1995

Catherine Palmer, *Prairie Rose*, 1997
Lori Wick, *As Time Goes By*, 1992

988

ALICE WALKER

The Color Purple: A Novel

(New York: Harcourt, 1982)

Category: Biographical Fiction
Subject(s): Racism; Sexual Abuse; Sisters
Age range(s): Young Adult-Adult
Major character(s): Celie, Abuse Victim, Sister (of Nettie), Spouse (of Mr.); Nettie, Sister (of Celie), Religious (missionary); Albert ''Mr.'', Spouse (of Celie); Shug Avery, Lover (of Mr.), Singer; Harpo, Son (of Mr.), Spouse (of Sophia); Sofia, Spouse (of Harpo)
Time period(s): 20th century
Locale(s): Georgia; Tennessee

Summary: Celie is only 14 when she is raped by her stepfather. She bears two children by him—children who disappear shortly after their birth. Her life doesn't get much easier when her mother dies in childbirth and she is wed to a man who physically abuses her. Despite her hardships Celie ultimately creates a full and satisfying life, largely due to her friendships with other women, especially her daughter-in-law, Sofia, and her husband's mistress, Shug Avery. Celie's story is told through her letters to God and, later, her correspondence with her sister, Nettie, who manages, through Celie's help and sacrifice, to escape the harsh experiences over which Celie ultimately triumphs.

Awards the book has won:
National Book Award, Fiction, 1983
Pulitzer Prize, Fiction, 1983

Other books by the same author:
Everyday Use, 1994
The Temple of My Familiar, 1989
You Can't Keep a Good Woman Down: Stories, 1981

Other books you might like:
Maya Angelou, *I Know Why the Caged Bird Sings*, 1970
Linda Beatrice Brown, *Crossing over Jordan*, 1995
J. California Cooper, *In Search of Satisfaction*, 1994
Terry McMillan, *Mama*, 1987
Toni Morrison, *Sula*, 1973
Gloria Naylor, *The Women of Brewster Place*, 1982

989

JIM WALKER

The Dreamgivers

(Minneapolis: Bethany House, 1994)

Category: Westerns
Series: Wells Fargo Trail
Subject(s): Frontier and Pioneer Life; Christian Life; Mystery and Detective Stories
Age range(s): Young Adult-Adult
Major character(s): Zachary Cobb, Veteran (Civil War), Detective—Private, Military Personnel (former)

Time period(s): 1860s
Locale(s): West

Summary: At the Civil War's end, Zachary Cobb returned home from Appomattox bitter and broken. Now he is an undercover agent working for the Wells Fargo company in the frontier West. He draws on his war experience to help him in his new line of work, and finds that the courage and cunning he developed on the battlefield are useful in cracking the mystery of holdups in the Mojave Desert. But something is missing in his life, and no show of courage will overcome the danger he finds himself in as love and faith work their way into his rough-and-tumble frontier life.

Other books by the same author:
The Warriors, 1997
The Desert Hawks, 1996
The Nightriders, 1994

Other books you might like:
Stephen Bly, *The Final Chapter of Chance McCall*, 1996
Stephen Bly, *Final Justice at Adobe Wells*, 1993
Al Lacy, *Circle of Fire*, 1996
Gilbert Morris, *Reno*, 1992

990
JIM WALKER

Murder on the Titanic: A Novel
(Nashville: Broadman & Holman Publishers, 1998)

Category: Mystery; Historical Fiction
Series: Mysteries in Time
Subject(s): Shipwrecks; Murder
Age range(s): Young Adult-Adult
Major character(s): Morgan Fairfield, Young Man (American); Margaret Hastings, Young Woman
Time period(s): 1910s (1912)
Locale(s): *Titanic*, At Sea

Summary: Morgan Fairfield is a young American who has recently graduated from Oxford University in England and is heading back to New York to take a newspaper job. Margaret Hastings is the young woman he has always loved but refused to marry until he could prove himself in the world. She, not willing to wait, accepted a proposal from someone else. Both are passengers on the *Titanic's* ill-fated voyage in 1912. Morgan, a man of faith and high character, is unexpectedly given a secret mission that coincides with his journey, and it involves him in adventure, suspense, and a mysterious murder. *Murder on the Titanic* is the story of men who will do whatever it takes to force their will on the world, and a man who, though questioning where his faith will lead him, does whatever he must to fulfill God's will in his life.

Other books by the same author:
Murder at Gettysburg, 1999
Voices From the Titanic, 1999
The Dreamgivers, 1994
The Nightriders, 1994

Other books you might like:
Beryl Bainbridge, *Every Man for Himself*, 1996
Terri Blackstock, *Blind Trust*, 1997
Terri Blackstock, *Justifiable Means*, 1996

Walter Lord, *The Night Lives On*, 1986
Walter Lord, *A Night to Remember*, 1958

991
LEW WALLACE

Ben-Hur: A Tale of the Christ
(New York: Harper & Brothers, 1880)

Category: Historical Fiction
Subject(s): Christianity; Jews; Roman Empire
Age range(s): Young Adult-Adult
Major character(s): Judah Ben Hur, Royalty (prince), Slave (galley); Messala, Military Personnel; Balthazar, Nobleman, Biblical Figure; Jesus, Historical Figure, Biblical Figure
Time period(s): 1st century (1-33)
Locale(s): Jerusalem, Israel; Antioch, Syria; Rome, Roman Empire

Summary: In this classic of religious fiction first published in 1880, Wallace connects the story of Jesus Christ with the family history of the Ben Hurs. Judah Ben Hur, son of a rich Jewish family, is accused of treason by his former friend, Messala. He becomes a galley slave and later is adopted by a Roman consul. When he returns to Antioch for revenge on Messala, he encounters Jesus' final days in Jerusalem.

Other books by the same author:
The Fair God; or, The Last of the 'Tzins: A Tale of the Conquest of Mexico, 1901

Other books you might like:
Lloyd C. Douglas, *The Robe*, 1942
Marjorie Holmes, *The Messiah*, 1987
Sonia Levitin, *Escape From Egypt*, 1994
Charles R. Swindoll, *Suddenly One Morning: The Shopkeeper's Story*, 1998

992
WALTER WANGERIN JR.

The Book of God: The Bible as a Novel
(Grand Rapids, Michigan: Zondervan, 1996)

Category: Historical Fiction
Subject(s): Scripture; Christianity; Bible
Age range(s): Young Adult-Adult

Summary: Walter Wangerin Jr.'s *The Book of God* is a storyteller's interpretation of the Old and New Testaments of the *Bible*. Rather than starting with the book of Genesis and ending with the book of Revelation, Wangerin focuses on the story that begins with Abraham and the ancestral line of David and leads to the coming of Jesus into the world and his life on Earth. Structured in an epic novel format, the stories of the Ancestors, the Covenant, the Wars of the Lord, the Kings, the Prophets, the years of exile, the anticipation of the Messiah, and the coming of the Messiah are brought to life in poetic language that preserves the spiritual significance of scriptural accounts while weaving them into a whole-cloth image of God's story on Earth.

Awards the book has won:
Gold Medallion Book Award, Fiction, 1997

Other books by the same author:
The Book of Sorrows, 1985
Potter, Come Fly to the First of the Earth, 1985
Ragman and Other Cries of Faith, 1984
The Book of the Dun Cow, 1978

Other books you might like:
Lynn N. Austin, *Among the Gods: A Novel*, 1998
Sigmund Brouwer, *The Weeping Chamber*, 1998
Paulo Coelho, *The Fifth Mountain*, 1998
Linn Creighton, *Beyond This Darkness*, 1993
Gene Edwards, *The Beginning*, 1992
    Chronicles of the Door
Gene Edwards, *The Escape*, 1993
    Chronicles of the Door
Ellen Gunderson Traylor, *Melchizedek*, 1997

993

WALTER WANGERIN JR.

The Book of the Dun Cow
(New York: Harper and Row, 1978)

Category: Fantasy
Subject(s): Animals; Good and Evil; Lutherans
Age range(s): Children-Young Adult
Major character(s): Chauntecleer, Rooster; John Wesley, Weasel; Mundo Cani, Dog; Wyrm, Monster
Time period(s): Indeterminate
Locale(s): Sularin, Fictional Country

Summary: In an imaginary kingdom called Sularin, a battle between good and evil rages. Chauntecleer and his subjects are fighting against the huge, evil Wyrm, who seeks freedom from his subterranean prison. The Dun Cow is a great-mother figure, who gives comfort and aid during the struggle. Written by Lutheran pastor Walter Wangerin Jr., this allegorical story for children and young adults depicts a world in which courage and selflessness fortify the forces for good. In Sularin, evil is not simplistically defeated in one fell swoop, and the animals come to know that the price of peace and security is watchfulness and sacrifice.

Awards the book has won:
National Book Award, Science Fiction, 1980

Other books by the same author:
Elisabeth and the Water Troll, 1991
The Book of Sorrows, 1985
Ragman and Other Cries of Faith, 1984

Other books you might like:
Richard Adams, *Watership Down*, 1972
Shirley Rousseau Murphy, *Medallion of the Black Hound*, 1989
Andre Norton, *Here Abide Monsters*, 1973
Pat O'Shea, *The Hounds of the Morrigan*, 1985

994

WALTER WANGERIN JR.
DANIEL SAN SOUCI, Illustrator

Potter, Come Fly to the First of the Earth
(Elgin, Illinois: Chariot Books, 1985)

Category: Gentle Reads
Subject(s): Death; Children; Afterlife
Age range(s): Children-Young Adult
Major character(s): Potter, Child, Friend (Jonathan's); Jonathan, Child, Friend (Potter's)

Summary: Potter is a young boy wracked by illness. While he is in bed with the Unstoppable Cough, his best friend, Jonathan, drowns in the flooded waters of the Red River. Potter is inconsolable at the loss of his companion and his parents are unable to help him understand death. One day, an oriole lands on his windowsill, and Potter's soul-in the form of a bird-begins a spiritual journey toward understanding the relationship between life and death, and the hope of the after-life that is part of the Christian faith.

Awards the book has won:
Gold Medallion Book Award, Children's Books, 1986

Other books by the same author:
The Book of God: The Bible as a Novel, 1996
The Book of Sorrows, 1985
Ragman and Other Cries of Faith, 1984
The Book of the Dun Cow, 1978

Other books you might like:
Louise Gish, *A Birthday Present for Daniel: A Child's Loss*, 1996
Sharon Greenlee, *When Someone Dies*, 1992
Sandy Lanton, *Daddy's Chair*, 1991
Benette W. Tiffault, *A Quilt for Elizabeth*, 1992

995

WALTER WANGERIN JR.

Ragman and Other Cries of Faith
(San Francisco: Harper & Row, 1984)

Category: Gentle Reads
Subject(s): Spirituality; Christianity; Interpersonal Relations
Age range(s): Young Adult-Adult

Summary: *Ragman and Other Cries of Faith* is an anthology of stories, allegories, essays, and meditations from storyteller Walter Wangerin, Jr. Based on Wangerin's interaction with people through pastoral work, the stories in *Ragman and Other Cries of Faith* celebrate the resiliency and dignity of human life and faith. The 26 tales explore the meaning of love—human and divine—in a secular world that is touched by the spiritual.

Other books by the same author:
The Book of God: The Bible as a Novel, 1996
The Book of Sorrows, 1985
Potter, Come Fly to the First of the Earth, 1985
The Book of the Dun Cow, 1978

Other books you might like:

Martin Bell, *The Way of the Wolf*, 1983
Chuck Fager, *The Best of Friends*, 1998
Nicholas Hagger, *A Spade Fresh with Mud: Collected Stories*, 1995
William R. White, *Stories for the Gathering: A Treasury for Christian Storytellers*, 1997

996

MARIAN WELLS

The Wedding Dress

(Minneapolis: Bethany House, 1982)

Category: Romance
Subject(s): Christianity; Marriage; Mormons
Major character(s): Rebecca Wolstone, Orphan, Young Woman; Joshua Smyth, Young Man
Time period(s): 19th century
Locale(s): Nauvoo, Illinois

Summary: Rebecca Wolstone remembers that when her mother died, she admonished Rebecca to take good care of the trunk that would be her inheritance, for ''There's in it your only hope.'' Inside the trunk was her mother's wedding dress and a small black book. Rebecca had always assumed that her hope was to one day wear that dress while marrying the man who would love her and take care of her forever. Her eye was on Joshua Smyth, a member of the family who had taken her in when she was newly orphaned. She decides to travel west with them from Illinois to a new Mormon settlement. Along the way, she begins to harbor doubts about their chosen religion, and she discovers some new truths in the trunk that is her mother's legacy.

Other books by the same author:
Jewel of Promise, 1990
Silver Highway, 1989
Colorado Gold, 1988
With This Ring, 1984

Other books you might like:
Rodello Hunter, *A Daughter of Zion*, 1972
Beverly LaHaye, *Seasons under Heaven*, 1999
Diane Noble, *The Veil*, 1998

997

FRANZ WERFEL

The Song of Bernadette

(New York: Viking, 1942)

Category: Historical Fiction
Subject(s): Catholicism; Religious Life; Saints
Age range(s): Young Adult-Adult
Major character(s): Bernadette Soubirous, Historical Figure, Religious; Dean Peyramale, Historical Figure, Religious (parish priest); Marie Therese, Historical Figure, Religious (nun)
Time period(s): 19th century (1858-1875)
Locale(s): Lourdes, France

Summary: This is the story of St. Bernadette's vision at Lourdes and the skepticism that resulted before many were convinced that a miracle had occurred. The author wrote the book in fulfillment of a vow he had made while hiding from the Nazis in the church of St. Bernadette at the beginning of World War II. He promised that if he escaped with his life, he would tell the story of Bernadette. More than a religious story or a testament of faith, the novel is a moving account of humans confronted by the unknown. This edition was translated by Ludwig Lewisohn.

Other books by the same author:
Embezzled Heaven, 1940
Hearken Unto the Voice, 1938
The Eternal Road: A Drama in Four Parts, 1936

Other books you might like:
Louis DeWohl, *The Restless Flame: A Novel about St. Augustine*, 1997
Madeline Pecora Nugent, *St. Anthony: Words of Fire, Life of Light*, 1995
Joan Ohanneson, *Scarlet Music: Hildegard of Bingen*, 1997

998

MORRIS L. WEST

The Shoes of the Fisherman

(New York: Morrow, 1963)

Category: Thrillers
Subject(s): Catholicism; Clergy; History
Age range(s): Adult
Major character(s): Kiril Lakota, Religious (Cardinal)
Time period(s): 1960s
Locale(s): Rome, Italy (Vatican)

Summary: Morris L. West's bestseller of the 1960s, *The Shoes of the Fisherman*, is the story of a Ukrainian cardinal who becomes the first non-Italian pope ever appointed. Kiril Lakota unexpectedly finds himself, in his role as Pope Kiril I, taking a central role in mediating political tensions between the United States and the Soviet Union to prevent the start of World War III. In narrative interspersed with journal entries from the new Pontiff, West captures the loneliness and sense of responsibility carried by the man who sits at the head of the Vatican. *The Shoes of the Fisherman* remarkably foreshadows the man who would, in reality, become the first Eastern European pope—Karol Wotyla, Pope John Paul II, who was appointed more than a decade after this novel was published.

Other books by the same author:
Eminence, 1998
Vanishing Point, 1996
The Clowns of God, 1981
The Devil's Advocate, 1959

Other books you might like:
Frederick J. Luhmann, *Millennium Pope: A Novel of Spiritual Journey*, 1999
Jerry Marcus, *The Last Pope*, 1997
Malachi Martin, *Vatican: A Novel*, 1986
Ralph McInerny, *The Red Hat: A Novel*, 1998
Edward R.F. Sheehan, *Cardinal Galsworthy: A Novel*, 1997

999

STEPHANIE GRACE WHITSON

Sarah's Patchwork

(Nashville: T. Nelson, 1998)

Category: Gentle Reads
Subject(s): Quilts; Family Life; Christianity
Age range(s): Young Adult-Adult
Major character(s): Sarah Biddle, Aunt (Lorna's); Lorna Biddle, Child, Relative (Sarah's niece)
Locale(s): United States

Summary: In a tale of family history and intergenerational love and faith, *Sarah's Patchwork* offers the story of one generation whose history is preserved in a patchwork quilt, and another whose future is tied to the quilt. One rainy afternoon, elderly Sarah Biddle shares her memories with young niece Lorna Biddle. Looking together at a patchwork quilt that has been hidden away in Sarah's blanket trunk, they trace the patches that represent episodes from Sarah's life. Lorna learns that Sarah and her brother, Tom, were sent west on an orphan train after they were abandoned by their penniless father. She hears how Sarah and Tom, too old to be adopted but too young to be on their own, nevertheless chose independence and managed to create a life for themselves in Lincoln, Nebraska. Lorna learns, through Sarah's quilt, that hardship and disappointment can lead to opportunity and faith, and Sarah discovers that the pain of her past is really a legacy to future generations.

Other books by the same author:
Karyn's Memory Box, 1999
Red Bird, 1997
Soaring Eagle, 1996
Walks the Fire: A Novel, 1995

Other books you might like:
T. Davis Bunn, *The Quilt*, 1993
Al Lacy, *The Perfect Gift*, 1999
Patricia McLachlan, *Sarah, Plain and Tall*, 1985
Catherine Palmer, *Prairie Rose*, 1997
Jane Peart, *The Pledge*, 1996

1000

LORI WICK

The Hawk and the Jewel

(Eugene, Oregon: Harvest House, 1993)

Category: Romance
Subject(s): Christian Life; Friendship; Love
Age range(s): Adult
Major character(s): Sunny, Teenager, Heiress; Brandon Hawkesbury, Sea Captain
Time period(s): 1840s
Locale(s): London, England; Darhabar, Fictional Country

Summary: Thirteen-year-old Sunny is believed to be dead. People thought she died in a shipwreck in her childhood. However, she is alive and well in the tiny country of Darhabar, where she has been raised and spoiled by royalty. Now Brandon Hawkesbury, a young sea captain, has been commissioned to bring the willful girl back to her family, to England, and to Christianity. Along the way, friendship and love emerge unexpectedly.

Other books by the same author:
Who Brings Forth the Wind, 1994
Wings of the Morning, 1994

Other books you might like:
Susan Kirby, *Prairie Rose*, 1997
Wendy Loggia, *Ever After: A Cinderella Story*, 1998
Janette Oke, *Heart of the Wilderness*, 1993

1001

LORI WICK

A Place Called Home

(Eugene, Oregon: Harvest House, 1990)

Category: Romance
Series: Place Called Home
Subject(s): Family Life; Christian Life; Love
Age range(s): Young Adult-Adult
Major character(s): Christine Bennett, Teenager; Luke Cameron, Young Man

Summary: When Christine Bennett's grandfather dies, she is not only in grief, she is in danger. Her grandfather's fortune makes her the target of one of his former associates who has already manipulated the old man's will. Now all that's left is to remove Christine from the picture—permanently. Acting on urgent advice, Christine diguises herself as a young boy and escapes during the night by train. When she finds herself hurt and in a small town all alone, Christine is at the mercy of the strangers she meets. Despite more dark times ahead, Christine finds more love than she ever thought possible in the heart of the Cameron family.

Other books by the same author:
A Gathering of Memories, 1991
The Long Road Home, 1990
A Song for Silas, 1990

Other books you might like:
Lawana Blackwell, *The Dowry of Miss Lydia Clark*, 1999
Lawana Blackwell, *Like a River Glorious*, 1995
Francine Rivers, *The Last Sin Eater*, 1998
Francine Rivers, *The Scarlet Thread*, 1996
Janette Oke, *Heart of the Wilderness*, 1993

1002

LORI WICK

Pretense

(Eugene, Oregon: Harvest House, 1998)

Category: Gentle Reads
Subject(s): Sisters; Family Relations; Christian Life
Age range(s): Young Adult-Adult
Major character(s): Mackenzie Bishop, Sister (of Delancey); Delancey Bishop, Sister (of Mackenzie)
Time period(s): 20th century (1976-1993)
Locale(s): United States

Summary: Mackenzie and Delancey Bishop are sisters. Since their father is a career Army officer, they have moved from base to base throughout their lives. They've become adept at being independent and self-sufficient, but will these characteristics be enough to help them deal with the circumstances they will encounter throughout their young lives? The first blow arrives when they are in junior high school and there is a sudden death in the family. Unresolved issues about religion and faith begin to surface and continue throughout the novel as the sisters grow up, form relationships with young men, select careers, and strike out on their own. Personal faith may help them stay together and survive the turmoil that is ahead, or their difficulties may push them further from God and each other.

Other books by the same author:
The Princess, 1999
Sophie's Heart, 1995
A Gathering of Memories, 1991

Other books you might like:
Jan Karon, *The Mitford Series*, 1994-
Janette Oke, *Return to Harmony: A Novel*, 1996
Francine Rivers, *The Atonement Child*, 1997
Francine Rivers, *Redeeming Love*, 1997

1003

LORI WICK

Whatever Tomorrow Brings

(Eugene, Oregon: Harvest House, 1992)

Category: Romance; Historical Fiction
Series: Californians
Subject(s): Family Life
Age range(s): Young Adult-Adult
Major character(s): Kaitlin Donovan, Daughter (of Patrick); Patrick Donovan, Father (of Kaitlin), Religious (missionary)
Locale(s): San Francisco, California

Summary: The Donovan family has been in Hawaii for fifteen years doing missionary work. It's the only home most of the Donovan children remember, but Kaitlin, at 20, remembers people and places from her early childhood in California. Now the family is returning to San Francisco to visit relatives, but the real reason for the trip is that Mrs. Donovan is ill. Not long after they arrive, she dies of untreatable tuberculosis. Patrick Donovan must return to the mission field, leaving Kaitlin alone to care for her teen-aged brother and nine-year-old sister. After a short stay with relatives, the Donovan children head to Santa Monica, where Kaitlin has received an invitation to teach school, and their new life begins. God provides for their needs and brings people into their lives to encourage and support them, and Kaitlin finds a special friend-perhaps one who will be by her side for a lifetime.

Other books by the same author:
Donovan's Daughter, 1994
Sean Donovan, 1993
As Time Goes By, 1992

Other books you might like:
Lawana Blackwell, *The Dowry of Miss Lydia Clark*, 1999

Lawana Blackwell, *Like a River Glorious*, 1995
Francine Rivers, *The Last Sin Eater*, 1998
Francine Rivers, *The Scarlet Thread*, 1996

1004

BRENDA WILBEE

Sweetbriar Summer

(Grand Rapids, Michigan: F. H. Revell, 1997)

Category: Gentle Reads
Subject(s): Frontier and Pioneer Life; Family Life; Marriage
Age range(s): Young Adult-Adult
Major character(s): Louisa Boren Denny, Settler, Spouse (of David); David Thomas Denny, Settler, Spouse (of Louisa)
Time period(s): 19th century
Locale(s): Pacific Northwest; Seattle, Washington

Summary: David and Louisa are a young couple who have settled in the Pacific Northwest with several other families. They have worked hard to create a community and they are enjoying the benefits of their labors, but news of Indian unrest bodes ill for the residents of the Sweetbriar settlement. How will this change their lives of love, hard work, and faith?

Other books by the same author:
Sweetbriar Autumn, 1998

Other books you might like:
Stephen Bly, *Sweet Carolina*, 1998
Catherine Marshall, *Christy*, 1967
Janette Oke, *They Called Her Mrs. Doc*, 1992
Lori Wick, *Promise Me Tomorrow*, 1997

1005

JAMES WILCOX

Modern Baptists

(Garden City, New York: Dial Press, 1983)

Category: Comedy
Subject(s): Christianity; Small Town Life; Baptists
Age range(s): Adult
Major character(s): Bobby Pickens, Businessman
Time period(s): 20th century
Locale(s): Tula Springs, South (a small town)

Summary: Bobby Pickens works at the Sonny Boy Bargain Store in Tula Springs. Life seems to have dealt him a bad break, and sinces he believes he won't be living long, he asks his recently paroled half-brother to come live with him. From that point on, life gets complicated and, for the reader, quite humorous. The girl Bobby has his eye on is making moves on his half-brother. The one who loves Bobby is engaged to someone else. The folks of Tula Springs are an odd and lovable assortment of people who might be found anywhere and nowhere. Running through the ups and downs of everyday life is the constancy of the local Baptist church. Modern sinners they may be, but the roots of down-home sensibilities and habits still tug at the hearts of Tula Springs' inhabitants.

Other books by the same author:
Plain and Normal, 1998
Guest of a Sinner, 1993

North Gladiola, 1985

Other books you might like:
Henry A. Buchanan, *And the Goat Cried: Southern Tales and Other Chance Meetings*, 1998
  Susan Sammons, illustrator
Clyde Edgerton, *Killer Diller: A Novel*, 1991
Clyde Edgerton, *Raney: A Novel*, 1985
T.R. Pearson, *Gospel Hour*, 1991
Bailey White, *Mama Makes Up Her Mind: And Other Dangers of Southern Living*, 1993

1006

A.N. WILSON

The Vicar of Sorrows

(New York: W.W. Norton, 1994)

Category: Mainstream Fiction
Subject(s): Clergy; Conduct of Life; Faith
Age range(s): Adult
Major character(s): Francis Kreer, Religious (vicar); Mrs. Spittle, Housewife
Locale(s): Thames Valley, England

Summary: The Reverend Francis Kreer, vicar of a church in Thames Valley, is definitely on a downward spiral. Two decades after his ordination, he is stuck in a small London suburban vicarage with petty parishioners such as the gossipy Mrs. Spittle and her husband. He is stuck in a marriage with a wife he hardly knows or cares about any longer, and he is stuck with a vocation for which he is ill-suited—he is now an atheist. Can things get worse? In A.N. Wilson's *The Vicar of Sorrows*, they certainly can. When Kreer's mother dies, after reducing his inheritance through an addition to her will, he really falls apart. As Kreer's weaknesses begin to show publicly, the Spittles take aim and begin to undermine him through gossip, innuendo, and outright falsehoods. And the vicar does himself no favors by taking up with a beautiful itinerant musician. Wilson's darkly witty novel portrays a ''man of faith'' in the absolute grip of a loss of faith, unable to find solid footing in any corner of his life.

Other books by the same author:
A Watch in the Night, 1996
Hearing Voices, 1995
The Rise and Fall of the House of Windsor, 1993

Other books you might like:
Georges Bernanos, *The Diary of a Country Priest*, 1937
Gail Godwin, *Evensong*, 1999
Gail Godwin, *Father Melancholy's Daughter*, 1991
Jon Hassler, *North of Hope: A Novel*, 1990

1007

CHERYL WOLVERTON

A Father's Love

(New York: Steeple Hill Books, 1998)

Category: Romance
Subject(s): Twins; Parenthood; Faith
Age range(s): Young Adult-Adult

Major character(s): Max Stevens, Businessman; Kaitland, Young Woman
Time period(s): 1990s

Summary: Max Stevens is suddenly the father of twins and not the least bit ready for the job. Though he believes his former fiancee, Kaitland, betrayed him, he calls on her to help out, not knowing where else to turn. God uses the circumstances to open Max's heart to love and forgiveness. This title is one of Harlequin's Love Inspired Christian romances.

Other books by the same author:
A Mother's Love, 1999
This Side of Paradise, 1998
A Matter of Trust, 1997

Other books you might like:
Irene Brand, *Child of Her Heart*, 1998
Loree Lough, *Suddenly Mommy*, 1998
Virginia Myers, *The Dad Next Door*, 1999
Penny Richards, *Unanswered Prayers*, 1997
Ruth Scofield, *In God's Own Time*, 1998

1008

CHERYL WOLVERTON

A Mother's Love

(New York: Harlequin, 1999)

Category: Romance
Subject(s): Pregnancy; Self-Acceptance; Love
Age range(s): Young Adult-Adult
Major character(s): Maggie Gardere, Young Woman; Jake Mathison, Religious (pastor)
Time period(s): 1990s
Locale(s): United States

Summary: Unemployed and pregnant, Maggie doesn't know which way to turn. In her confusion, she prays for direction and emotional support. Her prayers are answered in the guise of an attractive young pastor, Jake Mathison, whose spiritual guidance helps Maggie learn to offer and accept forgiveness. Both faith and love grow in Maggie's life when Jake accepts her as she is.

Other books by the same author:
For Love of Zach, 1999
The Best Christmas Ever, 1998
This Side of Paradise, 1998

Other books you might like:
Irene Brand, *A Groom to Come Home To*, 1999
Virginia Myers, *The Dad Next Door*, 1999
Anna Schmidt, *Caroline and the Preacher*, 1999

1009

JAMES D. YODER

Black Spider over Tiegenhof

(Scottdale, Pennsylvania: Herald Press, 1995)

Category: Historical Fiction
Subject(s): Holocaust; Nazis; Mennonites
Age range(s): Young Adult-Adult

Fiction

Major character(s): Esther Claassen, Mother; Gerhard Claassen, Father
Time period(s): 1930s; 1940s
Locale(s): Tiegenhof, Germany

Summary: Esther and Gerhard Claassen and their sons live peacefully in a community of German Mennonites in Tiegenhof, Germany. Hopeful about the economic prosperity Hitler has promised, they-like most of their German neighbors-are not fully aware of the ways in which Hitler plans to create the ''New Germany.'' Before long, however, the terror of the swastika, the Black Spider, becomes all too clear to them. Putting their faith and commitment to God and peace before family security, they agree to shelter a young Jewish girl from the Nazis. But this is a risk with potentially deadly consequences for everyone involved, if they should fail.

Other books by the same author:
Barbara: Sarah's Legacy, 1994
Sarah of the Border Wars, 1993

Other books you might like:
Anne Frank, *The Diary of a Young Girl*, 1952
Boris Pahor, *Pilgrim Among Shadows*, 1995
Bronka Schneider, *Exile: A Memoir of 1939*, 1998
Corrie ten Boom, *The Hiding Place*, 1971
Elie Wiesel, *Night*, 1960

1010

RICHARD ZIMLER

The Last Kabbalist of Lisbon

(Woodstock, New York: Overlook Press, 1998)

Category: Mystery; Mainstream Fiction

Subject(s): Mysticism; Murder
Major character(s): Abraham, Religious (Kabbalist mystic); Berekiah Zarco, Businessman, Artisan, Narrator
Time period(s): 16th century
Locale(s): Lisbon, Portugal

Summary: *The Last Kabbalist of Lisbon* is the story of a murder that takes place in Lisbon, Portugal during the 16th century. The narrator is Berekiah Zarco, a manuscript illuminator and local businessman whose Uncle Abraham is the murdered kaballah master of the title. The novel is set during a period of time when Jews were freely killed for not converting to Christianity and when an active secret group had evolved to preserve the orthodox traditions of mysticism that were threatened with extinction during the persecution of the Jews. The narrative is supposed to be the long-lost manuscript written by Berekiah during the period of time before and after his uncle's death. Richard Zimler graphically and accurately recreates an unfamiliar culture from the distant past for modern audiences. Some particularly graphic descriptions of violence may be offensive to some readers.

Other books by the same author:
The Angelic Darkness: A Novel, 1999
Unholy Ghosts, 1996

Other books you might like:
Aron Appelfeld, *The Conversion: A Novel*, 1998
Allegra Goodman, *Kaaterskill Falls: A Novel*, 1998
Abraham B. Yehoshua, *A Journey to the End of the Millennium*, 1999

Series Index

This index alphabetically lists series to which books featured in the entries belong. Beneath each series name, book titles are listed alphabetically with author names. Numbers refer to the entries that feature each title.

Award Index

This index lists major awards given to books featured in the entries. Books are listed alphabetically beneath the name of the award, with author name and entry number also indicated.

Time Period Index

This index chronologically lists the time settings in which the featured books take place. Main headings refer to a century; where no specific time is given, the headings INDETERMINATE PAST, INDETERMINATE FUTURE, and INDETERMINATE are used. The 18th through 21st centuries are broken down into decades when possible. (Note: 1800s, for example, refers to the first decade of the 19th century.) Featured titles are listed alphabetically beneath time headings, with author names, and entry numbers also provided.

20th CENTURY

Geographic Index

This index provides access to all featured books by geographic settings, such as countries and continents. States and provinces are indicated for the United States and Canada. Also interfiled are headings for fictional place names (Mythical Places, Imaginary Planets, etc.). Sections are further broken down by city or the specific name of the imaginary locale. Book titles are listed alphabetically under headings, and author names and entry numbers are also provided.

AFRICA

Of Water and the Spirit: Ritual, Magic, and Initiation in the Life of an African Shaman - Malidoma Patrice Some 547

AMERICAN COLONIES

MASSACHUSETTS

Plymouth
The Captive Bride - Gilbert Morris 864
The Honorable Imposter - Gilbert Morris 867

Salem
The Captive Bride - Gilbert Morris 864

VIRGINIA

Valiant Bride - Jane Peart 903

ARABIA

The Big Fisherman - Lloyd C. Douglas 747

AT SEA

Mayflower
The Honorable Imposter - Gilbert Morris 867

Titanic
Murder on the Titanic: A Novel - Jim Walker 990

AUSTRALIA

Code of Honor - Sandra Dengler 743
Lambs of God - Marele Day 742

AUSTRIA

Danzig Passage - Bodie Thoene 960
Munich Signature - Bodie Thoene 964
Vienna Prelude - Bodie Thoene 967

BRAZIL

Bahia
The War of the Saints - Jorge Amado 681

CANADA

Arctic Dreams: Imagination and Desire in a Northern Landscape - Barry Lopez 369

Prairie Provinces
The Calling of Emily Evans - Janette Oke 881

ALBERTA

They Called Her Mrs. Doc - Janette Oke 892
When Calls the Heart - Janette Oke 893

BRITISH COLUMBIA

Eclipse of the Sun: A Novel - Michael D. O'Brien 876

Kingcome
I Heard the Owl Call My Name - Margaret Craven 739

QUEBEC

Montreal
They Called Her Mrs. Doc - Janette Oke 892

CENTRAL AMERICA

The Religions of the American Indians - Ake Hultkrantz 292

CHINA

The Good Earth - Pearl S. Buck 706
It's My Turn - Ruth Bell Graham 252
A Time for Remembering: The Story of Ruth Bell Graham - Patricia Cornwell 140

EARTH

Angelwalk: A Modern Fable - Roger Elwood 755

EGYPT

A Prophetical Walk through the Holy Land - Hal Lindsey 365
Saint Francis: A Novel - Nikos Kazantzakis 812
Stone Tables: A Novel - Orson Scott Card 723

Cairo
Tourmaline - Jon Henderson 783

ENGLAND

Alpha Centauri - Robert Siegel 946
C.S. Lewis: Through the Shadowlands - Brian Sibley 538
Heart of Allegiance - Jake Thoene 970
Heart of Joy - Mother Teresa 588
The Honorable Imposter - Gilbert Morris 867
The Lion, the Witch, and the Wardrobe - C.S. Lewis 829
The Return of Merlin - Deepak Chopra 730
Taken on Trust - Terry Waite 623
Taliesin - Stephen R. Lawhead 827
The Wanderings of Clare Skymer - George MacDonald 839

Bedford
The Pilgrim's Progress - John Bunyan 714

Canterbury
Murder in the Cathedral - T.S. Eliot 192

Finchale
Godric - Frederick Buechner 708

Kingsdene
Priscilla's Promise - L.T. Meade 854

London
Bright Captivity - Eugenia Price 921
Gaudy Night - Dorothy L. Sayers 940
The Hawk and the Jewel - Lori Wick 1000
The Satanic Verses - Salman Rushdie 934
Warsaw Requiem - Bodie Thoene 968

Starbridge
Absolute Truths: A Novel - Susan Howatch 797

Thames Valley
The Vicar of Sorrows - A.N. Wilson 1006

Yorkshire
The James Herriot Series - James Herriot 280
The Secret Garden - Frances Hodgson Burnett 716

EUROPE

The Dark Is Rising Sequence - Susan Cooper 734
Gibraltar Passage - T. Davis Bunn 711
Madame Blavatsky's Baboon: A History of the Mystics, Mediums, and Misfits who Brought Spiritualism to America - Peter Washington 629

Angels in America: A Gay Fantasia on National Themes - Tony Kushner 345
Another Homecoming - Janette Oke 880
The Atonement Child - Francine Rivers 930
Billy: A Personal Look at Billy Graham, the World's Best-Loved Evangelist - Sherwood Eliot Wirt 654
Black Elk Speaks: Being the Life Story of a Holy Man of the Ogalala Sioux - Black Elk 52
Born Again - Charles Colson 130
The Call to Conversion: Recovering the Gospel for These Times - Jim Wallis 625
A Closer Walk - Catherine Marshall 390
Conjectures of a Guilty Bystander - Thomas Merton 414
A Covenant of Love - Gilbert Morris 865
Ellie - Mary Christopher Borntrager 698
Elmer Gantry - Sinclair Lewis 830
Encyclopedic Handbook of Cults in America - J. Gordon Melton 411
The Gospel According to Peanuts - Robert L. Short 536
Hawk, I'm Your Brother - Byrd Baylor 690
Heart of Joy - Mother Teresa 588
The Illuminati - Larry Burkett 715
Illusions: The Adventures of a Reluctant Messiah - Richard Bach 686
In My Father's House - Bodie Thoene 962
It's My Turn - Ruth Bell Graham 252
Joni - Joni Eareckson 184
Joshua and the City - Joseph F. Girzone 768
Light From Heaven - Christmas Carol Kauffman 809
Madame Blavatsky's Baboon: A History of the Mystics, Mediums, and Misfits who Brought Spiritualism to America - Peter Washington 629
Modern American Religion - Martin E. Marty 396
A Month of Sundays - John Updike 983
A Mother's Love - Cheryl Wolverton 1008
My Brother Joseph: The Spirit of a Cardinal and the Story of a Friendship - Eugene Kennedy 328
Nana's Gift - Janette Oke 887
Not My Will - Francena H. Arnold 683
Of Water and the Spirit: Ritual, Magic, and Initiation in the Life of an African Shaman - Malidoma Patrice Some 547
Practicing Catholic: The Search for a Livable Catholicism - Penelope Ryan 509
Pretense - Lori Wick 1002
The Red Geranium - Janette Oke 889
Religion in America: An Historical Account of the Development of American Religious Life - Winthrop S. Hudson 289
Religious Bodies in the United States: A Directory - J. Gordon Melton 413
The Sacred Journey - Frederick Buechner 88
Sarah's Patchwork - Stephanie Grace Whitson 999
Searching for God in America - Hugh Hewitt 282
Soul Harvest: The World Takes Sides - Tim LaHaye 819
A Step Further - Joni Eareckson 185
Still Me - Christopher Reeve 490
The Story of My Life - Helen Keller 324
The Tender Years - Janette Oke 891
A Time for Remembering: The Story of Ruth Bell Graham - Patricia Cornwell 140
The War Romance of the Salvation Army - Evangeline Booth 66
What Really Matters: Searching for Wisdom in America - Tony Schwartz 528
When the Almond Tree Blossoms - David Aikman 677
When Time Shall Be No More: Prophecy Belief in Modern American Culture - Paul Boyer 74

Ashton
This Present Darkness - Frank E. Peretti 912

Bacon's Corner
Piercing the Darkness - Frank E. Peretti 911

Blessing
The Reapers' Song - Lauraine Snelling 953

Camp Juniper
The Tongues of Angels - Reynolds Price 925

Hope
Prairie Rose - Catherine Palmer 895

Pacific Northwest
Sweetbriar Summer - Brenda Wilbee 1004

Salt Lake
The Letter - Richard Paul Evans 759

Smoky Mountains
The Last Sin Eater - Francine Rivers 931

"The Valley"
Reno - Gilbert Morris 868

ALABAMA

Sand Mountain
Salvation on Sand Mountain: Snake Handling and Redemption in Southern Appalachia - Dennis Covington 143

ARIZONA

S. - John Updike 984

ARKANSAS

Brookdale
The Heart's Lonely Secret - Jane Peart 900

CALIFORNIA

A New Frontier: Saga of the Sierras - Brock Thoene 969
Sign of the Carousel - Jane Peart 902
Westward the Dream - Judith Pella 907

Los Angeles
House Made of Dawn - N. Scott Momaday 860
In the House of My Pilgrimage - Julia Shuken 945
Millennium's Eve - Ed Stewart 958
The Scarlet Thread - Francine Rivers 932

Miracle Springs
A Home for the Heart - Michael Phillips 915

Newport Beach
The Third Millennium: A Novel - Paul Meier 856

Oak Hill
With Wings as Eagles - Elaine Schulte 941

Oregon Trail
The Scarlet Thread - Francine Rivers 932

Pasadena
Saint Ben - John Fischer 762

Redondo Beach
Beloved Stranger - Judith Pella 905

Sacramento
Sea to Shining Sea - Michael Phillips 918

San Francisco
Sea to Shining Sea - Michael Phillips 918
Whatever Tomorrow Brings - Lori Wick 1003

Shadow Ridge
The Man From Shadow Ridge - Bodie Thoene 963

Whittier
Beloved Stranger - Judith Pella 905

COLORADO

In the Beauty of the Lilies - John Updike 982

CONNECTICUT

A Circle of Quiet - Madeleine L'Engle 355

DELAWARE

In the Beauty of the Lilies - John Updike 982

DISTRICT OF COLUMBIA

Washington
Ceremony of the Innocent - Taylor Caldwell 718
The Red Hat: A Novel - Ralph McInerny 853
The Strand: A Novel - Ellen Vaughn 986

FLORIDA

Armadillo
Lion Country - Frederick Buechner 709

GEORGIA

The Color Purple: A Novel - Alice Walker 988
Lamb in His Bosom - Caroline Miller 858

Atlanta
The Temple Bombing - Melissa Fay Greene 257

Enigma
Gospel Singer - Harry Crews 740

Plains
Living Faith - Jimmy Carter 109

St. Simons Island
The Beloved Invader - Eugenia Price 920
Bright Captivity - Eugenia Price 921
Lighthouse - Eugenia Price 922
New Moon Rising - Eugenia Price 923

Savannah
Savannah - Eugenia Price 924

ILLINOIS

In Love's Own Time - Susan Feldhake 761

Chicago
The Letter - Richard Paul Evans 759
Sacred Hoops: Spiritual Lessons of a Hardwood Warrior - Phil Jackson 298
Years of Grace - Margaret Ayer Barnes 689

Nauvoo
The Wedding Dress - Marian Wells 996

INDIANA

Bethel Lake
Threshold - Bill Myers 875

KANSAS

Council Grove
The Enchanted Prairie - Esther Loewen Vogt 987

KENTUCKY

The Hermitage Journals: A Diary Kept While Working on the Biography of Thomas Merton - John Howard Griffin 259

Cutter Gap
Christy - Catherine Marshall 849

LOUISIANA

New Orleans
A Confederacy of Dunces - John Kennedy Toole 975

WASHINGTON

Seattle
Sweetbriar Summer - Brenda Wilbee   1004

WEST

The Dreamgivers - Jim Walker   989
Love Comes Softly - Janette Oke   883
Love's Enduring Promise - Janette Oke   884
Love's Long Journey - Janette Oke   885

Broken Arrow Crossing
Hard Winter at Broken Arrow Crossing - Stephen
Bly   697

WYOMING

Jackson
The Final Chapter of Chance McCall - Stephen
Bly   696

WALES

Body and Soul - Marcelle Bernstein   693

Taliesin - Stephen R. Lawhead   827

YUGOSLAVIA

Hidden Rainbow - Christmas Carol Kauffman   808

ZAIRE

*Caught in the Crossfire: The Trials and Triumphs of
African Believers through an Era of Tribulation* -
Levi Keidel   813

Category Index

This index lists the books featured as main entries in *What Inspirational Literature Do I Read Next?* by categories (Autobiography, Devotionals, Morality Tales, New Age (Fiction), Scripture, etc.). The categories are listed alphabetically, and titles appear alphabetically under each category heading. The name of the primary author and the book entry number also appear with each title.

Comedy

Devotionals

Doctrine

History

Journals/Letters

Self-Help

Sermons

Theology

Subject Index

This index lists subjects that are covered in the featured titles. These can include such things as denomination or religious body, personal and social problems, historical events, and faith. Beneath each subject heading, titles are arranged alphabetically with author names and entry numbers also indicated.

Birth

Blind

Boats and Boating

Brothers

Brothers and Sisters

Buddhism

Christian Science

Christianity

Conspiracies

Courage

Creation

Creationism

Crime and Criminals

Criticism

Crusades

Crystals

Cults

Culture

Customs

Evangelism

Evolution

Extrasensory Perception

Fairy Tales

Faith

Family

Family Life

Family Problems

Family Relations

Religious Communes

Religious Conflict

Religious Life

Religious Traditions

Resistance Movements

Retirement

Reunions

Revenge

Character Name Index

This index alphabetically lists the major characters in each featured title. Each character name is followed by a description of the character. Citations also provide titles of the books featuring the character—listed alphabetically if there is more than one title—author names, and entry numbers.

A

Aaron (Biblical Figure; Brother)
Stone Tables: A Novel - Orson Scott Card   723

Abel (Indian; Convict; Relative)
House Made of Dawn - N. Scott Momaday   860

Abernathy, Clarence (Journalist)
Dominion - Randy Alcorn   679

Abraham (Bastard Son)
In Abraham's Bosom - Paul Green   254

Abraham (Religious)
The Last Kabbalist of Lisbon - Richard Zimler   1010

Absalom (Historical Figure; Royalty; Biblical Figure)
David, Warrior and King: A Biblical Biography - Frank G. Slaughter   949

Adalgisa (Aunt; Guardian)
The War of the Saints - Jorge Amado   681

Adso (Assistant)
The Name of the Rose - Umberto Eco   750

Afton (Young Woman)
Afton of Margate Castle - Angela Elwell Hunt   799

Albert "Mr." (Spouse)
The Color Purple: A Novel - Alice Walker   988

Alden, John (Historical Figure; Leader)
The Honorable Imposter - Gilbert Morris   867

Alicia (Musician)
A Month of Sundays - John Updike   983

Allison (Orphan)
The Heart's Lonely Secret - Jane Peart   900

Anderson, Burke (Religious)
Death Stalks a Holiday: Sequel to Beyond a Reasonable Doubt - Gary E. Parker   896

Andre (Artist)
Years of Grace - Margaret Ayer Barnes   689

Andrei (Religious)
Eclipse of the Sun: A Novel - Michael D. O'Brien   876

Anna (Orphan; Religious)
The Christmas Tree - Julie Salamon   937

Anna (Traveler)
The Holy Man - Susan Trott   980

Antipas, Herod (Historical Figure; Ruler; Biblical Figure)
The Big Fisherman - Lloyd C. Douglas   747

The Last Temptation of Christ - Nikos Kazantzakis   811

Aramus (Wolf)
A Wolf Story - James Byron Huggins   798

Armstrong, Joseph (Young Man)
Light From Heaven - Christmas Carol Kauffman   809

Ashby, Devora (Daughter)
Captive Heart - Linda Chaikin   726

Ashworth, Charles (Religious)
Absolute Truths: A Novel - Susan Howatch   797

Aslan (Lion)
The Lion, the Witch, and the Wardrobe - C.S. Lewis   829

Auntie Lou (18-Year-Old)
Once upon a Summer - Janette Oke   888

Austin, Ivy (Orphan)
The Heart's Lonely Secret - Jane Peart   900

Austin, Lynda Dawn (Editor)
The Final Chapter of Chance McCall - Stephen Bly   696

Avery, Shug (Lover; Singer)
The Color Purple: A Novel - Alice Walker   988

B

Baalkor (Wolf)
A Wolf Story - James Byron Huggins   798

Bach, Richard (Writer; Pilot)
Illusions: The Adventures of a Reluctant Messiah - Richard Bach   686

Baggins, Bilbo (Mythical Creature)
The Hobbit; or, There and Back Again - J.R.R. Tolkien   973

Baggins, Frodo (Mythical Creature; Traveler)
The Lord of the Rings Trilogy - J.R.R. Tolkien   974

Bailey, Moses (Spouse)
The Devil's Dream - Lee Smith   952

Baldwin, Brenton (Brother; Photographer; 18-Year-Old)
Westward the Dream - Judith Pella   907

Baldwin, Jordana (Sister; 16-Year-Old)
Westward the Dream - Judith Pella   907

Balthazar (Nobleman; Biblical Figure)
Ben-Hur: A Tale of the Christ - Lew Wallace   991

Baptiste, Mariette (17-Year-Old; Religious)
Mariette in Ecstasy - Ron Hansen   778

Barbara (Saint)
The War of the Saints - Jorge Amado   681

Barlowe, Dooley (Abandoned Child)
At Home in Mitford - Jan Karon   803

Barlowe, Dooley (Child)
A Light in the Window - Jan Karon   804

Barlowe, Dooley (Student—Boarding School; Son)
Out to Canaan - Jan Karon   806

Barlowe, Dooley (Child)
These High, Green Hills - Jan Karon   807

Barnabas (Dog)
At Home in Mitford - Jan Karon   803
A Light in the Window - Jan Karon   804
These High, Green Hills - Jan Karon   807

Barrett, Williston Bibb "Will" (Young Man; Recluse)
The Last Gentleman - Walker Percy   908

Basil of Antioch (Artisan; Slave)
The Silver Chalice: A Novel - Thomas Bertram Costain   736

Bathsheba (Historical Figure; Royalty; Biblical Figure)
David, Warrior and King: A Biblical Biography - Frank G. Slaughter   949

Baylor, Breanna (Heroine)
Legacy - Al Lacy   815

Bebb, Leo (Con Artist)
The Book of Bebb - Frederick Buechner   707

Bebb, Leo (Con Artist; Spouse)
Lion Country - Frederick Buechner   709

Bebb, Lucille (Spouse)
Lion Country - Frederick Buechner   709

Becky (Teenager)
Alpha Centauri - Robert Siegel   946

Bedloe, Danny (Postal Worker)
Saint Maybe - Anne Tyler   981

Bedloe, Ian (Student—College; Carpenter)
Saint Maybe - Anne Tyler   981

Bedloe, Lucy (Waiter/Waitress)
Saint Maybe - Anne Tyler   981

C

Character Description Index

This index alphabetically lists descriptions of the major characters in featured titles. The descriptions may be occupations (archaeologist, police officer, rancher, etc.) or may describe persona (psychic, biblical figure, angel, etc.). For each description, character names are listed alphabetically. Also provided are book titles, author names, and entry numbers.

9-YEAR-OLD

Jennifer
Dead Air - Bob Larson   822

10-YEAR-OLD

Cadi
The Last Sin Eater - Francine Rivers   931

Craven, Colin
The Secret Garden - Frances Hodgson Burnett   716

Lennox, Mary
The Secret Garden - Frances Hodgson Burnett   716

12-YEAR-OLD

Dickon
The Secret Garden - Frances Hodgson Burnett   716

Grietkirk, Carrie
I Read It in the Wordless Book: A Novel - Betty Smartt Carter   725

Joshua
Once upon a Summer - Janette Oke   888

McDoogle, Wally
My Life as a Smashed Burrito with Extra Hot Sauce - Bill Myers   872

14-YEAR-OLD

Huff, Ninah
The Rapture of Canaan - Sheri Reynolds   928

16-YEAR-OLD

Baldwin, Jordana
Westward the Dream - Judith Pella   907

Jackson, Vernon
Killer Diller: A Novel - Clyde Edgerton   751

Ried, Julia
Julia Ried - Isabella Macdonald Alden   680

Temple, Barbara
The Enchanted Prairie - Esther Loewen Vogt   987

Zorn, Chase
Evensong - Gail Godwin   770

17-YEAR-OLD

Baptiste, Mariette
Mariette in Ecstasy - Ron Hansen   778

Duncan, Maggie
The Heather Hills of Stonewycke - Michael Phillips   914

McPhee, B.T.
Rebel Glory - Sigmund Brouwer   703

18-YEAR-OLD

Auntie Lou
Once upon a Summer - Janette Oke   888

Baldwin, Brenton
Westward the Dream - Judith Pella   907

Wallace, Julie Paige
Julie - Catherine Marshall   850

19-YEAR-OLD

Huddleston, Christy
Christy - Catherine Marshall   849

Kallahan, Faith
Faith - Lori Copeland   735

Peel, Priscilla
Priscilla's Promise - L.T. Meade   854

21-YEAR-OLD

Boatner, Bridge
The Tongues of Angels - Reynolds Price   925

ABANDONED CHILD

Barlowe, Dooley
At Home in Mitford - Jan Karon   803

ABUSE VICTIM

Celie
The Color Purple: A Novel - Alice Walker   988

Hogan, Billy
Sons of an Ancient Glory - B.J. Hoff   793

Nelson, Melissa
Justifiable Means - Terri Blackstock   695

Potter, Sharon
Sharon's Hope - Neva Coyle   737

Turner, Lacey
These High, Green Hills - Jan Karon   807

ACTOR

Chamcha, Saladin
The Satanic Verses - Salman Rushdie   934

Farishta, Gibreel
The Satanic Verses - Salman Rushdie   934

ACTRESS

Jordan, Ginger
I Read It in the Wordless Book: A Novel - Betty Smartt Carter   725

Saunders, Sasha
Mazel - Rebecca Goldstein   772

Wilmot, Esther
In the Beauty of the Lilies - John Updike   982

ADMINISTRATOR

Reichner, Helmut
Threshold - Bill Myers   875

ADVENTURER

Bull-Roar, Harold
Byzantium - Stephen R. Lawhead   823

Gelly
Flight to Hollow Mountain - Mark Sebanc   942

Kalaquinn
Flight to Hollow Mountain - Mark Sebanc   942

Seagull, Jonathan Livingston
Jonathan Livingston Seagull - Richard Bach   687

AGED PERSON

Kirshner, Rav
Kaaterskill Falls: A Novel - Allegra Goodman   773

Parkin, Mary
The Christmas Box - Richard Paul Evans   758

Rigsbee, Mattie
Walking Across Egypt: A Novel - Clyde Edgerton   753

Shea, Simon Peter
Simon's Night - Jon Hassler   781

Stephens, Marta
I Heard the Owl Call My Name - Margaret Craven   739

Turpin, Daniel
In Heaven as on Earth: A Vision of the Afterlife - M. Scott Peck   904

ANGEL

Chamberlain, Michael
An Angel for Emily - Jude Deveraux   745

Darien
Angelwalk: A Modern Fable - Roger Elwood   755

Farishta, Gibreel
The Satanic Verses - Salman Rushdie   934

Gabriel
Meetings with the Archangel - Stephen Mitchell   859

Michael
The Third Millennium: A Novel - Paul Meier   856

Observer
Fallen Angel: A Novel - Roger Elwood   756

Raphael
On the Road with the Archangel: A Novel - Frederick Buechner   710

Raphaella
Angel Light: An Old-Fashioned Love Story - Andrew M. Greeley   775

Stedfast
Stedfast: Guardian Angel - Roger Elwood   757

APPRENTICE

Melchior
The Return of Merlin - Deepak Chopra   730

ARCHAEOLOGIST

Livingstone, Adam
A Rift in Time - Michael Phillips   917

Weber, Jon
A Skeleton in God's Closet: A Novel - Paul L. Maier   841

ART DEALER

Stacy
Sign of the Carousel - Jane Peart   902

ARTISAN

Basil of Antioch
The Silver Chalice: A Novel - Thomas Bertram Costain   736

Joshua
Joshua - Joseph F. Girzone   766
Joshua and the Children - Joseph F. Girzone   767
Joshua and the City - Joseph F. Girzone   768
Joshua in the Holy Land - Joseph F. Girzone   769

Zarco, Berekiah
The Last Kabbalist of Lisbon - Richard Zimler   1010

ARTIST

Andre
Years of Grace - Margaret Ayer Barnes   689

Coppersmith, Cynthia
At Home in Mitford - Jan Karon   803
A Light in the Window - Jan Karon   804

Ives, Edward
Mr. Ives' Christmas - Oscar Hijuelos   786

Kavanaugh, Cynthia
A New Song - Jan Karon   805
Out to Canaan - Jan Karon   806
These High, Green Hills - Jan Karon   807

ASSISTANT

Adso
The Name of the Rose - Umberto Eco   750

Jim
I Heard the Owl Call My Name - Margaret Craven   739

Steadman, Lee
Gospel Fever: A Novel about America's Most Beloved TV Evangelist - Frank G. Slaughter   950

AUNT

Adalgisa
The War of the Saints - Jorge Amado   681

Biddle, Sarah
Sarah's Patchwork - Stephanie Grace Whitson   999

BABY

Canaan
The Rapture of Canaan - Sheri Reynolds   928

BACHELOR

More, Tom
Love in the Ruins: The Adventures of a Bad Catholic at a Time Near the End of the World - Walker Percy   909

BASTARD SON

Abraham
In Abraham's Bosom - Paul Green   254

Smerdyakov
The Brothers Karamazov - Fyodor Dostoevsky   746

BIBLICAL FIGURE

Aaron
Stone Tables: A Novel - Orson Scott Card   723

Absalom
David, Warrior and King: A Biblical Biography - Frank G. Slaughter   949

Antipas, Herod
The Big Fisherman - Lloyd C. Douglas   747
The Last Temptation of Christ - Nikos Kazantzakis   811

Balthazar
Ben-Hur: A Tale of the Christ - Lew Wallace   991

Bathsheba
David, Warrior and King: A Biblical Biography - Frank G. Slaughter   949

David
David, Warrior and King: A Biblical Biography - Frank G. Slaughter   949
Leap over a Wall: Earthy Spirituality for Everyday Christians - Eugene H. Peterson   474

Elijah
The Fifth Mountain - Paulo Coelho   732

Iscariot, Judas
I, Judas - Taylor Caldwell   721
The Last Temptation of Christ - Nikos Kazantzakis   811

Jesus
According to Mary Magdalene - Marianne Fredriksson   764
Ben-Hur: A Tale of the Christ - Lew Wallace   991
The Big Fisherman - Lloyd C. Douglas   747
The Crown and the Cross: The Life of Christ - Frank G. Slaughter   948
The Gospel According to the Son - Norman Mailer   842
The Gospel of the Beloved Disciple - James P. Carse   724
Great Lion of God - Taylor Caldwell   720
The Greatest Story Ever Told: A Tale of the Greatest Life Ever Lived - Fulton Oursler   894
I Came to Love You Late - Joyce Landorf   821
I, Judas - Taylor Caldwell   721
The Last Temptation of Christ - Nikos Kazantzakis   811
Mary Magdalene - Ellen Gunderson Traylor   977
The Messiah - Marjorie Holmes   794
Quarantine - Jim Crace   738
Three From Galilee: The Young Man From Nazareth - Marjorie Holmes   795

John
John, Son of Thunder - Ellen Gunderson Traylor   976
The Messiah - Marjorie Holmes   794

John the Baptist
The Big Fisherman - Lloyd C. Douglas   747
I, Judas - Taylor Caldwell   721
The Last Temptation of Christ - Nikos Kazantzakis   811
The Messiah - Marjorie Holmes   794

Joseph
The Birth - Gene Edwards   754
The Last Temptation of Christ - Nikos Kazantzakis   811
Three From Galilee: The Young Man From Nazareth - Marjorie Holmes   795
Two From Galilee: A Love Story - Marjorie Holmes   796

Joseph of Arimathea
Great Lion of God - Taylor Caldwell   720
The Nazarene - Sholem Asch   685

Judas
The Gospel According to the Son - Norman Mailer   842

Lazarus
The Last Temptation of Christ - Nikos Kazantzakis   811
The Messiah - Marjorie Holmes   794

Luke
Dear and Glorious Physician - Taylor Caldwell   719
The Silver Chalice: A Novel - Thomas Bertram Costain   736

Martha
I Came to Love You Late - Joyce Landorf   821

Mary
The Birth - Gene Edwards   754
Dear and Glorious Physician - Taylor Caldwell   719
I Came to Love You Late - Joyce Landorf   821
I, Judas - Taylor Caldwell   721
The Last Temptation of Christ - Nikos Kazantzakis   811
Three From Galilee: The Young Man From Nazareth - Marjorie Holmes   795
Two From Galilee: A Love Story - Marjorie Holmes   796

Mary Magdalene
According to Mary Magdalene - Marianne Fredriksson   764
I, Judas - Taylor Caldwell   721
The Last Temptation of Christ - Nikos Kazantzakis   811
Mary Magdalene - Ellen Gunderson Traylor   977
The Messiah - Marjorie Holmes   794

HEIRESS

Helena
Swords & Scimitars - Linda Chaikin   728

Kendall, Coral
Silk - Linda Chaikin   727
Under Eastern Stars - Linda Chaikin   729

Sunny
The Hawk and the Jewel - Lori Wick   1000

HERO

Merriman
The Dark Is Rising Sequence - Susan Cooper   734

Stranger, John
Legacy - Al Lacy   815

HEROINE

Baylor, Breanna
Legacy - Al Lacy   815

HISTORIAN

Dobson, Wayne
The Celestine Prophecy: An Adventure - James Redfield   927

HISTORICAL FIGURE

Absalom
David, Warrior and King: A Biblical Biography - Frank G. Slaughter   949

Alden, John
The Honorable Imposter - Gilbert Morris   867

Antipas, Herod
The Big Fisherman - Lloyd C. Douglas   747
The Last Temptation of Christ - Nikos Kazantzakis   811

Bathsheba
David, Warrior and King: A Biblical Biography - Frank G. Slaughter   949

Bradford, William
The Honorable Imposter - Gilbert Morris   867

Caligula
The Robe - Lloyd C. Douglas   748

David
David, Warrior and King: A Biblical Biography - Frank G. Slaughter   949
Leap over a Wall: Earthy Spirituality for Everyday Christians - Eugene H. Peterson   474

Dodge, Anna
The Beloved Invader - Eugenia Price   920

Dodge, Anson
The Beloved Invader - Eugenia Price   920

Dodge, Ellen
The Beloved Invader - Eugenia Price   920

Elijah
The Fifth Mountain - Paulo Coelho   732

Flambard, Ranulf
Godric - Frederick Buechner   708

Francis of Assisi
Saint Francis: A Novel - Nikos Kazantzakis   812

Godric
Godric - Frederick Buechner   708

Gould, Deborah
New Moon Rising - Eugenia Price   923

Gould, Horace
New Moon Rising - Eugenia Price   923

Gould, James
Lighthouse - Eugenia Price   922

Gould, Jane Harris
Lighthouse - Eugenia Price   922

Grant, Ulysses S.
A City Not Forsaken - Lynn Morris   869

Iscariot, Judas
I, Judas - Taylor Caldwell   721
The Last Temptation of Christ - Nikos Kazantzakis   811

Jesus
According to Mary Magdalene - Marianne Fredriksson   764
Ben-Hur: A Tale of the Christ - Lew Wallace   991
The Big Fisherman - Lloyd C. Douglas   747
The Crown and the Cross: The Life of Christ - Frank G. Slaughter   948
The Gospel According to the Son - Norman Mailer   842
The Gospel of the Beloved Disciple - James P. Carse   724
Great Lion of God - Taylor Caldwell   720
The Greatest Story Ever Told: A Tale of the Greatest Life Ever Lived - Fulton Oursler   894
I Came to Love You Late - Joyce Landorf   821
I, Judas - Taylor Caldwell   721
The Last Temptation of Christ - Nikos Kazantzakis   811
Mary Magdalene - Ellen Gunderson Traylor   977
The Messiah - Marjorie Holmes   794
Quarantine - Jim Crace   738
Three From Galilee: The Young Man From Nazareth - Marjorie Holmes   795

John
John, Son of Thunder - Ellen Gunderson Traylor   976
The Messiah - Marjorie Holmes   794

John the Baptist
The Big Fisherman - Lloyd C. Douglas   747
I, Judas - Taylor Caldwell   721
The Last Temptation of Christ - Nikos Kazantzakis   811
The Messiah - Marjorie Holmes   794

Joseph
The Birth - Gene Edwards   754
The Last Temptation of Christ - Nikos Kazantzakis   811
Three From Galilee: The Young Man From Nazareth - Marjorie Holmes   795
Two From Galilee: A Love Story - Marjorie Holmes   796

Joseph of Arimathea
Great Lion of God - Taylor Caldwell   720
The Nazarene - Sholem Asch   685

Judas
The Gospel According to the Son - Norman Mailer   842

Lazarus
The Last Temptation of Christ - Nikos Kazantzakis   811
The Messiah - Marjorie Holmes   794

Luke
Dear and Glorious Physician - Taylor Caldwell   719
The Silver Chalice: A Novel - Thomas Bertram Costain   736

Magus, Simon
The Silver Chalice: A Novel - Thomas Bertram Costain   736

Martha
I Came to Love You Late - Joyce Landorf   821

Mary
The Birth - Gene Edwards   754
Dear and Glorious Physician - Taylor Caldwell   719
I Came to Love You Late - Joyce Landorf   821

I, Judas - Taylor Caldwell   721
The Last Temptation of Christ - Nikos Kazantzakis   811
Three From Galilee: The Young Man From Nazareth - Marjorie Holmes   795
Two From Galilee: A Love Story - Marjorie Holmes   796

Mary Magdalene
According to Mary Magdalene - Marianne Fredriksson   764
I, Judas - Taylor Caldwell   721
The Last Temptation of Christ - Nikos Kazantzakis   811
Mary Magdalene - Ellen Gunderson Traylor   977
The Messiah - Marjorie Holmes   794

Moses
Stone Tables: A Novel - Orson Scott Card   723

Nero
The Silver Chalice: A Novel - Thomas Bertram Costain   736

Paul
The Silver Chalice: A Novel - Thomas Bertram Costain   736

Peter
The Big Fisherman - Lloyd C. Douglas   747
Great Lion of God - Taylor Caldwell   720
The Messiah - Marjorie Holmes   794
The Robe - Lloyd C. Douglas   748
The Silver Chalice: A Novel - Thomas Bertram Costain   736

Peyramale, Dean
The Song of Bernadette - Franz Werfel   997

Pilate, Pontius
Dear and Glorious Physician - Taylor Caldwell   719
Great Lion of God - Taylor Caldwell   720
I, Judas - Taylor Caldwell   721
The Last Temptation of Christ - Nikos Kazantzakis   811
The Robe - Lloyd C. Douglas   748

Salome
The Robe - Lloyd C. Douglas   748

Samson
Samson - Ellen Gunderson Traylor   978

Samuel
David, Warrior and King: A Biblical Biography - Frank G. Slaughter   949

Saul
David, Warrior and King: A Biblical Biography - Frank G. Slaughter   949

Saul of Tarsus
Great Lion of God - Taylor Caldwell   720

Scott, Walter
Bright Captivity - Eugenia Price   921

Solomon
David, Warrior and King: A Biblical Biography - Frank G. Slaughter   949

Soubirous, Bernadette
The Song of Bernadette - Franz Werfel   997

Standish, Miles
The Honorable Imposter - Gilbert Morris   867

Therese, Marie
The Song of Bernadette - Franz Werfel   997

Tiberius
Dear and Glorious Physician - Taylor Caldwell   719
The Robe - Lloyd C. Douglas   748

Yeshua
The Nazarene - Sholem Asch   685

HOSTAGE

Ileeta
The Kiowa - Elgin Groseclose   777

HOUSEWIFE

Spittle
The Vicar of Sorrows - A.N. Wilson   1006

IMMIGRANT

Connolly, Linnet
Code of Honor - Sandra Dengler   743

Connolly, Margaret
Code of Honor - Sandra Dengler   743

Connolly, Samantha
Code of Honor - Sandra Dengler   743

IMPOSTER

Spina, Pietro
Bread and Wine - Ignazio Silone   947

INDIAN

Abel
House Made of Dawn - N. Scott Momaday   860

Crow
Crow and Weasel - Barry Lopez   832

Francisco
House Made of Dawn - N. Scott Momaday   860

Sanjak
The Kiowa - Elgin Groseclose   777

Weasel
Crow and Weasel - Barry Lopez   832

INVALID

Fitzgerald, Morgan
Dawn of the Golden Promise - B.J. Hoff   792

INVENTOR

More, Tom
Love in the Ruins: The Adventures of a Bad Catholic at a Time Near the End of the World - Walker Percy   909

JOURNALIST

Abernathy, Clarence
Dominion - Randy Alcorn   679

Bertelli, Carla
The Mind Invaders: A Novel - Dave Hunt   800

Hollister, Corrie Belle
A Home for the Heart - Michael Phillips   915
Sea to Shining Sea - Michael Phillips   918

MacIntyre, Jake
Tourmaline - Jon Henderson   783

Marlow, Josie
The Twilight of Courage: A Novel - Bodie Thoene   966

Scibelli, Beth
Millennium's Eve - Ed Stewart   958

Wallace, Julie Paige
Julie - Catherine Marshall   850

Warne, Ellie
The Gates of Zion - Bodie Thoene   961

Williams, Cameron "Buck"
Apollyon: The Destroyer Is Unleashed - Tim LaHaye   816
Left Behind: A Novel of the Earth's Last Days - Tim LaHaye   817
Nicolae: The Rise of Antichrist - Tim LaHaye   818
Soul Harvest: The World Takes Sides - Tim LaHaye   819
Tribulation Force: The Continuing Drama of Those Left Behind - Tim LaHaye   820

Woods, Jake
Deadline: A Novel - Randy Alcorn   678
Dominion - Randy Alcorn   679

JUDGE

McBride, Neal
October Holiday: A Novel - Stephen P. Adams   676

KIDNAP VICTIM

Jennifer
Dead Air - Bob Larson   822

KNIGHT

Redwan, Tancred
Swords & Scimitars - Linda Chaikin   728

LANDLORD

Tyndall
Julia Ried - Isabella Macdonald Alden   680

LANDOWNER

Gould, Horace
New Moon Rising - Eugenia Price   923

Gould, James
Lighthouse - Eugenia Price   922

Karamazov, Fyodor
The Brothers Karamazov - Fyodor Dostoevsky   746

McCranie
In Abraham's Bosom - Paul Green   254

LAWYER

Cohn, Roy
Angels in America: A Gay Fantasia on National Themes - Tony Kushner   345

Grubeshov
The Fixer - Bernard Malamud   844

Mantle, Julian
The Monk Who Sold His Ferrari: A Fable about Fulfilling Your Dreams and Reaching Your Destiny - Robin S. Sharma   534

Murray, Gordon
The Iron Lance - Stephen R. Lawhead   825

LEADER

Alden, John
The Honorable Imposter - Gilbert Morris   867

Bradford, William
The Honorable Imposter - Gilbert Morris   867

Carpathia, Nicolae
Apollyon: The Destroyer Is Unleashed - Tim LaHaye   816
Left Behind: A Novel of the Earth's Last Days - Tim LaHaye   817
Nicolae: The Rise of Antichrist - Tim LaHaye   818

Soul Harvest: The World Takes Sides - Tim LaHaye   819
Tribulation Force: The Continuing Drama of Those Left Behind - Tim LaHaye   820

Cone, Alleluia
The Satanic Verses - Salman Rushdie   934

Ponomarev, Alexei Ilyich
When the Almond Tree Blossoms - David Aikman   677

Servais, Patrique
Gibraltar Passage - T. Davis Bunn   711

Standish, Miles
The Honorable Imposter - Gilbert Morris   867

LIBRARIAN

Shepherd, Charles
Raney: A Novel - Clyde Edgerton   752

Todd, Emily
An Angel for Emily - Jude Deveraux   745

LINGUIST

Mac Cainnech, Aidan
Byzantium - Stephen R. Lawhead   823

LION

Aslan
The Lion, the Witch, and the Wardrobe - C.S. Lewis   829

LOVER

Avery, Shug
The Color Purple: A Novel - Alice Walker   988

LUMBERJACK

Huff, Donnie
Gospel Hour - T.R. Pearson   898

MAGICIAN

Magus, Simon
The Silver Chalice: A Novel - Thomas Bertram Costain   736

MAIL ORDER BRIDE

Kallahan, Faith
Faith - Lori Copeland   735

MILITARY PERSONNEL

Buckley, Jace
Under Eastern Stars - Linda Chaikin   729

Canfield, Jefferson
In My Father's House - Bodie Thoene   962

Cobb, Zachary
The Dreamgivers - Jim Walker   989

Fraser, John
Bright Captivity - Eugenia Price   921

Gallio, Marcellus
The Robe - Lloyd C. Douglas   748

Grant, Ulysses S.
A City Not Forsaken - Lynn Morris   869

Karamazov, Dmitri
The Brothers Karamazov - Fyodor Dostoevsky   746

Bull-Roar, Harold
Byzantium - Stephen R. Lawhead   823

Caligula
The Robe - Lloyd C. Douglas   748

Nero
The Silver Chalice: A Novel - Thomas Bertram
Costain   736

Saul
David, Warrior and King: A Biblical Biography -
Frank G. Slaughter   949

Solomon
David, Warrior and King: A Biblical Biography -
Frank G. Slaughter   949

Tiberius
Dear and Glorious Physician - Taylor Caldwell   719
The Robe - Lloyd C. Douglas   748

SAINT

Barbara
The War of the Saints - Jorge Amado   681

SCHOLAR

Gilles, Lewis
The Paradise War - Stephen R. Lawhead   826

Rawnson, Simon
The Paradise War - Stephen R. Lawhead   826

Viadomsky, Pan
The Nazarene - Sholem Asch   685

SCIENTIST

Benson, Steve
The Oath - Frank E. Peretti   910

Reichner, Helmut
Threshold - Bill Myers   875

Saunders, Phoebe
Mazel - Rebecca Goldstein   772

Stewart, Eleanor
Not My Will - Francena H. Arnold   683

Weintraub, Sarah
Threshold - Bill Myers   875

SEA CAPTAIN

Hawkesbury, Brandon
The Hawk and the Jewel - Lori Wick   1000

SECRETARY

Lorrimer, Amory
Silver Wings - Grace Livingston Hill   789

SERVANT

Berenin, Anna Yevnovna
A House Divided - Michael Phillips   916
Travail and Triumph - Michael Phillips   919

Gamgee, Sam
The Lord of the Rings Trilogy - J.R.R. Tolkien   974

SETTLER

Denny, David Thomas
Sweetbriar Summer - Brenda Wilbee   1004

Denny, Louisa Boren
Sweetbriar Summer - Brenda Wilbee   1004

Howland, Robert
The Captive Bride - Gilbert Morris   864

Hunter, Seth
Prairie Rose - Catherine Palmer   895

Kelly, Chris Beth
The Journey West: Love Is a Gentle Stranger - June
Masters Bacher   688

Winslow, Gilbert
The Captive Bride - Gilbert Morris   864
The Honorable Imposter - Gilbert Morris   867

SHEPHERD

Manolios
The Greek Passion - Nikos Kazantzakis   810

SINGER

Avery, Shug
The Color Purple: A Novel - Alice Walker   988

Cocker, Katie
The Devil's Dream - Lee Smith   952

Gospel Singer
Gospel Singer - Harry Crews   740

Tremayne, Vali
The Captive Voice - B.J. Hoff   791

SINGLE MOTHER

Lynn
Body and Soul - Marcelle Bernstein   693

Potter, Sharon
Sharon's Hope - Neva Coyle   737

SISTER

Baldwin, Jordana
Westward the Dream - Judith Pella   907

Bishop, Delancey
Pretense - Lori Wick   1002

Bishop, Mackenzie
Pretense - Lori Wick   1002

Celie
The Color Purple: A Novel - Alice Walker   988

Connolly, Linnet
Code of Honor - Sandra Dengler   743

Connolly, Margaret
Code of Honor - Sandra Dengler   743

Connolly, Samantha
Code of Honor - Sandra Dengler   743

Hunter, Melissa
Phantom of the Haunted Church - Bill Myers   873

Mary
I Came to Love You Late - Joyce Landorf   821

Miriam
Stone Tables: A Novel - Orson Scott Card   723

Nelson, Melissa
Justifiable Means - Terri Blackstock   695

Nettie
The Color Purple: A Novel - Alice Walker   988

Voloshin, Nadya
In the House of My Pilgrimage - Julia Shuken   945

SKIER

Bishop, Keegan
Snowboarding—To the Extreme—Rippin' - Sigmund
Brouwer   704

SLAVE

Basil of Antioch
The Silver Chalice: A Novel - Thomas Bertram
Costain   736

Ben Hur, Judah
Ben-Hur: A Tale of the Christ - Lew Wallace   991

Demetrius
The Robe - Lloyd C. Douglas   748

Hadassah
A Voice in the Wind - Francine Rivers   933

SOCIALITE

Whitney
Silver Wings - Grace Livingston Hill   789

SON

Barlowe, Dooley
Out to Canaan - Jan Karon   806

Canaan
The Rapture of Canaan - Sheri Reynolds   928

Craven, Colin
The Secret Garden - Frances Hodgson Burnett   716

Davis, Claridge Luke "Clare"
Love's Enduring Promise - Janette Oke   884

Harpo
The Color Purple: A Novel - Alice Walker   988

Isaiah, Nathan
Love's Long Journey - Janette Oke   885

Jonathan
Saint Ben - John Fischer   762

Lawrence, Laramie
A Gown of Spanish Lace - Janette Oke   882

Lazlo, Clark
In the Beauty of the Lilies - John Updike   982

McCranie, Lonnie
In Abraham's Bosom - Paul Green   254

Shepherd, Nicholas
Faith - Lori Copeland   735

Wilmot, Teddy
In the Beauty of the Lilies - John Updike   982

SPORTS FIGURE

McPhee, B.T.
Rebel Glory - Sigmund Brouwer   703

SPOUSE

Albert "Mr."
The Color Purple: A Novel - Alice Walker   988

Bailey, Moses
The Devil's Dream - Lee Smith   952

Bebb, Leo
Lion Country - Frederick Buechner   709

Bebb, Lucille
Lion Country - Frederick Buechner   709

Bonner, Adrian
Evensong - Gail Godwin   770

Bonner, Margaret Gower
Evensong - Gail Godwin   770

Browning, Caroline
Savannah - Eugenia Price   924

Browning, Mark
Savannah - Eugenia Price   924

Carver, Cean
Lamb in His Bosom - Caroline Miller 858

Carver, Jane Ward
Years of Grace - Margaret Ayer Barnes 689

Carver, Stephen
Years of Grace - Margaret Ayer Barnes 689

Celie
The Color Purple: A Novel - Alice Walker 988

Davis, Clark
Love Comes Softly - Janette Oke 883
Love's Enduring Promise - Janette Oke 884

Davis, Marty Claridge
Love Comes Softly - Janette Oke 883
Love's Enduring Promise - Janette Oke 884

Denny, David Thomas
Sweetbriar Summer - Brenda Wilbee 1004

Denny, Louisa Boren
Sweetbriar Summer - Brenda Wilbee 1004

Dodge, Anna
The Beloved Invader - Eugenia Price 920

Dodge, Ellen
The Beloved Invader - Eugenia Price 920

Duncan
Nana's Gift - Janette Oke 887

Feldstein, Shimon
Vienna Prelude - Bodie Thoene 967

Gould, Deborah
New Moon Rising - Eugenia Price 923

Gould, Horace
New Moon Rising - Eugenia Price 923

Gould, James
Lighthouse - Eugenia Price 922

Gould, Jane Harris
Lighthouse - Eugenia Price 922

Harpo
The Color Purple: A Novel - Alice Walker 988

Isa
Vipers' Tangle - Francois Mauriac 851

Ives, Annie
Mr. Ives' Christmas - Oscar Hijuelos 786

Ives, Edward
Mr. Ives' Christmas - Oscar Hijuelos 786

J.B.
''J.B.'': A Play in Verse - Archibald MacLeish 840

Judah
Sotah - Naomi Ragen 926

Kaine, Daniel
The Captive Voice - B.J. Hoff 791

Kaine, Jennifer
The Captive Voice - B.J. Hoff 791

Kavanaugh, Cynthia
A New Song - Jan Karon 805
Out to Canaan - Jan Karon 806
These High, Green Hills - Jan Karon 807

Kavanaugh, Tim
A New Song - Jan Karon 805
Out to Canaan - Jan Karon 806
These High, Green Hills - Jan Karon 807

Keri
The Christmas Box - Richard Paul Evans 758

LaHaye, Missie
Love's Long Journey - Janette Oke 885

LaHaye, Willie
Love's Long Journey - Janette Oke 885

Lizzie
Nana's Gift - Janette Oke 887

Lorelli, Anne
The Strand: A Novel - Ellen Vaughn 986

Lorelli, Paul
The Strand: A Novel - Ellen Vaughn 986

Louis
Vipers' Tangle - Francois Mauriac 851

Madrid, Alex
The Scarlet Thread - Francine Rivers 932

Madrid, Sierra
The Scarlet Thread - Francine Rivers 932

Malone, Kate
The Devil's Dream - Lee Smith 952

McGraw, Diane
The Makeshift Husband - Hilda Stahl 956

McGraw, Seth
The Makeshift Husband - Hilda Stahl 956

O-lan
The Good Earth - Pearl S. Buck 706

Parkin, David
The Letter - Richard Paul Evans 759

Parkin, Mary Anne
The Letter - Richard Paul Evans 759

Porter, Ellen Watson
Ceremony of the Innocent - Taylor Caldwell 718

Porter, Jeremy
Ceremony of the Innocent - Taylor Caldwell 718

Reich, Dina
Sotah - Naomi Ragen 926

Richard
The Christmas Box - Richard Paul Evans 758

Sara
''J.B.'': A Play in Verse - Archibald MacLeish 840

Shulman, Elizabeth
Kaaterskill Falls: A Novel - Allegra Goodman 773

Smith, Lonzo
Lamb in His Bosom - Caroline Miller 858

Sofia
The Color Purple: A Novel - Alice Walker 988

Stewart, Chad
Not My Will - Francena H. Arnold 683

Winslow, Rachel
The Captive Bride - Gilbert Morris 864

SPY

Richfield, Douglas
When the Almond Tree Blossoms - David Aikman 677

Sarafian, Tatul "The Fox"
Deliver Us From Evil - Clint Kelly 814

STUDENT

Carey, Dynah
The Atonement Child - Francine Rivers 930

Rutherford, John Wesley
The Pledge - Jane Peart 901

Zorn, Chase
Evensong - Gail Godwin 770

STUDENT—BOARDING SCHOOL

Barlowe, Dooley
Out to Canaan - Jan Karon 806

STUDENT—COLLEGE

Bedloe, Ian
Saint Maybe - Anne Tyler 981

Boatner, Bridge
The Tongues of Angels - Reynolds Price 925

Deirdre
The Water Is Wide: A Novel of Northern Ireland - Elizabeth Gibson 765

Jack
The Water Is Wide: A Novel of Northern Ireland - Elizabeth Gibson 765

Kate
The Water Is Wide: A Novel of Northern Ireland - Elizabeth Gibson 765

Liam
The Water Is Wide: A Novel of Northern Ireland - Elizabeth Gibson 765

Peel, Priscilla
Priscilla's Promise - L.T. Meade 854

Roger
The Water Is Wide: A Novel of Northern Ireland - Elizabeth Gibson 765

Sheila
The Water Is Wide: A Novel of Northern Ireland - Elizabeth Gibson 765

TEACHER

Bennett, Laurel
Blossoming Love - Hilda Stahl 954

Benson, Ariana
A Gown of Spanish Lace - Janette Oke 882

Huddleston, Christy
Christy - Catherine Marshall 849

Ives, Annie
Mr. Ives' Christmas - Oscar Hijuelos 786

Kelly, Chris Beth
The Journey West: Love Is a Gentle Stranger - June Masters Bacher 688

Martin, Shelby
Beloved Stranger - Judith Pella 905

Talbot, Betsy
With Wings as Eagles - Elaine Schulte 941

Thatcher, Beth
When Calls the Heart - Janette Oke 893

TEENAGER

Becky
Alpha Centauri - Robert Siegel 946

Benfield, Wesley
Walking Across Egypt: A Novel - Clyde Edgerton 753

Benjamin, Rachel
The Romance Reader - Pearl Abraham 675

Bennett, Christine
A Place Called Home - Lori Wick 1001

Gelly
Flight to Hollow Mountain - Mark Sebanc 942

Huff, Ninah
The Rapture of Canaan - Sheri Reynolds 928

Jenny
The Tender Years - Janette Oke 891

Kalaquinn
Flight to Hollow Mountain - Mark Sebanc 942

Sunny
The Hawk and the Jewel - Lori Wick 1000

Character Description Index

Weasel
Crow and Weasel - Barry Lopez   832

YOUNG WOMAN

Afton
Afton of Margate Castle - Angela Elwell Hunt   799

Bell, Raney
Raney: A Novel - Clyde Edgerton   752

Carmichael, Eva
Unanswered Prayers - Penny Richards   929

Feldstein, Leah
Munich Signature - Bodie Thoene   964
Vienna Prelude - Bodie Thoene   967

Gallus, Diana
The Robe - Lloyd C. Douglas   748

Gardere, Maggie
A Mother's Love - Cheryl Wolverton   1008

Graham, Deborah
Frontier Lady - Judith Pella   906

Halsay, Juliet
A Rift in Time - Michael Phillips   917

Hastings, Margaret
Murder on the Titanic: A Novel - Jim Walker   990

Ibsen, Lori
Danzig Passage - Bodie Thoene   960
Warsaw Requiem - Bodie Thoene   968

Kaitland
A Father's Love - Cheryl Wolverton   1007

Lapp, Katie
The Shunning - Beverly Lewis   828

Lindheim, Elisa
Vienna Prelude - Bodie Thoene   967

Marsh, Noramary
Valiant Bride - Jane Peart   903

Mary
The Banks of the Boyne: A Quest for a Christian Ireland - Donna Fletcher Crow   741

Murphy, Elisa
Munich Signature - Bodie Thoene   964

Olesh, Anna
Hidden Rainbow - Christmas Carol Kauffman   808

O'Shea, Quinn
Sons of an Ancient Glory - B.J. Hoff   793

Reich, Dina
Sotah - Naomi Ragen   926

Roe, Sally Beth
Piercing the Darkness - Frank E. Peretti   911

Stone, Sue Ellen
In Love's Own Time - Susan Feldhake   761

Warren, Marion
Crimson Roses - Grace Livingston Hill   788

Winston, Cassandra Dell
They Called Her Mrs. Doc - Janette Oke   892

Wolstone, Rebecca
The Wedding Dress - Marian Wells   996

Author Index

This index alphabetically lists authors of books featured in entries and those listed under "Other books by the same author" and "Other books you might like." For each author, the titles of books written and entry numbers are also provided. Editors, co-authors, and adaptors are interfiled with author names. Bold numbers indicate a featured main entry; other numbers refer to books recommended for further reading.

A

Aaseng, Nathan
Explorers for God   657, 658, 659

Abanes, Richard
Journey Into the Light: Exploring Near-Death Experiences   145

Abbey, Lynn
Unicorn and Dragon   973

Abbott, Edwin
Flatland   **674**

Abegg, Martin Jr.
The Dead Sea Scrolls: A New Translation   **655**

Abelar, Taisha
The Sorcerers' Crossing   110, 111, 112

Abraham, Pearl
Giving Up America   675, 772, 773, 926
The Romance Reader   **675**, 752, 772, 773, 926, 928

Abrams, Elliott
Faith or Fear: How Jews Can Survive in a Christian America   235

Abrams, Judith Z.
A Beginner's Guide to the Steinsaltz Talmud   556

Abrams, Richard I.
An Illustrated Life of Jesus: From the National Gallery of Art Collection   430

Achtemeier, Paul J.
HarperCollins Bible Dictionary   223

Ackland, Donald F.
Day by Day with the Master   549

Ackroyd, Peter R.
The Cambridge History of the Bible   **1**

Adams, Georgie
The First Christmas   939

Adams, Richard
Watership Down   798, 993

Adams, Stephen P.
The Hofburg Treasures   676
October Holiday: A Novel   **676**
The Temple Scroll   676

Adelman, Penina V.
The Bible From Alef to Tav   344

Adiccabuandhu, Padmasri
Siddhartha and the Swan   784

Adkins, Jan
A Storm Without Rain   946

Adler, Bill
Growing Up Jewish: An Anthology   235

Adler, Margot
Drawing Down the Moon: Witches, Druids, Goddess-Worshippers and Other Pagans in America Today   **2**, 550
Heretic's Heart: A Journey through Spirit and Revolution   2

Adler, Mortimer J.
The Angels and Us   **3**
Desires, Right and Wrong: The Ethics of Enough   3, 4
How to Think about God: A Guide for the 20th-Century Pagan   **4**, 239, 476
Reforming Education: The Opening of the American Mind   3, 4
Six Great Ideas: Truth, Goodness, Beauty, Liberty, Equality, Justice: Ideas We Judge by, Ideas We Act On   3, 4
Truth in Religion: The Plurality of Religions and the Unity of Truth   3, 4

Agee, James
A Death in the Family   143

Agnon, S.Y.
Days of Awe: A Treasury of Jewish Wisdom for Reflection, Repentance, and Renewal on the High Holy Days   297

Ahlstrom, Sydney
A Religious History of the American People   397

Ahmed, Akbar S.
Islam Today: A Short Introduction to the Muslim World   436

Ahmed, Leila
Women and Gender in Islam: Historical Roots of a Modern Debate   522

Aikman, David
Great Souls: Six Who Changed the Century   677
When the Almond Tree Blossoms   **677**

Aitken, Molly Emma
Meeting the Buddha: On Pilgrimage in Buddhist India   **5**

Aitken, Robert
The Dragon Who Never Sleeps: Adventures in Zen Buddhist Practice   6
The Ground We Share: Everyday Practice, Buddhist and Christian   440
The Mind of Clover: Essays in Zen Buddhist Ethics   6
Taking the Path of Zen   **6**, 566, 567, 568, 569

Ajahn Sumano, Bhikkhu
Questions From the City, Answers From the Forest: Simple Lessons You Can Use From a Western Buddhist Monk   64

Akhtar, Shabbir
A Faith for All Seasons: Islam and the Challenge of the Modern World   432

Akong Tulku, Rinpoche
Taming the Tiger: Tibetan Teachings on Right Conduct, Mindfulness, and Universal Compassion   153

Albom, Mitch
Fab Five: Basketball, Trash Talk, the American Dream   7
The Live Albom: The Best of Detroit Free Press Sports Columnist Mitch Albom   7
Tuesdays with Morrie: An Old Man, a Young Man, and Life's Greatest Lesson   **7**, 141

Alcorn, Randy
Deadline: A Novel   677, **678**, 679, 755, 756, 757, 855, 856, 910, 911
Dominion   677, 678, **679**, 755, 756, 757, 910, 911
Edge of Eternity   678, 679

Alcott, Louisa May
Little Women; or Meg, Jo, Beth, and Amy   849

Alden, Isabella Macdonald
Ester Ried Yet Speaking   680
Ester Ried's Awakening   680
Julia Ried   **680**, 683, 854
The Sunset Gate   680

Aldridge, Marion D.
The Changing Shape of Protestantism in the South   283

Alexander, Cecil Francis
All Things Bright and Beautiful   362

Alexander, Hannah
Sacred Trust   951

Alexander, Jon
American Personal Religious Accounts, 1600-1980: Toward an Inner History of America's Faiths   247

Alexander, Lloyd
The Castle of Llyr   734
The Remarkable Journey of Prince Jen   973
Taran Wanderer   734

Alexander, Pat
Amazing Bible Mysteries   8
Eerdmans' Book of Christian Poetry   **8**
Eerdman's Family Encyclopedia of the Bible   8
My Own Book of Bible Stories   8
What a Wonderful World   8

Ali-Shah, Omar
Sufism for Today   198

Alighieri, Dante
The Divine Comedy   **9**, 360, 421
La Vita Nuova   9

Allen, Carlton
Stories of Falling Toward Grace   666

Allen, Charlotte
The Human Christ: The Search for the Historical Jesus   304, 537, 650

Allen, James
As a Man Thinketh   137, 845, 846, 847

Allen, Ronald B.
Lord of Song: The Messiah Revealed in the Psalms   662

Allenbaugh, Kay
Chocolate for a Lover's Heart: Soul-Soothing Stories That Celebrate the Power of Love   103

G

Q

R

Raver, Miki
Listen to Her Voice: Women of the Hebrew Bible 320

Rawl, Miriam Freeman
From the Ashes of Ruin 815, 865

Rawlings, Maurice
Beyond Death's Door 423, 904
To Hell and Back: Life After Death—Startling New Evidence 145, 183

Rawlins, C.L.
The Daily Bible Study Series 31

Raymo, Chet
Honey From Stone: A Naturalist's Search for God 321
Skeptics and True Believers: The Exhilarating Connection between Science and Religion 478

Raynolds, John
The Halo Effect 378

Read, Piers Paul
On the Third Day 810, 841

Reardon, Bernard M.G.
Religious Thought in the Victorian Age: A Survey From Coleridge to Gore 471

Redfield, James
The Celestine Prophecy: An Adventure 489, 649, 699, **927**
The Celestine Vision: Living the New Spiritual Awareness **489**, 927
The Song of Celestine 489
The Tenth Insight: Holding the Vision 489, 927

Reese, Thomas J.
Inside the Vatican: The Politics and Organization of the Catholic Church 428

Reeve, Christopher
Still Me 184, 185, **490**

Regrut, Brian
Stolen Identity: A Suspense Thriller 908

Reid, Daniel G.
Dictionary of Christianity in America 146, 407

Reid, David
New Wine: The Cultural Shaping of Japanese Christianity 186

Reimer, Gail Twersky
Beginning Anew: A Woman's Companion to the High Holy Days **491**
Reading Ruth: Contemporary Women Reclaim a Sacred Story **320**

Reis, Elizabeth
Damned Women: Sinners and Witches in Puritan New England 319

Reiser, William
To Hear God's Word, Listen to the World: The Liberation of Spirituality 214

Reps, Paul
Ten Ways to Meditate 492
Unknot the World in You 492
Zen Flesh, Zen Bones: A Collection of Zen and Pre-Zen Writings 207, **492**
Zen Telegrams 492

Reynolds, Sheri
Bitterroot Landing 928
A Gracious Plenty 928

The Rapture of Canaan 725, 752, **928**

Rhie, Marilyn M.
Worlds of Transformation: Tibetan Art of Wisdom and Compassion 151

Rhodes, Tricia McCary
A Pilgrimage of Prayer 376

Rice, Edward
Eastern Definitions: A Short Encyclopedia of Religions of the Orient 598

Rice, Helen Steiner
A Book of Prayer **493**, 494
Helen Steiner Rice's Poems of Faith 493, 494
Life Is Forever 493, 494
Somebody Loves You 493, **494**
Someone Cares: The Collected Poems of Helen Steiner Rice 493, 494

Richards, Chris
The Illustrated Encyclopedia of World Religions 189, 598

Richards, Penny
Eden 929
Passionate Kisses 929
Unanswered Prayers **929**, 1007
Where Dreams Have Been 929

Richardson, Alan
The Westminster Dictionary of Christian Theology 146

Richardson, Arleta
Prairie Homestead 888

Richey, Russell E.
Reimagining Denominationalism: Interpretive Essays 445

Riddell, Carol
The Findhorn Community: Creating a Human Identity for the 21st Century 205

Rigaud, Milo
Secrets of Voodoo 582

Rinehart, Stacy T.
Upside Down: The Paradox of Servant Leadership 574

Ring, Kenneth
Lessons From the Light: What We Can Learn From the Near-Death Experience 669

Rivers, Francine
As Sure as the Dawn 933
The Atonement Child **930**, 931, 932, 1002
An Echo in the Darkness 930, 933
The Last Sin Eater 712, 930, **931**, 932, 1001, 1003
The Mark of the Lion 976, 978
Redeeming Love 985, 1002
The Scarlet Thread 930, 931, **932**, 1001, 1003
A Voice in the Wind 867, 932, **933**

Roads, Michael J.
Journey into Nature: A Spiritual Adventure 367
Talking with Nature: Sharing the Energies and Spirit of Trees, Plants, Birds, and Earth 321

Robb, Candace M.
The Nun's Tale 778

Robbins, Anthony
Awaken the Giant Within: How to Take Immediate Control of Your Mental, Emotional, Physical, & Financial Destiny **495**
Ebony Power Thoughts: Inspirational Thoughts From Outstanding African-Americans 495
Giant Steps: Small Changes to Make a Big Difference: Daily Lessons in Self-Mastery 495
Notes From a Friend: A Quick and Simple Guide to Taking Charge of Your Life 495
Unlimited Power: A Black Choice 495
Unlimited Power: The New Science of Personal Achievement 495

Robbins, Thomas
Millennium, Messiahs, and Mayhem: Contemporary Apocalyptic Movements 74

Roberts, Elizabeth
Earth Prayers From around the World: 365 Prayers, Poems, and Invocations for Honoring the Earth 19

Roberts, J. Aelwyn
Holy Ghostbuster: A Parson's Encounters with the Paranormal 260

Roberts, Oral
Expect a Miracle: My Life and Ministry 496

Robertson, Pat
The Autobiography of Pat Robertson: Shout It From the Housetops! **496**
Beyond Reason: How Miracles Can Change Your Life 496
The End of the Age: A Novel 496
The Secret Kingdom 496

Robin, Uri
The Eye of the Beholder: The Life of Muhammad as Viewed by the Early Muslims 23

Robinson, Francis
The Cambridge Illustrated History of the Islamic World 199

Robinson, James M.
The Nag Hammadi Library in English 354, 457, **497**
A New Quest of the Historical Jesus 529
Trajectories through Early Christianity 497, 545

Robinson, John A.T.
Honest to God 73, **498**
Truth Is Two-Eyed 498

Rochman, Ed Hazel
Somehow Tenderness Survives: Stories of Southern Africa 897

Rock, Lois
Glimpses of Heaven: Poems and Prayers of Mystery and Wonder 8, 58

Rockwood, Joyce
Groundhog's Horse 690

Rodeheaver, Homer A.
Singing Black: Twenty Thousand Miles with a Music Missionary 813

Roetzel, Calvin J.
The Letters of Paul: Conversations in Context 273

Rogers, Dale Evans
Angel Unaware 244, **499**

Rogers, Fred
Dear Mister Rogers, Does It Ever Rain in Your Neighborhood?: Letters to Mr. Rogers 500
Mister Rogers' Playbook: Insights and Activities for Parents and Children 500
Mister Rogers Talks with Families about Divorce 500
Mister Rogers Talks with Parents 115, 406, 500
You Are Special: Words of Wisdom From America's Most Beloved Neighbor 115, **500**

Rogers, Rosemary
Saints Preserve Us!: Everything You Need to Know about Every Saint You'll Ever Need **327**

Rogerson, John
The Atlas of the Bible 70
The Cambridge Companion to the Bible **322**

Rohan, Michael Scott
The Forge in the Forest 974

Rohr, Richard
Discovering the Enneagram: An Ancient Tool for a New Spiritual Journey **501**
Enneagram II: Advancing Spiritual Discernment 501
Simplicity: The Art of Living 501
The Wild Man's Journey: Reflections on Male Spirituality 501

Roiphe, Anne Richardson
Lovingkindness 772, 773

Rol, Ruud van der
Anne Frank, Beyond the Diary: A Photographic Remembrance 219

Rolfe, Randy
The Seven Secrets of Successful Parents 115

Rosen, Norma
Biblical Women Unbound: Counter-Tales 724

Rosenbaum, Ray
Condors 783

Rosenberg, Arnold S.
Jewish Liturgy as a Spiritual System: A Prayer-by-Prayer Explanation of the Nature and Meaning of Jewish Worship 267

Rosenberg, David
The Book of David: A New Story of the Spiritual Warrior and Leader Who Shaped Our Inner Consciousness 474, 949
The Book of J **57**
Communion: Contemporary Writers Reveal the Bible in Their Lives **502**, 503
Genesis as It Is Written: Contemporary Writers on Our First Stories 429, **503**
Job Speaks: Interpreted From the Original Hebrew Book of Job 503
The Lost Book of Paradise: Adam and Eve in the Garden of Eden 502
The Movie That Changed My Life 502
A Poet's Bible: Rediscovering the Voices of the Original Text 502, 503
Testimony: Contemporary Writers Make the Holocaust Personal 503

Author Index

S

Title Index

This index alphabetically lists all titles featured in entries and those listed under "Other books by the same author" and "Other books you might like." Each title is followed by the author's name and the number of the entry of that title. Bold numbers indicate featured main entries; other numbers refer to books recommended for further reading.

Title Index

Title Index

O

Title Index